The Opening of Hegel's *Logic*

The Opening of Hegel's *Logic*

From Being to Infinity

Stephen Houlgate

Purdue University Press
West Lafayette, Indiana

Printed in the United States of America

Library of Congress Cataloging-in-Publication Data

Houlgate, Stephen.
The opening of Hegel's logic : from being to infinity / Stephen Houlgate.-- 1st ed.
p. cm. -- (Purdue University series in the history of philosophy)
Includes bibliographical references and index.
ISBN 1-55753-257-5 (pbk.) -- ISBN 1-55753-256-7 (hard)
1. Hegel, Georg Wilhelm Friedrich, 1770-1831. Wissenschaft der Logik. 2. Logic. I. Title. II. Series.

B2942.Z7H68 2005
160--dc22

2004028121

For my mother, Margaret Houlgate,

and in memory of my father, Raymond Houlgate (1919–1987)

Contents

Part Two: Text

Part Three: Commentary and Discussion

Preface

Hegel's *Science of Logic* cannot be said to enjoy huge popularity at present, either among philosophers or the public at large. One sometimes catches snippets of Nietzsche or Wittgenstein on the radio, but one is extremely unlikely to overhear a colleague or a neighbor extolling the virtues of an especially memorable passage from Hegel's *Logic*. This text remains completely unknown to many and is deemed by most of those who have heard of it to be too abstract and impenetrable to warrant serious study. Yet the *Logic* is regarded by many of those who do take the time and trouble to read it attentively as one of the greatest works of philosophy ever written. For them, it is a veritable treasure-house of insights, comparable to Spinoza's *Ethics* or Kant's *Critique of Pure Reason.* This study aims to help readers who are interested in exploring Hegel's complex work, but who feel in need of a guiding hand in approaching it, to discover some of those insights for themselves. It is designed primarily for use by graduate students and upper-level undergraduates (and other interested readers), and for that reason I have tried hard to make Hegel's arguments as accessible as I can. I hope, however, that Hegel scholars will also find something of benefit in this study. I believe that it presents an original interpretation of the *Logic,* and I look forward to reading or hearing just how persuasive other experts in the field judge that interpretation to be.

During the last fifteen years I have had the privilege of teaching Hegel's *Logic* on various occasions to students at DePaul and at Warwick. I feel privileged not only to have been able to devote time to what I consider to be a text of extraordinary subtlety and intelligence, but also to have worked together with students who have themselves brought to that text extraordinary subtlety and intelligence. Some of these students have gone on to write PhD dissertations and theses devoted wholly or in part to Hegel's *Logic*. Others have pursued other lines of research, but have preserved an interest in, and perhaps even affection for, Hegel's "obscure" text. To all who worked so hard to bring Hegel's ideas alive in seminars on and discussions of the *Logic,* and who have helped hone my own understanding of those ideas, I offer my hearty thanks. Much of this study was written with their perceptive comments and criticisms in mind. In particular, I would like to thank the following for their enthusiasm, insight, and intellectual companionship: Darren Ambrose, Tom Bailey, Tom Brugger, Kelly Coble, Rod Coltmann, Chris Groves, Wendell Kisner, Hector Kollias, Kathy Dow Magnus, George Matthews, John Protevi, Paul Schafer, Dennis Schulting, Bob Vallier, and Anna Vaughn.

I have also benefited greatly from conversations with other friends and col-

leagues who have themselves published on or taught Hegel's *Logic*. We have not always agreed on the merits of Hegel's analysis of a particular category or on the extent to which the *Logic* is presuppositionless; but I have always come away from our conversations enlightened, enriched and attentive to features of Hegel's text that I had previously overlooked. For their encouragement and companionship, I should like to thank in particular: Michael Baur, John Burbidge, Ardis Collins, Will Dudley, David Kolb, Joseph Flay, William Maker, John McCumber, Sally Sedgwick, Robert Stern, Robert Williams, and Richard Winfield.

My mother, Margaret Houlgate, has—wisely, most would say—so far resisted the temptation to try to read Hegel's *Logic*. She has, however, expressed an interest in learning more about Hegel, and I hope that at least parts of this study might prove illuminating to her. My father, Raymond Houlgate, who died in 1987, once bravely read through a long manuscript on Karl Jaspers written by a friend and might, I think, have tried his hand at this book on Hegel. My father always gave me, and my mother continues to give me, the most generous and loving support in my work. In gratitude for all they have done for me over the years, I dedicate this book to them.

Adriaan Peperzak deserves thanks for inviting me many years ago to write this study. Finally, I wish thank my wife, Mary, and our children, Mark, Michael, Margaret, and Christopher, for all the love, generosity and patience they have shown me during the genesis of the book. Writing about Hegel is not easy; it places considerable demands not only on the writer but also on his or her nearest and dearest. That doors were closed and music was turned down, so that much of this book could be written in a house both quiet and calm, is something for which I am deeply grateful. Indeed, I thank my family for all the incalculable ways in which they have helped to give birth to this study.

Acknowledgements

The German text of the opening of Hegel's *Science of Logic*, reprinted in part 2 of this study, is the same as that found in G. W. F. Hegel, *Wissenschaft der Logik I*, ed. E. Moldenhauer and K. M. Michel, *Werke in zwanzig Bänden*, vol. 5 (Frankfurt am Main: Suhrkamp Verlag, 1969). It is taken from the following CD-ROM: G. W. F. Hegel, *Werke*, ed. Hegel-Institut Berlin (Berlin: Talpa Verlag, 2000). The English translation is taken from *Hegel's Science of Logic*, trans. A. V. Miller (Amherst, NY: Humanity Books, 1999). For permission to reprint this material, I should like to thank the respective publishers.

List of Abbreviations

A G. W. F. Hegel, *Aesthetics. Lectures on Fine Art*, trans. T. M. Knox, 2 vols. (Oxford: Clarendon Press, 1975).

CPR I. Kant, *Critique of Pure Reason*, trans. P. Guyer and A. Wood (Cambridge: Cambridge University Press, 1997).

EL G. W. F. Hegel, *The Encyclopaedia Logic*, trans. T. F. Geraets, W. A. Suchting, and H. S. Harris (Indianapolis: Hackett, 1991).

EPN *Hegel's Philosophy of Nature. Being Part Two of the Encyclopaedia of the Philosophical Sciences (1830)*, trans. A. V. Miller (Oxford: Clarendon Press, 1970).

EPM *Hegel's Philosophy of Mind. Being Part Three of the Encyclopaedia of the Philosophical Sciences (1830)*, trans. W. Wallace, together with the *Zusätze* in Boumann's text (1845), trans. A. V. Miller (Oxford: Clarendon Press, 1971).

LHP G. W. F. Hegel, *Lectures on the History of Philosophy. The Lectures of 1825–1826*, ed. R. F. Brown, trans. R. F. Brown and J. M. Stewart with the assistance of H. S. Harris, vol. 3: *Medieval and Modern Philosophy* (Berkeley: University of California Press, 1990).

PhS *Hegel's Phenomenology of Spirit*, trans. A. V. Miller (Oxford: Oxford University Press, 1977).

PR G. W. F. Hegel, *Elements of the Philosophy of Right*, ed. A. W. Wood, trans. H. B. Nisbet (Cambridge: Cambridge University Press, 1991).

SL *Hegel's Science of Logic*, trans. A.V. Miller (Amherst, NY: Humanity Books, 1999).

VGP G. W. F. Hegel, *Vorlesungen über die Geschichte der Philosophie*, ed. E. Moldenhauer and K.M. Michel, 3 vols., *Werke in zwanzig Bänden*, vols. 18, 19, 20 (Frankfurt am Main: Suhrkamp Verlag, 1971).

VLM G. W. F. Hegel, *Vorlesungen über Logik und Metaphysik.* Heidelberg 1817, ed. K. Gloy, *Ausgewählte Nachschriften und Manuskripte*, vol. 11 (Hamburg: Felix Meiner, 1992).

Note on Hegel's *Science of Logic*

Hegel's *Science of Logic* (usually referred to in this study simply as the *Logic*) was published in three parts between 1812 and 1816. The first part, containing the Objective Logic. Book One: The Doctrine of Being, appeared in 1812. The second part, containing the Objective Logic. Book Two: The Doctrine of Essence, appeared in 1813. The third part, containing the Subjective Logic. The Doctrine of the Concept, appeared in 1816. Towards the end of his life, Hegel revised and greatly extended the first part of the *Logic* (on the Doctrine of Being). He may also have started work on revising the second part (on the Doctrine of Essence), but, if this is the case, he did not complete his revision. A second edition of the first part of the *Logic* was published in 1832 after Hegel's death.

The text of Hegel's *Logic* included in this study is from the second edition. This edition has recently been republished in: G. W. F. Hegel, *Wissenschaft der Logik. Erster Teil: Die Objektive Logik. Erster Band: Die Lehre vom Sein (1832)*, ed. F. Hogemann and W. Jaeschke, *Gesammelte Werke*, vol. 21 (Hamburg: Felix Meiner Verlag, 1985). This volume forms part of the new historical-critical edition of Hegel's collected works.

The most popular (if that is the right word) German edition of the *Science of Logic* is: G. W. F. Hegel, *Wissenschaft der Logik*, ed. E. Moldenhauer and K. M. Michel, 2 vols., *Werke in zwanzig Bänden*, vols. 5, 6 (Frankfurt am Main: Suhrkamp Verlag, 1969), the first volume of which contains the second edition version of the Doctrine of Being. Since the Suhrkamp edition is the one with which most students able to read German are likely to be familiar, I have made use of it, rather than the Felix Meiner edition, in this study.

The English translation of Hegel's *Science of Logic* used in this study is: *Hegel's Science of Logic*, trans. A. V. Miller (Amherst, NY: Humanity Books, 1999). Miller translates the second edition version of The Doctrine of Being. When quoting from the *Logic*, I cite the relevant page numbers from the Miller translation, the Suhrkamp edition and (where appropriate) part 2 of this study: e.g., Hegel, *SL* 109/I: 116 (203).

The principal difference between the two versions of the Doctrine of Being concerns the ordering of the categories. In chapter 17, "Something and Other," I have commented on the different position of the category of "otherness" in the two editions. For the first edition of the Doctrine of Being, see G. W. F. Hegel, *Wissenschaft der Logik. Erster Band: Die Objektive Logik (1812/1813)*, ed. F. Hogemann and W. Jaeschke, *Gesammelte Werke*, vol. 11 (Hamburg: Felix Meiner Verlag, 1978). As far as I know, this is not available in an English translation.

Besides the first edition of the *Logic* and the second edition of the Doctrine of Being, Hegel produced several other versions of his logical science. These include:

(1) the Jena *Logic* (1804–5), which is considerably shorter than either edition of the *Science of Logic* and rests on a somewhat different conception of logical science. It was not published in Hegel's lifetime, but can be found in: G. W. F. Hegel, *Jenaer Systementwürfe II: Logik, Metaphysik, Naturphilosophie*, ed. R.-P. Horstmann, *Gesammelte Werke*, vol. 7 (Hamburg: Felix Meiner, 1971) and G. W. F. Hegel, *Jena System of 1804–1805: Logic and Metaphysics*, ed. J. Burbidge and G. di Giovanni (Montreal: McGill-Queen's University Press, 1986). The Jena *Logic* contains very few pages on the Doctrine of Being.

(2) the *Philosophical Encyclopedia* (1808ff) and four other versions of the *Logic* (1808–1811), which are similar in conception to the first edition of the *Science of Logic*. These were all written during Hegel's years as rector of a secondary school or *Gymnasium* in Nuremberg and were used in teaching school children. None was published in Hegel's lifetime, but they can be found in: G. W. F. Hegel, *Nürnberger und Heidelberger Schriften. 1808–1817*, ed. E. Moldenhauer and K. M. Michel, *Werke in zwanzig Bänden*, vol. 4 (Frankfurt am Main: Suhrkamp Verlag, 1970) and (with the exception of Logic for the Middle Class [1808–9]) in G. W. F. Hegel, *The Philosophical Propaedeutic*, trans. A. V. Miller, ed. M. George and A. Vincent (Oxford: Blackwell, 1986). A few pages on the Doctrine of Being can be found in the *Philosophical Encyclopedia*, Logic for the Middle Class (1808–9) and Logic for the Middle Class (1810–11).

(3) the *Encyclopedia Logic* (1817), which also follows the first edition of the *Science of Logic*. This was published during Hegel's lifetime and has been republished in: G. W. F. Hegel, *Enzyklopädie der philosophischen Wissenschaften (1817)*, ed. W. Bonsiepen and K. Grotsch, *Gesammelte Werke*, vol. 13 (Hamburg: Felix Meiner, 2000). It is available in English in: G. W. F. Hegel, *Encyclopedia of the Philosophical Sciences in Outline (1817) and Critical Writings*, ed. E. Behler (New York: Continuum, 1990).

In the summer of 1817 Hegel delivered lectures on logic and metaphysics at the University of Heidelberg based on his 1817 *Encyclopedia Logic*. A student's transcript of these lectures has been published in: G. W. F. Hegel, *Vorlesungen über Logik und Metaphysik. Heidelberg 1817*, ed. K. Gloy, *Ausgewählte Nachschriften und Manuskripte*, vol. 11 (Hamburg: Felix Meiner, 1992).

There is much material on the Doctrine of Being in both the 1817 *Encyclopedia Logic* and the lectures.

(4) the *Encyclopedia Logic* (1827) and *Encyclopedia Logic* (1830),

which are very similar to one another and overlap in the Doctrine of Being with the second edition of the *Science of Logic*. Both were published in Hegel's lifetime and have been republished in: G. W. F. Hegel, *Enzyklopädie der philosophischen Wissenschaften im Grundrisse (1827)*, ed. W. Bonsiepen and H.-C. Lucas, *Gesammelte Werke*, vol. 19 (Hamburg: Felix Meiner, 1989) and G.W.F. Hegel, *Enzyklopädie der philosophischen Wissenschaften (1830)*, ed. W. Bonsiepen and H.-C. Lucas, *Gesammelte Werke*, vol. 20 (Hamburg: Felix Meiner, 1992). The 1830 edition has been translated into English in: G.W.F. Hegel, *The Encyclopaedia Logic*, trans. T.F. Geraets, W.A. Suchting, and H.S. Harris (Indianapolis: Hackett, 1991). There is a considerable amount of material on the Doctrine of Being in these two editions of the *Encyclopedia* and I would recommend reading the *Encyclopedia Logic* alongside the *Science of Logic* itself. It is important, however, not to think of the *Encyclopedia Logic* as a substitute for the *Science of Logic*. The former offers merely an outline of the logical science and, as Hegel himself points out, "the nature of an outline not only rules out any exhaustive discussion of ideas in respect of their *content*, but also particularly cramps the tracing out of their systematic derivation" (*EL* 1 [Preface to the First Edition]). That systematic derivation is provided only by the *Science of Logic* itself.

Since most students able to read German will be more familiar with the Suhrkamp edition of the 1830 *Encyclopedia Logic* than the Meiner edition, I make reference to the former in this study; see G.W.F. Hegel, *Enzyklopädie der philosophischen Wissenschaften im Grundrisse (1830). Erster Teil: Die Wissenschaft der Logik*, eds. E. Moldenhauer and K.M. Michel, *Werke in zwanzig Bänden*, vol. 8 (Frankfurt am Main: Suhrkamp Verlag, 1970). Note that the *Zusätze* or Additions in this edition of the *Encyclopedia Logic* (and in the Hackett translation) were not written by Hegel himself, but are based on students' transcripts of his lectures. A transcript of Hegel's 1831 lectures on the *Encyclopaedia Logic* has recently been published in: G.W.F. Hegel, *Vorlesungen über die Logik. Berlin 1831*, ed. U. Rameil in cooperation with H.-C. Lucas, *Ausgewählte Nachschriften und Manuskripte*, vol. 10 (Hamburg: Felix Meiner, 2001).

Most commentaries on Hegel's logic focus on the *Science of Logic* and, in particular, the second edition of the Doctrine of Being. Two notable exceptions are the works by J. Biard et al. (who concentrate on the first edition of the *Logic*) and Bernhard Lakebrink (who focuses on the 1830 *Encyclopedia Logic*). (For bibliographical details, see the Bibliography at the end of this book.)

Introduction

Georg Wilhelm Friedrich Hegel (1770–1831) is one of the most important, most influential, and least read of all the philosophers in the Western tradition. Some of those whom Hegel has influenced—such as Marx, Adorno, Gadamer and Derrida—know his texts and lectures well and have written with great subtlety about them. Yet others who acknowledge a debt to Hegel—including, for example, Nietzsche—have little firsthand knowledge of his philosophy, preferring instead to rely on commentaries or histories of philosophy or to read only selected passages by Hegel himself. Furthermore, a great many of those who work consciously against Hegel—such as Russell, Popper, and Deleuze—have almost no direct knowledge of his texts and lectures. Hegel thus finds himself in the unenviable position of being admired (perhaps for his emphasis on the historicity of human life) or reviled (for his alleged hostility to reason, liberty, or difference) by people who often have little idea of what he actually wrote or said.

In the second half of the twentieth century Hegel's *Phenomenology of Spirit* and *Philosophy of Right* began to reach and be read carefully by a much broader audience than ever before, thanks to the labors of commentators such as Jean Hyppolite and Charles Taylor. But many of Hegel's works still remain largely unexplored even when, as in the case of the lectures on aesthetics, they contain insights (for example, that art is essentially historical) that have become part of the common stock of modern ideas.

One Hegelian text that still languishes in particular obscurity is the monumental *Science of Logic* (1812–16, second edition 1832). Lenin, Heidegger, Gadamer, McTaggart, and Hyppolite all read the *Logic* and recognized its enormous importance for Hegel's system and for philosophy generally. Yet for most people today, and even for many Hegelians, the *Logic* remains both figuratively and literally a firmly closed book. It is rarely taught at either the undergraduate or graduate level, and it is rarely referred to by anyone other than the specialist. Devotees of the *Logic* may insist that thorough knowledge of the text is indispensable if one is to understand the rest of Hegel's system properly and that it offers unparalleled insights into the structure of being and human thought. But the *Logic* nevertheless continues to be (with the *Philosophy of Nature*) one of the least studied parts of Hegel's all-too-little-studied philosophy.

It is not difficult to see why this should be. The *Logic* is ferociously abstract, largely eschewing the concrete examples that make the lectures on the philosophy of history or aesthetics so engagingly readable and that even leaven the at times indigestible text of the *Phenomenology*. In the *Logic*, if we leave aside Hegel's frequent digressions, we are given nothing to think except highly abstract categories which turn (miraculously, it appears to some) into other ab-

stract categories that are even harder to understand than those that preceded them. For those like Hegel's contemporary Arthur Schopenhauer, who are of an empirical cast of mind and insist that "every concept has its value and its existence only in reference to a representation from perception," the *Logic* is thus bound to appear empty and vacuous, lacking any valuable or intelligible thoughts at all.[1] Consequently, it is understandable why they should have avoided taking it seriously. (For Schopenhauer, indeed, all Hegel's *Logic* does is "disorganize" young heads by offering them "frantic word-combinations in which the mind torments and exhausts itself in vain to conceive something").[2]

But even readers who are attracted by the very abstractness and purity of thought that so frustrates and angers Schopenhauer—those, for example, who prefer Plato's *Parmenides* to his *Republic*—are likely to find Hegel's *Logic* intractable due to its formidable density and complexity (which greatly exceeds anything found in Plato). There are sentences in the *Logic* that are quite straightforward, indeed arresting, such as Hegel's Beckettian judgment on finite things that "the hour of their birth is the hour of their death".[3] But there are also sentences such as this that can bring the most eager reader to a sudden and dispiriting halt:

> Determination is affirmative determinateness as the in-itself with which something in its determinate being remains congruous in face of its entanglement with the other by which it might be determined, maintaining itself in its self-equality, and making its determination hold good in its being-for-other. (*SL* 123/1: 132 [221])

As I will try to show in part 3 of this study, this sentence is in fact quite intelligible when read in context and indeed gives wonderfully concise (if not especially elegant) expression to a highly important idea. Like Wagner, Hegel is a master of economy who does not waste his words and who produces long works only because he has a lot to say. Yet one has to acknowledge that the sentence just quoted is unlikely to be as immediately accessible or memorable to the uninitiated as "I think, therefore I am" or "reason is, and ought only to be the slave of the passions" and that someone reading Hegel for the first time and encountering page after page of such dense Hegelese may be forgiven for deciding that his or her time would be better spent rereading Descartes or Hume.

Of course, density and complexity need not automatically dissuade someone

---

1. A. Schopenhauer, *The World as Will and Representation*, trans. E. F. J. Payne, 2 vols. (New York: Dover Publications, 1969), 1: 65.

2. Schopenhauer, *The World as Will and Representation*, 1: xxiv.

3. *Hegel's Science of Logic*, trans. A. V. Miller (Amherst, N.Y.: Humanity Books, 1999), p. 129; G. W. F. Hegel, *Wissenschaft der Logik*, ed. E. Moldenhauer and K. M. Michel, 2 vols., *Werke in zwanzig Bänden*, vols. 5 and 6 (Frankfurt am Main: Suhrkamp Verlag, 1969), 1: 140; see also below, p. 231. Further references to the *Science of Logic* will be given in the following form: *SL* 129/1: 140 (231).

from reading a philosopher's works. Students of Kant's *Critique of Pure Reason*, for example, are also accustomed to being confronted with and deeply discouraged by obscure sentences and paragraphs (especially in the Transcendental Deduction). But they are encouraged to persevere by the knowledge that Kant's First *Critique* is generally held to be an important, indeed essential, text for any self-respecting philosopher to study and that the mental torment inevitably caused by studying Kant is generally considered to be worthwhile. The problem with Hegel's *Logic* is that it is not generally recognized to be of comparable merit or importance. Indeed, it is thought by most philosophers (if they give any thought to it at all) to be of *no* obvious merit or importance whatsoever. As Allen Wood puts it with some slight (but only slight) exaggeration, "there is no generally accepted interpretation even of what Hegelian logic is about, not to mention matters of finer detail" and "on no interpretation does Hegelian speculative logic have any credibility at all for philosophers today."[4] There are in fact a few "incorrigible enthusiasts" who believe that speculative, dialectical logic is the "only proper form of philosophical thinking" (as Wood himself notes elsewhere), so the claim that Hegelian logic has no credibility *at all* today is a little overblown.[5] But Wood's point is nevertheless well taken: contemporary philosophers on the whole clearly do not accept that Hegel's *Logic* sets out the proper method of philosophizing or, indeed, that it is even worthy of serious study. They consider many of the philosophical paradoxes that provide the motor for Hegel's logic to be based on "shallow sophistries," and they regard his resolution of those paradoxes as "artificial and unilluminating".[6] Students of philosophy are thus very unlikely ever to be steered by their teachers in the specific direction of the *Logic* even if they are studying Hegel, and those who do embark on reading the *Logic* for whatever reason but find that it takes up far more time and causes many more headaches than they expected are unlikely to be urged to continue with their labors at the expense of other work. But this means that very few students ever learn to read and understand the *Logic* intelligently and that the familiar tradition of neglect (and, in some cases, disdain) continues unchecked. The *Logic* thus remains largely uncharted territory for all but a happy few quite simply because not enough people are convinced that it is worth their while to study it in detail and to invest the time and effort that such study would inevitably cost them.

The purpose of this introductory study is to try to remedy this situation by explaining in clear and accessible terms what Hegel is actually doing in the *Logic* and by arguing that it is indeed very much worthwhile—perhaps even es-

---

4. A. W. Wood, "Reply," *Bulletin of the Hegel Society of Great Britain* 25 (Spring/Summer 1992): 34.

5. A. W. Wood, *Hegel's Ethical Thought* (Cambridge: Cambridge University Press, 1990), pp. 4–5.

6. Wood, *Hegel's Ethical Thought*, p. 4.

sential—for philosophers to study Hegel's difficult text. This book is by no means the first to endeavor to make Hegel's *Logic* intelligible to a wider audience. It is profoundly indebted to invaluable studies by Dieter Henrich, Michael Theunissen, John Burbidge, Robert Pippin, and others, many of which are discussed at various points in the chapters that follow. But the book presents an original interpretation of Hegel's *Logic* that aims to complement and improve on the work that has gone before.

The first part of the book places the *Logic* in relation to Kant's critical philosophy and Hegel's own *Phenomenology* and argues that the *Logic* should be understood at once as a presuppositionless analysis of the basic categories of thought and as a post-Kantian ontology. The second part contains the text (in German and English) of the opening two chapters of Hegel's *Logic*. The third part then provides a commentary on these chapters designed to help prospective readers understand the detailed arguments with which Hegel's text begins. The aim of this introduction is thus not only to shed light on the general project of the *Logic* but also to show students how to read and understand individual sentences and paragraphs of Hegel's text that are all too often dismissed as obscure and unintelligible.

The ground covered in this book is not great. It extends from Hegel's initial analysis of the category of "being" to the end of his account of the concept of "infinity." This encompasses merely the first two-thirds of the first third of the first third of the *Logic*, or two twenty-sevenths of the whole text. This may not appear to be very much: one would, after all, expect to study more than four pages of Descartes' *Meditations* or twenty propositions from Spinoza's *Ethics*. My experience, however, is that, if one is reading the *Logic* carefully and seeking to understand all the twists and turns of the argument, then two twenty-sevenths of Hegel's text is more than enough to tackle in one term. If one takes on any more, there is a great danger that one will begin to skip individual arguments and content oneself with acquiring a general sense of the whole. But that would be to miss what is most important and most exciting in Hegel's text: the *details*.

It is clearly very tempting when approaching Hegel to think that the whole picture is actually of primary importance and that the details of individual arguments are secondary or even incidental—mere "moments" of a totality that constitutes the real truth or mere "examples" of some universal, omnipotent dialectical principle. After all, Hegel himself says in the preface to the *Phenomenology* that "the True is the whole."[7] Is it not reasonable, therefore, that students (with limited time and many other philosophers to study besides Hegel) be given a gen-

---

7. *Hegel's Phenomenology of Spirit*, trans. A. V. Miller (Oxford: Oxford University Press, 1977), p. 11; G. W. F. Hegel, *Phänomenologie des Geistes*, ed. E. Moldenhauer and K. M. Michel, *Werke in zwanzig Bänden*, vol. 3 (Frankfurt am Main: Suhrkamp Verlag, 1969), p. 24. Further references to the *Phenomenology* will be given in the following form: *PhS* 11/24.

eral overview of his whole philosophy and introduced to basic ideas such as "dialectic," rather than dragged through the dense thickets of a few Hegelian analyses (which are probably incomprehensible anyway) and left with a fragmentary grasp of a system that can only be comprehended as a totality? Many who teach a little Hegel appear to think so. But this leads to a curious imbalance in the way different philosophers are treated. When we read Descartes' *Meditations* and Spinoza's *Ethics*, we are urged to weigh individual arguments very carefully and consider whether or not they are valid. But when it comes to Hegel, the main point in the eyes of many seems to be to get a rough sense of the whole forest and not to worry too much about the trustworthiness of the individual trees. Hence the relative popularity (among those who teach any Hegel at all) of Hegel's introductions, prefaces, and closing chapters, from which, it is believed, an overview of the whole Hegelian system can be gained without too much pain.

According to Hegel, however, the mode of thought that insists on "forever surveying the whole and standing above the particular existence of which it is speaking" is not philosophical thought, or "scientific cognition," but mere "formal understanding" (*formeller Verstand*). Truly philosophical thought, he suggests, "*forgets* about that general survey" and demands, rather, that we be "immersed in the material" and "surrender [ourselves] to the life of the object" (*PhS* 32/52, my emphasis). That is to say, philosophy requires that we actually stop generalizing about the "whole" and pay close attention instead to the particular details of the subject matter at hand. Hegel acknowledges that a whole picture will eventually emerge through study of the details and that it constitutes the truth finally disclosed by philosophy. Yet he insists that the whole we come to understand is nothing but the organized pattern formed by the *particular* concepts or the *particular* natural or historical phenomena that we consider.

If we are to follow Hegel himself, therefore, the properly philosophical way to approach his texts is not to look in the prefaces and introductions for intimations of his general conception of dialectic or spirit, but to look in the main body of his texts at the many particular analyses of specific concepts or natural or historical phenomena and to discern the overall pattern that emerges *through* those particular analyses. This is the way that we are taught to read Descartes, Spinoza, and Kant, and it should also be the way that we are taught to read Hegel. Yet as we know, the details of Hegel's analyses are at times extraordinarily hard to understand, especially in the *Logic*. They demand considerable investment of time and effort and cannot be rushed through. If we are to encourage students to study Hegel's *Logic* carefully and philosophically, therefore, we cannot ask them to read very much in a term. In my view, the opening of the *Logic*—from "being" to "infinity"—reproduced in part 2 of this book contains about as much material as can reasonably be managed within such a time.

This book will inevitably leave its readers with a fragmentary understanding of Hegel's *Logic*. But my hope is that by learning how to read and understand well the few pages from that text reprinted here students will acquire the ability

to read the rest of the text for themselves and go on to discover on their own the extraordinary subtleties of Hegel's varied analyses that inevitably remain hidden from those whose only concern is to gain an "overview."

Precisely what Hegel is doing in the *Logic* and why we should take the trouble to study that work are topics I propose to discuss in subsequent chapters. Suffice it to say at this point that I believe the *Logic* to be one of the richest, most challenging, and most illuminating philosophical texts ever written. It provides an account of the basic categories of thought and the basic structures of being that matches in subtlety and sophistication those given by Aristotle in his *Metaphysics*, Spinoza in his *Ethics*, and Kant in his *Critique of Pure Reason* and that deserves to be studied with just as much care and attention. The aim of this introduction is to open Hegel's *Logic* to as wide an audience as possible in the hope that many more philosophers than is currently the case might recognize it to be as important and valuable as the texts of Aristotle, Spinoza, and Kant.

This book does not seek to convince its readers that Hegel is right in everything he says. Its aim, rather, is to help its readers begin to understand a text that they might otherwise have simply ignored or abandoned in frustration and to determine for themselves whether Hegel is right. Inevitably, some of the material in this book is difficult; there is just no way to avoid complex, convoluted arguments when dealing with Hegel. I have made every effort, however, to make my account as clear and intelligible as I can. I have also refrained from presupposing on the part of the reader any previous knowledge of Hegel, of the background to his philosophy, or of philosophical German. All the book presupposes is an interest in philosophy, an ability to handle abstract concepts, a willingness to reread passages more than once, and a readiness to recognize that there may after all be some merit in an unfashionable Hegelian work that most have found dark and obscure but from which a few "incorrigible enthusiasts" have drawn enlightenment and inspiration. That is to say, this book presupposes little more on the part of its reader than a willingness to concentrate and an attitude of openness toward the difficult but immensely rewarding text it endeavors to open to view.

Part One

The Project of the *Science of Logic*

Chapter One

The Categories of Thought

What Is Hegel's Logic *About?*

Hegel's *Science of Logic* may not be the easiest book in the world to read, but there is, to my mind, no mystery surrounding its purpose. It provides an extensive analysis of the basic categories of thought. These categories permeate our consciousness and language and give structure to all that we perceive. They turn the flow of our sensations into an intelligible experience of *things* that *exist*, that have *form* and *content*, and that enter into *causal* relations with one another. Categories are not themselves sensations or perceptions: they do not involve any awareness of red or blue, hard or sweet. They are, rather, abstract concepts by means of which we understand the red we see to be *something real* or the hardness we feel to be the *cause* of some effect. Such categories are not merely words that allow us to talk in a certain way. They are forms of thought that allow us to understand and experience in different ways what we perceive—concepts, such as "reality," "something," "quantity," "form," "content," "existence," "thing," and "cause."

It may not seem obvious to everyone that human experience rests on such concepts. Surely we just open our eyes and see what we see: the sky, trees, houses, people. For Hegel, experience is not quite that simple. All we actually see, in his view, are colors and shapes, and all we hear are sounds. It is only because we entertain the *concept* of "being real" or "being a cause" that we can understand what we see and hear to be "something real" or to "cause" something to happen. Without such concepts or categories, we would be incapable of understanding—and so of experiencing—what we perceive in either of these ways. Indeed, we would be incapable of experiencing it as *being* anything at all; in fact, we might well be quite unaware of it. Abstract categories are thus what make it possible for us to have concrete experiences of things in the world rather than a mere flow of (possibly unconscious) sensations, and Hegel believes that such categories inform every aspect of our conscious life:

> Into all that becomes something inward for men, an image or conception as such, into all that [man] makes his own, language has penetrated, and everything that he has transformed into language and expresses in it contains a category (*Kategorie*)—concealed, mixed with other forms or

> clearly determined as such, so much is logic his natural element, indeed his own peculiar *nature.* (*SL* 31/1: 20)[1]

As a rule, however, we are not directly aware of the role that the categories of thought play in forming our experience. For the most part, Hegel says, "the activity of thought which is at work in all our ideas, purposes, interests and actions is . . . unconsciously busy (*bewußtlos geschäftig*)" (*SL* 36/1: 26). We find ourselves asking whether something *really* happened or what *caused* a certain event, without reflecting on the fact that only the possession of the categories of "reality" and "cause" allows us to ask such questions. Similarly, we find ourselves talking about *something* we saw in town the other day or about that *object* under the table without considering whether we understand properly what such concepts mean. Indeed, we do not normally imagine that there might be a "proper" (or "improper") understanding of terms such as "something" and "object." For us, these are familiar, unproblematic words that we use without thinking.

In Hegel's view, however, such unreflective use of categories may be more problematic than we think. For it may leave us caught in a network of concepts that are in fact improperly formed and thereby distort our view of the world. In other words, it might leave us "in bondage to unclarified and therefore unfree thinking" (*SL* 38/1: 28). Take, for example, the concept of "something." We might assume that to be "something" is to be quite separate from and unrelated to "something else," and that whatever we think of as "something" has an identity of its own that is unaffected by interaction with other things. We might then apply this concept to human beings—who, after all, must be thought of as at least *something*—and come to think of individual men and women as having a core identity that remains unaffected by their relations to other people. Thus our apparently innocuous conception of what it is to be something might lead us to conceive of human beings as distinct individuals with a character and "free will" that is independent of social relations and conditions. We might then formulate moral principles or political policies on the basis of that conception and punish people for actions that otherwise would be judged to have a broader social cause and to be beyond an individual's control. Of course, if this is in fact the proper way to understand "something," then we have nothing to worry about. But if this is *not* the way to understand "something," then our unreflective use of a seemingly innocent category may actually prove to be deeply problematic, even

---

1. See also G. W. F. Hegel, *The Encyclopaedia Logic*, trans. T. F. Geraets, W. A. Suchting, and H. S. Harris (Indianapolis: Hackett, 1991), p. 27 (§3); G. W. F. Hegel, *Enzyklopädie der philosophischen Wissenschaften im Grundrisse (1830). Erster Teil: Die Wissenschaft der Logik*, ed. E. Moldenhauer and K. M. Michel, *Werke in zwanzig Bänden*, vol. 8 (Frankfurt am Main: Suhrkamp Verlag, 1970), pp. 44–5. Further references to the *Encyclopaedia Logic* will be given in the following form: *EL* 27/44–5 (§3).

dangerous: for it may lead us to profoundly misunderstand ourselves and our world, with all the practical, political, as well as theoretical, problems that this can entail.

The task of philosophy, for Hegel—in particular that of the *Logic*—is to free us from such possible misunderstanding and to render our theoretical and practical activity more intelligent and clear-headed by determining in a rigorous and disciplined way how the basic categories of thought are to be conceived. As "impulses," Hegel says, "the categories are only instinctively active." Consequently "they afford to mind only a fragmentary and uncertain actuality; the loftier business of logic therefore is to clarify these categories and in them to raise mind to freedom and truth" (*SL* 37/1: 27). Paul Owen Johnson puts the point well:

> Philosophy makes us conscious of the way the categories dominate our thought and helps to clarify them so that we can think more clearly. In attaining to this consciousness we liberate ourselves from the prevailing prejudices of the day.[2]

The *Logic* does not undertake to clarify all the concepts with which we operate. It does not address empirical concepts, such as "chair" or "table" (which can vary widely in their meaning according to local linguistic usage), nor does it deal with concepts that apply specifically to nature (such as "space" and "time") or to history (such as "the state" or "society"). It sets out to examine the simplest and most basic *general* categories with which we think, such as "being," "reality," "something," "limit," "form," "content," "cause"—concepts through which we formulate our minimal understanding of anything at all.

It is important to remember, therefore, that, even though the *Logic* may appear to be an obscure text that moves in a rarified realm of abstraction, it actually analyzes categories with which all of us (from the most to the least philosophically minded) are intimately familiar—"those determinations of thought which we employ on every occasion, which pass our lips in every sentence we speak" (*SL* 33/1: 22; see also *EL* 45/67 [§19]). One should also remember, however, that the *Logic* proceeds from the assumption that what is familiar (*bekannt*) is *not* thereby truly understood or known (*erkannt*) (*SL* 33/1: 22; see also *PhS* 18/35). The task of the *Logic* for Hegel is thus to provide us with a proper understanding of our familiar categories so that we can determine whether or not the way we are used to understanding them is indeed correct.

---

2. P. O. Johnson, *The Critique of Thought: A Re-Examination of Hegel's Science of Logic* (Aldershot: Avebury, 1988), p. 10. Hegel believes, however, that some realms of experience—for example, religion—already recognize the truths disclosed by philosophy and so do not need philosophical "clarification" to the same degree as others; see S. Houlgate, *An Introduction to Hegel: Freedom, Truth and History* (1991) (Oxford: Blackwell, 2005), pp. 244–5.

Hegel's Relation to Kant

It will not have escaped the notice of those conversant with German philosophy that some of the views I have attributed to Hegel are remarkably similar to those put forward by his great Enlightenment predecessor, Immanuel Kant (1724–1804). It was, after all, Kant who first argued, in the *Critique of Pure Reason* (1781, second edition 1787), that categories allow us to conceive as an *object* that which we perceive through the senses and that such categories are therefore the necessary conditions of objective experience. Hegel readily acknowledges his debt to Kant in this and many others areas of philosophy; indeed, he praises Kant for providing "the base and the starting-point of recent German philosophy" (by which he means primarily the thought of Fichte and Schelling out of which his own speculative philosophy developed) (*SL* 61/1: 59).

Plato and Aristotle win Hegel's approval for being the first to point out that the human mind thinks in terms of abstract categories, or "forms" (such as "one" and "many"), and for separating them from the complex array of intuitions, representations, and desires in which they are normally submerged and so making them objects of contemplation in their own right (*SL* 33/1: 22). Kant merits particular praise from Hegel, however, for noting the special role categories play in lending *objectivity* to our perceptions. Categories for Kant (as later for Hegel) are what permit us to say of what we see, hear and touch, not just that it is a collection of sensations (colors, sounds, and tactile impressions) but that it is a real object with identifiable properties and of measurable size standing in causal relations with other similar objects. Categories thus constitute the conditions of the possibility of experience because "only by means of them can any *object* of experience be thought at all."[3]

Kant's other great insight, in Hegel's view, is that the fundamental general categories, through which what we perceive "become[s] an object for me" (*CPR* 249/149 [B 138]), are a priori concepts generated "spontaneously" and independently by pure thought. In other words, Kant saw (as Hegel himself puts it), that "the thought-determinations have their source in the I (*Ich*)" and in the I alone (*EL* 84/117 [§42 Add. 1]).[4] Categories, such as "reality," "quantity," "substance," and "cause" are thus not abstracted from what is given to the senses in the manner of empirical concepts: we do not first encounter a variety of colors and sounds, gradually notice that they all have in common the quality of being "real," and then formulate the general concept "reality" as we formulate (or at

3. I. Kant, *Critique of Pure Reason*, trans. P. Guyer and A. Wood (Cambridge: Cambridge University Press, 1997), p. 224 (B 126), my emphasis; I. Kant, *Kritik der reinen Vernunft*, ed. R. Schmidt (Hamburg: Felix Meiner Verlag, 1990), p. 134. Further references to the *Critique of Pure Reason* will be given in the following form: *CPR* 224/134 (B 126). See also Hegel, *EL* 81/113 (§40).

4. The translators of the Hackett edition of the *Encyclopaedia Logic* render *Ich* in this passage as "Ego" rather than "I," though elsewhere they also render it as "I."

least might be said to formulate) the empirical concept "red" by comparing and contrasting the various shades of red that we see. Rather, the category of "reality" is produced spontaneously and independently by thought and then employed to understand as real the red that is given to us.

Kant exercised an enormous influence on Hegel, especially in the areas of moral philosophy, aesthetics, and the philosophy of history. In the area of theoretical philosophy, however, one of the Kantian ideas that most impressed Hegel is clearly this claim that "the *original identity* of the 'I' within thinking (the transcendental unity of self-consciousness) [constitutes] the determinate *ground* of the concepts of the understanding" (*EL* 83/116 [§42]). Hegel will take up this idea and make it the cornerstone (albeit in an amended form) of his whole philosophy.

One important difference between Kant and Hegel is that Hegel in his lectures on the philosophy of history and the history of philosophy argues—*contra* Kant—that the categories are not all produced at the same time by thought or employed together in every period of history. Kant understands the categories discussed in the *Critique of Pure Reason* to be the universal conditions of the possibility of objective experience for *any* rational being endowed with a discursive, finite intellect. For Hegel, by contrast, human thought generates the basic categories over a period of time, so they are not all to be found—or at least not all given the same prominence—in every epoch of history or in every culture. Consequently, although Hegel believes that all the categories discussed in the *Logic* will be familiar to the inhabitants of our post-Reformation Western world, they would not necessarily all be familiar to ancient Egyptians or Greeks. Yet Hegel agrees with Kant that the source of the categories is always and only the spontaneous activity of pure thought itself. Thought certainly produces its categories in response to changing situations, but the categories with which it responds are wholly its own and a priori.

As I remarked above, Hegel sees it as the task of the *Logic* to provide in a rigorous and disciplined manner a proper understanding of the familiar categories of thought whose meanings we normally take for granted. The purpose of the *Logic* is not just to describe and analyze how we understand categories in everyday life but to determine how they are supposed to be understood, how they are to be understood *in truth*. Hegel thus will not describe the way concepts operate in concrete speech situations or given language games (in the manner of J. L. Austin or Wittgenstein), nor will he examine the way concepts operate in given texts (in the manner of Derrida). Such descriptions may well reveal that we do not actually understand and employ concepts as we imagine we do. But as descriptions of the way concepts happen to be used in *given* verbal or textual practices, they would not be able to establish how concepts *should* be understood.

How, then, is Hegel to proceed in his task? The way forward is indicated by Kant. If, as Kant argues, the categories have their source in and are generated by

pure thought alone, then *pure thought* alone must determine how those categories are properly to be conceived (just as it must explain our ordinary understanding of the categories, which may or may not overlap with the proper understanding). The way to determine the proper understanding of the categories is thus to consider how pure thought itself *requires* categories to be conceived. This is what Hegel will endeavor to do in the *Logic*: that text will seek to determine which categories are necessitated by, and so are inherent in, thought, as well as the form that these categories must take. In this way, it will set up a standard—the proper understanding of the categories—in relation to which we can determine to what extent our ordinary understanding is rational and appropriate. Hegel's *Logic* will thus not only clarify the categories of thought for thought but also offer a thorough *critique* of our ordinary conception of them to the extent that that conception falls short of what the *Logic* reveals them to be.

Hegel is aware that Kant also set out to discover the principal categories of thought (and how to conceive them) by determining which ones are inherent in thought. As is evident from both the *Logic* and the *Encyclopedia Logic* (1830), however, Hegel believes that Kant's attempt to discover the categories is vitiated by the fact that he took for granted rather too readily what is to be regarded as the essential character of thought. From Hegel's perspective, Kant's procedure for identifying the principal categories of thought rests on the unwarranted *assumption* that thought is fundamentally the activity of judgment and that the various kinds of judgment with which we are familiar from traditional (Aristotelian) formal logic yield the categories. Hegel's view of Kant's method of discovering the categories is set out in this passage from the *Encyclopedia Logic:*

> We are all well aware that Kant's philosophy took the easy way in its *finding* of the categories. "I," the unity of self-consciousness, is totally abstract and completely undetermined. So how are we to arrive at the *determinations* of the I, or at the categories? Fortunately, we can find the *various kinds of judgment* (*Arten des Urteils*) already specified empirically in the traditional logic. To judge, however, is to *think* a determinate object. So, the various modes of judgment that have already been enumerated give us the various *determinations of thinking*. (*EL* 84/116–17 [§42]; see also *SL* 47/1: 40–1)

The core of Hegel's complaint here is clear: Kant "discovers" the categories by simply examining "the *various kinds of judgment* already specified *empirically* in the traditional logic." It is important, however, not to be misled by the word "empirically." As we know, Hegel is well aware that Kant believes the categories are generated *a priori* by the understanding and are not produced in the manner of empirical concepts by comparing and generalizing from empirical perceptions. In the passage just quoted, Hegel is not accusing Kant himself of simply gleaning the principal categories from our empirical experience in a haphazard way as we might gather sea-shells on a beach. *Pace* Rolf-Peter Horstmann, he is thus not

maintaining that Kant's procedure for discerning the categories "is lacking a convincing principle which guides it."[5]

Hegel understands that Kant's procedure is indeed guided by a principle: namely, that the categories are determined by the basic intellectual activity of judgment. But he has two specific concerns about that procedure.

First, Kant—in common with many other philosophers—does not investigate fully *whether* the basic activity of thought is in fact judgment or "*whether* the form of the judgment could be the form of truth" (*EL* 66/94 [§28], my emphasis). He simply assumes that it is because it is deemed to be such by traditional formal logic. Second, Kant simply accepts the various kinds of judgment that he *finds* in formal logic. That is to say, he takes over the different kinds of judgment (and therewith the categories) "*from formal logic* as *given*" (*SL* 789/2: 505). In the doctrine of the concept (part 3 of the *Logic*), Hegel claims that formal logicians themselves simply *found* certain kinds of judgment and categories to be fundamental to thought (*SL* 613/2: 289). He thus understands Kant to base his account of the categories on various kinds of judgment that he *finds* in formal logic after they had themselves been *found* by formal logicians in thought. It is this reliance on what he *assumes* thought to be and on what he *finds* in formal logic, not any alleged recourse to empirical, sensuous experience, that makes Kant's procedure in Hegel's eyes "empirical."[6]

Kant's "empirical" approach to thought, judgments, and the categories falls short of what is demanded in a science of logic, Hegel believes, because it does not demonstrate that thought itself requires the categories to be conceived in a particular way. It does not prove that thought *by its very nature* is the activity of judging and that the categories thus have to be taken from the various kinds of judgment, but it simply assumes the primacy of judgment. Furthermore, Kant does not show that the specific kinds of judgment that he takes to underlie the categories inhere in thought necessarily. Kant thus fails to determine the proper way to conceive of the categories because his own account lacks necessity. In-

---

5. R.-P. Horstmann, "What's Wrong with Kant's Categories, Professor Hegel?" in *Proceedings of the Eighth International Kant Congress*, ed. H. Robinson, 2 vols. (Milwaukee: Marquette University Press, 1995), 1.3: 1009. For my reply to this paper, see S. Houlgate, "Response to Professor Horstmann," in *Proceedings of the Eighth International Kant Congress*, 1.3: 1017–23.

6. See G. W. F. Hegel, *Lectures on the History of Philosophy. The Lectures of 1825–1826*, ed. R. F. Brown, trans. R. F. Brown and J. M. Stewart with the assistance of H. S. Harris, vol. 3: *Medieval and Modern Philosophy* (Berkeley: University of California Press, 1990), p. 229; G. W. F. Hegel, *Vorlesungen über die Geschichte der Philosophie. Teil 4: Philosophie des Mittelalters und der neueren Zeit*, ed. P. Garniron and W. Jaeschke, *Ausgewählte Nachschriften und Manuskripte*, vol. 9 (Hamburg: Felix Meiner, 1986), p. 157. Further references to the *Lectures on the History of Philosophy* will be given in the following form: *LHP* 229/157.

deed, it simply follows in the footsteps of ordinary, everyday consciousness by *taking for granted* what it is to think and how to understand the categories.

If we are to determine how the categories have to be conceived, our conception of them must be based not just on what thought is found or assumed to be but on what thought *proves itself* or *determines itself* to be. In other words, our conception of the categories has to be derived or deduced from—and so necessitated by—thought's own self-determination. According to Hegel, such a deduction would involve demonstrating that certain categories understood in a certain way arise directly from the very nature of thought as such; that is to say, it would entail "the exposition of the *transition* of that simple unity of self-consciousness *into* these its determinations and distinctions" (*SL* 789/2: 505, my emphasis). But, Hegel laments, "Kant spared himself the trouble of demonstrating this genuinely synthetic progress" by simply taking the basic character of thought (and therefore of its categories) for granted.

Kant's Account of the Categories

In my view, Hegel's criticisms of Kant are insightful and acute. Kant does ultimately take it for granted that thought—or at least the understanding (*Verstand*)—is essentially the activity of judgment, and he does seek to discover the categories by examining the kinds of judgment he finds in formal logic. The process whereby he identifies the categories is set out in the so-called "Metaphysical Deduction" in the *Critique of Pure Reason.* There Kant notes (a) that the categories "spring pure and unmixed from the understanding," and (b) that "the *understanding* in general can be represented as a *faculty for judging* (*Vermögen zu urteilen*)" (*CPR* 204-5/107–9 [B 92–4]). He clearly indicates thereby that the categories originate in, or at least are closely related to, the activity of judgment and that the way to discover them is to examine the distinctive forms that judgment can take (see *CPR* 213/119 [B 106]).[7]

It could be argued, however, that Kant does not merely assume that understanding is the activity of judgment but derives that conclusion from consideration of another, more fundamental feature of thought. At the start of the Metaphysical Deduction, Kant makes no explicit mention of judgment but notes simply that "the understanding is . . . not a faculty of intuition" (*CPR* 205/108 [B 92]). This means that through understanding we are not made aware of the immediate presence of objects, as we are through vision or touch. (Merely

7. Note that Kant does not refer to his "derivation" of the categories from the activity of judgment as a "metaphysical deduction" until later in the text; see *CPR* 261/177 (B 159). Judgment (*Urteilen*), or the logical activity of connecting concepts with one another, should not, of course, be confused with the "power of judgment" (*Urteilskraft*), which is the activity of subsuming intuitions under concepts or rules; see *CPR* 268/193 (B 171).

thinking of a hundred dollars does not place us in "immediate" relation to them in the way that seeing them does; see *CPR* 172, 567/63, 572 [B 33, 627].) Knowledge yielded by understanding thus can only be *discursive*. That is to say, all that understanding can do is give us "mediate knowledge" of, or tell us "about," what is (or can be) brought before the mind by nonintellectual, sensuous intuition or perception: it tells us *that* what we are seeing is "one hundred dollars" or *that* what we touch is "something real" or "something measurable." The concepts employed by understanding thus cannot yield knowledge by themselves but only insofar as they are used to determine or characterize something given in sensuous intuition. It is for this reason, Kant maintains, that "the understanding can make no other use of these concepts than that of judging by means of them"—judging *that* this intuited or perceived X is to be characterized as Y or as Z. Concepts, indeed, are nothing but "predicates of possible judgments" (*CPR* 205/108–9 [B 93–4]).

It therefore appears that, strictly speaking, Kant does not just assume that understanding is the activity of judgment but derives that conclusion from the supposition that understanding is fundamentally nonintuitive or discursive. It has to be said, however, that there is not really any *derivation* of judgment here: for the assertion that understanding is the activity of judgment is actually just another way of saying that understanding is discursive and can only tell us "about" things by means of concepts. Kant thus can be defended against the charge that he simply assumes understanding to be judgment only if it can be shown that he does not just assume that understanding is discursive.

Prima facie it seems that a case can be made for saying that Kant does not just assume this: for Kant's assertion that our spontaneous, active understanding cannot be a faculty of intuition, and so must be discursive, itself rests on the prior claim that human beings cannot intuit anything without *sensibility*—that is, without being passively affected by something. Furthermore, it would seem from a passage at the end of the Transcendental Aesthetic in the *Critique of Pure Reason* that this claim is not just taken for granted either but is based on a prior argument.

Kant maintains at the end of the Transcendental Aesthetic that *intellectual* intuition would be able to give us "the existence of the object of intuition," that is, would be able to bring an actual object before the mind merely by conceiving of it. He also maintains that "so far as we can have insight" the only being for whom an object would actually be given merely by being thought would be God. Accordingly, "intellectual intuition . . . seems to pertain only to the original being." A human being, for Kant, is not self-sufficient like God but a finite dependent being—"dependent as regards both its existence and its intuition." Our mode of intuition thus cannot bring an actual object before the mind by itself but "is dependent on the existence of the object": it is "possible only insofar as the representational capacity of the subject is affected through that [object]" and so is *sensible* (*CPR* 191–2/92–3 [B 72]). Kant therefore does not just as-

sume that our mode of intuition is sensible; he argues that it must be because only God is capable of intellectual intuition, and we are not God.

This conclusion, as we have already suggested, supports the further claim that our understanding is discursive and thus a faculty of judgment. For if we are capable only of sensible, not intellectual, intuition, then our understanding cannot intuit anything or be aware of the immediate presence of an object purely through its own spontaneous activity; it can only think "about," and characterize, what is brought before us through sensible intuition. Finite, human understanding thus *has* to be discursive because it can yield knowledge only by determining something that it has been *given* to think: "the understanding . . . demands first that something be given (at least in the concept) in order to be able to determine it in a certain way" (*CPR* 370/314 [B 323]).

But this "proof" that human intuition must be sensible and that human understanding must thus be discursive in fact takes for granted the very thing that is at issue. For the premise from which Kant starts (namely, that "intellectual intuition . . . seems to pertain *only* to the original being") already contains the claim that the human intellect cannot be intuitive and so must be discursive—provided, of course, one assumes, as Kant does, that human beings are quite distinct from God. Kant thus does not prove that human understanding is nonintuitive and discursive by deriving that claim from some independent premise; he takes it for granted in the very premise from which he starts. Now, as I indicated above, the assertion that understanding is the activity of judgment is simply another way of saying that understanding is discursive. In taking for granted that human understanding is discursive, Kant thus takes for granted that understanding is fundamentally *judgment*, just as Hegel claims. One could also point out that Kant's assumption that human beings are quite separate from God is contestable and, indeed, is contested by Spinoza. The idea that human understanding is irreducibly finite and discursive is thus by no means as obvious as Kant seems to believe.

On the surface Hegel's charge that Kant simply assumes that understanding is judgment appears to be too hasty. But closer examination of Kant's position in the *Critique of Pure Reason* proves Hegel to be right. Indeed, one of Kant's strongest advocates, Reinhard Brandt, confirms Hegel's view. In the First *Critique*, Brandt writes, "it is *assumed as obvious* that the understanding is a faculty of knowledge through concepts, [and] that concepts can be used to obtain knowledge only through judgments."[8] Hegel is also right to claim that Kant simply takes over the various kinds of judgment with which he is familiar from formal logic and does not derive them from the nature of understanding itself. Indeed, Kant states explicitly that such a derivation is impossible to provide:

8. R. Brandt, *The Table of Judgments: Critique of Pure Reason A 67–76; B 92–101*, trans. E. Watkins (Atascadero, Calif.: Ridgeview Publishing, 1995), p. 6, my emphasis.

> for the peculiarity of our understanding, that it is able to bring about the unity of apperception *a priori* only by means of the categories and only through precisely this kind and number of them, a further ground may be offered just as little as one can be offered for *why we have precisely these and no other functions for judgment* or for why space and time are the sole forms of our possible intuition. (*CPR* 254/159 [B145–6], my emphasis)

All Kant can say, therefore, is that "if we abstract from all content of a judgment . . . , we *find* (*finden*) that the function of thinking in that can be brought under four titles" (*CPR* 206/110 [B 95], my emphasis).

Note that, whereas Hegel speaks of various "kinds of judgment" (*Arten des Urteils*) (*EL* 84/116–17 [§42]), Kant himself talks of different "functions" for (or of) judgment. For Kant, the *general* functions of judgment (or functions of thought in judgment)—quantity, quality, relation, and modality—are actually found in all kinds of judgment and in every individual judgment we make.[9] All judgments thus involve a certain quantitative determination (and state, for example, that "all Xs are Y" or that "some Xs are Y"); all have a certain quality (and state that "X is Y" or that "X is not Y"); all give expression to a certain relation (for example, between subject and predicate: "X is Y," or between ground and consequent: "if X, then Y"); and all have a certain modality (and state that "X just is Y," that "X might be Y," or that "X must be Y"). Different kinds of judgment (to use Hegel's phrase) are distinguished by the specific function of thought—the specific kind of quantity, quality, relation, or modality—they exhibit, that is, by whether they are qualitatively affirmative ("X is Y") or negative ("X is not Y"), or whether they give expression to a subject-predicate or a ground-consequent relation. Nevertheless, it remains true that Kant derives neither the general functions nor the various kinds of judgment from the very nature of understanding itself but simply takes them as given, at least in their essentials, in formal logic. It is also true that Kant understands the categories to be based on these given functions of judgment. In this sense, Hegel's charge is perfectly accurate.

Kant defines categories as "concepts of an object in general, by means of which its intuition is regarded as *determined* with regard to one of the *logical functions* for judgments" (*CPR* 226, 252, 344/136, 156, 295 [B 128, 143, A 245]). This sounds somewhat intimidating, but Kant's idea is actually relatively simple. Consider first the specific logical function that a judgment may express. A judgment may, for example, attribute a predicate to a subject (rather than connect a ground and its consequent) and be a "categorical" judgment. The example Kant gives (on B 128) is "all bodies are divisible," in which divisibility is

9. See H. Allison, *Kant's Transcendental Idealism: An Interpretation and Defense* (New Haven: Yale University Press, 1983), p. 117.

predicated of the subject, "all bodies." Now, we can reverse the order of the two concepts in this judgment and formulate a second judgment that states the immediate consequence of the first: "something divisible is a body." In this case, "being a body" is predicated of the subject, "something divisible." The concepts of "body" and "divisibility" can thus each occupy the position of logical subject or logical predicate in the judgment; either way the judgment is intelligible and well formed. From a purely logical point of view, therefore, it remains "undetermined which of these two concepts will be given the function of the subject and which will be given that of the predicate" (*CPR* 226/136 [B 128]).

The fact that the *logical* role that can be played by the concept of body in a judgment is not fixed does not mean, however, that the *objective* status of the bodies we actually see around us also has to remain indeterminate. That is to say, it need not leave us unsure whether those bodies themselves constitute the fundamental reality or whether "being a body" is merely a quality that is predicated of some other, more fundamental reality, such as "divisibility." In Kant's view, we can avoid all such ambiguity and definitely understand bodies to constitute the fundamental reality in our world even if the concept that refers to them in a judgment is given the role of logical predicate (as in the judgment "something divisible is a body"). But we can understand bodies in this way only if we think of their perceived or intuited presence as always constituting the *actual* subject of our discourse, whatever the logical role of the concept "body" may be. In Kant's words, bodies can be conceived as the fundamental reality, if each body's "empirical intuition in experience [is] always . . . considered as subject, never as mere predicate."

Now, according to Kant, the concept of "something that can be thought as a subject (without being a predicate of something else)" is the concept or category of *substance* (*CPR* 277/204 [B 186]). We thus protect the bodies we actually experience from the logical ambiguity attaching to the concept of "body" by understanding those perceived bodies to be substances. Similarly, we can understand the divisibility which we experience to be a definite *accident* of those bodily substances even when the concept of divisibility forms the logical subject of the judgment. In Kant's view, all logical subjects for which there is a corresponding empirical intuition or perception must be conceived in this way as referring either to real substances or to their accidents. Otherwise, we can never fix the *objective* status of the perceived "things" which those logical subjects denote.[10]

Two things should be noticed here. First, Kant understands the category of substance to be a thought by means of which our empirical *intuition* of bodies is rendered determinate. Subsuming the concept of body under the category of

---

10. Ultimately for Kant the only real substances in experience are movable particles of matter. Empirical objects, such as chairs and tables are in fact "accidental" constellations of such particles; see Allison, *Kant's Transcendental Idealism*, p. 211.

substance enables intuited bodies to be understood as substances, but it does not remove the logical indeterminacy attaching to the concept of body itself: that concept can still function as a logical subject or predicate. Second, Kant understands the category of substance to be a thought by means of which our empirical intuition of bodies is rendered determinate *in respect of one of the logical functions of judgment*. Subsuming the concept of body under the category of substance determines the bodies we experience to be real *subjects* rather than predicates and so introduces into our intuitions a determinacy that is specifically derived from the categorical function of judgment.

Kant's definition of a category on B 128 thus captures precisely the way in which he understands the category of substance, namely as the "concept of an object in general, by means of which its intuition is regarded as determined with regard to one of the logical functions for judgments."[11] Indeed, this definition reveals how every Kantian category is to be generated (though Kant does not explicitly define every category himself). In each case, we simply take a specific function (or kind) of judgment (such as "if X, then Y," "X is Y," or "all Xs are Y"), introduce a thought such as "object" or "something" or "that which," and then form the thought of that which is *determined* in respect of the specific function of judgment concerned.[12] This thought or category is then used to render determinate what is given to us in intuition—and so to understand it—in some specific way. That is to say, the category is used to understand what we perceive to be definitely this kind of thing rather than that.

A *cause* is thus something that is definitely a ground rather than consequence (an "if," rather than a "then"); the category of *reality* signifies that which is definitely affirmative rather than negative; the category of *totality* signifies that which is determined to be "all" rather than "some"; and so on. Even *negation* is to be conceived in this way. Negation is thus that which is determined to be negative rather than affirmative: nonbeing, absence rather than being, reality, presence. This is not to say that the concept of negation refers to some *positive* object called "the negative." But it is to say that the concept is not simply without any referent whatsoever: for the category of negation signifies a definite and determinate *lack* of positive reality. To understand what it is to be cold, therefore, one must be able to form the thought not of some positive quality but of the *identifiable* lack of heat.[13] To be sure, categories are fully meaningful only when they are "schematized" or understood in temporal terms: substance is to be understood as that which is permanent, and cause as that which can never come after its effect (*CPR* 272, 341/197, 290 [B 177, 299]). Nevertheless, Kant rec-

11. See also Allison, *Kant's Transcendental Idealism*, p. 126.

12. For Kant "all the categories . . . constitute the thinking of an *object (Objekt) in general*" (*CPR* 260/176 [B 158]; see also *CPR* 193/94 [B 75]).

13. See Kant, *CPR* 274, 382, 555/201, 332, 553–4 (B182, 347, 602).

ognizes that each category also has a meaning of its own in abstraction from its temporal sense, and in each case the definition of a category given on B 128 provides the key to that purely logical meaning.

As we have seen from this brief account of the way Kant discovers the categories, Hegel is absolutely right that, for Kant, "the various modes of judgment (*Urteilsweisen*) that have already been enumerated [in traditional logic] give us the various *determinations of thinking*" (*EL* 84/117 [§42]). We can also see why this should matter: Kant's manner of establishing the categories has a direct bearing on the number of categories he regards as fundamental and on how they are to be conceived. Since there are twelve specific functions of judgment, in Kant's view, there can be only twelve basic categories: the categories of quantity (unity, plurality, totality), of quality (reality, negation, limitation), of relation (substance, causality, reciprocity), and of modality (possibility, actuality, and necessity)—though further "predicables," such as force, action, passion, and resistance can be "derived" from these (*CPR* 212–14/118–20 [B 106–8]). But, of course, this leaves open the following question: how many categories would thought prove to have if they were not taken from the twelve functions of judgment that Kant simply *finds* there to be?

Similarly, the fact that Kant bases the categories on distinct functions and kinds of judgment (and, indeed, the fact that each category is the thought of something *determined* in one way rather than another) means that he conceives the categories themselves as logically distinct from one another (even though they are all needed for determinate cognition of what is given in intuition and so are epistemically interdependent). The category of reality, for example, is quite distinct from that of negation—which is what allows Kant to formulate the idea of God as the most real being or *ens realissimum*, which has no negation or lack originally in itself (*CPR* 557/556–7 [B 606–7]).[14] The (meta-)category of quantity is quite distinct from that of quality—which is what allows Kant to regard the proposition that "the straight line between two points is the shortest" as a synthetic one in which the predicate adds something that is not already contained in the subject (CPR 145/49 [B 16]). And the category of substance is quite distinct from that of causality—which is what allows Kant to reject Spinoza's conception of substance as causa sui and to see in substance solely that in which accidents inhere.[15] But once again we must ask whether the cate-

14. See also S. Houlgate, "Hegel, Kant, and the Formal Distinctions of Reflective Understanding," in *Hegel on the Modern World*, ed. A. Collins (Albany: SUNY Press, 1995), p. 132.

15. I. Kant, *Schriften zur Metaphysik und Logik*, ed. W. Weischedel, 2 vols. (Frankfurt am Main: Suhrkamp Verlag, 1968), 1: 340–1 (note). See also S. Houlgate, "Substance, Causality, and the Question of Method in Hegel's *Science of Logic*," in *The Reception of Kant's Critical Philosophy: Fichte, Schelling, and Hegel*, ed. Sally Sedgwick (Cambridge: Cambridge University Press, 2000), pp. 247–8.

gories would still have to be conceived as logically distinct from one another in this way if they were not based on distinct kinds of judgment (or generated by thinking of something as determined in respect of a logical function of judgment—as this rather than that). Might not categories derived in a different way prove to be logically much more closely interrelated than Kant allows?

Whatever one may think generally about the merits (and occasional distortions) in Hegel's critique of Kant, it is important to recognize that he comes to his distinctive conception of the categories in the *Logic* for one very simple reason: he endeavors to base his understanding of those categories not, as Kant does, on what formal logicians have simply *found* thought to be but on what thought itself *proves* to be. Hegel's aim in the *Logic* is thus to avoid making any unwarranted assumptions about thought, such as Kant makes, and to derive the categories from what thought minimally has to be. By determining in this way which categories are inherent in thought *as such* (and how they are to be conceived), Hegel hopes to provide the immanent deduction (*Ableitung*) of the categories that he believes Kant was obliged but failed to deliver (*SL* 47/1: 40).

Fichte's Contribution

Before Hegel, another great German Idealist, Johann Gottlieb Fichte (1762–1814), made the charge that Kant failed to provide a proper deduction or derivation of the categories. Fichte acknowledges Kant to be the founder of Critical (or Transcendental) Idealism, the philosophy according to which the fundamental concepts and laws of thought—or "determinations of consciousness"—are generated by the spontaneous activity of the intellect itself rather than imposed on the intellect from some outside source. Yet Fichte maintains that Kant himself "does not derive the presumed laws of the intellect from the very nature of the intellect," but abstracts these laws from our empirical experience of objects, albeit via a "detour through logic" (which itself abstracts its laws from our experience of objects).[16] In Fichte's view, therefore, Kant may assert that the categories and laws of thought have their source in the spontaneity of the intellect, but—because of the way he proceeds—"he has no way to confirm that the laws of thought he postulates actually are laws of thought and that they are really nothing else but the immanent laws of the intellect." The only way to confirm this, Fichte tells us, would be to start from the simple premise that the intellect *acts*—that the intellect is "a kind of *doing* and absolutely nothing more"—and to show how the laws of thought can be derived from this premise alone. By proceeding in this way, he suggests, "Critical idealism allows the entire range of our representations to come into being gradually before the eyes of the reader or

16. J.G. Fichte, *Introductions to the Wissenschaftslehre and Other Writings*, trans. D. Breazeale (Indianapolis: Hackett, 1994), pp. 25, 27–8.

listener" and so reconstructs for the reader the logical *genesis* of the categories and laws of thought from the activity of thought itself.[17]

Hegel leaves no doubt about the tremendous importance he attributes to Fichte's critical development of Kantian thought. "It remains the profound and enduring merit of *Fichte's* philosophy," he writes in the *Encyclopedia Logic,* "to have reminded us that the *thought-determinations* must be exhibited in their *necessity,* and that it is essential for them to be *deduced* (*daß sie wesentlich abzuleiten seien*)" (*EL* 84/117 [§42]). Indeed, in his lectures on the history of philosophy, Hegel claims that apart from Fichte "no-one else since Aristotle has thought about how to exhibit the determinations of thinking in their necessity, their derivation, their construction."[18] Furthermore, he praises Fichte for attempting to provide such a derivation by "letting reason itself exhibit its own determinations" (*SL* 47/1: 41). Nevertheless, Hegel believes that Fichte himself takes too much for granted in his derivation of the categories by assuming that the pure thought or intellectual activity with which philosophy is to begin is to be understood from the outset as *I* (*Ich*), or immediate, abstract *self-consciousness.* The possibility of self-consciousness may be implicit in thought but self-consciousness for Hegel is not the most basic feature of thought (see *SL* 75–8/1: 76–9 [183–7]). Pure self-consciousness, or I, thus should not provide the starting point from which to derive the categories, and the task of philosophy should not be (as Fichte puts it), to define the categories *"by showing how each category is determinately related to the possibility of self-consciousness."*[19] The task of philosophy, in Hegel's view, is rather to establish which categories are immanent in thought conceived simply as *thought* as such. (The proper deduction of the categories, which "Kant spared himself" and which was referred to earlier [p. 16], thus actually involves "the exposition of the transition of thought"—rather than the simple unity of self-consciousness—"into these its determinations and distinctions.")

Radical Self-Criticism

So far I have suggested that what motivates Hegel in the *Logic* is the desire for necessity. Like Fichte, Hegel wants to find out how basic categories have to be understood, not just how they have in fact been understood. This can only be discovered, he believes, if we demonstrate which categories are inherent in thought as such, and we can only do this if we allow pure thought to determine *itself*—and so to generate its own determinations—"before our very eyes" (to use Fichte's expression).[20] The study of thought will inevitably lack such neces-

17. Fichte, *Introductions to the Wissenschaftslehre*, pp. 26–8.
18. Hegel, *LHP* 234/160.
19. Fichte, *Introductions to the Wissenschaftslehre*, p. 63.
20. Fichte, *Introductions to the Wissenschaftslehre*, p. 28.

sity if it begins not from thought as such but from what we merely assume, find, or assert thought to be. This is because, as Fichte puts it, "it is hard to see why we should place any more credence in the unproven assertions of the one than in the unproven assertions of the other"; or as Hegel himself writes in the introduction to the *Phenomenology*, "one bare assurance is worth just as much as another."[21] An account of the categories—such as Kant's (or indeed Fichte's own) —that is based upon unproven assumptions can thus never demonstrate how the categories have to be understood *schlechthin* but only how they are to be understood *given* those assumptions. Accordingly, we can determine the necessary character of the categories only if we avoid all such unproven assumptions about thought and derive the categories from what thought itself minimally *is*. Hegel's concern to begin the *Logic* by suspending all our familiar views about thought is thus a direct consequence of his search for an account of the categories that is completely necessary.

Yet—though it may come as a surprise to some to learn this—it is also the consequence of his desire to be utterly *self-critical*. The conviction that only the suspension of one's cherished assumptions will lead to what is necessary and true is, as Hegel well knows, a central pillar of Descartes's philosophy. Hegel traces the demand for a thoroughly critical study of the *categories* back to Kant, however, rather than to the "father" of modern philosophy. Prior to Kant, Hegel tells us, metaphysical and empiricist philosophers employed categories, such as substance and causality, to understand the world, but they did not prove that it was actually legitimate to do so. This is true of Aristotle, Leibniz, Locke, and indeed—despite his pledge to demolish all his previous opinions—Descartes.[22] In his *Critique of Pure Reason* Kant put an end to such "naive thinking" by "investigating just how far the forms of thinking are in general capable of helping us reach the cognition of truth" (*EL* 81–2/114 [§41 Add. 1]). Hegel maintains that "Kant's subjection of knowing to examination in this way was a great and important step."[23] Yet, at the same time, he claims that Kant himself did not take his critical investigation of the legitimacy of the categories anything like far enough.

For Hegel, Kant's concern was to determine the epistemic status of the categories—that is, whether categories, such as substance or causality, can justifiably be used to understand objects in the world (*EL* 81–2/114 [§41 Add. 1]). Kant concluded that such categories can be employed to understand objects as they are given to us in spatio-temporal intuition but that they cannot be used to determine objects as they might be "in themselves," that is, apart from the way they appear to intuition. As we shall see later, Hegel rejects the idea that the

---

21. See Fichte, *Introductions to the Wissenschaftslehre*, p. 28, and Hegel, *PhS* 49/71.

22. For Hegel's views on pre-Kantian metaphysics and empiricism, see *EL* 65–80/93–112 (§§26–39).

23. Hegel, *LHP* 218/149.

categories do not apply to things themselves.[24] More importantly, however (at least for our current discussion), Hegel points out that in undertaking this critical examination of the *epistemic* status of the categories Kant neglects to carry out a similar critical investigation of the *logical* meaning of the categories themselves. Kant's "critique does not involve itself with the *content*, . . . or with the determinate mutual relationship of these thought-determinations to each other" (*EL* 81/113 [§41]).[25] Instead, as we have seen, Kant simply bases his understanding of the categories on the functions of judgment traditionally assumed in formal logic. As Hegel recognizes, Kant insists against some of his predecessors that the categories have to be understood in temporal terms (or "schematized") in order to be fully meaningful.[26] But this does not affect Kant's understanding of the purely logical meaning of the categories, which remains governed by the accepted functions of judgment. Kant thus does not subject the categories themselves to critical examination but retains—without proving that it is necessary to do so—what Hegel regards as a quite traditional (Aristotelian) understanding of them. In this respect, Kant's critique of pure reason remains, for Hegel—like the thought of the "older metaphysicians," Leibniz and Wolff—"an *uncritical* thinking" (*EL* 82/115 [§41 Add. 1], my emphasis). A properly critical thinking, by contrast, would suspend the traditional conception of the categories and determine anew how the categories are to be understood.

Hegel will show in the *Logic* that the traditional understanding of the categories—found in both pre-Kantian metaphysics and ordinary consciousness—does not in fact correspond fully to the way those categories should be understood. The *Logic*—or at least the first part, entitled the "Objective Logic"—thus provides a "genuine critique" of the categories of metaphysics (and of ordinary thought) (*SL* 64/1: 62). Kant's critique, on the other hand, "has not produced any alteration in [the categories]": they are deemed to be applicable only to what is given in sensuous experience, not to things in themselves, but they are "left in the same shape for the subject knower as they formerly possessed for the object" (*SL* 46-7/1: 40). Hegel's *Logic* thus proves to be an even more thoroughly critical text than Kant's own *Critique of Pure Reason.*

It is clear, then, that Hegel regards his *Logic* as a refinement of Kant's theoretical philosophy in two ways. On the one hand, the *Logic* perfects the genetic

---

24. See chapter 6, below, pp. 131–7.

25. See also Houlgate, "Hegel, Kant, and the Formal Distinctions of Reflective Understanding," p. 131 and "Response to Professor Horstmann," *Proceedings of the Eighth International Kant Congress*, 1.3: 1019.

26. See G. W. F. Hegel, *Vorlesungen über die Geschichte der Philosophie*, ed. E. Moldenhauer and K. M. Michel, 3 vols., *Werke in zwanzig Bänden*, vols. 18, 19, and 20 (Frankfurt am Main: Suhrkamp Verlag, 1971), 3: 347–8, and Kant *CPR* 271–7, 341/196–205, 290 (B 176–87, 299). Further references to the *Vorlesungen über die Geschichte der Philosophie* will be given in the following form: *VGP* 3: 347–8.

derivation of the categories that (according to Fichte) is made necessary by Kant's insight that the categories have their source in the understanding alone. On the other hand, the *Logic* presents the thorough critique of the traditional conception of the categories that Hegel thinks is demanded by Kant's critical turn but never delivered by Kant himself. These two projects dovetail, of course, because Hegel can derive the proper conception of the categories from thought as such only after he has critically suspended all that thought has traditionally been found to be.

I have great sympathy with Hegel's demand for a thoroughly critical derivation of the categories. I have to admit, however, that Hegel is wrong to believe that Kant's own emphasis on *critique* itself implies such a demand. The word "critique," for Kant, has quite a narrow and restricted meaning. If metaphysics is the body of synthetic a priori principles that constitutes knowledge through pure reason, the task of critique for Kant is simply "to display the sources and conditions of its possibility" (*CPR* 105/13 [A xxi]). Critique thus shows how metaphysics is possible; it does not call for anything like thoroughgoing self-criticism, either explicitly or implicitly. That is a Cartesian, not a Kantian aim. Yet Hegel interprets it as implicit in Kant's critical project. Hegel thus interprets his own critique of Kant as an immanent critique insofar as he sees his own philosophy as fulfilling the demand for radical self-criticism implicit in Kant's critical philosophy better than Kant himself. But Hegel's critique of Kant clearly is not immanent in *that* sense.

Yet in another admittedly rather extended sense, I think that Hegel's critique of Kant can be interpreted as immanent: for I agree with Hegel (and Fichte) that a rigorous *derivation* of the categories of the kind Kant fails to provide is made necessary by Kant's own claim that the categories "spring pure and unmixed from the understanding" (*CPR* 204/107 [B 92]). As we have seen, such a derivation must demonstrate that the categories follow necessarily from what thought itself *is*, not merely from what thought has been found to be. But this means that the philosopher must first suspend all unproven assumptions about thought and so be thoroughly *self-critical*. The demand for a thoroughgoing "Cartesian" critique, or suspension of the traditional conception, of the categories can thus be said to be implicit in Kant's philosophy after all, as Hegel suggests. It is implicit, however, not in Kant's own conception of critique as such but in the demand for a rigorous *derivation* of the categories that is itself implicit in Kant's recognition that they have their source in the intellect.[27]

The requirement that philosophy make no unwarranted assumptions about thought in its derivation of the categories is the requirement that philosophy be *presuppositionless*. Philosophy, in Hegel's view, should not presuppose that thought is judgment or that it is self-conscious intellectual activity (the work of

27. This revises slightly the conclusion I came to in my "Response to Professor Horstmann"; see *Proceedings of the Eighth International Kant Congress*, 1.3: 1022.

the "I"); indeed, it should not presuppose anything about thought at all. This demand for radical presuppositionlessness is easily misunderstood, and we shall consider later some of the things it definitely does *not* mean. It is essential that we take it seriously, however, even if we are initially tempted to think that it is an impossible demand to fulfil (or perhaps quite insane). For if we do not take it seriously, we will be unable to understand precisely what Hegel is doing in the *Logic* and we will miss what is most exciting and original about that text. In the next chapter we shall examine more closely what presuppositionless thinking entails for Hegel.

Chapter Two

Presuppositionless Thinking

Beginning with Pure Being

By no means does every modern commentator on Hegel accept that he really meant his philosophy to be presuppositionless. Yet it is quite clear from several passages in his texts and from the testimony of his earliest critics that he did. In the *Encyclopedia Logic*, for example, he writes that

> All . . . presuppositions or assumptions (*Voraussetzungen oder Vorurteile*) must equally be given up when we enter into the Science, whether they are taken from representation or from thinking; for it is this Science, in which all determinations of this sort must first be investigated, and in which their meaning and validity like that of their antitheses must be [re]cognised. . . . Science should be preceded by *universal doubt*, i.e., by total *presuppositionlessness* (*die gänzliche Voraussetzungslosigkeit*). (*EL* 124/167–8 [§78])[1]

In the *Science of Logic* itself the same point is made:

> the beginning must be an *absolute*, or what is synonymous here, an *abstract* beginning; and so it *may not presuppose anything*, must not be mediated by anything nor have a ground; rather it is to be itself the ground of the entire science. (*SL* 70/1: 68–9 [175])

The great importance of this idea to Hegel was also clearly recognized by his most significant nineteenth-century critics. Schelling, for example, remarks in the 1830s that "Hegelian philosophy boasts of being a philosophy which presupposes nothing, absolutely nothing"; Trendelenburg makes reference in 1843 to Hegel's "proud doctrine of the presuppositionless pure thinking"; and Kierkegaard introduces his discussion of Hegel in his *Concluding Unscientific Postscript* (1846) by noting that "the System begins with the immediate, and hence without any presuppositions." None of these figures believed that Hegel's philosophy is actually presuppositionless (or that presuppositionlessness is even

1. See also Hegel, *LHP* 137–8/92.

desirable), but they all took seriously his *claim* that he avoids taking anything for granted. Indeed, that is precisely why they are so eager to refute it.[2]

But what exactly does it mean to philosophize "without presuppositions"? As we saw in the last chapter, it means that we do not take for granted any particular conception of thought and its categories at the outset of philosophy or assume (with Kant) that concepts are "predicates of possible judgments" (*CPR* 205/109 [B 94]). It also means, however, that we do not assume that thought should be governed by the rules of Aristotelian logic or that the law of noncontradiction holds, or that thought is regulated by any principles or laws whatsoever. In short, it means that we give up everything we have learned about thought from Plato, Aristotle, Leibniz, or Kant (or twentieth-century symbolic logic)—that we "abstract from everything" (*EL* 124/168 [§78]). This is not to say that we ourselves assume that the principles of Aristotelian (or post-Fregean) formal logic are simply wrong (Hegel maintains that the rules of syllogizing will eventually be shown in the *Logic* to be valid—albeit for a limited range of thought that excludes philosophy). It is to say that we may not assume at the outset that such principles are clearly correct and determine in advance what is to count as rational. We should thus not look to formal logic to provide a standard by which to establish whether Hegel's arguments in the *Logic* are rational (or, more likely, by which to judge that they are sophistical). As G. R. G. Mure remarks, "to exempt a principle from criticism and presuppose it as a criterion by which to condemn a logical method is grossly and barbarously to beg the question"; and if there is one thing that a truly *critical* philosopher may not do, in Hegel's view, it is "beg the question."[3]

To philosophize without presuppositions is thus not to reject in advance all that traditionally counts as "thought," "concept," or "rationality." It is merely to suspend our familiar assumptions about thought and to look to discover in the course of the science of logic *whether or not* they will prove to be correct. A science of logic has to set our familiar assumptions to one side at the beginning because *it* is to be the very discipline that determines what it is to think and

---

2. See F. W. J. von Schelling, *On the History of Modern Philosophy,* trans. A. Bowie (Cambridge: Cambridge University Press, 1994), p. 148; F. A. Trendelenburg, *The Logical Question in Hegel's System,* in G. W. F. Hegel: *Critical Assessments,* ed. R. Stern, 4 vols. (London: Routledge, 1993), 1: 205; and S. Kierkegaard, *Concluding Unscientific Postscript,* trans. D. F. Swenson and W. Lowrie (Princeton: Princeton University Press, 1968), p. 101.

3. See G. R. G. Mure, *A Study of Hegel's Logic* (1950) (Westport, Conn.: Greenwood Press, 1984), p. 33. See also J. Burbidge, *On Hegel's Logic: Fragments of a Commentary* (Atlantic Highlands, N.J.: Humanities Press, 1981), p. 4: "To evaluate Hegel's logic against the conventional standards of formal logic begs the question. For Hegel is asking about the grounds of all logical validity."

which categories and laws (if any) are inherent in thought as such. Critics of Hegel from Schopenhauer to Popper may rail against him for deliberately violating the law of noncontradiction (and muddling young heads in the process), but Hegel does not have it in mind deliberately to reject any of the traditional laws of thought. In fact, he is himself extremely critical of what he perceives to be the "crude rejection of all method" in the work of Romantics such as Friedrich Schlegel (*SL* 53/1: 49). His point is simply that "logic . . . cannot *presuppose* any of these forms of reflection and laws of thinking, for these constitute part of its own content and have first to be established within the science" (*SL* 43/1: 35, my emphasis). Consequently, he has to be open at the start of the *Logic* to the possibility that the traditional laws of thought may, *or may not*, govern thought, properly understood. If Hegel's *Logic* does turn out to violate the law of noncontradiction, therefore—and I am not here assuming that it does—it will be because thought *proves* not to be completely governed by that law, not because Hegel has simply decided to abandon it.

At this point, we need to consider one obvious question. If we are to examine thought without presupposing that it has any particular structure, operates with any particular concepts, or is governed by any particular rules, what are we to understand thought to be? What is to be the object of our examination? What is thought *minimally*? Hegel's answer is indicated by his statement in §78 of the *Encyclopedia Logic* that the "freedom that abstracts from everything . . . grasps its own pure abstraction, the simplicity of thinking" (*EL* 124/168). In Hegel's view, free, self-critical thought that suspends all its presuppositions about itself is left with nothing to think but itself, its own simple *being*. To put it another way (suggested by a perceptive comment by Ute Guzzoni), thought that sets aside all its assumptions about *what* it is, is left with nothing to think but the simple thought *that* it is.[4] Hegel's presuppositionless science of logic begins, therefore, with the thought of thought itself as simply *being*—not being anything in particular but simply *be-ing* as such. Consequently, the first category considered by Hegel in the *Logic* is that of sheer indeterminate being *tout court*. At the outset, Hegel says, all that is present

> is simply the resolve . . . that we propose to consider thought as such (*das Denken als solches*). Thus the beginning . . . *may not presuppose anything* . . . Consequently, it must be purely and simply *an* immediacy, or rather merely *immediacy* itself. . . . The beginning therefore is *pure being* (*das reine Sein*). (*SL* 70/1: 68–9 [175])

The path of "universal doubt" that leads into Hegel's science of logic is clearly very similar to that taken by Descartes. Hegel's conclusion, however, is

---

4. U. Guzzoni, *Werden zu sich. Eine Untersuchung zu Hegels "Wissenschaft der Logik"* (Freiburg/München: Verlag Karl Alber, 1963), p. 35.

not "I think, therefore I am" but rather "thinking, therefore *is*."[5] From this pure being of thought, Hegel believes, the necessary categories of thought have to be derived.

Does Hegel Have a Method?

We will look at the beginning of Hegel's *Logic* in more detail later in this study. What I now wish to draw attention to is another important—and potentially rather disturbing—consequence of Hegel's commitment to radical presuppositionlessness. Not only must we begin by conceiving thought itself as wholly indeterminate being, but we must also conduct our own examination of thought without assuming that it should take any particular course or follow any particular rule of procedure. As Richard Winfield puts it, our examination of thought "cannot be guided or legitimated by any propositional calculus, rules of syllogism, logic of discovery, semantic analysis, or doctrine of intentionality," for none of these can be assumed at the outset to have any validity.[6] This is not to say that Hegel should adopt no *method* whatsoever in his *Logic*. But his method can consist in nothing more than considering indeterminate being itself and setting out what, if anything, the thought of such being involves. That is to say, after he has "abstracted" from everything, his method must be simply "to take up *what is there before us*" and calmly "observe" it (*zusehen*).[7] Hegel may not assume, however, that we are to proceed beyond that initial consideration of indeterminate being according to any prescribed rules, nor indeed that we are to proceed beyond that thought at all, for to do so would be to take too much for granted.

This means—though it may surprise some to hear it—that Hegel may not presuppose that we are to proceed *dialectically* in the *Logic* by showing, say, how one category passes over into, or contains, its opposite and then is taken up with that opposite into a third category that synthesizes the first two. The indeterminate concept of being may well prove on further examination to be dialectical and to disappear into the concept of nothing, but we may not assume at the outset that this will be the case or that our method should be to look for such dialectical slippage in other categories. All we may do is consider the concept of indeterminate being and note what, if anything, that concept *itself* turns out to be or do.

---

5. See *The Philosophical Writings of Descartes*, trans. J. Cottingham, R. Stoothoff, D. Murdoch, 3 vols. (Cambridge: Cambridge University Press, 1984–91), 1: 196 (*Principles of Philosophy*, 1: 10)

6. R. Winfield, *Reason and Justice* (Albany: SUNY Press, 1988), p. 142.

7. Hegel, *SL* 69/1: 68 (175), and G. W. F. Hegel, *Vorlesungen über Logik und Metaphysik. Heidelberg 1817*, ed. K. Gloy, *Ausgewählte Nachschriften und Manuskripte*, vol. 11 (Hamburg: Felix Meiner, 1992), p. 21. Further references to the *Vorlesungen über Logik und Metaphysik* will be given in the following form: *VLM* 21. Phenomenology, for Hegel, also requires us "simply to look on (*zusehen*)" while consciousness develops itself immanently; see *PhS* 85/77.

William Maker is thus right, in my view, to maintain that Hegel does not have a dialectical or speculative method, "insofar as one uses the term 'method' in its traditional philosophical sense" to mean a rule of procedure that can be specified *prior* to its application to a given content:

> Insofar as method is that which can—even if only in principle—be justified, formulated or learned in abstraction from the subject matter to which it is to be applied, Hegel does not have a method. . . . Insofar as one can speak of there being, in the sense just outlined, a phenomenological method, a scientific method, a transcendental method, an analytical method, a speculative method, and so on, Hegel does not have a method.[8]

Many commentators on Hegel—both friendly and not so friendly—find it very hard indeed to believe such a claim. Surely, they say, the discovery of dialectical method is one of Hegel's great achievements, the lasting legacy he passed on (albeit in a modified form) to Marx, Engels, Adorno, and many others. Is it possible that the very idea of a definite Hegelian dialectical method is misconceived? Michael Forster, to name but one, seems quite convinced that Hegel devises a general philosophical method whose structure can be described in abstraction from, and prior to, any particular Hegelian analysis and which can then be "applied" to all manner of natural and spiritual phenomena. "Beginning from a category A," Forster tells us,

> Hegel seeks to show that upon conceptual analysis, category A proves to contain a *contrary* category, B, and conversely that category B proves to contain category A, thus showing both categories to be self-contradictory. He then seeks to show that this negative result has a positive outcome, a new category, C . . . This new category unites—as Hegel puts it—the preceding categories A and B.[9]

Forster claims that the analysis of the category of being at the beginning of the *Logic* provides a "textbook example" of this "general model" but that we can also draw on that model to highlight the inadequacies of many of Hegel's other analyses.[10] For "over large stretches of his texts," Forster maintains, Hegel "deviates from the intended general structure of the method in more or less extreme ways." This is already noticeable in the transition from the category of becoming to that of determinate being,

> where, instead of showing Becoming and a contrary category to be mutually implying and then showing them to be unified in Determinate Be-

---

8. W. Maker, *Philosophy Without Foundations: Rethinking Hegel* (Albany: SUNY Press, 1994), pp. 99–100.

9. M. Forster, "Hegel's Dialectical Method," in *The Cambridge Companion to Hegel*, ed. F. C. Beiser (Cambridge: Cambridge University Press, 1993), p. 132.

10. Forster, "Hegel's Dialectical Method," p. 133.

> ing, Hegel tries to find a contradiction between two component concepts contained in the category Becoming and then argues that these two component concepts are unified in Determinate Being.[11]

Later in the *Logic*, we are told, in the discussion of the forms of judgment and syllogism, "there is hardly even a trace of the official method." Forster thus belongs to that well-established tradition of commentators who seek to criticize and correct Hegel's specific analyses of concepts by measuring them against what they take to be his general philosophical method.[12] In my view, however, if Hegel's philosophy is to be genuinely presuppositionless, as he proclaims it to be, then it cannot presuppose at the outset any general conception of dialectical (or any other kind of) method that is to be "applied" in particular cases. It is thus wholly illegitimate to criticize specific Hegelian analyses by reference to such a general method. As we shall see, Forster is quite right to note that Hegel's analysis of becoming does not proceed in exact accordance with the model that Forster himself sets up. But he is quite wrong to believe that matters: for in a genuinely presuppositionless philosophy we have no right to assume in advance any general model as a standard by which to evaluate Hegel's particular arguments. We are not to assume, therefore, that the *Logic* is structured according to the famous pattern of thesis, antithesis, and synthesis, nor indeed that Hegel arranges concepts in any other, more subtle, triadic sequence. We have simply to consider indeterminate being and observe how, if at all, it develops.

Now, as I have indicated, to insist that Hegel presupposes no dialectical method in his *Logic* is not to deny that indeterminate being may itself *prove* to be dialectical and to give rise to further categories that themselves turn dialectically into yet others. Dialectic may well *turn out*, therefore, to be the proper method for philosophical thought. Indeed, as we shall see, Hegel believes this to be the case—but this is only because thought is required to become dialectical by the concepts it is led to consider, not because dialectic is assumed in advance to be a "higher" way of thinking. Dialectic is thus "not brought to bear on the thought-determinations from outside; on the contrary, it must be considered as dwelling within them" (*EL* 82/114 [§41 Add. 1]). As we shall see, Hegel's *Logic* does proceed in accordance with dialectical method after all, but such method is not a "'method' in its traditional philosophical sense" (to quote Maker), because it is not a manner of thinking that is *applied* by Hegel to a given subject matter, such as thought, and that could be applied by someone else (for example, Engels) to nature or human history. It is, rather, the manner in

11. Forster, "Hegel's Dialectical Method," p. 155.

12. In a similar spirit Gerhard Martin Wölfle proposes to revise Hegel's doctrine of essence in light of what he believes Hegel *should* be doing; see G. M. Wölfle, *Die Wesenslogik in Hegels "Wissenschaft der Logik"* (Stuttgart-Bad Cannstatt: Frommann-Holzboog, 1994). For my review of Wölfle's book, see *Bulletin of the Hegel Society of Great Britain* 32 (Autumn/Winter 1995): 40–7.

which concepts themselves develop and demand to be thought—"the method proper to every subject matter" (*SL* 826/2: 552). Dialectical method thus is not *Hegel's* method but the method or manner of development that proves to be inherent in presuppositionless thought itself: "the nature of the content itself which spontaneously develops itself in a scientific method of knowing" (*SL* 27/1: 16).[13]

Since dialectical "method" is nothing but the manner in which the category of being develops into further categories, we can only understand what that method is supposed to be as we come to understand that course of development. There can be no *prior* understanding of that method, such as Michael Forster pretends to offer. In other words, the method of dialectic cannot be anticipated or predicted; it can only be discovered as we follow the movement from the category of being to that of becoming, determinate being, and so on. "What logic is cannot be stated beforehand, rather does this knowledge of what it is first emerge as the final outcome and consummation of the whole exposition" (*SL* 43/1: 35).[14] This means that prior to any particular transition in the *Logic,* we have no model available by which to judge how that transition *should* proceed. All we know is how previous transitions have proceeded; but we do not know that future transitions should take a similar course. Nor, of course, are we allowed to judge any particular transition in the *Logic* by reference to traditional criteria of rationality. We cannot fault a transition for violating the law of non-contradiction or for failing to meet the traditional standards required for valid deduction or induction because we are not permitted to take any such criteria for granted in a fully self-critical philosophy.

But if we cannot evaluate Hegel's arguments by reference to traditional standards of rationality or by reference to any preconceived notion of dialectic, how is it possible to criticize what he says at all? Can presuppositionless thought be criticized, or is it simply beyond all reproach by definition? What is so disturbing about Hegel's insistence on presuppositionlessness is that it appears to render his philosophy invulnerable to any rational critique.

Hegel's Rejection of External Criticism

As we shall see in a moment, Hegel by no means puts his philosophy beyond all criticism. He clearly recognizes that his derivation of the categories of thought in the *Logic* might need improvement, and indeed he laments the fact that he does not have the leisure to revise the text himself "seven and seventy times"

---

13. See also Hegel, *SL* 53, 830/1: 49, 2: 556, and A. White, *Absolute Knowledge: Hegel and the Problem of Metaphysics* (Athens, Ohio: Ohio University Press, 1983), p. 51.

14. See also D. Henrich, "Hegels Logik der Reflexion. Neue Fassung," in *Die Wissenschaft der Logik und die Logik der Reflexion*, ed. D. Henrich, *Hegel-Studien* Beiheft 18 (Bonn: Bouvier Verlag, 1978), pp. 223–5.

(*SL* 42/1: 33; see also *SL* 31, 54/1: 19, 50). He does, however, unequivocally reject all criticisms levelled at his philosophy from a standpoint other than that of presuppositionless thought itself. That is to say, he rejects what has come to be called all "external criticism" of his philosophy. Hegel does not, therefore, recognize as legitimate any criticism that charges him with riding roughshod over basic conceptual distinctions (for example, between what is finite and what is infinite), with confusing the "is" of predication with the "is" of identity, or with simply contradicting himself, if the critics concerned base those charges on the authority of formal logic or tradition and fail to show that the development of presuppositionless thought itself leads to the prohibiting of contradiction or conceptual "confusion."

Hegel's rejection of external criticism of his system is sometimes taken to rest on his own unjustified *assumptions* about philosophical thought. Hegel (so the story goes) simply takes it for granted that thought is dialectical or "absolute," erects an entire philosophical system on that assumption, and rejects in advance any criticisms that are not made from within the "superior" standpoint of that dialectical system. Michael Rosen, for example, claims that Hegel only overcomes the challenge of skepticism by integrating it (in the *Phenomenology*) "into the course of an exposition which *presupposes* determinate negation [the thesis that negation always has a positive result] for its very possibility."[15] Similarly, Jürgen Habermas maintains that Hegel's rejection of Kant's critical limitation of human knowledge "already *presupposes* precisely what this for its part calls into question: the possibility of absolute knowing."[16] This interpretation also dominates much contemporary French reading of Hegel. In *Writing and Difference,* for example, Jacques Derrida insists that "the Hegelian *Aufhebung* is produced entirely from *within* discourse, from *within* the system or the work of signification" and that it thus "belongs to restricted economy."[17]

In my view, however, the interpretation of Hegel put forward by writers such as Rosen, Habermas, and Derrida, though popular, is in fact quite wrong. Hegel does not reject external criticism of his philosophy from *within* a dialectical system whose validity he presupposes, nor does he reject such criticism simply because its proponents fail to acknowledge some "higher" principle of dialectic that he himself takes for granted. He cannot be doing this because he does

---

15. M. Rosen, *Hegel's Dialectic and its Criticism* (Cambridge: Cambridge University Press, 1982), p. 42, my emphasis; on determinate negation, see p. 31. For my review of Rosen's book, see S. Houlgate, "Some Notes on Michael Rosen's *Hegel's Dialectic and its Criticism*," *Hegel-Studien* 20 (1985): 213–19.

16. J. Habermas, *Erkenntnis und Interesse* (Frankfurt am Main: Suhrkamp Verlag, 1968), p. 21, my emphasis, my translation.

17. J. Derrida, *Writing and Difference*, trans. A. Bass (London: Routledge and Kegan Paul, 1978), p. 275, my emphasis. On the relation between Hegel and Derrida more generally, see S. Houlgate, "Hegel, Derrida, and Restricted Economy: The Case of Mechanical Memory," *Journal of the History of Philosophy* 34, 1 (January 1996): 79–93.

not begin by *presupposing* the viewpoint of dialectic, determinate negation or the "system" at all; he begins, rather, by *suspending* all presuppositions and assumptions about thought. For Hegel, if philosophical thought is to be fully self-critical and free, it can accept nothing on authority or as simply given and so can take nothing for granted about thought itself except its sheer indeterminate being; it must, in other words, be radically presuppositionless. But if thoroughly self-critical thinking suspends all presuppositions in this way, then any criticism levelled at Hegel from a position other than that of radically presuppositionless thought will necessarily stem from a thinking that is *less* self-critical and so more dogmatic than presuppositionless thought itself. This is the case because any such thinking by definition will uncritically presuppose some principle or other. It is for this reason, and this reason alone, that Hegel rejects all external criticism of his philosophy.

It can be very frustrating for someone approaching Hegel for the first time to be told constantly that this or that criticism made from an Aristotelian, Kantian, or Derridean point of view, or from the viewpoint of formal or symbolic logic, is illegitimate. (I am acutely aware of the evident frustration of some of my own students every time I teach the *Logic*.) But it is important to recognize that Hegel rules such criticism out of order *not* in the name of certain principles of nontraditional thinking that he has simply assumed—uncritically—to be authoritative but in the name of the most radical and thorough self-criticism he can conceive. In other words, Hegel rejects external criticism of his philosophy because he believes that one cannot legitimately criticize fully self-critical thinking from a position that is itself necessarily *less* than fully self-critical.

This explanation of, and justification for, Hegel's rejection of all external criticism of his philosophy is not the one that is usually found in the secondary literature. More common is the claim made by Michael Rosen that Hegel dismisses or "overcomes" alternative points of view on the basis of his own conviction or assumption that thought is in truth dialectical or speculative. Yet it is clear on any attentive reading of the *Logic* that Hegel does not charge his critics with being insufficiently dialectical or with failing to raise themselves to the position of the "absolute." He charges them only with being insufficiently *critical* of the presuppositions on the basis of which they formulate their own criticisms of him—that is to say, with taking too much for granted themselves. For example, in the preface to the second edition of the *Logic*, he charges certain unnamed critics with presupposing that the basic categories of thought are set in a fixed, determinate relation to one another and that categories (such as "reality" and "negation" or "finitude" and "infinity"), which are usually held to be opposed to one another, are indeed definitively opposed. In ordinary discourse such assumptions would be unobjectionable. Hegel considers them to be inappropriate for critics of the *Logic*, however, because the whole point of the *Logic* is to seek to discover—without taking anything for granted—*whether* the presumed opposition between categories such as "finitude" and "infinity" is defini-

tive or not. To criticize a philosophy whose task is precisely to find out how the categories are to be conceived on the basis of the uncritical assumption that they are to be conceived in a certain way is, from Hegel's point of view, to miss the point of the exercise he is undertaking and to bring dogmatic prejudgment—indeed prejudice—to bear on an enterprise that demands complete openness of mind. Remember that Hegel is not claiming that his critics are obviously wrong in their understanding of the categories and laws of thought. He is simply pointing out that such critics are less self-critical in their approach to the categories than he is (and than they should and could be) because they do not first set their assumptions about thought to one side and then seek to derive an understanding of the categories from the simple being of thought. He is also claiming that it is illegitimate for such insufficiently self-critical philosophers to criticize his efforts to *discover* the true character of the categories on the basis of what they in advance *assume* the categories to be.

Hegel admits that his critics are often unaware that they are taking a great deal for granted in their criticisms of him, but he still takes them to task for presupposing what he is seeking without prejudgment to discover:

> I have been only too often and too vehemently attacked by opponents who were incapable of making the simple reflection that their opinions and objections contain categories which are presuppositions and which themselves need to be criticized first before they are employed. Ignorance in this matter reaches incredible lengths. . . . Such presuppositions as that infinity is different from finitude, that content is other than form, that the inner is other than the outer, also that mediation is not immediacy (as if anyone did not know these things), are brought forward by way of information and narrated and asserted rather than proved. But there is something stupid (*eine Albernheit*)——I can find no other word for it—about this didactic behaviour; technically it is unjustifiable simply to presuppose and straightway assume (*vorauszusetzen und geradezu anzunehmen*) such propositions; and, still more, it reveals ignorance of the fact that it is the requirement and the business of logical thinking to enquire into just this, whether such a finite without infinity is something true, or whether such an abstract infinity, also a content without form and a form without content, an inner by itself which has no outer expression, an externality without an inwardness, whether any of these is *something true* or *something actual*. (*SL* 40–2/1: 31–3)

In his detailed and meticulous study of the criticisms levelled at the *Logic* by Hegel's contemporaries Schelling, Weisse, I. H. Fichte, Fries, Herbart, Schubarth, and Carganico, Bernd Burkhardt has shown that Hegel is quite right to accuse his critics of failing to call their own presuppositions into question. Those critics all dismissed as impossible Hegel's project of a "consideration of the thought-determinations in and for themselves," but in so doing, Burkhardt

points out, they "showed no readiness to submit the presuppositions . . . in their objections to a critical examination and so, at least formally, to take Hegel's claim to presuppositionlessness and immanent self-criticism seriously."[18] To my mind, Hegel's charge can be levelled as well at those who have continued to criticize him after his death. To the extent that they proceed from some tacit or explicitly acknowledged assumptions about thought and so do not suspend all such assumptions, they necessarily fall short of what, according to Hegel, is demanded of a modern, self-critical philosophy. Whether they part company with Hegel because they assume (with Marx) that thought is conditioned by social and economic practices or (with Nietzsche) that thought is an expression of the will to power or (with many contemporary analytic philosophers) that thought is governed by the rules of formal or symbolic logic makes little difference. In every case they base their criticisms of Hegel (and their own further philosophizing) on *presuppositions* that they do not call into question or suspend and in this respect remain less self-critical than Hegel in his *Logic*. Strange though it will seem to many to say so, most, if not all, post-Hegelian philosophy is thus in fact logically *pre-Hegelian* in that it has still to carry out the radical self-criticism that is demanded of any modern philosophy and that Hegel endeavors to carry out in his *Logic*.

On my reading, Hegel's *Logic* is not some relic from a bygone age of naive metaphysical speculation or grandiose system-building but *the* quintessentially modern philosophy and the model for all post-Hegelian thinkers. It is the open-minded, thoroughly self-critical enquiry into the nature of thought that seeks to discover, without prejudging the issue, what it is to think. The radicality of the challenge posed by Hegel's *Logic* to modern philosophers has, however, all too often been obscured by interpreters, such as Rosen and Habermas, who insist—against the clear evidence of Hegel's own text—that Hegel's *Logic* is in fact a closed system founded on questionable and now outdated assumptions of its own.

My aim in this study is to draw attention once more to the radicality of Hegel's project. Furthermore, it is to explain how, according to Hegel, a fully self-critical, presuppositionless philosophy proceeds and what it reveals about the basic categories of thought. If readers of this study are to understand the significance, indeed the revolutionary import, of Hegel's philosophy, they must take seriously his demand that thought suspend its assumptions about itself. They do not have to disengage their critical faculty altogether; they do not simply have to give themselves over to the authority of Hegel or of anyone else. But they do need to be as self-critical as possible in their reading of Hegel. This means that they must continually ask themselves whether their objections to a given Hegelian claim are based on an informed understanding of what Hegel, on

18. B. Burkhardt, *Hegels "Wissenschaft der Logik" im Spannungsfeld der Kritik* (Hildesheim: Georg Olms, 1993), p. 527, my translation.

his own terms, is or is not entitled to say or whether they simply rest on assumptions made from an external (e.g., an Aristotelian, Kantian, or Wittgensteinian) point of view. Those who are tempted to dismiss the very idea of a presuppositionless philosophy as preposterous must also ask themselves whether their anti-Hegelian conviction that assumptions and presuppositions are unavoidable is itself anything more than an uncritical presupposition.

We should also be on our guard against the assumptions that are hidden in what appear to be the simplest and most innocent of questions—questions that any rational person might raise, such as "*what* is 'being,' according to Hegel?" This question is natural, but it is by no means as innocent and neutral as it appears. In Hegel's view, "the question: *what*?" actually contains a very significant assumption because it "demands that *determinations* be assigned" (*SL* 121/1: 130 [217]). It demands that something at hand be determined in one way or another (as this or that) and so presupposes that what is asked about can in fact be so determined. Being, however, is initially understood by Hegel not to be something *determinate*—not to be a "what" or an "it"—but to be sheer *indeterminacy* or utterly "indeterminate immediacy" (*SL* 82/1: 82 [193]). The simple question "*what* is 'being,' according to Hegel?" thus always risks distorting the very thing it asks after, for it presupposes in its very form that being is not sheer indeterminacy but rather *something determinate*. Now, to point to this presupposition in the question "*what*?" is not to say that the question should never be posed; that question is, as I have suggested, perfectly natural. But it is to urge self-critical caution on those who pose this question and to enjoin them to bracket out in their minds the assumption the question contains. In other words, it is to enjoin them to ask the question "*what*?" without automatically assuming that what is asked after is necessarily a "what" itself.

If readers of Hegel's *Logic* are to be thoroughly self-critical, they have no alternative but to set aside *all* their presuppositions about thought, its categories, and rules. This means that no external critique of Hegel's *Logic* based on such presuppositions can have legitimacy. But it does not mean that Hegel's work is beyond all criticism whatsoever, for that work remains vulnerable to criticism that is based on the requirements of presuppositionless thought itself, that is, *immanent* criticism. The method followed by presuppositionless thought is simply to render explicit or "unfold" what—if anything—is implicit in or entailed by the thought of sheer indeterminate being with which it begins. As Hegel insists in the *Encyclopedia Logic*, "the whole course of philosophising, being methodical, i.e., *necessary*, is nothing else but the mere *positing* of what is already contained in a concept" (*EL* 141/188 [§88]). No special intuition or privileged insight is needed to carry out this task. What is required is simply the ability to comprehend the definition of a concept and draw out what is implied in its definition. That is to say, what is required is *understanding*, of which Hegel thinks we are all capable. Philosophy, for Hegel, is thus an exoteric, public activity in which any rational person can participate; it is not the "esoteric possession of a

few individuals" (*PhS* 7, 43/20, 65) and certainly not the private property of G. W. F. Hegel. Consequently, any rational person can examine Hegel's account of what is implicit in the initial category of being (and the subsequent categories) and consider whether or not that account is correct. To the extent that Hegel does not in fact render explicit what is implicit in a specific category, he is open to criticism and correction by the reader. It is essential to remember, however, that the criterion to be employed in formulating such a criticism must be provided by the relevant category as it has been determined by presuppositionless thought and by that category alone. Such a criterion must thus be wholly *immanent* to presuppositionless thought.

The task of the fully self-critical reader of the *Logic* is thus not to adduce alternative arguments against which to test Hegel's own but to follow the course of and "advance together with" (*mitfortschreiten*) what is immanent in each category, making sure that Hegel adheres rigorously to what is required by presuppositionless thought (*EL* 17/31). If Hegel does not do this and either fails to draw out the evident implications of a category or moves from one category to another on the basis of extraneous considerations (such as metaphorical association or the simple desire to press on), then he is subject to criticism. But if Hegel does in fact keep rigorously to these requirements, then he can claim to have demonstrated successfully without taking anything for granted at the outset what it is to think and to have completed the task (bequeathed to him by Kant and Fichte) of deriving the basic categories and laws of thought from the very nature of thought. As Richard Winfield writes:

> So long as examination shows that not one of the development's determinations owes its character or order of presentation to introductions of extraneously given material or the stipulating of an extraneous determiner, the development can be said to exhibit the radically independent immanence that alone can signal its freedom from arbitrary direction and dogmatic foundations.[19]

Hegel remarks at the beginning of the Subjective Logic, concerning his own critique of Spinoza, that "genuine refutation must penetrate the opponent's stronghold and meet him on his own ground" (*SL* 581/2: 250). It is clear also that legitimate criticism of Hegel can be made only by one who is prepared to meet Hegel (or rather presuppositionless thought) on his (its) own ground. Such criticism can thus only be advanced by someone who accepts the demand for presuppositionlessness, recognizes what it requires of the thinker, and carries this out better than Hegel himself. Although Hegel has sometimes been accused of "Teutonic arrogance," he never claims that his presentation of the progressive development of presuppositionless thinking in the *Logic* is beyond improvement by himself or by others. "I could not pretend," he writes, "that the method which

---

19. Winfield, *Reason and Justice*, p. 130. See also White, *Absolute Knowledge*, p. 36.

I follow in this system of logic—or rather which this system in its own self follows—is not capable of greater completeness, of much elaboration in detail" (*SL* 54/1: 50). But, he goes on, "at the same time I know that it is the only true method"—because he sees no alternative for philosophy in the modern world than to undertake a fully self-critical study of thought that suspends all previous assumptions about thought and draws out patiently and carefully the categories that are immanent and implicit in the sheer indeterminate *being* of thought itself. For Hegel, therefore, this "altogether new concept of scientific procedure" is the one on which philosophy "in future must always be based" (*SL* 27, 48/1: 16, 42).

Dialectic and Immanent Development

The details of Hegel's new scientific procedure will be examined later in this study, as we discover how the indeterminate thought of being develops, but for the benefit of new readers of the *Logic*, I shall outline its principal features in advance. It should be obvious that my remarks are intended not to set out the way in which Hegel's *Logic should* proceed but merely to provide a general description for the newcomer of how the *Logic* does actually proceed.

The first thing to note is that this procedure shows the categories of thought to be dialectical. That is to say, it demonstrates that, when properly understood, each category (starting with the initial indeterminate thought of being) turns before our very eyes into its own negation. As Hegel puts it, each category or "universal . . . , *considered in and for itself*, shows itself to be the other of itself" (*SL* 833–4/2: 561). The thought of sheer *being* immediately vanishes into the thought of *nothing*, the thought of *something* passes over into the thought of what is *other*, and the category of *finitude* turns into the category of *infinity*. No category simply is what it is, therefore, but each negates itself through what it is into its negation. Such dialectical slippage is not imported into the categories by the philosopher, according to Hegel, but is revealed to be the truth of each category by close and careful study of its structure. It is thus the dialectic that is inherent in thought itself—"the inwardness of the content, the dialectic which it possesses within itself" (*SL* 54/1: 50; see also *EL* 128/172 [§81]).

There is little doubt that Hegel's insistence that the categories are dialectical is one of the things that most offends his critics about his philosophical system. This is because it so clearly runs counter to what Western philosophy has held to be true since Plato. Plato affirms that any individual thing can take on a form that is opposed to the one it already has. A thing can come to exhibit "beauty," for example, and thereby shed the form of "ugliness," or it can come to be the "same" as something else and cease being "different" from it. Indeed, it is only in this way, according to Plato, that individual things can change. But Plato insists that the forms taken on or shed by things cannot themselves change or turn into their opposites. The very form of beauty itself—what it is to be beautiful—cannot turn into or turn out to be the form of ugliness, and sameness cannot turn

into or turn out to be difference. Such forms are thus opposed to one another and simply are what they are. As Socrates puts it in the *Phaedo*, "the opposite itself could never come to be opposite to itself."[20] This understanding of forms and of universal concepts and categories has largely governed Western philosophy since Plato's day and also coincides with our ordinary intuitions about opposites.

In Hegel's view, however, even though Plato's position seems to be incontrovertible, we should not simply take it for granted in a fully self-critical philosophy. After all, the obvious may be misleading. Indeed, according to Hegel, presuppositionless thought actually shows that Plato's position is wrong, or rather only half right, for when it is properly understood, each "universal" or category *does* actually "sublate itself in itself and is in its own self the opposite of itself" (*SL* 106/1: 112 [199]). There is certainly a difference between the categories of being and nonbeing or between the categories of finitude and infinity; Hegel never denies that. (This is the respect in which Plato is half right.) But the remarkable insight provided by presuppositionless philosophy is that this difference is not absolute because being *itself* invests things with nonbeing (in the form of determinacy and finitude); to be something is *itself* always to be other than something else; and finitude *itself* turns out to constitute true infinity. This insight may well disturb many readers of Hegel, but if Hegel is to be believed, such readers can only turn their backs on his findings by clinging uncritically to what Plato and the tradition have *assumed* to be true.

The precise reason why a specific category entails its own opposite varies in each case, but the general idea remains the same: each category in *being* what it is contains within itself its *negative* (*SL* 55/1: 51). The moment of nonbeing or negation is thus not simply opposed to being or "external" to it but is immanent in being itself. To *be* such and such is at the same time and in the same respect *not* to be such and such. In this sense for Hegel, the concept of being is profoundly contradictory, but it is no less valid for that. The insight generated by presuppositionless thought thus not only challenges the Platonic orthodoxy (which governs any thinking, however anti-Platonic it may deem itself, that considers beauty to be simply different from ugliness or sameness to be simply different from difference); it also challenges the even more ancient assumption of Parmenides that being simply *is* and does not in any way involve nonbeing.

For Parmenides, "what is there to be said and thought must needs be: for it is there for being, but nothing is not."[21] True being is thus purely affirmative with no trace of negation or indeed change in it; it is "uncreated and imperishable."[22] This conception of being as purely affirmative continues to cast its shadow over

20. Plato, *Phaedo*, trans. D. Gallop (Oxford: Oxford University Press, 1993), p. 60 [103b]).

21. *The Presocratic Philosophers*, eds. G. S. Kirk, J. E. Raven, and M. Schofield (1957) (Cambridge: Cambridge University Press, 1983), p. 247.

22. *The Presocratic Philosophers*, p. 248.

subsequent philosophy right up to the modern period. It is to be seen, for example, in Spinoza's assertion that "the definition of any thing affirms, and does not deny, the thing's essence," and that consequently, "while we attend only to the thing itself, and not to external causes, we shall not be able to find anything in it which can destroy it."[23] (Spinoza talks here of "things" rather than being as such, but he remains recognizably Parmenidean to the extent that he thinks that things are not consigned to nonbeing and death through their very own being but can only be destroyed by something else outside them.)[24] Parmenides' conception of the purely affirmative character of being is also to be encountered in Descartes's idea of God as the supremely perfect being from whom no error, falsity, or defect can arise and in Kant's idea of God as the *ens realissimum*.[25]

This Parmenidean conception of being is undermined, however, by the whole course of presuppositionless thought. According to Hegel's account, the category of being proves to harbor within itself the moment of negation in several forms: the concept of reality entails negation in the form of determinacy and difference; being something entails negation in the form of otherness and finitude; and infinite being also contains negation insofar as it lives in and through self-negating, finite being.

Recall that in insisting on the immanence of negation in the category of being Hegel is not deliberately or wilfully rejecting the legacy of Parmenides or flouting the law of noncontradiction. He is simply claiming that if we are prepared to suspend our cherished assumptions about thought (and about being) and follow the course laid down by presuppositionless thought itself, we will *discover* that the Parmenidean opposition between being and nonbeing is in fact unsustainable. The dialectical movement whereby a category turns through its very own structure into its opposite and so "shows itself to be the other of itself" (*SL* 833–4/2: 561) will certainly bewilder or annoy the reader of Hegel's *Logic* who wishes to maintain as absolute and unsurpassable the conceptual distinctions drawn by Parmenides and Plato (and common sense). For those, however, who are prepared to be guided, surprised, and transformed by the course of presuppositionless thinking, that dialectical movement proves to be the profound truth that such thinking brings to the fore but that the tradition of Western philosophy has largely overlooked.

It cannot be emphasized enough that that dialectical movement, dynamism, and "life-pulse" (*SL* 37/1: 27), is, in Hegel's view, inherent in the categories themselves. It is not some generalized "Heraclitean" flux attributed to the cate-

---

23. *A Spinoza Reader. The Ethics and Other Works*, ed. E. Curley (Princeton: Princeton University Press, 1994), p. 159 (*Ethics* III P4 Dem).

24. See Hegel, *SL* 94–5/1: 98: "with Parmenides as with Spinoza, there is no progress from being or absolute substance to the negative."

25. See *The Philosophical Writings of Descartes*, 1: 130, and Kant, *CPR* 556–8/555–8 (B604–8).

gories by Hegel but "the spontaneous movement of the moments" (*die eigene Bewegung der Momente*) (*SL* 75/1: 75 [183])[26]—the movement whereby each category turns into its negation simply by virtue of what it is *itself*. True, it falls to the philosopher to render explicit the self-negation that is implicit in a specific category, but the activity of the philosopher in so doing is determined by the nature of the categories themselves. Progress in the *Logic* is thus generated by nothing other than the tension intrinsic to the initial indeterminate thought of being and the subsequent categories to which it gives rise, and in this sense, it is nothing but the immanent unfolding or (self-) development of the opening category—the "movement of *being* itself" (*SL* 79/1: 80 [191]).

We do not advance in the *Logic*, therefore, by simply replacing an initial incorrect definition of being with a more adequate one or substituting different categories for a concept of being that proves to be too abstract (though it can appear to the untrained eye that that is what is going on). We advance in the *Logic* by specifying more clearly what is entailed by the initial indeterminate thought of being itself. That is to say, "the *progress* from that which forms the beginning is to be regarded as only a *further determination* (*weitere Bestimmung*) of it" (*SL* 71/1: 71 [177], my emphasis). In the course of this further determination of being (or, indeed, self-determination of being), new concepts do arise that go beyond the mere thought of being as such. The thought of being is not simply replaced by those new concepts, however, but itself becomes more complex and concrete in them (see *SL* 48, 840/1: 41, 2: 569). The thought of being thus itself gains what Hegel calls "extension" and "intensity" as what "being" actually means becomes more and more apparent in the new concepts that arise (*SL* 841/2: 570). We learn, for example, that to be is not just to *be* but to be *determinate*, to be *something*, to be *limited*, to be *finite*, to be part of the process of *infinity*, and so on. Each thought is a new thought that has not been entertained before by presuppositionless thought, but each new thought or category arises by simply refining the initial indeterminate conception of being. In the course of the *Logic*, therefore, the thought of being *itself* turns into all the other categories of thought through its own internal dynamic.

The most striking characteristic of Hegel's *Logic* is thus that the initial category of being is actually *transformed* as it comes to be understood. Each new category or determination of being casts the thought of being in a new light and reveals it to be somewhat different from the way it was previously thought. Initially, the thought of being is taken to be just that—the thought of simple, immediate *being*. But on closer examination, the thought of being turns out not just to be that after all but to be the thought of determinacy, finitude, infinity, quantity, specificity, reflexivity, and eventually at the end of the *Logic*, self-determining reason (or "absolute Idea") and nature. In the course of being un-

26. Translation revised.

derstood, therefore, the concept of being becomes steadily more complex and gradually *changes into* the concept of nature.

This process of conceptual (self-) transformation clearly distinguishes Hegel's *Logic* from a more conventional philosophical text, such as Leibniz's *Monadology*. In Leibniz's text, we begin with a definition of a monad (namely, that it is a "simple substance"), and we proceed through ninety paragraphs to learn more about the nature of such monads. At the end of Leibniz's analysis, we know much more than we did at the beginning, but in the process monads never cease being understood as monads; they do not turn out in the end to be anything other than they were first thought to be. They remain the fixed subjects of Leibniz's discourse, and his philosophical procedure is to provide us with a more sophisticated account of such fixed subjects. Hegel's procedure is different, for we begin with the concept of being, but the thought of being transforms itself in the process into the thought of becoming, infinity, and so on. We thus do not simply learn more about a subject that is clearly identified to begin with; on the contrary, the true subject matter of the *Logic* only becomes apparent *through* Hegel's analysis. (It is because the subject matter of Hegelian philosophy is not given at the outset but unfolds itself and emerges in the course of philosophy itself that it has to be presented by means of curious verbal nouns such as "coming-to-self" [*Zu-sich-selbst-Kommen*] [*SL* 841/2: 571].)[27]

Many philosophers talk about the omnipresence of change and flux in the world, but few enact that process in their own texts. The distinctive feature of Hegel's thought is that it does not merely describe but actually articulates before our very eyes the process whereby concepts change into one another. In my view, unless one is prepared to move *with* that change and allow one's understanding to be constantly challenged and revised by these concepts themselves, one will never appreciate fully what Hegel discloses about thought.

In the process of conceptual (self-) transformation that Hegel articulates, earlier determinations of being are not simply left behind or set to one side but are taken up, or *aufgehoben*, into the more complex determinations that emerge. The concept of finitude thus incorporates the concepts of immediate being, determinacy, something, and limit (to be finite, after all, is to be limited, to be something, to be determinate, and indeed, to *be*). Similarly, the thought of infinity incorporates the thought of finitude, and the thought of the absolute Idea incorporates all the previous categories set out in the *Logic*. Thus, not only does "that which forms the starting point of the development [the category of 'being'] remain at the base of all that follows and . . . not vanish from it" (*SL* 71/1: 71 [177]), but in the case of every categorical transition "the first [category] is essentially *preserved* and *retained* even in the other" (*SL* 834, 840/2: 561, 569).

27. Miller's translation actually dispenses with the verbal noun and has "because truth only comes to be itself." The German text is: "weil die Wahrheit nur das Zu-sich-selbst-kommen. . . ist."

What becomes apparent in the course of the *Logic*, therefore, is that each category constitutes an irreducible element of our fundamental "conceptual scheme" yet none by itself defines or exhausts what it is to think. To think *is* to think in terms of being, determinacy, finitude, and infinity; it cannot be anything less or other than that. Yet it is not to think *just* of sheer being or *just* of determinacy, finitude or infinity, because none of these thoughts stands alone; each proves to be an aspect or a "moment" of a further, more complex thought, and all prove to be aspects of the thought with which the *Logic* culminates, that of the absolute Idea. The concluding insight of the *Logic*, therefore, is that thought, properly understood, entails *all* the general categories—taken together as a unity—that prove to be inherent in the initial thought of being.

As the category of sheer being gradually mutates into the concept of self-determining reason (or the "absolute Idea") and then into the concept of nature, two important things happen, according to Hegel. The first is that the initial category of being comes to be seen as an inadequate determination of what is being thought. Through the movement of thought, Hegel says, "the subject matter has obtained for itself a *determinateness* that is a *content*, . . . [and] as this determinateness is the proximate truth of the indeterminate beginning, it condemns the latter as something imperfect" (*SL* 838–9/2: 567). Hegel's language is not especially elegant, but his point is simple: insofar as the thought of being shows itself in truth to be the thought of the absolute Idea, it becomes clear that being is not thought properly insofar as it is thought merely *as* sheer being. The initial category of being is imperfect, therefore, because it fails to render explicit all that is entailed by the very thought of being itself. As Stace puts it, "in thinking of it simply as being we have not as yet seen the full truth about it, for we have not seen all that it contains."[28]

Indeed, not only is the opening category of being imperfect, but every category is imperfect compared to the more concrete determinations that emerge from it. This is not to say that we are simply in error to think in terms of relatively simple categories, such as "determinacy," "something," and "finitude." Being does entail being determinate, being something, and being finite, but as we learn from the rest of the *Logic*, that is not all it entails. For being also entails being quantitative, having proportion, form, content, appearing, being rational, being mechanical, chemical, and organic, and so on. The defect of categories, such as "determinacy" and "something," therefore, is that they *underdetermine* what it is to be or, in the words of Errol Harris, that they possess "a sort of vagueness or indeterminacy characteristic of the more primitive and rudimentary."[29] Indeed, compared to the thought of being as self-determining reason or

28. W. T. Stace, *The Philosophy of Hegel* (1924) (New York: Dover Publications, 1955), p. 109.

29. E. E. Harris, *An Interpretation of the Logic of Hegel* (Lanham, Md.: University Press of America, 1983), pp. 32–3.

Idea, *all* the categories of the *Logic* underdetermine being (just as the concept of being as rational Idea will prove to be an underdetermination of the concept of being as nature and as history).

The *error*, for Hegel, consists not in employing less determinate categories as such, but in regarding them as exhaustive or definitive conceptions of being and as exhausting what it is to think. The error, therefore, consists in claiming that being is finitude to the exclusion of infinity or that being is sheer quantity or that it is merely the expression of force or the work of power. Such errors are, of course, all too frequently encountered in both pre- and post-Hegelian philosophy. In exposing such errors, Hegel's *Logic* thus exercises a *critical*, as well as a revelatory, function.

Although earlier categories prove to be imperfect in comparison with later categories, the disclosure of such relative imperfection is *not* what drives thought on from one category to another in the first place. Thought does not compare a specific category with the absolute Idea, judge that category to be deficient, and then move on to a new category that better approximates to the Idea. Some commentators, however, have interpreted Hegel's *Logic* in precisely this way. J. M. E. McTaggart, for example, maintains that

> the motive force of the process lies in the discrepancy between the concrete and perfect idea implicitly in our own minds and the abstract and imperfect idea explicitly in our minds, and the essential characteristic of the process is in the search of this abstract and imperfect, not after its negation as such, but after its complement as such.[30]

But it is clear that this cannot be the way in which Hegel proceeds. The *Logic*, after all, sets out the course of *presuppositionless* thought. This means that no "concrete and perfect idea" can be presupposed at the outset as the standard against which to determine the relative adequacy or inadequacy of a specific category. The truth, Hegel says, cannot serve from the start of philosophy as the (implicit or explicit) criterion of judgment because "truth only comes to be itself through the negativity of immediacy" (*SL* 841/2: 571) and so is not present "in our minds" (either consciously or unconsciously) at the start. Consequently, the only thing that can drive thought forward in the *Logic* is the tension inherent *within* the specific category itself that is under consideration. As Hegel writes, "the immediate of the beginning must be *in its own self* deficient and endowed with the *urge* to carry itself further" (*SL* 829/2: 555). Similarly, each further category must develop into a new one through its own immanent dialectic. In this way, the categories must "investigate themselves, [and] they must determine their own limits and point out their own defects" (*EL* 82/114 [§41 Add. 1]).

---

30. J. M. E. McTaggart, "The Changes of Method in Hegel's Dialectic," in *G. W. F. Hegel. Critical Assessments*, 2: 70.

The progress of thought in the *Logic* must thus be a wholly immanent one. Once a more concrete conception of being has emerged, however, the one from which it emerged is automatically determined—retrospectively—to be an *underdetermination* of that more concrete concept. Categories *are* judged to be deficient in relation to subsequent categories, therefore, but this only occurs as a consequence of the development to which they first independently give rise. A later category, of which an earlier category proves to be an underdetermination, is itself nothing but a further determination *of* that earlier category.

The second thing that emerges as the category of sheer being mutates into the concept of reason or Idea is the insight that the concrete thought of the Idea is itself the ultimate logical *ground* of the initial indeterminate thought of being. What one might call the historical ground of the thought of pure being is the act of abstraction undertaken at the beginning of the *Logic* by the thinker who wishes to suspend all his or her assumptions about thought and discover from scratch what it is to think. (This historical ground is itself rational insofar as it follows logically from the modern demand for radical self-criticism, but it is still an historical act.) However, the ultimate (and purely) *logical* ground of the category of being—what makes that category absolutely necessary—is the thought of the Idea (or the concrete, rational unity of all the categories) that thought ultimately proves to be.

The important point to note about this thought of the Idea is that it can only emerge after all the other basic general (or pure) categories have been derived, because it is the unity of all those categories. It is thus not a thought with which philosophy can begin but one that can only be the *result* of the process of conceptual (self-) transformation that philosophy articulates. Since such a thought can only be a result, it must arise from a beginning in which it is not already present or presupposed, that is to say, from a beginning in which the various categories of thought that it incorporates are not yet explicitly conceived. Such a beginning must be the beginning of *thought* but can be no more than the *beginning* of thought. It is to be found, of course, in the thought of sheer indeterminate being. The very fact that the true, concrete character of thought can only *emerge as a result* through a process of conceptual derivation and so can never be understood immediately thus requires that it be derived from the least that thought can be: the simple thought of being. "The method of truth," Hegel writes, "knows the beginning to be incomplete, because it is a beginning; but at the same time it knows this incompleteness to be a necessity, because truth only comes to be itself through the negativity of immediacy" (*SL* 841/2: 571). It is in this sense that the true character of thought—as the unity of all its intrinsic categories, or the "Idea"—is the logical *ground* of the initial thought of indeterminate being. The (rational) historical requirement that we suspend our presuppositions and the logical requirement that the true, concrete character of thought be understood to emerge from thought itself thus coincide: for both make it necessary for the *Logic* to begin with sheer being.

According to Hegel, therefore, "the advance [in the *Logic*] is a *retreat into the ground*, to what is *primary* and *true*, on which depends and, in fact, from which originates, that with which the beginning is made" (*SL* 71/1: 70 [177]). Yet, unlike the historical ground of the thought of sheer being, the logical ground of that thought does not and cannot precede it precisely because that logical ground—the true character of thought as the unity of all its categories—can only emerge through the (self-) transformation *of* the thought of sheer being. The logical ground of that empty category of being grounds it, therefore, by *requiring it to come first*. It presupposes that category but is not its prior cause. But, of course, the true character of thought can in fact only *come to* presuppose the thought of pure being because it itself has to emerge as that which requires the thought of pure being as its point of origin.

Precisely because the true, concrete character of thought does require—or rather comes to require—the category of pure being to come first, "it is equally necessary to consider as *result* that into which the movement returns as into its *ground*." In this respect, Hegel comments, "the first is equally the ground, and the last a derivative; since the movement starts from the first and by correct inferences arrives at the last as the ground, this latter is a result" (*SL* 71/1: 70–1 [177]). The thought of sheer indeterminate being thus itself *gives rise* to the thought of the absolute Idea, which in turn *requires* the thought of sheer being to precede it.

For this reason, presuppositionless thought proves to be a self-constituting circle. It begins with sheer indeterminacy and immediacy, then draws itself out, as it were, as the various categories are unfolded, and finally comes to be the whole circle—the unity of all the categories—*of which* sheer indeterminacy is retrospectively understood to be the necessary, but mere, beginning. This circle proves to be the ground of the initial category because that category itself proves to be required *by* that circle and to be nothing but a moment *of* that circle. But this ground—the circle—is not, and cannot be, presupposed at the outset of the development. Rather, the ground only *emerges*—and the circle only *constitutes itself*—through the self-negation of the sheer immediacy of the beginning. Accordingly, Hegel maintains, "the method, which thus winds itself into a circle, cannot *anticipate* (*antizipieren*) in a development in time that the beginning is, as such, already something derived; it is sufficient for the beginning in its immediacy that it is simple universality" (*SL* 841/2: 570, my emphasis). That is to say, the presuppositionless philosopher cannot, and does not, *start out* by understanding the category of being to be required by the thought of the Idea—or the circle of all the categories—as its abstract beginning. The philosopher has to begin with the thought of sheer, indeterminate being in the abstract and *discover* in the course of the (self-) transformation of that thought into the thought of the Idea that it is the category from which the thought of the Idea must proceed.

This holds true even for those who have read Hegel's prefaces and introduc-

tion to the *Logic* (and introductory studies of the *Logic*, such as this one) and who, consequently, have already been told before they study the *Logic* itself that the category of being is the beginning of the thought of the Idea. For what such readers have also been told is that the category of being leads to the Idea and so constitutes the beginning *of* the thought of the Idea only insofar as it is understood initially as sheer indeterminate being and is not taken explicitly at the outset *as* the beginning of the truth. The only way for such readers to proceed, therefore, if they are to be fully responsible and self-critical, is to set aside the thought of the Idea, begin with the thought of sheer indeterminate being alone, and *discover for themselves* whether that thought leads immanently to the thought of the Idea or not. Hegel's own anticipatory assurance that the category of being is the beginning of the thought of the Idea therefore should not simply be taken for granted; rather, it should be interpreted as a call to readers to determine for themselves whether or not his claim is true. Winfield explains the matter well:

> In order for all assumptions to be precluded, the point at which philosophy begins must involve no preconceptions of what it is a beginning of, no indication that it is a commencement, nor any given whatsoever. At its start, philosophy can only be an empty word, which is precisely why indeterminacy is all with which the quest for truth can begin. . . . Indeterminacy would not even stand as the beginning of what finally results until the very conclusion of the entire development. Then alone would what indeterminacy is a beginning of first come into view.[31]

The presuppositionless philosopher must begin with the category of pure being alone, without assuming in advance that that category is in fact the beginning of the thought of the Idea, the Absolute, or infinity. Indeed, he or she may not assume that the category of being leads to any further categories at all but must wait and see *whether* any such categories arise. The aim of the presuppositionless philosopher is thus not to set out to demonstrate that the thought of being generates a more complex—dialectical or nondialectical—view of the world; it is simply to consider the indeterminate thought of being itself, to dwell with that category for its own sake, and to observe where, if anywhere, it takes us. In this sense, presuppositionless philosophy is radically *nonteleological*: it presupposes and aims at no particular result, pursues no projected goal, and follows no prescribed path. Accordingly, as Alan White remarks, "the speculative thinker in the process of determining the categories, as they arise, for the first time does not know where, if anywhere, he is headed."[32] Indeed, he does not know if he is *headed* anywhere at all. All he knows is that he is thinking sheer indeterminate being without any further presuppositions or determinations.

31. Winfield, *Reason and Justice*, pp. 127, 129.
32. White, *Absolute Knowledge*, p. 57.

Nevertheless, as White puts it, the *Logic* does "make its own way" and create a path of its own.[33] As we shall see later, this is because the thought of pure being slips away of its own accord into the thought of nothing, and the thought of nothing itself slips away into the thought of pure being, thereby generating the new thought of this very slippage or "vanishing," which Hegel names *becoming*. It is further because this thought in turn passes into those of determinacy, finitude, infinity, and so on. Even though no systematic development is presupposed or anticipated at the outset, therefore, Hegel argues that such a development does occur and a system does emerge precisely because of the initial indeterminacy of sheer being itself.

This systematic development is necessary, because it is simply the unfolding of that which is immanent in each category and so cannot not display itself. It is generated not by any arbitrary associations or stipulations made by the philosopher but by pure thought's "own immanent activity" (*SL* 31, 55/1: 19, 51). Moreover, precisely because it is generated solely by pure thought's own activity, the development set out in the *Logic* is not only necessary but also wholly self-determining and *free*.[34]

The crucial thing to emphasize is that the systematic development of thought is *not* presupposed from the outset as the "truth" that philosophy is to disclose or as the "horizon" of all philosophical enquiry or as the "straitjacket" into which all thought and life are forced by Hegel. Rather, the system is what *emerges* when thought suspends all its assumptions about itself, considers nothing but the sheer indeterminate thought of being, and holds itself open to what that thought shows itself to be. Hegel stresses this in both the *Logic* and the *Phenomenology*. In the *Logic*, as we have already seen, he clearly states that "truth only comes to be itself through the negativity of immediacy" and that philosophy thus presents "the *immanent coming-to-be* (*Entstehung*) of the distinctions" (*SL* 841, 55/2: 571, 1: 51). The *Logic* thus traces the "self-constructing path" of thought; it does not follow a route that has been marked out for it in advance (*SL* 28/1: 17).[35] The preface to the *Phenomenology* strikes the same chord: the whole cannot be presupposed at the outset of philosophy because it only arises *as* determinations (i.e., shapes of consciousness or categories) turn into other determinations and so constitute a continuity, of which each determination is but a moment. "Through this process," Hegel writes, "the simple, self-surveying whole itself *emerges* (*emergiert*) from the wealth in which its reflection seemed to be lost" (*PhS* 33/53, my emphasis).

In letting the category of indeterminate being determine itself and the whole

33. White, *Absolute Knowledge*, p. 57.

34. On the intimate connection between self-determining necessity and freedom, see Hegel, *EL* 73/102–3 (§35 Add.).

35. Translation revised. Miller's translation has "self-construing" for *sich selbst konstruierend*.

system emerge in this way, Hegel thus completes the task he believes is bequeathed to him by Kant and Fichte: to derive the basic categories of thought from the very nature of thought itself. Furthermore, he completes that task by following Fichte in particular and "allow[ing] the entire range of our representations to *come into being gradually* before the eyes of the reader or listener."[36] Hegel's presuppositionless derivation of the whole array of categories that are intrinsic to thought is not completed until the end of the third part of his system, the *Philosophy of Spirit.* By the end of the *Logic,* however, immediately prior to the discovery that the thought of being is actually the thought of nature, all of the basic general (or pure) categories of thought—what Kant would call the "unschematized" categories—have been derived and properly determined. By that point, therefore, the true character of thought has been disclosed—at least in its essentials—and we have begun to think *properly* (even if we do not yet know all that that will entail). We can now draw on this new understanding of true or proper thinking to render our nonphilosophical activity (both theoretical and practical) more intelligent. In this sense, for Hegel, "the study of this science [of logic], to dwell and labour in this shadowy realm, is the absolute culture and discipline of consciousness" (*SL* 58/1: 55).

36. Fichte, *Introductions to the Wissenschaftslehre*, p. 27, my emphasis.

Chapter Three

The Presuppositions of Presuppositionless Thinking

The Orthodox View of Hegel

I have argued that Hegel's *Logic* does not presuppose at the outset that thought constitutes a dialectical system of categories, but starts with the utterly indeterminate concept of pure being and simply lets such a system emerge. This interpretation has been rejected or ignored by many of the most influential commentators on Hegel despite all the textual evidence in its favor. Indeed, the prevailing assumption has been that the beginning of Hegel's *Logic* is shot through with unwarranted presuppositions.

Schelling, for example, is in no doubt that the development in the *Logic* beyond the initial abstract category of pure being depends upon the prior assumption that the truth to be attained is not actually abstract but concrete. We find the category of pure being to be deficient, and so move on from it to other, more determinate categories because we are

> already used to a more concrete being, a being more full of content, and thus cannot be satisfied with that meagre diet of pure being in which only content in the abstract but no determinate content is thought; in the last analysis, then, what does not allow him [the philosopher] to remain with that empty abstraction is only the fact that there really *is* a more rich being which is more full of content, and the fact that the thinking spirit itself is already such a being . . . what always tacitly leads this progression is always the *terminus ad quem*, the real world, at which science finally is to arrive.[1]

Hegel may pretend that thought is moved forward by a necessity immanent within its most indeterminate category, but Schelling maintains, "it obviously has a goal that it is striving towards."[2]

---

1. Schelling, *On the History of Modern Philosophy*, p. 138.

2. Schelling, *On the History of Modern Philosophy*, p. 139. See also R. Pippin, *Hegel's Idealism: The Satisfactions of Self-Consciousness* (Cambridge: Cambridge University Press, 1989), p. 236. For a more extensive discussion of Schelling's critique of Hegel, see White, *Absolute Knowledge,* and S. Houlgate, "Schelling's Critique of Hegel's *Science of Logic,*" *The Review of Metaphysics* 53, 1 (September 1999): 99–128.

A similar view is adopted by McTaggart (as we saw in chapter 2) and has been endorsed more recently by Klaus Hartmann. For Hartmann, "the sequential forward reading [of Hegel's *Logic*] cannot be the whole story," because a presuppositionless beginning by itself would never lead to anything: "how could the absence of determination lead to richness?" Hegel's *Logic* must, therefore, already presuppose at the start "the ordered richness of granted content," and his procedure must be to arrange the categories applicable to such content in a sequence—from the least to the most determinate—such that each category (apart from the first) can be regarded as made necessary or "justified" by its antecedent. The linear progression from "being" to the "absolute Idea" set out in the *Logic* is thus not the pure derivation or "deduction" of the determinate from the indeterminate but the logical "reconstruction" of categories that are *already* presupposed: "what it [the linear progression] is heading for is granted."[3]

For Feuerbach, too, Hegel's *Logic* presupposes from the very start what is to be proved: namely (in Feuerbach's view), the existence of the Absolute, or the Absolute Idea. "That the Absolute existed was beyond all doubt. All it needed was to prove itself and be known *as such*." Moreover, Feuerbach maintains, the stages of this proof are made necessary by the Absolute Idea itself. At the beginning of the *Logic*, therefore, "Hegel does not step outside the Idea, nor does he forget it. Rather, he already thinks the antithesis out of which the Idea should produce itself *on the basis of its having been taken for granted* (*unter ihrer Voraussetzung*)."[4] The true starting point of the *Logic* is thus not the category of pure being with which the text formally begins but the Absolute Idea itself, "because it was already a certainty, an immediate truth for Hegel before he wrote the *Logic*." Indeed, Feuerbach claims that the Idea's apparent "lack of self-knowledge" (*das Nichtwissen der Idee von sich*) at the beginning of the *Logic*—the fact that Hegel's text officially starts not with the Idea as such but with pure being—is actually "ironical" (*ironisches Nichtwissen*). The Idea pretends to emerge from an indeterminate concept in which it is utterly absent, but in fact "it posits itself in advance as true" (*sie setzt sich selbst als wahr voraus*).[5]

At the start of the *Logic*, Hegel does not, therefore, critically suspend all his assumptions in order to embark on a voyage of intellectual discovery; for Feuerbach, "there was nothing of the critic or the skeptic in him." On the contrary, in

---

3. K. Hartmann, "Hegel: A Non-Metaphysical View," in *Hegel: A Collection of Critical Essays,* ed. A. MacIntyre (1972) (Notre Dame: University of Notre Dame Press, 1976), p. 105.

4. L. Feuerbach, *Towards a Critique of Hegel's Philosophy*, in *The Young Hegelians: An Anthology,* ed. L. Stepelevich (Cambridge: Cambridge University Press, 1983), p. 111; L. Feuerbach, "Zur Kritik der Hegelschen Philosophie" (1839), in *Philosophische Kritiken und Grundsätze,* ed. W. Bolin and F. Jodl, *Sämtliche Werke,* vol. 2 (Stuttgart-Bad Cannstatt: Frommann-Holzboog, 1959), p. 181.

5. Feuerbach, *Towards a Critique of Hegel's Philosophy*, p. 112; "Zur Kritik der Hegelschen Philosophie," pp. 182–3.

his "heart of hearts" Hegel was "convinced of the certainty of the Absolute Idea" right from the beginning. Consequently, from the outset, he "can anticipate (*übergreifen*) that which is yet to be presented because everything is already settled for him (*ausgemacht*)."[6]

The interpretation of Hegel's *Logic* offered by Feuerbach and Schelling shortly after Hegel's death has been hugely influential on later readers of Hegel, particularly (though not exclusively) among Continental philosophers. Indeed, it has become something of an orthodoxy among such philosophers. Heidegger, for example, claims (albeit in his study of the *Phenomenology*, but with reference to Hegel's system as a whole) that "Hegel understood being as absolute, in advance and without question" and that "this absoluteness and infinity never became a problem for him because they *could* never become a problem." What is posited from the start in Hegelian speculative cognition is thus "the absolute, in which the manner, extent, and the range of the first point of departure and of the concluding sentence of speculation (which returns to that starting point) are determined." The reason why this is the case is that Hegel's thought is essentially ontotheological: "it is the essence of God as spirit in general that pre-scribes the essence of the concept and thus the character of the logical."[7]

Levinas similarly discerns no self-critical openness at the heart of Hegel's philosophy, but sees rather a philosopher who from the start is "*assured* . . . of being able to complete the cycle of thought." Derrida (though he talks more about "spirit" in Hegel than the Absolute Idea) continues the Schellingian-Feuerbachian-Heideggerian line of interpretation. Hegelian spirit, for Derrida, is that which "in advance interiorizes all content." "Spirit," he writes, "will always have preceded or accompanied itself up to the procession's end"; "everything that is, all time, *precomprehends* itself, strictly, in the circle of *Sa* [*savoir absolu,* or absolute knowing]."[8]

Now, I am well aware that there are many significant differences between all these interpreters of Hegel that should not be overlooked. What I wish to point out, however, is that all of them take for granted "in advance and without question" that Hegel himself takes for granted "in advance and without question" the goal and outcome of his philosophy. None of them takes seriously Hegel's clear insistence that the beginning of the *Logic "may not presuppose anything"* (*SL*

6. Feuerbach, *Towards a Critique of Hegel's Philosophy*, p. 112; "Zur Kritik der Hegelschen Philosophie," p. 182.

7. M. Heidegger, *Hegel's Phenomenology of Spirit*, trans. P. Emad and K. Maly (Bloomington: Indiana University Press, 1988), pp. 74, 100, 98.

8. E. Levinas, *Basic Philosophical Writings*, ed. A. T. Peperzak, S. Critchley and R. Bernasconi (Bloomington: Indiana University Press, 1996), p. 126, my emphasis, and J. Derrida, *Glas,* trans. J. P. Leavey and R. Rand (Lincoln: University of Nebraska Press, 1986), pp. 22–3, 226, my emphasis. See also Houlgate, "Hegel, Derrida, and Restricted Economy: The Case of Mechanical Memory," p. 82.

70/1: 69 [175])—or at least none accepts that Hegel lives up to his own demands—but each of them confidently assumes that Hegel in fact begins to philosophize from *within* a dialectical system whose completion or "closure" he takes for granted, explicitly or implicitly, at the outset. Through being interpreted in this way, Hegel has become for many today the quintessential philosopher of "totality," whose system allows nothing to fall outside it—no "otherness" or radical "alterity"—but always aims to "assimilate," "absorb," or "digest" whatever might seek to criticize or resist it and confronts everyone after Hegel with the (possibly impossible) task of trying to "elude," "subvert," or "disrupt" it.

This view of Hegel—though in my view profoundly misguided—is extraordinarily widespread and is espoused by those whose readings of other philosophers are models of rigor and subtlety. To take one recent example, Christina Howells—a highly perspicacious reader of Sartre and Derrida—talks in her recent book on Derrida (without any hint of irony) of "the all-devouring rigour of Hegel's search for *Savoir Absolu*," of "Hegel's totalizing encyclopaedic project," and even (in unfortunate complicity with Karl Popper) of "Hegelian totalitarianism."[9] Hegel, we are told, is "a predatory philosopher, infinitely hard to escape," whose dialectic "engulfs contradiction and recuperates subversion as error to be transcended."[10] Clearly, for Howells, as for Feuerbach, Hegel's philosophy is the product not of self-critical openness but of an Absolute Idea that "posits itself in advance as true."[11]

The reading presented in this study aims to counter the orthodox Schellingian-Feuerbachian interpretation and thereby to dispel the myth of "Hegel the Totalitarian" that underlies—indeed gives life and critical purpose to—much post-Hegelian thought. What the implications for contemporary Continental philosophy will be, I am not sure. My concern here is simply to join such commentators as Richard Winfield, William Maker, and Alan White in reminding people that there is an alternative to the orthodox interpretation that has been neglected—one is tempted to say *systematically*—for most of the last 170 years.

The cornerstone of this alternative is that Hegel's *Logic* begins not with the presupposed idea of the Absolute but with the radical suspension of all our presuppositions about thought and being. At the outset of the *Logic*, all we are given to think is the sheer indeterminate being of thought itself—that is, thought understood *as* sheer indeterminate being. Nothing is determined or decided in advance about whether or how such a thought of being will develop into further determinations. No ultimate goal beyond this thought of being is presupposed, nor is any method of logical progression assumed. Hegel does, indeed, argue

9. C. Howells, *Derrida: Deconstruction from Phenomenology to Ethics* (Cambridge: Polity Press, 1999), pp. 84–5, 90.

10. Howells, *Derrida: Deconstruction from Phenomenology to Ethics,* p. 85.

11. Feuerbach, *Towards a Critique of Hegel's Philosophy,* p. 112; "Zur Kritik der Hegelschen Philosophie," p. 182.

that this concept of pure being develops into a system of categories culminating in that of the Absolute Idea. But the fact that the concept of pure being develops in this way is demonstrated in the course of the *Logic* itself; it is not assumed at the outset. About this Hegel is absolutely clear:

> Not only the account of scientific method, but even the concept (*Begriff*) itself of the science as such belongs to its content, and in fact constitutes its final result; *what logic is cannot be stated beforehand* (*was sie ist, kann sie daher nicht voraussagen*), rather does this knowledge of what it is first emerge as the final outcome and consummation of the whole exposition. (*SL* 43/1: 35, my emphasis)[12]

At the beginning of the Logic, therefore, thought does not aim to reach any preset goal, to follow any preestablished method, or to absorb all alternative positions "within" the Absolute Idea; its task is simply to "stand back from its content, allowing it to have free play [or hold sway] (*gewähren zu lassen*) and not determining it further" (SL 73/1: 72 [179]).

My concern in this study of the opening of Hegel's *Logic* is thus not only to open up to new readers a formidably dense and complex text. It is also to show readers who are already familiar with Hegel that his philosophy begins from self-critical *openness* to being rather than from the assumption of absolute closure. Indeed, in my view, Hegelian "absolute knowing" is precisely such openness to what pure being shows itself to be. It is marked not by the certainty in advance that being is always already the Absolute Idea but by the simple readiness to *let* pure being as such hold sway in thought. To my mind, such radical openness of mind and willingness to let be is the real, hermeneutic presupposition of Hegel's thought.

Before we look in more detail at what such openness of mind entails, however, we must consider one obvious objection to the interpretation I am recommending—namely, that in the preface to the *Phenomenology* Hegel appears to understand his own system in precisely the way in which Feuerbach and Derrida interpret it. Hegel states that the true (*das Wahre*)

> is the process of its own becoming, the circle that presupposes its end as its goal (*der Kreis, der sein Ende als seinen Zweck voraussetzt*), having its end also as its beginning; and only by being worked out to its end, is it actual. (*PhS* 10/23)

This remark is made in the *Phenomenology*, not in the *Logic*, but it is clear from the context that it describes the structure of absolute knowing as such, which is

---

12. Miller's translation has "Notion" for Begriff, instead of "concept." In quotations from Hegel included in parts 1 and 3 of this study, I have replaced "Notion" with "concept." In the text of the Logic included in part 2, I have left the word "Notion" unchanged.

at work in both of Hegel's major texts. I do not wish, therefore, to defend the presuppositionless interpretation of the *Logic* presented here by claiming that this problematic passage applies only to the *Phenomenology*. In my view, it applies equally to the *Logic*. But, then, does it not confirm that the orthodox reading of Hegel is correct and that Hegel does indeed presuppose the goal of philosophy from the very start?

Careful attention to the passage under consideration reveals that it does not confirm the orthodox reading of Hegel. This is because it does not describe what happens at the *start* of philosophy but explains what is entailed by philosophy's being a *circle*. Insofar as philosophy is circular, Hegel says, its beginning points forward to, and so presupposes, its end (indeed, as we learn from a similar passage at the end of the *Phenomenology* and as we saw in the last chapter, its end points back to, and so presupposes, its beginning [see *PhS* 488/585]). The important thing to remember, however, is that, for Hegel, *philosophy does not start out as a circle;* it develops into, and so *becomes*, a circle. At the start of philosophy, all we have is sheer immediacy—in the *Phenomenology*, the immediacy of sense-certainty, and in the *Logic*, the immediacy of pure being. That immediacy, we eventually learn, develops, through its own inner dialectic into the circle of consciousness or thought. Before that circle has emerged, however, there is nothing about that immediacy that marks it as the beginning, or indeed the promise, *of* such a circle; it is pure and simple *immediacy*. Hegel states this explicitly in a passage from the *Logic* cited in the last chapter (see *SL* 841/2: 570, and p. 50 above).

The problematic passage from the *Phenomenology* should thus be read as a statement of what comes to be true of philosophy at the *completion* of philosophy (or at the end of a particular region of philosophy), not as a statement of what is true at the *start* of philosophy. Once philosophy has finally become a circle, then we can say of it that its beginning points toward, and so presupposes, its goal. But we cannot say this at the start of philosophy, *before* it has become a circle, because there is nothing in sheer immediacy as such to suggest that it will give rise to, and so form the beginning of, such a circle. At the beginning, philosophy does not, and cannot, "presuppose its end as its goal."

The error of the orthodox interpretation of Hegel thus consists in failing to recognize that speculative philosophy *comes to be* the circle of absolute knowing and for that reason cannot already be such a circle at the outset. In other words, the orthodox interpretation of Hegel misses the point of one of Hegel's most famous statements: "Of the Absolute it must be said that it is essentially a *result*, that only in the *end* is it what it truly is; and that precisely in this consists its nature, viz. to be actual, subject, the spontaneous becoming of itself" (*PhS* 11/24).

Passivity and Activity in Presuppositionless Thought

Orthodox interpreters of Hegel are perhaps also misled by his generous habit of providing in his prefaces and introductions and at various points in the main texts overviews of what is to be disclosed. These overviews let the reader know that philosophy will develop dialectically or turn out to be circular and often anticipate the details of a specific analysis. They thus inform the reader in advance of what he or she should expect based on what the philosopher has discovered and may create the impression in the minds of some interpreters that the reader's own ability to make progress in philosophy depends on being so informed. Hegel makes it clear, however, that such overviews are designed solely to satisfy the demands of those who are overly eager to know where they are to be taken by presuppositionless philosophy but should play no constructive role in moving thought on from the category of pure being to further categories. Overviews afford "nothing more than a picture for *ordinary thinking* (*Vorstellung*) . . . to meet the subjective needs of unfamiliarity and its impatience" (*SL* 842/2: 571; see also *SL* 43/1: 35–6); they do not constitute founding preconditions of doing philosophy. When we begin to philosophize, therefore, we are not to consider the category of pure being to be deficient by comparing it with the anticipated concept of the absolute Idea or by regarding it as a mere "moment" of what we already know to be a dialectical development toward the absolute. We are simply to attend to the thought of pure being and to follow its immanent self-transformation.

Indeed, as I noted in the introduction, Hegel maintains in the preface to the *Phenomenology* that the precondition of doing philosophy is that the reader *forget* any general overview he or she may have gained and simply enter into the immanent content of the matter at hand. The presupposition of speculative philosophy is thus not that we know in advance where we are headed but that in a spirit of radical openness we simply *let* the thought of pure being take us where it will.

Presuppositionless philosophy does, therefore, have a presupposition after all. It presupposes no goal, method, or principle that would orient its development and so in that sense is presupposition*less*. But it requires a self-critical openness of mind on the part of the philosopher and in that sense has a definite presupposition. Indeed, it presupposes precisely a readiness on the part of the reader to suspend all his or her presuppositions about thought and being. Such readiness, Hegel maintains, involves the willingness to *let go* of our cherished certainties, assumptions, and prejudices—to "giv[e] up the *fixity* of [our] self-positing" (*PhS* 20/37)—and the willingness to *let* our thinking be guided and determined by what is immanent in the matter at hand. Such willingness can be considered the *hermeneutic* presupposition of speculative philosophy since without it we could not understand or follow the course of such philosophy. But it is not to be regarded as a *founding* presupposition of speculative philosophy

since it does not determine in advance the course that that philosophy will take. Indeed, it cannot do so since it is precisely the willingness to let thought take the course that follows immanently from the concept of pure being.

The word "let" (*lassen*) is not always recognized to be a distinctively Hegelian word. It is more often associated with Heidegger, the philosopher of *Gelassenheit*, or letting-be.[13] Careful reading of Hegel's texts reveals, however, that Hegel employs the word *lassen* frequently, especially when characterizing the basic attitude of mind required of the philosopher. In previously cited lines from the *Logic*, for example, Hegel writes that pure knowing must "stand back from its content, allowing it to have free play (*gewähren zu lassen*) and not determining it further" (*SL* 73/1: 72 [179]). In the preface to the *Phenomenology* we are told that "what is looked for here [in philosophy] is the effort . . . to sink [one's] freedom in the content, letting it move spontaneously of its own nature (*ihn durch seine eigne Natur . . . sich bewegen zu lassen*), . . . and then to contemplate this movement" (*PhS* 35–6/56). In the *Encyclopedia Logic*, Hegel further states boldly that "when I think, I give up (*gebe auf*) my subjective particularity, sink myself in the matter, let thought follow its own course (*lasse das Denken für sich gewähren*); and I think badly whenever I add something of my own" (*EL* 58/84 [§24 Add. 2]). In my view, these and many other passages clearly show that for Hegel the most important hermeneutic presupposition of presuppositionless philosophy is quite simply the willingness to *let*.

But what exactly does this mean? It means first of all that one give up the aspiration to control the path of thinking. We are not to be the ones who decide that this or that concept should now be considered, nor are we responsible for marshalling arguments in favor of or against a particular idea. We are simply to follow wherever presuppositionless thought takes us and to attend to and think through whatever concepts it leads us to. Through this process we uncover the ultimately dialectical character of thought. But as David Kolb astutely notes, "that does not make us lords of its motion."[14] Hegel is as aware as Nietzsche that understanding can serve our interest in power and control. But in contrast to Nietzsche, he does not regard all thought as an expression of the will to power: to seek to understand is not by its very nature to seek to dominate. Rather, genuine philosophical thought begins only when we relinquish the desire to dominate through understanding and *let* ourselves be guided by thought itself (*SL* 35–6/1: 25).

To let the matter at hand hold sway is, secondly, to refrain from raising objections to speculative philosophy that are based on one's personal convictions, preferences, or presumed experiences. As we saw in chapter 2, Hegel by no means excludes criticism of speculative philosophy, provided that it takes the

13. See M. Heidegger, *Gelassenheit* (Pfullingen: Verlag Günther Neske, 1959).

14. D. Kolb, *The Critique of Pure Modernity: Hegel, Heidegger, and After* (Chicago: University of Chicago Press, 1986), p. 81.

form of drawing out more carefully and accurately than Hegel himself does the implications of a certain concept. What is ruled out, however, is charging speculative philosophy with neglecting or downplaying such phenomena as difference, time, gender, or language on the prior *assumption* that one or other is ontologically, epistemologically, or politically fundamental. For many readers of Hegel this prohibition on external criticism is the hardest thing to accept and abide by; indeed, it is firmly rejected by most. Hegel, however, insists on that prohibition since presuppositionless philosophy presupposes the willingness to "rid oneself of all . . . reflections and opinions whatever, [and] simply to take up *what is there before us*" (*SL* 69/1: 68 [175]). If one believes, as many critics do, that Hegel's system actually has founding presuppositions of its own (such as, for example, a bias in favor of identity over difference), then Hegel's prohibition on external criticism will mean excluding from the start alternative points of view through an act of concealed violence. If on the other hand one takes seriously the presupposition*less* character of Hegel's philosophy, then such a prohibition is the only way to allow a truly self-critical understanding of thought and being to emerge that does not itself simply take for granted how they are to be conceived.

It is important to note that Hegel's radically self-critical philosophy requires a profound *passivity* on the part of those who are to enter into it. Hegel is not denying that a good philosopher should be perceptive and imaginative and possess good judgment. But the principal quality he looks for is the ability, without prejudice, to *let* one's thinking be guided by what is immanent in the thought of pure being.

> Philosophical thinking proceeds analytically in that it simply takes up its object, the Idea, and lets it go its own way (*dieselbe gewähren läßt*), while it simply watches the movement and development of it, so to speak. To this extent philosophising is wholly passive (*passiv*). (*EL* 305/390 [§238 Add.])

Yet Hegel points out that this very passivity requires us to exercise the greatest vigilance and restraint and in that sense demands that we be *active*—active precisely in keeping ourselves passive and holding ourselves to what is necessitated by the matter at hand. As he puts it, passivity "requires the effort to beware of our own inventions and particular opinions which are forever wanting to push themselves forward" (*EL* 305/390 [§238 Add.]). Hegel recognizes that "the peculiar restlessness and distraction of our modern consciousness" actually make it very hard for modern readers to "calmly suppress *their own* reflections and opinions." All manner of counter-examples and objections beset us when we begin to read a philosophical text, engendered in part by the "noisy clamour" we hear all around us and in part by our impatient desire to demonstrate our own originality and independence of mind (*SL* 40, 42/1: 31, 34). This does not mean that the modern age altogether lacks readers able to approach presuppositionless

philosophy in the right spirit of passivity and open-mindedness. But it means that modern readers must work particularly hard and exercise considerable self-discipline if they are to let the truth rather than prejudice and contingent opinion hold sway in their thinking and if they are to participate in what Hegel calls "the passionless calm of a knowledge which is in the element of pure thought alone" (*SL* 42/1: 34).

Hegel believes that readers of the *Logic*—that is, those who wish to *think* speculatively—must also be active in another sense. For we can only let categories transform themselves into further categories insofar as we ourselves render explicit, or "posit," what is implicit in each category. We are passive insofar as we allow the categories to determine what is to be rendered explicit and to take us where they will, but equally we are active insofar as *we* are the ones who actually have to draw out the implications inherent in each category and hold fast to the new categories that emerge (see *EL* 141/188 [§88]).

Readers who succeed in exercising self-discipline and in letting reason govern their thought do not, therefore, cease to think for *themselves*. They have to keep focused on the matter at hand through their own efforts, and they have to render explicit for themselves what is implicit in and necessitated by a given category. (As Hegel rather acidly remarks, no one can think for someone else any more than anyone can eat or drink for someone else; we always think for ourselves [*EL* 55/80 (§23)].) Yet such readers allow their thinking to be guided by the matter at hand rather than their own particular ideas and foibles, and in that sense their attitude is one of passivity. Consequently, as Stace recognizes, "it is, in fact, not *we* who deduce the categories at all. They deduce themselves"—though they do so in and through *our* thinking of them.[15]

The fact that philosophical passivity—letting the categories of thought develop immanently by themselves—itself requires us to be active is indicated by a striking juxtaposition in the preface to the first edition of the *Science of Logic* (1812). Hegel concludes one paragraph with a clear statement that the matter at hand in the *Logic* transforms itself:

> It can be only the nature of the content itself which spontaneously develops itself in a scientific method of knowing, since it is at the same time the reflection of the content itself which first posits and *generates* its determinate character (*SL* 27/1: 16).

At the start of the following paragraph, Hegel then distinguishes the two forms of human thought that nevertheless have to be actively at work in philosophy: understanding (*Verstand*) and reason (*Vernunft*). Unlike Kant, Hegel does not regard understanding and reason as separate faculties of the mind; they are for him different aspects of *one* activity of thought. But he does consider them to be distinct operations of thought with their own specific character.

---

15. Stace, *The Philosophy of Hegel*, p. 85.

> The understanding *determines*, and holds the determinations fixed; reason is negative and *dialectical*, because it resolves the determinations of the understanding into nothing; it is positive because it generates the universal and comprehends the particular therein. (*SL* 28/1: 16)

By juxtaposing this passage with the one cited above, Hegel clearly implies that unless we are active in employing our understanding and reason we shall not be in a position to follow passively the immanent development of the categories.

A somewhat more detailed account of these operations of thought is given in the *Encyclopedia Logic*. There we are told that "*understanding* stops short at the fixed determinacy and its distinctness vis-à-vis other determinacies." Understanding thus differentiates one concept from another (say, finitude and infinity) and holds fast to that distinction. Dialectical reason, by contrast, discerns "the self-sublation of these finite determinations on their own part, and their passing into their opposites." That is to say, it recognizes that the distinctions drawn by understanding undermine themselves as each concept turns into its opposite. Positive, or "speculative," reason then "apprehends the unity of the determinations in their opposition" (*EL* 125–31/169–76 [§§80–2]).

Hegel insists that each of these operations of thought is needed throughout the whole course of the *Logic* and should not be thought of as corresponding to just one of the three parts of the text: the doctrine of being, essence, or concept. Each stage of the analysis in each part requires us (a) to form a precise understanding of a concept and its difference from other concepts, (b) to appreciate why distinctions between ostensibly opposed concepts break down, and (c) to recognize how ostensibly opposed concepts can be thought together as a unity of different determinations. All three operations are indeed evident in the opening pages of the *Logic*. We understand the initial categories of being and nothing to be immediately different, and we also discern their immediate slippage into one another by virtue of which each one is seen to be the *becoming* of the other. We then recognize how these two ostensibly opposed concepts settle into the single thought of their unity—determinate being (*Dasein*)—in which being is inseparable from not-being and not-being is inseparable from being. Becoming, in this account, is nothing but the *dialectical* passage into one another of being and nothing, and determinate being is nothing but their speculative *unity*. Hegel's opening analysis thus simply traces the process whereby our *understanding* of being and nothing turns into *rational* comprehension. (*Pace* Michael Forster, whose interpretation of Hegel we considered in chapter 2, nothing in this analysis requires that the concept of becoming itself generate its own opposite, with which it would then need to be reconciled. Forster's expectation that becoming should generate such an opposite stems from the unwarranted assumptions he makes about Hegel's "dialectical method" [see pp. 33–4 above].)

A word of caution is, however, due at this point. It is clear that we can fol-

low the immanent development of the category of pure being into further categories only if we exercise understanding and allow such understanding to become speculative, rational insight. But we must not take Hegel's introductory comments about understanding and reason in the *Logic* and *Encyclopedia* to lay down a consistent *method* that is to be applied throughout the science of logic strictly as it has been laid down. Such comments simply provide us with a general, descriptive outline of the activity of thought at work at each stage of the *Logic*. In the main body of the text itself, how concepts are actually to be understood and distinguished and how distinctions between such concepts undermine themselves vary according to the *specific* concepts under discussion. There is no uniform pattern of development exhibited at every stage of the analysis. The difference between being and nothing is different from the difference between something and other, and the difference between finitude and infinity is different again—and so are the speculative consequences that follow from such differences.

Indeed, many concepts are not initially understood to be explicitly differentiated from another concept at all. Something and other are explicitly contrasted with one another from the outset, but being and finitude are initially understood purely by themselves and only come to be related to their opposites (nothing and infinity, respectively) once they have been seen to turn autonomously *into* those opposites. In these cases, therefore, dialectic is responsible not just for undermining a distinction between concepts but also for generating that distinction in the first place. Being is certainly understood to be distinct from nothing, but it *comes to be* distinguished from nothing in the very dialectical slippage through which that distinction is undermined. In the analysis of being, the operations of understanding-as-distinguishing and dialectical reason thus actually coincide.

This means that the operation of *pure* understanding at the very start of the *Logic* does not actually consist in holding fast to a fixed *distinction* between being and nothing (as it would have to do if the account of understanding provided in §80 of the *Encyclopedia Logic* were to set out the first stage of a consistent logical method). To begin with, understanding simply suspends or abstracts from all its presuppositions—lets go of all its assumptions—and lets pure being *alone* hold sway. It is "the freedom that abstracts from everything, and grasps its own pure abstraction, the simplicity of thinking—. . . the resolve of *the will to think purely*" (*EL* 124/168 [§78]).

It is important to recognize that the *Logic* progresses not because of the mechanical repetition of identical acts of understanding and dialectical and speculative reason but because thought attends to the *specific* character of concepts—beginning with that of pure being—and lets them develop and determine themselves immanently according to their unique specificity. It is equally important, however, to recognize that understanding and reason are nonetheless at work in the *Logic*. Indeed, understanding and reason are precisely the operations through which we discern the specific character and development of the catego-

ries: understanding holds fast to the specific character of pure being, determinate being, something, finitude, and infinity, and reason recognizes that those concepts turn into further categories through their own immanent dialectic. Understanding and reason are thus, for Hegel, the operations of the mind through which we hold ourselves open to, and allow to hold sway, whatever is implicit in the category of pure being and subsequent categories—the operations through which we are *passive* in our thinking.

Philosophy, in Hegel's view, does not presuppose any definite, clearly articulated method of understanding and reasoning or any prior knowledge of the way concepts are to be manipulated. It presupposes rather the *readiness* to understand and be rational—that is, the readiness to keep in view what is contained in a concept and to let the implications of that concept take us where they will. Contrary to what one might imagine, this is not a recipe for conceptual chaos because for Hegel "philosophising requires, above all, that each thought should be grasped in its full precision (*Präzision*) and that nothing should remain vague and indeterminate" (*EL* 127–8/171 [§80 Add.]).[16] Precision is not just the prerogative of Descartes and twentieth-century analytic philosophers but is also a characteristic of Hegelian speculative philosophy. The paradox, of course, is that the first category to which we must devote our precise attention in Hegel's *Logic* is the utterly indeterminate category of pure being.

In Hegel's view, it is the precise attention to detail that ensures the intelligibility of speculative philosophy. Hegel's comment in the preface to the *Phenomenology* applies just as much to the *Logic:*

> Only what is completely determined is at once exoteric, comprehensible, and capable of being learned and appropriated by all. The intelligible (*verständig*) form of Science is the way open and equally accessible to everyone, and consciousness as it approaches Science justly demands that it be able to attain to rational knowledge by way of the ordinary understanding (*durch den Verstand zum vernünftigen Wissen zu gelangen*). (*PhS* 7–8/20)

Hegel's *Logic* is difficult, but nothing about it is meant to be esoteric; it is not to be the province of a privileged few who are gifted with some mysterious power of dialectical insight or intuition. It is intended to be a rigorous, disciplined study of the categories of thought that can be followed by anyone who seeks to understand what it is to think and what it is to be, without assuming in advance that they already know.[17]

---

16. See also R. Bubner, "Die 'Sache selbst' in Hegels System," in *Seminar: Dialektik in der Philosophie Hegels,* ed. R.-P. Horstmann (Frankfurt am Main: Suhrkamp Verlag, 1978), p. 117.

17. On the role of the understanding in speculative philosophy, see also J. Burbidge, "Where Is the Place of Understanding?", and S. Houlgate, "A Reply to John Burbidge," both in *Essays on Hegel's Logic,* ed. G. di Giovanni (Albany: SUNY Press, 1990).

The Historical Conditions of Hegelian Logic

Presuppositionless philosophy does, therefore, have certain presuppositions. Its hermeneutic presuppositions include the readiness to suspend or let go of what we have assumed to be true of thought and being and the readiness to focus one's attention and understanding on, and to be moved by, the minimal thought of pure being that results from letting go of all our assumptions. Indeed, Hegel's *Logic* requires of us not only such readiness and willingness but also "a trained ability (*Kraft und Geübtheit*) to withdraw into pure thought, hold onto it and move within it" (*EL* 45/67 [§19]).[18] This ability is reinforced through actually studying the *Logic* itself and *doing* presuppositionless philosophy: as we work through the *Logic*, we obviously become more practiced in thinking abstractly (*SL* 42/1: 33). But we also need to become used to thinking abstractly—to holding in mind pure logical form—*before* we embark on presuppositionless philosophy. For if we were not used to thinking abstractly and always had to picture something in order to understand it, we would not even be able to follow the opening dialectic of pure being, much less the rest of the analysis.

We first acquire this ability to abstract, Hegel maintains, by studying previous philosophers, such as Plato and Aristotle, and through the discipline of traditional *formal* (i.e., nondialectical) logic:

> There is no doubt that working on this formal logic has its use. Through it, as people say, we sharpen our wits [or "clean out our head"] (*wird . . . der Kopf ausgeputzt*); we learn to collect our thoughts, and to abstract. For in ordinary consciousness we deal with sensible representations, which cut across one another and cause confusion; but in abstraction what happens is that the mind concentrates on *one* point, and we acquire in that way the habit of occupying ourselves with what is inward. (*EL* 52/75–6 [§20 Add.])[19]

Without acquiring this habit of thinking abstractly, Hegel notes wryly (in the *Encyclopedia Philosophy of Mind*), we will find that, when we do engage in abstract thought, it will invariably cause us headaches.[20]

---

18. Translation revised.

19. See also W. Wieland, "Bemerkungen zum Anfang von Hegels Logik," in *Seminar: Dialektik in der Philosophie Hegels*, p. 201.

20. *Hegel's Philosophy of Mind. Being Part Three of the Encyclopaedia of the Philosophical Sciences (1830)*, trans. W. Wallace, together with the *Zusätze* in Boumann's text (1845), trans. A. V. Miller (Oxford: Clarendon Press, 1971), p. 143 (§410); G. W. F. Hegel, *Enzyklopädie der philosophischen Wissenschaften im Grundrisse (1830). Dritter Teil: Die Philosophie des Geistes*, ed. E. Moldenhauer and K. M. Michel, *Werke in zwanzig Bänden*, vol. 10 (Frankfurt am Main: Suhrkamp Verlag, 1970), p. 186. Further references to Hegel's *Philosophy of Mind* will be given in the following form: *EPM* 143/186 (§410). See also *EL* 27, 142/44, 190 (§§3, 88).

Philosophy not only demands certain abilities and dispositions on the part of the individual, it also presupposes certain broader social conditions. According to Hegel, these include above all the liberation from pressing material need. "In the silent regions of thought which has come to itself and communes only with itself, the interests which move the lives of races and individuals are hushed" (or at least do not cry out loudly for attention), and, Hegel writes (following Aristotle), for the philosopher to enjoy such quietude, "everything requisite for human comfort and intercourse" must be available in society at large (*SL* 33–4/1: 22–3).

Not being exposed to grave material hardship is a hermeneutic precondition of speculative philosophy (indeed of any philosophizing) since it enables us to attend patiently and rigorously to, and comprehend, what philosophy has to say. It is also one of the *historical* preconditions of speculative philosophy (indeed of any philosophizing) since it is an important feature of the context that gives birth to philosophy. In the case of speculative philosophy in particular, this historical context also includes the distinctive conditions of European (especially, German) modernity—"the new spirit which has arisen in the sciences no less than in the world of actuality," that is, "the higher standpoint reached by spirit in its awareness of itself" (*SL* 25–6/1: 15, 13). This spirit incorporates the spirit of Kantian critique, which demands that the categories underlying metaphysics be subjected to scrutiny; the "instinct of healthy reason," found in such writers as Hamann, Herder, Jacobi, and the Romantics, who turned against "the baldness of the merely formal categories" (but who also failed to appreciate the positive value of strict logical reasoning and all too often resorted to the "crude rejection of all method") (*SL* 38, 53/1: 28, 49)[21]; Fichte's demand for a rigorous derivation of the categories from the very nature of thought; and the challenge to traditional conceptual distinctions and the recovery of the idea of the "identity of opposites," in the work of Schelling.

From none of these thinkers does Hegel take over a determinate conception of thought or being on which to base, and from which to begin, his own philosophy. As we have seen, Hegel insists that the beginning of the *Logic* may not presuppose any rules of thought or any definite understanding of the categories. (Hegel may not, therefore, start from the Schellingian idea of the identity of the finite and the infinite, even though he is clearly attracted to this idea and comes to endorse it explicitly later in the *Logic*.)[22] Nevertheless, each of the philosophers just mentioned reinforces the demand to examine anew the categories in which we are wont to think and thereby contributes to the modern spirit of free self-criticism, which finds its most complete expression in Hegel's presuppositionless logic.

---

21. Miller's translation has "healthy common sense." The German is *gesunde Vernunft*.

22. See Hegel, *VLM* 65, and chapter 22, below.

Hegel's philosophy presupposes as its historical precondition not only the extraordinary developments in German intellectual life since 1770 but also the general modern interest in freedom, self-determination, and critical self-scrutiny, which Hegel traces back to the Reformation and to Cartesian thought (indeed to the emergence of scientific enquiry and civic freedom in cities in the late Middle Ages), and which he believes suffuses modern political, economic, aesthetic, religious, and philosophical life.[23] This is not to say, of course, that Martin Luther or the honorable burghers of sixteenth-century Nuremberg would have had the remotest interest in or sympathy with presuppositionless philosophy. But—strange as it may seem—it is to say that presuppositionless philosophy is the fruit of the powerful modern movement toward freedom that they helped initiate.

Presuppositionless philosophy is therefore a historical necessity—not in the sense that it could not fail to arise but in the sense that it alone is the philosophical fulfillment of the modern historical demand for freedom. Later in the philosophical system that emerges dialectically from the category of pure being, history will itself prove to be the *rational* development of the human spirit toward freedom and self-consciousness. Presuppositionless philosophy will thus turn out to be required not just by historical contingency but by reason at work in history. At the start of philosophy, however—before being has been determined as reason and before history has been revealed to be rational—all we can say is that presuppositionless philosophy is necessitated by the given *historical* interests of modernity.[24]

The Role of Religion

In the *Phenomenology* Hegel points to one further presupposition of his philosophy: religion. It is unclear whether he believes that one must be a religious believer in order to be capable of understanding and doing speculative philosophy (and so whether he regards religion as an essential hermeneutic precondition of such philosophy). But he clearly considers religion to have played an important historical role in the emergence of such philosophy, and he is convinced that in individuals without religious belief the intellectual enterprise of philosophy will lack any real connection to their hearts and souls. Individuals embarking on speculative philosophy must be ready and able to think abstractly—that is, in terms of pure logical categories rather than concrete visible or tangible examples—and they must also be prepared to let go of their firmly

23. See, for example, G. W. F. Hegel, *Vorlesungen über die Philosophie der Weltgeschichte, Zweite Hälfte,* ed. G. Lasson (1919) (Hamburg: Felix Meiner, 1923), pp. 842, 856–7; and *EL* 48/71 (§19 Add. 3).

24. On the relation between reason and contingency in Hegel's philosophy, see S. Houlgate, "Necessity and Contingency in Hegel's *Science of Logic*," *The Owl of Minerva* 27, 1 (Fall 1995): pp. 47–9. See also chapter 6, below, p. 118.

held assumptions. If, however, that willingness to let go intellectually is to be an integral part of people's lives, then prospective philosophers must be able to *feel* what it is to let go, too. This feeling, Hegel suggests, is gained through religion, specifically through imbibing the Christian spirit of forgiveness and reconciliation, which enjoins us to let go of our own entrenched positions and recognize our common purpose with others. Religion thus lends support to and prepares the way for presuppositionless philosophizing, even if it is not necessarily an indispensable hermeneutic precondition of such philosophizing.

This view of religion is particularly evident in the *Phenomenology*, where Hegel understands true religion to begin from and to rest on "the reconciling *Yea*, in which . . . two I's let go their antithetical *existence* (*von ihrem entgegengesetzten Dasein ablassen*)" and forgive one another (*PhS* 409/494). This "reconciling Yea," we are told, is itself the manifestation of God—of divine love—in the human community. For Hegel, therefore, true religion prepares the way for presuppositionless philosophy by fostering in us at the level of feeling the very willingness to *let go of* (*ablassen von*) what we hold most dear, which we have to exhibit in our philosophical activity.[25]

This is not to deny that religion consists in much more than such willingness: Hegel is well aware that religion tells a rich and subtle story about God's creative and redeeming work in the lives of individuals and in history. But he also insists that a free, *presuppositionless* philosophy cannot begin from any determinate vision of the divine order of things inherited from religion. "Scholasticism," Hegel points out, "adopted its content as something given . . . by the Church" (*EL* 69/98 [§31 Add.]), but scholasticism consequently was unfree thinking and so is no longer appropriate in the modern world. Hegel's own philosophy therefore cannot be a new scholasticism that *bases itself* on a religious conception of the world.

Once presuppositionless philosophy has completed its account of being and thought, it will become clear that philosophy and religion (in particular, Christianity) tell the same story: namely, that being as such ("God") comes to full self-consciousness (becomes incarnate "spirit") in human beings. The difference between the two forms of experience will be simply that religion pictures and feels what philosophy understands. Philosophy cannot, however, presuppose the truth of that story—in either its religious or its fully developed philosophical form—at the start. It cannot, therefore, begin from the determinate principle that "divine" being is the process of becoming self-conscious spirit in humanity. As Hegel puts it, "philosophy on its own, peculiar ground leaves theology completely behind as far as its principle is concerned."[26] Heidegger is thus wrong to claim that the theological idea of "God as spirit in general . . . pre-scribes the essence of the concept and thus the character of the logical," because this interpre-

25. See Houlgate, *An Introduction to Hegel,* p. 41.

26. Hegel, *VGP* 3: 123, my translation.

tation—which is shared by, among others, Derrida—turns Hegel into precisely the latter-day scholastic that he cannot be.[27]

Religion certainly prepares us for presuppositionless philosophy—this is the grain of truth in Heidegger's reading—but it does so by teaching us to "let go of our antithetical existence," *not* by giving us a determinate vision of spirit on which to base philosophy. For Hegel, indeed, the historical significance of the Protestant Reformation is that by freeing people from subservience to the Church and teaching them to find God within their own faith it encouraged them (wittingly or unwittingly) to free themselves from and so to let go of religious doctrine *itself* in their intellectual activity and to pursue the unrestricted freedom of thought. "To Protestantism alone," Hegel claims, "the important thing is to get a sure footing in the prose of life, to make it absolutely valid in itself independently of religious associations, and to let it develop in unrestricted freedom."[28] The role of presuppositionless philosophy, as we saw in chapter 1, is to clarify the categories that inform our ordinary experience. What we see now is that an important dimension of ordinary experience itself—namely, religion—prepares us "spiritually" to undertake that very activity of clarification without prejudice.

To recapitulate: Hegel's *Logic* does have certain historical and hermeneutic presuppositions, but these do not predetermine the course or the outcome of speculative logic. They cannot do so because they require philosophers, or enable them, to consider nothing beyond the indeterminate being of thought. Insofar as speculative philosophy begins from such indeterminacy, it has no *founding* presupposition and is thus in Hegel's sense presuppositionless. Paradoxical though it may seem, therefore, the various features we have examined in this chapter—the readiness to let, training in formal logic, and the historical circumstances that characterize modernity—constitute the presuppositions of genuinely presupposition*less* philosophy.

27. Heidegger, *Hegel's Phenomenology of Spirit*, p. 98.

28. G. W. F. Hegel, *Aesthetics: Lectures on Fine Art*, trans. T. M. Knox, 2 vols. (Oxford: Clarendon Press, 1975), 1: 598; G. W. F. Hegel, *Vorlesungen über die Ästhetik,* ed. E. Moldenhauer and K. M. Michel, 3 vols., *Werke in zwanzig Bänden,* vols. 13, 14, and 15 (Frankfurt am Main: Suhrkamp Verlag, 1969), 2: 225–6. Further references to the *Aesthetics* will be given in the following form: *A* 1: 598/2: 225–6.

Chapter Four

Language, Reflection, and the Beginning of the *Logic*

The Linguistic Challenge to Hegel

Almost from the moment the first volume of the *Science of Logic* was published in 1812, Hegel has been accused of ignoring, or failing to take full account of, what many regard as the most significant presupposition of his philosophy: namely, *language*. In particular, so the charge goes, Hegel neglects to notice the extent to which his very use of language vitiates the claim of his philosophy to be presuppositionless and immanent.

In a series of private letters to Hegel, the Nuremberg professor of mathematics (and Hegel's colleague at the time) J. W. A. Pfaff takes Hegel to task for employing, in his explanation of dialectical transitions, categories that are not derived and justified but rather "presupposed" and "*borrowed* from some other theory." The unfortunate consequence of such "borrowing," in Pfaff's view, is that Hegel's system falls into vicious circularity: categories examined in later sections of the *Logic*, which are said to be developed from what is discussed earlier, are themselves assumed in those earlier discussions. Pfaff locates the source of this vicious circularity in the fact that Hegel undertakes his "presuppositionless" derivation of the categories in a natural language containing a host of unproven assumptions and concepts. Pfaff's own discipline, mathematics, is said to avoid such circularity by employing an artificial system of notation with a limited number of postulates and premises and by openly admitting to being based on such premises and so not pretending to be presuppositionless in the first place. Philosophy, however, will inevitably lapse into vicious circularity to the extent that it endeavors to derive—and so not to take for granted—the fundamental categories of thought by employing a rich natural language in which categories are simply taken for granted.[1]

Twenty years later Schelling continues this line of criticism when he accuses Hegel of presupposing at the beginning of the *Logic* "virtually *all* concepts

1. See *Hegel: The Letters*, trans. C. Butler and C. Seiler (Bloomington: Indiana University Press, 1984), pp. 265–6.

which we use in everyday life."[2] In 1839 Feuerbach then repeats the charge when he suggests that in Hegel's initial account of pure being in the *Logic* the notions of immediacy, indeterminacy, and identity are presupposed.[3]

In the twentieth century Gadamer also pointed out that Hegel's *Logic* "must already presuppose and use the categories of reflection which it then claims to deduce dialectically."[4] This is due not to the unique character and circumstances of Hegel's philosophy but to an ineliminable feature of language as such. In Gadamer's view, "one must always use the categories of Essence, e.g., the determinations of Reflection, if one wants to make any statement at all. One cannot utter a sentence without bringing the categories of identity and difference into play."[5] Hegel's dependence on language means not only that certain words and concepts have to be presupposed at the outset of his *Logic* but also that the whole course of his logical derivation of the categories is guided, at least in part, by the ordinary historical meanings and associations that words have come to acquire over time. "With words," Gadamer writes, "there is no beginning ex nihilo": all words have inherited meanings that we cannot simply disavow. "Nor is it the case," he continues, "that a concept could be determined as a concept without the usage of the word with all of its many meanings playing a role."[6] The dialectical development of thought presented in the *Logic* is thus not driven purely by the immanent logical implications of the concepts considered but is also moved along by "the speculative power lying in the connotations of the German words."[7]

As examples of Hegel's dependence on language, Gadamer draws attention to the way that "Hegel is able to conjure up speculative truths out of the simplest turns of speech in German, e.g., *an sich, für sich, an und für sich,* or from words like *Wahr-nehmung and Bestimmung*."[8] Indeed, when he turns to Hegel's account of the transition from "becoming" to "determinate being" (*Dasein*), Gadamer appears to ignore altogether what Hegel claims is the *logical* ground of that transition—which we will consider in part 3 of this study—and to present it as following purely from the inherited meaning of the word "becoming":

---

2. Schelling, *On the History of Modern Philosophy*, p. 148.

3. Feuerbach, *Towards a Critique of Hegel's Philosophy*, p. 108; "Zur Kritik der Hegelschen Philosophie," p. 177. The English translation leaves out the word "indeterminacy." Hegel does not define or describe pure being in terms of "identity" in either the *Logic* or the *Encyclopedia Logic*, but he does talk of its "indeterminate immediacy," so Feuerbach's criticism cannot simply be dismissed on the grounds of textual inaccuracy; see *SL* 82/1: 82 (193).

4. H.-G. Gadamer, *Hegel's Dialectic: Five Hermeneutical Studies*, trans. P. C. Smith (New Haven: Yale University Press, 1976), p. 93.

5. Gadamer, *Hegel's Dialectic*, p. 82.

6. Gadamer, *Hegel's Dialectic*, p. 93.

7. Gadamer, *Hegel's Dialectic*, p. 112.

8. Gadamer, *Hegel's Dialectic*, p. 114.

> All becoming is a becoming of something which exists as a result of having become. That is an ancient truth, one already formulated by Plato in the *Philebus*. . . . It lies in the very meaning of Becoming itself that it reaches determinacy in that which finally has become.[9]

Gadamer accepts that Hegel acknowledges a connection between thought and language. But he believes that for Hegel language is nothing more than "a self-effacing and temporary medium of thought or merely its 'casing.'"[10] That is to say, the function of language is "limited to merely making plain what is being thought of *beforehand*" (my emphasis). It gives external expression to thought that has become "transparent to itself" through its own, internal, purely logical development. As Rod Coltman puts it, for Gadamer's Hegel, "even though thought is inseparable from the word, language . . . does not determine the course of 'true thinking' within it, but remains at the surface as its mere outward manifestation"—as if thought or spirit "in itself" were actually "something entirely other than language."[11]

For Gadamer himself, by contrast, language is the permanent "abode" of thought and infuses thought through and through.[12] There is thus no purely logical structure to concepts, such as "becoming" or "finitude," that is independent of the historical meanings that the *words* "becoming" and "finitude" have acquired through years of human dialogue and interpretation. Rather, in Gadamer's view, the apparently autonomous development of thought depends upon a "*natural* logic" of language that incorporates dialectic but is also much richer, more complex, and more open-ended than Hegel recognizes.[13]

Language, for Gadamer, is thus that which "breathes life into Hegel's philosophy." At the same time it is that which ultimately eludes the grasp of that philosophy because Hegel's rationalism can see nothing more in language than "an instinctive *logic* waiting to be penetrated by thought and conceptualized."[14] In other words, Gadamer finds in language what virtually all of Hegel's subsequent critics in the Continental tradition—including Schelling, Feuerbach, Kierkegaard, Marx, Nietzsche, Heidegger, Deleuze, Levinas, and Derrida—believe they have found: "a condition for the possibility of Hegel's system . . . that Hegel cannot recognize [or at least fully acknowledge] within that system."[15]

---

9. Gadamer, *Hegel's Dialectic*, p. 87. P. C. Smith translates Hegel's term *Dasein* as "existence" rather than "determinate being."

10. Gadamer, *Hegel's Dialectic*, p. 94.

11. R. Coltman, *The Language of Hermeneutics: Gadamer and Heidegger in Dialogue* (Albany: SUNY Press, 1998), pp. 102–3.

12. Gadamer, *Hegel's Dialectic*, p. 94.

13. Gadamer, *Hegel's Dialectic*, p. 99, my emphasis. See Coltman, *The Language of Hermeneutics*, p. 109.

14. Gadamer, *Hegel's Dialectic*, pp. 112, 92, my emphasis.

15. Kolb, *The Critique of Pure Modernity*, p. 219.

Hegel's Views on Language

The first thing to be said in response to these charges is that Hegel is fully aware that all thought is indeed linguistic. Thought is not reducible to language: thought is understanding and reasoning—consciousness of the nature or form of what there is and of what follows therefrom—whereas language is the system of signs in which such understanding is articulated. But Hegel insists that we can think and understand only *in language*. Language is no more a merely temporary "casing" for thought in Hegel's view than it is in Gadamer's, but it is the very abode of thought. We can form mental images of visible things without explicitly employing words, but we can frame thoughts—and so become conscious of what is not evident to our senses (such as the form or causes of things)—only through the explicit use of words. "It is in names that we *think*," Hegel says.[16] This is because it is only through words that our thoughts come to be something objective and determinate for us. Thoughts cannot be pictured or felt but need to be named and explained if they are to become something definite.

> We only know our thoughts, only have definite, actual thoughts, when we give them the form of objectivity, of a being distinct from our inwardness, and therefore the shape of externality, and of an externality, too, that at the same time bears the stamp of the highest inwardness. The articulated sound, the *word*, is alone such an inward externality.[17]

This is not to deny that thoughts can also be given *inadequate* articulation in language. "Language," Hegel maintains, "is exposed to the fate of serving just as much to conceal as to reveal human thoughts."[18] We do not, however, judge that a thought has been inadequately articulated by comparing what we say with some putative perfectly formed thought residing "behind" language in the inner depths of our mind (as we might compare our verbal description of someone with our mental image of him). We can justify such a judgment only by giving more adequate articulation to the thought concerned in *words*.

This is how we are to understand the relation between Hegel's account of the categories in his *Logic* and our ordinary understanding of those categories as it finds expression in everyday language. Hegel maintains that "the forms of thought [or categories] are, in the first instance, displayed and stored in human *language*" (*SL* 31/1: 20); they are given expression in the things we say, such as "this leaf *is* green" (*EL* 27/45 [§3]). In ordinary discourse, however, categories such as "being," "quantity," and "cause" are often employed without a full understanding of all they imply. The role of the *Logic*, as we have seen, is to bring us to a full understanding of such categories by drawing out their immanent im-

---

16. Hegel, *EPM* 220/278 (§462), translation revised. See also *SL* 31/1: 20.

17 Hegel, *EPM* 221/280 (§462 Add.). See also S. Houlgate, *Hegel, Nietzsche, and the Criticism of Metaphysics* (Cambridge: Cambridge University Press, 1986), pp. 141–5.

18. Hegel, *EPM* 151/197 (§411 Add.).

plications. This immanent exposition of the true structure of our categories cannot, however, bypass language. Rather, it will use language to give us a more precise and more developed grasp of the categories than we ordinarily employ in our discourse.

Indeed, Hegel's exposition will use the resources of *ordinary* language itself to take us beyond our ordinary understanding of the categories. For Hegel, of course, this means that it will use the resources of everyday German. Not only is German Hegel's native tongue, but it is also particularly suited, in his view, to articulating the true, speculative character of the categories. This is because (so Hegel believes) more categories find explicit expression in German as ordinary nouns and verbs (such as *Maß* or *sein*) than in many other languages and also because German is endowed with a distinctive "speculative spirit." "Some of its words," Hegel writes, "possess the . . . peculiarity of having not only different but opposite meanings" (*SL* 32/1: 20), and as we saw in chapter 3, speculative reason is reason that comprehends "the unity of the determinations [such as being and nothing] in their opposition" (*EL* 131/176 [§82]). Speculative philosophy thus does not need to adopt a specialized, technical vocabulary (though it can, and does, employ non-German words, such as *Reflexion*), but can exploit the resonances of everyday German words (*SL* 32, 708/1: 21, 2: 406).

In fact, Hegel thinks that only in this way can philosophy avoid alienating its students and be understood as clarifying and extending their *own* understanding: "when they are expressed in one's own language (for example, *Bestimmtheit* instead of *Determination*, *Wesen* instead of *Essenz*, etc.), it is immediately apparent to consciousness that these concepts are its ownmost—that with which it is always concerned—and not something alien."[19] A philosophy written in the vernacular can thereby become the property of a people as a whole and be seen as the public enterprise of self-clarification in which the participants find freedom in being released to the true implications of their own thoughts, rather than being subordinated to the dictates of an alien intellectual authority. In choosing to use German vocabulary wherever possible, like Fichte before him and Heidegger after him, and to avoid the Latin terminology favored by Kant (and often Adorno), Hegel thus continues in the area of philosophy the work begun by Martin Luther, who enabled people to find truths about their *own* lives more easily in Christianity through his translation of the Bible into German.[20]

At this point, those who know Hegel's work only through English translations may be forgiven a distinctly skeptical smile. Hegel uses *ordinary* vocabulary? Can that be true? Do Germans really go around talking about "determinateness" (*Bestimmtheit*) and "being in and for itself" (*Anundfürsichsein*)? Well, perhaps not precisely in the way Hegel does, but they do use related expressions in everyday speech. Ask a German if he or she thinks national reunification was

19. Hegel, *VGP* 3: 259, my translation.

20. Hegel, *VGP* 3: 16, 53.

a good thing, and you may hear in response "*bestimmt*" ("definitely") or "*an und für sich, schon*" ("in principle, sure"). These are quite straightforward German expressions and do not simply indicate that the speakers spent too many ill-judged hours in their youth wading through Hegel's *Logic*. One should remember, therefore, that although Hegel's vocabulary may seem strange to our ears when translated into English, he is deliberately using *familiar* German words and turns of phrase to articulate his speculative comprehension of the categories. He clarifies his aim in a famous letter to J. H. Voss written in 1805: "I may say of my endeavor that I wish to try to teach philosophy to speak German"—just as Luther had made the Bible speak German and Voss had done the same for Homer.[21]

There is no doubt that Hegel's syntax is strange to ordinary speakers of German, but to the extent that Hegel employs a predominantly German vocabulary, Gadamer is right to claim that the German language "breathes life into Hegel's philosophy."[22] Where I disagree with Gadamer, however, is in his claim that Hegel—despite his intention to produce a purely logical account of the categories—in fact "conjures up" speculative truths *out of* German words and idioms and that the ordinary meanings of words thus play a significant role in determining how Hegel understands the categories and their development.[23] In my view, Hegel certainly exploits the resources of German in order to render his dialectical account of the categories as intelligible and as engaging to his audience as he can, but as I will try to show later in this study, his understanding of the categories themselves is determined solely by the way they are derived *logically* from the initial category of pure being, not by the ordinary meanings and associations of the words he uses. As Wolfgang Wieland puts it, "although the logic must always manifest itself in a given language, it is not therefore a mere function of this language."[24] Hegel's philosophy is clearer and more accessible in German than in English, but his arguments do not depend on peculiarities of the German language. It can consequently be translated into, or rewritten in, other languages than German.

Hegel's claim is that the categories he sets out are derived from the sheer being of thought as such, not from the contingent qualities of any particular way of thinking or any specific language. This does *not* mean that people in all civilizations of the past or present necessarily employ all these categories or that every language has an appropriate expression for each category. Many categories may be latent in the understanding of certain cultures and not yet have become explicit categories of thought. If Hegel is right, however, all the categories set out

21. *Hegel: The Letters*, p. 107.

22. Gadamer, *Hegel's Dialectic*, p. 112.

23. Gadamer, *Hegel's Dialectic*, pp. 114, 93.

24. Wieland, "Bemerkungen zum Anfang von Hegels Logik," p. 207, my translation.

in the *Logic* must at least be *implicit* in the understanding of everyone, and where a civilization does not employ a category that Hegel has derived, its members must, like Meno's slave, be able to be brought to an explicit understanding of it. In such cases, new expressions may have to be coined in the relevant languages, and as a result, the speakers of those languages may find themselves less able to feel at home in Hegel's *Logic* than speakers of German. But there is nothing in principle to prevent Hegel's *Logic* from being translated into those other languages and to preclude the speakers of those languages following his arguments. In that sense, although the German language does "breathe through it," Hegel's philosophy is in principle *universally* intelligible.

The German language constitutes a historical presupposition of Hegel's speculative philosophy since it forms part of the historical and cultural context that gave birth to that philosophy. It does not, however, constitute an ineliminable hermeneutic precondition of speculative philosophy since one does not have to speak German in order to understand that philosophy or to philosophize speculatively oneself (though Hegel's *Logic* is certainly easier to read and understand, and—as it were—more homey, if one does speak German). Language as such, by contrast, is a necessary hermeneutic precondition of speculative philosophy insofar as all thought must occur in words. Moreover, since we do not just speak "language as such," but rather one or more specific languages, the speculative philosopher must presuppose the vocabulary and idioms of at least one of those languages. Such a philosopher must also presuppose whatever "concepts of reflection," such as identity (or sameness) and difference, may be operative in all languages. To this extent, then, Pfaff, Schelling, Feuerbach, and Gadamer are right: Hegel cannot begin his *Logic* without taking for granted and employing concepts that are only derived and justified *later* in the *Logic*.

Yet neither language as such nor any specific language constitutes the *founding* presupposition of speculative philosophy in the sense in which I have been using the term. This is because the ordinary meanings of the words and concepts that Hegel must presuppose and employ do not themselves determine the course of his derivation of categories from the thought of pure being. That is determined by the thought of pure being alone. Hegel's *Logic* does not, therefore, fall into vicious circularity: he certainly uses words and concepts at the start of his account that are justified only later, but that process of justification is not determined in advance by those words and concepts. As Richard Winfield aptly puts it, language (and the concepts of reflection it entails) constitutes nothing more than the "enabling condition" of speculative philosophy: it makes it possible for us to do philosophy but does not predetermine, or set prior limits to, what we can think and understand.[25] For Gadamer's Hegel (though not for Gadamer himself), pure thought develops autonomously *apart from* language

25. R. Winfield, *Overcoming Foundations: Studies in Systematic Philosophy* (New York: Columbia University Press, 1989), pp. 63, 87–8.

and is then merely encased in words. For the Hegel I am presenting in this study, by contrast, pure thought develops autonomously *in* language and *thanks to* language.

But how can language play such an enabling role? How can it *not* predetermine in some way what we are to think? In other words, how can philosophy be immersed in language and yet be moved forward not by the ordinary meanings of words but by the immanent development of the category of pure being alone?

The Beginning of the **Logic**: *Henrich's Insight*

Language plays this enabling role by allowing us to formulate *negative* or *self-canceling* expressions through which we hold at bay or eliminate the ordinary connotations of certain pivotal words we use to characterize each category. This is what permits us at the start of the *Logic* to form the purely abstract and indeterminate concept of being and to focus solely on what follows from that indeterminate concept rather than from the more familiar meanings of the word "being." Hegel's distinctive use of language at the beginning of the *Logic* has been analyzed with considerable subtlety by Dieter Henrich in his seminal article, "Anfang und Methode der Logik." What follows here is based on, though also expands on, Henrich's account. The claim I am making, by the way, is not that Hegel's *Logic* presupposes a theory about language, which might itself be open to dispute, but that it presupposes a distinctive *use* of language that is shown to be possible by Hegel's very practice. In order to appreciate how a presuppositionless, immanent philosophy is possible, the reader of Hegel's *Logic* needs to understand not so much what Hegel believes about language but how he actually employs it to think pure being.

Henrich distinguishes two types of expression employed by Hegel that are especially important. On the one hand, some of Hegel's expressions "have an unmistakenly negative character and clearly just have the task of keeping every further determination away from the purity of being."[26] Henrich says nothing more about such expressions, but it is obvious which ones he has in mind: for instance, at the very start of the *Logic*, being is described as being "*without* (*ohne*) any further determination" and as having "*no* (*keine*) diversity within itself nor any with a reference outwards" (*SL* 82/1: 82 [193], my emphasis).

On the other hand, according to Henrich, two expressions in particular attribute a positive character to pure being by means of "categories of reflection" whose own reflexive meaning is at the same time cancelled. The expressions to which Henrich refers are those in which Hegel describes pure being as enjoying "indeterminate immediacy" (*unbestimmte Unmittelbarkeit*) and as being "equal

26. D. Henrich, "Anfang und Methode der Logik," in D. Henrich, *Hegel im Kontext* (Frankfurt am Main: Suhrkamp Verlag, 1971), p. 85. All translations from Henrich's article are my own.

only to itself" (*nur sich selbst gleich*). These expressions are intended by Hegel to explicate and help us focus on precisely what is meant by *pure*, rather than determinate, being.

Take the first of these, according to which being is understood not as visible or tangible being, nor as existence, reality, or nature, but as sheer *indeterminate immediacy*. We know what the word "indeterminate" normally means: it means "lacking all definition and specificity that comes from being contrasted with something else," that is, "lacking the determinacy of being *this* rather than *that*." We also know what "immediacy" means: it means "that which is simply, directly or straightaway what it is and is not mediated (or there by virtue of) something else." By putting these two terms together, we can thus formulate the thought of pure or sheer being—being that just *is* and that lacks any further defining characteristic.

Henrich notes, however, that these terms focus our minds on pure being only to the extent that their juxtaposition cancels certain aspects of their meaning. Strictly speaking, the word "immediacy" means "unmediatedness," "not-being-mediated," or "the negation of mediation." To think of *immediacy* as such is thus, paradoxically, to think of a concept that is not itself *immediate* but rather "*mediated* and *determined* by this concept [of mediation]."[27] The fact that the term "immediacy" has meaning only through the contrast with "mediation" is, indeed, what makes it a *reflexive* term.[28] In Hegel's expression, however, the immediacy we are to think of is characterized as indeterminate; that is to say, as *not* determined or specified by means of a contrast with anything else. If immediacy is to be understood as indeterminate in this way, it cannot therefore be conceived in explicit contrast to mediation. In other words, it cannot be understood explicitly as *im*-mediacy (*Un-mittelbarkeit*). The effect of qualifying the word "immediacy" with the adjective "indeterminate" is thus to cancel part of the normal meaning of the word. Accordingly, Hegel's expression focuses our attention on an immediacy lacking in determinacy to such a degree that it cannot be thought *as* "immediacy" at all but can only be thought as pure *being*.

But if Hegel wants us to think of pure being, not "im-mediacy" as such, why does he use the term "immediacy" here at all? In my view, he needs to use this term because he is addressing an audience that usually thinks of being (to the extent that it does so at all) not just as pure but as specified and qualified in a variety of ways and so as *mediated* by all manner of differences and contrasts—as tangible being, rather than visible being, or as historical rather than natural existence, and so on. He thus has to make it clear to this audience that at the start of the *Logic* being is *not* to be thought of in any of these normal ways—as

27. Henrich, "Anfang und Methode der Logik," p. 85, my emphasis.

28. In this study I use the word "reflexive" to refer to meanings or logical structures that are defined by opposition to other such meanings, and I use the word "reflection" to refer to the form of thought that employs reflexive words or concepts.

mediated or specified—but is to be conceived as sheer and utter *immediacy*. Hegel's use of the word "immediacy" is rendered necessary, therefore, by the fact that he aims to bring readers, accustomed to certain ways of thinking about what there is, to a much more abstract way of conceiving of being.

At the same time, Hegel does not want his readers to focus on the thought of *im-mediacy* as such because, as he points out, "simple immediacy is itself an expression of reflection and contains a reference to its distinction from what is mediated" (*SL* 69/1: 68 [175]). He goes on to note that "this simple immediacy . . . in its true expression is *pure being*."[29] At the beginning of the *Logic*, therefore, in order to help his readers form the thought of pure being, he directs them to think of an immediacy that is quite *indeterminate*. By naming the object of thought "indeterminate immediacy," Hegel thus employs ordinary, reflexive words in such a way that the reflexive connotations of those words are cancelled leaving his readers focused on pure being alone.

As Henrich notes, the same result is achieved by describing pure being as "equal only to itself." Normally, something is regarded as equal to something *else*. By speaking of being's equality only with itself, therefore, Hegel makes it clear that the normal connotation of *equality* is being negated here. Pure being, after all, is not initially conceived in relation to or in contrast to anything else with which it could be equal. Equality is not, however, a redundant notion to invoke, for pure being *is* equal to itself in the sense that it has no internal division or diversity. Hegel describes pure being as equal only with itself, therefore, in order to direct the attention of the reader to the sheer simplicity of pure being.

In both these cases, Henrich points out, the thought of being is articulated by means of "negated determinations of reflection." That is to say, "a category of reflection ['immediacy' or 'equality'] is qualified by a determination ['indeterminate' or 'only with itself'], which is meant precisely to *cancel* (*aufheben*) the reflexive character of that category" (and thereby part of the ordinary meaning of the term). These categories—and the self-canceling expressions of which they form a part—thus do not identify reflexive structures in pure being; on the contrary, they "point (*verweisen*) to the thought that is meant by 'being,' by declaring it to be completely free of reflexive structures." In other words, they bring the thought of pure being to mind by way of the negation of reflection (*via negationis*). Yet they do not lead us to conceive of pure being *as* the explicit *negation* of the many ordinary and reflexive senses of being (as the negation of existence, actuality, and so on). They direct us toward the thought of being as "something unanalysable . . . in its simple, unfilled immediacy" (*SL* 75/1: 75 [183]) and so lead us to think of pure *being* alone.[30]

The overtly negative expressions employed by Hegel to characterize pure being (such as "*without* any further determination" and "has *no* diversity within

---

29. See also Hegel, *VLM* 73.

30. Henrich, "Anfang und Methode der Logik," pp. 85–7.

itself") are also designed to bring to mind the sheer purity and simplicity of being. They are not intended, despite their negative form, to make us think of being *as* explicitly *negative* itself. The opening words of the first paragraph on being—"*being, pure being*, without any further determination"—should therefore be taken as a description, rather than a definition, of being: they tell us *that* pure being lacks all further determination, but they do not define being *as* the explicit lack, absence, or negation of determinacy.[31] Indeed, one can actually read Hegel's phrase as an injunction: it enjoins us to think of pure being alone and not to determine it any further. Similarly, Hegel's statement that being has no internal diversity should not lead us to think of pure being *as* that which lacks such diversity. It should lead us to think of pure being alone and, at the same time, to leave any thought of internal diversity to one side.

This may seem to be a rather obscure and trivial point on which to insist, but it is not: for it demonstrates—*contra* Schelling, Feuerbach, and Gadamer—how *language* does, indeed, enable us to bring to mind an utterly *presuppositionless* conception of being (and to think the purely autonomous, logical development of that conception into further categories). Hegel believes that self-critical philosophy should begin by suspending all presuppositions about, and determinate conceptions of, thought and being. All we may begin from is the sheer being of thought: the thought of thought *as* sheer being. What is meant by such being is not nature, existence, actuality or the being expressed in the copula, but utterly indeterminate, immediate being as such. Hegel is aware, however, that if such being is defined explicitly *as* in-determinacy and im-mediacy, it is invested with a determinacy of its own through being contrasted with determinacy and mediation and is thereby mediated—constituted as a concept—by the very concepts it excludes. It is thus not understood to be utterly *indeterminate* and *immediate* being, after all. Paradoxically, being can be thought to be utterly indeterminate, immediate being only when it is not conceived *as* indeterminacy and immediacy but is thought—through a distinctive use of language—as pure being alone.[32]

This, I believe, is the point Hegel is seeking to make in these lines from the *Encyclopedia Logic:*

> When thinking is to begin, we have nothing but thought in its pure lack of determination (*Bestimmungslosigkeit*); for determination requires both one and another, but at the beginning we have as yet no other. That which lacks determination, as we have it here, is the immediate, not a

31. See H.-P. Falk, *Das Wissen in Hegels "Wissenschaft der Logik"* (Freiburg/München: Verlag Karl Alber, 1983), p. 25.

32. Heidegger appears to ignore this important point completely. In his view, being is understood by Hegel explicitly "als das *Un*-bestimmte, *Un*-vermittelbare, genauer: die *Un-bestimmtheit und Un-vermitteltheit schlechthin*." See M. Heidegger, *Hegel*, ed. I. Schübler, *Gesamtausgabe*, vol. 68 (Vittorio Klostermann: Frankfurt am Main, 1993), p. 19; see also p. 30: "Das Sein begriffen als *Unbestimmtheit und Unmittelbarkeit*."

> mediated lack of determination, *not the sublation of all determinacy* (*nicht die Aufhebung aller Bestimmtheit*), but the lack of determination in all its immediacy, what lacks determination prior to all determinacy, what lacks determinacy because it stands at the very beginning. But this is what we call "being." (*EL* 137/184 [§86 Add. 1], my emphasis)

Hegel's meaning here is surely clear: we are to think of being "in its pure lack of determination" as pure being, *not* as the explicit "*sublation* [or *negation*] of determinacy."

We can see now more clearly what it means to "suspend" or "abstract from" all our ordinary assumptions about being. It means setting such assumptions to one side and leaving them out of the thought of being altogether; it does *not* mean thinking of them as explicitly excluded by the thought of pure being itself. A purely abstract thought, for Hegel, is one that simply lacks any determinacy whatsoever; it is not one that is *defined* and *determined as* lacking all determinacy and that thereby explicitly includes within itself the idea that all determinacy is excluded from it.

Later in the *Logic* more concrete, determinate concepts will be defined as explicitly excluding other concepts ("something," for example, will be thought as the limit or "non-being" of what is other [*SL* 126/1: 136 (225)]), but that is not the case with the initial utterly abstract and indeterminate concept of pure being. Nor is it the case with the equally abstract thought of pure nothing into which the thought of pure being immediately vanishes. Nothing is not to be thought of as the "nothing of a particular something," Hegel writes, but is to be thought of as "nothing . . . in its indeterminate simplicity": that is, as "nothing, purely on its own account, negation devoid of any relations—what could also be expressed if one so wished merely by 'not'" (*SL* 83/1: 84 [195]).

Language and Abstraction

Purely abstract thought requires us to suspend the ordinary connotations of the words "being" and "nothing," but it requires us to do so in language and through the use of ordinary words. Indeed, it is only through the precise use of negative and self-canceling expressions (and, of course, ordinary words, such as *all, further, has, within,* etc.) that abstract thought is possible at all. It is *in language*, therefore, that ordinary thought or reflection becomes the pure *abstract* understanding that sets the ordinary connotations of words to one side, holds fast to the thought of indeterminate being, and lets it hold sway.[33]

The result of such abstraction is that right at the start of the *Logic* two levels of thought emerge.[34] Hegel writes and speaks in a specific language—modern German—whose words are infused with all the determinate connotations and

---

33. See chapter 3, above, pp. 65–6.
34. See Wieland, "Bemerkungen zum Anfang von Hegels Logik," p. 200.

associations of everyday usage (though he does also make occasional use of Greek and Latin words as well). But in that language Hegel forms the indeterminate thought of pure being and unfolds what follows immanently from that thought. He thus uses (or "operates" with) ordinary *determinate* words with rich and varied meanings to bring to mind (and "thematize") an utterly *indeterminate* thought. This is what generates the two different levels of thought. It needs to be stressed that these two levels are not simply assumed to be present from the start. They are *generated* by the process of abstraction—the process in which ordinary thought uses ordinary words and concepts to become self-critical and speculative. It also needs to be emphasized that the "thematization" and logical development of the thought of indeterminate being does not take place *outside* or *behind* language. It is a development that is articulated *in* language but that (*pace* Gadamer) is not governed *by* the contingencies of language itself.

These two levels persist throughout the *Logic*, since Hegel never ceases to employ the words and concepts of his natural language—unlike Leibniz, he eschews any attempt to create a purely formal, symbolic language in which to express speculative insights—and, equally, he never ceases to focus on or "thematize" what is immanent in the thought of pure being and the subsequent categories that are derived from it. This, I take it, is what Henrich has in mind when he asserts that "the *science* of logic must be distinguished from the process of the logical thought-determinations."[35] The concept of pure being gives rise to an autonomous, linear development of thought (an "*einsinnige Entwicklung*"), but the scientific account of that development is an activity of thought undertaken by concrete human beings living in definite historical circumstances and utilizing the words and reflexive concepts of ordinary language.

Hegel accepts that even though our thought is focused on the immanent implications of the category of pure being we remain throughout *reflective* beings who are able to describe the concepts that arise in various ways and comment on their similarities with and differences from other concepts that have been considered already or that have yet to be discussed. In theory, Hegel remarks, the exposition presented in the *Logic* "would demand that at no stage of the development should any thought-determination or reflection occur which does not immediately emerge at this stage and that has not entered this stage from the one preceding it" (*SL* 40/1: 30–1). However, he continues, "such an abstract perfection of exposition must, I admit, in general be dispensed with." The reason why is that we have not only to unfold the dialectical implications of the thematized categories but also to explain the dialectical development, in a language shot through with contingent, historical assumptions about the very concepts that are being derived, to an audience that may find it hard to keep on suspending such assumptions and so needs to be reminded repeatedly to set them aside.

The fact that the science of logic must begin with "what is absolutely sim-

---

35. Henrich, "Anfang und Methode der Logik," p. 92.

ple," Hegel notes, would (or should) "restrict the exposition solely to these same quite simple expressions of the simple without any further addition of a single word." In other words, all we should be permitted to do is name each category as it arises and give a minimal account of why it emerges and why it gives rise to further concepts. Hegel points out, however, that in fact we also need to inject into our account "negative reflections (*negierende Reflexionen*) . . . to ward off and banish any heterogeneous elements which otherwise might be introduced by pictorial thought or unregulated thinking." He concedes that "it is futile to try to deal with *all* of them," but he also acknowledges that "the peculiar restlessness and distraction of our modern consciousness compel us to take some account of the more readily suggested reflections and opinions" (*SL* 40/1: 31; see also *SL* 94/1: 97).[36] For this reason, Hegel's *Logic* provides not only a rigorous logical derivation of the categories, but also frequent digressions, remarks, reviews, and anticipatory comments in order to facilitate our understanding and to counter certain foreseeable misunderstandings.

Hegel recognizes, however, that "such reflections . . . have the disadvantage of appearing as unjustified assertions, grounds and foundations for what is to follow." To state, for example, that being will turn out to be becoming, determinate being, and finitude *before* this has been proven dialectically, may well help readers orient themselves, but it is nevertheless to make an unwarranted assertion (as later critics, such as Schelling and Feuerbach are eager to point out). Such reflections, Hegel insists, "should therefore not be taken for more than they are supposed to be and should be distinguished from what is a moment in the development of the subject matter itself" (*SL* 110/1: 117 [205]). They are included, as Alan White points out, "for pedagogical rather than for logical reasons."[37] The logical derivation of the categories should not be based on such reflections or on the ordinary associations of the words used to describe and define the categories being thematized but should follow immanently from those thematized categories themselves: "only that which is *posited* (*gesetzt*) in a concept belongs in the dialectical development of that concept" (*SL* 110/1: 117 [205]). In part 3 of this study, I will try to show that, *pace* Gadamer, the development of categories in the *Logic* is indeed wholly immanent and is not dependent at all on the contingent associations of the ordinary words used to describe them or on any reflective comparisons that Hegel may draw between concepts.

The logical development of the concept of becoming, for example, thus has to be generated by what is immanent in the fact that becoming proves to be the vanishing of being into nothing and of nothing into being; it may not be based on the ordinary assumption that becoming is always the coming-to-be of *something*. Equally, the logical development of the category of determinate being has

36. Miller translates *negierende Reflexionen* as "negative considerations."

37. White, *Absolute Knowledge*, p. 52.

to follow solely from the fact that determinate being proves to be the settled unity of being and nothing; it may not be determined or influenced by the fact that the German word Hegel uses, *Dasein*, implies existence in space, or being-*there*.

Provided that we focus our attention on the explicit definition of each category and on what is implicit in such definitions, then the absolute immanence of our account will not be vitiated or compromised in any way by the fact that we use ordinary, reflexive concepts to describe the thematized categories and to situate them in relation to others that have not yet been derived. Clearly, whether or not Hegel's derivation of each category is strictly immanent can only be established in each specific case: we should not take it for granted in advance that Hegel is always successful in deriving categories solely from what is implicit in their predecessors. What I do wish to claim, however, is that there is no *a priori* reason why Hegel's inevitable reliance on the given words and concepts of ordinary language should prevent him from deriving the categories immanently and presuppositionlessly from the concept of pure being.

It is quite true that the reflexive concepts, such as equality, diversity, immediacy, and indeterminacy, operative at the start of the *Logic* (as well as all the vocabulary Hegel employs) make possible, and so *mediate*, our initial conception of pure being. At the same time, however, one must recognize that the mediation they provide is a *self-negating* or *self-sublating* one, because such words and concepts are employed precisely to hold at bay their own ordinary connotations and to leave thought with the indeterminate thought of pure being. Hegel's description of the role played by the *Phenomenology* in preparing the way for, or mediating, the beginning of the *Logic* (which we will look at in chapter 7) applies equally, in my view, to the role played by language and the concepts of reflection: "the beginning is made with being which is represented as having come to be through mediation, a mediation which is also a sublating of itself (*Vermittlung . . . welche zugleich Aufheben ihrer selbst ist*)" (*SL* 69/1: 68 [175]).

Hegel is thus well aware—as we should be—that the thought of pure being is produced by, and is thus the *mediated* result of, a process of abstraction undertaken in ordinary language.[38] At the outset of the *Logic*, however, when we are to suspend all our assumptions and convictions about thought and being, we have to set aside this idea that being is a mediated abstraction and take it in its *immediacy* as pure being alone:

> *Pure being*, this absolute immediacy[,] has equally the character of something absolutely mediated. But it is equally essential that it be taken only in the one-sided character in which it is pure immediacy, *precisely because* here it is the beginning. If it were not this pure indeterminate-

38. See Hegel, *VLM* 71: "Dieser Begriff [des Seins] ist der leichteste, weil man nur alles andere *weggelassen* hat, um diesen Begriff zu haben," my emphasis.

> ness, if it were determinate, it would have been taken as something mediated, something already carried a stage further. . . . Therefore, it lies in the *very nature of a beginning* that it must be being and nothing else. (*SL* 72/1: 72 [179])

In other words, if we are truly to suspend our assumptions at the beginning of the *Logic*, and to start *from scratch*, we must even abstract from and set aside—indeed deliberately forget—the very fact that pure being is the product of abstraction. We are not to think of it *as* an abstraction from—*as* the negation of—being as it is usually conceived, but simply *as* pure being.[39]

Hegel's point here is important: the only way genuinely to let go of all we take for granted about being and to conceive it *in* its utterly abstract indeterminacy and immediacy is to stop thinking of it *as* the abstraction we know it to be. For if we think of pure being *as* an abstraction, we think of it as mediated and therefore determined by the process of abstracting and by that from which it has been abstracted. But that, paradoxically, is to think of it as having a determinate, concrete (albeit barely concrete), and not utterly *abstract* character. Consequently, Hegel writes, "when being is taken in this simplicity and immediacy, the recollection that it is the result of complete abstraction, and so for that reason alone is abstract negativity, nothing, is left behind, outside the science" (*SL* 99/1: 104). Indeed, the moment we allow that recollection to determine our thought of being, we no longer think of pure being as such but rather of something that has been mediated and produced, that is, something "essential" (*SL* 389/2: 13–14).

It should be clear from what we have said that Hegel is by no means as naive as he is sometimes taken to be. He is not suggesting that we can or should blot out from our minds all that we know about ourselves and the world we live in. As presuppositionless philosophers, we remain well aware that being includes natural and historical existence and that "pure being" is an abstraction. We remain well aware of the complex experience of things from which the idea of pure being has been abstracted and of the mediating role played by language in that work of abstraction. Yet at the same time, we focus our attention, with the help of various negative and self-canceling *linguistic* expressions, on the abstract thought of pure being itself and hold at bay everything else of which we are "well aware." That means that we even abstract from the fact that pure being is the result of abstraction and focus on *what* has been abstracted rather than on the fact of its *having been abstracted*. This work of keeping in mind yet holding at bay all that we take to be true is what the self-critical suspension of our pre-

39. In contrast to Pippin, therefore, I think that Hegel does believe that we arrive at the concept of pure being by "*abstracting* from every concrete determination and think[ing] the result" (Pippin, *Hegel's Idealism*, p. 184). I agree with Pippin, however, that Hegel does not conceive of pure being explicitly *as* that which has been abstracted from, or *as* the negation of, determinacy.

suppositions consists in. In one sense, it involves "emptying our mind" of concrete, determinate thoughts (in the manner of Meister Eckhart). But such emptying entails focusing our explicit *attention* on sheer empty, indeterminate being, not eliminating every single word or thought from our mind. It means becoming "dull, empty consciousness" that "says inwardly only *Om*, *Om*, *Om*"—or *being*, *being*, *being*—in and through a rich and varied language that one continues to speak (*SL* 97/1: 101). As Hegel makes clear in the preface to the *Phenomenology*, such emptying and self-restraint demands considerable effort:

> What, therefore, is important in the *study* of *Science*, is that one should take on oneself the strenuous effort of the concept (*die Anstrengung des Begriffs*). This requires attention (*Aufmerksamkeit*) to the concept as such, to the simple determinations, e.g. of Being-in-itself, Being-for-itself, Self-identity, etc. (*PhS* 35/56)

An essential precondition of our making this effort, in Hegel's view, is that we employ ordinary, familiar words, such as *without* and *no*.

Kierkegaard's Critique of Hegel

The claim that rational thought can, indeed, suspend the idea that pure being is the result of abstraction is firmly denied by one of Hegel's subtlest critics, Kierkegaard. In his *Concluding Unscientific Postscript*, Kierkegaard points out that Hegel's *Logic* begins with what is immediate but that it does not begin immediately with the immediate because the beginning is—or, at least, is supposed to be—"*reached by means of a process of reflection*." The immediate is construed by Hegel as simply the "most abstract content remaining after an exhaustive reflection." Kierkegaard believes, however, that this process of reflection and abstraction is much more problematic than Hegel is prepared to admit. Indeed, he believes that it cannot actually give way to the thought of purely immediate being at all because it cannot bring itself to an end. The activity of reflection and abstraction is "infinite," in Kierkegaard's view, for the simple reason that "in attempting to stop itself it must use itself" and so cannot in fact put a stop to itself at all.[40]

In his comments on Hegel in the *Postscript*, Kierkegaard does not provide a full explanation of what he means, but his point is clear enough: the very act of trying to put a stop to reflection and to think of sheer immediacy is itself an act of reflection; in trying to put a stop to itself, reflection thus remains at work and so cannot but regard the immediacy, which it comes to think, as the mediated result of its own activity. Similarly, the activity of abstraction can bring itself to an

40. Kierkegaard, *Concluding Unscientific Postscript*, pp. 102–3. Since the activity of reflection and abstraction repeats itself endlessly, for Kierkegaard, it is "infinite" in the sense of Hegel's bad infinite or, more precisely, his progress to infinity, not in the sense of his true infinite. See chapters 21 and 22, below.

end only by abstracting from itself and so continuing to be carried on, but that means that it again faces the task of bringing itself to an end and abstracting from itself, and so on *ad infinitum*. By itself, therefore, the activity of reflection and abstraction, which is meant to issue in the thought of purely immediate being with which the *Logic* is to begin, is in fact incapable of leading to such a thought and so fails to get Hegel's system going.

In Kierkegaard's view, however, this endless activity of reflection and abstraction can be interrupted by an arbitrary "resolve" or "resolution of the will" through which the philosopher simply *decides* to think of what is immediate. Kierkegaard thus acknowledges that Hegel's system can get going after all, but he insists that the precondition of its so doing is a subjective decision by the individual, *not* an act of self-suspension by reflective thought. Since it depends upon such an arbitrary decision or existential "leap," Kierkegaard concludes, Hegel's system is not as absolute and presuppositionless, or as purely logical and rational, as Hegel pretends it is.[41]

Kierkegaard's reading of Hegel is significant because it points to a frequently overlooked feature of the *Logic:* namely, that it does indeed presuppose a resolve or decision on the part of the philosopher to consider pure being. As we have seen, the *Logic* is made necessary historically by the modern spirit of free self-criticism. Yet however necessary it may be that the categories of thought be derived presuppositionlessly, someone still has to take the decision to set aside his or her assumptions about thought and being and undertake such a derivation. Hegel is quite explicit about this: at the beginning of logic

> all that is present is simply the resolve (*Entschluß*), which can also be regarded as arbitrary (*eine Willkür*), that we propose to consider thought as such. . . . To enter into philosophy . . . calls for no other preparations, no further reflections or points of connection. (*SL* 70, 72/1: 68, 72 [175, 179])

In this respect, Kierkegaard's interpretation of Hegel is right on the mark. Furthermore, as Kierkegaard points out, this prevents the beginning of Hegel's *Logic* from being presuppositionless and "absolute" in one sense because it means that the beginning presupposes and is conditioned by a subjective decision. What Kierkegaard fails to recognize, however, is that drawing attention to this fact does not constitute a telling criticism of Hegel since Hegel never denies that the *Logic* is conditioned in this sense. He is well aware that the *Logic* presupposes certain historical conditions and certain hermeneutical abilities on the part of the philosopher, and the decision to think of pure being is simply a further, indispensable precondition of doing philosophy as Hegel understands it.

In addition, Kierkegaard fails to recognize that nothing he has said prevents the *Logic* from being presuppositionless in the one sense that matters to Hegel because, as Alan White writes, "the development of thought following the deci-

41. Kierkegaard, *Concluding Unscientific Postscript*, pp. 103–5.

sion is not conditioned by whatever course of reflection led to the decision."[42] In other words, the decision made by the thinker to focus on pure being does not constitute a *founding* presupposition of the *Logic*: one that determines in advance the path that the *Logic* will take.

Kierkegaard also fails to note that, for Hegel, the decision to think of pure being does not simply interrupt the process of reflection and abstraction but is itself an act *of* abstract thought. What is described in the *Logic* as a "resolve" is described in the *Encyclopedia Logic* as "the free act of thinking" (*der freie Akt des Denkens*) (*EL* 41/63 [§17]); the intimate connection between deciding and willing, on the one hand, and thinking, on the other, is further reinforced in the *Philosophy of Right*. The will, Hegel tells us, makes choices and initiates actions, but it only does so by first freeing us from what we are determined to be by our *given* drives and desires. This act of liberation by the will is, according to Hegel, an act of thought—of thought that *abstracts* from the natural character of the mind:

> The will (*Wille*) contains (a) the element of *pure indeterminacy* or of the "I"'s pure reflection (*Reflexion*) into itself, in which every limitation, every content, whether present immediately through nature, through needs, desires, and drives, or given and determined in some other way, is dissolved; this is the limitless infinity of *absolute abstraction* (*der absoluten Abstraktion*) or *universality*, the pure thinking of oneself (*das reine Denken seiner selbst*).[43]

The decision to think pure being at the start of the *Logic* initiates a study of the basic categories of thought rather than action in the world. Nevertheless, as a decision or act of will, it is the same as the act described in the *Philosophy of Right:* an act of abstraction by thought.

This is not the place to conduct an exhaustive comparison of the relative merits of Kierkegaard's and Hegel's conceptions of willing and deciding in general. All I wish to point out is that for Hegel, in contrast to Kierkegaard, the particular resolve or decision presupposed by the *Logic* is a free act *of* thought, not an act that interrupts thought from a position "outside" thought. Furthermore, it is motivated by the rational desire to be fully self-critical and to take nothing for granted about thought and being. In Hegel's view, therefore, the fact that the *Logic* presupposes a decision does not prevent it from being a *logical* undertaking.

---

42. White, *Absolute Knowledge*, p. 26.

43. G. W. F. Hegel, *Elements of the Philosophy of Right*, ed. A. W. Wood, trans. H. B. Nisbet (Cambridge: Cambridge University Press, 1991), p. 37 (§5); G. W. F. Hegel, *Grundlinien der Philosophie des Rechts*, ed. E. Moldenhauer and K. M. Michel, *Werke in zwanzig Bänden*, vol. 7 (Frankfurt am Main: Suhrkamp Verlag, 1970), p. 49. Further references to the *Elements of the Philosophy of Right* will be given in the following form: *PR* 37/49 (§5).

The decision concerned is described as "arbitrary" by Hegel not—as Kierkegaard suggests—because it is the product of a willful intention to break out of an endless circle of reflection (or, indeed, the product of weariness with endless reflection) but because it is a *free* act. As White notes, "the task of thinking pure thought is not an absolutely compelling one": we do not need to philosophize speculatively in the way that we need to eat.[44] Nevertheless, that task is one that a rational, self-critical person should undertake. The decision to philosophize may certainly be free and "arbitrary," but it is also a logical decision to take—a decision made by rational thought.

Yet the mere fact that Hegel interprets the decision presupposed by the *Logic* in a different way from Kierkegaard does not mean that he is right to do so. From Kierkegaard's point of view, this decision must be an irrational act of willfulness (or weariness) because reflective, rational thought can never lead by itself to the decisive act of thinking of pure being alone. The activity of reflection and abstraction continues *endlessly* and never ceases being aware that the thought of pure being is the mediated result of reflection and abstraction itself. For Kierkegaard, therefore, the decision to think of pure being can only be an act that interrupts the circle of reflection and abstraction; it cannot be an act *of* reflection and abstraction. Kierkegaard may well fail to take account of the way in which Hegel interprets that decision, but that may be irrelevant since Kierkegaard's interpretation may be the only one that explains what is actually going on when we decide to think of pure being.

Yet Kierkegaard's interpretation of this decision depends completely on his assumption that the activity of abstraction is endless, and to my mind at least, it is far from clear that abstraction is necessarily endless in Kierkegaard's sense. To abstract from the fact that we are abstracting, and so to suspend the thought that what we end up with is the product of abstraction, is still to engage in the activity of *abstracting*. In that sense, Kierkegaard is right: we continue the activity of abstracting in the very act of deliberately forgetting that that is what we are doing. What Kierkegaard fails to note, however, is that abstracting by its very nature is the activity of leaving something out and ignoring it. Yes, we engage in the act of abstracting when we suspend the idea that we are abstracting; but precisely for that reason what we do is *leave out of consideration* the fact that we are abstracting. That is what it *means* to abstract. The act of abstraction does not have to be infinite in the way Kierkegaard describes, therefore, because it can suspend and set to one side its own consciousness of itself.

Abstraction will be regarded as infinite only if we disregard what abstracting actually involves. That is to say, abstraction will be regarded as infinite only if we add a further layer of abstraction and abstract from what is actually going on when we abstract from the fact that we are abstracting. Obviously, we *can* always perform that further act of abstraction and ignore what abstracting in-

44. White, *Absolute Knowledge*, p. 23.

volves, but we do not *need* to do so. We can perform the first act of abstraction and leave out of consideration all that "thought" and "being" normally mean. We can then perform a second act of abstraction and leave out of consideration the fact that the thought of pure being *results* from leaving out of consideration all that "thought and "being" normally mean. We can then stop there and consider what, if anything, is entailed by or implicit in the thought of pure being as such. That is what Hegel does at the start of his *Logic*.

It is always possible, however, to perform a third act of abstraction that leaves out of consideration what the second act actually involves; we are always free to ignore the true character of abstraction. In that case, we will come to believe that the second act of abstraction—the act of completely setting to one side the thought that pure being is the result of abstraction—is actually impossible. The fact of abstracting and of having abstracted will then be understood to be something that it is impossible to ignore, however much we try to ignore it, and the task of abstraction will be regarded as endless. Yet one arrives at that conception of infinite abstraction only by ignoring—*needlessly*—what abstraction actually entails. This, I would maintain, is what Kierkegaard does.

To recapitulate: we can abstract from all we usually take thought and being to be and so produce the thought of pure being; we can then abstract from the fact that this thought of pure being is the result of abstraction, and so leave ourselves thinking of nothing but pure being as such. Indeed, if we are to take seriously what it means to abstract—namely, to "leave out" or "look away from"—then the result of our activity of abstraction can be nothing but the thought of sheer immediate being from which the idea of its being a result has been left out.

As we have seen, Hegel does not believe that this act of abstraction requires us to eliminate from our minds *altogether* the idea that pure being is the mediated product of abstraction. We remain fully aware of this fact, but we leave it out of *our thought of pure being*. As philosophers, we know that pure being is the result of abstraction on our part, but we attend only to its purity as *being*. To abstract, for Hegel, is thus not to empty our mind completely of everything we know but to leave out from the specific thought on which we are focusing all we know about how we arrived at it. It is to hold before our mind's eye what it is for being to be immediate being, not what it is for it to be the mediated result of abstraction.

To employ Kierkegaard's terminology, one might say that reflection is in one sense infinite or endless, for Hegel, insofar as we remain throughout the *Logic* aware of the historical and hermeneutic conditions that make it necessary and possible for the derivation of the categories to take place. But it is also true that reflection understood as the specific activity of *abstraction* is not infinite because it entails successfully leaving out of the explicit object of our attention—pure being—everything of which we remain reflectively aware.

Kierkegaard's insistence that the *decision* presupposed by the *Logic* is irra-

tional rests on his conviction that the rational activity of abstract thought is necessarily endless. It is evident, however, that if we are to take seriously what it means to abstract, abstraction does not have to be endless in Kierkegaard's sense. But this means that there is no compelling reason to regard the decision of which Hegel speaks as a willful or weary *interruption* of an endless circle of thought. Indeed, there is no reason not to accept Hegel's claim that that decision is a free act of abstract, rational thought itself—that is, that the decision to think pure being is nothing but the very act of abstraction itself through which we think such being.

In my view, Kierkegaard misunderstands what is going on at the start of Hegel's *Logic*. His misunderstanding is highly instructive, however, because it forces us to clarify what Hegel is and is not claiming about the beginning of his logical enterprise. My response to Kierkegaard may itself be rather too abstract for some. But the abstractness of that response is inevitable: for what Kierkegaard forces us to do is specify exactly what *abstraction* itself—the condition of Hegel's *Logic*—entails.

The Speculative Proposition

As I have suggested, Hegel's method in the *Logic* is to focus on the initial abstraction of pure being and to articulate whatever is entailed or implied by that concept (insofar as it is understood precisely as *pure being* rather than as the *result of abstraction*). Our activity as speculative philosophers thus consists in simply rendering explicit what is implicit: "the whole course of philosophising, being methodical, i.e., *necessary*, is nothing else but the mere *positing* (*Setzen*) of what is already contained in a concept" (*EL* 141/188 [§88]). As reflective beings, we may occasionally depart from this strict method of immanent development and examine objections that have been, or might be, leveled at the conception of the categories to which that method leads. Anyone who has read more than a few pages into the main body of the *Logic* knows that Hegel cannot resist defending his account against all manner of charges. Such reflections must not, however, drive the logical development forward and carry us from one category to another. A new category may only be understood to emerge from what is implicit in a previous category—that is, may only emerge as one category *turns into* another one.

Unlike, say, J. S. Mill, Hegel does not and may not advance his main argument by means of addressing and countering the objections of others. He recognizes that this is one way of proceeding in philosophical texts, but it is ruled out by his strictly immanent approach. As he writes in the *Phenomenology*, "it is not difficult to see that the way of asserting a proposition, adducing reasons for it, and in the same way refuting its opposite by reasons, is not the form in which truth can appear" (*PhS* 28/47). Some readers will no doubt be frustrated by Hegel's refusal to argue "normally," but given his commitment to presupposi-

tionless philosophy, he has no choice in the matter, and in my view, Hegel's way of proceeding lends his texts an austere elegance that many other works of philosophy lack.

Hegel's immanent method requires that we use negative or self-undermining expressions to keep our attention focused on the categories being derived. It also requires us to employ a special kind of proposition to articulate the character of each category. Hegel calls these "speculative propositions" (*spekulative Sätze*) (*PhS* 38/59; *EL* 142/190 [§88]). Such propositions have the outward form of ordinary judgments, but as he tells us in the *Phenomenology*, the relation between subject and predicate in them is logically different.[45]

In an ordinary judgment, such as "the rose is red," the subject is assumed to be identified first of all by the subject-term (as a rose) and then to be characterized in a particular way by the predicate (as red). The subject is thus regarded as an "*objective*, fixed self" (*PhS* 37/58) whose identity has been established once and for all, and the judgment as a whole is held to tell us something *about* that subject: what we are dealing with is a rose—nothing more, nothing less—and we say *of* the rose that it is red.

In a speculative proposition, by contrast, the subject-term names something that only comes to be properly understood and identified through the predicate itself. The predicate does not characterize a subject which has already been definitively identified; it articulates or unfolds what the subject actually is in truth: "the Substance, the essence and the concept of what is under discussion." We may well think that what we are dealing with has been established, but that is not in fact the case, since the true character of the subject is first articulated in the very act of predication itself. The predicate thus names "the being or *essence* which exhausts (*erschöpft*) the nature of the Subject" (*PhS* 37–8/58–9).

In the *Phenomenology* Hegel gives two examples of speculative propositions: "God is being" and "the *actual* is the *universal*" (*PhS* 38–9/59–60). In each case, the subject appears to have a clear, fixed identity (as "God" or the "actual"), which is then qualified in a particular way, but in fact the subject only *comes to be* properly identified and understood through the predicate itself. Consequently, Hegel writes, "thinking . . . loses the firm objective basis it had [or thought it had] in the subject": "God ceases to be what he is from his position in the proposition, viz. a fixed subject" and comes to be identified *as* being. Similarly, "the actual as subject disappears in its predicate" as it becomes clear that "the universal is meant to express the essence of the actual" (*PhS* 38–9/59–60).

This is not to say that the subject-term in a speculative proposition always turns out to be a meaningless place marker. The word "God," taken by itself, Hegel claims, is indeed "a meaningless sound, a mere name," and "it is only the

45. See also Houlgate, *Hegel, Nietzsche, and the Criticism of Metaphysics*, pp. 145–56.

predicate that says *what God is*, gives him content and meaning" (*PhS* 12/26). The word "actual" (*wirklich*), by contrast, as is apparent throughout Hegel's philosophy, has a specific, clearly articulable meaning of its own that differs from those of such words as "real" and "existing." The point is that what it means to be actual is not exhausted by the meaning of the word "actual" itself but implies much more than is explicitly covered by that word or concept. Hegel's speculative proposition makes this clear by stating that the actual is in fact not just the actual but the universal. This proposition does not, however, destroy the concept of the "actual" altogether; it simply reveals more clearly what is to be understood by the actual. What it is to be universal thus incorporates (but also exceeds) what it is to be actual. Consequently, what "disappears" in the proposition is not the concept of actuality as such but merely the idea that the actual as such is the *fixed*, definitive subject of discourse.

In the *Logic* Hegel does not discuss the speculative proposition in detail, nor does he pick out any propositions or sentences as specifically speculative. It is clear, however, that many sentences in that book should be read as speculative propositions rather than ordinary judgments. Some of these define the category in question *as* this or that: for example, "something is the *first negation of negation*, as simple self-relation in the form of being" (*SL* 115/1: 123 [207]). Others *redefine* a particular category and so carry us forward from one category to another: for example, "being . . . is in fact *nothing*, and neither more nor less than *nothing*," or "something with its immanent limit . . . is the *finite*" (*SL* 82, 129/1: 83, 139 [195, 229]). In some cases, there may be a series of sentences that together give expression to one complex speculative proposition: for example,

> *Pure being* and *pure nothing* are therefore the same. . . . But it is equally true that they are . . . absolutely distinct, and yet that they are unseparated and inseparable and that each immediately *vanishes in its opposite*. Their truth is, therefore, this movement of the immediate vanishing of the one in the other: *becoming*. (*SL* 82–3/1: 83 [195])

In each of these cases, the proposition is speculative because it tells us how a category is properly to be understood; it does not merely point to one particular characteristic of a category whose meaning has already been definitively established. Speculative propositions are thus the appropriate vehicle for gradually *unfolding* the meaning of thought's basic categories. They are the form of expression best suited to a method of philosophizing in which the subject matter is not simply *given* at the start but *comes to be* fully what it is.

Having briefly considered the structure of speculative propositions, we are now in a position to look more closely at one of the charges that Schelling levels at Hegel. Schelling writes that "Hegel uses without thinking the form of the proposition, the copula, the *is*, before he has explained anything at all about the

meaning of this *is*."[46] From Schelling's following remarks, it becomes clear that his objection is not simply that Hegel presupposes the form of the proposition as such. Schelling's complaint is that initially one cannot tell whether Hegel's proposition, "pure being is nothing," is a mere tautology (in which case "pure being and nothing are only two different expressions for one and the same thing") or a judgment (in which case "pure being is the *subject*, that which carries nothingness"). That is to say, Hegel leaves it unclear whether the *is* in that proposition is the *is* of identity or the *is* of predication. Schelling eventually comes to the conclusion that Hegel's proposition must be a tautology: in saying that "pure being is nothing" Hegel is thus actually saying that "nothing is nothing." Schelling draws this conclusion, by the way, because he believes that Hegel's concept of pure being is in fact one in which "nothing is thought," not because he concludes that Hegel goes on to make the meaning of *is* clear after all.[47]

I have claimed that Hegel's proposition is not a predicative judgement but a speculative proposition. As such, however, it cannot be a mere tautology, despite Schelling's assertion to the contrary. This is because speculative propositions posit not only an identity between subject and predicate but also the non-identity of the two. Speculative propositions are identity statements, insofar as what is named by the subject-term is only properly identified by the predicate: what is to be understood by *being* is revealed in the predicate *nothing*, just as the meaning of *bachelor* is revealed in the predicate *married man*. But in a speculative proposition a moment of negation is also implied: "if the content is speculative, the *non-identical* aspect of subject and predicate is also an essential moment" (*SL* 91/1: 93).

That moment of negation may be veiled (when a category is simply being described or defined), or it may be stated overtly (when a category is redefined as its opposite or as a new category). For example, something is defined as "simple self-relation in the form of being" (*SL* 115/1:123 [207]), but it is also *not* just that since, as we go on to discover, something entails "otherness" and "finitude" as well. Similarly, being is redefined as nothing; but it is also *not* just that since it is *being* that *vanishes* into nothing and so is becoming. Either way, the *is* of the speculative proposition is not reducible to the ordinary *is* of identity because it implies "is not" as much as "is" and so is *dialectical*. This is why one speculative proposition necessarily leads on to a further speculative proposition in which the subject is explicitly identified as the negation of what it was previously stated to be (see *SL* 90/1: 92–3). It is also why simple speculative propositions often give way in Hegel's text to complex ones (such as the one cited above from the paragraph on "becoming") in which Hegel tries to articulate the very process through which categories come into their true identity by *negating* themselves.

---

46. Schelling, *On the History of Modern Philosophy*, p. 140.

47. Schelling, *On the History of Modern Philosophy*, pp. 139–40.

One might, of course, claim that the ordinary *is* of identity harbors a concealed moment of negation, too, since bachelors are not just unmarried men but have many other qualities besides this, such as nationality, eye-color, height, weight, and so on. But there is nothing in the very statement that a bachelor is an unmarried man that implies that the opposite is equally true or that the definition of a bachelor as an unmarried man is actually an inadequate determination of what it is to be a bachelor *as such*. That statement is thus not a speculative proposition in Hegel's sense.

Hegel's *Logic* abounds in ordinary sentences of many kinds (not all of which by any means are simple, affirmative judgments). He also endeavors to employ as many ordinary German words as possible—though he does use foreign words, too, and turn familiar German words into unfamiliar German nouns, such as *Anderssein* ("otherness" or "being other") or *Aufgehobensein* ("being sublated") (*SL* 119, 123/1: 127, 133 [214, 220]).[48] His immanent unfolding of the category of pure being is, however, carried forward in a series of speculative propositions, the syntax of which is neither that of the ordinary predicative judgment nor that of the ordinary identity statement and may indeed be highly complex. The lack of clarity Schelling finds at the start of the *Logic* is thus not due to any failure on Hegel's part to make clear how the *is* in speculative propositions should be understood. It is because that speculative *is* fits into neither of the two categories of *is* with which Schelling is familiar but is *sui generis*. In other words, Schelling's confusion arises from presupposing that Hegel's speculative *is* must overlap with one of the *ordinary* senses of *is* and his consequent failure to discern the new and distinctive role that that *is* actually plays in Hegel's speculative propositions.

Remember that Hegel may not *presuppose* at the outset that the *is* in speculative propositions is dialectical (but must discover this in the course of the *Logic*) because he may not presuppose that being will entail negation. For that reason, he is not obliged—or, indeed, entitled—to explain (as Schelling demands) how the speculative *is* is to be understood *before* he actually uses it. Hegel does, however, presuppose that we should suspend the assumption that the word "is" as it is used in speculative philosophy will invariably mean one of the things it ordinarily means. In my view, it is this suspension that Schelling fails to carry out. He remains wedded to the ordinary senses of *is* and so cannot see that Hegel's speculative *is* is actually something quite new.

In the *Logic* we must begin with the category of pure being because that is what we are left with after we have abstracted from all that it means to think and to be. We must also go on to say that "being is . . . " (rather than just continue to utter the single word *being*) because the category of being itself requires us to articulate—in language—all that is implicit in being. But we must refrain from assuming that that *is* is simply the *is* of predication or of identity. To assume the

48. Miller has "in . . . sublated form" for *Aufgehobensein*.

former would commit us, as Schelling notes, to regard being as the bearer of properties. To assume the latter would condemn us in advance to repeating endlessly—with Parmenides—that "being is being is being" (or—if we agree with Schelling that Hegel's "pure being" actually means nothing whatsoever—to repeating that "nothing is nothing is nothing"). In either case, what we understand by *being* would be predetermined, and we would thus be prevented from ever *discovering* how "being" and "is" are actually to be conceived.

Philosophy and Ordinary Language

Hegel maintains that we should not assume that "being," or any other category derived in the *Logic*, means what it is ordinarily taken to mean. As Alan White notes, "the signification of each thought must in every case be determined by the movement leading to it."[49] The ordinary meanings of words thus play no foundational role in determining how categories are to be understood. They do, however, constitute the hermeneutic conditions of doing speculative philosophy, for as we have seen, we need to understand the everyday meanings of words in our language—be it German or any other language—in order to formulate sentences that focus our attention on the pure categories and their immanent development. We also need to understand the ordinary meanings of words in order to be able to *name* each category as it arises logically during the course of our analysis.

The philosopher chooses names for the categories, Hegel explains, by "select[ing] from the language of common life . . . such expressions as *seem to approximate* (*nahekommen*) to the determinations of the concept" (*SL* 708/2: 406). He does this in order to make it clear that the immanent derivation of the categories in the *Logic* clarifies the structure of the concepts with which we *ordinarily* operate. Hegel is adamant that the logical derivation of the categories is presuppositionless and immanent. Precisely because it is a purely immanent deduction, however, it demonstrates that the categories that are derived inhere in thought as such. They belong to what it *is* to think, to the very *being* of thought itself. But that means that they must find expression in ordinary thought and language, too—albeit in different ways and with varying degrees of explicitness (or varying degrees of obscurity) in different cultures and at different times in history.

Philosophy derives the categories from the abstract thought of pure being. That concept is not, however, hauled down from some remote intellectual heaven; it is generated by abstracting from all that we ordinarily take thought and being to be. Indeed, the concept of pure being is simply our ordinary concept of being, stripped down to its absolute minimum. Pure being, in other words, is the *least* that we can understand ordinary, everyday being—the only being we know—to be.

49. White, *Absolute Knowledge*, p. 36. See also Hegel, *SL* 582/2: 252.

In order to show that his *Logic* provides a radically self-critical derivation and clarification of the categories that inform (with different degrees of obscurity) *ordinary* thought, Hegel names each category as it arises after the one it resembles most in everyday language. To be able to do this, the philosopher must obviously understand the ordinary meanings of words such as *becoming, quantity,* and *concept*. Furthermore, he or she must also be able to recognize that the derived category is a purified version of, and so corresponds to, a category we ordinarily employ. In this way, the philosopher makes it clear that the task of the *Logic* is not merely to present a formal system of abstract concepts unrelated to our everyday experience but to "know the concept *of* that which is otherwise a mere pictorial representation" (*SL* 708/2: 406).[50] The *Logic*, therefore, provides a logical "reconstruction" of our ordinary categories or "representations" (*SL* 39/1: 30). It does not do so, however, by simply arranging "a *given* set of categories" in a dialectical sequence, as Klaus Hartmann suggests; it does so by deriving the true structure of our ordinary categories—that is largely hidden from ordinary thought itself—immanently and purely a priori from the empty thought of pure, indeterminate being.[51]

In Hegel's *Logic* the meaning of a category is first determined by pure logic alone and then associated with a corresponding ordinary concept and given its name. The logical derivation, *pace* Gadamer, is not dependent in any way on the ordinary connotations of the names that are chosen. "One usually begins with the word and then seeks to know the concept," Hegel is reported as saying in his 1817 lectures on logic. "We, however, proceed here from the concept first and then seek the human name (*Bezeichnung*) for the concept."[52]

Often it is obvious why Hegel chooses a certain name for a category. The opening category is named "being" because that is the name we give to simple immediacy and the opening category is just the thought of the very least that our ordinary conception of "being" implies. In some cases, such as that of being-for-self (*Fürsichsein*), Hegel explicitly examines our ordinary usage of a concept or expression to see if it does actually correspond to the category that has been derived:

> We have arrived at the general concept of being-for-self. All that is now necessary to justify our use of the term for this concept is to demonstrate that the representation (*Vorstellung*) associated with the expression, "being-for-self," corresponds to that concept. And so indeed it seems. (*SL* 157–8/1: 174–5).[53]

In many cases, however, Hegel leaves it up to us to recognize that his a pri-

50. Translation revised, my emphasis.
51. See Hartmann, "Hegel: A Non-Metaphysical View," p. 110, my emphasis.
52. Hegel, *VLM* 82, my translation.
53. Translation revised.

ori account of a category clarifies a concept in everyday use and that the name he has selected for it is thus appropriate. One of the questions students of Hegel's *Logic* will therefore have to consider—in addition to determining whether the derivation of a category is truly immanent—is whether the name Hegel chooses always fits the category concerned.

Hegel's remarks about naming categories are important because they help us resolve two of the most troubling problems in the interpretation of his philosophy. First of all, if Hegel's philosophy is meant to be rigorously a priori, how can it tell us about our ordinary experience? Second, how can Hegel demand both that philosophy be presuppositionless and that it presuppose familiarity with all the concepts concerned?

As far as the first question is concerned, it should be noted that some commentators deny that Hegel intends his philosophy to be a priori at all. They believe, like Hartmann, that Hegel is providing a philosophical account of concepts that are *given* to it (by, for example, natural science) and that changes in his philosophy are determined by changes in those given concepts. If this is the case, Hegel's philosophy cannot be purely a priori and immanent because its structure depends upon factors outside of philosophy itself. To my mind, however, this interpretation cannot be right. Hegel insists over and over again that his derivation of concepts is a priori, immanent, and necessary. In the *Logic*, for example, he writes that "in the science of the concept its content and character can be guaranteed solely by the *immanent deduction* which contains its genesis" (*SL* 582/2: 252). In the *Philosophy of Right* he is equally explicit:

> in philosophical cognition . . . the chief concern is the *necessity* of a concept, and the route by which it has become a *result* [is] its proof and deduction. Thus, given that its *content* is necessary *for itself*, the second step is to look around for what corresponds to it in our ideas [*Vorstellungen*] and language.[54]

To emphasize that Hegel aims to provide a purely immanent deduction of concepts is *not* to deny that he may, and does, frequently revise his understanding of the way that deduction must proceed. Hegel never claimed that every detail of his immanent deduction was beyond criticism or improvement (see *SL* 54/1: 50). With each revision, however, Hegel endeavored to present an im-

---

54. Hegel, *PR* 27/31–2 (§2). See also *Hegel's Philosophy of Nature. Being Part Two of the Encyclopaedia of the Philosophical Sciences (1830)*, trans. A. V. Miller (Oxford: Clarendon Press, 1970), pp. 6–7, 29, 87 (§§246, 254 Add., 275 Add.); G. W. F. Hegel, *Enzyklopädie der philosophischen Wissenschaften im Grundrisse (1830). Zweiter Teil: Die Naturphilosophie*, ed. E. Moldenhauer and K. M. Michel, *Werke in zwanzig Bänden*, vol. 9 (Frankfurt am Main: Suhrkamp Verlag, 1970), pp. 15, 42, 111. Further references to *Hegel's Philosophy of Nature* will be given in the following form: *EPN* 6–7/15 (§246).

proved *immanent* and *necessary* deduction. There is thus no fundamental incompatibility between Hegel's aim of producing an a priori system and his evident practice of frequent self-criticism and revision. Nor can Hegel's revisions count as evidence for the thesis that his system was never intended to be a priori in the first place.

Hegel's *a priori* system enables us better to understand the concepts informing our *ordinary* thought and experience for the reason I have already suggested: that system unfolds categories that are inherent in thought and being *as such*, and ordinary thought is one of the forms that thought as such takes. Assuming that they are properly derived and conceived, these categories must therefore inform—implicitly or explicitly, with distortion or without—our ordinary thought and experience. Hegel's purely logical account of what it is to be "something" or to be "finite" *as such* must thus illuminate what it is to be a finite thing in *our* world. "We usually suppose," Hegel says, "that the Absolute must lie far beyond; but it is precisely what is wholly present, what we, as thinkers, always carry with us and employ, even though we have no express consciousness of it. It is in language that these thought-determinations are primarily deposited" (*EL* 59/85 [§24 Add. 2]). This, in my view, is the great value of Hegel's *Logic*: it does not describe a putative noumenal realm "beyond" everyday experience but reveals the ultimate structure *of* the very world we inhabit every day of our lives.

This leads us directly to the answer to the second of our two questions: how can Hegel insist that philosophy be presuppositionless and that it presuppose familiarity with the concepts to be derived? Philosophy makes both these demands because its very aim is to provide a rigorously *self-critical* derivation and clarification *of* concepts with which we are already familiar. Hegel proceeds from the assumption that what is familiar is not for that reason well understood and that philosophy's role is to develop a proper understanding of the familiar (*SL* 33/1: 22; *PhS* 18/35). The fact that philosophy is to be radically self-critical means, as we have seen, that we must begin by suspending all we assume thought and being to be and derive an understanding of the categories of thought and being from scratch. At the same time, however, we must retain our familiarity with the basic categories as they are ordinarily conceived; otherwise, we could never recognize that philosophy is indeed providing a clearer understanding of *familiar* concepts.

Hegel insists upon such familiarity at several places. In the *Encyclopedia Logic*, for example, he writes:

> Philosophy can, of course, presuppose some *familiarity* (*Bekanntschaft*) with its objects; in fact it *must* presuppose this, as well as an interest in these objects. The reason is that in the order of time consciousness produces *representations* (*Vorstellungen*) of objects before it produces *concepts* (*Begriffe*) of them. (*EL* 24/41 [§1])

He goes on later to say that logic is the easiest science precisely because the concepts with which it deals are "what we are *most familiar* with: being, nothing, etc.; determinacy, magnitude, etc.; being-in-itself, being-for-itself, one, many, and so on" (*EL* 45/67 [§19]). At the same time, he argues, it is the hardest science because we are required to consider these categories in themselves as purely logical forms and because our very familiarity with them often gets in the way of our achieving this. Everyone knows—or, rather, can picture—what it is to be "something," so it is often deemed to be not worth one's while to think about such a basic category philosophically. Moreover, if we do turn our attention to such concepts, we frequently find it hard to let go of our familiar understanding of them and to understand them anew: we are used to thinking of "something" as something visible or tangible, and it is hard to get one's mind around the idea that something must be understood logically as the "negation of negation." It is certainly possible to train oneself to abstract from the familiar meanings of words and to learn to understand concepts in purely logical terms. However, Hegel never overlooks the fact that it takes considerable and continuous effort.

This is an inevitable pitfall of doing speculative philosophy: for as a philosopher one may not, and cannot, obliterate the familiar meanings of words, such as *becoming* and *something*, from one's mind altogether. We are to suspend our ordinary assumptions about the categories and undertake a presuppositionless derivation of them from scratch. Yet we are to do so while continuing to speak a language and remaining familiar with the ordinary meanings of the very categories being derived. We will, therefore, always have to be on our guard against allowing those ordinary meanings to govern our understanding of the categories. Critics, such as Gadamer, doubt that we can actually prevent that from happening. In my view, however, we can prevent that from happening because we can use the resources of ordinary language *itself*—especially negative words, such as *no* and *without*—to loosen the very hold that ordinary language exercises on our understanding.

Chapter Five

Immanent and Quasi-Transcendental Thought

Quasi-Transcendental Approaches to Being

After our discussion of the presuppositions of Hegel's *Logic*, we are now in a position to consider the principal difference between Hegel's radically immanent analysis of the concept of being and the transcendental, or "quasi-transcendental," approach to the concept (or meaning or question) of being adopted by many of his critics and successors.[1]

As we have seen, Hegel is well aware that certain historical and hermeneutic conditions make possible or mediate the thought of being. His concern in the main body of the *Logic*, however, is to focus on the thought of pure being itself and what may be immanent in it, not on the mediating conditions that make this thought possible. He examines those conditions themselves in the lectures on the philosophy of history and the history of philosophy, the introductory paragraphs of the *Encyclopedia Logic*, and of course, in the prefaces and introduction to the *Logic*.

Many of Hegel's critics take a strikingly different approach to the idea of "being." In his lectures *On the History of Modern Philosophy*, Schelling evinces no interest whatsoever in unfolding what is immanent in the thought of pure being because he denies that such a thought is possible: "it is an impossibility to think *being in general*, because there is no being *in general*, there is no being without a subject." For Schelling, the thought of pure being with which Hegel claims to begin the *Logic* is in fact one in which "nothing is thought"—indeed,

---

1. The term "quasi-transcendental" is borrowed from Rodolphe Gasché's superb study of Derrida, *The Tain of the Mirror: Derrida and the Philosophy of Reflection* (Cambridge, Mass.: Harvard University Press, 1986), p. 316. Gasché uses the term to refer to the "infrastructures" (such as *différance*) that Derrida takes to constitute the conditions of possibility and impossibility of philosophical discourse. I use the term in a somewhat broader sense than Gasché to refer to any approach that considers the "conditions" or "presuppositions" of being (or of the thought of being) rather than being itself. Quasi-transcendental thought should be distinguished from *transcendental* thought in the strict, Kantian sense that focuses specifically on the *a priori* epistemic conditions of experience and its objects; see Kant, *CPR* 133/55 (A 11–12).

it is an "un-thought"—and Hegel's assertion that "pure being is nothing" is just an empty tautology stating that "nothing is nothing."[2]

This concept, or "un-thought," is generated according to Schelling by a process of abstraction from the concrete being—the "real world"—in which we live. Furthermore, Schelling insists that the progression in Hegel's *Logic* from pure being to the Idea and nature is driven not by the autonomous, immanent development of pure being itself but rather by the philosopher's desire to leave behind empty abstraction and recover "the complete content of the world and of consciousness"; that is, by the philosopher's "need to progress from the empty to the full."[3] Schelling not only dismisses Hegel's immanent approach to pure being, therefore; he also points to what he understands to be the existential factors that actually determine the course of the *Logic* but are overlooked, ignored, or suppressed by Hegel, namely the philosopher's own desires and needs. Since these factors both explain how thought can progress from "being" to "becoming" and beyond and also make it impossible for that progression to be understood as immanent in the way Hegel understands it, we might refer to them (borrowing an expression from Derrida) as conditions of the possibility and impossibility of the development described in Hegel's *Logic*.[4] It is Schelling's interest in these existential *conditions* of what seems (but only seems) to be an autonomous logical development that marks his approach to the concept of pure being as "quasi-transcendental."

Nietzsche famously launches one of the most sustained assaults on the concept of "being" in the history of philosophy. The decisive feature of a Dionysian philosophy, he proclaims, is "saying Yes to opposition and war; *becoming*, along with a radical repudiation of the very concept of *being*."[5] Yet Nietzsche's interest in the concept of being does not end with this repudiation because he wants to uncover "how the illusion of being could have arisen (was bound to arise)."[6] One of his many (and often contradictory) answers to this question is that man "derived the concept 'being' only from the concept 'ego,' he posited 'things' as possessing being according to his own image."[7] Nietzsche does not have in mind Hegel's concept of being in particular, nor does he understand the concept in the same way as Hegel (he associates being with stasis, rigidity, and

---

2. Schelling, *On the History of Modern Philosophy*, pp. 139–40.

3. Schelling, *On the History of Modern Philosophy*, pp. 138, 143.

4. See J. Derrida, *Margins of Philosophy*, trans. A. Bass (Brighton: Harvester Press, 1982), p. 328, and Gasché, *The Tain of the Mirror*, pp. 316–17.

5. F. Nietzsche, *On the Genealogy of Morals*, trans. W. Kaufmann and R. J. Hollingdale, and *Ecce Homo*, trans. W. Kaufmann (New York: Vintage Books, 1969), p. 273.

6. F. Nietzsche, *The Will to Power*, trans. W. Kaufmann and R. J. Hollingdale (New York: Vintage Books, 1968), p. 377 (§708).

7. F. Nietzsche, *Twilight of the Idols/The Antichrist*, trans. R. J. Hollingdale (Harmondsworth: Penguin Books, 1968), p. 49.

the denial of becoming rather than indeterminate immediacy).[8] Nevertheless, his approach to that concept is clearly quasi-transcendental rather than immanent. This is because he is not interested in unpacking the intrinsic implications of the concept of being itself (and finding out, for example, whether it turns out to mean something more or other than rigidity and stasis), but is concerned, rather, to uncover the historical, psychological, and physiological *conditions* that he believes gave rise to that concept in the first place.

Heidegger's approach to being is considerably more subtle than that of Nietzsche. He does not regard the concept of being as settled or dismiss that concept as illusory but wants to revive the question of the *meaning* of "being." In the introduction to *Being and Time*, he protests that a "dogma" in Western philosophy (of which Nietzsche is a modern heir) "not only declares the question about the meaning of Being to be superfluous, but sanctions its complete neglect."[9] It does so because it regards being as universal, indefinable, and self-evident. For Heidegger, however, these supposed qualities of being are precisely what require us to *enquire* into being's meaning. If "being" is the most universal concept, "this cannot mean that it is the one which is clearest or that it needs no further discussion. It is rather the darkest of all." Similarly, "the indefinability of Being does not eliminate the question of its meaning; it demands that we look that question in the face." We all live in an understanding of being—"everyone understands, 'The sky *is* blue,' 'I *am* merry,' and the like"—but the *meaning* of being is at the same time "veiled in darkness," and this fact, Heidegger contends, proves the fundamental necessity of recovering the question of the meaning of "being."[10]

Hegel makes a similar point in the *Encyclopedia Logic*. "What is well-known . . . is usually what is most unknown," he remarks. "Thus, *Being*, for example, is a pure thought-determination; but it never occurs to us to make 'is' the subject matter of our inquiry" (*EL* 59/85 [§24 Add. 2]). As we have seen, Hegel's response to this failure of critical intelligence is to suspend all assumptions about being and to examine what is immanent in the thought of sheer being as such. Heidegger, by contrast, having raised the question of the meaning of being, steps back from considering being itself and examines first of all the ontological structure of the one who poses the question: namely, *Dasein*.[11]

There appear to be two reasons for this move. First, Heidegger—for all his declared openness to the *question* of the meaning of being—takes it for granted

8. Nietzsche, *Twilight of the Idols/The Antichrist*, p. 35.

9. M. Heidegger, *Being and Time*, trans. J. Macquarrie and E. Robinson (Oxford: Blackwell, 1962), p. 21.

10. Heidegger, *Being and Time*, p. 23.

11. Note that the word "Dasein," for Heidegger, refers not just to determinate being (as it does for Hegel) but to "an entity which, in its very Being, comports itself understandingly towards that Being." See Heidegger, *Being and Time*, p. 78.

in *Being and Time* that "'Being' means the Being of entities" and that entities themselves are thus what is "interrogated" in the question concerning being: entities are, so to speak, "questioned as regards their Being." The following questions thus arise, for Heidegger: "From which entities is the disclosure of Being to take its departure?" and "Which entity shall we take for our example, and in what sense does it have priority?" His contention is that *Dasein* is this "exemplary" being.[12]

Second (and, for our purposes, more importantly), Heidegger believes that, before the question of the meaning of being can be answered, it must be properly formulated and posed. In order to formulate and "work out the question of Being," he writes, "we must make an entity—the inquirer—transparent in his own Being."[13] We need to consider the structure of the questioner if we are to understand why the question itself arises, how it is to be asked, and what might provide the "horizon" of any possible answer. That horizon, as is well known, proves to be time: "whenever *Dasein* tacitly understands and interprets something like Being, it does so with time as its standpoint." Consequently, for Heidegger, "*time* must be brought to light—and genuinely conceived—as the horizon for all understanding of Being and for any way of interpreting it."[14]

Like Hegel, Heidegger is interested in enquiring after the meaning of being. It is apparent, however, that in contrast to Hegel, Heidegger's transcendental instincts deflect him away from considering being directly and toward a prior consideration of the *question* of being and of the questioner himself. Now Hegel agrees that the philosopher must be properly prepared to think being, but that preparation for him takes the form of *suspending* all determinate presuppositions that may serve as the "horizon" for understanding being and opening oneself to being as such. Heidegger, by contrast, prepares himself for his enquiry into the meaning of being by establishing what he regards as the *irreducible* horizon or prior condition of any such enquiry. The principal fault of previous philosophers (including Hegel), according to Heidegger, has thus been not just their neglect of the question of being in general but their failure "to provide an ontology with *Dasein* as its theme or (to put this in Kantian language) to give a preliminary ontological analytic of the subjectivity of the subject."[15]

A possible Hegelian equivalent to such an analysis might be thought to be found in the *Phenomenology*, which examines the structure of ordinary consciousness as a prelude to the *Logic*. As we shall see, however, Hegel's *Phenomenology* demonstrates how the various "horizons" of understanding taken for granted by consciousness break down and lead logically to the radical openness of absolute knowing; it does not, like *Being and Time*, establish a definitive

12. Heidegger, *Being and Time*, pp. 26, 28.
13. Heidegger, *Being and Time*, p. 27.
14. Heidegger, *Being and Time*, p. 39.
15. Heidegger, *Being and Time*, p. 45.

horizon of understanding within which all thought of being (including absolute knowing) must occur. Hegel's *Phenomenology* is, indeed, nothing but the systematic process of suspending the assumptions of ordinary consciousness, a process that complements and supports the simple resolve to suspend such assumptions stated to be the precondition of speculative thought in the *Logic* itself. Hegel's *Phenomenology* and Heidegger's *Being and Time* thus perform very different functions.

Like Hegel, and unlike Nietzsche, Heidegger does not believe that "being as such" is an illusion or a fiction. But like both Nietzsche and Schelling, and unlike Hegel, Heidegger (in *Being and Time*) is clearly a quasi-transcendental thinker insofar as he believes that the first (and, perhaps, principal) task of the philosopher is to uncover the existential and historical conditions that unavoidably predetermine how "being" is—and is to be—understood.

Heidegger well knows that most philosophers do not understand being in light of the "genuine" conception of temporality developed in *Being and Time*. Yet every philosopher, in his view, understands being within the horizon of some conception of time: the Greeks, for example, understood being as "presence," and even the idea that being is atemporal or supratemporal is still a *temporal* conception of being.[16] Hegel's philosophy is no exception to this and is governed by what Heidegger calls the "vulgar" conception of time, specifically by the conception of time as the "negation of a negation."[17] In his writings on negativity in Hegel (from 1938–41), Heidegger does not, therefore, see Hegel's *Logic* as the product of a thinking that is radically open to being but as the product of a thinking that already *presupposes* that being is negativity (and becoming, actuality, concept, and self-knowing spirit): "Hegel's concept of being thus stands under *pre-suppositions that are wholly its own* (*unter ganz eigenen Voraus-setzungen*), . . . though these are at the same time those of western metaphysics."[18] Indeed, Hegel's initial, abstract concept of being as such—which, we are told, is not the "*essential* concept of being" (*der* wesentliche *Begriff des Seins*)—only arises through the "dismantling" or "de-construction" (*Ab-bau*) of the governing idea of absolute actuality. The real beginning of Hegel's *Logic*—that is to say, its principle or "supporting ground"—is thus *not* the concept of pure being but that of becoming (as actuality); "pure being" is merely the *Logic's* "point of departure" (*Ausgang*).[19]

Like Schelling, Nietzsche, and many other post-Hegelians, Heidegger concludes that the appropriate way to engage with Hegel's philosophy is not simply to "follow every step of Hegelian thought in every region of his system." Such an immanent approach, he argues, would simply entail pointing repeatedly to

16. Heidegger, *Being and Time*, pp. 47, 40.
17. Heidegger, *Being and Time*, p. 484.
18. Heidegger, *Hegel*, p. 30, my translation; see also pp. 12–13.
19. Heidegger, *Hegel*, pp. 11, 14, 12, my translation.

the same principle at work in each region.[20] A more appropriate way of engaging with Hegel, for Heidegger, is to subject that principle itself to critical scrutiny; that is, to call into question the inadequate conception of time as becoming and actuality that serves as the *condition* determining the character and course of Hegelian thought.[21]

A similar quasi-transcendental approach to Hegel's philosophy, and to the concept (or meaning or question) of being as such, is adopted by many subsequent philosophers influenced by Heidegger. Gadamer, as we have already seen, finds the condition of all thought of being, including Hegel's, in language and dialogue, and Derrida names (among other things) the play of "*différance*"—of differing and deferring—as that which is "'older' than Being itself" and "makes possible the presentation of the being-present."[22] Not all post-Hegelian thinkers by any means have rejected Hegel's call to follow the immanent unfolding of the concept of being: several prominent commentators on Hegel, including Burbidge and Winfield, have reconstructed with great insight the immanent logic of Hegel's analysis of being. The predominant concern of post-Hegelian Continental philosophers, however, has been to eschew such an immanent unfolding of the concept of pure being and to examine what they regard as the conditions of the possibility of the thought of being. Only in this way, they believe, can they develop a viable alternative to Hegel's philosophy.

It is easy to see why this should be. To confront Hegel head-on and to assert that philosophy should begin with a different, more convincing or "realistic" conception of being—say, Spinoza's conception of substance—and to develop the implications of that conception is to risk losing the argument against Hegel from the start because it is immediately to expose oneself to the charge of taking too much for granted about being, or at least of taking more for granted than Hegel. That is to say, it is to run the risk of being less self-critical than he is. Yet, the alternative of simply thinking through Hegel's conception of being strikes many post-Hegelians as deeply unattractive. Feuerbach regards such a task as condemning him "to go on reading [Hegel's *Logic*] or to memorize it as a 'paternoster,'" when he has other, more practical goals to achieve in life.[23] Heidegger, as we have just seen, believes that such an approach would simply reveal more fully how Hegel's basic ideas (such as negativity, actuality, and spirit) operate in various fields of philosophy without ever loosening the hold of those ideas over our thinking. The worry shared by many post-Hegelian thinkers seems to be that once you begin to think along with Hegel, you will be drawn

20. Heidegger, *Hegel*, pp. 5–6, my translation.

21. See Heidegger, *Being and Time*, pp. 480–6.

22. Derrida, *Margins of Philosophy*, pp. 26, 6.

23. Feuerbach, *Towards a Critique of Hegel's Philosophy*, p. 102; "Zur Kritik der Hegelschen Philosophie," p. 168.

inexorably into a system of thought from which there is no escape and yet which fails to do justice to existence, life, or difference.

In view of this worry, one can see why the quasi-transcendental approach to the concept of being and to Hegel's analysis of that concept might seem attractive: it appears to offer the option of avoiding a possibly fruitless head-on confrontation with Hegelian philosophy *without* having to be drawn inescapably into Hegel's system. The proponents of the quasi-transcendental approach to being tread this middle path by pointing to what they believe is *presupposed* by the very thought of being itself and thus by Hegel's philosophy and also by arguing that such presuppositions necessarily elude the grasp of Hegel's system or are misinterpreted by him as expressions of reason or the Idea. This is not to suggest that their interest in "presuppositions" is motivated solely by a concern to circumvent Hegel but simply that such a concern is part of what promotes that interest.

Some quasi-transcendental thinkers, such as Schelling, base their account of these (alleged) presuppositions on their own experience of, or insight into, existence, life, or philosophy. Nietzsche often seems to base his account on his preference or "taste" for physiology and genealogy. Heidegger and Derrida, by contrast, endeavor to uncover such presuppositions surreptitiously at work *within* the very texts of Hegel and other thinkers; they thus seek to combine an immanent and quasi-transcendental approach in one (and, for that reason, offer, in my view, more interesting and illuminating interpretations of Hegel than Schelling or Nietzsche).

Each of these thinkers points to different preconditions of the thought of being—existence, will to power, *différance*, *Dasein*'s temporality (and changing understanding of time)—and construes in very different ways the relation between those presuppositions and the thinking they make possible. They do not all understand the concept of being in the same way, nor do they read Hegel in the same way. Nevertheless, there are clear family resemblances between the approaches they take. They are all interested in the conditions of the possibility (and, sometimes, impossibility) of the thought of being, and they all refuse to open themselves, as Hegel does, to the thought of being as such and to unfold what is *immanent* in it. The question we now have to consider is why Hegel's immanent approach to the concept of being should be preferred to the quasi-transcendental approach.

Why the Immanent Approach to Being Is to Be Preferred

The principal reason, in my view, why Hegel's immanent approach to being should be preferred to the quasi-transcendental approach is simply that the immanent approach takes less for granted about what it is to think and what it is to be than the quasi-transcendental approach. The immanent approach begins from the simple being of thought—from thought *as* sheer being—and requires of the

philosopher that he or she do no more than focus on what, if anything, is implicit in that idea of sheer being. We are not to perform any particular operation of our own devising on that idea—such as analyzing it into its supposed constituent parts or synthesizing it with other ideas—but are simply to observe what, if anything, happens to the idea as we attend to it in thought. Our approach, as I have already argued, is one of radical openness to whatever being shows itself to be.

The quasi-transcendental approach, by contrast, assumes from the outset that the more intelligent, critical (and less naive) thing to do is to reflect on the conditions that give rise to—and possibly also render impossible—the thought of being. This is clearly to assume much more than the immanent approach, for it presupposes that we as thinkers are to do more than merely hold ourselves *open* to being. We are to discern what makes the thought of being possible (and, perhaps, impossible) and thus to regard being from the start not just as *being* but as *conditioned* being or being-that-bears-the-trace-of-its-conditions-of-possibility.

But what warrants this assumption? From a Hegelian point of view, at the start of philosophy nothing can warrant it; it is simply taken for granted. For many post-Hegelian philosophers, indeed, thinking quasi-transcendentally—existentially, historically, genealogically—is quite instinctive, an unquestioned response to whatever they encounter. Being (and whatever is regarded as "in being") is automatically taken to presuppose possibility or processes of production or hidden operations of differentiation and deferral, and the thought of being is assumed to presuppose some prior horizon of interpretation. The idea of being (to the extent that it is considered at all) is not considered in itself but always in light of what it *pre*-supposes. Quasi-transcendental thought thus follows Kant in being governed by the unquestioned concern for what is *prior*, for what is *already* operative in any thinking of being, and such thought cannot, or will not, set that concern aside in the interest of self-critical openness.[24]

For Hegel, the step back from the thought of being into the preconditions of that thought is a *reflective* move. One of the principal features of reflection is that it does not accept that what appears to be immediate is actually immediate but focuses on what it believes *mediates* such "immediacy" (especially difference). The problem is that reflection takes for granted *immediately* that the reflective move is the first one to make. This is what motivates Hegel's criticism of his quasi-transcendental critics: they immediately assume that our primary task as thinkers is to point out the presuppositions of thought, but they do not consider the very nature or being of thought and prove this to be the case, nor do they derive a proper understanding of the concepts of "presupposition," "condition," and "possibility" from the thought of pure being itself. Hegel does not deny that thought *turns out* to entail, among other things, disclosing the condi-

---

24. On the difference between quasi-transcendental thought and Kantian transcendental thought, see chapter 5, note 1, above (p. 103).

tions of thought—indeed, the second part of the *Logic*, the doctrine of essence, will prove precisely this—but he does not take thought's orientation toward conditions and presuppositions for granted at the start.[25]

Nor, indeed, does Hegel assume that our very use of *language*, with its many concepts of reflection, inevitably embroils us in the search for preconditions since, as we saw in chapter four, he thinks that language can be used negatively to focus our attention on pure being alone. We may well find it impossible to speak and think without talking about "presuppositions," but we can nevertheless prevent ourselves from focusing on them by stating explicitly that philosophy "*may not presuppose anything*" (*SL* 70/1: 69 [175]).

Since Hegel's *Logic* goes on to set out the proper understanding of the categories of reflection (in the doctrine of essence), it might appear as if his critique of the reflective assumptions of his opponents at the start of the *Logic* itself presupposes what will only be proven later in the text. The specter of vicious circularity seems to raise its ugly head once again. This is certainly suggested by Dieter Henrich. Henrich accepts that the development of the categories from the thought of pure being is immanent and linear, but at the same time he claims that the full justification for the *science* of speculative logic as a whole can only be "retrospective" (*rückläufig*).[26] Henrich's reasons for making this claim are to my mind far from clear. As far as I can tell, his point is this: the reason why we should free our thought from domination by reflection in the first place and attend to pure being alone only becomes apparent *after* we have actually done so—that is, after we have derived the concepts of reflection from the thought of pure being.

Assuming that this is Henrich's view, it is one aspect of his interpretation with which I strongly disagree. It is true that Hegel accuses his opponents of basing their objections to him on reflexive categories whose meaning can only be clarified through presuppositionless logic itself:

> those who are most prolific with such objections straightway launch their reflections (*Reflexionen*) against the first propositions [of the *Logic*] without first acquiring or having acquired, by a further study of logic, an awareness of the nature of these crude reflections. (*SL* 94/1: 98)

Yet Hegel's critique of his opponents does not depend on his later account of the categories of reflection: for his principal complaint is not that his opponents misunderstand the structure of a presupposition or condition and should understand it in the way he does later in the *Logic*. To argue in that way is certainly to be guilty of vicious circularity. Hegel's main complaint against his opponents is simply that they presuppose *any* categories of reflection *at all* as the

---

25. For Hegel's account of the ideas of "presupposition" and "condition," see *SL* 400–4, 469–72/2: 25–30, 113–15.

26. Henrich, "Anfang und Methode der Logik," p. 92.

basis of their criticisms of him: "that their opinions and objections contain categories which are presuppositions (*Voraussetzungen*) and which themselves need to be criticized first before they are employed" (*SL* 40–1/1: 31). This criticism by Hegel of his opponents is justified by the modern demand for radical self-criticism that requires us to suspend all our (founding) presuppositions about thought and being; it is not dependent in any way on Hegel's later account of the categories of reflection themselves. *Pace* Henrich, therefore, the project of Hegel's *science* of logic is not justified merely retrospectively, and there is no suspicion of vicious circularity surrounding his enterprise.

From a Hegelian point of view, it is not altogether wrong to think reflectively and to interest oneself in presuppositions. Nor can any Hegelian know from the start that thought does *not* presuppose existence, will to power, time, or *différance.* All the Hegelian can claim is that it is un-self-critical to *assume* at the outset of philosophy that the principal task of thought is to focus on the possible preconditions of thought and to base one's understanding of being (as an illusion or as always already temporal) on one's understanding of those preconditions. For the philosopher interested in radically self-critical openness of mind, therefore, the immanent approach to the thought of being has to be preferable to the quasi-transcendental approach, however the latter is conceived (and I acknowledge once again that Nietzsche, Heidegger, and Derrida are *not* all saying or doing exactly the same thing).

A second reason for preferring the immanent approach is that it alone is able to *discover*—without prejudging the issue—what being as such is and entails. Nietzsche assumes that "being" means "rigidity" and "stasis" and that consequently the concept of being is a fiction. But does "being" mean this? Certain philosophers in the past may have believed that "what is, does not *become*," but were they right?[27] And how will Nietzsche ever find out if he refuses to consider the bare idea of being and to hold himself open to whatever it shows itself to be? Similarly, how can Heidegger ever determine the meaning of being as such if he assumes that the horizon of all understanding of being is time? We all use the word "being" and we assume thereby that we know what it means. In my view, however, it is only the radically presuppositionless approach to being that can *learn* what the word does mean and imply.

Another way of putting the same point is to say that only the presuppositionless approach can discover whether the idea of sheer *being* is or is not sustainable. Only this approach can set to one side the conditions that make the thought of being possible—including the fact that "pure being" is the product of abstraction—and discover the immanent fate of that abstraction, "pure being," *itself.*

A third reason for preferring the immanent over the quasi-transcendental approach to being—which is not apparent at the outset but becomes apparent later

27. Nietzsche, *Twilight of the Idols/The Antichrist*, p. 35.

in the *Logic*—is that the immanent approach actually undermines the idea of *pure* being much more profoundly than any other approach. This is precisely because it begins with the idea of pure being and shows that the purity of being undoes, or "deconstructs," *itself*.

It has become a commonplace among many Continental philosophers that there is no "purity" in the world—no pure immediacy, no pure self-presence, no pure reason—but that everything is in some way conditioned, contaminated, and compromised by what it appears to exclude. Such arguments depend upon showing that a certain irreducible, prior "alterity" always inhabits or haunts self-consciousness or reason and prevents it from being purely what it "is." Similar arguments can be adduced to show that there is no such thing as pure being because being is always conditioned by, for example, difference or time. Such arguments fall short of Hegel's, however, to the extent that they do not show difference or time to be immanent in the very purity of being itself but to be a condition of the possibility of being—a condition that informs all being and every idea of being but that is logically prior to being. The reason these arguments fall short of Hegel's is that they unwittingly leave open the possibility that being *would* remain pure if difference or time—*per impossibile* (their proponents would claim)—were left out of account. According to Hegel, by contrast, it is absolutely impossible for being to remain pure under any circumstances because the purity of being undermines itself, causes itself to vanish. This is a much more profound challenge to the Parmenidean conception of sheer being than that mounted by Nietzsche, Heidegger, or Derrida because it does away with even the impossible dream of an enduring purity of being.

The paradox, of course, is that Hegel can show that the purity of being undermines itself only by beginning with the idea of pure being in total abstraction from time and difference. The assumption prevalent among quasi-transcendental critics, however, is that it is impossible to think of being in the abstract in this way because our thought of being is always already conditioned at some level by time or difference (and so is implicitly thought of as presence or as differential). From this perspective, Hegel's claim that one can begin with pure being appears to be naive. But there is a price to pay for avoiding Hegelian "naiveté" because without beginning from the idea of pure being as such it is impossible to prove that the purity of being is *intrinsically* and *necessarily* unsustainable and that being is *intrinsically* and *necessarily* inseparable from difference and time. Without proving that, however, one cannot prove that it is impossible to think of being in the first place in abstraction from time and difference and that Hegel's *Logic* thus cannot begin with the thought of pure being. Furthermore, there remains the lingering possibility that pure being might be a sustainable idea after all if it were to be considered in the abstract.

The point I wish to emphasize here is that Hegel's quasi-transcendental critics are caught in a double-bind. *Either* they deny that pure being can be thought in the abstract without reference to difference or time, in which case they are

unable to prove that being is *intrinsically* differential and temporal and so leave open the possibility that it is not—a possibility, presumably, they do not wish to leave open; *or* they accept Hegel's argument that pure being turns out to be intrinsically differential and temporal, in which case they have to allow that pure being can be thought in complete abstraction from difference and time as the first stage of proving that this very abstraction is unsustainable—an option, presumably, they also do not wish to countenance.

Hegel faces no such problem because he does not assume in advance that the very idea of *pure* being is problematic. On the contrary, he suspends all assumptions about being and just begins with the thought of being as such, without incorporating into the thought of being the ideas of difference, time, nonbeing, or anything else. His analysis of being then shows that the idea of pure being undermines itself and turns itself into the ideas of negation, finitude, quantity, difference, space, time, matter, and eventually, history. Many of these things are also regarded as fundamental features of our world by non-Hegelians. But in Hegel's philosophy they are derived from, and so shown to be immanent in, the very idea of *pure being*. They are not simply taken for granted at the start. For this reason, I would contend, Hegel's immanent, presuppositionless approach to being is the one to be preferred.[28]

---

28. For a similar Hegelian critique of (quasi-)transcendental philosophy, see Winfield, *Overcoming Foundations*, pp. 16ff., and *Reason and Justice*, pp. 60ff. For an excellent Hegelian critique of Derrida in particular, see W. Kisner, "*Erinnerung*, *Retrait*, Absolute Reflection: Hegel and Derrida," *The Owl of Minerva* 26, 2 (Spring 1995): 171–86.

Chapter Six

Logic and Ontology

Hegel's Logic *as Ontology*

In the preceding chapters I have argued that Hegel's *Logic* provides a presuppositionless account of thought and its fundamental categories. The *Logic*'s task, on this view, is to determine, without taking anything for granted, what it is to think; it fulfills this task by "exhibit[ing] the realm of thought philosophically, that is, in its own immanent activity or what is the same, in its necessary development" (*SL* 31/1: 19). The *Logic* is thus Hegel's alternative to Kant's "Metaphysical Deduction" in the *Critique of Pure Reason*—the analysis through which Kant aims to discover the basic categories of thought prior to determining in the "Transcendental Deduction" whether or not they apply to the objects of experience.

At various points in the preceding chapters, however, I have indicated that Hegel's *Logic* provides an account of the basic structure of *being*, as well as of thought. Interpreted in this way, the *Logic* is not only a logic but also an ontology or metaphysics—Hegel's alternative to, say, Spinoza's *Ethics* (or at least part 1 thereof). In recent years it has become popular to deny that Hegel's *Logic* makes any metaphysical claims.[1] The purpose of this chapter is to defend the view that Hegel's *Logic* is a metaphysics or ontology and to explain precisely how Hegel's onto-logical science differs from ontology and metaphysics as Hegel believes they were undertaken before Kant.

Hegel states explicitly in both the *Logic* and the *Encyclopedia Logic* that his speculative logic is a metaphysics. In the preface to the first edition of the *Logic*, for example, he talks of "the logical science which constitutes metaphysics proper, or pure, speculative philosophy" (*SL* 27/1: 16).[2] In §24 of the *Encyclopedia Logic* he claims that "*logic* coincides with *metaphysics*, with the science of *things* grasped in *thoughts*" (*EL* 56/81), and in the introduction to the *Logic* he maintains that "the objective logic . . . takes the place . . . of former *metaphysics* which was intended to be the scientific construction of the world in terms of *thoughts* alone" (*SL* 63/1: 61). Hegel also emphasizes the metaphysical character of the *Logic* by asserting that its subject matter is the *logos*, "the rea-

1. See, for example, Pippin, *Hegel's Idealism*, p. 6.
2. Translation revised.

son of that which is": "it is least of all the logos which should be left outside the science of logic" (*SL* 39/1: 30).

Now it is true that according to the passage just cited from the introduction to the *Logic,* only the "Objective Logic" (which includes the doctrines of being and essence) "takes the place" of the former metaphysics and so by implication constitutes Hegel's ontology. André Doz argues, however, that the whole of the *Logic* is to be regarded as ontology, since all the concepts analyzed in it—including the concepts of "concept," "judgment," and "syllogism" examined in the "Subjective Logic" (the doctrine of the concept)—are "nothing but more developed forms or modes of being."[3] Doz's interpretation is confirmed, in my view, by passages from Hegel's own texts. In the doctrine of the concept, for example, Hegel explains that the "concept" (*Begriff*) analyzed in the *Logic* is to be regarded "not as the act of the self-conscious understanding, not as the *subjective understanding*, but as the concept in and for itself which constitutes a *stage of nature* as well as of *spirit*" (*SL* 586/2: 257)[4]; in the *Encyclopedia Logic* he states that the "syllogistic form is a universal form of all things (*aller Dinge*)" (*EL* 59/84 [§24 Add. 2]). These passages clearly indicate that the words "concept," "judgment," and "syllogism" name structures in nature, and so in *being itself*, not just forms of human understanding and reason. They are, therefore, ontological as well as logical structures—structures of being, as well as categories of thought.

Hegel does not claim that ontological structures are known in the *Logic* precisely as they occur in nature. The *Logic* conceives such structures in abstraction from space, time, and matter first of all, and the *Philosophy of Nature* then examines how such structures manifest themselves in space and time. Hegel's claim that conceptual and syllogistic form is to be found in nature (or in "all things") should not therefore be taken to blur the distinction between the *Logic* and the *Philosophy of Nature*. What that claim does make clear, however, is that for Hegel "concept" and "syllogism" are forms inhering in what there is and are not just forms in terms of which we think; they are ontological and not merely logical structures.

As the *Logic* takes us from the categories of being (such as being, becoming, something, finitude) through the determinations of essence (such as difference, form, content, substance, causality) to the determinations of concept (such as concept, judgment, syllogism, Idea), it does not suddenly shift from being an account of what there is to being an account of our own mental activity but remains throughout an account of the basic categories of thought *and* of the basic forms of being. It is from beginning to end an ontological logic that renders ex-

---

3. A. Doz, *La logique de Hegel et les problèmes traditionnels de l'ontologie* (Paris: Vrin, 1987), pp. 22–3, my translation. See also O. Pöggeler, ed. *Hegel* (Freiburg/München: Verlag Karl Alber, 1977), p. 78.

4. Translation revised.

plicit what is implicit in the indeterminate *thought* of being and in *being* itself. Indeed, the *Logic* presupposes from the start that the structure of thought—of our own *certainty* of being—is identical with the structure of being itself. We will examine later whether a philosophy that prides itself on being presuppositionless is entitled to make this Platonic or Spinozan assumption (especially after Kant's critical turn). Let us first confirm that Hegel does indeed argue for the identity of thought and being and consider how such an identity is—and is not—to be understood.

The Identity of Thought and Being

The identity of thought and being is proclaimed at various points by Hegel. In the introduction to the *Logic*, he declares that the *Logic* presupposes "liberation from the opposition of consciousness" (between subject and object) and that this liberation commits the speculative logician to the view that "the absolute truth of being is the known concept [*Begriff*] and the concept as such is the absolute truth of being" (*SL* 49/1: 43). Later in the text, Hegel claims that in the *Logic* "being is known to be the pure concept in its own self, and the pure concept to be the true being" (*SL* 60/1: 57; see also *SL* 51/1: 45).

This does *not* mean that being is simply an idea in the mind of God or of human beings. Hegel is not a quasi-Berkeleyan subjective idealist who denies the reality of the world around us and believes it to exist only for or in finite or infinite consciousness. For Hegel, being and all that it entails exists in its own right without having to be thought or "represented" by a conscious mind.[5] Hegel does not take the view, either, that beings have independent existence but are all endowed with a consciousness of their own. The identity of thought and being does not mean that all things, including stones and chairs, are thinking, imagining beings. Spinoza endorses a diluted version of this position, but Hegel patently does not.[6]

So what does it mean to say that thought and being are "identical"? It means neither that beings exist only for conscious thought nor that they are all capable of conscious thought themselves but that they exhibit a logical *form* or structure that is intelligible to thought and is the same as the structure of our basic categories. Indeed, it means that being *is* in itself intelligible logical form and that thought is the direct awareness of such intelligible being. Being is immediacy, or sheer "that-ness," prior to consciousness or "spirit." But immanent in such immediacy are various ways or modes or forms of being—being determinate, being something, being finite, being infinite—that have a definite logical struc-

5. See Hegel, *EPN* 7/16 (§246 Add.): "natural objects do not think, and are not presentations (*Vorstellungen*) or thoughts," and J. N. Findlay, *Hegel: A Re-Examination* (1958) (New York: Oxford University Press, 1976), p. 22.

6. *A Spinoza Reader*, p. 124 (*Ethics* II P13 Schol.), and Hegel, *EL* 56/81 (§24 Add. 1). See also *EL* 144/192 (§88 Add.).

ture of their own (characterized, for example, by negation or self-relation). Hegel's claim is that the logical structure of, say, "something" constitutes what it is to *be* something. Anything we encounter in the world that is "something" thus necessarily exhibits that logical structure. This pen, for example—whatever other qualities it may have—*is* itself self-relating negation because self-relating negation is the logical structure of any "something." For Hegel, therefore, being is intelligible because the "pure concept" is "the innermost nature (*das Innerste*) of things" (*SL* 37/1: 27).[7]

To understand the nature of being, Hegel maintains, all we need to do is understand what is implied by the category of "being" because the structure of that category is identical to that of being itself. The nature of being can thus be determined *a priori* by examining the basic concepts of thought. This is not to deny that there are many contingent features of the world of nature and history that can only be discovered *a posteriori* by empirical experience. Hegel's most famous example of such contingency is the fact that there are—or apparently were in Hegel's day—over sixty species of parrot (*SL* 682/2: 375). Thought cannot derive this fact from the nature of being but must discover it through observation and reflection on what we observe. Thought can, however, demonstrate a priori from the nature of being that there must be contingencies and why. Furthermore, thought can determine a priori the logical structure of contingency in general and its relation to necessity. The fact that all contingent things are subject to change and eventual destruction can be known a priori, therefore, even though pure thought cannot predict precisely how any given thing will change or when it will be destroyed. Indeed, Hegel never claims that the exact course of the world can be predicted by pure thought: "the future is not absolute, and it remains exposed to contingency."[8] What Hegel claims is that, whatever contingencies await us in the future, pure thought can determine with absolute certainty what it is to be "something," to be "finite," to be "quantitative," to have "form" and "content," to exercise "causality," and so on. Pure thought is thus able to set certain limits on the range of possible future contingencies because it knows that, whatever happens, nothing can be "something" or be "finite"—or indeed *be* at all—without exhibiting the corresponding logical structure. Pure thought, therefore, can predict what will happen insofar as that is governed by the logical structure of "something" or "finitude," but it is not in a position to foresee everything that will happen and in that sense does not lay claim to a "total" vision of things.[9]

---

7. Translation revised. In the doctrine of the concept Hegel describes the *Logic* as the "science of the *absolute form*" (*Wissenschaft der absoluten Form*) (*SL* 592/2: 265).

8. Hegel, *PR* 155/241 (§127 Add.). See Houlgate, "Necessity and Contingency in Hegel's *Science of Logic*," p. 44.

9. On Hegel's view of the "limits" of philosophy, see Houlgate, "Necessity and Contingency in Hegel's *Science of Logic*," p. 42.

The task of the *Logic* is not to predict all the specific contingent changes that will happen to being and to beings but to disclose and understand the general ways or forms of being (such as being something or being finite) that are logically entailed by, and so inherent in, being as such. It is to discover through pure thought all that being *logically* proves to be. The presupposition behind the *Logic* is the same as that associated by Hegel with pre-Kantian metaphysics: namely, that "thinking in its immanent determinations and the true nature of things form one and the same content" (*SL* 45/1: 38; see *EL* 66/94 [§28]). This presupposition is strikingly at odds with Kant's conviction that understanding is incapable of disclosing the character of things as they may be in themselves and is restricted to determining objects as they appear to us in the pure, subjective forms of intuition, space, and time (*CPR* 361/302–3 [B308–9]). Even though Hegel's *Logic* is written in the wake of Kant's critical turn, therefore, it remains a metaphysical or ontological text. Yet the *Logic* presents a new, modern metaphysics that departs in certain significant ways from pre-Kantian metaphysics as Hegel conceives it. Indeed, the metaphysics contained in the *Logic* is the direct result of Hegel's own *critique* of pre-Kantian metaphysics—a critique prompted by Kant's critical turn or at least by what Hegel takes to be the implications of that critical turn.[10]

As we have seen, Hegel endorses the metaphysical conviction that pure thought can determine by itself the inner nature of things. He is critical, however, of two further assumptions made by pre-Kantian metaphysicians. The first such assumption is that the objects addressed by metaphysics—the soul, the world, God—are given entities, or "*completed given subjects*" (*fertige gegebene Subjekte*) standing, as it were, "over there," quite separate from the mind "over here" that knows them (*EL* 68/97 [§30]).[11] Pre-Kantian metaphysics thus draws a sharp line between the *truth* (or object) that is known and the *certainty* enjoyed by the knowing mind. Another way to put the point is to say that pre-Kantian metaphysics assumes from the start that its objects are indeed *objects*—distinct, determinate entities that stand over against us—and that the task of the metaphysician is to gain access to and to tell us *about* such objects. It presupposes that the mind stands in *relation* to its objects but that the "space" between thought and things can be bridged by pure thought itself.

The second assumption made by pre-Kantian metaphysics, according to Hegel, is that thought tells us about things in the world by attributing properties or "predicates" to them in *judgments*.

> This metaphysics presupposed that cognition of the Absolute could come about through the *attaching of predicates to it. . . . Being there* (*Dasein*), for instance, is a predicate of this kind like in the proposition

10. See chapter 1, above, pp. 25–7. On Hegel's critique of pre-Kantian metaphysics, see also Houlgate, *Hegel, Nietzsche, and the Criticism of Metaphysics*, pp. 96–112.

11. Translation revised.

> "God is there"; or *finitude* and *infinity*, in the question whether the world is finite or infinite; or *simple* and *composite*, in the proposition, "The soul is *simple*" (*EL* 66/94 [§28]).

Truth was thus conceived to lie in the correspondence between our judgments (and their constituent concepts) and what there is—a correspondence that had to be verified by pure reason alone.[12]

In determining whether its judgments were true, Hegel maintains, pre-Kantian metaphysics took for granted that reason had to abide by the laws of formal logic and syllogistic reasoning. It also presupposed that the concepts with which it operated were mutually exclusive—that the soul was either simple or composite, and the universe either finite or infinite. Metaphysics was thus a form of "dogmatism" governed by the understanding (*Verstand*), because "it had to assume that of *two opposed assertions* . . . one must be *true*, and the other *false*" (*EL* 69, 65/98, 93 [§§32, 27]).

In the *Encyclopedia Logic* Hegel explicitly identifies such pre-Kantian metaphysics with the philosophies of Christian Wolff and the Scholastics (*EL* 76, 299/106, 383 [§§36 Add., 231]). According to the *Lectures on the History of Philosophy* (delivered in the 1820s), Descartes, Leibniz, and Spinoza also fall within the "period of metaphysics."[13] It would be hard to claim, however, that these philosophers are all completely "metaphysical" in Hegel's sense: Scholastics often denied that God could be adequately understood by human beings, and it is not obvious that Spinoza conceived of substance as a "completed, given subject" separate from human thought since he thought of human beings as modes *of* substance itself. But none of these philosophers—with the possible

12. As we saw in chapter 1, Hegel argues that Kant retains this idea that thought is above all the activity of judgment, even though he denies that we can come to know the true nature of things through our judgments. In this sense, for Hegel, there is a continuity between pre-Kantian thought and Kant's own critical philosophy. Kant insists that human understanding must be the activity of judgment because—unlike divine understanding—it is not intuitive but discursive; that is to say, it has to be *given* something to think about. Since human understanding is not intuitive, human intuition, for Kant, cannot be intellectual but must be *sensuous*; that is to say, it must arise through our being affected by things. Kant's conclusion is that human judgment can only be given something to think about through sensation. Note that Hegel's pre-Kantian metaphysicians do not share Kant's view that the activity of judgment is dependent on sensuous intuition. They believe that the objects of metaphysics—the soul, the cosmos, and God—can be brought before the mind, or "represented," by reason itself (see *EL* 68/97 [§30]). They thus appear to believe that human beings are capable both of judgment *and* of a form of "intellectual intuition" because they take their judgments to be about objects that are (somehow) given to us by the *intellect*. For Kant, by contrast, human understanding is the discursive activity of judgment to the exclusion of any intellectual intuition (see chapter 1, above, pp. 16–18).

13. Hegel, *VGP* 3: 122–267.

exception of Wolff—is actually reduced to being a metaphysician by Hegel. All Hegel claims is that Leibniz, Wolff, and others are to be considered metaphysicians to the extent that they aim to understand the true nature of objects through pure concepts (such as "substance" and "cause") and believe that their judgments tell us *about* a separate reality.[14]

Hegel challenges both of the presuppositions of pre-Kantian metaphysics mentioned above because he regards them as taken for granted uncritically; as we know, he believes that after Kant's critical turn the one thing we must avoid above all else is taking things for granted. Of course, Hegel may not assume himself that being is *not* made up of objects and that thought does *not* involve forming judgments about such objects, but he may, and does, object to the fact that (as he sees it) metaphysicians before Kant simply assumed from the outset that thought is essentially the activity of judgment. His complaint is that "there was no investigation of *whether* predicates of this kind are something true in and for themselves, nor of *whether* the form of the judgment could be the form of truth" (*EL* 66/94 [§28], my emphasis). In Hegel's view, the properly self-critical thing to do after Kant is not to reject outright but initially to suspend the idea that metaphysics is a *relation* of the knowing mind to *given objects* and that it tells us from a position, as it were, "over here" *about* things that are, as it were, "over there."

As we have seen, Hegel acknowledges that there *is* being; being is not just a figment of our imagination or a "construct" of thought. He insists, however, that we may not assume from the start that being is a separate realm of objectivity *to which* we stand in relation. Initially, all we may assume is the minimal idea that being is the sheer immediacy of which thought is immediately aware. Being may well—and, as we shall see in part 3, does—turn out to constitute a world of objects, but we should not *presuppose* that it does. We must wait to find out whether that is the case starting from the indeterminate thought of sheer immediacy. Hegelian metaphysics will thus not face the task of having to gain "access" to and form judgments "about" a realm of objectivity that is assumed from the beginning to be separate from us—a task notoriously fraught with epistemological difficulties—but will simply have to unfold whatever is implicit in the immediacy of which thought is aware—that is to say, whatever is implicit in the bare *thought* (or *certainty*) of such immediacy. Such metaphysics will accordingly take the form of *logic*: it will provide an account of being by examining the thought of being and the various categories that are inherent in it. In Hegel's ontological logic,

> what we are dealing with . . . is not a thinking *about* (*über*) something which exists independently as a base for our thinking and apart from it,

14. It is interesting to note that Hegel does not regard Plato and Aristotle as metaphysicians in this sense, but sees them as close in spirit to his own speculative philosophy; see *EL* 76/106 (§36 Add.).

> nor forms which are supposed to provide mere signs or distinguishing marks of truth; on the contrary, the necessary forms and self-determinations of thought are the content and the ultimate truth itself (*SL* 50/1: 44).

It is important to bear this in mind when considering Hegel's well-known claim in the *Encyclopedia Logic* that the categories analyzed in speculative logic can be regarded as "definitions of the Absolute" (*EL* 135/181 [§85]). This has been taken by some commentators as clear evidence that Hegel understood his *Logic* to tell us "about" a cosmic entity called the "Absolute" or "Absolute Spirit." Indeed, Frederick Beiser maintains that "one basic, straightforward and indisputable fact about Hegel's philosophy" is that "its aim is to know the absolute, the infinite or the unconditioned."[15]

It is true that Hegel argues in the doctrine of essence that being proves to be the Absolute or what there absolutely is.[16] But it is important to recognize that being is not conceived in this way by Hegel from the start. The Absolute is not the enduring subject (or object) of Hegelian discourse—it is not an infinite being or entity "about" which Hegelian metaphysics informs us throughout its course. It is rather what sheer immediate being as such eventually *turns out to be*. (Indeed, later in the *Logic*, such absolute being itself proves to be not just absolute being but self-determining reason, "concept," or "Idea.") Hegel concedes that, retrospectively, from the perspective of the end of the *Logic*, "it may indeed be said that every beginning must be made *with the absolute* (*dem Absoluten*), just as all advance is merely the exposition of it." He also points out, however, that "because the absolute is at first only *in itself* (*an sich*)[,] it is equally *not* the absolute nor the posited concept, and also not the Idea" but sheer immediate *being* (*SL* 829/2: 555). If we take this remark seriously and also recognize that Hegelian ontology arises from the critique of pre-Kantian metaphysics, we can see that Hegel's claim in the *Encyclopedia Logic* is actually misleading: speculative logic does not, and cannot, provide a series of "definitions of the Absolute" in any straightforward sense.

Hegelian ontology cannot provide such "definitions of the Absolute" because it does not start out by assuming that there is an Absolute (or substance or God or spirit) and see its task as that of providing an account of such a "thing" (and of having to justify its claim to direct access to that "thing"). Indeed, it does not start out from any determinate conception of what there is at all. It

---

15. F. C. Beiser, "Hegel, A Non-Metaphysician? A Polemic Review of H. T. Engelhardt and Terry Pinkard, eds. *Hegel Reconsidered*," *Bulletin of the Hegel Society of Great Britain* 32 (Autumn/Winter 1995): 3. A similar position is adopted by Charles Taylor, for whom Hegel's basic ontological thesis is "that the universe is posited by a Spirit whose essence is rational necessity"; see C. Taylor, *Hegel* (Cambridge: Cambridge University Press, 1975), p. 538.

16. See Hegel, *SL* 530–40/2: 187–200.

starts out from the utterly indeterminate awareness or thought of being as such and sees its task as the onto-*logical* one of simply unfolding what is implicit in that bare thought itself. In Hegel's view, such a developmental onto-logic is required by Kant's critical turn because it follows directly from self-critically suspending the pre-Kantian assumption that being is a determinate *object* to which we relate and from adopting the minimal idea that being is, at least initially, merely the immediacy of which we are aware in thought.[17]

Similarities and Differences Between Kant and Hegel

Hegel's ontology is indebted to Kant in another sense because it is prefigured in Kant's transcendental logic. In the *Critique of Pure Reason* Kant distinguishes transcendental logic from general logic in the following way. General logic sets out the rules of valid thinking in general—the rules (such as the law of noncontradiction) that all thought must observe if it is to be logical and formally valid at all. Transcendental logic, by contrast, sets out the rules governing the thought of objects (*Gegenstände*)—the rules we are to observe if what we are conscious of is to count as an *object* rather than a mere succession of subjective images or perceptions.[18] This latter logic stipulates, for example, that what we perceive can only be understood as an object if it is conceived of as a quantifiable unity, as a substance (or as an accident thereof), and as having a cause. In this way, such logic demonstrates that categories such as quantity, substance, and cause are the "transcendental" conditions of any consciousness or experience of objects (*CPR* 224/134 [B 126]). Consequently, Kant claims, we know *a priori* that any object we encounter in experience must have a definite magnitude and a cause even if we are unable to determine in every specific case precisely how big an object is or what caused it to be as it is.

Categories, Kant argues, are generated a priori by the spontaneous activity of our understanding and are not abstracted from our experience of things. Furthermore, we are justified in employing such categories not because they accurately "mirror" the true nature of things but because they stipulate what is to be understood by the term "object" and so define what is to count as an object for us. This is Kant's famous Copernican Revolution: to argue that our fundamental concepts do not have to be shown to conform or correspond to the objects we encounter because nothing can be encountered as an object in the first place unless it already conforms to our fundamental concepts (*CPR* 110/19–20 [B xvi]).

Accordingly, after Kant's revolution, if we are to undertake a philosophical study of the objective structure of things, we no longer need to try to gain "ac-

---

17. See also Doz, *La logique de Hegel et les problèmes traditionnels de l'ontologie*, p. 44.

18. Kant, *CPR* 195–6/98 (B 79–80). See also Hegel, *SL* 62/1: 59.

cess" from a position "over here" to things "over there" (and to explain how we are able to gain such access). All we need to do is study the basic categories of our own understanding and the rules that govern their use. This is because the objective structure of things—at least, of anything that can count as an object for us—is contained *in* our own understanding itself, specifically in such categories as quantity and cause. As Kant puts it,

> the proud name of an ontology, which presumes to offer synthetic *a priori* cognitions of things in general in a systematic doctrine (e.g., the principle of causality), must give way to the modest one of a mere analytic of the pure understanding. (*CPR* 358–9/296 [B 303])

Or as Hegel puts it, "the critical philosophy . . . turned metaphysics into logic," specifically, *transcendental* logic—the study of objects via the examination of the *categories* (and their conditions of use) that are required for any consciousness of objects (*SL* 51/1: 45).

As we have seen, Hegel follows Kant's lead by developing an ontological logic that also circumvents the need to gain "access" to things—in Hegel's case by rendering explicit what is implicit in the sheer immediacy of which thought is immediately aware. Kant's transcendental logic thus directly anticipates Hegel's ontological logic. It falls short of that onto-logic, however, for two reasons. First, it takes itself to be determining a priori the structure of *objects* rather than immediate being as such. Second, it only tells us what "objectivity" means (and must mean) *for us*, not how the world (or being) *itself* is to be understood. Kant argues that categories, such as quantity and causality, can only be used to conceive as a realm of objects what is given to us in sensuous intuition. Furthermore, he believes that the forms that characterize everything we intuit—space and time—are merely the *subjective* forms in which we intuit things, not forms that belong to things themselves (*CPR* 185/83–4 [B 59–60]). Categories can only be used, therefore, to interpret the *appearance* (*Erscheinung*) of things—what *we* intuit—as an ordered objective world; they do not grant us any insight into the fundamental nature of things in themselves or being itself (*CPR* 234, 356–65/162, 291–308 [A 111, B 300–15]). In Hegel's words, Kant thereby gave "the logical determinations . . . an essentially subjective significance" with the result that the critical philosophy remained burdened with "the residue of a thing-in-itself, an infinite obstacle, as a beyond" (*SL* 51/1: 45). Kant's groundbreaking transformation of metaphysics into logic thus does not earn Hegel's unequivocal endorsement, for it sacrifices the one feature of pre-Kantian metaphysics that Hegel wants to preserve: the conviction that thought can disclose the innermost nature of things—of being—as such.[19]

Hegel is profoundly influenced by Kant's conception of transcendental

19. On the close proximity, but also difference, between Kantian transcendental logic and Hegelian ontology, see Taylor, *Hegel*, pp. 226–7.

logic, but he dismisses the restrictions Kant places on the categories. For Hegel, "thoughts are not merely our thoughts, but at the same time the *In-itself* of things" (*EL* 83/116 [§41 Add. 2]). This is not to say that Hegel thinks we can after all reach a realm of being beyond our sensuous experience that Kant deems to be inaccessible. It is to say, rather, that Hegel rejects the idea that what is "in itself" transcends our experience. For Hegel, the "in-itself of things" is here, all around us; it is present *in* our experience and its true nature is disclosed *in* our thought. What is revealed through the logical study of our basic categories is thus the structure not just of objectivity *for us* but of *being itself*. Hegel's logic is not merely a transcendental logic, therefore, but an ontological logic that determines what it is *to be* by determining what it is to think.

For Hegel, pure thought is indeed the intellectual intuition of being. It is directly aware *that* there is being and it understands by itself what being is. This is why, at the beginning of the main text of the *Logic*, Hegel speaks of the category of nothing as "the same empty *intuition or thought* (*Anschauen oder Denken*) as pure being" (*SL* 82/1: 83 [195], my emphasis).[20] This is not to say that Hegel believes pure thought is able to intuit the immediate existence of *individual* things by itself without the aid of sensation. I can only determine whether, for example, there is a squirrel in my garden by looking and listening and reflecting on what I see and hear. Hegel insists that I am conscious through *thought* of the squirrel's actually *being there*, of its *immediacy*: I see certain colors and shapes and hear certain sounds, but I *understand* what I see and hear to be an existing object there before me.[21] Nevertheless, he also recognizes that, in order to determine that there is a squirrel rather than a cat scampering around on my lawn, I must perceive certain colors and sounds and understand what I actually *see* and *hear* to be an existing thing. Thought can thus only intuit the existence of individual things with the assistance of perception; it cannot establish by itself that specific things exist.

Hegel does not accept that space and time are merely subjective forms in which *we* perceive things rather than forms of what there is.[22] The fact that our consciousness of individual things is tied to sense perception does not mean, therefore, that we are conscious only of the way such things *appear* to us. In Hegel's view, perception or sensuous intuition discerns colors and sounds in space and time, and thought determines those spatio-temporal qualities actually to be there. There is no further reason to deny that what we are conscious of thereby are things as they are in themselves. Hegel's claim is simply that thought cannot intuit the existence of individual things themselves without the aid of perception.

---

20. See Hegel, *SL* 827-8/2: 553, and Doz, *La logique de Hegel et les problèmes traditionnels de l'ontologie*, p. 39.

21. Hegel, *EPM* 159, 224/206, 283 (§§418, 465).

22. Hegel, *EPM* 198/253 (§448 Add.).

Hegel insists, however, that thought can know through purely intellectual intuition that *there is being as such* and that being takes (and must take) the form of finitude, quantitative and causally determined being, self-determining reason, and ultimately, nature. In this sense, pure thought by itself can make certain general existence claims.[23] For Kant, by contrast, thought—at least, human thought—is irreducibly and exclusively discursive (as we saw in chapter 1). Thought is incapable of determining by itself that there *is* anything at all but can only tell us how something given in sensuous intuition is to be understood. It can tell us that what we see and hear is something *objective*—a quantifiable object that has a cause and produces an effect—and (in its empirical form) it can identify that object's empirical characteristics; but it cannot bring to mind by itself the *immediacy* of anything. Only sensuous intuition can do that. "Intuition," Kant writes, is "that through which [knowledge] relates immediately (*unmittelbar*) to [objects], and at which all thought as a means is directed." Intuition, however, takes place "only insofar as the object is given to us (*uns gegeben*); but this, in turn, is possible only if it affects the mind in a certain way" (*CPR* 155/63 [B 33]). Accordingly, all human intuition is sensuous intuition.

Kant thus distinguishes between our consciousness of the *immediacy* of a thing and our consciousness of the *objectivity* of that thing. The former is made possible by sensation and the pure forms of intuition (space and time), and the latter is made possible by understanding and its categories. As is well known, Kant believes that we are never conscious of the immediacy of a thing without judging it to be objective in some way (that is, to be a thing or an event): perceiving and judging always occur together. Intuitions without concepts are "blind" for Kant, just as thoughts without content are "empty" (*CPR* 193–4/94–

---

23. This is another respect in which my interpretation of Hegel differs from that of Klaus Hartmann. Hartmann accepts that Hegel's account of the basic categories of thought is also "an account of the determinations of the real, or of what is" ("Hegel: A Non-Metaphysical View," p. 103). For Hartmann, the *Logic* is thus an ontology: categories are "stances of grasped being, or of being grasped in various degrees of coincidence with thought" and accordingly entail "an identity of being and thought" (pp. 106, 108). Hartmann denies, however, that Hegel's ontological logic can provide any independent philosophical demonstration that anything must exist. Hegelian ontology accepts the findings of ordinary, nonphilosophical consciousness that there is a world and that there is being, but it is "devoid of existence claims" of its own (p. 110). Hegel's *Logic* thus does not itself prove that there is and must be a world of finite beings or anything at all. It simply describes the logical, categorial structure of the world that is *given* to us through ordinary experience; it tells us *what* that world is in truth (p. 114). The fact that Hegel's *Logic* does not prove by itself *that* anything exists but merely renders *what* is given intelligible explains why Hartmann considers Hegel's *Logic* to be a *nonmetaphysical* ontology (pp. 117–18). For other differences between my reading of Hegel and Hartmann's, see chapters 3 and 4, above, pp. 55, 99–100.

5 [B 74–5]).[24] It is important, however, to note the radically different contributions that sensuous intuition and understanding make to our experience of things. It is especially important to recognize that understanding does not itself entail any consciousness of the *immediacy* or actual presence of things. It simply judges that what is immediately before our eyes is an *object* of a certain kind.[25] The categorial structure conceived spontaneously by thought is thus not known by thought itself to be the structure of anything that is actual and immediate but is understood merely to be the structure of *possible* objects—objects that can only be known through sensuous intuition actually to exist.

This, I believe, is a fundamental difference between Kant and Hegel. For Kant, as he explains in the *Critique of Judgment*, "concepts . . . deal with the mere possibility of an object," whereas "sensible intuitions . . . give us something actual, yet without allowing us to cognize it as an object."[26] Concepts, in other words, tell us what it is or *would be* to be something: pure concepts or categories stipulate what it would be to be an object in general; schemata lay down what it would be to be a spatio-temporal object in general; and empirical concepts tell us what it would be to be a determinate thing, such as a squirrel or a cat. Intuition, on the other hand, constitutes direct awareness of the immediacy of the thing. Entertaining the mere concept of something—be it of an empirical object, an object in general, or indeed a "thing in itself"—can thus never assure us *that* such a thing exists. It can only tell us *what* that thing would be if it were to exist. We can only know that something we have conceived actually exists when we are given intuitions that can be subsumed under, and so be rendered intelligible by, our concepts.

In Kant's view, as we have seen, such intuitions can be given to human beings only by means of sensation. Furthermore, they presuppose the subjective forms of human sensibility, space, and time. We can thus only confirm the existence of objects—of quantifiable substances causally related to one another—in the realm of sensuous experience. That is to say, pure understanding, which by itself is restricted to conceiving of possibility, can only know a priori the structure of *actual* objects in the sphere of empirical appearance. By contrast, the idea that things have an existence "in themselves" apart from the way they ap-

---

24. See also Kant, *CPR* 211/117 (B 105). This is not to deny that we can form conceptions of the categories in abstraction from intuitions. But, for Kant, categories only yield knowledge of objects in conjunction with sensuous intuitions.

25. For Kant, the copulative "is" in judgments (which are formed by the understanding) thus confers objectivity, not immediacy, on to our intuitions (see *CPR* 251–2/152–5 [B 141–2]). Later in the *Critique of Pure Reason* Kant notes that the copula also "posits" the existence of a thing (or "posits" certain qualities as being in a thing) (*CPR* 567/572 [B 626]). It remains the case, however, that the thing we posit as existing cannot be known to exist unless it is capable of being intuited sensuously.

26. I. Kant, *Critique of Judgment*, trans. W. S. Pluhar (Indianapolis: Hackett, 1987), pp. 284–5 (§76).

pear to us must remain a purely logical possibility—albeit one that we *must* entertain—that can never be definitively confirmed or disproven. The concept of the "thing in itself" is thus considered by Kant to be necessarily "problematic" (*CPR* 362/304 [B 310]).

For the metaphysician Hegel, on the other hand, thought is not primarily the conceiving of possible objectivity but is above all the direct awareness of immediate *being*—the intuitive understanding *that* there is being and of what being is. The forms of being set out in the *Logic* are thus not just forms of possible being, but forms that actually inhere in being itself—forms that being must and does take on: being finite, being quantitative, being rational, and so on. As far as these general ways of being are concerned, Kant's judgment is therefore correct: "if our understanding were intuitive, it would have no objects except actual [ones]."[27] *Pace* Kant, however, this does not mean that an intuitive intellect can never entertain possibilities. It means, rather, that genuine possibilities must be rooted in actuality itself; they must be *actual* rather than merely formal, "logical" possibilities.[28]

As we have seen, Hegel does not argue that an intuitive understanding by itself can intuit the existence of individual things. For Hegel, as for Kant, the existence of individual things can only be established in conjunction with sense perception. There are certainly differences in the ways the two thinkers explain our consciousness of individual things. For Kant, we are conscious through sensuous intuition that something is there, and thought merely identifies what it is; for Hegel, by contrast, thought both identifies what we are perceiving *and* understands it to *be there*. In Hegel's view, thought thus confers both objectivity and immediacy on to what we perceive. (In the *Logic*, as we shall see, Hegel shows that the logical categories constitutive of being an *object*, such as "something" and "finitude," are actually implicit in the thought of immediate being itself.) Both Kant and Hegel acknowledge, however, that understanding and sensation must work together if we are to be conscious of the existence of any particular thing. Furthermore, both acknowledge that it is possible to misidentify what one perceives and so to assert that something exists when it does not. The two philosophers thus end up giving very similar accounts of our knowledge of individual things.

Where they differ is in their understanding of what pure thought by itself can know of being as such. For Kant, pure thought can know nothing of being as such, but can only conceive of what is possible. For Hegel, by contrast, pure thought can intuit the true nature of being itself. Indeed, provided that the logical derivation of the pure categories in speculative logic properly unfolds the immanent implications of the concept of being, such logic cannot fail to disclose

---

27. Kant, *Critique of Judgment*, p. 284 (§76).

28. See Houlgate, "Necessity and Contingency in Hegel's *Science of Logic*," pp. 40–5.

the nature of being because the nature of being is identical with the structure that being is *understood* to have.

Hegel's "Transcendental Deduction"

In the *Critique of Pure Reason* Kant's argument justifying the claim that the categories of pure thought apply to objects of experience is called the Transcendental Deduction of the categories. Hegel's arguments in support of the claim that thought understands not just the objects of our experience but being itself can be regarded as forming his own Transcendental Deduction. I now want briefly to review that Hegelian "deduction" so that it is quite clear what justifies Hegel's neo-Spinozan or neo-Platonic confidence that thought can determine from within itself the true character of being. It should be noted, by the way, that Hegel's Transcendental Deduction is not undertaken within the main body of the *Logic* but is presupposed by it. This is made clear by Hegel's statement that the "unity" of thought and being constitutes from the start the "element" of the *Logic* itself—the subject matter that speculative logic is to determine (*SL* 60/1: 57).

There are two intimately related arguments at the heart of Hegel's Transcendental Deduction, both of which should now be familiar. The first is extraordinarily simple. After Kant's critical turn, Hegel maintains, the logician is no longer justified in taking for granted any rules, laws, or concepts of thought (*SL* 43/1: 35). Indeed, the logician cannot take for granted anything at all about thought except thought's own simple being. In the science of logic, therefore, we may begin from nothing more determinate than the sheer being of thought itself—thought *as* sheer being.

> The beginning must be an *absolute* . . . beginning; and so it *may not presuppose anything*. . . .Consequently, it must be purely and simply *an* immediacy, or rather merely *immediacy* itself. . . . The beginning therefore is *pure being*. (*SL* 70/1: 69 [175])

For Hegel, then, thought must be minimally the thought of being—not of objects, or nature, or even possibility—because *being* is all that is left once thought has self-critically suspended all its presuppositions about itself. This argument obviously echoes Descartes's at the start of the second Meditation, according to which, by doubting everything it knows, including itself, thought discovers that its own being is irreducible.[29] The principal difference between Descartes and Hegel, of course, is that for Hegel the process of suspending all that thought has previously taken for granted about itself leaves us not with the recognition that *I* am but with the indeterminate thought of thought itself as sheer *being*.

---

29. See *The Philosophical Writings of Descartes*, 2: 17.

Hegel's second argument is equally simple but starts from the idea of "being" rather than from thought. If we are to be thoroughly self-critical, we cannot initially assume that being is anything beyond the being of which thought is minimally aware. We may not assume that being stands over against thought or eludes thought but must take being to be the sheer immediacy *of which* thought is minimally aware—because that is all that the self-critical suspension of our presuppositions about being and thought leaves us with. A thoroughly self-critical philosopher has no choice, therefore, but to equate being with what is thought and understood. Any other conception of being—in particular, one that regards being as possibly or necessarily transcending thought—is simply not warranted by the bare idea of being as the "sheer-immediacy-of-which-thought-is-minimally-aware" from which we must begin. At the beginning of logic, therefore, we do not yet know all that being will turn out to be, but we do know that the structure of being will be the structure of the thought of being. That is to say, we know that "the matter (*Sache*) can be for us nothing other than our concepts of it" (*SL* 36/1: 25).[30]

These two Hegelian arguments, sketched in the prefaces and introduction to the *Logic*, yield two principles that underlie the *Logic*. First, we are aware of being for no other reason than that we *think*; thought is thus the "condition" of our awareness of being. This is Hegel's quasi-Kantian principle. Second, thought is minimally the awareness or intuition of *being itself*. This is Hegel's quasi-Spinozan principle. These two principles dovetail in the single principle that the structure of being is the structure of the thought of being and cause Hegel to collapse ontology and logic into the new science of *ontological logic*.[31]

Hegel acknowledges that there is a difference between thought and being: being *is* what it is in its own right and is not there only *for* conscious thought. Moreover, as we learn in the course of the *Logic*, being does, after all, turn out to constitute a realm of objects ("over there" and all around us). Hegel insists, however, that we may not begin by assuming that being is quite separate from thought. We must begin from the idea that being and thought are in fact *inseparable* (*untrennbar*): for we must start from the idea that thought is initially nothing but the thought of sheer, immediate being, that being is initially nothing but the simple immediacy of which thought is minimally aware, and that both thought and being thus have the same categorial form. This is the "identity" or "unity" of thought and being that forms the "element" of Hegel's *Logic* (see *SL* 60/1: 57). We do not, therefore, need to gain "access" to being in order to understand its nature. All we need to do is to render explicit whatever is implicit in the *thought* of simple, immediate being. In this way, we will discover a priori

30. Translation revised.

31. See S. Houlgate, "Hegel and Fichte: Recognition, Otherness, and Absolute Knowing," *The Owl of Minerva* 26, 1 (Fall 1994): 16–17, and S. Houlgate, "Absolute Knowing Revisited," *The Owl of Minerva* 30, 1 (Fall 1998): 59.

from within thought itself all that being is and must be (including what it is to be "something" or to be an "object").

Note that Hegel's "Spinozan" (or "Platonic") conviction that thought is ontological results from his radically *self-critical* suspension of previous assumptions about thought and being, including Kant's assumption that thought is restricted to conceiving of what is merely possible rather than what is. Hegel does not turn his back on Kantian critique (as he understands it) and revert to Spinozan metaphysics as if Kant had never existed. Nor does he follow Hölderlin and Schelling and overcome the Kantian separation of thought from being by simply *presupposing* that the Spinozan unity of thought and being is the precondition of any such separation. (Hegel took this latter course in early texts, such as the *Differenzschrift*, but does not do so in mature works, such as the *Logic*.) Hegel is driven to his reformed Spinozism by what he takes to be Kant's own call to radical self-criticism: for that call leads him to regard Kant's assertion that pure thought is limited to thinking what is merely possible, rather than actual, as itself quite uncritical and unwarranted.

Hegel, Kant, and the "Thing in Itself"

Hegel's rejection of Kant's notorious concept of the "thing in itself" (*Ding an sich*) is also rooted to a large degree in his belief that Kant does not live up to what Hegel takes to be Kant's own demand for thorough self-criticism. In this section I shall consider the critique of Kant's concept provided by Hegel prior to the beginning of the science of logic itself. Within the main body of the *Logic* Hegel offers a further critique of Kant's concept, which we shall examine in chapter 18.

A "thing in itself," for Kant, is a thing as it might be apart from the way it appears to us and is experienced by us. Kant insists that we can never know whether there is actually anything to things beyond what we experience of them, but he maintains that we can and indeed must entertain the *thought* that there is. Hegel also talks of the "*In-itself* of things" (*EL* 83/116 [§41 Add. 2]), but he does not conceive of it in the same way as Kant. What Hegel has in mind is not some possible dimension of things beyond what we experience them to be but the actual nature of being that is disclosed in our experience and fully articulated by pure, speculative thought. Hegel does not, therefore, accept the idea that there is a dimension to things *beyond* our experience and argue against Kant that we can gain access to that dimension after all. He rejects the idea that what a thing—or being—is "in itself" transcends our experience and instead conceives of being "in itself" as the intelligible, ontological structure *of* the very things we experience. From the Hegelian point of view, Kant fails to develop a proper understanding of the concept of being *in itself* because he does not derive it from consideration of the bare concept of being. Rather, he clings dogmatically to the idea that the fundamental orientation of thought is toward *things* or *objects* and then forms the concept of a thing in itself, in abstraction from our experience of

it—a concept that (as we shall see in chapter 18 especially) ends up being too abstract to count as a concept of a possible *thing* at all.

As far as Hegel is concerned, Kant's legacy is thus an ambiguous one. On the positive side, Kant inaugurates the era of philosophical critique and sets Hegel on the path of radical self-criticism. This prompts Hegel to suspend the assumption of pre-Kantian metaphysics that thought's task is to form true judgments "about" objects and leads him to the view that metaphysics after Kant must take the form of ontological logic—the discovery of what being entails through simply rendering explicit what is implicit in the *thought* of being. Furthermore, Kant's own transcendental logic frees us from the idea that thought must somehow gain *access* from "over here" to objects "over there." Transcendental logic achieves this liberation by arguing that we can understand a priori the fundamental structure of things—albeit only of the objects of "appearance"—through examining the categories of our *own* understanding. Hegel turns Kantian transcendental logic into ontological logic by contending that an examination of our basic categories discloses not just the structure of things as they appear to us but the structure of being itself. Hegel reaches this conclusion, as we have seen, by directing philosophical criticism—under the inspiration of Kant himself—against Kant's claim that thought by itself is restricted to understanding merely *possible* objectivity rather than being as such. Kant thus moves Hegel to develop an original position that goes beyond both pre-Kantian metaphysics and Kant's own critical, transcendental philosophy.

On the other hand, Kant still adheres to the assumption, shared by pre-Kantian metaphysics and ordinary consciousness, that thought is fundamentally a *relation* of the knowing mind (and of judgment) to *things* and *objects*. Unlike metaphysics and ordinary consciousness, Kant believes that the understanding itself stipulates what is to count as an object of experience and so can know a priori the necessary structure of any such objects without needing to gain "access" to them (through pure thought or perception). Furthermore—again in contrast to metaphysics and ordinary consciousness—Kant denies that we can ever know the true nature of things in themselves. He never suspends the assumption, however, that thought is essentially concerned with objects and so never sees that thought is minimally the understanding not of objects but of *immediate being*. Accordingly, Kant never reaches the point from which Hegel thinks a thoroughly self-critical philosophy must begin. In Hegel's view, Kant's unquestioning insistence that thought is primarily directed toward objects is particularly evident in his conception of the "thing in itself."

Some of Hegel's comments, however, fail to make his precise reasons for criticizing Kant's conception of the "thing in itself" apparent. In the *Logic*, for example, Hegel twice refers to the concept of the "thing in itself" as a product of abstraction calling it a "product of . . . merely abstractive thought" and a "thought-thing" (*Gedankending*) (*SL* 62, 36/1: 60, 26). These remarks do not, in my view, adequately explain why Hegel disapproves of Kant's concept. Indeed,

a Kantian might argue that by themselves they do not actually constitute criticisms of Kant at all. After all, Kant himself acknowledges that the concept of the "thing in itself" is produced by the understanding when it *abstracts* from the sensuous conditions under which alone we can experience objects and considers what objects might be like in themselves apart from such conditions.

> The understanding (*Verstand*), when it calls an object in a relation mere phenomenon, simultaneously makes for itself, beyond this relation, another representation of an *object in itself* (*Gegenstand an sich selbst*) and hence also represents itself as being able to make *concepts* of such an object. (*CPR* 360/302 [B 306-7])

If Kant himself explicitly understands the concept of the "thing in itself" to be the product of abstraction, then why should Hegel's comment that this is the case be regarded as a criticism? It can only count as a criticism of Kant if thought is not supposed to produce such abstractions. But it is not immediately clear by Hegel's own criteria that self-critical thought should avoid acts of abstraction. Indeed, does Hegel not recommend that self-critical thought should suspend, and so *abstract from*, all that it takes for granted about itself, and does he not insist that the beginning of the *Logic* should be "an *abstract* beginning" (*SL* 70/1: 68 [175])? Could one not argue, therefore, that the concept of the "thing in itself" is actually the result of Kant's taking self-criticism seriously since it is generated when thought sets to one side, and so *abstracts* from, the traditional metaphysical assumption that the world is as we know it to be and considers that things might differ from the way we experience them?

If we turn to Hegel's discussion of Kant in the *Encyclopedia Logic*, however, we see more clearly why Hegel regards the concept of the "thing in itself" as a sign of Kant's failure to be thoroughly self-critical rather than an indication of his self-critical intent. In §44 of the *Encyclopedia Logic* Hegel repeats his charge that the concept of the "thing in itself" is the product of abstraction: it is, he says, "the *product* of thinking . . . that has gone to the extreme of pure abstraction." But then he adds a significant remark. The concept of the "thing in itself," he tells us, is the "product of the empty 'I' that makes its own empty self-*identity* into its *object* (*Gegenstand*)" (*EL* 87/121). What this remark makes clear is that, in Hegel's view, the concept of the "thing in itself" results from an act of abstraction that *preserves* the idea that all thought relates to objects and that does not in any way suspend or abstract from that conviction. The problem with Kant, therefore, is that he does not actually abstract enough from the way we ordinarily conceive of things.

The assumption that thought is fundamentally a relation to objects that stand over against us rather than an awareness of the immediacy of being as such is one that is made by pre-Kantian metaphysics and by ordinary consciousness. As we know, Kant shares the view that our ordinary, sensuous experience is fundamentally an experience of objects. According to Hegel, Kant retains the idea

that thought fundamentally relates to objects even when formulating the thought of things as they might be in themselves apart from the conditions under which they are ordinarily experienced by us. The fact that Kant regards things in themselves as quite beyond the reach of our knowledge—and, indeed, the fact that he regards their very existence as problematic, as no more than logically possible—makes no real difference to Hegel's point. The fact remains that Kant conceives of things in themselves as logically possible *objects* transcending our experience. Nor does it matter that Kant admits that "it . . . remains completely unknown whether such an object is to be encountered within or without us, whether it would be canceled out along with sensibility or whether it would remain even if we took sensibility away." For, wherever the "thing in itself" might be thought to reside—even if within the mind itself—it is conceived by Kant as a "transcendental *object*" (*transzendentales Objekt*) that is "the cause (*Ursache*) of appearance (thus not itself appearance)" and to that extent is conceived as quite distinct from the field of objects of which alone *we* can be aware.[32]

The core of Hegel's charge against Kant prior to the start of the science of logic itself is thus that the concept of the "thing in itself" is the result of an act of abstraction by thought that remains mired in the perspective of ordinary consciousness insofar as it retains the idea that all thought relates to objects—even though it points to that which might possibly transcend ordinary experience.

---

32. Kant's claim that "the concept of the noumenon is . . . not the concept of an object" does not contradict the argument of this paragraph. Kant's point in making this claim, as I understand it, is that in the absence of sensibility no object is *given* to us to which the concept of "noumenon" could apply. This claim is quite compatible with the further assertion made by Kant that the understanding "*thinks* of an object in itself . . . as a transcendental object," and that "if we want to call this object a noumenon . . . we are free to do so" (*CPR* 380–1/330 [B 343–5], my emphasis). I assume in this discussion that the concepts of the "thing in itself," "transcendental object," and (negative) "noumenon" are all essentially the same concept: the bare concept of "something" or of "something in general = X" (*etwas überhaupt = X*) (*CPR* 231/151 [A 104]). On the identity of the thing in itself and the noumenon, see *CPR* 362–4/304–8 (B 310, 312, 315); on the identity of the thing in itself and the transcendental object, see *CPR* 424/395 (A 366). I recognize, however, that these concepts often perform different functions in Kant's philosophy. The concepts of the "thing in itself" and (negative) "noumenon" serve primarily to "limit the pretension of sensibility" by allowing us to think of things as being different in themselves from the way in which they are known under the conditions of human sensibility (*CPR* 362/305 [B 311]). The concept of the "transcendental object," by contrast, often serves a more constructive role as a condition of experience itself. On the one hand, it is the thought of "something" embedded in every category that allows us to think of what we intuit as *something* real, *something* with size, or *something* that exercises causality (*CPR* 233, 347–8/159, 299 [A 109, 250]). On the other hand, it is the thought of "something" that allows us to understand our sensations to be the result of being affected by *something* beyond our experience (*CPR* 381/330 [B 344]). It has to be said, however, that Kant is not always consistent in his use of these concepts.

This is confirmed by a passage from the introduction to the *Logic* where Hegel first states explicitly that Kant's point of view "remains confined within consciousness and its opposition," and then immediately associates this fact with Kant's concept of the "thing in itself." "Besides the empirical element of feeling and intuition," Hegel writes, Kant's point of view "has something else left over which is not posited and determined by thinking self-consciousness, a *thing-in-itself*, something alien and external to thought" (*SL* 62/1: 59–60).[33] What concerns Hegel, therefore, is not just that the concept of the "thing in itself" is an *abstract* concept but that it is an abstract concept of a *thing* or *object* of consciousness. His objection is that "the *thing-in-itself* . . . expresses the *object* (*Gegenstand*), inasmuch as abstraction is made of all that it is *for consciousness*" (*EL* 87/120–1 [§44], my emphasis). From Hegel's point of view, Kant's philosophy falls short of what radical self-criticism demands, however critical it may purport to be, because it fails to suspend our *ordinary* assumption that we are essentially subjects standing over against, and in relation to, an objective world.

From Kant's point of view, of course, the concept of the "thing in itself" (or "negative noumenon") is itself a *critical* concept that "limits the pretension of sensibility" by keeping us mindful of the idea that the world should not simply be reduced to what we experience it to be (*CPR* 350/305 [B 311]). It reminds us that we should not overestimate the powers of natural science or metaphysics and believe that they can tell us about anything more than the structure of the world we experience. We should not pretend that they reveal the inner nature of things (including natural objects, human beings, and God) themselves.

To the Hegelian eye, however, Kant's apparently modest acceptance that things should not be thought to be reducible to the way we experience them is not modest at all. On the contrary, it rests on two dogmatic assertions. The first is that ordinary consciousness is right to insist that thought is fundamentally a relation to a realm of things or objects. The second is that the forms of space and time through which we ordinarily perceive things are the *a priori* forms of *our* intuiting alone and so—contrary to what ordinary consciousness believes—cannot characterize objects "in themselves," and that human thought can thus do no more than determine the character of objects as they *appear*. This second point is particularly important. Kant maintains that we must entertain the *thought*—the logical possibility—that the objects of experience have a dimension to them that exceeds our cognition and that therefore things in themselves exist, but he insists that we cannot *know* that they do. (Herein lies his apparent modesty.) At the same time, he confidently maintains that such things in themselves must be thought to differ radically from the way we perceive them because the forms of human intuition are a priori and so (according to Kant) can only be the subjective conditions of our experience, *not* the ontological condi-

33. See also Hegel, *EPM* 161/209 (§420).

tions of things. I remarked above that Kant's thought of the "thing in itself" could be said to make space for the idea that things "might differ" in themselves from the way we perceive them (p. 133). It is important to remember, however, that Kant's claim is not that things in themselves definitely exist yet *might differ* from the way we experience them. It is that things in themselves *might exist* yet, whether or not they do, *must be thought to differ* from the way we experience them. It is their existence that is problematic, not the idea that they differ from our experience of them. Indeed, this idea is put forward by Kant without the slightest hesitation.

From a Hegelian point of view, the claim that the *a priori* forms of our intuition definitely cannot belong to the world in itself as well (whether or not such a dimension to the world exists) is never properly justified by Kant and is indeed asserted quite dogmatically. The claim that human cognition is limited by virtue of being conditioned by a priori forms of intuition is thus also a dogmatic one.[34] For Hegel, indeed, Kant's insistence that human cognition is limited is an uncritical insistence that needs to be challenged. "People speak of the limits of human reason as a sign of humility (*Demut*)," Hegel notes in his 1817 lectures on logic, but "reason knows itself to be something finite according to the assertion (*Behauptung*) of those who say that man can know nothing of anything higher, of God." Consequently, he adds, "their humility becomes proud (*stolz*) because they assert this."[35]

The genuinely self-critical thing to do, according to Hegel, is to suspend all the assumptions about thought made by ordinary consciousness and Kantian "critical" philosophy and to start from scratch. This means giving up the ordinary assumption (shared by Kant and pre-Kantian metaphysics) that thought is fundamentally a relation to objects. It also means setting to one side Kant's distinctive further assertion that we must frame the thought of a hidden dimension to objects—what they are in themselves—that differs fundamentally from the way we experience them. The result of giving up such assumptions, as we have seen, is that thought is left with nothing to think to begin with except sheer indeterminate being. Suspending Kant's apparently critical but in fact dogmatic restrictions on thought thus leads us to the quasi-Spinozan idea that thought is minimally ontological: the thought not just of *possibility* but of *being*. Hegel is a reformed Spinozist, in other words, because he is more of a critical philosopher than Kant himself.

Hegel is sometimes thought to have put us back in touch with "things in themselves" after Kant had separated us from them. But to present Hegel's chal-

---

34. For Hegel's critique of Kant's subjectivization of space and time, see *EPM* 198/253 (§448 Add.). For Kant's dogmatic statement that space and time are a priori, subjective forms of intuition and *therefore* cannot be properties of things themselves, see *CPR* 176, 180, 185/70, 76, 83 (B 42, 49, 59).

35. Hegel, *VLM* 7, my translation.

lenge to Kant in this way is somewhat misleading. Hegel's response to Kant is not to say "yes, we can know things in themselves beyond experience, after all." It is to *give up* the very idea that there might be a realm of being "beyond" our "limited" experience—together with all other preconceptions about being—and to attend to whatever may be implicit in the simple thought of being as such.

Pippin's Hegel

Perhaps the most significant recent nonmetaphysical interpretation of Hegel's *Logic* is that offered by Robert Pippin in his book *Hegel's Idealism*. To end this chapter, I wish to indicate the principal ways in which his interpretation overlaps with and differs from mine.

For Pippin, Hegel does not attempt to prove the existence of a Divine Mind, nor does he aim to offer "a deduction of the content of the actual universe or of world history." Rather, he preserves—indeed, radicalizes—Kant's "transcendental break with the metaphysical tradition." What Hegel's *Logic* provides is a "full 'scientific' account by thought of the basic categorial distinctions involved in . . . self-understanding."[36] Yet Pippin does not see Hegel as a pure category theorist. Pippin's Hegel does not just "establish that there are peculiar sorts of relations among primitive and somehow basic concepts" and so give "an account by thought of itself." He seeks to determine the categories through which "a subject could take itself to be in relation to *objects*." Indeed, he proposes to disclose "the conceptual conditions required for there to be possibly determinate objects of cognition in the first place."[37] Pippin's Hegel is thus overtly committed to continuing the project of transcendental logic as Kant himself conceived it: namely, to establish not just the rules that govern thinking in general but the particular rules, or "categories," that are required if we are to understand something to be an *object*.

Pippin's Hegel differs from Kant, however, in two important ways. First, he does not rely on a table of judgments to work out which concepts are needed for cognition of objects but derives the categories by reflecting on the bare thought of "being" and determining its conceptual "conditions."[38] Second, he holds that these categories do not merely render intelligible our sensuous experience and leave a putative realm of things in themselves beyond our comprehension. For Hegel, the categories cannot be contrasted in this way with what there ultimately is or might be because they themselves contain "all that 'being' could intelligibly be." Whatever is judged to be determinate, actual, or possible—to be *anything* at all—can only be so judged with the help of the categories. The categories thus structure "any possible world that a self-conscious judger could

---

36. Pippin, *Hegel's Idealism*, pp. 5, 39, 16, 169.
37. Pippin, *Hegel's Idealism*, pp. 177, 171, 176, my emphasis.
38. Pippin, *Hegel's Idealism*, pp. 39–40.

determine."[39] Nothing can be judged to lie "outside" or "beyond" their range of validity.

For Pippin's Hegel, therefore, metaphysics and ontology give way to transcendental logic: for being can be understood only by examining the *categories* through which it is necessarily conceived. Determining what it is to be, or to be an object, actually means establishing what it is to be an "apprehensible object" or an "object of thought."[40] Truth is reached, on this view, by understanding properly what it *means* to be an object of thought, not by trying to match our categories to something "out there."[41]

To the extent that Pippin interprets Hegel's *Logic* as an account of the basic categories of thought and as a revised transcendental logic, his reading overlaps with one side of the interpretation offered in this study. Pippin's interpretation of Hegel differs from mine, however, in three ways. First, Pippin takes it for granted that Hegel, like Kant, is seeking to establish the conceptual conditions under which there can be *objects* of thought. He believes that Hegel—like Kant—does away with the need to prove that thought corresponds to objects "out there" by showing that thought can determine from out of itself a priori what it means to be an object. He never doubts, however, that for Hegel thought is always oriented toward objects rather than sheer immediate being.

Second, Pippin takes a strikingly different view of the course of the *Logic* from the one I adopt in this study. As I see it, the task of the *Logic* requires us simply to unfold the initial indeterminate thought of being. In so doing, we see the thought of being turn into—or turn out to be—the thought of quality, quantity, reflexivity, causality, concept, judgment, syllogism, and self-determining reason, or Idea. The *Logic* thus shows an initial indeterminate thought mutate into further categories in terms of which we must think and must understand being.

For Pippin, by contrast, as we pass from the doctrine of being to the doctrines of essence and concept, we move on to consider not just further categories but also the fundamental *operations* or *activities* of self-conscious thought, which he contends are the preconditions of there being determinate objects of thought. The doctrine of being, according to Pippin, reveals the problems that arise when one tries to conceive of determinacy in terms of simple negation; namely, that things end up being conceived "in a spuriously infinite relation with all other things" as not this, not this, not this, and so on. The doctrine of essence then shows that the employment of categories of reflection, such as "essence," "form," and "content," allows us to identify things more successfully. It also shows that "there is and must be a kind of spontaneous, positing reflection necessary for the determinacy of any determinate being to be accounted for."

39. Pippin, *Hegel's Idealism*, pp. 98, 250.

40. Pippin, *Hegel's Idealism*, pp. 227, 200.

41. Pippin, *Hegel's Idealism*, p. 187.

(This, Pippin notes, is Hegel's idealism "in a nutshell.")[42] The doctrine of the concept demonstrates further that the activity of reflection itself presupposes a total conceptual scheme generated by the self-conscious spontaneity of thought. Pippin identifies such self-conscious spontaneous thought, together with the system of categories it produces, as the "Notion" or concept (*Begriff*). The "Notion" is thus not just a complex concept in terms of which we must think; it is the "necessary subjective activity"—the "process of 'thought's autonomous development'"—that is presupposed by all thought of determinacy.[43] Hegel's *Logic* thus tells a story that is strongly indebted to Kant: namely that cognition of objects presupposes subjective activity that is at least implicitly self-conscious or "apperceptive."[44]

The problem, to my mind, is that the text of Hegel's *Logic* simply does not support this aspect of Pippin's interpretation. In the doctrine of essence, Hegel states unequivocally that "what is under discussion here is neither reflection at the level of consciousness, nor the more specific reflection of the understanding, . . . but reflection generally (*Reflexion überhaupt*)" (*SL* 404/2: 30–1); in the doctrine of the concept, as was noted at the start of this chapter, Hegel writes that "here . . . the concept is to be regarded not as the act of the self-conscious understanding, not as the *subjective understanding*, but as the concept in and for itself" (*SL* 586/2: 257).[45] What is described in the *Logic* are thus the ontological structures of "reflexivity" and "concept," not the *operations* of self-conscious reflecting and conceiving.

Pippin justifies his interpretation by referring to two passages in which Hegel appears to equate the concept, or "Notion," with self-consciousness. Hegel comments at one point that "the concept, when it has developed into a *concrete existence* that is itself free, is none other than the *I* or pure self-consciousness" (*SL* 583/2: 253); he goes on to say that "the object . . . has its objectivity in the *concept* and this is the *unity of self-consciousness* into which it has been received" (*SL* 585/2: 255).[46] Pippin neglects to point out, however, that the second of these passages is not actually Hegel's own position but is Hegel's restatement in his own words of *Kant's* position. Nor does Pippin point out that the first passage equates self-consciousness with the concept only insofar as the concept has "developed into a concrete *existence* (*Existenz*) that is itself free." As we learn later in Hegel's system, the concept or reason exists as self-conscious reason in space, time, and history. In the *Logic*, however, the concept

42. Pippin, *Hegel's Idealism*, pp. 197, 201, 216.

43. Pippin, *Hegel's Idealism*, pp. 224–5, 232–4.

44. Pippin, *Hegel's Idealism*, pp. 19–21, and R. Pippin, "Hegel's Idealism: Prospects," *Bulletin of the Hegel Society of Great Britain* 19 (Spring/Summer 1989): 31.

45. Translation revised.

46. Pippin, *Hegel's Idealism*, p. 232.

is understood not as existing in this concrete form but as a purely *logical* structure or category. The lesson of the *Logic* is thus not that the thought of determinate being presupposes self-conscious activity but that the concept of being turns into the concept of "concept" and that being itself thus turns out in truth to be reason. Provocative though Pippin's reading is, it is in my view based on a misreading of Hegel's *Logic*.

The third difference between Pippin's interpretation and mine is that Pippin does not consider the *Logic* to be an ontology in a strong sense. On my reading, the categories articulated in the *Logic*—including those of "reflexivity" and "concept"—are forms or ways of *being* as well as categories of thought. Speculative logic is accordingly not merely transcendental but ontological logic. For Pippin, by contrast, transcendental logic has altogether replaced ontology. We can no longer talk of being or reality *tout court* but can only talk of what it is to be an "object of a possibly self-conscious judgment."[47] Pippin's point is not that ontology is impossible because things are somehow unreachable in themselves. His claim is that ontology is no longer an intelligible undertaking because we now realize that being an object of *thought* is "all that 'being' could intelligibly be."[48] For this reason, after Kant (and Fichte) ontology must give way to transcendental logic.

To my mind, however, this overlooks an important fact about thought: thought opens up—and takes itself to open up—not just the space of "being as it is for thought" but the space of *being as such*—being that has its own immediacy and character. That is to say, thought is aware—and takes itself to be aware—not merely of what is *intelligible* but also of intelligible *being*. If we take transcendental logic seriously, therefore, and set out what thought must understand there to be, we inevitably find ourselves doing ontology, for we necessarily provide an account of the thought of *being tout court* and all that it entails.

Pippin is clearly not moved by this line of reasoning. Yet by protecting transcendental logic against what he regards as "confusion" with ontology, he reintroduces a distinction between being as it *is* and being as it is *thought*, which, on my reading, Hegel's revised "transcendental logic" was meant to set aside. This is not to say that Pippin revives the precise Kantian distinction between "appearance" and "things in themselves." He consistently maintains that it is unintelligible to hold that there is anything beyond what we understand and know there to be. What we understand there to be, as far as we are concerned, *is* what there is; the objects all around us, which we regard as determinate, exhaust what we mean by "being." Nevertheless, Pippin draws a distinction between the conditions needed for these objects to exist and be whatever they are and the conditions needed for them to be picked out and identified by thought *as* determinate

47. Pippin, *Hegel's Idealism*, p. 250.
48. Pippin, *Hegel's Idealism*, p. 98.

things.[49] The categories presented in the *Logic* serve only the latter function. They are concepts in terms of which we think and determinations that must characterize objects if they are to be determinate objects of thought; but they are *not* ontological forms, or ways of being of things themselves.

Pippin makes this eminently clear in the course of chastising Hegel for transgressing what Pippin regards as the proper limits of transcendental logic:

> Hegel . . . "forces his argument beyond what it can strictly yield," by confusing the requirement that any being be characterized "contrastively," in a way that will distinguish it from some other, with the claim that *beings* actually oppose and negate each other and, in their opposition and negation, are essentially related, could not be what they are outside such a relation. The latter claim, then, not only represents a conflation with the first, but is itself suspect, since it again confuses logical with ontological issues. It appears to claim that a thing's not being something else is a property of it, part of what make[s] it what it is.[50]

At numerous other points in his book Pippin warns Hegel and his commentators against "confusing the conditions of thought with the conditions of existence" or "carelessly confusing the conceptual with the real order." In the doctrine of being above all, Pippin complains, Hegel "slips frequently from a 'logical' to a 'material' mode" and makes "a claim . . . , on the supposed basis of logical necessity, about things."[51]

It is clear from these remarks that Pippin assigns a considerably more limited role to Hegelian logic than I do. In Pippin's view, such logic sets out "all that 'being' could *intelligibly* be," but it does not set out "all that 'being' could intelligibly *be*." It determines the categorial structure that things must be understood to have if they are to be picked out as intelligible, determinate objects of thought, but it does not show us the structure they must have in order to *be* at all. To my mind, however, Pippin misses the essential lesson of transcendental logic as Hegel conceives it: namely, that *being* can no longer be distinguished at all from what it is *understood* to be. The whole point of Hegel's radicalized "transcendental turn" is to do away with the very distinction between the structure of being or existence and the structure of intelligibility on which Pippin continues to insist. *Pace* Pippin, Hegel is not and cannot be guilty of "confusing" logical and ontological issues; on the contrary, he shows that they are intrinsically inseparable. This is because "being" is simply what we are aware of through thought and its categories, and an account of the basic categories of thought thus has to be an account of *being*. Pippin's claim that for Hegel there

---

49. For the idea of "picking out" an object of thought, see Pippin, *Hegel's Idealism*, p. 204.

50. Pippin, *Hegel's Idealism*, p. 188.

51. Pippin, *Hegel's Idealism*, pp. 207, 193, 187.

should still be difference between the determinacy things must be thought to have and the determinacy they must exhibit as existing things suggests that his Hegel is actually closer to Kant than to Hegel himself (or at least to the Hegel presented in this study).

Pippin may be motivated to retain the distinction between logical and existential determinacy by his worry that if things really did "oppose and negate each other" they would be caught up "in a spuriously infinite relation with all other things."[52] It is not clear to me, however, that Pippin has good reason to be worried here. On my reading, Hegel does indeed argue that negative relations to other things form part of what it is to be something. He concludes from this (a) that things are intrinsically vulnerable to being changed and reconstituted by other things and (b) that they necessarily differ from and are limited by those other things. These conclusions do not, however, strike me as obviously problematic. What would be problematic is the claim that *we* cannot identify a thing at all until we have distinguished it from everything else—for such a task would clearly be impossible for us to fulfil. But Hegel is not making *that* claim.[53] He is simply arguing that each thing itself differs from and is open to being affected by other things and that such difference and determinability are *intrinsic* features of things. From a Hegelian point of view, Pippin's resistance to the idea that negative relations to other things are co-constitutive of the very being of things means that he must deny that things are intrinsically vulnerable to external determination. It also suggests that, like Kant, Pippin would prefer to keep being free of negation and contradiction and to understand it as pure positivity. But does this not mean that, like Kant, Pippin perhaps exhibits an "excessive tenderness for the world" (*SL* 237/1: 276)?

Another reason why Pippin continues to keep logical and ontological claims apart might be that he wants to avoid turning Hegel into a subjective idealist. If he were to admit that logical determinations, such as negation, do actually constitute the ontological or existential conditions of things, then he would be forced by his own reading of Hegel's text to regard existing things as also conditioned by the *activities* of self-conscious reflection and conceiving. This, however, would turn Hegel into an unacceptable neo-Berkeleyan. To claim by contrast that the activities of reflection and conceiving are merely the transcendental conditions of any object's being determinate for us is much less objectionable since it is an "idealist" claim that is quite compatible with the idea that objects exist independently of their being conceived.

On my reading of the *Logic*, there is no such risk of turning Hegel into a subjective idealist. This is, first, because the *Logic* is understood to be an account of the basic categories, not the self-conscious operations, of thought (there is thus no danger that we might be misled into thinking of being itself as condi-

52. Pippin, *Hegel's Idealism*, pp. 197, 201.

53. See chapter 16, below, note 23 (p. 311).

tioned by self-consciousness) and, second, because the *Logic* shows being to have the same logical form or determinacy as the categories of thought but not actually to be constituted by *our* concepts and categories. Hegel's claim is far removed from that of Berkeley. It is the neo-Platonic or neo-Spinozan claim that being is what it is in its own right but is constituted by formal determinations, such as "negation" and self-relation," that are intelligible from within thought. What Pippin does not see is that Hegel is led to that neo-Spinozan position precisely by his radicalization of Kant's transcendental turn. In Hegel's eyes, being itself must be intelligible to thought because "being" is precisely what we *understand* there to be—the "space" that thought itself opens up to view and intuits.

Chapter Seven

Phenomenology and Logic

The Role of the Phenomenology

In the *Logic* Hegel tells us that nothing is needed to begin doing speculative philosophy except "the resolve (*Entschluß*), which can also be regarded as arbitrary, that we propose to consider thought as such" (*SL* 70/1: 68 [175]). Such a resolve requires that one "rid oneself of all other reflections and opinions whatever," and simply "take up *what is there before us*"—namely, the sheer being of thought, or thought *as* sheer being (*SL* 69/1: 68 [175]).[1] Hegel's Transcendental Deduction, as I described it in the previous chapter, involves nothing more than this act of ridding oneself of all assumptions; for that act leaves us with the thought that thought is minimally the thought of being and that being is initially nothing beyond what thought is immediately aware of. For Hegel, presuppositionless logic must be *ontological* logic because it can only begin with the utterly indeterminate thought of sheer immediacy or *being*. Indeed, he writes, "it lies in the *very nature of a beginning* that it must be being and nothing else" (*SL* 72/1: 72 [179]).

Anyone can embark on the study of ontological logic, therefore, provided he or she is willing to suspend all assumptions about thought and being, start from scratch, and let the indeterminate thought of being unfold. "To enter into philosophy . . . , calls for no other preparations, no further reflections or points of connection" (*SL* 72/1: 72 [179]). Moreover, anyone who is alert to the modern demand for radical self-criticism and self-determining freedom should be willing to suspend his or her assumptions in this way. In this sense, Hegel believes, the modern historical situation—after Kant, Fichte, and the French Revolution—*requires* of all philosophically educated people "the resolve . . . to consider thought as such." This resolve is "arbitrary," as I suggested in chapter 4, because it is a free decision that, although rational, one does not have to take. It is also arbitrary from another perspective, however: namely, from the perspective of ordinary, everyday, *non-philosophical* consciousness, which is not moved by the modern spirit of free self-criticism but firmly wedded to the certainties of everyday life. Ordinary consciousness is surrounded by objects and people of whose existence it is in no doubt, and it adheres to beliefs and engages

1. See also Hegel, *EL* 124/168 (§78).

in habitual practices whose validity and utility it sees no reason to challenge. It feels no imperative, therefore, to cast aside all its cherished assumptions and begin with sheer being but is more likely to regard the call to suspend one's presuppositions as dangerous or mad.

Hegel maintains that ordinary consciousness shares the conviction of the speculative philosopher and the pre-Kantian metaphysician (a belief repudiated by Kant) that we can know the true nature of things themselves.[2] He notes, however, that like the pre-Kantian metaphysician and Kant himself, and *unlike* the speculative philosopher, ordinary consciousness takes it for granted that all thought relates to *things* and never just to pure being as such. Specifically, it holds that we are always conscious of *these* particular objects of experience—these particular trees, animals, houses, and people. Consciousness, he tells us, is caught up in "externality" (*SL* 28/1: 17); its standpoint is that it "knows objects in their antithesis (*Gegensatz*) to itself, and itself in antithesis to them" (*PhS* 15/30).[3] It thus does not accept Hegel's claim that philosophy can divine the nature of things by simply unfolding the indeterminate thought of being but insists that one only discovers what things are like by going over and looking at them or listening to them and by reflecting on what one sees and hears. From the perspective of ordinary or "natural" consciousness, therefore, being asked to embark on the presuppositionless study of pure being is like being invited "to walk on [one's] head." Consciousness regards the demand made of it by speculative philosophy as a "violence (*Gewalt*) it is expected to do to itself, all unprepared and seemingly without necessity." Ordinary consciousness, Hegel writes, is characterized not by the commitment to radical self-criticism but by "the certainty of itself"; from its point of view, speculative philosophy simply looks "wrong" (*verkehrt*) (*PhS* 15/30).[4]

If ordinary consciousness is to be persuaded to take speculative logic seriously, it needs to be shown that such a logic is in fact an intelligent, not a perverse, enterprise. It needs to be given what Hegel calls a "ladder" to the standpoint of speculative logic. Indeed, Hegel notes, the individual has the right to demand such a ladder—a right rooted in the "absolute independence" of ordinary consciousness, its certainty of itself, that is, its unshakable confidence that its own view of the world is the norm and that any alternative views need to be justified in its terms (*PhS* 14–16/29–31).

The *Phenomenology of Spirit* is intended by Hegel to provide this justification by demonstrating that the standpoint of speculative logic or "absolute knowing" is actually made necessary by the certainties of ordinary consciousness itself:

---

2. See Hegel, *EL* 54, 65/79, 93 (§§22 Add., 26).
3. See also Hegel, *SL* 62–3/1: 60.
4. Miller translates *verkehrt* as "inverted."

> In the *Phenomenology of Spirit* I have exhibited consciousness in its movement onwards from the first immediate opposition of itself and the object (*Gegenstand*) to absolute knowing. The path of this movement goes through every form of the *relation of consciousness to the object* and has the concept (*Begriff*) of science for its result. (*SL* 48/1: 42; see also *PhS* 15/31)

Hegel insists, indeed, that only a phenomenological analysis of consciousness itself can justify the standpoint of absolute knowing to ordinary consciousness: logic "cannot be justified in any other way than by this emergence in consciousness, all the forms of which are resolved into this concept as into their truth" (*SL* 48/1: 42).[5]

As we have seen, the *Phenomenology* does not provide the only possible route into speculative philosophy. Those who are prepared to suspend their ordinary certainties can bypass the *Phenomenology* and proceed directly to the *Logic*. Hegel believes that many people can be persuaded to give up their "presuppositions and prejudices" by studying the history of modern philosophy.[6] I suggested at the close of chapter 3 that true religion can also prepare the way for presuppositionless philosophy by teaching us to "let go of our antithetical existence." Those who take to heart St. Paul's call to be "not conformed to this world" but "transformed by the renewing of your mind" (Rom. 12:2) may therefore be open to Hegel's call to set aside the certainties of everyday life in favor of an openness to being as such.

Those, however, who are not persuaded by philosophy or religion that the ordinary view of the world should be treated with skepticism but who nevertheless want to learn what speculative philosophy might reveal about the world must take the phenomenological path to absolute knowing: for only the *Phenomenology* can prove that the speculative standpoint is necessitated by ordinary consciousness itself.

Note that ordinary consciousness does not need to be persuaded that we can know the true nature of things or of being. For Hegel, as we have seen, consciousness already is, and knows itself to be, the awareness of what is. The *Phenomenology* does not, therefore, constitute an alternative, systematic Hegelian "Transcendental Deduction" since it does not set out to convince the skeptic that the categories of thought do after all apply to what there is. (Hegel's way of dealing with the skeptic, as we saw in the previous chapter, is to challenge the assumptions on which skepticism rests.) The aim of the *Phenomenology* is to

---

5. Two of the best studies of Hegel's *Phenomenology*, in my view, are J. Hyppolite, *Genesis and Structure of Hegel's Phenomenology of Spirit*, trans. S. Cherniak and J. Heckman (Evanston, Ill.: Northwestern University Press, 1974), and Q. Lauer, *A Reading of Hegel's Phenomenology of Spirit* (New York: Fordham University Press, 1976).

6. This, I take it, is the main purpose behind Hegel's review of the history of philosophy in §§26–78 of the *Encyclopedia Logic*; see *EL* 65–124/93–168.

teach ordinary consciousness—and philosophers wedded to the convictions of ordinary consciousness—that being is not simply something *objective* to which we stand in relation but exhibits one and the same logical form as thought itself and thus can be understood a priori from *within* thought.

The precise role of the *Phenomenology* is explained at various places by Hegel, and the account he gives of the relation between that text and the *Logic* is remarkably consistent.[7] The role of the *Phenomenology* is simply to free us from the "opposition of consciousness" between what is known and the knowing subject itself. In the introduction to the *Logic*, for example, Hegel writes the following:

> The concept of pure science and its deduction is therefore presupposed in the present work in so far as the *Phenomenology of Spirit* is nothing other than the deduction of it. Absolute knowing is the *truth* of every mode of consciousness because, as the course of the *Phenomenology* showed, it is only in absolute knowing that the separation of the *object* (*Gegenstand*) from the *certainty of oneself* (*Gewißheit seiner selbst*) is completely eliminated: truth is now equated with certainty and this certainty with truth.
>
> Thus pure science presupposes liberation from the opposition of consciousness. It contains *thought in so far as this is just as much the matter* (*Sache*) *in itself, or the matter in itself in so far as it is equally pure thought.* (SL 49/1: 43)[8]

The same point is made in the *Phenomenology* itself:

> Whereas in the phenomenology of Spirit each moment is the difference of knowledge and Truth, and is the movement in which that difference is cancelled, Science on the other hand does not contain this difference and the cancelling of it. On the contrary, since the moment has the form of the concept (*Begriff*), it unites the objective form of Truth and of the knowing self *in an immediate unity* (*in unmittelbarer Einheit*). (*PhS* 491/589, my emphasis)[9]

For consciousness, the object—though knowable—is clearly distinct from the knowing mind. What is more important for speculative philosophy is that being has the same logical structure as our own thought or certainty of it and in that sense is immediately identical to, or in "immediate unity" with, thought. As we have seen, philosophy will not deny altogether that being takes the form of things "over there." It will start, however, from the idea that being is simply the *immediacy* of which thought is minimally aware and then proceed to demon-

7. See Houlgate, "Absolute Knowing Revisited," p. 61.
8. Translation revised.
9. See also Hegel, *PhS* 21–2/39, and *SL* 28, 60, 62, 68/1: 17, 57, 60, 67 (173).

strate that such being turns out to be (among other things) a realm of *things*. Philosophy thus no longer regards things as simply "over there," but understands them to be concrete modes of being as such, whose logical structure can be determined from within thought simply by examining the category of being. In this sense, philosophy is freed not from all difference but from the *presupposed* "opposition" between thought and being that characterizes consciousness.

Phenomenological Method

Hegel's procedure in the *Phenomenology* is to show that consciousness's own experience of things eventually leads it to the standpoint of speculative thought. This procedure involves examining various "shapes" of consciousness and asking whether they experience and understand their objects quite as they claim they do. Hegel maintains that consciousness in fact never does so and that, as each shape of consciousness becomes aware of the way it actually experiences things rather than the way it claims to understand them, it comes to be a new shape of consciousness. In this way, he argues, consciousness's own experience leads it to recognize that what it is aware of is not just "over there" after all, but is informed by a categorial structure comprehensible from *within* consciousness—or thought—itself (*SL* 69/1: 67–8 [173–5]).

Consciousness's initial experience will not be "disproved" in this process. Hegel will not argue that consciousness is simply wrong to think of the world as made up of perceivable things or self-conscious agents or forms of social and historical organization. He will argue that the experience of consciousness shows the world not *merely* to be determined in these ways. When consciousness realizes this, it ceases to be mere *consciousness* of a world over against it and becomes the *thought* of the universal, categorial structure immanent in that world and in thought (*SL* 62–3/1: 60).

The method of Hegel's phenomenological analysis is elaborated in the introduction to the *Phenomenology*. This method entails initially accepting the distinction consciousness draws between its own awareness of the object and the object of which it is aware. Consciousness takes itself to be directly aware of what there is, but for precisely this reason, it takes the object of which it is aware to be real and independent of consciousness (*PhS* 52–3/76). Hegel maintains that this distinction requires consciousness to consider whether its awareness always matches the nature of the object itself. This question might seem to be redundant. After all, the "object" is simply that of which consciousness is aware, so how could there fail to be a correspondence between the object and our knowledge of it? The question is not redundant, however: for even though consciousness equates the object with what it knows, it also distinguishes its *knowledge* of that object from the *object* known and thereby opens up the possibility that it may not actually know *properly* the very object it knows. "The object," Hegel writes, "seems only to be for consciousness in the way that con-

sciousness knows it." But "the distinction between the in-itself and knowledge is already present in the very fact that consciousness knows an object at all" (*PhS* 54/78). Since consciousness distinguishes in this way between its own knowledge of the object and the object itself, it cannot but ask itself whether these two elements always correspond to one another. Although there is no principle of radical self-criticism in ordinary consciousness, therefore, there is a need to assure ourselves that we do actually understand our object properly. The very structure of our ordinary certainty itself—the fact that we are certain of what is distinct from us—requires that we examine that certainty in order to *make certain* we are getting things right.

In seeking this assurance, consciousness cannot step outside its own perspective and compare its understanding of the object with the object viewed, as it were, "from nowhere." Consciousness has to consider whether its understanding corresponds to the object as this latter is *for consciousness* itself. The standard, or "measure" (*Maßstab*), that consciousness must use to assess the adequacy of its knowledge is thus "what consciousness affirms from within itself as *being-in-itself* or the *True*" (*PhS* 53/77). Consciousness is required by the distinction it draws between its own knowledge and the object itself to consider whether it properly understands that which it itself regards as its object.

Hegel believes that this is a question consciousness is perfectly capable of answering:

> Consciousness is, on the one hand, consciousness of the object, and, on the other, consciousness of itself; consciousness of what for it is the True, and consciousness of its knowledge of the truth. Since both are *for* the same consciousness, this consciousness is itself their comparison; it is for this same consciousness to know whether its knowledge of the object corresponds to the object or not. (*PhS* 54/77–8)

Furthermore, Hegel believes that consciousness invariably discovers that it does *not* actually understand its own object adequately. Consciousness's object is nothing but that of which it is conscious, but the way consciousness actually understands that object does not always overlap with what it initially takes or declares its object to be.

To the extent that consciousness's actual understanding or knowledge of its object diverges from what it initially takes its object to be, "it would seem that consciousness must alter its knowledge to make it conform to the object"; that is, to make it consistent with its initial, stated conception of its object (*PhS* 54/78). However, the understanding consciousness has reached arises, in Hegel's account, not through any arbitrary fancy but through consciousness's attention to what its own object shows itself to be. That understanding cannot, therefore, simply be rejected or revised because it constitutes *new knowledge of the object itself:* it discloses what the object of consciousness is in truth. What has to be revised, therefore, is the initial conception of the object since consciousness

now recognizes, in light of what it has learned, that that conception was not completely adequate and only presented the object as it initially appears to consciousness: "it comes to pass for consciousness that what it previously took to be the *in-itself* is not an *in-itself*, or that it was only an in-itself *for consciousness*" (*PhS* 54/78). Accordingly, consciousness now declares itself certain that the object has a new character—disclosed by its experience—and it thereby comes to be a new shape of consciousness.

Each subsequent shape of consciousness undertakes a similar examination of its knowledge claims by measuring them against its own distinctive conception of its object and eventually comes to revise that conception. Throughout the *Phenomenology*, therefore, consciousness continues to try to make certain that it is understanding its object properly, but it does so by measuring its understanding against a standard that constantly changes (*PhS* 54/78).

Hegel's analysis continues until consciousness discovers that its understanding of its object does not actually correspond to the stated definition of an object of *consciousness* at all. An object of consciousness is stated to be something known by, but standing over against, consciousness. Consciousness eventually discovers, however, that it actually understands its object to have one and the same categorial structure as itself and so not simply to stand over against consciousness after all. At that point, consciousness realizes that it is no longer mere consciousness but has become speculative *thought,* or absolute knowing.

The dialectical movement through which a new understanding of its object—and so a new object—constantly arises for consciousness is understood by Hegel to constitute the *experience* (*Erfahrung*) of consciousness (*PhS* 55/78). This experience is not an historical experience that every individual necessarily makes in his or her own life but the experience that is *logically* entailed by the structure of ordinary consciousness itself. It is the experience through which ordinary consciousness is taken by its own internal logic from its most primitive shape of sense-certainty through perception, understanding, self-consciousness, reason, spirit, and religion to philosophy or absolute knowing, albeit an experience that concrete historical individuals all too often fail to comprehend.

From Sense-Certainty to Absolute Knowing

Hegel's specific analyses in the *Phenomenology* clearly exemplify the process of self-discovery described in the introduction. Each shape of consciousness initially takes its object in a certain way but comes through experience to a fuller understanding of that object. In this process, Hegel says, "we learn by experience that we [actually] mean something other than we meant to mean" (*PhS* 39/60).[10]

To begin with, sense-certainty takes itself to be conscious of the pure particularity of things without the mediation of concepts or language. It under-

10. Translation revised.

stands what it has before it simply as *this*, *here*, *now*. Its own experience shows, however, that its object is actually much more complex than it initially believes. Consciousness is not just aware of a pure and simple *this* after all but of a complex unity and continuity of different moments—"a Now which is an absolute plurality of Nows" and a *here* that is a "simple complex of many heres, . . . a Before and Behind, an Above and Below, a Right and Left" (*PhS* 64/89–90). When consciousness accepts this new conception of its object, it ceases being mere sense-certainty and becomes a new shape of consciousness: perception.

Perception discovers in turn that its object is not merely a unified thing with multiple moments or "properties" but the concrete expression of invisible inner force. At this point, perception becomes understanding (*Verstand*). Understanding discovers that the inner character of things is not just force but force governed by law—the same lawfulness that governs understanding itself. Understanding thus finds a dimension of itself in the things it encounters and so becomes *self*-consciousness. Self-consciousness then discovers that the objects to which it relates are not just law-governed objects in nature but other living, self-conscious beings—self-conscious beings who confirm our own consciousness of ourselves by recognizing us but whose recognition of us we in turn have to recognize (*PhS* 111/145).

In this way, self-consciousness acquires a sense that an individual's identity does not belong to that individual alone but is constituted by his or her social interaction with others. Self-consciousness comes to regard itself as part of a "unity of . . . different independent self-consciousnesses which, in their opposition, enjoy perfect freedom and independence." That is to say, it begins to think of itself as an "*I* that is *We* and *We* that is *I*" (*PhS* 110/145).[11] This social (and historical) unity of different self-consciousnesses is named by Hegel *spirit* (*Geist*) and is understood to constitute the "absolute substance" of those individuals who belong to it.

The relation between the "master" and the "slave" is a social-spiritual one in that each is tied inextricably to the other: the slave takes his direction from the master, and the master needs the slave to prepare natural objects for his consumption. But the master and slave do not yet acknowledge any common identity or purpose. Their relation is thus not yet a fully spiritual one but one in which each focuses primarily on himself and his superiority over or subordination to the other. Only when there emerges an explicit, shared recognition of a common identity between people embodied in the laws and institutions of the society they form does self-consciousness become spirit proper. The simplest and most basic shape of such spirit, Hegel maintains, is that found in the Greek world depicted in Sophocles' *Antigone*.

At this point the phenomenology of consciousness becomes the phenomenology of *spirit*. Consciousness does not suddenly disappear from Hegel's book,

11. Emphasis in German text but not in Miller's translation.

however, but remains an important moment of spirit itself. This is evident from the fact that the spirit Hegel examines remains *conscious* of itself as spirit. That is to say, it continues to regard its own social, historical, and spiritual character at least to some extent as something "over there"—for example, as constituting the *world* into which individuals are born.

Spiritual consciousness does not, however, just understand itself to be social and historical. It also comes to understand itself as ontologically grounded, as the self-consciousness that being itself—"substance" or the "Absolute"—comes to exhibit. The shape of consciousness or spirit that understands both being and itself in this way is religion. In religion—in particular in Christianity—consciousness is not just aware of natural objects or its own social-spiritual character; it understands being as such to become self-conscious—or "substance" to become "subject"—in and as *human* self-consciousness (*PhS* 459/552; see also *PhS* 10/23). Christianity gives expression to this idea by picturing being or substance as "God" and understanding God to become "incarnate" in Jesus Christ and, after Christ's death and resurrection, to become Holy Spirit within—indeed *as*—the community of Christian believers. This process of becoming incarnate and then becoming spirit is regarded by Christianity not as contingent but as unfolding the very nature of God. As Hegel puts it, "in this religion the divine Being (*das göttliche Wesen*) is *revealed*. Its being revealed obviously consists in this, that what it is, is known. But it is known precisely in its being known as Spirit (*Geist*), as a Being that is essentially *self-consciousness*" (*PhS* 459/552).[12]

In Christianity, consciousness thus finds itself included in absolute, "divine" being as the medium through which being itself becomes self-conscious. Religious consciousness also finds itself in being in another way, however. For it understands "divine" being or God to be (as well as love) infinite, eternal "essence" or *reason* (*Begriff*) (*PhS* 459, 464–5/552, 558–9). For religion, therefore, absolute, "divine" being not only becomes self-conscious in and through human beings; it has the same logical structure as human thought, albeit in an infinite rather than finite form. This is the structure of dialectical reason or *negativity*, of coming to be truly what one is through negating or "dying to" what one is initially. As Hegel puts it, "the object has the form of *Self* (*Selbst*) in its relation to consciousness." This means that "consciousness knows itself immediately in the object, or is manifest to itself in the object," insofar as "the divine nature is the *same* (*dasselbe*) as the human, and it is this unity that is beheld" (*PhS* 459–60/552–3).

Yet consciousness still conceives of "divine" being itself—infinite reason, *logos*, or God—as the "*object* (*Gegenstand*) of consciousness," as that which initially at least is quite distinct from human consciousness itself (*PhS* 459/552, my emphasis). Yes, God realizes himself (or, rather, itself) in humanity and has

12. Translation revised.

the same logical structure as human thought, but the process of divine self-realization is understood to be the work of God, not of man. It is conceived of as "the deed of an *alien* (*fremd*) satisfaction." In other words, the power through which divine being develops into human being is understood to reside in divine being alone; the conscious, human self "does not find it in its *own* action as such" (*PhS* 477–8/573).

Religious consciousness changes into absolute knowing, however, when it recognizes that this power is not actually alien to us at all but is the power of dialectical reason, or the "concept" (*Begriff*), that is operative in both being as such *and* human consciousness itself. At this point, consciousness ceases to be *consciousness* as such and becomes speculative thought: for its "object" is no longer simply being "over there" but *universal* reason immanent in being and in thought itself (*PhS* 490–1/588–9).

Religion and Speculative Philosophy

Hegel insists that speculative philosophy and revealed—that is, Christian—religion have the same content. They both disclose the same truth about being: namely, that it is the process of becoming self-conscious spirit in and as humanity. Philosophy understands this process to be the work of universal dialectical reason—of being *as* dialectical reason. It knows the truth to be "*Thought* (*Denken*) or pure Essence, and knows this Thought as simple Being (*Sein*) and Existence (*Dasein*), and Existence as the negativity of itself, hence as Self (*Selbst*)." Hegel adds that "it is precisely this that the revealed religion knows" (*PhS* 461/554).

Religion, however, conceives—or, rather, pictures (*vorstellt*)—being, absolute reason, or negativity as divine reason, or *God*, who is essentially *other* than we are but who becomes spirit in and through us. In Hegel's view, therefore, religion is still burdened by the "opposition of consciousness": "the Spirit of the revealed religion has not yet surmounted its consciousness as such." It is *conscious* of "absolute-reason-that-becomes-spirit" as its *object*. "Spirit itself as a whole, and the self-differentiated moments within it, fall," we are told, "within the sphere of picture-thinking (*Vorstellen*) and in the form of objectivity (*Gegenständlichkeit*)" (*PhS* 479/575). Religion gives expression before philosophy to the truth that being is the process of becoming self-conscious spirit, but Hegel argues "only [philosophical] Science is its true knowledge of itself" (*PhS* 488/586).

In contrast to religion, speculative philosophy does not regard absolute reason as simply the *object* of consciousness but understands such reason to be the inherent nature of being *and* of human thought itself. Being develops rationally and dialectically, and human thought (when it thinks properly) follows the same dialectic. Furthermore, it is only through its own rational activity that thought can determine the precise structure of the rational activity of being itself. That is to say, thought can only establish what it is to be by working out—in specula-

tive logic—what it is to think properly. As soon becomes clear in the *Logic*, thought does not control the path of its rational, dialectical development; nor does it receive dialectical insight as a gift from another "on high." It discovers its own dialectical structure—and thereby also the dialectical structure of being—by rendering explicit what is immanent in, and so necessitated by, its *own* activity of thinking. Being is thus known through our own rational activity to be essentially the same rational activity as we are.[13]

This is the point behind Hegel's assertion toward the end of the *Phenomenology* that "what in religion was *content* or a form for presenting (*Vorstellen*) an *other*, is here the *Self's* own *act*" (*PhS* 485/582). It is easy to misread Hegel here as simply replacing the religious idea of God with the idea of our own activity—as if we, not God, were the real creators of the world. Hegel is not, however, a subjective idealist of that kind, and he does not deny that human thought is itself the product of being or "substance." Rational knowledge is certainly "the self's own act," but Hegel immediately notes that rational knowledge is also knowledge of "*substance*," indeed of substance as itself the "knowledge of its act." Hegel is not, therefore, obliterating all difference between substance or being, on the one hand, and the knowing self, on the other, or reducing the former to something created by the latter. His point is that rational thought through its *own* activity knows itself to be identical in form to substance or being—and so, as he puts it, knows "subject as substance"—and also understands substance or being itself to issue in the very knowing that we ourselves are. Once again, Hegel brilliantly combines quasi-Kantian and quasi-Spinozan insights into one: we know the structure of being through our *own* conceptual activity, and through that activity we know *being itself* to become conscious of itself in us.

The fact that being is known through our own reason to be universal, dialectical reason that achieves self-consciousness in us—and so is known to be *one and the same* reason as we are—distinguishes speculative philosophy from religion for Hegel. In religion, the object—"God"—is only implicitly (*an sich*) identical with human being. That is to say, "God" exhibits the same dialectical structure as we do and becomes incarnate in a human being, but he is originally *other* than us. In religion, therefore, we take ourselves to relate to and to be graced by something distinct from ourselves: "Truth . . . in religion is still not identical with its certainty" (*PhS* 485/583). In philosophy, by contrast, we see in being itself nothing but the very same rationality that immanently structures our own thinking, and the idea that being is essentially something *other* than us falls away (though, of course, being remains irreducible to us in the sense that it pre-

---

13. To say that being is rational activity is not, of course, to deny the place of contingency in being (in both nature and history). For Hegel, it is rational that there be contingency, and the rational development of being to self-consciousness is mediated by such contingency; see chapter 6, above, p. 118.

cedes us and will continue when human beings are no more). By thus dissolving the residual otherness of being that is still retained in religion, philosophy understands fully the truth that religion merely pictures and feels.

The transition from religion to speculative philosophy involves nothing more than overcoming the idea that absolute reason is the "divine" *object* of consciousness and releasing the thought that such reason is actually *universal* and immanent in both being and thought itself (see *PhS* 416/502–3). This overcoming is made necessary by the whole development of the *Phenomenology* insofar as the whole analysis—from sense-certainty onwards—serves to undermine the conviction of consciousness that it fully understands its object. The transition to philosophy is, however, also motivated by revealed religion in particular. This is because Christianity itself undermines the very difference between God and humanity from which it proceeds. This occurs above all in the doctrine that God becomes Holy Spirit as the community of religious believers. For in knowing God as spirit, such believers actually know themselves to be spirit, too. True, they are conscious of themselves as what *God* has become, but they are conscious that *they* are the concrete self-consciousness, or spirit, of God. In Hegel's view, this is not just a philosophical reinterpretation of Christian belief but essential Christian doctrine itself. For Hegel, the Christian religion itself overcomes the idea that God is simply other than humanity and leads us to recognize that our consciousness of God as spirit is at the same time our own consciousness of *ourselves*. Spirit is not merely the "content" or "object" of our consciousness, therefore, but what we know ourselves to be. "The concept of spirit," Hegel writes, "is *intuited* by the religious consciousness to which the absolute Being is revealed, and this consciousness dissolves (*aufhebt*) the *difference* between *itself* and *that which it intuits*" (*PhS* 477/572).[14]

But if Christianity already overcomes the standpoint of consciousness, why move on to philosophy? Because Christianity as a form of religious consciousness still thinks of the absolute power as "God," who *comes to* unite himself with humanity but is nevertheless originally other than humanity itself. It does not recognize explicitly that what it pictures as "God" is in fact *universal* reason, which exists both as being (or the "world") *and* as self-conscious humanity. Religion thus retains a lingering sense that God is separate from us even in reconciling himself with us. Consequently, the satisfaction felt by religious consciousness in knowing itself to be one with God "remains burdened with the antithesis of a beyond," and humanity's final reconciliation with God is projected into an indefinitely deferred future (*PhS* 478/574). Philosophy, by contrast, is the understanding that we are completely "reconciled with God" *now*, since God is not in truth something other than us after all but universal reason that immanently structures both being *and* our own thought. Philosophy understands, there-

14. Translation revised.

fore, that "reason . . . is the absolute power," or to cite one of Hegel's most famous lines, that "what is rational is actual, and what is actual is rational."[15]

Hegel's claim is not, of course, that human beings abide by the dictates of reason in everything they do. We have to learn what reason is, what it does, and what it requires of us, and we can always fail to learn this or to pay heed to what we have learned; crime, poverty, and war are thus always possibilities even in modern, rational societies. The point, however, is that in committing crimes or acting irrationally, we are failing to abide by the demands of reason that is as much our *own* as it is immanent in being itself. Furthermore, our failure to act in accordance with (our own) reason has *rational* consequences that we cannot disavow. In this sense, reason is always "actual," whatever we do. Or, as religious consciousness would put it, God is at work in everything we undertake.

I suggested earlier in this chapter that the task of the *Phenomenology* is to show those who are not persuaded by the history of philosophy or by religion to suspend the certainties of ordinary life and to take up speculative philosophy that such philosophy is actually the logical outcome of the very certainties they hold dear. What becomes clear in the process of Hegel's phenomenological analysis is that the religious—specifically, Christian—understanding of the world is itself made necessary by our ordinary certainties and that consciousness is required to become philosophical (in Hegel's sense) by the implications of Christian belief. From Hegel's point of view, therefore, ordinary consciousness errs as much in resisting religion as it does in resisting speculative philosophy (and, indeed, as it does in resisting the idea that consciousness is fundamentally social, historical, moral, and aesthetic). As we know, religion is not the only route into speculative philosophy—all one needs is the *resolve* to consider thought as such without presuppositions—but it does provide one way into philosophy: for it teaches us that truth comes to those who are prepared to give up, or "die to," their dearest convictions, or in the words of Luke's Gospel, that "whosoever shall lose his life shall preserve it" (Luke 17: 33). The *Phenomenology* shows that consciousness is pointed in the direction of speculative philosophy by religious belief that is itself made necessary by the instability of our own secular certainties.

I should point out, by the way, that Hegel's phenomenological account of religion should not be confused with his later philosophy of religion. Hegel's phenomenology of religion considers religion insofar as it is a relation of *consciousness* to an *object* (God), albeit one that undermines the perspective of consciousness itself through the idea that God and humanity come to form one self-knowing spirit. Hegel's philosophy of religion, on the other hand, considers religion insofar as it is a way of knowing the *truth*, albeit through consciousness, "picture-thinking," and feeling. It will show that religion complements philosophy by picturing as "love," and believing in, the very power of universal

15. Hegel, *VGP* 3: 372, my translation, and *PR* 20/24. See also *EL* 29/47 (§6).

reason and negativity that we fully understand only in philosophy. The philosophy of religion thus emphasizes more than the phenomenology of religion the enduring positive significance of religion for our spiritual lives.[16] The phenomenology of religion, by contrast, stresses that we need to let go of the religious viewpoint if we are to become speculative philosophers. It shows that religion points beyond itself to philosophy by conceiving of God and humanity as "reconciled." It also shows that religion itself helps us to let go of the very form of religious consciousness—though only for the purposes of doing philosophy, not in our everyday lives (in which religion remains central, for Hegel)—by conceiving of the willingness to *let go* as the spirit of true forgiveness.

As I remarked in chapter 3, religious consciousness emerges in the *Phenomenology* at the point where the "self-certain Spirit which forgives evil . . . lets go of (*abläßt von*) its own simple unitary nature and rigid unchangeableness" (*PhS* 477/572).[17] In Hegel's view, this readiness to let go—for example, of the opposition between God and humanity—suffuses fully developed religious consciousness as a whole and eventually leads logically to the move to philosophy or absolute knowing.

Letting Go

Absolute knowing is not religious consciousness, but it, too, requires the readiness to let go because consciousness can become philosophical, onto-logical thought only if the "I" refrains from "cling[ing] (*festhalten*) to itself in the *form* of *self-consciousness* as against the form of substantiality and objectivity" (*PhS* 490/588). Absolute knowing, one should recall, does not bridge the gap between consciousness and things by showing how we can gain access to them; it suspends or gives up the idea that consciousness and being are fundamentally separate in the first place. Absolute knowing does not, however, "suspend" the opposition of subject and object by simply "cast[ing] the differences back into the abyss of the Absolute" in the manner of Schelling. Hegel's mature approach to all oppositions—in the *Phenomenology* and beyond—is not to assert that they presuppose a unified Absolute in which they are dissolved but to let such oppositions dissolve themselves. Absolute knowing, he says, consists in "this seeming inactivity which merely contemplates how what is differentiated spontaneously moves in its own self (*sich an ihm selbst bewegt*) and returns into its unity" (*PhS* 490/588).

This readiness to let go of oppositions by letting them undermine themselves is required if we are to follow the detailed arguments of both the *Logic* and the *Phenomenology*, which are both the work of absolute knowing.[18] The *Logic* proceeds not by overcoming or "sublating" oppositions in a presupposed "higher

16. See Houlgate, *An Introduction to Hegel,* pp. 242–75.
17. Translation revised. See also Hegel, *PhS* 409, 484/494, 581.
18. See Houlgate, "Absolute Knowing Revisited," p. 64.

unity" but by allowing concepts to demonstrate their own "finitude and the untruth of their supposed independent self-subsistence (*die Unwahrheit ihres Für-sich-sein-Sollens*)" (*SL* 39/1: 30).[19] Concepts become fluid, therefore,

> when the pure certainty of self . . . giv[es] up the *fixity* (*das Fixe*) of its self-positing, by giving up not only the fixity of the pure concrete, which the "I" itself is, in contrast with its differentiated content, but also the fixity of the differentiated moments . . . posited in the element of pure thinking [i.e., of the categories]. (*PhS* 20/37)

We will see in part 3 precisely what it means for concepts to become "fluid." It is important to recognize, however, that progress is made in the *Logic* by watching the assumed independence of concepts, such as "being" and "nothing," undermine itself and *not* by assuming in advance that such concepts are mere moments of some overarching, synthetic whole.

Progress is made in the *Phenomenology* in the same way. One shape of consciousness develops logically into another by depriving *itself* of the very certainty of which it is initially so assured and so doing "violence" to itself (*PhS* 51/74). Consciousness progresses, therefore, by *losing* its certainty of itself—letting go of its initial conception of itself and its object—and coming to understand itself in a new way. Progress is certainly made; it would be absurd to deny that Hegel's thought is progressive. But consciousness moves forward purely because it loses the apparently firm ground on which it believes it stands, not because it is pulled forward teleologically by the lure of absolute knowing or driven forward by some presupposed power of dialectic. For natural consciousness, Hegel writes, the path of the *Phenomenology* "has negative significance . . . , and what is in fact the realization of the concept [the emergence of absolute knowing], counts for it rather as the loss of its own self; for it does lose its truth on this path" (*PhS* 49/72).

The *Phenomenology* is thus above all a skeptical, deconstructive work that brings about a "despair about all the so-called natural ideas, thoughts, and opinions" (*PhS* 50/73). In this sense, it resembles Descartes's First Meditation, which also serves to lead the reader to a philosophical understanding of truth through first loosening the hold that ordinary preconceptions have on us. Unlike the skepticism of the First Meditation, however, which is driven by the strategic energy of the philosopher, the skepticism at work in the *Phenomenology* is deployed by the very shapes of consciousness that are the subject of phenomenological study. Moreover, such skepticism is deployed by consciousness against itself *unintentionally* as each shape endeavors to assure itself that it does actually understand its object as it thinks it does. Each shape of consciousness is thus forced to let go of its certainty by its own act of trying to confirm it.

19. See also Hegel, *EL* 82/114 (§41 Add. 1): "they must determine their own limits and point out their own defects."

Consciousness is not trying to become anything other than it is or to reach some predetermined goal, such as absolute knowing. It is trying to stand still and to *be* what it takes itself to be: to be immediately certain of *this* or to be in control of the slave, and so on. In so doing, however, consciousness undermines itself and forces itself to become something new. This is the "cunning" whereby the reason immanent in consciousness itself—consciousness's own inherent logic—turns consciousness into something other than it takes itself to be. For Hegel, indeed, phenomenological knowing is itself a form of cunning because it simply *lets* each shape of consciousness undermine itself through its own efforts, just as the speculative logician will let each category turn itself into a new one through its own intrinsic logic. In Hegel's own words, phenomenological and philosophical knowing are

> the cunning (*List*) which, while seeming to abstain from activity, looks on and watches how determinateness, with its concrete life, just where it fancies it is pursuing its own self-preservation and particular interest, is in fact doing the very opposite, is an activity that results in its own dissolution, and makes itself a moment of the whole. (*PhS* 33/53–4)

The *Phenomenology* sets out a systematic, immanent skepticism that is clearly different from the "external" skepticism of the radically self-critical philosopher who urges ordinary consciousness, from a position not shared by consciousness itself, to suspend its assumptions. Such external skepticism may, of course, succeed in moving ordinary consciousness on toward speculative philosophy. Through the *Phenomenology*, however, it becomes clear that the certainties of ordinary consciousness necessarily undermine themselves and that absolute knowing is in fact the logical outcome of all that such consciousness holds dear.

For Whom Is the Phenomenology *Written?*

The *Phenomenology* shows how shapes of consciousness logically entail, or "develop into," one another. It is possible, however, for ordinary consciousness to refuse to accept the lessons of the *Phenomenology*, just as it is able to resist the imperative of radical self-criticism. From Hegel's perspective, individuals and societies who do so will still be subject to the tensions he discerns within their own certainties, but they are nonetheless free to hold on to those certainties and to resist new ones. No one can be forced to become a religious believer or a pure philosopher, not even by the logic of his or her own position.

It is perfectly possible, therefore, for people to insist that the ordinary distinction between subject and object is irreducible, however convincing the phenomenologist's arguments may seem; if they do so, they effectively "bar the entrance to philosophy" as a presuppositionless discipline (*SL* 45/1: 38). This is unfortunate, but if people insist on their ordinary certainties, there is ultimately

nothing to be done except to leave them to their own devices. In Hegel's view, people who refuse to consider the arguments of others and declare themselves "finished and done with anyone who does not agree" ultimately "trample underfoot the roots of humanity" (*PhS* 43/64–5). Like the "barren ego" that "gloats over its own understanding," they exhibit a "satisfaction which we must leave to itself, for it flees from the universal, and seeks only to be for itself" (*PhS* 52/75). The *Phenomenology* is clearly not written for them.

For whom is it written then? Do the potential readers of Hegel's text already have to be predisposed to agree with him? No, but they must at least be open to the suggestion that the certainties of everyday life might prove to be problematic and lead consciousness in a direction in which it does not expect to go. As I understand it, the readers of the *Phenomenology* are intended to be ordinary people (and philosophers tied to ordinary beliefs) who are unmoved by the modern spirit of philosophical self-criticism and so need to be persuaded that Hegel's presuppositionless, ontological logic is a justified and relevant science. Such people will be firmly immersed in the world of everyday experience. But they cannot be completely bull-headed; they must have some interest in what Hegelian speculative philosophy might disclose about the world and be open to what it may show them about their own everyday beliefs. The *Phenomenology* is thus directed at readers who although steeped in the certainties of everyday life share in the openness of mind that characterizes true philosophy itself. Such openness of mind may come from a basic ethical decency and intelligence, or indeed, it may stem from religion. In the case of such readers, one must assume, religion does not cause them actually to suspend their ordinary certainties and begin philosophizing without presuppositions, but it does encourage them at least to consider the idea that their ordinary certainties might undermine themselves.

The consciousness of the *Phenomenology*'s intended readers anticipates the perspective of absolute knowing, but it is not absolute knowing in the fullest sense. It shares the readiness of absolute knowing to let the matter at hand develop but does not yet have the confidence that thought can know the true nature of being purely from within itself. The philosophical thought that undertakes the *phenomenological* study of consciousness is not absolute knowing in the fullest sense either. However, it is absolute knowing that has *suspended* its claim to know the form of being from within thought rather than open-minded ordinary consciousness that is *yet* to be convinced that it can make that claim. Philosophy must set aside its own ontological convictions in this way because it cannot simply take its own standpoint for granted in its education of consciousness. The *Phenomenology* does not, therefore, set out a *philosophy* of consciousness: it is not the study by pure thought of what consciousness ultimately *is*. It is simply a study of the way consciousness experiences itself and the world, a study of consciousness's own multiple certainties—a logical account of what is *apparent* to consciousness about itself and its world, rather than a presentation of the full truth of being or consciousness itself. This, indeed, is why

Hegel names his study *phenomenology*—the logic of appearance—rather than philosophy. The *Phenomenology* demonstrates, however, that the certainties of consciousness themselves lead to absolute knowing—the mode of thought that is responsible for both philosophical ontology *and* phenomenology itself.[20]

From the Phenomenology *to the* Logic

The *Phenomenology* leads to the standpoint of the *Logic*. Yet absolute knowing at the end of the *Phenomenology* does not collapse directly into the thought of pure being with which the *Logic* begins. The *Phenomenology* ends with the recognition that being is essentially universal, dialectical reason, or *Begriff*—the *same* reason as that which informs our own thinking (*PhS* 491/589). This changes our relation to being because being is no longer regarded as the *object* of consciousness, as something fundamentally distinct from our knowledge or thought of it. On the contrary, we now understand that we can determine the true nature of being merely by determining the true character of thought itself—that is, by becoming properly *self*-conscious. Absolute knowing is thus

> the certainty which, on the one hand, no longer has the object over against it but has internalized it, knows it as its own self—and, on the other hand, has given up the knowledge of itself as of something confronting the object of which it is only the annihilation, has divested itself of this subjectivity and is at one with its self-alienation. (*SL* 69/1: 68 [175])[21]

The opposition between consciousness and its object dissolves because both are discovered to have the same *determinate* character: both are negativity, dialectical reason, *Begriff*. With the collapse of that opposition, however, comes a new task: that of determining in detail the true nature of being now that being is no longer to be regarded merely as the object of consciousness but as structurally identical to thought and as comprehensible from within thought itself. As Hegel puts it in the *Phenomenology*, "Spirit, . . . having won the concept (*Begriff*), unfolds existence and movement (*entfaltet . . . das Dasein und Bewegung*) in this ether of its life and is *Science*" (*PhS* 491/589).[22]

Now if this new understanding of being is not to be governed by the various

20. Unlike Kantian appearance, Hegelian "appearance" is not experience that is conditioned by irreducibly *subjective* forms of intuition and so cut off from being as it might be in itself. Hegelian "appearance" is experience that is directly conscious of *being as such* but that does not fully comprehend the being of which it is aware. Ordinary consciousness, for Hegel, can be brought to a true, untrammeled understanding of being itself, but this is not possible for Kant.

21. See D. S. Stern, "The Immanence of Thought: Hegel's Critique of Foundationalism," *The Owl of Minerva* 22, 1 (Fall 1990): 33.

22. Translation revised.

conceptions of it previously formed by consciousness, these must obviously be set to one side. We must retain an ethical, religious, or simply intelligent willingness to let thought unfold immanently, but we must actively *forget* that being comprises perceivable natural objects and social and historical life.[23] We must also leave behind the conception of being entertained by religion and taken over by absolute knowing at the close of the *Phenomenology*: namely, that being is the dialectical process of becoming self-conscious in us. This means that we must hold to the simple idea that being is determinable by thought while suspending any determinate conceptions consciousness has of either (see *SL* 69/1: 68 [175]).

The *Phenomenology* thus does not end directly where the *Logic* begins—with the pure thought of being as such. It ends with a determinate conception of being as universal reason (*Begriff*) that marks the disappearance of the opposition between consciousness and its object. This collapse of the standpoint of consciousness then confronts thought with the task of determining a priori the nature of being *without* bringing into consideration any of the conceptions that consciousness forms of being or thought. The immanent skepticism of the *Phenomenology* leaves us, therefore, with the same task as the skepticism of radically self-critical thought. If we come to this task from the *Phenomenology*, however, we can carry it out only by first suspending the determinate conception of being with which the *Phenomenology* itself ends and which initially generated the task.

The project of the *Logic* is not to analyze what is involved in the determinate idea of being as "reason" (or "spirit"), even though absolute knowing in the *Phenomenology* culminates in this idea. Whichever route we take to it, the project of the *Logic* is simply to unfold what is implicit in pure or absolute knowing as such; that is, in the simple *unity* of thought and being—a unity that is initially no more than the indeterminate thought of sheer, immediate being.[24]

---

23. See M. Theunissen, *Sein und Schein. Die kritische Funktion der Hegelschen Logik* (Frankfurt am Main: Suhrkamp Verlag, 1980), p. 113.

24. See Hegel, *SL* 69/1: 68 (175). In denying that, at the end of the *Phenomenology*, absolute knowing collapses directly into the thought of pure being with which the *Logic* begins, I take issue with William Maker's reading of Hegel. I fully endorse Maker's view that "the *Phenomenology* does not serve to deduce the concept of science by in any way predetermining or grounding the method, manner or nature of scientific cognition" and that the *Logic* itself "begins neither in nor with . . . any *structure* of knowing at all." In contrast to Maker, however, I believe that between the end of the *Phenomenology* and the beginning of the *Logic* there must occur an act of abstraction in which we specifically set aside the determinate conception of being and spirit reached at the close of the *Phenomenology*. See Maker, *Philosophy without Foundations*, pp. 72–3.

Chapter Eight

Preparing to Read Hegel's *Logic*

In the preceding chapters I have explained what I take to be Hegel's project in the *Logic* and contrasted my interpretation of that project with certain other important interpretations. Hegel's *Logic*, as I understand it, is a post-Kantian ontology. It does not give us a description of some assumed object, such as Spirit or the Absolute, but starts from the indeterminate immediacy of being and unfolds all that is logically entailed by such being—all that it *is* to be. After Kant, however, we can only discover what it is to be by understanding what it *means* to be—that is, by unpacking all that is implicit in the thought or category of being; there is no alternative route to knowledge of the fundamental nature of being, such as mystical intuition, divine revelation, or empirical observation. Post-Kantian ontology must, therefore, take the form of *logic*. Hegel's *Logic* thus continues the work of Kant's Metaphysical Deduction in the *Critique of Pure Reason* in seeking to determine the basic categories of thought and, *in so doing*, continues the work of Spinoza's *Ethics* in seeking to determine what there is and must be.

I mention Spinoza in particular here, as he is the metaphysician who, in my view, anticipates Hegel most closely (and who least resembles the typical "pre-Kantian metaphysician" identified by Hegel himself). This is because "substance" is understood by Spinoza not as *a* being or *an* entity but as being itself, and his method is simply to determine all that follows necessarily from the nature of substance. What separates Hegel from Spinoza is his view that "substance" is too determinate a concept from which to start philosophy and that Spinoza takes too much for granted about its structure—namely, that it excludes negation and has "attributes" and "modes." Hegel, I have argued, differs from both Spinoza and Kant by beginning from no determinate conception of being or thought whatsoever. He does not assume from the outset that being is self-grounding substance or that thought is essentially judgment but begins from the idea of both being and thought as sheer indeterminate being. In this sense, Hegel's *Logic* is presuppositionless.

This does not mean that the *Logic* lacks historical or hermeneutic presuppositions. On the contrary, presuppositionless logic is made necessary by the modern demand for radical self-criticism and freedom from the "given"; it presupposes a readiness to let go of our guiding assumptions about thought and being. The *Logic* is presuppositionless, however, because it rests on no *founding* prin-

ciples. Hegel takes for granted no rules of procedure, axiomatic definitions, or anticipated conclusions but begins from a purely indeterminate thought and simply lets it develop where it will.

Readers of the *Logic* thus do not need to master any special philosophical technique before embarking on the study of thought and being. They do not need to know in advance how to "synthesize" a "thesis" with an "antithesis" or how to reconcile opposites. All they have to do is focus, with an open mind, on the category under consideration and draw out whatever may be implicit in that category.

Before we proceed to part 2 and the text of the *Logic*, however, I have five things to ask of the reader. First, consider the *logical* structure of the categories or modes of being themselves and try to avoid relying on empirical examples to make sense of what Hegel is saying. One of the habits of mind that makes it particularly difficult to follow the argument of the *Logic* is that of taking a category and then thinking "*something other* than the category itself" (*SL* 41/1: 32)—that is, picturing something or imagining a thing actually being destroyed instead of understanding the logical structure of being "something" or of being "finite." There is, as Hegel puts it, "nothing to be thought with a concept save the concept itself" (*EL* 27/45 [§3]). All we should consider, therefore, are the relations between abstract determinations, such as "being," "not-being," and "self-relation," that constitute a particular concept. Later concepts are distinguished from earlier concepts not by the addition of any empirical content that can be pictured but purely by the fact that they are the logical "concretion of these abstract determinations" (*SL* 48/1: 41). That is to say, they represent more complex configurations of abstract terms than do earlier concepts. Our job is simply to understand that logical complexity.

Second, be prepared to let concepts and modes of being change as they are being thought. Do not assume in advance that they will retain a fixed identity but be open to the possibility that they might turn out to be somewhat different from they way they are initially conceived. Be prepared to think what Hegel calls the "movement" of concepts and the logical "movement" of being itself (*PhS* 28/47).

Third, avoid the desire to look eagerly for general principles of logical development but attend, rather, to the specific reasons why one concept might transform itself into another. That is to say, look to the details rather than the "total picture," and let the structure of the whole process *emerge* from those subtly varying and often surprising details. (This is not to deny that during the course of the *Logic* being will indeed prove to be *universal*, self-determining reason, or the "concept." One should bear in mind, however, that each moment of such universal reason—each category or form of being—will have its own distinctive structure. It is that distinctive structure that should be the main focus of one's concern.)

Fourth, hold Hegel to strict immanence and keep a critical eye out for places

where the logical development may be moved forward by external factors, such as metaphorical association or an eagerness to reach some projected conclusion. If Hegel is guilty of forcing a concept to develop in a direction that is not implied by the concept's own logical structure, do not rush to dismiss the whole enterprise of presuppositionless logic but consider where the immanent unfolding of that concept would and should take us.

Fifth, do not suspect in advance that speculative logic is a predetermined system from which one will never escape once one has been "sucked in." Remember that Hegel is trying to work out what is entailed by being radically *open-minded*. His account of the development of open-minded thought certainly should not be placed beyond all criticism, but readers who are wary from the start that they are going to be led to conclusions they do not like are effectively saying that they would prefer to remain secure in their own assumptions and not to *open* themselves at all to the risk of being surprised by being.

Now, to the text of the *Logic* itself.

Part Two

Text

Note on the Text

The German text of the opening of Hegel's *Science of Logic*, reprinted here in part 2, is the same as that found in G. W. F. Hegel, *Wissenschaft der Logik I*, ed. E. Moldenhauer and K. M. Michel, *Werke in zwanzig Bänden*, vol. 5 (Frankfurt am Main: Suhrkamp Verlag, 1969). It is taken from the following CD-ROM: G. W. F. Hegel, *Werke*, ed. Hegel-Institut Berlin (Berlin: Talpa Verlag, 2000). Additions in square brackets have been made by the German editors, Moldenhauer and Michel.

The English translation is taken from *Hegel's Science of Logic*, trans. A. V. Miller (Amherst, NY: Humanity Books, 1999). I have occasionally altered Miller's translation, but in each case his original version can be found in an accompanying note. Additions in square brackets have been made both by Miller and by me. The notes are all mine.

Womit muß der Anfang der Wissenschaft gemacht werden?

In neueren Zeiten erst ist das Bewußtsein entstanden, daß es eine Schwierigkeit sei, einen *Anfang* in der Philosophie zu finden, und der Grund dieser Schwierigkeit sowie die Möglichkeit, sie zu lösen, ist vielfältig besprochen worden. Der Anfang der Philosophie muß entweder ein *Vermitteltes* oder *Unmittelbares* sein, und es ist leicht zu zeigen, daß er weder das eine noch das andere sein könne; somit findet die eine oder die andere Weise des Anfangens ihre Widerlegung.

Das *Prinzip* einer Philosophie drückt wohl auch einen Anfang aus, aber nicht sowohl einen subjektiven als *objektiven*, den Anfang *aller Dinge*. Das Prinzip ist ein irgendwie bestimmter *Inhalt*: das Wasser, das Eine, Nus, Idee, — Substanz, Monade usf.; oder wenn es sich auf die Natur des Erkennens bezieht und damit mehr nur ein Kriterium als eine objektive Bestimmung sein soll — Denken, Anschauen, Empfinden, Ich, die Subjektivität selbst —, so ist es hier gleichfalls die Inhaltsbestimmung, auf welche das Interesse geht. Das Anfangen als solches dagegen bleibt als ein Subjektives in dem Sinne einer zufälligen Art und Weise, den Vortrag einzuleiten, unbeachtet und gleichgültig, somit auch das Bedürfnis der Frage, womit anzufangen sei, unbedeutend gegen das Bedürfnis des Prinzips, als in welchem allein das Interesse *der Sache* zu liegen scheint, das Interesse, was das *Wahre*, was der *absolute Grund* von allem sei.

Aber die moderne Verlegenheit um den Anfang geht aus einem weiteren Bedürfnisse hervor, welches diejenigen noch nicht kennen, denen es dogmatisch um das Erweisen des Prinzips zu tun ist oder skeptisch um das Finden eines subjektiven Kriteriums gegen dogmatisches Philosophieren, und welches diejenigen ganz verleugnen, die wie aus der Pistole aus ihrer inneren Offenbarung, aus Glauben, intellektueller Anschauung usw. anfangen und der *Methode* und Logik überhoben sein wollten. Wenn das früher abstrakte Denken zunächst nur für das Prinzip als *Inhalt* sich interessiert, aber im Fortgange der Bildung auf die andere Seite, auf das Benehmen des *Erkennens* zu achten getrieben ist, so wird auch das *subjektive* Tun als wesentliches Moment der objektiven Wahrheit erfaßt, und das Bedürfnis führt sich herbei, daß die *Methode* mit dem Inhalt, die Form mit dem Prinzip vereint sei. So soll das Prinzip auch Anfang und das, was das *Prius* für das Denken ist, auch das *Erste* im *Gange* des Denkens sein.

Es ist hier nur zu betrachten, wie der *logische* Anfang erscheint; die beiden Seiten, nach denen er genommen werden kann, sind schon genannt,

Chapter Nine

Beginning Logic: Text

With What Must Science Begin?

It is only in recent times that thinkers have become aware of the difficulty of finding a beginning in philosophy, and the reason for this difficulty and also the possibility of resolving it has been much discussed. What philosophy begins with must be either *mediated* or *immediate,* and it is easy to show that it can be neither the one nor the other; thus either way of beginning is refuted.

The *principle* of a philosophy does, of course, also express a beginning, but not so much a subjective as an *objective* one, the beginning of *everything.* The principle is a particular determinate *content*—water, the one, *nous,* idea, substance, monad, etc. Or, if it refers to the nature of cognition and consequently is supposed to be only a criterion rather than an objective determination—thought, intuition, sensation, ego, subjectivity itself. Then here too it is the nature of the content which is the point of interest. The beginning as such, on the other hand, as something subjective in the sense of being a particular, inessential way of introducing the discourse, remains unconsidered, a matter of indifference, and so too the need to find an answer to the question, With what should the beginning be made? remains of no importance in face of the need for a principle in which alone the interest of the matter in hand seems to lie, the interest as to what is the *truth,* the *absolute ground.*

But the modern perplexity about a beginning proceeds from a further requirement of which those who are concerned with the dogmatic demonstration of a principle or who are sceptical about finding a subjective criterion against dogmatic philosophising, are not yet aware, and which is completely denied by those who begin, like a shot from a pistol, from their inner revelation, from faith, intellectual intuition, etc., and who would be exempt from *method* and logic. If earlier abstract thought was interested in the principle only as content, but in the course of philosophical development has been impelled to pay attention to the other side, to the behaviour of the cognitive process, this implies that the *subjective* act has also been grasped as an *essential* moment of objective truth, and this brings with it the need to unite the method with the content, the form with the principle. Thus the principle ought also to be the beginning, and what is the first for thought ought also to be the first in the *process* of thinking.

Here we have only to consider how the *logical* beginning appears; the two sides from which it can be taken have already been named, to wit, either as a

entweder als Resultat auf vermittelte oder als eigentlicher Anfang auf unmittelbare Weise. Die in der Bildung der Zeit so wichtig erscheinende Frage, ob das Wissen der Wahrheit ein unmittelbares, schlechthin anfangendes Wissen, ein Glauben, oder aber ein vermitteltes Wissen sei, ist an diesem Orte nicht zu erörtern. Insofern solche Betrachtung *vorläufig* angestellt werden kann, ist dies anderwärts (in meiner *Enzyklopädie der philosophischen Wissenschaften*, 3. Ausgabe [1830] im "Vorbegriff", § 61 ff.) geschehen. Hier mag daraus nur dies angeführt werden, daß es Nichts *gibt*, nichts im Himmel oder in der Natur oder im Geiste oder wo es sei, was nicht ebenso die Unmittelbarkeit enthält als die Vermittlung, so daß sich diese beiden Bestimmungen als *ungetrennt* und *untrennbar* und jener Gegensatz sich als ein Nichtiges zeigt. Was aber die *wissenschaftliche Erörterung* betrifft, so ist es jeder logische Satz, in welchem die Bestimmungen der Unmittelbarkeit und der Vermittlung und also die Erörterung ihres Gegensatzes und ihrer Wahrheit vorkommt. Insofern dieser Gegensatz in Beziehung auf Denken, Wissen, Erkennen die konkretere Gestalt von unmittelbarem oder vermitteltem *Wissen* erhält, wird die Natur des Erkennens überhaupt sowohl innerhalb der Wissenschaft der Logik betrachtet, als dasselbe in seiner weiteren konkreten Form in die Wissenschaft vom Geiste und in die Phänomenologie desselben fällt. *Vor* der Wissenschaft aber schon über das Erkennen ins reine kommen wollen, heißt verlangen, daß es *außerhalb* derselben erörtert werden sollte; *außerhalb* der Wissenschaft läßt sich dies wenigstens nicht auf wissenschaftliche Weise, um die es hier allein zu tun ist, bewerkstelligen.

Logisch ist der Anfang, indem er im Element des frei für sich seienden Denkens, im *reinen Wissen* gemacht werden soll. *Vermittelt* ist er hiermit dadurch, daß das reine Wissen die letzte, absolute Wahrheit des *Bewußtseins* ist. Es ist in der Einleitung bemerkt, daß die *Phänomenologie des Geistes* die Wissenschaft des Bewußtseins, die Darstellung davon ist, daß das Bewußtsein den *Begriff* der Wissenschaft, d. i. das reine Wissen, zum Resultate hat. Die Logik hat insofern die Wissenschaft des erscheinenden Geistes zu ihrer Voraussetzung, welche die Notwendigkeit und damit den Beweis der Wahrheit des Standpunkts, der das reine Wissen ist, wie dessen Vermittlung überhaupt enthält und aufzeigt. In dieser Wissenschaft des erscheinenden Geistes wird von dem empirischen, *sinnlichen* Bewußtsein ausgegangen, und dieses ist das eigentliche *unmittelbare* Wissen; daselbst wird erörtert, was an diesem unmittelbaren Wissen ist. Anderes Bewußtsein, wie der Glaube an göttliche Wahrheiten, innere Erfahrung, Wissen durch innere Offenbarung usf., zeigt sich bei geringer Überlegung sehr uneigentlich als unmittelbares Wissen aufgeführt zu werden. In jener Abhandlung ist das unmittelbare Bewußtsein auch das in der Wissenschaft Erste und Unmittelbare, somit die Voraussetzung; in der Logik aber ist dasjenige die Voraussetzung, was aus jener Betrachtung sich als das Resultat erwiesen hatte, — die Idee als reines Wissen. Die *Logik ist die reine Wissenschaft*, d. i. das reine Wissen in dem ganzen Umfange seiner Entwicklung. Diese Idee aber hat sich in jenem

mediated result or as a beginning proper, as an immediacy. This is not the place to deal with the question apparently so important in present-day thought, whether the knowledge of truth is an immediate knowledge having a pure beginning, a faith, or whether it is a mediated knowledge. In so far as this can be dealt with *preliminarily* it has been done elsewhere.[1] Here we need only quote from it this, that there is nothing, nothing in heaven, or in nature or in mind or anywhere else which does not equally contain both immediacy and mediation, so that these two determinations reveal themselves to be *unseparated* and inseparable and the opposition between them to be a nullity. But as regards the philosophical discussion of this, it is to be found in every logical proposition in which occur the determinations of immediacy and mediation and consequently also the discussion of their opposition and their truth. Inasmuch as this opposition, as related to thinking, to knowing, to cognition, acquires the more concrete form of immediate or mediated *knowledge*, it is the nature of cognition simply as such which is considered within the science of logic, while the more concrete form of cognition falls to be considered in the philosophy of spirit and in the phenomenology of spirit. But to want the nature of cognition clarified *prior* to the science is to demand that it be considered *outside* the science; *outside* the science this cannot be accomplished, at least not in a scientific manner and such a manner is alone here in place.

The beginning is *logical* in that it is to be made in the element of thought that is free and for itself, in *pure knowing*. It is *mediated* because pure knowing is the ultimate, absolute truth of *consciousness*. In the Introduction it was remarked that the phenomenology of spirit is the science of consciousness, the exposition of it, and that consciousness has for result the *Notion* [or concept] of science, i.e. pure knowing.[2] Logic, then, has for its presupposition the science of manifested spirit, which contains and demonstrates the necessity, and so the truth, of the standpoint occupied by pure knowing and of its mediation.[3] In this science of manifested spirit the beginning is made from empirical, *sensuous* consciousness and this is *immediate* knowledge in the strict sense of the word; in that work there is discussed the significance of this immediate knowledge. Other forms of consciousness such as belief in divine truths, inner experience, knowledge through inner revelation, etc., are very ill-fitted to be quoted as examples of immediate knowledge as a little reflection will show. In the work just mentioned immediate consciousness is also the first and that which is immediate in the science itself, and therefore the presupposition; but in logic, the presupposition is that which has proved itself to be the result of that phenomenological consideration—the Idea as pure knowledge.[4] *Logic*

---

1. See Hegel, *EL* 108–22/148–66 (§§61–76).
2. See Hegel, *SL* 48/1: 42. Miller translates *Begriff* as "Notion," rather than "concept." In quotations from Hegel included in parts 1 and 3 of this study I have replaced "Notion" with "concept." In the text of the *Logic* included in part 2, however, I have left the word "Notion" unchanged.
3. On the precise relation of the *Phenomenology of Spirit* to the *Science of Logic*, see chapter 7, above.
4. Note that this "Idea" is initially thought in the *Logic* only as pure, indeterminate *being*, not as *Idea* as such. It is not thought explicitly as *Idea* until near the end of the *Logic*. See chapter 2, above, pp. 49–51.

Resultate dahin bestimmt, die zur Wahrheit gewordene Gewißheit zu sein, die Gewißheit, die nach der einen Seite dem Gegenstande nicht mehr gegenüber ist, sondern ihn innerlich gemacht hat, ihn als sich selbst weiß, — und die auf der andern Seite das Wissen von sich als von einem, das dem Gegenständlichen gegenüber und nur dessen Vernichtung sei, aufgegeben [hat], dieser Subjektivität entäußert und Einheit mit seiner Entäußerung ist.

Daß nun von dieser Bestimmung des reinen Wissens aus der Anfang seiner Wissenschaft immanent bleibe, ist nichts zu tun, als das zu betrachten oder vielmehr mit Beiseitsetzung aller Reflexionen, aller Meinungen, die man sonst hat, nur aufzunehmen, *was vorhanden ist.*

Das reine Wissen, als in diese *Einheit zusammengegangen*, hat alle Beziehung auf ein Anderes und auf Vermittlung aufgehoben; es ist das Unterschiedslose; dieses Unterschiedslose hört somit selbst auf, Wissen zu sein; es ist nur *einfache Unmittelbarkeit* vorhanden.

Die einfache Unmittelbarkeit ist selbst ein Reflexionsausdruck und bezieht sich auf den Unterschied von dem Vermittelten. In ihrem wahren Ausdrucke ist daher diese einfache Unmittelbarkeit das *reine Sein*. Wie das *reine* Wissen nichts heißen soll als das Wissen als solches, ganz abstrakt, so soll auch reines Sein nichts heißen als das *Sein* überhaupt; Sein, sonst nichts, ohne alle weitere Bestimmung und Erfüllung.

Hier ist das Sein das Anfangende, als durch Vermittlung und zwar durch sie, welche zugleich Aufheben ihrer selbst ist, entstanden dargestellt; mit der Voraussetzung des reinen Wissens als Resultats des endlichen Wissens, des Bewußtseins. Soll aber keine Voraussetzung gemacht, der Anfang selbst *unmittelbar* genommen werden, so bestimmt er sich nur dadurch, daß es der Anfang der Logik, des Denkens für sich, sein soll. Nur der Entschluß, den man auch für eine Willkür ansehen kann, nämlich daß man das *Denken als solches* betrachten wolle, ist vorhanden. So muß der Anfang a*bsoluter* oder, was hier gleichbedeutend ist, abstrakter Anfang sein; er darf so *nichts voraussetzen*, muß durch nichts vermittelt sein noch einen Grund haben; er soll vielmehr selbst Grund der ganzen Wissenschaft sein. Er muß daher schlechthin ein Unmittelbares sein oder vielmehr nur *das Unmittelbare* selbst. Wie er nicht gegen Anderes eine Bestimmung haben kann, so kann er auch keine in sich, keinen Inhalt enthalten, denn dergleichen wäre Unterscheidung und Beziehung von Verschiedenem aufeinander, somit eine Vermittlung. Der Anfang ist also das *reine Sein.*

Nach dieser einfachen Darlegung dessen, was zunächst nur zu diesem selbst Allereinfachsten, dem logischen Anfang gehört, können noch folgende weitere Reflexionen beigebracht werden; doch können sie nicht sowohl zur Erläuterung und Bestätigung jener Darlegung, die für sich fertig ist, dienen sollen, als sie vielmehr nur durch Vorstellungen und Reflexionen veranlaßt werden, die uns zum voraus in den Weg kommen können, jedoch, wie alle anderen vorangehenden Vorurteile, in der Wissenschaft selbst ihre Erledigung finden müssen, und daher eigentlich zur Geduld hierauf zu verweisen wäre.

is pure science, that is, pure knowledge in the entire range of its development. But in the said result, this Idea has determined itself to be the certainty which has become truth, the certainty which, on the one hand, no longer has the object over against it but has internalised it, knows it as its own self—and, on the other hand, has given up the knowledge of itself as of something confronting the object of which it is only the annihilation, has divested itself of this subjectivity and is at one with its self-alienation.

Now starting from this determination of pure knowledge, all that is needed to ensure that the beginning remains immanent in its scientific development is to consider, or rather, ridding oneself of all other reflections and opinions whatever, simply to take up, *what is there before us.*

Pure knowing as concentrated into this unity has sublated all reference to an other and to mediation; it is without any distinction and as thus distinctionless, ceases itself to be knowledge; what is present is only *simple immediacy.*

Simple immediacy is itself an expression of reflection and contains a reference to its distinction from what is mediated. This simple immediacy, therefore, in its true expression is *pure being*. Just as *pure* knowing is to mean knowing as such, quite abstractly, so too pure being is to mean nothing but *being* in general: being, and nothing else, without any further specification and filling.

Here the beginning is made with being which is represented as having come to be through mediation, a mediation which is also a sublating of itself; and there is presupposed pure knowing as the outcome of finite knowing, of consciousness. But if no presupposition is to be made and the beginning itself is taken *immediately,* then its only determination is that it is to be the beginning of logic, of thought as such. All that is present is simply the resolve, which can also be regarded as arbitrary, that we propose to consider thought as such. Thus the beginning must be an *absolute*, or what is synonymous here, an *abstract* beginning; and so it *may not presuppose anything*, must not be mediated by anything nor have a ground; rather it is to be itself the ground of the entire science. Consequently, it must be purely and simply *an* immediacy, or rather merely *immediacy* itself. Just as it cannot possess any determination relatively to anything else, so too it cannot contain within itself any determination, any content; for any such would be a distinguishing and an interrelationship of distinct moments, and consequently a mediation. The beginning therefore is *pure being*.

To this simple exposition of what is only directly involved in the simplest of all things, the logical beginning, we may add the following further reflections; yet these cannot be meant to serve as elucidations and confirmations of that exposition—this is complete in itself—since they are occasioned by preconceived ideas and reflections and these, like all other preliminary prejudices, must be disposed of within the science itself where their treatment should be awaited with patience.

The insight that absolute truth must be a result, and conversely, that a result

Die Einsicht, daß das Absolut-Wahre ein Resultat sein müsse, und umgekehrt, daß ein Resultat ein erstes Wahres voraussetzt, das aber, weil es Erstes ist, objektiv betrachtet nicht notwendig und nach der subjektiven Seite nicht erkannt ist, — hat in neueren Zeiten den Gedanken hervorgebracht, daß die Philosophie nur mit einem *hypothetischen* und *problematischen* Wahren anfangen und das Philosophieren daher zuerst nur ein Suchen sein könne, eine Ansicht welche *Reinhold* in den späteren Zeiten seines Philosophierens vielfach urgiert hat und der man die Gerechtigkeit widerfahren lassen muß, daß ihr ein wahrhaftes Interesse zugrunde liegt, welches die spekulative Natur des philosophischen *Anfangs* betrifft. Die Auseinandersetzung dieser Ansicht ist zugleich eine Veranlassung, ein vorläufiges Verständnis über den Sinn des logischen Fortschreitens überhaupt einzuleiten; denn jene Ansicht schließt die Rücksicht auf das Fortgehen sogleich in sich. Und zwar stellt sie es so vor, daß das Vorwärtsschreiten in der Philosophie vielmehr ein Rückwärtsgehen und Begründen sei, durch welches erst sich ergebe, daß das, womit angefangen wurde, nicht bloß ein willkürlich Angenommenes, sondern in der Tat teils das *Wahre*, teils das *erste Wahre* sei.

Man muß zugeben, daß es eine wesentliche Betrachtung ist — die sich innerhalb der Logik selbst näher ergeben wird —, daß das Vorwärtsgehen ein *Rückgang* in den *Grund*, zu dem *Ursprünglichen* und *Wahrhaften* ist, von dem das, womit der Anfang gemacht wurde, abhängt und in der Tat hervorgebracht wird. — So wird das Bewußtsein auf seinem Wege von der Unmittelbarkeit aus, mit der es anfängt, zum absoluten Wissen als seiner innersten *Wahrheit* zurückgeführt. Dies Letzte, der Grund, ist denn auch dasjenige, aus welchem das Erste hervorgeht, das zuerst als Unmittelbares auftrat. — So wird noch mehr der absolute Geist, der als die konkrete und letzte höchste Wahrheit alles Seins sich ergibt, erkannt, als am *Ende* der Entwicklung sich mit Freiheit entäußernd und sich zur Gestalt eines *unmittelbaren* Seins entlassend, — zur Schöpfung einer Welt sich entschließend, welche alles das enthält, was in die Entwicklung, die jenem Resultate vorangegangen, fiel und das durch diese umgekehrte Stellung mit seinem Anfang in ein von dem Resultate als dem Prinzip Abhängiges verwandelt wird. Das Wesentliche für die Wissenschaft ist nicht so sehr, daß ein rein Unmittelbares der Anfang sei, sondern daß das Ganze derselben ein Kreislauf in sich selbst ist, worin das Erste auch das Letzte und das Letzte auch das Erste wird.

Daher ergibt sich auf der andern Seite als ebenso notwendig, dasjenige, in welches die Bewegung als in seinen *Grund* zurückgeht, als *Resultat* zu betrachten. Nach dieser Rücksicht ist das Erste ebensosehr der Grund und das Letzte ein Abgeleitetes; indem von dem Ersten ausgegangen und durch richtige Folgerungen auf das Letzte als auf den Grund gekommen wird, ist dieser Resultat. Der *Fortgang* ferner von dem, was den Anfang macht, ist nur als eine weitere Bestimmung desselben zu betrachten, so daß das Anfangende allem Folgenden zugrunde liegen bleibt und nicht daraus verschwindet. Das Fortgehen besteht nicht darin, daß nur ein *Anderes* abgeleitet oder daß in ein wahrhaft Anderes übergegangen würde; — und insofern dies Übergehen vor-

presupposes a prior truth which, however, because it is a first, objectively considered is unnecessary and from the subjective side is not known—this insight has recently given rise to the thought that philosophy can only begin with a *hypothetical* and *problematical* truth and therefore philosophising can at first be only a quest. This view was much stressed by Reinhold in his later philosophical work and one must give it credit for the genuine interest on which it is based, an interest which concerns the speculative nature of the philosophical *beginning*.[5] The detailed discussion of this view is at the same time an occasion for introducing a preliminary understanding of the meaning of progress in logic generally; for that view has a direct bearing on the advance; this it conceives to be such that progress in philosophy is rather a retrogression and a grounding or establishing by means of which we first obtain the result that what we began with is not something merely arbitrarily assumed but is in fact the *truth,* and also the *primary truth.*

It must be admitted that it is an important consideration—one which will be found in more detail in the logic itself—that the advance is a *retreat into the ground,* to what is *primary* and *true*, on which depends and, in fact, from which originates, that with which the beginning is made. Thus consciousness on its onward path from the immediacy with which it began is led back to absolute knowledge as its innermost truth. This last, the ground, is then also that from which the first proceeds, that which at first appeared as an immediacy. This is true in still greater measure of absolute spirit which reveals itself as the concrete and final supreme truth of all being, and which at the *end* of the development is known as freely externalising itself, abandoning itself to the shape of an *immediate being*—opening or unfolding itself into the creation of a world which contains all that fell into the development preceding that result and that, through this reversal of its position relatively to its beginning, is transformed into something dependent on the result as principle.[6] The essential requirement for the science of logic is not so much that the beginning be a pure immediacy, but rather that the whole of the science be within itself a circle in which the first is also the last and the last is also the first.

We see therefore that, on the other hand, it is equally necessary to consider as *result* that into which the movement returns as into its *ground.* In this respect the first is equally the ground, and the last a derivative; since the movement starts from the first and by correct inferences arrives at the last as the ground, this latter is a result. Further, the *progress* from that which forms the beginning is to be regarded as only a further determination of it, hence that which forms the starting point of the development remains at the base of all that follows and does not vanish from it. The progress does not consist merely in the derivation of an other,

---

5. Karl Leonhard Reinhold (1758–1823).

6. Miller has "a world which contains all that fell into the development which preceded that result and which through this reversal of its position relatively to its beginning." I have modified the translation slightly in order to make the sense of the lines clearer: "contains all that fell into the development […] and that […] is transformed."

kommt, so hebt es sich ebensosehr wieder auf. So ist der Anfang der Philosophie die in allen folgenden Entwicklungen gegenwärtige und sich erhaltende Grundlage, das seinen weiteren Bestimmungen durchaus immanent Bleibende.

Durch diesen Fortgang denn verliert der Anfang das, was er in dieser Bestimmtheit, ein Unmittelbares und Abstraktes überhaupt zu sein, Einseitiges hat; er wird ein Vermitteltes, und die Linie der wissenschaftlichen Fortbewegung macht sich damit *zu einem Kreise*. — Zugleich ergibt sich, daß das, was den Anfang macht, indem es darin das noch Unentwickelte, Inhaltslose ist, im Anfange noch nicht wahrhaft erkannt wird und daß erst die Wissenschaft, und zwar in ihrer ganzen Entwicklung, seine vollendete, inhaltsvolle und erst wahrhaft begründete Erkenntnis ist.

Darum aber, weil das *Resultat* erst als der absolute Grund hervortritt, ist das Fortschreiten dieses Erkennens nicht etwas Provisorisches noch ein problematisches und hypothetisches, sondern es muß durch die Natur der Sache und des Inhaltes selbst bestimmt sein. Weder ist jener Anfang etwas Willkürliches und nur einstweilen Angenommenes noch ein als willkürlich Erscheinendes und bittweise Vorausgesetztes, von dem sich aber doch in der Folge zeige, daß man recht daran getan habe, es zum Anfange zu machen; nicht wie bei den Konstruktionen, die man zum Behuf des Beweises eines geometrischen Satzes zu machen angewiesen wird, es der Fall ist, daß von ihnen es sich erst hinterher an den Beweisen ergibt, daß man wohlgetan habe, gerade diese Linien zu ziehen und dann in den Beweisen selbst mit der Vergleichung dieser Linien oder Winkel anzufangen; für sich an diesem Linienziehen oder Vergleichen begreift es sich nicht.

So ist vorhin der *Grund*, warum in der reinen Wissenschaft vom reinen Sein angefangen wird, unmittelbar an ihr selbst angegeben worden. Dies reine Sein ist die Einheit, in die das reine Wissen zurückgeht, oder wenn dieses selbst noch als Form von seiner Einheit unterschieden gehalten werden soll, so ist es auch der Inhalt desselben. Dies ist die Seite, nach welcher dies *reine Sein*, dies Absolut-Unmittelbare, ebenso absolut Vermitteltes ist. Aber es muß ebenso wesentlich nur in der Einseitigkeit, das Rein-Unmittelbare zu sein, genommen werden, *eben weil* es hier als der Anfang ist. Insofern es nicht diese reine Unbestimmtheit, insofern es bestimmt wäre, würde es als Vermitteltes, schon Weitergeführtes genommen; ein Bestimmtes enthält ein *Anderes* zu einem Ersten. Es liegt also in der *Natur des Anfangs selbst*, daß er das Sein sei und sonst nichts. Es bedarf daher keiner sonstigen Vorbereitungen, um in die Philosophie hineinzukommen, noch anderweitiger Reflexionen und Anknüpfungspunkte.

Daß der Anfang Anfang der Philosophie ist, daraus kann eigentlich auch keine *nähere Bestimmung* oder ein *positiver* Inhalt für denselben genommen werden. Denn die Philosophie ist hier im Anfange, wo die Sache selbst noch nicht vorhanden ist, ein leeres Wort oder irgendeine angenommene ungerechtfertigte Vorstellung. Das reine Wissen gibt nur diese negative Bestimmung, daß er der *abstrakte* Anfang sein soll. Insofern das reine Sein als *Inhalt* des reinen Wissens genommen wird, so hat dieses von seinem Inhalte zurückzutreten, ihn für sich selbst gewähren zu lassen und nicht weiter zu

or in the effected transition into a genuine other; and in so far as this transition does occur it is equally sublated again. Thus the beginning of philosophy is the foundation which is present and preserved throughout the entire subsequent development, remaining completely immanent in its further determinations.

Through this progress, then, the beginning loses the one-sidedness which attaches to it as something simply immediate and abstract; it becomes something mediated, and hence the line of the scientific advance becomes a *circle.* It also follows that because that which forms the beginning is still undeveloped, devoid of content, it is not truly known in the beginning; it is the science of logic in its whole compass which first constitutes the completed knowledge of it with its developed content and first truly grounds that knowledge.

But because it is the *result* which appears as the absolute ground, this progress in knowing is not something provisional, or problematical and hypothetical; it must be determined by the nature of the subject matter itself and its content. The said beginning is neither an arbitrary and merely provisional assumption, nor is it something which appears to be arbitrarily and tentatively presupposed, but which is subsequently shown to have been properly made the beginning; not as is the case with the constructions one is directed to make in connection with the proof of a theorem in geometry, where it becomes apparent only afterwards in the proof that one took the right course in drawing just those lines and then, in the proof itself, in beginning with the comparison of those lines or angles; drawing such lines and comparing them are not an essential part of the proof itself.

Thus the *ground,* the *reason,* why the beginning is made with pure being in the pure science [of logic] is directly given in the science itself. This pure being is the unity into which pure knowing withdraws, or, if this itself is still to be distinguished as form from its unity, then being is also the content of pure knowing. It is when taken in this way that this *pure being,* this absolute immediacy has equally the character of something absolutely mediated. But it is equally essential that it be taken only in the one-sided character in which it is pure immediacy, *precisely because* here it is the beginning. If it were not this pure indeterminateness, if it were determinate, it would have been taken as something mediated, something already carried a stage further: what is determinate implies an other to a first. Therefore, it lies in the *very nature of a beginning* that it must be being and nothing else. To enter into philosophy, therefore, calls for no other preparations, no further reflections or points of connection.

We cannot really extract any further determination or *positive* content for the beginning from the fact that it is the beginning of philosophy. For here at the start, where the subject matter itself is not yet to hand, philosophy is an empty word or some assumed, unjustified conception. Pure knowing yields only this negative determination, that the beginning is to be *abstract.* If pure being is taken as the *content* of pure knowing, then the latter must stand back from its content, allowing it to have free play and not determining it further. Or again, if pure being is to be considered as the unity into which knowing has collapsed at the extreme point of its union with the object, then knowing itself has vanished in that unity, leaving behind no difference from the unity and

bestimmen. — Oder indem das reine Sein als die Einheit zu betrachten ist, in die das Wissen auf seiner höchsten Spitze der Einigung mit dem Objekte zusammengefallen, so ist das Wissen in diese Einheit verschwunden und hat keinen Unterschied von ihr und somit keine Bestimmung für sie übriggelassen. — Auch sonst ist nicht etwas oder irgendein Inhalt vorhanden, der gebraucht werden könnte, um damit den bestimmteren Anfang zu machen.

Aber auch die bisher als Anfang angenommene Bestimmung *des Seins* könnte weggelassen werden, so daß nur gefordert würde, daß ein reiner Anfang gemacht werde. Dann ist nichts vorhanden als der *Anfang* selbst, und es wäre zu sehen, was er ist. — Diese Stellung könnte zugleich als ein Vorschlag zur Güte an diejenigen gemacht werden, welche teils damit, daß mit dem Sein angefangen werde, aus welchen Reflexionen es sei, sich nicht beruhigen und noch weniger mit dem Erfolge, den das Sein hat, in das Nichts überzugehen, teils [es] überhaupt nicht anders wissen, als daß in einer Wissenschaft mit der *Voraussetzung* einer *Vorstellung* angefangen werde — einer Vorstellung, welche hierauf *analysiert* werde, so daß nun das Ergebnis solcher Analyse den ersten bestimmten Begriff in der Wissenschaft abgebe. Indem wir auch dies Verfahren beobachteten, so hätten wir keinen besonderen Gegenstand, weil der Anfang, als des *Denkens,* ganz abstrakt, ganz allgemein, ganz Form ohne allen Inhalt sein soll; wir hätten somit gar nichts als die Vorstellung von einem bloßen Anfang als solchem. Es ist also nur zu sehen, was wir in dieser Vorstellung haben.

Es ist noch Nichts, und es soll Etwas werden. Der Anfang ist nicht das reine Nichts, sondern ein Nichts, von dem Etwas ausgehen soll; das Sein ist also auch schon im Anfang enthalten. Der Anfang enthält also beides, Sein und Nichts; ist die Einheit von Sein und Nichts, — oder ist Nichtsein, das zugleich Sein, und Sein, das zugleich Nichtsein ist.

Ferner: Sein und Nichts sind im Anfang als *unterschieden* vorhanden; denn er weist auf etwas anderes hin; — er ist ein Nichtsein, das auf das Sein als auf ein Anderes bezogen ist; das Anfangende *ist* noch nicht; es geht erst dem Sein zu. Der Anfang enthält also das Sein als ein solches, das sich von dem Nichtsein entfernt oder es aufhebt, als ein ihm Entgegengesetztes.

Ferner aber *ist* das, was anfängt, schon; ebensosehr aber *ist* es auch noch *nicht.* Die Entgegengesetzten, Sein und Nichtsein, sind also in ihm in unmittelbarer Vereinigung; oder er ist ihre *ununterschiedene Einheit.*

Die Analyse des Anfangs gäbe somit den Begriff der Einheit des Seins und des Nichtseins — oder, in reflektierterer Form, der Einheit des Unterschieden- und des Nichtunterschiedenseins — oder der Identität der Identität und Nichtidentität. Dieser Begriff könnte als die erste, reinste, d. i. abstrakteste Definition des Absoluten angesehen werden, — wie er dies in der Tat sein würde, wenn es überhaupt um die Form von Definitionen und um den Namen des Absoluten zu tun wäre. In diesem Sinne würden, wie jener abstrakte Begriff die erste, so alle weiteren Bestimmungen und Entwicklungen nur bestimmtere und reichere Definitionen dieses Absoluten sein. Aber die, welche mit dem *Sein* als Anfang darum nicht zufrieden sind, weil es in Nichts übergeht und daraus die Einheit des Seins und Nichts entsteht, mögen zusehen, ob sie mit diesem Anfange, der mit

hence nothing by which the latter could be determined. Nor is there anything else present, any content which could be used to make the beginning more determinate.

But the determination of *being* so far adopted for the beginning could also be omitted, so that the only demand would be that a pure beginning be made. In that case, we have nothing but the *beginning* itself, and it remains to be seen what this is. This position could also be suggested for the benefit of those who, on the one hand, are dissatisfied for one reason or another with the beginning with being and still more so with the resulting transition of being into nothing, and, on the other hand, simply know no other way of beginning a science than by *presupposing some general idea,* which is then *analysed,* the result of such analysis yielding the first specific concept in the science. If we too were to observe this method, then we should be without a particular object, because the beginning, as the beginning of *thought,* is supposed to be quite abstract, quite general, wholly form without any content; thus we should have nothing at all beyond the general idea of a mere beginning as such. We have therefore only to see what is contained in such an idea.

As yet there is nothing and there is to become something. The beginning is not pure nothing, but a nothing from which something is to proceed; therefore being, too, is already contained in the beginning. The beginning therefore contains both, being and nothing, is the unity of being and nothing; or is non-being which is at the same time being, and being which is at the same time non-being.

Further, in the beginning, being and nothing are present as *distinguished* from each other; for the beginning points to something else—it is a non-being which carries a reference to being as to an other; that which begins, as yet *is* not, it is only on the way to being. The being contained in the beginning is, therefore, a being which removes itself from non-being or sublates it as something opposed to it.

But again, that which begins already *is,* but equally, too, *is not* as yet. The opposites, being and non-being are therefore directly united in it, or, otherwise expressed, it is their *undifferentiated unity.*

The analysis of the beginning would thus yield the notion of the unity of being and nothing—or, in a more reflected form, the unity of differentiatedness and non-differentiatedness, or the identity of identity and non-identity. This concept could be regarded as the first, purest, that is, most abstract definition of the absolute—as it would in fact be if we were at all concerned with the form of definitions and with the name of the absolute. In this sense, that abstract concept would be the first definition of this absolute and all further determinations and developments only more specific and richer definitions of it. But let those who are dissatisfied with *being* as a beginning because it passes over into nothing and so gives rise to the unity of being and nothing, let them see whether they find this beginning, which begins with the general idea of a *beginning* and

der Vorstellung des *Anfangs* anfängt, und mit deren Analyse, die wohl richtig sein wird aber gleichfalls auf die Einheit des Seins und Nichts führt, zufriedener sein mögen als damit, daß das Sein zum Anfange gemacht wird.

Es ist aber noch eine weitere Betrachtung über dieses Verfahren zu machen. Jene Analyse setzt die Vorstellung des Anfangs als bekannt voraus; es ist so nach dem Beispiele anderer Wissenschaften verfahren worden. Diese setzen ihren Gegenstand voraus und nehmen bittweise an, daß jedermann dieselbe Vorstellung von ihm habe und darin ungefähr dieselben Bestimmungen finden möge, die sie durch Analyse, Vergleichung und sonstiges Räsonnement von ihm da- und dorther beibringen und angeben. Das aber, was den absoluten Anfang macht, muß gleichfalls ein sonst Bekanntes sein; wenn es nun ein Konkretes, somit in sich mannigfaltig Bestimmtes ist, so ist diese *Beziehung*, die es in *sich* ist, als etwas Bekanntes vorausgesetzt; sie ist damit als etwas *Unmittelbares* angegeben, *was sie aber nicht ist,* denn sie ist nur Beziehung als von Unterschiedenen, enthält somit die *Vermittlung* in sich. Ferner tritt am Konkreten die Zufälligkeit und Willkür der Analyse und des verschiedenen Bestimmens ein. Welche Bestimmungen herausgebracht werden, hängt von dem ab, was jeder in seiner unmittelbaren zufälligen Vorstellung *vorfindet*. Die in einem Konkreten, einer synthetischen Einheit enthaltene Beziehung ist eine *notwendige* nur, insofern sie nicht vorgefunden, sondern durch die eigene Bewegung der Momente, in diese Einheit zurückzugehen, hervorgebracht ist, — eine Bewegung, die das Gegenteil des analytischen Verfahrens ist, eines der Sache selbst äußerlichen, in das Subjekt fallenden Tuns.

Hierin ist auch das Nähere enthalten, daß das, womit der Anfang zu machen ist, nicht ein Konkretes, nicht ein solches sein kann, das eine Beziehung *innerhalb seiner selbst* enthält. Denn ein solches setzt ein Vermitteln und Herübergehen von einem Ersten zu einem Anderen innerhalb seiner voraus, wovon das einfachgewordene Konkrete das Resultat wäre. Aber der Anfang soll nicht selbst schon ein Erstes *und* ein Anderes sein; ein solches, das ein Erstes *und* ein Anderes in sich ist, enthält bereits ein Fortgegangensein. Was den Anfang macht, der Anfang selbst, ist daher als ein Nichtanalysierbares, in seiner einfachen unerfüllten Unmittelbarkeit, also *als Sein*, als das ganz Leere zu nehmen.

Wenn man etwa, gegen die Betrachtung des abstrakten Anfangs ungeduldig, sagen wollte, es solle nicht mit dem Anfange angefangen werden, sondern geradezu mit der *Sache*, so ist diese Sache nichts als jenes leere Sein; denn was die Sache sei, dies ist es, was sich eben erst im Verlaufe der Wissenschaft ergeben soll, was nicht vor ihr als bekannt vorausgesetzt werden kann.

Welche Form sonst genommen werde, um einen anderen Anfang zu haben als das leere Sein, so leidet er an den angeführten Mängeln. Diejenigen, welche mit diesem Anfange unzufrieden bleiben, mögen sich zu der Aufgabe auffordern, es anders anzufangen, um dabei diese Mängel zu vermeiden.

Ein origineller Anfang der Philosophie aber kann nicht ganz unerwähnt

with its analysis (which, though of course correct, likewise leads to the unity of being and nothing), more satisfactory than the beginning with being.

But there is a still further observation to be made about this procedure. The said analysis presupposes as familiar the idea of a beginning, thus following the example of other sciences. These presuppose their subject-matter and take it for granted that everyone has roughly the same general idea of it and can find in it the same determinations as those indicated by the sciences which have obtained them in one way or another through analysis, comparison and other kinds of reasoning. But that which forms the absolute beginning must likewise be something otherwise known; now if it is something concrete and hence is variously determined within itself, then this *internal relation* is presupposed as something known; it is thus put forward as an *immediacy* which, however, it is not; for it is a relation only as a relation of distinct moments, and it therefore contains *mediation* within itself. Further, with a concrete object, the analysis and the ways in which it is determined are affected by contingency and arbitrariness. Which determinations are brought out depends on what each person just *finds* in his own immediate, contingent idea. The relation contained in something concrete, in a synthetic unity, is *necessary* only in so far as it is not just given but is produced by the spontaneous movement of the moments back into this unity—a movement which is the opposite of the analytical procedure, which is an activity belonging to the subject-thinker and external to the subject matter itself.[7]

The foregoing shows quite clearly the reason why the beginning cannot be made with anything concrete, anything containing a relation *within itself.* For such presupposes an internal process of mediation and transition of which the concrete, now become simple, would be the result. But the beginning ought not itself to be already a first *and* an other; for anything which is in its own self a first *and* an other implies that an advance has already been made. Consequently, that which constitutes the beginning, the beginning itself, is to be taken as something unanalysable, taken in its simple, unfilled immediacy, and therefore *as being,* as completely empty being.[8]

If impatience with the consideration of the abstract beginning should provoke anyone to say that the beginning should be made not with the beginning, but straightway with the subject matter itself, well then, this subject matter is nothing else but the said empty being; for what this subject matter is, that will be explicated only in the development of the science and cannot be presupposed by it as known beforehand.

Whatever other form the beginning takes in the attempt to begin with something other than empty being, it will suffer from the defects already specified. Let those who are still dissatisfied with this beginning tackle the problem of avoiding these defects by beginning in some other way.

But we cannot leave entirely unmentioned an original beginning of phi-

---

7 Translation revised. Miller translates *die eigene Bewegung der Momente* as "the spontaneous return of the moments."

8 Miller has "as the completely empty being."

gelassen werden, der sich in neuerer Zeit berühmt gemacht hat, der Anfang mit *Ich.* Er kam teils aus der Reflexion, daß aus dem ersten Wahren alles Folgende abgeleitet werden müsse, teils aus dem Bedürfnisse, daß das erste Wahre ein Bekanntes und noch mehr ein *unmittelbar Gewisses* sei. Dieser Anfang ist im allgemeinen nicht eine solche Vorstellung, die zufällig ist und in einem Subjekte so, in einem anderen anders beschaffen sein kann. Denn Ich, dies unmittelbare Selbstbewußtsein, erscheint zunächst selbst teils als ein Unmittelbares, teils als ein in einem viel höheren Sinne Bekanntes als eine sonstige Vorstellung; etwas sonst Bekanntes gehört zwar dem Ich an, aber ist noch ein von ihm unterschiedener, damit sogleich zufälliger Inhalt; Ich hingegen ist die einfache Gewißheit seiner selbst. Aber Ich überhaupt ist auch *zugleich* ein Konkretes, oder Ich ist vielmehr das Konkreteste, — das Bewußtsein seiner als unendlich mannigfaltiger Welt. Daß Ich Anfang und Grund der Philosophie sei, dazu wird die Absonderung dieses Konkreten erfordert, — der absolute Akt, wodurch Ich von sich selbst gereinigt wird und als abstraktes Ich in sein Bewußtsein tritt. Allein dies reine Ich ist nun *nicht* ein unmittelbares, noch das bekannte, das gewöhnliche Ich unseres Bewußtseins, woran unmittelbar und für jeden die Wissenschaft angeknüpft werden sollte. Jener Akt wäre eigentlich nichts anderes als die Erhebung auf den Standpunkt des reinen Wissens, auf welchem der Unterschied des Subjektiven und Objektiven verschwunden ist. Aber wie diese Erhebung so *unmittelbar* gefordert ist, ist sie ein subjektives Postulat; um als wahrhafte Forderung sich zu erweisen, müßte die Fortbewegung des konkreten Ichs vom unmittelbaren Bewußtsein zum reinen Wissen an ihm selbst, durch seine eigene Notwendigkeit, aufgezeigt und dargestellt worden sein. Ohne diese objektive Bewegung erscheint das reine Wissen, auch als *die intellektuelle Anschauung* bestimmt, als ein willkürlicher Standpunkt oder selbst als einer der empirischen *Zustände* des Bewußtseins, in Rücksicht dessen es darauf ankommt, ob ihn der eine in sich *vorfinde* oder hervorbringen könne, ein anderer aber nicht. Insofern aber dies reine Ich das wesentliche reine Wissen sein muß und das reine Wissen aber nur durch den absoluten Akt der Selbsterhebung im individuellen Bewußtsein gesetzt wird und nicht unmittelbar in ihm vorhanden ist, geht gerade der Vorteil verloren, der aus diesem Anfange der Philosophie entspringen soll, daß er nämlich etwas schlechthin Bekanntes sei, was jeder unmittelbar in sich finde und daran die weitere Reflexion anknüpfen könne; jenes reine Ich ist vielmehr in seiner abstrakten Wesenheit etwas dem gewöhnlichen Bewußtsein Unbekanntes, etwas, das es nicht darin vorfindet. Damit tritt vielmehr der Nachteil der Täuschung ein, daß von etwas Bekanntem, dem Ich des empirischen Selbstbewußtseins die Rede sein solle, indem in der Tat von etwas diesem Bewußtsein Fernem die Rede ist. Die Bestimmung des reinen Wissens als Ich führt die fortdauernde Rückerinnerung an das subjektive Ich mit sich, dessen Schranken vergessen werden sollen, und erhält die Vorstellung gegenwärtig, als ob die Sätze und Verhältnisse, die sich in der weiteren Entwicklung vom Ich ergeben, im gewöhnlichen Bewußtsein, da es ja das sei, von dem sie

losophy which has recently become famous, the beginning with the *ego* [or the *I*].[9] It came partly from the reflection that from the first truth the entire sequel must be derived, and partly from the requirement that the *first* truth must be something with which we are acquainted, and still more, something of which we are *immediately certain*. This beginning is, in general, not a contingent idea which can be differently constituted in different subjects. For the ego, this immediate consciousness of self, at first appears to be itself both an immediacy and also something much more familiar to us than any other idea; anything else known belongs to the ego, it is true, but is still a content distinguished from it and therefore contingent; the ego, on the contrary, is the simple certainty of its own self. But the ego as such is *at the same time* also concrete, or rather, the ego is the most concrete of all things—the consciousness of itself as an infinitely manifold world. Before the ego, this concrete Being, can be made the beginning and ground of philosophy, it must be disrupted—this is the absolute act through which the ego purges itself of its content and becomes aware of itself as an abstract ego. Only this pure ego now is *not* immediate, is not the familiar, ordinary ego of our consciousness to which the science of logic could be directly linked for everyone. That act, strictly speaking, would be nothing else but the elevation to the standpoint of pure knowing where the distinction of subject and object has vanished. But as thus *immediately* demanded, this elevation is a subjective postulate; to prove itself a genuine demand, the progression of the concrete ego from immediate consciousness to pure knowing must have been indicated and exhibited through the necessity of the ego itself. Without this objective movement pure knowing, even in the shape of intellectual intuition, appears as an arbitrary standpoint, or even as one of the empirical *states* of consciousness with respect to which everything turns on whether or not it is found or can be produced in each and every individual. But inasmuch as this pure ego must be essential, pure knowing, and pure knowing is not *immediately* present in the individual consciousness but only as posited through the absolute act of the ego in raising itself to that standpoint, we lose the very advantage which is supposed to come from this beginning of philosophy, namely that it is something thoroughly familiar, something everyone finds in himself which can form the starting point for further reflection; that pure ego, on the contrary, in its abstract, essential nature, is something unknown to the ordinary consciousness, something it does not find therein. Instead, such a beginning brings with it the disadvantage of the illusion that whereas the thing under discussion is supposed to be something familiar, the ego of empirical self-consciousness, it is in fact something far removed from it. When pure knowing is characterised as ego, it acts as a perpetual reminder of the subjective ego whose limitations should be forgotten, and it fosters the idea that the propositions and relations resulting from the further development of the ego are present and can already be found in the ordinary consciousness—for in fact it is this of which they are asserted. This confusion, far from clarifying the problem of a beginning, only adds to the

9. This is a reference to Fichte.

behauptet werden, vorkommen und darin vorgefunden werden können. Diese Verwechslung bringt statt unmittelbarer Klarheit vielmehr nur eine um so grellere Verwirrung und gänzliche Desorientierung hervor; nach außen hat sie vollends die gröbsten Mißverständnisse veranlaßt.

Was ferner die *subjektive* Bestimmtheit des Ich überhaupt betrifft, so benimmt wohl das reine Wissen dem Ich seine beschränkte Bedeutung, an einem Objekte seinen unüberwindlichen Gegensatz zu haben. Aus diesem Grunde wäre es aber wenigstens *überflüssig*, noch diese subjektive Haltung und die Bestimmung des reinen Wesens als Ich beizubehalten. Allein diese Bestimmung führt nicht nur jene störende Zweideutigkeit mit sich, sondern sie bleibt auch, näher betrachtet, ein subjektives Ich. Die wirkliche Entwicklung der Wissenschaft, die vom Ich ausgeht, zeigt es, daß das Objekt darin die perennierende Bestimmung eines *Anderen* für das Ich hat und behält, daß also das Ich, von dem ausgegangen wird nicht das reine Wissen, das den Gegensatz des Bewußtseins in Wahrheit überwunden hat, sondern noch in der Erscheinung befangen ist.

Es ist hierbei noch die wesentliche Bemerkung zu machen, daß, *wenn an sich wohl Ich* als das reine Wissen oder als intellektuelle Anschauung bestimmt und als Anfang behauptet werden könnte, es in der Wissenschaft nicht um das zu tun ist, was *an sich* oder *innerlich* vorhanden sei, sondern um das Dasein des Innerlichen *im Denken* und um die *Bestimmtheit*, die ein solches in diesem Dasein hat. Was aber von der intellektuellen Anschauung oder — wenn ihr Gegenstand das Ewige, das Göttliche, das Absolute genannt wird — was vom Ewigen oder Absoluten im *Anfange* der Wissenschaft *da* ist, dies kann nichts anderes sein als erste, unmittelbare, einfache Bestimmung. Welcher reichere Name ihm gegeben werde, als das bloße Sein ausdrückt, so kann nur in Betracht kommen, wie solches Absolute in das *denkende* Wissen und in das Aussprechen dieses Wissens eintritt. Die intellektuelle Anschauung ist wohl die gewaltsame Zurückweisung des Vermittelns und der beweisenden, äußerlichen Reflexion. Was sie aber mehr ausspricht als einfache Unmittelbarkeit, ist ein Konkretes, ein in sich verschiedene Bestimmungen Enthaltendes. Das Aussprechen und die Darstellung eines solchen jedoch ist, wie schon bemerkt, eine vermittelnde Bewegung, die von *einer* der Bestimmungen anfängt und zu der anderen fortgeht, wenn diese auch zur ersten zurückgeht; — es ist eine Bewegung, die zugleich nicht willkürlich oder assertorisch sein darf. Von was daher in solcher Darstellung *angefangen* wird, ist nicht das Konkrete selbst, sondern nur das einfache Unmittelbare, von dem die Bewegung ausgeht. Außerdem fehlt, wenn ein Konkretes zum Anfange gemacht wird, der Beweis, dessen die Verbindung der im Konkreten enthaltenen Bestimmungen bedarf.

Wenn also im Ausdrucke des Absoluten oder Ewigen oder Gottes (und das unbestrittenste Recht hätte *Gott*, daß mit ihm der Anfang gemacht werde), wenn in deren Anschauung oder Gedanken *mehr liegt* als im reinen Sein, so soll das, was darin *liegt*, ins Wissen als denkendes, nicht vorstellendes, erst *hervortreten*; das, was darin liegt, sei so reich, als es wolle, so ist die Bestimmung, die ins

difficulties involved and tends completely to mislead; among the uninitiated it has given rise to the crudest misunderstandings.

Further, as regards the *subjective* determinateness of the ego in general, it is true that pure knowing frees the ego from the restricted meaning imposed on it by the insuperable opposition of its object; but for this reason it would be *superfluous* at least to retain this subjective attitude and the determination of pure knowing as ego. This determination, however, not only introduces the disturbing ambiguity mentioned, but closely examined it also remains a subjective *ego*. The actual development of the science which starts from the ego shows that in that development the object has and retains the perennial character of an other for the ego, and that the ego which formed the starting point is, therefore, still entangled in the world of appearance and is not the pure knowing which has in truth overcome the opposition of consciousness.

In this connection a further essential observation must be made, namely that although the ego could *in itself* or *in principle* [*an sich*] be characterised as pure knowing or as intellectual intuition and asserted as the beginning, we are not concerned in the science of logic with what is present only in *principle* or as something *inner*, but rather with the determinate reality *in thought* of what is inner and with the *determinateness* possessed by such an inner in this reality. But what, at the *beginning* of the science, is *actually present* of intellectual intuition—or of the eternal, the divine, the absolute, if its object be so named—cannot be anything else than a first, immediate, simple determination. Whatever richer name be given to it than is expressed by mere *being*, the consideration of such absolute must be restricted solely to the way in which it enters into our knowing as *thought* and is enunciated as such. True, intellectual intuition is the forcible rejection of mediation and the ratiocinative, external reflection; but what it enunciates above and beyond simple immediacy is something concrete, something which contains within itself diverse determinations. However, as we have remarked, the enunciation and exposition of such concrete beginning is a process of mediation which starts from *one* of the determinations and advances to the other, even though the latter returns to the first; it is a movement which at the same time may not be arbitrary or assertoric. Consequently, it is not the concrete something itself with which that exposition begins but only the simple immediacy from which the movement starts. And further, if something concrete is taken as the beginning, the conjunction of the determinations contained in it demands proof, and this is lacking.

If, therefore, in the expression of the absolute, or eternal, or God (and *God* has the absolutely undisputed right that the beginning be made with him)—if in the intuition or thought of these there is *implied more* than pure being—then this *more* must make its *appearance* in our knowing only as something *thought*, not as something imagined or figurately conceived; let what is present in intuition or figurate conception be as rich as it may, the determination which *first* emerges in knowing is simple, for only in what is simple is there

Wissen *zuerst* hervortritt, ein Einfaches, denn nur im Einfachen ist nicht mehr als der reine Anfang; nur das Unmittelbare ist einfach, denn nur im Unmittelbaren ist noch nicht ein Fortgegangensein von einem zu einem anderen. Was somit über das Sein ausgesprochen oder enthalten sein soll in den reicheren Formen des Vorstellens von Absolutem oder Gott, dies ist im Anfange nur leeres Wort und nur Sein; dies Einfache, das sonst keine weitere Bedeutung hat, dies Leere ist also schlechthin der Anfang der Philosophie.

Diese Einsicht ist selbst so einfach, daß dieser Anfang als solcher keiner Vorbereitung noch weiteren Einleitung bedarf; und diese Vorläufigkeit von Räsonnement über ihn konnte nicht die Absicht haben, ihn herbeizuführen, als vielmehr alle Vorläufigkeit zu entfernen.

nothing more than the pure beginning; only the immediate is simple, for only in the immediate has no advance yet been made from a *one* to an *other*. Consequently, whatever is intended to be expressed or implied beyond *being*, in the richer forms of representing the absolute or God, this is in the beginning only an empty word and only being; this simple determination which has no other meaning of any kind, this emptiness, is therefore simply as such the beginning of philosophy.

This insight is itself so simple that this beginning as such requires no preparation or further introduction; and, indeed, these preliminary, external reflections about it were not so much intended to lead up to it as rather to eliminate all preliminaries.

Allgemeine Einteilung des Seins

Das Sein ist *zuerst* gegen Anderes überhaupt bestimmt; *Zweitens* ist es sich innerhalb seiner selbst bestimmend; *Drittens*, indem diese Vorläufigkeit des Einteilens weggeworfen ist, ist es die abstrakte Unbestimmtheit und Unmittelbarkeit, in der es der Anfang sein muß.

Nach der *ersten* Bestimmung teilt das Sein sich gegen das *Wesen* ab, indem es weiterhin in seiner Entwicklung seine Totalität nur als *eine* Sphäre des Begriffs erweist und ihr als Moment eine andere Sphäre gegenüberstellt.

Nach der *zweiten* ist es die Sphäre, innerhalb welcher die Bestimmungen und die ganze Bewegung seiner Reflexion fällt. Das Sein wird sich darin in den drei Bestimmungen setzen:

I. als *Bestimmtheit* als solche; *Qualität*;
II. als *aufgehobene* Bestimmtheit; *Größe*, *Quantität*;
III. als *qualitativ* bestimmte *Quantität*; Maß.

Diese Einteilung ist hier, wie in der Einleitung von diesen Einteilungen überhaupt erinnert worden, eine vorläufige Anführung; ihre Bestimmungen haben erst aus der Bewegung des Seins selbst zu entstehen, sich dadurch zu definieren und zu rechtfertigen. Über die Abweichung dieser Einteilung von der gewöhnlichen Aufführung der Kategorien, nämlich als Quantität, Qualität, Relation und Modalität, was übrigens bei *Kant* nur die Titel für seine Kategorien sein sollen, in der Tat aber selbst — nur allgemeinere — Kategorien sind, ist hier nichts zu erinnern, da die ganze Ausführung das überhaupt von der gewöhnlichen Ordnung und Bedeutung der Kategorien Abweichende zeigen wird.

Nur dies kann etwa bemerkt werden, daß sonst die Bestimmung der *Quantität* vor der *Qualität* aufgeführt wird, und dies — wie das meiste — ohne weiteren Grund. Es ist bereits gezeigt worden, daß der Anfang sich mit dem Sein *als solchem* macht, daher mit dem qualitativen Sein. Aus der Vergleichung der Qualität mit der Quantität erhellt leicht, daß jene die der Natur nach erste ist. Denn die Quantität ist die schon negativ gewordene Qualität; die *Größe* ist die Bestimmtheit, die nicht mehr mit dem Sein eins, sondern schon von ihm unterschieden, die aufgehobene, gleichgültig gewordene Qualität ist. Sie schließt die Veränderlichkeit des Seins ein, ohne daß die Sache selbst, das Sein, dessen Bestimmung sie ist, durch sie verändert werde; dahingegen die qualitative Bestimmtheit mit ihrem Sein eins ist, nicht

Chapter Ten

Being: Text

General Division of Being

Being is determined, first, as against another in general;

Secondly, as immanently self-determining;

Thirdly, setting aside the preliminary character of this division, it is the abstract indeterminateness and immediacy in which it must be the beginning.

According to the first determination, *being* is classified as distinct from *essence,* for later in its development it proves to be in its totality only one sphere of the *Notion* and to this sphere as moment, it opposes another sphere.

According to the second determination, it is the sphere within which fall the determinations and the entire movement of its reflection. Here, *being* will posit itself in three determinations:

I. as *determinateness* as such: *quality*

II. as *sublated* determinateness: *magnitude, quantity*

III. as *qualitatively* determined *quantity: measure.*

At this stage, this division is, as was remarked of these divisions generally in the *Introduction,* a preliminary statement;[1] its determinations have first to arise from the movement of *being* itself and in so doing define and justify themselves. As regards the divergence of this classification from the usual presentation of the categories, namely, as *quantity, quality, relation* and *modality*—these moreover with Kant are supposed to be only titles for his categories though they are, in fact, themselves categories, only more general ones—this calls for no special comment here, as the entire exposition will show a complete divergence from the usual arrangement and significance of the categories.

This only perhaps can be remarked, that hitherto the determination of *quantity* has been made to precede *quality* and this—as is mostly the case—for no given reason. It has already been shown that the beginning is made with being *as such,* therefore, with qualitative being. It is easily seen from a comparison of quality with quantity that the former by its nature is first. For quantity is quality which has already become negative; *magnitude* is the determinateness which is no longer one with *being* but is already differentiated from it, sublated quality which has become indifferent. It includes the alterableness of being, although the category itself, namely being, of which it is the determination, is not altered by it. The qualitative determinateness, on the other hand, is one with its being:

1. See Hegel, *SL* 59/1: 56.

darüber hinausgeht noch innerhalb desselben steht, sondern dessen unmittelbare Beschränktheit ist. Die Qualität ist daher, als die *unmittelbare* Bestimmtheit, die erste und mit ihr der Anfang zu machen.

Das *Maß* ist eine *Relation*, aber nicht die Relation überhaupt, sondern bestimmt der Qualität und Quantität zueinander; die Kategorien, die Kant unter der Relation befaßt, werden ganz anderwärts ihre Stelle nehmen. Das Maß kann auch für eine Modalität, wenn man will, angesehen werden; aber indem bei *Kant* diese nicht mehr eine Bestimmung des Inhalts ausmachen, sondern nur die Beziehung desselben auf das Denken, auf das Subjektive, angehen soll, so ist dies eine ganz heterogene, hierher nicht gehörige Beziehung.

Die *dritte* Bestimmung des *Seins* fällt innerhalb des Abschnittes der Qualität, indem es sich als abstrakte Unmittelbarkeit zu einer einzelnen Bestimmtheit gegen seine anderen innerhalb seiner Sphäre herabsetzt.

Erster Abschnitt: Bestimmtheit (Qualität)

Das Sein ist das unbestimmte Unmittelbare; es ist frei von der Bestimmtheit gegen das Wesen sowie noch von jeder, die es innerhalb seiner selbst erhalten kann. Dies reflexionslose Sein ist das Sein, wie es unmittelbar nur an ihm selber ist.

Weil es unbestimmt ist, ist es qualitätsloses Sein; aber *an sich* kommt ihm der Charakter der Unbestimmtheit nur im Gegensatze gegen das *Bestimmte* oder Qualitative zu. Dem Sein überhaupt tritt aber das *bestimmte* Sein als solches gegenüber; damit aber macht seine Unbestimmtheit selbst seine Qualität aus. Es wird sich daher zeigen, daß das *erste* Sein an sich bestimmtes [ist], und hiermit

Zweitens, daß es in das *Dasein* übergeht, *Dasein* ist; daß aber dieses als endliches Sein sich aufhebt und in die unendliche Beziehung des Seins auf sich selbst,

Drittens in das *Fürsichsein* übergeht.

1. Sein

A. Sein

Sein, reines Sein, — ohne alle weitere Bestimmung. In seiner unbestimmten Unmittelbarkeit ist es nur sich selbst gleich und auch nicht ungleich gegen Anderes, hat keine Verschiedenheit innerhalb seiner noch nach außen. Durch irgendeine Bestimmung oder Inhalt, der in ihm unterschieden oder wodurch es als unterschieden von einem Anderen gesetzt würde, würde es nicht in seiner Reinheit festgehalten. Es ist die reine Unbestimmtheit und Leere. — Es ist *nichts* in ihm anzuschauen, wenn von Anschauen hier gesprochen werden kann; oder es ist nur dies reine, leere Anschauen selbst. Es ist ebensowenig etwas in ihm zu denken, oder es ist ebenso nur dies leere

it neither goes beyond it nor is internal to it, but is its immediate limitedness. Quality therefore, as the *immediate* determinateness, is primary and it is with it that the beginning must be made.

Measure is a *relation*, but not relation in general, for it is the specific relation between *quality* and *quantity*; the categories which Kant includes under relation will come up for consideration in quite another place. Measure can also, if one wishes, be regarded as a modality; but since with Kant modality is supposed no longer to constitute a determination of the content, but to concern only the relation of the content to thought, to the subjective element, it is a quite heterogeneous relation and is not pertinent here.[2]

The third determination of *being* falls within the section Quality, for as abstract immediacy it reduces itself to a single determinateness in relation to its other determinatenesses within its sphere.

Section One: Determinateness (Quality)

Being is the indeterminate *immediate*; it is free from determinateness in relation to *essence* and also from any which it can possess within itself. This reflectionless *being* is *being* as it is immediately in its own self alone.

Because it is indeterminate being, it lacks all quality; but *in itself*, the character of indeterminateness attaches to it only in contrast to what is *determinate* or qualitative. But *determinate* being comes to stand in contrast to being in general, so that the very indeterminateness of the latter constitutes its quality.[3] It will therefore be shown that the *first* being is in itself determinate, and therefore, *secondly*, that it passes over into *determinate being*—is *determinate being*—but that this latter as finite being sublates itself and passes over into the infinite relation of being to its own self, that is, *thirdly*, into *being-for-self*.

1. Being

A. Being

Being, pure being, without any further determination. In its indeterminate immediacy it is equal only to itself. It is also not unequal relatively to an other; it has no diversity within itself nor any with a reference outwards. It would not be held fast in its purity if it contained any determination or content which could be distinguished in it or by which it could be distinguished from an other. It is pure indeterminateness and emptiness. There is *nothing* to be intuited in it, if one can speak here of intuiting; or, it is only this pure intuiting itself. Just as little is anything to be thought in it, or it is equally only this

2. See Kant, *CPR* 322/266 (B 266).

3. Miller translates *tritt* [. . .] *gegenüber* as "stands in contrast." See chapter 15, below, p. 295, and chapter 16, below, p. 305.

Denken. Das Sein, das unbestimmte Unmittelbare ist in der Tat *Nichts* und nicht mehr noch weniger als Nichts.

B. Nichts

Nichts, das reine Nichts; es ist einfache Gleichheit mit sich selbst, vollkommene Leerheit, Bestimmungs- und Inhaltslosigkeit; Ununterschiedenheit in ihm selbst. — Insofern Anschauen oder Denken hier erwähnt werden kann, so gilt es als ein Unterschied, ob etwas oder *nichts* angeschaut oder gedacht wird. Nichts Anschauen oder Denken hat also eine Bedeutung; beide werden unterschieden, so *ist* (existiert) Nichts in unserem Anschauen oder Denken; oder vielmehr ist es das leere Anschauen und Denken selbst und dasselbe leere Anschauen oder Denken als das reine Sein. — Nichts ist somit dieselbe Bestimmung oder vielmehr Bestimmungslosigkeit und damit überhaupt dasselbe, was das reine *Sein* ist.

C. Werden

a. Einheit des Seins und Nichts

Das reine Sein und das reine Nichts ist also dasselbe. Was die Wahrheit ist, ist weder das Sein noch das Nichts, sondern daß das Sein in Nichts und das Nichts in Sein — nicht übergeht, sondern übergegangen ist. Aber ebensosehr ist die Wahrheit nicht ihre Ununterschiedenheit, sondern daß *sie nicht dasselbe*, daß sie *absolut unterschieden*, aber ebenso ungetrennt und untrennbar sind und unmittelbar *jedes in seinem Gegenteil verschwindet*. Ihre Wahrheit ist also diese *Bewegung* des unmittelbaren Verschwindens des einen in dem anderen: *das Werden*; eine Bewegung, worin beide unterschieden sind, aber durch einen Unterschied, der sich ebenso unmittelbar aufgelöst hat.

Anmerkungen

Nichts pflegt dem *Etwas* entgegengesetzt zu werden; Etwas aber ist schon ein bestimmtes Seiendes, das sich von anderem Etwas unterscheidet; so ist also auch das dem Etwas entgegengesetzte Nichts, das Nichts von irgend Etwas, ein bestimmtes Nichts. Hier aber ist das Nichts in seiner unbestimmten Einfachheit zu nehmen. — Wollte man es für richtiger halten, daß statt des Nichts dem Sein das *Nichtsein* entgegengesetzt würde, so wäre in Rücksicht auf das Resultat nichts dawider zu haben, denn im *Nichtsein* ist die Beziehung auf das *Sein* enthalten; es ist beides, Sein und die Negation desselben, in *einem* ausgesprochen, das Nichts, wie es im Werden ist. Aber es ist zunächst nicht um die Form der Entgegensetzung, d. i. zugleich der *Beziehung* zu tun, sondern um die abstrakte, unmittelbare Negation, das Nichts rein für sich, die beziehungslose Verneinung, — was man, wenn man will, auch durch das bloße *Nicht* ausdrücken könnte. […]

Diese Unbestimmtheit oder abstrakte Negation, welche so das Sein an ihm selbst hat, ist es, was die äußere wie die innere Reflexion ausspricht, indem sie es dem Nichts gleichsetzt, es für ein leeres Gedankending, für Nichts erklärt. — Oder, kann man sich ausdrücken, weil das Sein das Be-

empty thinking. Being, the indeterminate immediate, is in fact *nothing,* and neither more nor less than *nothing.*

B. Nothing

Nothing, pure nothing: it is simply equality with itself, complete emptiness, absence of all determination and content—undifferentiatedness in itself. In so far as intuiting or thinking can be mentioned here, it counts as a distinction whether something or *nothing* is intuited or thought. To intuit or think nothing has, therefore, a meaning; both are distinguished and thus nothing *is* (exists) in our intuiting or thinking; or rather it is empty intuition and thought itself, and the same empty intuition or thought as pure being. Nothing is, therefore, the same determination, or rather absence of determination, and thus altogether the same as, pure *being.*

C. Becoming

(a) Unity of Being and Nothing

Pure Being and *pure nothing* are, therefore, the same. What is the truth is neither being nor nothing, but that being—does not pass over but has passed over—into nothing, and nothing into being.[4] But it is equally true that they are not undistinguished from each other, that, on the contrary, they are not the same, that they are absolutely distinct, and yet that they are unseparated and inseparable and that each immediately *vanishes in its opposite.* Their truth is therefore, this movement of the immediate vanishing of the one in the other: *becoming,* a movement in which both are distinguished, but by a difference which has equally immediately resolved itself.

Remarks

Nothing is usually opposed to *something*; but the being of *something* is already determinate and is distinguished from another *something*; and so therefore the nothing which is opposed to the something is also the nothing of a particular something, a determinate nothing. Here, however, nothing is to be taken in its indeterminate simplicity. Should it be held more correct to oppose to being, *non-being* instead of nothing, there would be no objection to this so far as the result is concerned, for in *non-being* the relation to *being* is contained: both being and its negation are enunciated in a *single* term, nothing, as it is in becoming. But we are concerned first of all not with the form of opposition (with the form, that is, also of *relation)* but with the abstract, immediate negation: nothing, purely on its own account, negation devoid of any relations—what could also be expressed if one so wished merely by 'not'. [. . .]

It is this indeterminateness or abstract negation which being thus has present within it,[5] which reflection, both outer and inner, enunciates when it equates it with nothing, declares it to be an empty product of thought, to be nothing. Or it can be expressed thus: because being is devoid of all determination

---

4. See chapter 14, below, p. 271.
5. Miller renders this as "which thus has being present within it."

stimmungslose ist, ist es nicht die (affirmative) Bestimmtheit, die es ist, nicht Sein, sondern Nichts.

In der reinen Reflexion des Anfangs, wie er in dieser Logik mit dem *Sein* als solchem gemacht wird, ist der Übergang noch verborgen; weil das *Sein* nur als unmittelbar gesetzt ist, bricht das *Nichts* an ihm nur unmittelbar hervor. Aber alle folgenden Bestimmungen, wie gleich das *Dasein*, sind konkreter; es ist an diesem das schon *gesetzt*, was den Widerspruch jener Abstraktionen und daher ihr Übergehen enthält und hervorbringt. Beim Sein als jenem Einfachen, Unmittelbaren wird die Erinnerung, daß es Resultat der vollkommenen Abstraktion, also schon von daher abstrakte Negativität, Nichts ist, hinter der Wissenschaft zurückgelassen, welche innerhalb ihrer selbst, ausdrücklich vom *Wesen* aus, jene einseitige *Unmittelbarkeit* als eine vermittelte darstellen wird, wo das Sein als *Existenz* und das Vermittelnde dieses Seins, der Grund, *gesetzt* ist.

Mit jener Erinnerung läßt sich der Übergang vom Sein in Nichts als etwas selbst Leichtes und Triviales so vorstellen oder auch, wie man es nennt, *erklären* und *begreiflich* machen, daß freilich das Sein, welches zum Anfang der Wissenschaft gemacht worden, Nichts sei, denn man könne von allem abstrahieren, und wenn von allem abstrahiert worden, so bleibe Nichts übrig. Aber, kann man fortfahren, somit sei der Anfang nicht ein Affirmatives, nicht Sein, sondern eben Nichts, und Nichts sei dann auch das *Ende*, wenigstens sosehr als das unmittelbare Sein, und selbst noch vielmehr. Das Kürzeste ist, solches Räsonieren gewähren zu lassen und zuzusehen, wie denn die Resultate beschaffen sind, auf welche es pocht. Daß hiernach das Nichts das Resultat jenes Räsonnements wäre und nun der Anfang mit Nichts (wie in chinesischer Philosophie) gemacht werden sollte, so wäre darum nicht die Hand umzukehren, denn ehe man sie umkehrte, hätte sich ebensosehr dies Nichts in Sein verkehrt. […]

b. Momente des Werdens

Das Werden, Entstehen und Vergehen, ist die Ungetrenntheit des Seins und Nichts; nicht die Einheit, welche vom Sein und Nichts abstrahiert, sondern als Einheit *des Seins* und *Nichts* ist es diese *bestimmte* Einheit oder [die,] in welcher sowohl Sein als Nichts *ist*. Aber indem Sein und Nichts jedes ungetrennt von seinem Anderen ist, *ist es nicht*. Sie *sind* also in dieser Einheit, aber als Verschwindende, nur als *Aufgehobene*. Sie sinken von ihrer zunächst vorgestellten *Selbständigkeit* zu *Momenten* herab, *noch unterschiedenen*, aber zugleich aufgehobenen.

Nach dieser ihrer Unterschiedenheit sie aufgefaßt, ist jedes in *derselben* als Einheit mit dem *anderen*. Das Werden enthält also Sein und Nichts als *zwei solche Einheiten*, deren jede selbst Einheit des Seins und Nichts ist; die eine das Sein als unmittelbar und als Beziehung auf das Nichts; die andere das Nichts als unmittelbar und als Beziehung auf das Sein: die Bestimmungen sind in ungleichem Werte in diesen Einheiten.

Das Werden ist auf diese Weise in gedoppelter Bestimmung; in der einen ist das Nichts als unmittelbar, d. h. sie ist anfangend vom Nichts, das sich

whatsoever, it is not the (affirmative) determinateness which it is; it is not being but nothing.

In the pure reflection of the beginning as it is made in this logic with being as such, the transition is still concealed; because *being* is posited only as immediate, therefore *nothing* emerges in it only immediately. But all the subsequent determinations, like determinate being which immediately follows, are more concrete; in determinate being there is already *posited* that which contains and produces the contradiction of those abstractions and therefore their transition. When being is taken in this simplicity and immediacy, the recollection that it is the result of complete abstraction, and so for that reason alone is abstract negativity, nothing, is left behind, outside the science, which, within its own self, from *essence* onwards will expressly exhibit the said one-sided *immediacy* as a mediated immediacy where being is *posited* as *existence* and the mediating agent of this being is *posited* as *ground.*

In the light of such recollection, the transition from being into nothing can be represented, or, as it is said, *explained* and *made intelligible,* as something even easy and trivial; of course the being which is made the beginning of the science is *nothing,* for abstraction can be made from everything, and if abstraction is made from everything then *nothing* is left over. But, it may be continued, the beginning is thus not an affirmative, not being, but just nothing, and nothing is then also the *end,* at least as much as immediate being, and even more so. The shortest way is to let such reasoning take its course and then wait and see what is the nature of its boasted results. That *nothing* would be the result of such reasoning and that now the beginning should be made with nothing (as in Chinese philosophy), need not cause us to lift a finger, for before we could do so this nothing would no less have converted itself into being […].

(b) *Moments of Becoming: Coming-to-Be and Ceasing-to-Be*

Becoming is the unseparatedness of being and nothing, not the unity which abstracts from being and nothing; but as the unity of *being* and *nothing* it is this *determinate* unity in which there *is* both being and nothing. But in so far as being and nothing, each unseparated from its other, *is*, each *is not*. They *are* therefore in this unity but only as vanishing, sublated moments. They sink from their initially imagined *self-subsistence* to the status of *moments,* which are still *distinct* but at the same time are sublated.

Grasped as thus distinguished, each moment is in this *distinguishedness* as a unity with the *other.* Becoming therefore contains being and nothing as two such unities, *each* of which is itself a unity of being and nothing; the one is being as immediate and as relation to nothing, and the other is nothing as immediate and as relation to being; the determinations are of unequal values in these unities.

Becoming is in this way in a double determination. In one of them, *nothing* is immediate, that is, the determination starts from nothing which relates itself

auf das Sein bezieht, d. h. in dasselbe übergeht, in der anderen ist das Sein als unmittelbar, d. i. sie ist anfangend vom Sein, das in das Nichts übergeht, — *Entstehen* und *Vergehen*.

Beide sind dasselbe, Werden, und auch als diese so unterschiedenen Richtungen durchdringen und paralysieren sie sich gegenseitig. Die eine ist *Vergehen*; Sein geht in Nichts über, aber Nichts ist ebensosehr das Gegenteil seiner selbst, Übergehen in Sein, Entstehen. Dies Entstehen ist die andere Richtung; Nichts geht in Sein über, aber Sein hebt ebensosehr sich selbst auf und ist vielmehr das Übergehen in Nichts, ist Vergehen. — Sie heben sich nicht gegenseitig, nicht das eine äußerlich das andere auf, sondern jedes hebt sich an sich selbst auf und ist an ihm selbst das Gegenteil seiner.

c. Aufheben des Werdens

Das Gleichgewicht, worein sich Entstehen und Vergehen setzen, ist zunächst das Werden selbst. Aber dieses geht ebenso in *ruhige Einheit* zusammen. Sein und Nichts sind in ihm nur als Verschwindende; aber das Werden als solches ist nur durch die Unterschiedenheit derselben. Ihr Verschwinden ist daher das Verschwinden des Werdens oder Verschwinden des Verschwindens selbst. Das Werden ist eine haltungslose Unruhe, die in ein ruhiges Resultat zusammensinkt.

Dies könnte auch so ausgedrückt werden: Das Werden ist das Verschwinden von Sein in Nichts und von Nichts in Sein und das Verschwinden von Sein und Nichts überhaupt; aber es beruht zugleich auf dem Unterschiede derselben. Es widerspricht sich also in sich selbst, weil es solches in sich vereint, das sich entgegengesetzt ist; eine solche Vereinigung aber zerstört sich.

Dies Resultat ist das Verschwundensein, aber nicht als *Nichts*; so wäre es nur ein Rückfall in die eine der schon aufgehobenen Bestimmungen, nicht Resultat des Nichts *und des Seins*. Es ist die zur ruhigen Einfachheit gewordene Einheit des Seins und Nichts. Die ruhige Einfachheit aber ist *Sein*, jedoch ebenso nicht mehr für sich, sondern als Bestimmung des Ganzen.

Das Werden so [als] Übergehen in die Einheit des Seins und Nichts, welche als *seiend* ist oder die Gestalt der einseitigen *unmittelbaren* Einheit dieser Momente hat, ist *das Dasein*.

Anmerkung

Aufheben und das *Aufgehobene* (das *Ideelle*) ist einer der wichtigsten Begriffe der Philosophie, eine Grundbestimmung, die schlechthin allenthalben wiederkehrt, deren Sinn bestimmt aufzufassen und besonders vom Nichts zu unterscheiden ist. — Was sich aufhebt, wird dadurch nicht zu Nichts. Nichts ist das *Unmittelbare*; ein Aufgehobenes dagegen ist ein *Vermitteltes*, es ist das Nichtseiende, aber als *Resultat*, das von einem Sein ausgegangen ist; es hat daher die *Bestimmtheit*, *aus der es herkommt*, *noch an sich*.

Aufheben hat in der Sprache den gedoppelten Sinn, daß es soviel als

to being, or in other words changes into it; in the other, *being* is immediate, that is, the determination starts from being which changes into nothing: the former is coming-to-be and the latter is ceasing-to-be.

Both are the same, *becoming,* and although they differ so in direction they interpenetrate and paralyse each other. The one is *ceasing-to-be:* being passes over into nothing, but nothing is equally the opposite of itself, transition into being, coming-to-be. This coming-to-be is the other direction: nothing passes over into being, but being equally sublates itself and is rather transition into nothing, is ceasing-to-be. They are not reciprocally sublated—the one does not sublate the other externally—but each sublates itself in itself and is in its own self the opposite of itself.

(c) Sublation of Becoming

The resultant equilibrium of coming-to-be and ceasing-to-be is in the first place *becoming* itself. But this equally settles into a stable unity. Being and nothing are in this equilibrium[6] only as vanishing moments; yet becoming as such *is* only through their distinguishedness. Their vanishing, therefore, is the vanishing of becoming or the vanishing of the vanishing itself. Becoming is an unstable unrest which settles into a stable result.

This could also be expressed thus: becoming is the vanishing of being in nothing and of nothing in being and the vanishing of being and nothing generally; but at the same time it rests on the distinction between them. It is therefore inherently self-contradictory, because the determinations it unites within itself are opposed to each other; but such a union destroys itself.

This result is the vanishedness of becoming, but it is not *nothing*; as such it would only be a relapse into one of the already sublated determinations, not the resultant of *nothing and being.* It is the unity of being and nothing which has settled into a stable oneness. But this stable oneness is being, yet no longer as a determination on its own but as a determination of the whole.

Becoming, as this transition into the unity of being and nothing, a unity which is in the form of being or has the form of the one-sided *immediate* unity of these moments, is *determinate being.*

Remark: The Expression 'To Sublate'

To sublate, and the *sublated* (that which exists ideally as a moment), constitute one of the most important notions in philosophy. It is a fundamental determination which repeatedly occurs throughout the whole of philosophy, the meaning of which is to be clearly grasped and especially distinguished from *nothing.* What is sublated is not thereby reduced to nothing. Nothing is *immediate*; what is sublated, on the other hand, is the result of *mediation*; it is a non-being but as a *result* which had its origin in a being. It still has, therefore, *in itself* the *determinateness from which it originates.*

'*To sublate*' has a twofold meaning in the language: on the one hand it

6. Miller has "in this unity." The German, however, is "in ihm" not "in ihr."

aufbewahren, *erhalten* bedeutet und zugleich soviel als aufhören lassen, *ein Ende machen*. Das Aufbewahren selbst schließt schon das Negative in sich, daß etwas seiner Unmittelbarkeit und damit einem den äußerlichen Einwirkungen offenen Dasein entnommen wird, um es zu erhalten. — So ist das Aufgehobene ein zugleich Aufbewahrtes, das nur seine Unmittelbarkeit verloren hat, aber darum nicht vernichtet ist. — Die angegebenen zwei Bestimmungen des *Aufhebens* können lexikalisch als zwei *Bedeutungen* dieses Wortes aufgeführt werden. Auffallend müßte es aber dabei sein, daß eine Sprache dazu gekommen ist, ein und dasselbe Wort für zwei entgegengesetzte Bestimmungen zu gebrauchen. Für das spekulative Denken ist es erfreulich, in der Sprache Wörter zu finden, welche eine spekulative Bedeutung an ihnen selbst haben; die deutsche Sprache hat mehrere dergleichen. Der Doppelsinn des lateinischen *tollere* (der durch den Ciceronianischen Witz "tollendum esse Octavium" berühmt geworden) geht nicht so weit, die affirmative Bestimmung geht nur bis zum Emporheben. Etwas ist nur insofern aufgehoben, als es in die Einheit mit seinem Entgegengesetzten getreten ist; in dieser näheren Bestimmung als ein Reflektiertes kann es passend *Moment* genannt werden. *Gewicht* und *Entfernung* von einem Punkt heißen beim Hebel dessen mechanische *Momente*, um der *Dieselbigkeit* ihrer Wirkung willen bei aller sonstigen Verschiedenheit eines Reellen, wie das ein Gewicht ist, und eines Ideellen, der bloßen räumlichen Bestimmung, der Linie; s. *Enzyklopädie der philosophischen Wissenschaften*, 3. Ausgabe [1830], § 261 Anm. — Noch öfter wird die Bemerkung sich aufdrängen, daß die philosophische Kunstsprache für reflektierte Bestimmungen lateinische Ausdrücke gebraucht, entweder weil die Muttersprache keine Ausdrücke dafür hat oder, wenn sie deren hat wie hier, weil ihr Ausdruck mehr an das Unmittelbare, die fremde Sprache aber mehr an das Reflektierte erinnert.

Der nähere Sinn und Ausdruck, den Sein und Nichts, indem sie nunmehr *Momente* sind, erhalten, hat sich bei der Betrachtung des Daseins als der Einheit, in der sie aufbewahrt sind, zu ergeben. Sein ist Sein und Nichts ist Nichts nur in ihrer Unterschiedenheit voneinander; in ihrer Wahrheit aber, in ihrer Einheit sind sie als diese Bestimmungen verschwunden und sind nun etwas anderes. Sein und Nichts sind dasselbe; *darum weil sie dasselbe sind, sind sie nicht mehr Sein und Nichts* und haben eine verschiedene Bestimmung; im Werden waren sie Entstehen und Vergehen; im Dasein als einer anders bestimmten Einheit sind sie wieder anders bestimmte Momente. Diese Einheit bleibt nun ihre Grundlage, aus der sie nicht mehr zur abstrakten Bedeutung von Sein und Nichts heraustreten.

means to preserve, to maintain, and equally it also means to cause to cease, to put an end to. Even 'to preserve' includes a negative element, namely, that something is removed from its immediacy and so from an existence which is open to external influences, in order to preserve it. Thus what is sublated is at the same time preserved; it has only lost its immediacy but is not on that account annihilated. The two definitions of 'to sublate' which we have given can be quoted as two dictionary *meanings* of this word. But it is certainly remarkable to find that a language has come to use one and the same word for two opposite meanings. It is a delight to speculative thought to find in the language words which have in themselves a speculative meaning; the German language has a number of such. The double meaning of the Latin *tollere* (which has become famous through the Ciceronian pun: *tollendum esse Octavium*) does not go so far; its affirmative determination signifies only a lifting-up.[7] Something is sublated only in so far as it has entered into unity with its opposite; in this more particular signification as something reflected, it may fittingly be called a *moment.* In the case of the lever, weight and distance from a point are called its mechanical moments on account of the sameness of their effect, in spite of the contrast otherwise between something real, such as a weight, and something ideal, such as a mere spatial determination, a line.[8] We shall often have occasion to notice that the technical language of philosophy employs Latin terms for reflected determinations, either because the mother tongue has no words for them or if it has, as here, because its expression calls to mind more what is immediate, whereas the foreign language suggests more what is reflected.

The more precise meaning and expression which being and nothing receive, now that they are *moments,* is to be ascertained from the consideration of determinate being as the unity in which they are preserved. Being is being, and nothing is nothing, only in their contradistinction from each other; but in their truth, in their unity, they have vanished as these determinations and are now something else. Being and nothing are the same; *but just because they are the same they are no longer being and nothing,* but now have a different significance. In becoming they were coming-to-be and ceasing-to-be; in determinate being, a differently determined unity, they are again differently determined moments. This unity now remains their base from which they do not again emerge in the abstract significance of being and nothing.

---

7. "Octavius must be raised up/removed." Miller has *est* for *esse.*
8. See Hegel, *EPN* 41–2/56–7 (§261).

2. Das Dasein

Dasein ist *bestimmtes* Sein; seine Bestimmtheit ist *seiende* Bestimmtheit, *Qualität.* Durch seine Qualität ist *Etwas* gegen ein *Anderes*, ist *veränderlich* und *endlich*, nicht nur gegen ein Anderes, sondern an ihm schlechthin negativ bestimmt. Diese seine Negation dem endlichen Etwas zunächst gegenüber ist das *Unendliche;* der abstrakte Gegensatz, in welchem diese Bestimmungen erscheinen, löst sich in die gegensatzlose Unendlichkeit, in das *Fürsichsein* auf.

Die Abhandlung des Daseins hat so die drei Abteilungen:

A. das *Dasein als solches,*

B. *Etwas und Anderes*, die *Endlichkeit,*

C. die *qualitative Unendlichkeit.*

A. Dasein als solches

An dem Dasein

a) *als solchem* ist zunächst seine Bestimmtheit

b) als *Qualität* zu unterscheiden. Diese aber ist sowohl in der einen als in der anderen Bestimmung des Daseins zu nehmen, als *Realität* und als *Negation.* Aber in diesen Bestimmtheiten ist Dasein ebensosehr in sich reflektiert; und als solches gesetzt ist es

c) *Etwas*, Daseiendes.

a. Dasein überhaupt

Aus dem Werden geht das Dasein hervor. Das Dasein ist das einfache Einssein des Seins und Nichts. Es hat um dieser Einfachheit willen die Form von einem *Unmittelbaren.* Seine Vermittlung, das Werden, liegt hinter ihm; sie hat sich aufgehoben, und das Dasein erscheint daher als ein Erstes, von dem ausgegangen werde. Es ist zunächst in der einseitigen Bestimmung des *Seins*; die andere, die es enthält, das *Nichts*, wird sich gleichfalls an ihm hervortun, gegen jene.

Es ist nicht bloßes Sein, sondern *Dasein*; etymologisch genommen: Sein an einem gewissen *Orte*; aber die Raumvorstellung gehört nicht hierher. Dasein ist, nach seinem Werden, überhaupt *Sein* mit einem *Nichtsein*, so daß dies *Nichtsein* in einfache Einheit mit dem Sein aufgenommen ist. Das *Nichtsein* so in das Sein aufgenommen, daß das konkrete Ganze in der Form des Seins, der Unmittelbarkeit ist, macht die *Bestimmtheit* als solche aus.

Das *Ganze* ist gleichfalls in der Form, d. i. *Bestimmtheit* des Seins — denn Sein hat im Werden sich gleichfalls nur ein Moment zu sein gezeigt — ein

Chapter Eleven

Determinate Being: Text

2. *Determinate Being*

In considering determinate being [*Dasein*] the emphasis falls on its determinate [*bestimmt*] character; the determinateness is in the form of *being*, and as such it is *quality*. Through its quality, something is determined as opposed to an other, as *alterable* and *finite*; and as negatively determined not only against an other but also in its own self. This its negation as at first opposed to the finite something is the *infinite*; the abstract opposition in which these determinations appear resolves itself into the *infinity* which is free from the opposition, into *being-for-self*.

The treatment of determinate being falls therefore into three parts:

A. Determinate being as such
B. Something and other, finitude
C. Qualitative infinity.

A. Determinate Being as Such

In determinate being *(a) as such*, its determinateness is first of all *(b)* to be distinguished as *quality*. This, however, is to be taken as well in the one determination of determinate being as in the other—as *reality* and *negation*. But in these determinatenesses determinate being is equally reflected into itself; and posited as such it is *(c) something, a* determinate being.

(a) Determinate Being in General

From becoming there issues determinate being, which is the simple oneness of being and nothing. Because of this oneness it has the form of *immediacy*. Its mediation, becoming, lies behind it; it has sublated itself and determinate being appears, therefore, as a first, as a starting-point for the ensuing development. It is first of all in the one-sided determination of *being*; the other determination, *nothing*, will likewise display itself and in contrast to it.

It is not mere being, but determinate being [*Dasein*], etymologically taken, being in a certain *place*; but the idea of space is irrelevant here. Determinate being as the result of its becoming is, in general, being with a non-being such that this non-being is taken up into simple unity with being. *Non-being* thus taken up into being in such a way that the concrete whole is in the form of being, of immediacy, constitutes *determinateness* as such.

The *whole* is likewise in the form, that is, in the *determinateness* of being, for being has likewise shown itself in becoming to be only a moment—a sublated, negatively determined being; but it is such *for us in our reflection*, it is not yet

aufgehobenes, negativ-bestimmtes; aber so ist es *für uns in unserer Reflexion*, noch nicht *gesetzt* an ihm selbst. Aber die Bestimmtheit des Daseins als solche ist die gesetzte, die auch im Ausdruck "*Da*sein" liegt. — Beides ist immer sehr wohl voneinander zu unterscheiden; das nur, was *gesetzt* ist an einem Begriffe, gehört in die entwickelnde Betrachtung desselben, zu seinem Inhalte. Die noch nicht an ihm selbst gesetzte Bestimmtheit aber gehört unserer Reflexion, sie betreffe nun die Natur des Begriffs selbst oder sie sei äußere Vergleichung; eine Bestimmtheit der letzteren Art bemerklich zu machen, kann nur zur Erläuterung oder Vorausandeutung des Ganges dienen, der in der Entwicklung selbst sich darstellen wird. Daß das Ganze, die Einheit des Seins und des Nichts, in der *einseitigen Bestimmtheit* des Seins sei, ist eine äußerliche Reflexion; in der Negation aber, im Etwas und *Anderen* usf. wird sie dazu kommen, als *gesetzte* zu sein. — Es hat hier auf den angegebenen Unterschied aufmerksam gemacht werden sollen; über alles aber, was die Reflexion sich erlauben kann zu bemerken, Rechenschaft zu geben, würde in die Weitläufigkeit führen, das zu antizipieren, was sich an der Sache selbst ergeben muß. Wenn dergleichen Reflexionen dienen können, die Übersicht und damit das Verständnis zu erleichtern, so führen sie wohl auch den Nachteil herbei, als unberechtigte Behauptungen, Gründe und Grundlagen für das Weitere auszusehen. Man soll sie daher für nichts mehr nehmen, als was sie sein sollen, und sie von dem unterscheiden, was ein Moment im Fortgange der Sache selbst ist.

Das Dasein entspricht dem *Sein* der vorigen Sphäre; das Sein jedoch ist das Unbestimmte, es ergeben sich deswegen keine Bestimmungen an demselben. Aber das Dasein ist ein bestimmtes Sein, ein *konkretes*; es tun sich daher sogleich mehrere Bestimmungen, unterschiedene Verhältnisse seiner Momente an ihm auf.

b. Qualität

Um der Unmittelbarkeit willen, in der im Dasein Sein und Nichts eins sind, gehen sie nicht übereinander hinaus; soweit das Dasein seiend ist, soweit ist es Nichtsein, ist es bestimmt. Das Sein ist nicht das *Allgemeine*, die Bestimmtheit nicht das *Besondere*. Die Bestimmtheit hat sich noch *nicht* vom *Sein abgelöst*; zwar wird sie sich auch nicht mehr von ihm ablösen, denn das nunmehr zum Grunde liegende Wahre ist die Einheit des Nichtseins mit dem Sein; auf ihr als dem Grunde ergeben sich alle ferneren Bestimmungen. Aber die Beziehung, in der hier die Bestimmtheit mit dem Sein steht, ist die unmittelbare Einheit beider, so daß noch keine Unterscheidung derselben gesetzt ist.

Die Bestimmtheit so für sich isoliert, als *seiende* Bestimmtheit, ist die *Qualität*, — ein ganz Einfaches, Unmittelbares. Die *Bestimmtheit* überhaupt ist das Allgemeinere, das ebensosehr auch das Quantitative wie weiter Bestimmte sein kann. Um dieser Einfachheit willen ist von der Qualität als solcher weiter nichts zu sagen.

Aber das Dasein, in welchem ebensowohl das Nichts als das Sein enthalten, ist selbst der Maßstab für die Einseitigkeit der Qualität als nur *unmittelbarer* oder *seiender* Bestimmtheit. Sie ist ebensosehr in der Bestimmung

posited as such in its own self. But the determinateness as such of determinate being is the determinateness which is posited, and this is implied in the expression *Dasein* [*there*-being or being which is *there*]. The two are always to be clearly distinguished from each other; only that which is *posited* in a Notion belongs in the dialectical development of that Notion to its content; whereas the determinateness that is not yet posited in the Notion itself belongs to our reflection, whether it concerns the nature of the Notion itself or is an external comparison. To draw attention to a determinateness of the latter kind can only serve to elucidate or indicate in advance the course which will be exhibited in the development itself. That the whole, the unity of being and nothing, is in the one-sided determinateness of being is an external reflection; but in the negation, in *something* and *other* and so on, it will come to be *posited.* It was necessary here to draw attention to the distinction referred to; but to take account of all the remarks which may be prompted by reflection would lead to the prolixity of anticipating what must yield itself in the subject matter. Such reflections may facilitate a general view and thereby an understanding of the development, but they also have the disadvantage of appearing as unjustified assertions, grounds and foundations for what is to follow. They should therefore not be taken for more than they are supposed to be and should be distinguished from what is a moment in the development of the subject matter itself.

Determinate being corresponds to *being* in the previous sphere, but being is indeterminate and therefore no determinations issue from it. *Determinate* being, however, is *concrete*; consequently a number of determinations, distinct relations of its moments, make their appearance in it.

(b) Quality

Because of the immediacy of the oneness of being and nothing in determinate being, they do not extend beyond each other; so far as determinate being is in the form of being, so far is it non-being, so far is it determinate. Being is not the *universal,* determinateness not the *particular*. Determinateness has not yet severed itself from being; and indeed it will no more sever itself from being, for the truth which from now on underlies them as ground is the unity of non-being with being; on this as ground all further determinations are developed. But the relation in which determinateness here stands to being is the immediate unity of both, so that as yet no differentiation of this unity is posited.

Determinateness thus isolated by itself in the form of *being* is *quality*—which is wholly simple and immediate. *Determinateness* as such is the more universal term which can equally be further determined as quantity and so on. Because of this simple character of quality as such, there is nothing further to be said about it.

Determinate being, however, in which nothing no less than being is contained, is itself the criterion for the one-sidedness of quality as a determinateness which is only *immediate* or only in the form of *being.* It is equally to be posited in the determination of nothing, whereby then the immediate or *affirmative* [*seiend*] de-

des Nichts zu setzen, womit dann die unmittelbare oder die *seiende* Bestimmtheit als eine unterschiedene, reflektierte gesetzt wird; das Nichts so als das Bestimmte einer Bestimmtheit ist ebenso ein Reflektiertes, eine *Verneinung*. Die Qualität, so daß sie unterschieden als *seiende* gelte, ist die *Realität*; sie als mit einer Verneinung behaftet, *Negation* überhaupt, [ist] gleichfalls eine Qualität, aber die für einen Mangel gilt, sich weiterhin als Grenze, Schranke bestimmt.

Beide sind ein Dasein; aber in der *Realität* als Qualität mit dem Akzente, eine *seiende* zu sein, ist es versteckt, daß sie die Bestimmtheit, also auch die Negation enthält; die Realität gilt daher nur als etwas Positives, aus welchem Verneinung, Beschränktheit, Mangel ausgeschlossen sei. Die Negation als bloßer Mangel genommen wäre, was Nichts ist; aber sie ist ein Dasein, eine Qualität, nur mit einem Nichtsein bestimmt. [A]

c. Etwas

An dem Dasein ist seine Bestimmtheit als Qualität unterschieden worden; an dieser als daseiender *ist* der Unterschied — der Realität und der Negation. Sosehr nun diese Unterschiede an dem Dasein vorhanden sind, sosehr sind sie auch nichtig und aufgehoben. Die Realität enthält selbst die Negation, ist Dasein, nicht unbestimmtes, abstraktes Sein. Ebenso ist die Negation Dasein, nicht das abstrakt sein sollende Nichts, sondern hier gesetzt, wie es an sich ist, als seiend, dem Dasein angehörig. So ist die Qualität überhaupt nicht vom Dasein getrennt, welches nur bestimmtes, qualitatives Sein ist.

Dieses Aufheben der Unterscheidung ist mehr als ein bloßes Zurücknehmen und äußeres Wiederweglassen derselben oder als ein einfaches Zurückkehren zum einfachen Anfange, dem Dasein als solchem. Der Unterschied kann nicht weggelassen werden; denn er *ist*. Das Faktische, was also vorhanden ist, ist das Dasein überhaupt, Unterschied an ihm und das Aufheben dieses Unterschiedes; das Dasein nicht als unterschiedslos, wie anfangs, sondern als *wieder* sich selbst gleich, *durch Aufheben des Unterschieds*, die Einfachheit des Daseins *vermittelt* durch dieses Aufheben. Dies Aufgehobensein des Unterschieds ist die eigene Bestimmtheit des Daseins; so ist es *Insichsein*; das Dasein ist *Daseiendes, Etwas*.

Das Etwas ist die *erste Negation der Negation*, als einfache seiende Beziehung auf sich. Dasein, Leben, Denken usf. bestimmt sich wesentlich zum *Daseienden*, *Lebendigen*, *Denkenden* (Ich) usf. Diese Bestimmung ist von der höchsten Wichtigkeit, um nicht bei dem Dasein, Leben, Denken usf., auch nicht bei der Gott*heit* (statt Gottes) als Allgemeinheiten stehenzu-

terminateness is posited as a differentiated, reflected determinateness.[1] Nothing, as thus the determinate element of a determinateness, is equally something reflected, a *negative*.[2] Quality, taken in the distinct character of *being*, is *reality*; as burdened with a negative it is *negation* in general, likewise a quality but one which counts as a deficiency, and which further on is determined as limit, limitation.

Both are determinate being, but in *reality* as quality with the accent on *being*, the fact is concealed that it contains determinateness and therefore also negation. Consequently, reality is given the value only of something positive from which negation, limitation and deficiency are excluded. Negation taken as mere deficiency would be equivalent to nothing; but it is a *determinate* being, a quality, only determined with a non-being. [R][3]

(c) Something

In determinate being its determinateness has been distinguished as quality; in quality as determinately present, there *is* distinction—of reality and negation. Now although these distinctions are present in determinate being, they are no less equally void and sublated. Reality itself contains negation, is determinate being, not indeterminate, abstract being. Similarly, negation is determinate being, not the supposedly abstract nothing but posited here as it is in itself, as affirmatively present [*als seiend*], belonging to the sphere of determinate being. Thus quality is completely unseparated from determinate being, which is simply determinate, qualitative being.

This sublating of the distinction is more than a mere taking back and external omission of it again, or than a simple return to the simple beginning, to determinate being as such. The distinction cannot be omitted, for it *is*. What is, therefore, in fact present is determinate being in general, distinction in it, and sublation of this distinction; determinate being, not as devoid of distinction as at first, but as *again* equal to itself through sublation of the distinction, the simple oneness of determinate being *resulting* from this sublation. This sublatedness of the distinction is determinate being's *own* determinateness; it is thus *being-within-self*: determinate being is *a determinate being*, a *something*.

Something is the *first negation of negation,* as simple self-relation in the form of being. Determinate being, life, thought, and so on, essentially determine themselves to become a determinate being, a living creature, a thinker (ego) and so on. This determination is of supreme importance if we are not to remain at the stage of determinate being, life, thought, and so on—also the Godhead (instead of God)—as generalities. In our ordinary way of thinking, *something* is rightly credited with

---

1. Miller's translation has "when it will be posited as a differentiated, reflected determinateness, no longer as immediate or in the form of being." Hegel's point here is that, when quality is thought or posited "in the determination of nothing," a difference is introduced between negative and affirmative determinateness or quality. Immediate, affirmative determinateness thus comes to be thought not simply as immediate, but as a *differentiated*, reflected determinateness (i.e., as reality *in relation to* negation).

2. Miller's translation has "negation" for *Verneinung*. See chapter 16, below, note 16 (p. 306).

3. The insertions "[R]" in the English text and "[A]" in the German text indicate that a Remark (*Anmerkung*) by Hegel has been omitted at this point.

bleiben. *Etwas* gilt der Vorstellung mit Recht als ein *Reelles*. Jedoch ist *Etwas* noch eine sehr oberflächliche Bestimmung; wie *Realität* und *Negation*, das Dasein und dessen Bestimmtheit zwar nicht mehr die leeren — Sein und Nichts —, aber ganz abstrakte Bestimmungen sind. Deswegen sind sie auch die geläufigsten Ausdrücke, und die philosophisch nicht gebildete Reflexion gebraucht sie am meisten, gießt ihre Unterscheidungen darein und meint daran etwas recht gut und fest Bestimmtes zu haben. — Das Negative des Negativen ist als *Etwas* nur der Anfang des Subjekts; — das Insichsein nur erst ganz unbestimmt. Es bestimmt sich fernerhin zunächst als Fürsichseiendes und so fort, bis es erst im Begriff die konkrete Intensität des Subjekts erhält. Allen diesen Bestimmungen liegt die negative Einheit mit sich zugrunde. Aber dabei ist die Negation als *erste*, als Negation *überhaupt* wohl zu unterscheiden von der zweiten, der Negation der Negation, welche die konkrete, *absolute* Negativität, wie jene erste dagegen nur die *abstrakte* Negativität ist.

Etwas ist *seiend* als die Negation der Negation; denn diese ist das Wiederherstellen der einfachen Beziehung auf sich; — aber ebenso ist damit Etwas die *Vermittlung seiner mit sich selbst*. Schon in dem Einfachen des Etwas, dann noch bestimmter im Fürsichsein, Subjekt usf. ist die Vermittlung seiner mit sich selbst vorhanden, bereits auch im Werden nur die ganz abstrakte Vermittlung; die Vermittlung mit *sich* ist im Etwas *gesetzt*, insofern es als einfaches *Identisches* bestimmt ist. — Auf das Vorhandensein der Vermittlung überhaupt kann gegen das Prinzip der behaupteten bloßen Unmittelbarkeit des Wissens, von welcher die Vermittlung ausgeschlossen sein solle, aufmerksam gemacht werden; aber es bedarf weiterhin nicht, besonders auf das Moment der Vermittlung aufmerksam zu machen; denn es befindet sich überall und allenthalben, in jedem Begriffe.

Diese Vermittlung mit sich, die Etwas *an sich* ist, hat, nur als Negation der Negation genommen, keine konkreten Bestimmungen zu ihren Seiten; so fällt sie in die einfache Einheit zusammen, welche *Sein* ist. Etwas *ist* und *ist* denn auch Daseiendes; es ist *an sich* ferner auch *Werden*, das aber nicht mehr nur Sein und Nichts zu seinen Momenten hat. Das eine derselben, das Sein, ist nun Dasein und weiter Daseiendes. Das zweite ist ebenso ein *Daseiendes*, aber als Negatives des Etwas bestimmt, — ein *Anderes*. Das Etwas als Werden ist ein Übergehen, dessen Momente selbst Etwas sind und das darum *Veränderung* ist; — ein bereits *konkret* gewordenes Werden. — Das Etwas aber verändert sich zunächst nur in seinem Begriffe; es ist noch nicht so als vermittelnd und vermittelt *gesetzt*; zunächst nur als sich in seiner Beziehung auf sich einfach erhaltend, und das Negative seiner als ein ebenso Qualitatives, nur ein *Anderes* überhaupt.

reality. However, something is still a very superficial determination; just as reality and negation, determinate being and its determinateness, although no longer blank being and nothing, are still quite abstract determinations. It is for this reason that they are the most current expressions and the intellect which is philosophically untrained uses them most, casts its distinctions in their mould and fancies that in them it has something really well and truly determined. The negative of the negative is, as *something,* only the beginning of the subject—being-within-self, only as yet quite indeterminate. It determines itself further on, first, as *a being-for-self* and so on, until in the Notion it first attains the concrete intensity of the subject. At the base of all these determinations lies the negative unity with itself. But in all this, care must be taken to distinguish between the *first* negation as negation *in general,* and the second negation, the negation of the negation: the latter is concrete, *absolute* negativity, just as the former on the contrary is only *abstract* negativity.

Something is the negation of the negation in the form of *being*; for this second negation is the restoring of the simple relation to self; but with this, something is equally *the mediation of itself with itself.* Even in the simple form of *something,* then still more specifically in *being-for-self, subject,* and so on, self-mediation is present; it is present even in *becoming,* only the mediation is quite abstract. In *something,* mediation with self is *posited,* in so far as something is determined as a simple identity. Attention can be drawn to the presence of mediation in general, as against the principle of the alleged mere immediacy of knowledge, from which mediation is supposed to be excluded; but there is no further need to draw particular attention to the moment of mediation, for it is to be found everywhere, in every Notion.

This mediation with itself which something is *in itself,* taken only as negation of the negation, has no concrete determinations for its sides; it thus collapses into the simple oneness which is being. Something *is,* and *is,* then, also a determinate being; further, it is *in itself* also *becoming,* which, however, no longer has only being and nothing for its moments. One of these, being, is now determinate being, and, further, *a* determinate being. The second is equally a *determinate* being, but determined as a negative of the something—an *other.* Something as a *becoming* is a transition, the moments of which are themselves somethings, so that the transition *is alteration*—a becoming which has already become *concrete.* But to begin with, something alters only in its Notion; it is not yet *posited* as mediating and mediated, but at first only as simply maintaining itself in its self-relation, and its negative is posited as equally qualitative, as only an *other* in general.

B. Die Endlichkeit

a) Etwas *und* Anderes; sie sind zunächst gleichgültig gegeneinander; ein Anderes ist auch ein unmittelbar Daseiendes, ein Etwas; die Negation fällt so außer beiden. Etwas ist *an sich* gegen sein *Sein-für-Anderes.* Aber die Bestimmtheit gehört auch seinem *Ansich* an und ist

b) dessen *Bestimmung*, welche ebensosehr in *Beschaffenheit* übergeht, die, mit jener identisch, das immanente und zugleich negierte Sein-für-Anderes, die *Grenze* des Etwas ausmacht, welche

c) die immanente Bestimmung des Etwas selbst und dieses somit das *Endliche ist.*

In der ersten Abteilung, worin das *Dasein* überhaupt betrachtet wurde, hatte dieses, als zunächst aufgenommen, die Bestimmung des *Seienden*. Die Momente seiner Entwicklung, Qualität und Etwas, sind darum ebenso affirmativer Bestimmung. In dieser Abteilung hingegen entwickelt sich die negative Bestimmung, die im Dasein liegt, welche dort nur erst Negation überhaupt, *erste* Negation war, nun aber zu dem Punkte des *Insichseins* des Etwas, zur Negation der Negation bestimmt ist.

a. Etwas und ein Anderes

1. Etwas und Anderes sind beide *erstens Daseiende* oder *Etwas.*

Zweitens ist ebenso jedes ein *Anderes.* Es ist gleichgültig, welches zuerst und bloß darum *Etwas* genannt wird (im Lateinischen, wenn sie in einem Satze vorkommen, heißen beide *aliud*, oder "Einer den Anderen" *alius alium*; bei einer Gegenseitigkeit ist der Ausdruck *alter alterum* analog). Wenn wir ein Dasein *A* nennen, das andere aber *B*, so ist zunächst *B* als das Andere bestimmt. Aber *A* ist ebensosehr das Andere des *B*. Beide sind auf gleiche Weise *Andere.* Um den Unterschied und das als affirmativ zu nehmende Etwas zu fixieren, dient das *Dieses.* Aber *Dieses* spricht eben es aus, daß dies Unterscheiden und Herausheben des einen Etwas ein subjektives, außerhalb des Etwas selbst fallendes Bezeichnen ist. In dieses äußerliche Monstrieren fällt die ganze Bestimmtheit; selbst der Ausdruck *Dieses* enthält keinen Unterschied; alle und jede Etwas sind geradesogut *Diese*, als sie auch Andere sind. Man *meint*, durch "*Dieses*" etwas vollkommen Bestimmtes auszudrücken; es wird übersehen, daß die Sprache, als Werk des Verstandes, nur Allgemeines ausspricht, außer in dem *Namen* eines einzelnen Gegenstandes; der individuelle Name ist aber ein Sinnloses in dem Sinne, daß er nicht ein Allgemeines ausdrückt, und erscheint als ein bloß Gesetztes, Willkürliches aus demselben Grunde, wie denn auch

Chapter Twelve

Something and Other, Finitude: Text

B. Finitude

(*a*) Something *and* other are at first indifferent to one another; an other is also immediately a determinate being, a something; the negation thus falls outside both. Something is *in itself* as against its *being-for-other.* But the determinateness also belongs to its *in-itself* and is

(*b*) its *determination*; this equally passes over into *constitution* which, being identical with the determination, constitutes the immanent and at the same time negated being-for-other, the *limit* of the something. This limit is

(*c*) the immanent determination of the something itself, which latter is thus the *finite*.

In the first section, in which *determinate being* in general was considered, this had, as at first taken up, the determination of *being*. Consequently, the moments of its development, quality and something, equally have an affirmative determination. In this section, on the other hand, the negative determination contained in determinate being is developed, and whereas in the first section it was at first only negation in general, the *first* negation, it is now determined to the point of the *being-within-self* or the *inwardness* of the something, to the negation of the negation.

(a) Something and an Other

1. Something and other are, in the first place, both determinate beings or somethings.

Secondly, each is equally an other. It is immaterial which is first named and solely for that reason called *something*; (in Latin, when they both occur in a sentence, both are called *aliud,* or 'the one, the other', *alius alium*; when there is reciprocity the expression *alter alterum* is analogous). If of two things we call one A, and the other B, then in the first instance B is determined as the other. But A is just as much the other of B. Both are, in the same way, *others.* The word 'this' serves to fix the distinction and the something which is to be taken affirmatively. But 'this' clearly expresses that this distinguishing and signalizing of the one something is a subjective designating falling outside the something itself. The entire determinateness falls into this external pointing out; even the expression 'this' contains no distinction; each and every something is just as well a 'this' as it is also an other. By 'this' we *mean* to express something completely determined; it is overlooked that speech, as a work of the understanding, gives expression only to universals, except in the *name* of a single object; but the individual name is meaningless, in the sense that it does not express a universal, and for the same reason appears as something merely pos-

Einzelnamen willkürlich angenommen, gegeben oder ebenso verändert werden können.

Es erscheint somit das Anderssein als eine dem so bestimmten Dasein fremde Bestimmung oder das Andere *außer* dem einen Dasein; teils, daß ein Dasein erst durch das *Vergleichen* eines Dritten, teils, daß es nur um des Anderen willen, das außer ihm ist, als Anderes bestimmt werde, aber nicht für sich so sei. Zugleich, wie bemerkt worden, bestimmt sich jedes Dasein, auch für die Vorstellung, ebensosehr als ein anderes Dasein, so daß nicht ein Dasein bleibt, das nur als ein Dasein bestimmt, das nicht außerhalb eines Daseins, also nicht selbst ein Anderes wäre.

Beide sind sowohl als *Etwas* als auch als *Anderes* bestimmt, hiermit *dasselbe*, und es ist noch kein Unterschied derselben vorhanden. Diese *Dieselbigkeit* der Bestimmungen fällt aber ebenso nur in die äußere Reflexion, in die *Vergleichung* beider; aber wie das *Andere* zunächst gesetzt ist, so ist dasselbe für sich zwar in Beziehung auf das Etwas, aber auch *für sich außerhalb desselben.*

Drittens ist daher das *Andere* zu nehmen als isoliert, in Beziehung auf sich selbst; *abstrakt* als das Andere; τὸ ἕτερον des Platon, der es als eines der Momente der Totalität *dem Einen* entgegensetzt und *dem Anderen* auf diese Weise eine eigene *Natur* zuschreibt. So ist das *Andere*, allein als solches gefaßt, nicht das Andere von Etwas, sondern das Andere an ihm selbst, d. i. das Andere seiner selbst. — Solches seiner Bestimmung nach Andere ist die *physische Natur;* sie ist das *Andere des Geistes*; diese ihre Bestimmung ist so zunächst eine bloße Relativität, wodurch nicht eine Qualität der Natur selbst, sondern nur eine ihr äußerliche Beziehung ausgedrückt wird. Aber indem der Geist das wahrhafte Etwas und die Natur daher an ihr selbst nur das ist, was sie gegen den Geist ist, so ist, insofern sie für sich genommen wird, ihre Qualität eben dies, das Andere an ihr selbst, das *Außer-sich-Seiende* (in den Bestimmungen des Raums, der Zeit, der Materie) zu sein.

Das Andere für sich ist das Andere an ihm selbst, hiermit das Andere seiner selbst, so das Andere des Anderen, — also das in sich schlechthin Ungleiche, sich Negierende, das sich *Verändernde.* Aber ebenso bleibt es identisch mit sich, denn dasjenige, in welches es sich veränderte, ist das *Andere*, das sonst weiter keine Bestimmung hat; aber das sich Verändernde ist auf keine verschiedene Weise, sondern auf dieselbe, ein Anderes zu sein, bestimmt; es *geht* daher in demselben *nur mit sich zusammen.* So ist es gesetzt als in sich Reflektiertes mit Aufheben des Andersseins, mit sich *identisches* Etwas, von dem hiermit das Anderssein, das zugleich Moment desselben ist, ein Unterschiedenes, ihm nicht als Etwas selbst zukommendes ist.

2. Etwas *erhält* sich in seinem Nichtdasein; es ist wesentlich *eins* mit ihm und wesentlich *nicht eins* mit ihm. Es steht also *in Beziehung* auf

ited and arbitrary; just as proper names, too, can be arbitrarily assumed, given or also altered.

Otherness thus appears as a determination alien to the determinate being thus characterized, or as the other *outside* the one determinate being; partly because a determinate being is determined as other only through being *compared* by a Third, and partly because it is only determined as other on account of the other which is outside it, but is not an other on its own account. At the same time, as has been remarked, every determinate being, even for ordinary thinking, determines itself as an other, so that there is no determinate being which is determined only as such, which is not outside a determinate being and therefore is not itself an other.

Both are determined equally as something and as other, and are thus the same, and there is so far no distinction between them. But this self-sameness of the determinations likewise arises only from external reflection, from the *comparing* of them; but the other as at first posited, although an other in relation to the something, is nevertheless also an other on its own account, apart from the something.

Thirdly, therefore, the other is to be taken as isolated, as in relation to itself, *abstractly* as the *other*; the τὸ ἕτερον of Plato, who opposes it as one of the moments of totality to the One, and in this way ascribes to the other a *nature* of its own. Thus the other, taken solely as such, is not the other of something but the other in its own self, that is, the other of itself. Such an other, determined as other, is physical nature; it is the other of spirit. This its determination is thus at first a mere relativity by which is expressed, not a quality of nature itself, but only a relation external to it. However, since spirit is the true something and nature, consequently, in its own self is only what it is as contrasted with spirit, the quality of nature taken as such is just this, to be the *other* in its own self, that which is *external to itself* (in the determinations of space, time and matter).

The other simply by itself is the other in its own self, hence the other of itself and so the other of the other—it is, therefore, that which is absolutely dissimilar within itself, that which negates itself, *alters* itself.[1] But in so doing it remains identical with itself, for that into which it alters is the other, and this is its sole determination; but what is altered is not determined in any different way but in the same way, namely, to be an other; in this latter, therefore, it only unites with its own self. It is thus posited as reflected into itself with sublation of the otherness, as a self-identical something from which, consequently, the otherness, which is at the same time a moment of it, is distinct and does not appertain to the something itself.[2]

2. Something *preserves* itself in its negative determinate being [*Nichtdasein*];[3] it is essentially *one* with it and essentially *not one* with it. It stands, therefore, in a *relation* to its otherness and is not simply its otherness. The

---

1. The German word for "other" is *das Andere*, and the German word for "alteration" (or change) is *Veränderung*. Hegel thus understands alteration as the process whereby what is other "others" itself (*sich verändert*) into something else or comes to be other than it is.
2. Miller's translation has (redundantly) "from which [...] the otherness [...] is distinct from it."

sein Anderssein; es ist nicht rein sein Anderssein. Das Anderssein ist zugleich in ihm enthalten und zugleich noch davon *getrennt*; es ist *Sein-für-Anderes*.

Dasein als solches ist Unmittelbares, Beziehungsloses; oder es ist in der Bestimmung des *Seins*. Aber Dasein als das Nichtsein in sich schließend ist *bestimmtes*, in sich verneintes Sein und dann zunächst Anderes, — aber weil es sich in seiner Verneinung zugleich auch erhält, nur *Sein-für-Anderes*.

Es erhält sich in seinem Nichtdasein und ist Sein, aber nicht Sein überhaupt, sondern als Beziehung auf sich *gegen* seine Beziehung auf Anderes, als Gleichheit mit sich gegen seine Ungleichheit. Ein solches Sein ist *Ansichsein*.

Sein-für-Anderes und Ansichsein machen die *zwei Momente* des Etwas aus. Es sind *zwei Paare* von Bestimmungen, die hier vorkommen: 1. *Etwas* und *Anderes*; 2. *Sein-für-Anderes* und *Ansichsein*. Die ersteren enthalten die Beziehungslosigkeit ihrer Bestimmtheit; Etwas und Anderes fallen auseinander. Aber ihre Wahrheit ist ihre Beziehung; das Sein-für-Anderes und das Ansichsein sind daher jene Bestimmungen als *Momente* eines und desselben gesetzt, als Bestimmungen, welche Beziehungen sind und in ihrer Einheit, in der Einheit des Daseins bleiben. Jedes selbst enthält damit an ihm zugleich auch sein von ihm verschiedenes Moment.

Sein und Nichts in ihrer Einheit, welche Dasein ist, sind nicht mehr als Sein und Nichts, — dies sind sie nur außer ihrer Einheit; so in ihrer unruhigen Einheit, im Werden, sind sie Entstehen und Vergehen. — Sein im Etwas ist *Ansichsein*. Sein, die Beziehung auf sich, die Gleichheit mit sich, ist jetzt nicht mehr unmittelbar, sondern Beziehung auf sich nur als Nichtsein des Andersseins (als in sich reflektiertes Dasein). — Ebenso ist Nichtsein als Moment des Etwas in dieser Einheit des Seins und Nichtseins nicht Nichtdasein überhaupt, sondern Anderes und bestimmter nach der *Unterscheidung* des Seins von ihm zugleich *Beziehung* auf sein Nichtdasein, Sein-für-Anderes.

Somit ist *Ansichsein* erstlich negative Beziehung auf das Nichtdasein, es hat das Anderssein außer ihm und ist demselben entgegen; insofern Etwas *an sich* ist, ist es dem Anderssein und dem Sein-für-Anderes entnommen. Aber zweitens hat es das Nichtsein auch selbst an ihm; denn es selbst *ist das Nichtsein* des Seins-für-Anderes.

Das *Sein-für-Anderes* aber ist erstlich Negation der einfachen Beziehung des Seins auf sich, die zunächst Dasein und Etwas sein soll; insofern Etwas in einem Anderen oder für ein Anderes ist, entbehrt es des eigenen Seins. Aber zweitens ist es nicht das Nichtdasein als reines Nichts; es ist Nichtdasein, das auf das Ansichsein als auf sein in sich reflektiertes Sein hinweist, so wie umgekehrt das Ansichsein auf das Sein-für-Anderes hinweist.

3. Beide Momente sind Bestimmungen eines und desselben, nämlich des Etwas. *Ansich* ist Etwas, insofern es aus dem Sein-für-Anderes heraus,

otherness is at once contained in it and also still *separate* from it; it[4] is a *being-for-other.*

Determinate being as such is immediate, without relation to an other; or, it is in the determination of *being*; but as including within itself non-being, it is *determinate* being, being negated within itself, and then in the first instance an other—but since at the same time it also preserves itself in its negation, it is only a *being-for-other.*

It preserves itself in its negative determinate being[5] and is being, but not being in general, but as self-related in *opposition* to its relation to other, as self-equal in opposition to its inequality. Such a being is *being-in-itself.*

Being-for-other and being-in-itself constitute the two moments of the something. There are here present *two pairs* of determinations: 1. Something and other, 2. Being-for-other and being-in-itself. The former contain the unrelatedness of their determinateness; something and other fall apart. But their truth is their relation; being-for-other and being-in-itself are, therefore, the above determinations posited as *moments* of one and the same something, as determinations which are relations and which remain in their unity, in the unity of determinate being. Each, therefore, at the same time, also contains within itself its other moment which is distinguished from it.

Being and nothing in their unity, which is determinate being, are no longer being and nothing—these they are only outside their unity—thus in their unstable unity, in becoming, they are coming-to-be and ceasing-to-be. The being in something is *being-in-itself.* Being, which is self-relation, equality with self, is now no longer immediate, but is only as the non-being of otherness (as determinate being reflected into itself). Similarly, non-being as a moment of something is, in this unity of being and non-being, not negative determinate being in general, but an other, and more specifically—seeing that being is differentiated from it—at the same time a *relation* to its negative determinate being, a being-for-other.

Hence being-in-itself is, first, a negative relation to the negative determinate being, it has the otherness outside it and is opposed to it; in so far as something is *in itself* it is withdrawn from otherness and being-for-other. But secondly it has also present in it non-being itself, for it is itself the *non-being* of being-for-other.

But being-for-other is, first, a negation of the simple relation of being to itself which, in the first instance, is supposed to be determinate being and something; in so far as something is in an other or is for an other, it lacks a being of its own. But secondly it is not negative determinate being as pure nothing; it is negative determinate being which points to being-in-itself as to its own being which is reflected into itself, just as, conversely, being-in-itself points to being-for-other.

3. Both moments are determinations of what is one and the same, namely, the something. Something is *in itself* in so far as it has returned into itself out of the being-for-other. But something also has *in itself* (here the accent falls on *in*)

---

3. Miller's translation has "in the negative of its determinate being."
4. I.e., something.
5. Miller's translation has "in the negative of its determinate being."

in sich zurückgekehrt ist. Etwas hat aber auch eine Bestimmung oder Umstand *an sich* (hier fällt der Akzent auf *an*) oder *an ihm*, insofern dieser Umstand äußerlich *an ihm*, ein Sein-für-Anderes ist.

Dies führt zu einer weiteren Bestimmung. *Ansichsein* und Sein-für-Anderes sind zunächst verschieden; aber daß Etwas *dasselbe*, *was es an* sich ist, auch *an ihm* hat, und umgekehrt, was es als Sein-für-Anderes ist, auch an sich ist, — dies ist die Identität des Ansichseins und Seins-für-Anderes, nach der Bestimmung, daß das Etwas selbst ein und dasselbe beider Momente ist, sie also ungetrennt in ihm sind. — Es ergibt sich formell diese Identität schon in der Sphäre des Daseins, aber ausdrücklicher in der Betrachtung des Wesens und dann des Verhältnisses der *Innerlichkeit* und *Äußerlichkeit*, und am bestimmtesten in der Betrachtung der Idee als der Einheit des Begriffs und der Wirklichkeit. — Man meint, mit dem *Ansich* etwas Hohes zu sagen, wie mit dem *Inneren*; was aber Etwas *nur an sich* ist, ist auch *nur* an *ihm*; "an sich" ist eine nur abstrakte, damit selbst äußerliche Bestimmung. Die Ausdrücke "es ist nichts *an ihm*" oder "es ist etwas *daran*" enthalten, obgleich etwa[s] dunkel, daß das, was *an einem* ist, auch zu seinem *Ansichsein*, seinem inneren wahrhaften Werte gehöre.

Es kann bemerkt werden, daß sich hier der Sinn des *Dings-an-sich* ergibt, das eine sehr einfache Abstraktion ist, aber eine Zeitlang eine sehr wichtige Bestimmung, gleichsam etwas Vornehmes, so wie der Satz, daß wir nicht wissen, was die Dinge an sich sind, eine vielgeltende Weisheit war. — Die Dinge heißen an-sich, insofern von allem Sein-für-Anderes abstrahiert wird, das heißt überhaupt, insofern sie ohne alle Bestimmung, als Nichtse gedacht werden. In diesem Sinn kann man freilich nicht wissen, *was* das Ding-an-sich ist. Denn die Frage *Was*? verlangt, daß *Bestimmungen* angegeben werden; indem aber die Dinge, von denen sie anzugeben verlangt würde, zugleich *Dinge-an-sich* sein sollen, das heißt eben ohne Bestimmung, so ist in die Frage gedankenloserweise die Unmöglichkeit der Beantwortung gelegt, oder man macht nur eine widersinnige Antwort. — Das Ding-an-sich ist dasselbe, was jenes Absolute, von dem man nichts weiß, als daß Alles eins in ihm ist. Man weiß daher sehr wohl, was *an* diesen Dingen-an-sich ist; sie sind als solche nichts als wahrheitslose, leere Abstraktionen. Was aber das Ding-an-sich in Wahrheit ist, was wahrhaft an sich ist, davon ist die Logik die Darstellung, wobei aber unter *Ansich* etwas Besseres als die Abstraktion verstanden wird, nämlich was etwas in seinem Begriffe ist; dieser aber ist konkret in sich, als Begriff überhaupt begreiflich und als bestimmt und Zusammenhang seiner Bestimmungen in sich erkennbar.

Das Ansichsein hat zunächst das Sein-für-Anderes zu seinem gegenüberstehenden Momente; aber es wird demselben auch das *Gesetztsein*

or in *it* [*an ihm*], a determination or circumstance in so far as this circumstance is outwardly *in it,* is a being-for-other.[6]

This leads to a further determination. Being-in-itself and being-for-other are, in the first instance, distinct; but that something also has in *it*[7] the same character that it is *in itself,* and, conversely, that what it is as being-for-other it also is in itself—this is the identity of being-in-itself and being-for-other, in accordance with the determination that the something itself is one and the same something of both moments, which, therefore, are undividedly present in it. This identity is already formally given in the sphere of determinate being, but more expressly in the consideration of *essence* and of the relation of *inner and outer,* and most precisely in the consideration of the Idea as the unity of the Notion and *actuality*. People fancy that they are saying something lofty with the expression 'in itself', as they do in saying 'the inner'; but what something is *only in itself,* is also *only* in *it*;[8] 'in itself' is only an abstract, and so even external determination. The expressions: there is nothing *in it*, or, there is something *in it*, imply, though somewhat obscurely, that what is *in* a thing also belongs to the thing's *being-in-itself,* to its inner, true worth.

It may be observed that the meaning of the *thing-in-itself* is here revealed; it is a very simple abstraction but for some while it counted as a very important determination, something superior, as it were, just as the proposition that we do not know what things are in themselves ranked as a profound piece of wisdom. Things are called 'in themselves' in so far as abstraction is made from all being-for-other, which means simply, in so far as they are thought devoid of all determination, as nothings. In this sense, it is of course impossible to know *what* the *thing-in-itself* is. For the question: *what?* demands that *determinations* be assigned; but since the things to which they are to be assigned are at the same time supposed to be *things in-themselves,* which means, in effect, to be without any determination, the question is thoughtlessly made impossible to answer, or else only an absurd answer is given.[9] The thing-in-itself is the same as that *absolute* of which we know nothing except that in it all is one. What is *in* these things-in-themselves, therefore, we know quite well; they are as such nothing but truthless, empty abstractions. What, however, the thing-in-itself is in truth, what truly is in itself, of this logic is the exposition, in which however something better than an abstraction is understood by 'in-itself', namely, what something is in its Notion; but the Notion is concrete

6. Miller's translation has "within it" for *an ihm*. This is inappropriate, since that which something has *an ihm* does not specifically lie *within* the thing (as opposed to on the surface), but simply belongs to *it* rather than something else. Furthermore, it belongs to something *outwardly* and so is evident from an external point of view (or for another). That which lies *within* the thing is what something is *in itself* or *an sich*. In translating *an ihm* here as "in *it*", I am following the translation of Johnston and Struthers; see G.W.F. Hegel, *Science of Logic*, translated by W.H. Johnston and L.G. Struthers, 2 vols. (London: George Allen and Unwin, 1929), 1: 133. For a discussion of the differences between the terms *an sich* and *an ihm*, see chapter 18, below, pp. 337–8.

7. Miller's translation again has "within it" for *an ihm*.

8. And is *outwardly* evident in it.

9. Miller has "the things of which they are to be assigned."

gegenübergestellt; in diesem Ausdruck liegt zwar auch das Sein-für-Anderes, aber er enthält bestimmt die bereits geschehene Zurückbeugung dessen, was nicht an sich ist, in das, was sein Ansichsein, worin es *positiv* ist. Das *Ansichsein* ist gewöhnlich als eine abstrakte Weise, den Begriff auszudrücken, zu nehmen; *Setzen* fällt eigentlich erst in die Sphäre des Wesens, der objektiven Reflexion; der Grund *setzt* das, was durch ihn begründet wird; die Ursache noch mehr *bringt* eine Wirkung *hervor*, ein Dasein, dessen Selbständigkeit *unmittelbar* negiert ist und das den Sinn an ihm hat, in einem Anderen seine *Sache*, sein Sein zu haben. In der Sphäre des Seins *geht* das Dasein aus dem Werden nur *hervor*, oder mit dem Etwas ist ein Anderes, mit dem Endlichen das Unendliche gesetzt, aber das Endliche bringt das Unendliche nicht hervor, *setzt* dasselbe nicht. In der Sphäre des Seins ist das *Sichbestimmen* des Begriffs selbst nur erst *an sich*, — so heißt es ein Übergehen; auch die reflektierenden Bestimmungen des Seins, wie Etwas und Anderes oder das Endliche und Unendliche, ob sie gleich wesentlich aufeinander hinweisen oder als Sein-für-Anderes sind, gelten als *qualitative* für sich bestehend; das *Andere ist*, das Endliche gilt ebenso als *unmittelbar seiend* und für sich feststehend wie das Unendliche; ihr Sinn erscheint als vollendet auch ohne ihr Anderes. Das Positive und Negative hingegen, Ursache und Wirkung, sosehr sie auch als isoliert seiend genommen werden, haben zugleich keinen Sinn ohne einander; es ist *an ihnen selbst* ihr Scheinen ineinander, das Scheinen seines Anderen in jedem, vorhanden. — In den verschiedenen Kreisen der Bestimmung und besonders im Fortgange der Exposition oder näher im Fortgange des Begriffs zu seiner Exposition ist es eine Hauptsache, dies immer wohl zu unterscheiden, was noch *an sich* und was *gesetzt* ist, wie die Bestimmungen als im Begriffe und wie sie als gesetzt oder als seiend-für-Anderes sind. Es ist dies ein Unterschied, der nur der dialektischen Entwicklung angehört, den das metaphysische Philosophieren, worunter auch das kritische gehört, nicht kennt; die Definitionen der Metaphysik wie ihre Voraussetzungen, Unterscheidungen und Folgerungen wollen nur *Seiendes* und zwar *Ansichseiendes* behaupten und hervorbringen.

Das *Sein-für-Anderes* ist in der Einheit des Etwas mit sich, identisch mit seinem *Ansich*; das Sein-für-Anderes ist so *am* Etwas. Die so in sich reflektierte Bestimmtheit ist damit wieder *einfache seiende*, somit wieder eine Qualität, — die *Bestimmung*.

b. Bestimmung, Beschaffenheit und Grenze

Das *Ansich*, in welches das Etwas aus seinem Sein-für-Anderes in sich reflektiert ist, ist nicht mehr abstraktes Ansich, sondern als Negation seines Seins-für-Anderes durch dieses vermittelt, welches so sein Moment ist. Es ist nicht nur die unmittelbare Identität des Etwas mit sich, sondern die,

within itself, is comprehensible simply as Notion, and as determined within itself and the connected whole of its determinations, is cognizable.

Being-in-itself, in the first instance, has being-for-other as its contrasted moment; but *positedness,* too, is contrasted with it. This expression, it is true, includes also being-for-other, but it specifically contains the already accomplished bending back of that which is not *in itself* into that which is its being-in-itself, in which it is *positive.* Being-in-itself is generally to be taken as an abstract way of expressing the Notion; *positing,* properly speaking, first occurs in the sphere of *essence,* of objective reflection; the *ground posits* that which is grounded by it; still more, the *cause produces* or *brings forth* an *effect,* a determinate being whose self-subsistence is *immediately* negated and which carries the meaning of having its matter, its being, in an other. In the sphere of being, determinate being only *proceeds* from *becoming,* or, with the something an other is posited, with the finite, the infinite; but the finite does not bring forth the infinite, does not *posit* it. In the sphere of being, the *self-determining* even of the Notion is at first only *in itself* or *implicit*—as such it is called a transition; and the reflected determinations of being such as something and other, or finite and infinite, although they essentially refer to each other or are as a being-for-other, they too count as *qualitative,* as existing on their own account; the other *is,* the finite ranks equally with the infinite as an immediate, affirmative being, standing fast on its own account; the meaning of each appears to be complete even without its other. On the other hand positive and negative, cause and effect, however much they may be taken as isolated from each other, are at the same time meaningless one without the other. There is *present in them* their showing or reflection in each other, the showing or reflection in each of its other. In the different spheres of determination and especially in the progress of the exposition, or more precisely in the progress of the Notion towards the exposition of itself, it is of capital importance always clearly to distinguish what is still *in itself* and what is *posited,* the determinations as they are in the Notion, and as they are as posited, or as being-for-other. This is a distinction which belongs only to the dialectical development and which is unknown to metaphysical philosophising, which also includes the critical philosophy;[10] the definitions of metaphysics, like its presuppositions, distinctions and conclusions, seek to assert and produce only what comes under the category of *being,* and that, too, of *being-in-itself.*

Being-for-other is, in the unity of the something with itself, identical with its *in-itself;* the being-for-other is thus present *in* the something. The determinateness thus reflected into itself is, therefore, again in the simple form of *being,* and hence is again a quality: *determination.*

(b) Determination, Constitution and Limit

The *in-itself* into which something is reflected into itself out of its being-for-other is no longer an abstract in-itself, but as negation of its being-for-other is mediated by the latter, which is thus its moment. It is not only the immediate identity of the something with itself, but the identity through which there is

10. I.e., Kant's philosophy.

durch welche das Etwas das, was es *an sich* ist, auch *an ihm* ist; das Sein-für-Anderes ist *an ihm*, weil das *Ansich* das Aufheben desselben ist, *aus demselben* in sich ist; aber ebensosehr auch schon, weil es abstrakt, also wesentlich mit Negation, mit Sein-für-Anderes behaftet ist. Es ist hier nicht nur Qualität und Realität, seiende Bestimmtheit, sondern *an-sich-seiende* Bestimmtheit vorhanden, und die Entwicklung ist, sie als diese in sich reflektierte Bestimmtheit *zu setzen*.

1. Die Qualität, die das Ansich im einfachen Etwas wesentlich in Einheit mit dessen anderem Momente, dem *An-ihm-Sein* ist, kann seine *Bestimmung* genannt werden, insofern dieses Wort in genauer Bedeutung von *Bestimmtheit* überhaupt unterschieden wird. Die Bestimmung ist die affirmative Bestimmtheit als das Ansichsein, dem das Etwas in seinem Dasein gegen seine Verwicklung mit Anderem, wovon es bestimmt würde, gemäß bleibt, sich in seiner Gleichheit mit sich erhält, sie in seinem Sein-für-Anderes geltend macht. Es *erfüllt* seine Bestimmung, insofern die weitere Bestimmtheit, welche zunächst durch sein Verhalten zu Anderem mannigfaltig erwächst, seinem Ansichsein gemäß, seine Fülle wird. Die Bestimmung enthält dies, daß, was etwas *an sich* ist, auch *an ihm* sei.

Die *Bestimmung* des *Menschen* ist die denkende Vernunft: Denken überhaupt ist seine einfache *Bestimmtheit*, er ist durch dieselbe von dem Tiere unterschieden; er ist Denken *an sich*, insofern dasselbe auch von seinem Sein-für-Anderes, seiner eigenen Natürlichkeit und Sinnlichkeit, wodurch er unmittelbar mit Anderem zusammenhängt, unterschieden ist. Aber das Denken ist auch *an ihm*; der Mensch selbst ist Denken, er *ist da* als denkend, es ist seine Existenz und Wirklichkeit; und ferner, indem es in seinem Dasein und sein Dasein im Denken ist, ist es *konkret*, ist mit Inhalt und Erfüllung zu nehmen, es ist denkende Vernunft, und so ist es *Bestimmung* des Menschen. Aber selbst diese Bestimmung ist wieder nur *an sich* als ein *Sollen*, d. i. sie mit der Erfüllung, die ihrem Ansich einverleibt ist, in der Form des Ansich überhaupt *gegen* das ihr nicht einverleibte Dasein, das zugleich noch als äußerlich gegenüberstehende, unmittelbare Sinnlichkeit und Natur ist.

2. Die Erfüllung des Ansichseins mit Bestimmtheit ist auch unterschieden von der Bestimmtheit, die nur Sein-für-Anderes ist und außer der Bestimmung bleibt. Denn im Felde des Qualitativen bleibt den Unterschieden in ihrem Aufgehobensein auch das unmittelbare, qualitative Sein gegeneinander. Das, was das Etwas *an ihm* hat, teilt sich so und ist nach dieser Seite äußerliches Dasein des Etwas, das auch *sein* Dasein ist, aber nicht seinem Ansichsein angehört. — Die Bestimmtheit ist so *Beschaffenheit*.

So oder anders beschaffen ist Etwas als in äußerem Einfluß und Verhältnissen begriffen. Diese äußerliche Beziehung, von der die Beschaffenheit abhängt, und das Bestimmtwerden durch ein Anderes erscheint

present *in* the something that which it is *in itself*; being-for-other is present *in it* because the *in-itself* is the sublation of the being-for-other, has returned *out of* the being-for-other into itself; but equally, too, simply because it is abstract and therefore essentially burdened with negation, with being-for-other. There is present here not only quality and reality, determinateness in the form of simple being, but determinateness in the form of the *in-itself*; and the development consists in *positing* this determinateness as reflected into itself.

1. The quality which is constituted by the essential unity of the in-itself in the simple something with its other moment, being-in-it [*An-ihm-Sein*], can be called the *determination* of the something, in so far as this word in its exact meaning is distinguished from *determinateness* in general.[11] Determination is affirmative determinateness as the in-itself with which something in its determinate being remains congruous in face of its entanglement with the other by which it might be determined, maintaining itself in its self-equality, and making its determination hold good in its being-for-other. Something *fulfils* its determination in so far as the further determinateness which at once develops in various directions through something's relation to other, is congruous with the in-itself of the something, becomes its filling. Determination implies that what something is *in itself* [*an sich*], is also *present in* it [*an ihm*].

The *determination* of man is thinking reason; thought in general, thought as such, is his simple *determinateness*[12]—by it he is distinguished from the brute; *in himself* he is thought, in so far as this is also distinguished from his being-for-other, from his own natural existence and sense-nature through which he is directly connected with his other. But thought is also present *in* him; man himself is thought, he actually exists as thinking, it is his concrete existence and actuality; and, further, since thought is in his determinate being and his determinate being is in thought, it is to be taken as *concrete,* as having content and filling; it is thinking reason and as such the *determination* of man. But even this determination again is only *in itself* as something which *ought* to be, that is it, together with the filling which is incorporated in its in-itself, is in the form of the in-itself in general, *in contrast to* the determinate being not incorporated in it, which at the same time still confronts it externally as immediate sense-nature and nature.

2. The filling of the in-itself with determinateness is also distinct from the determinateness which is only being-for-other and remains outside the determination. For in the sphere of quality, the differences in their sublated form as moments also retain the form of immediate, qualitative being relatively to one another. That which something has *in it,* thus divides itself and is from this side an external

11. Miller translates *An-ihm-Sein* as "the *presence in it* of its being-for-other." Though inaccurate, this translation does have the virtue of reminding us that what something has in *it* is always evident to (and so in relation to) others. When Hegel says that the determination of something is the unity of the thing's being-in-itself and its being-in-*it*, what he means is thus that the determination is the way the thing's inner nature manifests itself in its relations to other things. (Note that Miller translates the words *seine Bestimmung* as "the *determination* of the in-itself," rather than as "the *determination* of the something.")

12. Miller has "in his simple *determinateness*."

als etwas Zufälliges. Aber es ist Qualität des Etwas, dieser Äußerlichkeit preisgegeben zu sein und eine *Beschaffenheit* zu haben.

Insofern Etwas sich verändert, so fällt die Veränderung in die Beschaffenheit; sie ist *am* Etwas das, was ein Anderes wird. Es selbst erhält sich in der Veränderung, welche nur diese unstete Oberfläche seines Andersseins, nicht seine Bestimmung trifft.

Bestimmung und Beschaffenheit sind so voneinander unterschieden; Etwas ist seiner Bestimmung nach gleichgültig gegen seine Beschaffenheit. Das aber, was Etwas *an ihm* hat, ist die sie beide verbindende Mitte dieses Schlusses. Das *Am-Etwas*-Sein zeigte sich aber vielmehr, in jene beiden Extreme zu zerfallen. Die einfache Mitte ist die *Bestimmtheit* als solche; ihrer Identität gehört sowohl Bestimmung als Beschaffenheit an. Aber die Bestimmung geht für sich selbst in Beschaffenheit und diese in jene über. Dies liegt im Bisherigen; der Zusammenhang ist näher dieser: Insofern das, was Etwas *an sich* ist, auch *an ihm* ist, ist es mit Sein-für-Anderes behaftet; die Bestimmung ist damit als solche offen dem Verhältnis zu Anderem. Die Bestimmtheit ist zugleich Moment, enthält aber zugleich den qualitativen Unterschied, vom Ansichsein verschieden, das Negative des Etwas, ein anderes Dasein zu sein. Die so das Andere in sich fassende Bestimmtheit, mit dem Ansichsein vereinigt, bringt das Anderssein in das Ansichsein oder in die Bestimmung hinein, welche dadurch zur Beschaffenheit herabgesetzt ist. — Umgekehrt das Sein-für-Anderes als Beschaffenheit isoliert und für sich gesetzt, ist es an ihm dasselbe, was das Andere als solches, das Andere an ihm selbst, d. i. seiner selbst ist; so ist es aber sich *auf sich beziehendes* Dasein, so Ansichsein mit einer Bestimmtheit, also *Bestimmung*. — Es *hängt* hiermit, insofern beide auch außereinanderzuhalten sind, die Beschaffenheit, die in einem Äußerlichen, einem Anderen überhaupt gegründet erscheint, auch von der Bestimmung *ab*, und das fremde Bestimmen ist durch die eigene, immanente des Etwas zugleich bestimmt. Aber ferner gehört die Beschaffenheit zu dem, was das Etwas an sich ist: mit seiner Beschaffenheit ändert sich Etwas.

Diese Änderung des Etwas ist nicht mehr die erste Veränderung des Etwas bloß nach seinem Sein-für-Anderes; jene erste war nur die an sich seiende, dem inneren Begriffe angehörige Veränderung; die Veränderung ist nunmehr auch die am Etwas gesetzte. — Das Etwas selbst ist weiter bestimmt und die Negation als ihm immanent gesetzt, als sein entwickeltes Insichsein.

Zunächst ist das Übergehen der Bestimmung und Beschaffenheit ineinander das Aufheben ihres Unterschiedes; damit ist das Dasein oder Etwas

determinate being of the something, which is also *its* determinate being, but does not belong to the something's in-itself. The determinateness is thus a *constitution.*

Constituted in this or that way, something is involved in external influences and relationships. This external connection on which the constitution depends, and the circumstance of being determined by an other, appears as something contingent. But it is the quality of something to be open to external influences and to have a *constitution.*

In so far as something alters, the alteration falls within its constitution; it is that *in* the something which becomes an other. The something itself preserves itself in the alteration which affects only this unstable surface of its otherness, not its determination.

Determination and constitution are thus distinguished from each other; something, in accordance with its determination, is indifferent to its constitution. But that which something has *in it,* is the middle term connecting them in this syllogism. Or, rather, *the being-in-the-something* showed itself as falling apart into these two extremes. The simple middle term is *determinateness* as such; to its identity belongs both determination and constitution.[13] But determination spontaneously passes over into constitution, and the latter into the former. This is implied in what has been said already; the connection is more precisely this: in so far as that which something is *in itself* is also present *in it,* it is burdened with being-for-other; hence the determination is, as such, open to relationship to other. The determinateness is at the same time a moment, but contains at the same time the qualitative distinction of being different from the in-itself, of being the negative of the something, another determinate being. The determinateness which thus holds the other within it, being united with the in-itself, brings the otherness into the latter or into the determination, which, consequently, is reduced to constitution. Conversely, being-for-other isolated as constitution and posited by itself, is in its own self the same as the other as such, the other in its own self, that is, the other of itself;[14] but thus it is *self-related* determinate being, the in-itself with a determinateness, and therefore a *determination.* Consequently, in so far as determination and constitution are also to be held apart, the latter, which appears to be grounded in something external, in an other in general, also *depends* on the former, and the determining from outside is at the same time determined by the something's own, immanent determination. But further, the constitution belongs to that which the something is in itself; something alters with its constitution.

This alteration of something is no longer the first alteration of something merely in accordance with its being-for-other; the first was only an intrinsic [*an sich seiend*] alteration belonging to the inner Notion;[15] now alteration is also

13. See chapter 19, below, p. 351.
14. See Hegel, *SL* 118/1:127 (213).
15. This is probably a reference back to Hegel's first discussion of alteration or change (see Hegel, *SL* 118/1:127 [213])— though that discussion occurred *before* the category of being-for-other was introduced. Since that first change was intrinsic to something (as a sheer other), rather than posited in something by something else, I have translated *an sich seiend* as "intrinsic." Miller, by contrast, translates it as "implicit."

überhaupt gesetzt, und indem es aus jenem Unterschiede resultiert, der das qualitative Anderssein ebenso in sich befaßt, sind Zwei Etwas, aber nicht nur Andere gegeneinander überhaupt, so daß diese Negation noch abstrakt wäre und nur in die Vergleichung fiele, sondern sie ist nunmehr als den Etwas *immanent*. Sie sind als *daseiend* gleichgültig gegeneinander, aber diese ihre Affirmation ist nicht mehr unmittelbare, jedes bezieht sich auf sich selbst *vermittels* des Aufhebens des Andersseins, welches in der Bestimmung in das Ansichsein reflektiert ist.

Etwas verhält sich so *aus sich selbst* zum Anderen, weil das Anderssein als sein eigenes Moment in ihm gesetzt ist; sein Insichsein befaßt die Negation in sich, vermittels derer überhaupt es nun sein affirmatives Dasein hat. Aber von diesem ist das Andere auch qualitativ unterschieden, es ist hiermit außer dem Etwas gesetzt. Die Negation seines Anderen ist nur die Qualität des Etwas, denn als dieses Aufheben seines Anderen ist es Etwas. Damit tritt erst eigentlich das Andere einem Dasein selbst gegenüber; dem ersten Etwas ist das Andere nur äußerlich gegenüber, oder aber, indem sie in der Tat schlechthin, d. i. ihrem Begriffe nach zusammenhängen, ist ihr Zusammenhang dieser, daß das Dasein in Anderssein, Etwas in Anderes *übergegangen*, Etwas sosehr als das Andere ein Anderes ist. Insofern nun das Insichsein das Nichtsein des Andersseins [ist], welches in ihm enthalten, aber zugleich als seiend unterschieden [ist], ist das Etwas selbst die Negation, *das Aufhören eines Anderen an ihm*; es ist als sich negativ dagegen verhaltend und sich damit erhaltend gesetzt; — dies Andere, das Insichsein des Etwas als Negation der Negation ist sein *Ansichsein*, und zugleich ist dies Aufheben als einfache Negation *an ihm*, nämlich als seine Negation des ihm äußerlichen anderen Etwas. Es ist *eine* Bestimmtheit derselben, welche sowohl mit dem Insichsein der Etwas identisch [ist], als Negation der Negation, als auch, indem diese Negationen als andere Etwas gegeneinander sind, sie aus ihnen selbst zusammenschließt und ebenso voneinander, jedes das Andere negierend, abscheidet, — die *Grenze*.

3. Sein-für-Anderes ist unbestimmte, affirmative Gemeinschaft von Etwas mit seinem Anderen; in der Grenze hebt sich das *Nichtsein*-für-Anderes hervor, die qualitative Negation des Anderen, welches dadurch von dem in sich reflektierten Etwas abgehalten wird. Die Entwicklung dieses Begriffs ist zu sehen, welche sich aber vielmehr als Verwicklung und Widerspruch zeigt. Dieser ist sogleich darin vorhanden, daß die Grenze als in sich reflektierte Negation des Etwas die Momente des Etwas und des Anderen in ihr *ideell* enthält, und diese als unterschiedene Momente zugleich in der Sphäre des Daseins als *reell*, *qualitativ unterschieden* gesetzt sind.

α) Etwas also ist unmittelbares sich auf sich beziehendes Dasein und hat eine Grenze zunächst als gegen Anderes: sie ist das Nichtsein des Anderen,

posited in the something. The something itself is further determined and the negation is posited as immanent in it, as its developed *being-within-self.*

In the first place, the transition of determination and constitution into each other is the sublation of their difference, resulting in the positing of determinate being or something in general; and since this latter results from that difference which equally includes within it qualitative otherness, there are *two* somethings which, however, are not opposed to each other only as others in general—for in that case this negation would still be abstract and would arise only from *comparing* them. But the negation is now *immanent* in the somethings. As *determinate beings* they are indifferent to each other, but this their affirmation is no longer immediate, each relates itself to itself only *by means of* the sublation of the otherness which, in the determination, is reflected into the in-itself.

Thus something *through its own nature* relates itself to the other, because otherness is posited in it as its own moment; its being-within-self includes the negation within it, by means of which alone it now has its affirmative determinate being. But the other is also qualitatively distinguished from this and is thus posited outside the something. The negation of its other is only[16] the quality of the something, for it is as this sublating of its other that it is something. It is only in this sublation that the other is really opposed to another determinate being; the other is only externally opposed to the *first* something, or rather, since in fact they are *directly* connected, that is in their Notion, their connection is this, that determinate being has *passed over* into otherness, something into other, and something is just as much an other as the other itself is.[17] Now in so far as the being-within-self is the non-being of the otherness which is contained in it but which at the same time has a distinct being of its own, the something is itself the negation, *the ceasing of an other in it*; it is posited as relating itself negatively to the other and in so doing preserving itself; this other, the being-within-self of the something as negation of the negation, is its *in-itself,*[18] and at the same time this sublation is *present in it* as a simple negation, namely, as its negation of the other something external to it. There is a *single* determinateness of both, which on the one hand is identical with the being-within-self of the somethings as negation of the negation, and on the other hand, since these negations are opposed to one another as other somethings, conjoins and equally disjoins them through their own nature, each negating the other: this determinateness is *limit.*

3. Being-for-other is the indeterminate, affirmative community of something with its other; in the limit the *non-being*-for-other becomes prominent, the qualitative negation of the other, which is thereby kept apart from the something which is reflected into itself. We must observe the development of this Notion, which manifests itself, however, rather as an entanglement and a contradiction. This contradiction is at once to be found in the circumstance that the limit, as

16. Miller has "now," reading *nun* for *nur*. In my view, "now" makes better sense here than "only," but both the Suhrkamp and the Meiner editions have *nur*, so I have revised the English translation accordingly.

17. See Hegel, *SL* 117–18/1: 125–6 (211–13).

18. For one possible reading of this unusually opaque statement, see chapter 19, below, p. 358.

nicht des Etwas selbst; es begrenzt in ihr sein Anderes. — Aber das Andere ist selbst ein Etwas überhaupt; die Grenze also, welche das Etwas gegen das Andere hat, ist auch Grenze des Anderen als Etwas, Grenze desselben, wodurch es das erste Etwas als *sein* Anderes von sich abhält, oder ist ein *Nichtsein jenes Etwas*; so ist sie nicht nur Nichtsein des Anderen, sondern des einen wie des anderen Etwas, somit des *Etwas* überhaupt.

Aber sie ist wesentlich ebenso das Nichtsein des Anderen, so *ist* Etwas zugleich durch seine Grenze. Indem Etwas begrenzend ist, wird es zwar dazu herabgesetzt, selbst begrenzt zu sein; aber seine Grenze ist, als Aufhören des Anderen an ihm, zugleich selbst nur das Sein des Etwas; *dieses ist durch sie das, was es ist*, hat *in ihr seine Qualität*. — Dies Verhältnis ist die äußere Erscheinung dessen, daß die Grenze einfache Negation oder die *erste* Negation, das Andere aber zugleich die Negation der Negation, das Insichsein des Etwas ist.

Etwas ist also als unmittelbares Dasein die Grenze gegen anderes Etwas, aber es hat sie *an ihm selbst* und ist Etwas durch die Vermittlung derselben, die ebensosehr sein Nichtsein ist. Sie ist die Vermittlung, wodurch Etwas und Anderes *sowohl ist* als *nicht ist*.

β) Insofern nun Etwas in seiner Grenze *ist* und *nicht ist* und diese Momente ein unmittelbarer, qualitativer Unterschied sind, so fällt das Nichtdasein und das Dasein des Etwas außereinander. Etwas hat sein Dasein *außer* (oder, wie man es sich auch vorstellt, *innerhalb*) seiner Grenze; ebenso ist auch das Andere, weil es Etwas ist, außerhalb derselben. Sie ist die *Mitte zwischen* beiden, in der sie aufhören. Sie haben das *Dasein jenseits* voneinander und *von ihrer Grenze*; die Grenze als das Nichtsein eines jeden ist das Andere von beiden.

Nach dieser Verschiedenheit des Etwas von seiner Grenze erscheint die *Linie* als Linie nur außerhalb ihrer Grenze, des Punktes; die *Fläche* als Fläche außerhalb der Linie; der *Körper* als Körper nur außerhalb seiner begrenzenden Fläche. — Dies ist die Seite, von welcher die Grenze zunächst in die Vorstellung — das Außersichsein des Begriffes — fällt, als vornehmlich auch in den räumlichen Gegenständen genommen wird.

γ) Ferner aber ist das Etwas, wie es außer der Grenze ist, das unbegrenzte Etwas, nur das Dasein überhaupt. So ist es nicht von seinem Anderen unterschieden; es ist nur Dasein, hat also mit seinem Anderen dieselbe Bestimmung, jedes ist nur Etwas überhaupt, oder jedes ist Anderes; beide sind so *dasselbe*. Aber dies ihr zunächst unmittelbares Dasein ist nun gesetzt mit der Bestimmtheit als Grenze, in welcher beide sind, was sie sind, unterschieden voneinander. Sie ist aber ebenso ihre *gemeinschaftliche* Unterschiedenheit, die Einheit und Unterschiedenheit derselben, wie das Dasein. Diese doppelte Identität beider, das Dasein und die Grenze, enthält dies, daß das Etwas sein Dasein nur in der Grenze hat und daß, indem die Grenze und das unmittelbare Dasein beide zugleich das Negative voneinander

something's negation reflected into itself, contains *ideally* in it the moments of something and other, and these, as distinguished moments, are at the same time posited in the sphere of determinate being as *really, qualitatively distinct.*

(α) Something, therefore, is immediate, self-related determinate being, and has a limit, in the first place, relatively to an other; the limit is the non-being of the other, not of the something itself: in the limit, something limits its other. But the other is itself a something in general, therefore the limit which something has relatively to the other is also the limit of the other as a something, its limit whereby it keeps the first something as *its* other apart from it, or is a *non-being of that something;* it is thus not only non-being of the other, but non-being equally of the one and of the other something, consequently of the something as such.

But the limit is essentially equally the non-being of the other, and so something at the same time *is* through its limit. It is true that something, in limiting the other, is subjected to being limited itself; but at the same time its limit is, as the ceasing of the other in it, itself only the being of the something; *through the limit something is what it is, and in the limit it has its quality.* This relationship is the outward manifestation of the fact that the limit is simple negation or the *first* negation, whereas the other is, at the same time, the negation of the negation, the being-within-itself of the something.

Something, as an immediate determinate being, is, therefore, the limit relatively to another something, but the limit is present in the something itself, which is a something through the mediation of the limit which is just as much the non-being of the something. Limit is the mediation through which something and other each as well *is,* as *is not.*

(β) Now in so far as something in its limit both *is* and *is not,* and these moments are an immediate, qualitative difference, the negative determinate being and the determinate being of the something fall outside each other. Something has its determinate being *outside* (or, as it is also put, on the *inside*) of its limit; similarly, the other, too, because it is a something, is outside it. Limit is the *middle between* the two of them in which they cease. They have their determinate being *beyond* each other and *beyond* their limit; the limit as the non-being of each is the other of both.

It is in accordance with this difference of something from its limit that the line appears as line only outside its limit, the point; the plane as plane outside the line; the solid as solid only outside its limiting surface. It is primarily this aspect of limit which is seized by pictorial thought—the self-externality of the Notion—and especially, too, in reference to spatial objects.

(γ) But further, something as it is outside the limit, the unlimited something, is only a determinate being in general. As such, it is not distinguished from its other; it is only determinate being and therefore has the same determination as its other; each is only a something in general, or each is an other; thus both are the *same.* But this their primarily immediate determinate being is now posited with the determinateness as limit, in which both are what they are, distinguished from each other. Limit is, however, equally their *common* distinguishedness, their unity and distinguishedness, like determinate being. This double identity of

sind, das Etwas, welches nur in seiner Grenze ist, ebensosehr sich von sich selbst trennt und über sich hinaus auf sein Nichtsein weist und dies als sein Sein ausspricht und so in dasselbe übergeht. Um dies auf das vorige Beispiel anzuwenden, so ist die eine Bestimmung, daß Etwas das, was es ist, nur in seiner Grenze ist. — So ist also der *Punkt* nicht nur so Grenze der *Linie*, daß diese in ihm nur aufhört und sie als Dasein außer ihm ist, — die *Linie* nicht nur so Grenze der *Fläche*, daß diese in der Linie nur aufhört, ebenso die *Fläche* als Grenze des *Körpers*. Sondern im Punkte *fängt* die Linie auch *an*; er ist ihr absoluter Anfang; auch insofern sie als nach ihren beiden Seiten unbegrenzt oder, wie man es ausdrückt, als ins Unendliche verlängert vorgestellt wird, macht der Punkt ihr *Element* aus, wie die Linie das Element der Fläche, die Fläche das des Körpers. Diese *Grenzen* sind *Prinzip* dessen, das sie begrenzen; wie das Eins, z. B. als Hundertstes, Grenze ist, aber auch Element des ganzen Hundert.

Die andere Bestimmung ist die Unruhe des Etwas in seiner Grenze, in der es immanent ist, der *Widerspruch* zu sein, der es über sich selbst hinausschickt. So ist der Punkt diese Dialektik seiner selbst, zur Linie zu werden, die Linie die Dialektik, zur Fläche, die Fläche die, zum totalen Raume zu werden. Von Linie, Fläche und ganzem Raum wird eine zweite Definition so gegeben, daß durch die *Bewegung* des Punktes die Linie, durch die Bewegung der Linie die Fläche entsteht usf. Diese *Bewegung* des Punktes, der Linie usf. wird aber als etwas Zufälliges oder nur so Vorgestelltes angesehen. Dies ist jedoch eigentlich darin zurückgenommen, daß die Bestimmungen, aus denen Linie usf. entstehen sollen, ihre *Elemente* und *Prinzipien* seien, und diese sind nichts anderes als zugleich ihre Grenzen; das Entstehen wird so nicht für zufällig oder nur so vorgestellt betrachtet. Daß Punkt, Linie, Fläche, für sich, sich widersprechend, Anfänge sind, welche selbst sich von sich abstoßen, und der Punkt somit aus sich durch seinen Begriff in die Linie übergeht, *sich an sich bewegt* und sie entstehen macht usf., — liegt in dem Begriffe der dem Etwas immanenten Grenze. Die Anwendung jedoch selbst gehört in die Betrachtung des Raums; um sie hier anzudeuten, so ist der Punkt die ganz abstrakte Grenze, aber *in einem Dasein*; dieses ist noch ganz unbestimmt genommen, es ist der sogenannte absolute, d. h. abstrakte *Raum*, das schlechthin kontinuierliche Außereinandersein. Damit, daß die Grenze nicht abstrakte Negation, sondern *in diesem Dasein*, daß sie *räumliche* Bestimmtheit ist, ist der Punkt räumlich, der Widerspruch der abstrakten Negation und der Kontinuität und damit das Übergehen und Übergegangensein in Linie usf., wie es denn keinen Punkt *gibt*, wie auch nicht eine Linie und Fläche.

Etwas mit seiner immanenten Grenze gesetzt als der Widerspruch seiner selbst, durch den es über sich hinausgewiesen und getrieben wird, ist das *Endliche*.

both, determinate being and limit, contains this:[19] that something has its determinate being only in the limit, and that since the limit and the determinate being are each at the same time the negative of each other, the something, which *is* only in its limit, just as much separates itself from itself and points beyond itself to its non-being, declaring this is to be its being and thus passing over into it. To apply this to the preceding example and taking first the determination that something is what it is only in its limit: as thus determined, the point is therefore the limit of the line, not merely in the sense that the line only ceases in the point, and as a determinate being is outside it; neither is the line the limit of the plane merely in the sense that the plane only ceases in it—and similarly with surface as limit of the solid; on the contrary, in the point the line also *begins*; the point is its absolute beginning. Even when the line is represented as unlimited on either side, or, as it is put, is produced to infinity, the point still constitutes its *element,* just as the line is the element of the plane, and the surface that of the solid. These limits are the *principle* of that which they limit; just as one, for example as hundredth, is the limit, but also the element, of the whole hundred.

The other determination is the unrest of the something in its limit in which it is immanent, an unrest which is the *contradiction* which impels the something out beyond itself. Thus the point is this dialectic of its own self to become a line, the line the dialectic to become a plane, and the plane the dialectic to become total space. A second definition is given of line, plane and total space: namely, that the line originates through the *movement* of the point, the plane through the movement of the line, and so on. But this *movement* of the point, line and so on, is regarded as something contingent or as only thus imagined. This point of view is, however, really retracted in so far as the determinations from which the line and so on are supposed to originate are their elements and principles which, at the same time, are nothing else but their limits; and so the origin is not considered as contingent or as only thus imagined. That point, line and plane by themselves are self-contradictory, are *beginnings* which spontaneously repel themselves from themselves, so that the point, through its Notion, passes out of itself into the line, *moves in itself* and gives rise to the line, and so on, lies in the Notion of limit which is immanent in the something. The application itself, however, belongs to the consideration of space; to give an indication of it here, the point is the wholly abstract limit, *but in a determinate being*; this is taken as still wholly abstract, it is so-called absolute, that is, abstract *space,* a purely continuous asunderness. But the limit is not abstract negation, but is *in this determinate being,* is a *spatial* determinateness; the point is, therefore, spatial, the contradiction of abstract negation and continuity, and is, therefore, the transition, the accomplished transition into the line, and so on; just as also, for the same reason, *there is* no such thing as a point, line or plane.

Something with its immanent limit posited as the contradiction of itself, through which it is directed and forced out of and beyond itself, is the *finite.*

---

19. Miller has "This double identity of both, of determinate being and limit." See chapter 19, below, note 24 (p. 368).

c. Die Endlichkeit

Das Dasein ist bestimmt; Etwas hat eine Qualität und ist in ihr nicht nur bestimmt, sondern begrenzt; seine Qualität ist seine Grenze, mit welcher behaftet es zunächst affirmatives, ruhiges Dasein bleibt. Aber diese Negation entwickelt, so daß der Gegensatz seines Daseins und der Negation als ihm immanenter Grenze selbst das Insichsein des Etwas und dieses somit nur Werden an ihm selbst sei, macht seine Endlichkeit aus.

Wenn wir von den Dingen sagen, *sie sind endlich*, so wird darunter verstanden, daß sie nicht nur eine Bestimmtheit haben, die Qualität nicht nur als Realität und ansichseiende Bestimmung, daß sie nicht bloß begrenzt sind —, sie haben so noch Dasein außer ihrer Grenze —, sondern daß vielmehr das Nichtsein ihre Natur, ihr Sein ausmacht. Die endlichen Dinge *sind*, aber ihre Beziehung auf sich selbst ist, daß sie als *negativ* sich auf sich selbst beziehen, eben in dieser Beziehung auf sich selbst sich über sich, über ihr Sein, hinauszuschicken. Sie *sind*, aber die Wahrheit dieses Seins ist ihr *Ende*. Das Endliche verändert sich nicht nur, wie Etwas überhaupt, sondern es *vergeht*, und es ist nicht bloß möglich, daß es vergeht, so daß es sein könnte, ohne zu vergehen. Sondern das Sein der endlichen Dinge als solches ist, den Keim des Vergehens als ihr Insichsein zu haben; die Stunde ihrer Geburt ist die Stunde ihres Todes.

α. Die Unmittelbarkeit der Endlichkeit. Der Gedanke an die Endlichkeit der Dinge führt diese Trauer mit sich, weil sie die auf die Spitze getriebene qualitative Negation ist, in der Einfachheit solcher Bestimmung ihnen nicht mehr ein affirmatives Sein *unterschieden* von ihrer Bestimmung zum Untergange gelassen ist. Die Endlichkeit ist um dieser qualitativen Einfachheit der Negation, die zum abstrakten Gegensatze des Nichts und Vergehens gegen das Sein zurückgegangen ist, die hartnäckigste Kategorie des Verstandes; die Negation überhaupt, Beschaffenheit, Grenze vertragen sich mit ihrem Anderen, dem Dasein; auch das abstrakte Nichts wird für sich als Abstraktion aufgegeben; aber Endlichkeit ist die als *an sich fixierte* Negation und steht daher seinem Affirmativen schroff gegenüber. Das Endliche läßt sich so in Fluß wohl bringen, es ist selbst dies, zu seinem Ende bestimmt zu sein, aber nur zu seinem Ende; — es ist vielmehr das Verweigern, sich zu seinem Affirmativen, dem Unendlichen hin affirmativ bringen, mit ihm sich verbinden zu lassen; es ist also untrennbar von seinem Nichts gesetzt und alle Versöhnung mit seinem Anderen, dem Affirmativen, dadurch abgeschnitten. Die Bestimmung der endlichen Dinge ist nicht eine weitere als ihr *Ende*. Der Verstand verharrt in dieser Trauer der Endlichkeit, indem er das Nichtsein zur Bestimmung der Dinge, es zugleich *unvergänglich* und *absolut* macht. Ihre Vergänglichkeit könnte nur in ihrem Anderen, dem Affirmativen, vergehen; so trennte sich ihre Endlichkeit von ihnen ab; aber sie ist ihre unveränderliche, d. i. nicht in ihr Anderes, d. i. nicht in ihr Affirmatives übergehende Qualität; *so ist sie ewig*.

Dies ist eine sehr wichtige Betrachtung; daß aber das Endliche absolut

(c) Finitude

The being of something [*Dasein*] is determinate; something has a quality and in it is not only determined but limited; its quality is its limit and, burdened with this, it remains in the first place an affirmative, stable being. But the development of this negation, so that the opposition between its determinate being and the negation as its immanent limit, is itself the being-within-self of the something, which is thus in its own self only a becoming, constitutes the finitude of something.

When we say of things that *they are finite,* we understand thereby that they not only have a determinateness, that their quality is not only a reality and an intrinsic determination, that finite things are not merely limited—as such they still have determinate being outside their limit—but that, on the contrary, non-being constitutes their nature and being. Finite things *are,* but their relation to themselves is that they are *negatively* self-related and in this very self-relation send themselves away beyond themselves, beyond their being. They *are*, but the truth of this being is their *end*. The finite not only alters, like something in general, but it *ceases to be*; and its ceasing to be is not merely a possibility, so that it could be without ceasing to be, but the being as such of finite things is to have the germ of decease as their being-within-self: the hour of their birth is the hour of their death.

(α) The Immediacy of Finitude. The thought of the finitude of things brings this sadness with it because it is qualitative negation pushed to its extreme, and in the singleness of such determination there is no longer left to things an affirmative being *distinct* from their destiny to perish. Because of this qualitative singleness of the negation, which has gone back to the abstract opposition of nothing and ceasing-to-be as opposed to being, finitude is the most stubborn category of the understanding; negation in general, constitution and limit, reconcile themselves with their other, with determinate being; and even nothing, taken abstractly as such, is given up as an abstraction; but finitude is the negation as *fixed in itself,* and it therefore stands in abrupt contrast to its affirmative. The finite, it is true, lets itself be brought into flux, it is itself this, to be determined or destined to its end, but *only* to its end—or rather, it is the refusal to let itself be brought affirmatively to its affirmative, to the infinite, and to let itself be united with it; it is therefore posited as inseparable from its nothing, and is thereby cut off from all reconciliation with its other, the affirmative. The determination or destiny of finite things takes them no further than their *end.* The understanding persists in this sadness of finitude by making non-being the determination of things and at the same time making it *imperishable* and *absolute.* Their transitoriness could only pass away or perish in their other, in the affirmative; their finitude would then be parted from them; but it is their unalterable quality, that is, their quality which does not pass over into its other, that is, into its affirmative; *it is thus eternal.*

This is a very important consideration; but certainly no philosophy or opinion, or understanding, will let itself be tied to the standpoint that the finite is

sei, solchen Standpunkt wird sich freilich irgendeine Philosophie oder Ansicht oder der Verstand nicht aufbürden lassen wollen; vielmehr ist das Gegenteil ausdrücklich in der Behauptung des Endlichen vorhanden; das Endliche ist das Beschränkte, Vergängliche; das Endliche ist *nur* das Endliche, nicht das Unvergängliche; dies liegt unmittelbar in seiner Bestimmung und Ausdruck. Aber es kommt darauf an, ob in der Ansicht *beim Sein der Endlichkeit* beharrt wird, die *Vergänglichkeit* bestehen bleibt, oder ob die *Vergänglichkeit* und das *Vergehen vergeht.* Daß dies aber nicht geschieht, ist das Faktum eben in derjenigen Ansicht des Endlichen, welche das *Vergehen* zum *Letzten* des Endlichen macht. Es ist die ausdrückliche Behauptung, daß das Endliche mit dem Unendlichen unverträglich und unvereinbar sei, das Endliche dem Unendlichen schlechthin entgegengesetzt sei. Dem Unendlichen ist Sein, absolutes Sein zugeschrieben; ihm gegenüber bleibt so das Endliche festgehalten als das Negative desselben; unvereinbar mit dem Unendlichen bleibt es absolut auf seiner eigenen Seite; Affirmation erhielte es vom Affirmativen, dem Unendlichen, und verginge so; aber eine Vereinigung mit demselben ist das, was für das Unmögliche erklärt wird. Soll es nicht beharren dem Unendlichen gegenüber, sondern vergehen, so ist, wie vorhin gesagt, eben sein Vergehen das Letzte, nicht das Affirmative, welches nur das Vergehen des Vergehens sein würde. Sollte aber das Endliche nicht im Affirmativen vergehen, sondern sein Ende als das *Nichts* gefaßt werden, so wären wir wieder bei jenem ersten, abstrakten Nichts, das selbst längst vergangen ist.

Bei diesem Nichts jedoch, welches *nur* Nichts sein soll und dem zugleich eine Existenz im Denken, Vorstellen oder Sprechen zugegeben wird, kommt derselbe Widerspruch vor, als soeben bei dem Endlichen angegeben worden, nur daß er dort nur *vorkommt*, aber in der Endlichkeit *ausdrücklich* ist. Dort erscheint er als subjektiv, hier wird behauptet, das Endliche *stehe perennierend* dem Unendlichen entgegen, das an sich Nichtige *sei*, und es sei *als* an sich Nichtiges. Dies ist zum Bewußtsein zu bringen; und die Entwicklung des Endlichen zeigt, daß es an ihm als dieser Widerspruch in sich zusammenfällt, aber ihn dahin wirklich auflöst, nicht daß es nur vergänglich ist und vergeht, sondern daß das Vergehen, das Nichts, nicht das Letzte ist, sondern vergeht.

β. Die Schranke und das Sollen. Dieser Widerspruch ist zwar abstrakt sogleich darin vorhanden, daß das *Etwas* endlich ist oder daß das Endliche *ist.* Aber *Etwas* oder das Sein ist nicht mehr abstrakt gesetzt, sondern in sich reflektiert und entwickelt als Insichsein, das eine Bestimmung und Beschaffenheit an ihm hat, und noch bestimmter, daß es eine Grenze an ihm hat, welche, als das dem Etwas Immanente und die Qualität seines Insichseins ausmachend, die Endlichkeit ist. In diesem Begriffe des endlichen Etwas ist zu sehen, was für Momente enthalten sind.

Bestimmung und Beschaffenheit ergaben sich als *Seiten* für die äußerliche Reflexion; jene enthielt aber schon das Anderssein als dem *Ansich* des Etwas angehörig; die Äußerlichkeit des Andersseins ist einerseits in der eigenen

absolute; the very opposite is expressly present in the assertion of the finite; the finite is limited, transitory, it is *only* finite, not imperishable; this is directly implied in its determination and expression. But the point is, whether in thinking of the finite one holds fast to the *being* of finitude and the *transitoriness* continues to be, or whether the *transitoriness* and the *ceasing-to-be cease to be*.[20] But it is precisely in that view of the finite which makes *ceasing-to-be* the *final* determination of the finite, that this does not happen. It is the express assertion that the finite is irreconcilable with the infinite and cannot be united with it, that the finite is utterly opposed to the infinite. Being, absolute being, is ascribed to the infinite; confronting it, the finite thus remains held fast as its negative; incapable of union with the infinite, it remains absolute on its own side; from the affirmative, from the infinite, it would receive affirmation, and would thus cease to be; but a union with the infinite is just what is declared to be impossible. If it is not to endure over against the infinite but is to cease to be, then, as we have already said, just this ceasing-to-be is its final determination, not the affirmative which would be only the ceasing to be of the ceasing-to-be.[21] If, however, the finite is not to pass way in the affirmative, but its end is to be grasped as the *nothing*, then we should be back again at that first, abstract nothing which itself has long since passed away.

With this nothing, however, which is supposed to be *only* nothing, and which at the same time is granted an existence in thought, imagination or speech, there occurs the same contradiction as has just been indicated in connection with the finite, but with this difference, that in the case of that first nothing it only *occurs*, whereas in finitude it is *explicitly stated*. There it appears as subjective; here it is asserted that the finite *stands perpetually* opposed to the infinite, that what is in itself null *is*, and is *as* in itself null. We have to become conscious of this; and the development of the finite shows that, having this contradiction present within it, it collapses within itself, yet in doing so actually resolves the contradiction, that not only is the finite transitory and ceases to be, but that the ceasing-to-be, the nothing, is not the final determination, but itself ceases to be.

(β) Limitation and the Ought [or the Should]. This contradiction is, indeed, abstractly present simply in the circumstance that the *something* is finite, or that the finite is. But *something* or being is no longer abstractly posited but reflected into itself and developed as being-within-self which possesses a determination and a constitution, and, still more specifically, a limit which, as immanent in the something and constituting the quality of its being-within-self, is finitude. It is to be seen what moments are contained in this Notion of the finite something.

Determination and constitution showed themselves as *sides* for external reflection; but the former already contained otherness as belonging to the something's

---

20. Miller has "whether in thinking of the finite one holds fast to the *being* of finitude and lets the transitoriness continue to be." This is inaccurate and misses the contrast Hegel draws here between holding fast to finitude and *letting* it cease to be sheer ceasing-to-be.

21. Miller translates *beharren dem Unendlichen gegenüber* as "remain fixed in its opposition to the infinite."

Innerlichkeit des Etwas, andererseits bleibt sie als Äußerlichkeit unterschieden davon, sie ist noch Äußerlichkeit als solche, aber *an* dem Etwas. Indem aber ferner das Anderssein als *Grenze*, selbst als Negation der Negation, bestimmt ist, so ist das dem Etwas immanente Anderssein als die Beziehung der beiden Seiten gesetzt, und die Einheit des Etwas mit sich, dem sowohl die Bestimmung als die Beschaffenheit angehört, [ist] seine gegen sich selbst gekehrte Beziehung, die seine immanente Grenze in ihm negierende Beziehung seiner an sich seienden Bestimmung darauf. Das mit sich identische Insichsein bezieht sich so auf sich selbst als sein eigenes Nichtsein, aber als Negation der Negation, als dasselbe negierend, das zugleich Dasein in ihm behält, denn es ist die Qualität seines Insichseins. Die eigene Grenze des Etwas, so von ihm als ein Negatives, das zugleich wesentlich ist, gesetzt, ist nicht nur Grenze als solche, sondern *Schranke*. Aber die Schranke ist nicht allein das als negiert Gesetzte; die Negation ist zweischneidig, indem das von ihr als negiert Gesetzte die *Grenze* ist; diese nämlich ist überhaupt das Gemeinschaftliche des Etwas und des Anderen, auch Bestimmtheit des *Ansichseins* der Bestimmung als solcher. Dieses Ansichsein hiermit ist als die negative Beziehung auf seine von ihm auch unterschiedene Grenze, auf sich als Schranke, *Sollen*.

Daß die Grenze, die am Etwas überhaupt ist, Schranke sei, muß es zugleich in sich selbst *über sie hinausgehen*, sich an ihm selbst *auf sie als auf ein Nichtseiendes* beziehen. Das Dasein des Etwas liegt ruhig gleichgültig gleichsam *neben* seiner Grenze. Etwas geht aber über seine Grenze nur hinaus, insofern es deren Aufgehobensein, das gegen sie negative Ansichsein ist. Und indem sie in der *Bestimmung* selbst als Schranke ist, geht Etwas damit *über sich selbst* hinaus.

Das Sollen enthält also die verdoppelte Bestimmung, *einmal* sie als an sich seiende Bestimmung gegen die Negation, das *andere Mal* aber dieselbe als ein Nichtsein, das als Schranke von ihr unterschieden, aber zugleich selbst ansichseiende Bestimmung ist.

Das Endliche hat sich so als die Beziehung seiner Bestimmung auf seine Grenze bestimmt; jene ist in dieser Beziehung *Sollen*, diese ist *Schranke*. Beide sind so Momente des Endlichen, somit beide selbst endlich, sowohl das Sollen als die Schranke. Aber nur die Schranke ist als das Endliche *gesetzt*; das Sollen ist nur an sich, somit für uns, beschränkt. Durch seine Beziehung auf die ihm selbst schon immanente Grenze ist es beschränkt, aber diese seine Beschränkung ist in das Ansichsein eingehüllt, denn nach seinem Dasein, d. i. nach seiner Bestimmtheit gegen die Schranke ist es als das Ansichsein gesetzt.

Was sein soll, *ist* und *ist* zugleich *nicht*. Wenn es *wäre*, so *sollte* es nicht bloß *sein*. Also das Sollen hat wesentlich eine Schranke. Diese Schranke ist nicht ein Fremdes; *das, was nur sein soll*, ist die *Bestimmung*, die nun gesetzt ist, wie sie in der Tat ist, nämlich zugleich nur eine Bestimmtheit.

Das Ansichsein des Etwas in seiner Bestimmung setzt sich also zum

in-itself; the externality of the otherness is on the one hand in the something's own inwardness, on the other hand it remains, as externality, distinguished from it, it is still externality as such, but present *in* the something. But further, since the otherness is determined as *limit,* as itself negation of the negation, the otherness immanent in the something is posited as the connection of the two sides, and the unity with itself of the something which possesses both determination and constitution, is its relation turned towards its own self, the relation of its *intrinsic* determination to the limit immanent in the something, a relation in which this immanent limit is negated.[22] The self-identical being-within-self thus relates itself to itself as [to] its own non-being, but as negation of the negation, as negating the non-being which at the same time retains in it determinate being, for determinate being is the quality of its being-within-self. Something's own limit thus posited by it as a negative which is at the same time essential, is not merely limit as such, but *limitation.* But what is posited as negated is not limitation alone; the negation is two-edged, since what is posited by it as negated is the *limit,* and this is in general what is common to both something and other, and is also a determinateness of the *in-itself* of the determination as such. This *in-itself,* therefore, as the negative relation to its limit (which is also distinguished from it), to itself as limitation, is the *ought.*

In order that the limit which is in something as such should be a limitation, something must at the same time in its own self transcend the limit, it must in its own self *be related to the limit as to that which is not.*[23] The determinate being of something lies inertly indifferent, as it were, *alongside* its limit. But something only transcends its limit in so far as it is the accomplished sublation of the limit, is the *in-itself* as negatively related to it. And since the limit is in the *determination* itself as a limitation, something transcends *its own self.*

The ought therefore contains the determination in double form: once as the *intrinsic* determination counter to the negation, and again as a non-being which, as a limitation, is distinguished from the determination, but is at the same time itself an intrinsic determination.[24]

The finite has thus determined itself as the relation of its determination to its limit; in this relation, the determination is an ought and the limit is a *limitation.* Both are thus moments of the finite and hence are themselves finite, both the ought and the limitation. But only the limitation is *posited* as finite; the ought is limited only in itself, that is, for us. It is limited through its relation to the limit which is already immanent in the ought itself, but this its restriction is enveloped in the in-itself, for, in accordance with its determinate being, that is, its determinateness relatively to the limitation, it is posited as the in-itself.

What ought to be *is,* and at the same time *is not.* If it *were,* we could not say that it *ought* merely *to be.* The ought has, therefore, essentially a limitation. This limitation is not alien to it; that which *only* ought to be is the *determination,* which is now posited as it is in fact, namely, as at the same time only a determinateness.

22. Miller translates *an sich seiende Bestimmung* as "implicit determination."

23. Miller has "*as to something which is not.*"

24. Miller again translates *an sich seiende Bestimmung* as "implicit determination."

Sollen herab dadurch, daß dasselbe, was sein Ansichsein ausmacht, in einer und derselben Rücksicht als *Nichtsein* ist; und zwar so, daß im Insichsein, der Negation der Negation, jenes Ansichsein als die eine Negation (das Negierende) Einheit mit der anderen ist, die zugleich als qualitativ andere Grenze ist, wodurch jene Einheit als *Beziehung* auf sie ist. Die Schranke des Endlichen ist nicht ein Äußeres, sondern seine eigene Bestimmung ist auch seine Schranke; und diese ist sowohl sie selbst als auch Sollen; sie ist das Gemeinschaftliche beider oder vielmehr das, worin beide identisch sind.

Als Sollen geht nun aber ferner das Endliche über seine Schranke *hinaus*; dieselbe Bestimmtheit, welche seine Negation ist, ist auch aufgehoben und ist so sein Ansichsein; seine Grenze ist auch nicht seine Grenze.

Als *Sollen* ist somit Etwas *über seine Schranke erhaben*, umgekehrt aber hat es nur *als Sollen* seine *Schranke*. Beides ist untrennbar. Etwas hat insofern eine Schranke, als es in seiner Bestimmung die Negation hat, und die Bestimmung ist auch das Aufgehobensein der Schranke. [A]

γ. Übergang des Endlichen in das Unendliche. Das Sollen für sich enthält die Schranke und die Schranke das Sollen. Ihre Beziehung aufeinander ist das Endliche selbst, das sie beide in seinem Insichsein enthält. Diese Momente seiner Bestimmung sind sich qualitativ entgegengesetzt; die Schranke ist bestimmt als das Negative des Sollens und das Sollen ebenso als das Negative der Schranke. Das Endliche ist so der Widerspruch seiner in sich; es hebt sich auf, vergeht. Aber dies sein Resultat, das Negative überhaupt, ist 1. seine *Bestimmung* selbst; denn es ist das Negative des Negativen. So ist das Endliche in dem Vergehen nicht vergangen; es ist zunächst nur ein *anderes* Endliches geworden, welches aber ebenso das Vergehen als Übergehen in ein anderes Endliches ist, und so fort etwa ins *Unendliche*. Aber 2. näher dies Resultat betrachtet, so hat das Endliche in seinem Vergehen, dieser Negation seiner selbst, sein Ansichsein erreicht, es ist darin *mit sich selbst zusammengegangen*. Jedes seiner Momente enthält eben dies Resultat; das Sollen geht über die Schranke, d. i. über sich selbst hinaus; über es hinaus aber oder sein Anderes ist nur die Schranke selbst. Die Schranke aber weist über sich selbst unmittelbar hinaus zu seinem Anderen, welches das Sollen ist; dieses aber ist dieselbe Entzweiung des *Ansichseins* und des *Daseins* wie die Schranke, ist dasselbe; über sich hinaus geht sie daher ebenso nur mit sich zusammen. Diese *Identität mit sich*, die Negation der Negation, ist affirmatives Sein, so das Andere des Endlichen, als welches die erste Negation zu seiner Bestimmtheit haben soll; — jenes Andere ist *das Unendliche*.

The being-in-itself of the something in its determination reduces itself therefore to an *ought-to-be* through the fact that the same thing which constitutes its in-itself is in one and the same respect a *non-being*; and that, too, in this way, that in the being-within-self, in the negation of the negation, this in-itself as one of the negations (the one that negates) is a unity with the other, which at the same time is a qualitatively distinct limit, through which this unity is a *relation* to it. The limitation of the finite is not something external to it; on the contrary, its own determination is also its limitation; and this latter is both itself and also the ought-to-be; it is that which is common to both, or rather that in which both are identical.

But now further, the finite as the ought *transcends* its limitation; the same determinateness which is its negation is also sublated, and is thus its in-itself; its limit is also not its limit.

Hence as the ought, something is *raised above its limitation*, but conversely, it is only as the *ought* that it has its *limitation*. The two are inseparable. Something has a limitation in so far as it has negation in its determination, and the determination is also the accomplished sublation of the limitation. [R]

(γ) Transition of the Finite into the Infinite. The ought as such contains limitation, and limitation contains the ought. Their relation to each other is the finite itself which contains them both in its being-within-self. These moments of its determination are qualitatively opposed; limitation is determined as the negative of the ought and the ought likewise as the negative of limitation. The finite is thus inwardly self-contradictory; it sublates itself, ceases to be. But this its result, the negative as such, is (α) its very *determination*; for it is the negative of the negative. Thus, in ceasing to be, the finite has not ceased to be; it has become in the first instance only *another* finite which, however, is equally a ceasing-to-be as transition into another finite, and so on to *infinity*.[25] But (b) closer consideration of this result shows that the finite in its ceasing-to-be, in this negation of itself has attained its being-in-itself, is *united with itself*. Each of its moments contains precisely this result; the ought transcends the limitation, that is, transcends itself; but beyond itself or its other, is only the limitation itself. The limitation, however, points directly beyond itself to its other, which is the ought; but this latter is the same duality of *being-in-itself* and *determinate being* as the limitation; it is the same thing; in going beyond itself, therefore, it equally only unites with itself. This *identity with itself*, the negation of negation, is affirmative being and thus the other of the finite, of the finite which is supposed to have the first negation for its determinateness; this other is the *infinite*.

25. For an analysis of this important transition, see chapter 21, below, pp. 394–6.

C. Die Unendlichkeit

Das Unendliche in seinem einfachen Begriff kann zunächst als eine neue Definition des Absoluten angesehen werden; es ist als die bestimmungslose Beziehung-auf-sich gesetzt als *Sein* und *Werden*. Die Formen des *Daseins* fallen aus in der Reihe der Bestimmungen, die für Definitionen des Absoluten angesehen werden können, da die Formen jener Sphäre für sich unmittelbar nur als Bestimmtheiten, als endliche überhaupt, gesetzt sind. Das Unendliche aber gilt schlechthin für absolut, da es ausdrücklich als Negation des Endlichen bestimmt ist, hiermit auf die Beschränktheit, derer das Sein und Werden, wenn sie auch an ihnen keine Beschränktheit haben oder zeigen, doch etwa fähig sein könnten, im Unendlichen ausdrücklich Beziehung genommen und eine solche an ihm negiert ist.

Damit aber selbst ist das Unendliche nicht schon in der Tat der Beschränktheit und Endlichkeit entnommen; die Hauptsache ist, den wahrhaften Begriff der Unendlichkeit von der schlechten Unendlichkeit, das Unendliche der Vernunft von dem Unendlichen des Verstandes zu unterscheiden; doch letzteres ist das *verendlichte* Unendliche, und es wird sich ergeben, daß, eben indem das Unendliche vom Endlichen rein und entfernt gehalten werden soll, es nur verendlicht wird.

Das Unendliche ist

a) in *einfacher Bestimmung* das Affirmative als Negation des Endlichen;

b) es ist aber damit in *Wechselbestimmung* mit dem *Endlichen* und ist das abstrakte, *einseitige Unendliche;*

c) das Sichaufheben dieses Unendlichen wie des Endlichen als *ein* Prozeß ist das *wahrhafte Unendliche.*

a. Das Unendliche überhaupt

Das Unendliche ist die Negation der Negation, das Affirmative, das *Sein*, das sich aus der Beschränktheit wieder hergestellt hat. Das Unendliche *ist*, und in intensiverem Sinn als das erste unmittelbare Sein; es ist das wahrhafte Sein, die Erhebung aus der Schranke. Bei dem Namen des Unendlichen *geht* dem Gemüt und dem Geiste sein Licht *auf*, denn er *ist* darin nicht nur abstrakt bei sich, sondern erhebt sich zu sich selbst, zum Lichte seines Denkens, seiner Allgemeinheit, seiner Freiheit.

Zuerst hat sich für den Begriff des Unendlichen ergeben, daß das Dasein in seinem Ansichsein sich als Endliches bestimmt und über die Schranke hinausgeht. Es ist die Natur des Endlichen selbst, über sich hinauszugehen, seine

Chapter Thirteen

Infinity: Text

C. Infinity

The infinite in its simple Notion can, in the first place, be regarded as a fresh definition of the absolute; as indeterminate self-relation it is posited as *being* and *becoming*. The forms of *determinate being* find no place in the series of those determinations which can be regarded as definitions of the absolute, for the individual forms of that sphere are immediately posited only as determinatenesses, as finite in general. The infinite, however, is held to be absolute without qualification for it is determined expressly as negation of the finite, and reference is thus expressly made to limitedness in the infinite—limitedness of which being and becoming could perhaps be capable, even if not possessing or showing it—and the presence in the infinite of such limitedness is denied.

But even so, the infinite is not yet really free from limitation and finitude; the main point is to distinguish the genuine Notion of infinity from spurious infinity, the infinite of reason from the infinite of the understanding; yet the latter is the *finitized* infinite, and it will be found that in the very act of keeping the infinite pure and aloof from the finite, the infinite is only made finite.

The infinite is:

(*a*) in its *simple determination,* affirmative as negation of the finite

(*b*) but thus it is in *alternating determination* with the *finite,* and is the abstract, *one-sided* infinite

(*c*) the self-sublation of this infinite and of the finite, as a *single* process—this is the *true* or *genuine infinite.*

(a) The Infinite in General

The infinite is the negation of the negation, affirmation, *being* which has restored itself out of limitedness. The infinite *is*, and more intensely so than the first immediate being; it is the true being, the elevation above limitation. At the name of the infinite, the heart and the mind light up, for in the infinite the spirit is not merely abstractly present to itself, but rises to its own self, to the light of its thinking, of its universality, of its freedom.

The Notion of the infinite as it first presents itself is this, that determinate being in its being-in-itself determines itself as finite and transcends the limitation. It is the very nature of the finite to transcend itself, to negate its negation and to become infinite. Thus the infinite does not stand as something finished and complete above or superior to the finite, as if the finite had an enduring

Negation zu negieren und unendlich zu werden. Das Unendliche steht somit nicht als ein für sich Fertiges *über* dem Endlichen, so daß das Endliche *außer* oder *unter* jenem sein Bleiben hätte und behielte. Noch gehen *wir* nur als eine subjektive Vernunft über das Endliche ins Unendliche hinaus. Wie wenn man sagt, daß das Unendliche der Vernunftbegriff sei und wir uns durch die Vernunft über das Zeitliche erheben, so läßt man dies ganz unbeschadet des Endlichen geschehen, welches jene ihm äußerlich bleibende Erhebung nichts angeht. Insofern aber das Endliche selbst in die Unendlichkeit erhoben wird, ist es ebensowenig eine fremde Gewalt, welche ihm dies antut, sondern es ist dies seine Natur, sich auf sich als Schranke, sowohl als Schranke als solche wie als Sollen, zu beziehen und über dieselbe hinauszugehen oder vielmehr als Beziehung-auf-sich sie negiert zu haben und über sie hinaus zu sein. Nicht im Aufheben der Endlichkeit überhaupt wird die Unendlichkeit überhaupt, sondern das Endliche ist nur dies, selbst durch seine Natur dazu zu werden. Die Unendlichkeit ist seine *affirmative Bestimmung*, das, was es wahrhaft an sich ist.

So ist das Endliche im Unendlichen verschwunden, und was *ist*, ist nur das *Unendliche*.

b. Wechselbestimmung des Endlichen und Unendlichen

Das Unendliche *ist*; in dieser Unmittelbarkeit ist es zugleich die *Negation* eines *Anderen*, des Endlichen. So als *seiend* und zugleich als *Nichtsein* eines *Anderen* ist es in die Kategorie des Etwas als eines bestimmten überhaupt, näher — weil es das in sich reflektierte, vermittels des Aufhebens der Bestimmtheit überhaupt resultierende Dasein, hiermit als das von seiner Bestimmtheit unterschiedene Dasein *gesetzt* ist — in die Kategorie des Etwas mit einer Grenze zurückgefallen. Das Endliche steht nach dieser Bestimmtheit dem Unendlichen als *reales Dasein* gegenüber; so stehen sie in qualitativer *Beziehung* als außereinander *bleibende*; das *unmittelbare Sein* des Unendlichen erweckt das *Sein* seiner Negation, des Endlichen wieder, das zunächst im Unendlichen verschwunden schien.

Aber das Unendliche und Endliche sind nicht nur in diesen Kategorien der Beziehung; die beiden Seiten sind weiter bestimmt, als bloß *Andere* gegeneinander zu sein. Die Endlichkeit ist nämlich die als Schranke gesetzte Schranke, es ist das Dasein mit der *Bestimmung* gesetzt, in sein *Ansichsein* überzugehen, unendlich *zu werden*. Die Unendlichkeit ist das Nichts des Endlichen, dessen *Ansichsein* und *Sollen*, aber dieses zugleich als in sich reflektiert, das ausgeführte Sollen, nur sich auf sich beziehendes, ganz affirmatives Sein. In der Unendlichkeit ist die Befriedigung vorhanden, daß alle Bestimmtheit, Veränderung, alle Schranke und mit ihr das Sollen selbst verschwunden, als aufgehoben, das Nichts des Endlichen gesetzt ist. Als diese Negation des Endlichen ist das Ansichsein bestimmt, welches so als Negation der Negation in sich affirmativ ist. Diese Affirmation jedoch ist als qualitativ *unmittelbare* Beziehung auf sich, *Sein*; hierdurch ist das Unendliche auf die Kategorie zurückgeführt, daß es das Endliche als ein *Anderes* sich gegenüber hat; seine negative Natur ist als die *seiende*, hiermit erste und unmittelbare Negation gesetzt. Das Unendliche ist auf diese Weise mit dem

being *apart from* or *subordinate to* the infinite. Neither do *we* only, as subjective reason, pass beyond the finite into the infinite; as when we say that the infinite is the Notion of reason and that through reason we rise superior to temporal things, though we let this happen without prejudice to the finite which is in no way affected by this exaltation, an exaltation which remains external to it. But the finite itself in being raised into the infinite is in no sense acted on by an alien force; on the contrary, it is its nature to be related to itself as limitation—both limitation as such and as an ought—and to transcend the same, or rather, as self-relation to have negated the limitation and to be beyond it. It is not in the sublating of finitude in general that infinity in general comes to be; the truth is rather that the finite is only this, through its own nature to become itself the infinite. The infinite is its *affirmative determination,* that which it truly is in itself.

Thus the finite has vanished in the infinite and what *is,* is only the *infinite.*

(b) Alternating Determination of the Finite and the Infinite

The infinite *is*; in this immediacy it is at the same time the *negation* of an other, of the finite. As thus in the form of simple being and at the same time as the *non-being* of an *other,* it has fallen back into the category of *something* as a determinate being in general—more precisely, into the category of something with a limit, because the infinite is determinate being reflected into itself, resulting from the sublating of determinateness in general, and hence is determinate being *posited* as distinguished from its determinateness. In keeping with this determinateness, the finite stands opposed to the infinite as a *real determinate being*; they stand thus in a qualitative relation, each *remaining* external to the other; the *immediate being* of the infinite resuscitates the *being* of its negation, of the finite again which at first seemed to have vanished in the infinite.

But the infinite and the finite are not in these categories of relation only; the two sides are determined beyond the stage of being merely *others* to each other. Finitude, namely, is limitation posited as limitation; determinate being is posited with the *determination* to pass over into its *in itself,* to *become* infinite. Infinity is the nothing of the finite, it is what the latter is *in itself,* what it *ought to be,* but this ought-to-be is at the same time reflected into itself, is *realized*; it is a purely self-related, wholly affirmative being. In infinity we have the satisfaction that all determinateness, alteration, all limitation and with it the ought itself, are posited as vanished, as sublated, that the nothing of the finite is posited. As this negation of the finite the in-itself is determinate and thus, as negation of the negation, is affirmative within itself. But this affirmation as qualitative, is *immediate* self-relation, is *being*; and thus the infinite is reduced to the category of a being which has the finite confronting it as an other; its negative nature is posited as the simply *affirmative,* hence as the first and immediate negation. The infinite is in this way burdened with the opposition to the finite which, as an other, remains at the same time a determinate reality although in its in-itself, in the infinite, it is at the same time posited as sublated; this infinite

Gegensatze gegen das Endliche behaftet, welches, als Anderes, das bestimmte, reale Dasein zugleich bleibt, obschon es in seinem Ansichsein, dem Unendlichen, zugleich als aufgehoben gesetzt ist; dieses ist das Nicht-Endliche, — ein Sein in der Bestimmtheit der Negation. Gegen das Endliche, den Kreis der seienden Bestimmtheiten, der Realitäten, ist das Unendliche das unbestimmte Leere, das Jenseits des Endlichen, welches sein Ansichsein nicht an seinem Dasein, das ein bestimmtes ist, hat.

So das Unendliche gegen das Endliche in qualitativer Beziehung von *Anderen* zueinander gesetzt, ist es das *Schlecht-Unendliche*, das Unendliche des *Verstandes* zu nennen, dem es für die höchste, für die absolute Wahrheit gilt; ihn zum Bewußtsein darüber zu bringen, daß, indem er seine Befriedigung in der Versöhnung der Wahrheit erreicht zu haben meint, er in dem unversöhnten, unaufgelösten, absoluten Widerspruche sich befindet, müßten die Widersprüche bewirken, in die er nach allen Seiten verfällt, sowie er sich auf die Anwendung und Explikation dieser seiner Kategorien einläßt.

Dieser Widerspruch ist sogleich darin vorhanden, daß dem Unendlichen das Endliche als Dasein gegenüberbleibt; es sind damit *zwei* Bestimmtheiten; es *gibt* zwei Welten, eine unendliche und eine endliche, und in ihrer Beziehung ist das Unendliche nur *Grenze* des Endlichen und ist damit nur ein bestimmtes, *selbst endliches Unendliches*.

Dieser Widerspruch entwickelt seinen Inhalt zu ausdrücklicheren Formen. — Das Endliche ist das reale Dasein, welches so verbleibt, auch indem zu seinem Nichtsein, dem Unendlichen, übergegangen wird; — dieses hat, wie gezeigt, nur die erste, unmittelbare Negation zu seiner Bestimmtheit gegen das Endliche, so wie dieses gegen jene Negation als Negiertes nur die Bedeutung eines *Anderen* hat und daher noch Etwas ist. Wenn somit der sich aus dieser endlichen Welt erhebende Verstand zu seinem Höchsten, dem Unendlichen, aufsteigt, so bleibt ihm diese endliche Welt als ein Diesseits stehen, so daß das Unendliche nur *über* dem Endlichen gesetzt, von diesem *abgesondert* und eben damit das Endliche von dem Unendlichen *abgesondert* wird, — beide an einen *verschiedenen Platz gestellt*: das Endliche als das hiesige Dasein, das Unendliche aber, zwar das *Ansich* des Endlichen, doch als ein Jenseits in die trübe, unerreichbare Ferne, *außerhalb* welcher jenes sich befinde und dableibe.

So abgesondert sind sie ebenso wesentlich eben durch die sie abscheidende Negation aufeinander *bezogen*. Diese sie, die in sich reflektierten Etwas, beziehende Negation ist die gegenseitige Grenze des Einen gegen das Andere, und zwar so, daß jedes derselben sie nicht bloß gegen das Andere *an ihm* hat, sondern die Negation ist ihr *Ansichsein*, jedes hat die Grenze so an ihm selbst für sich, in seiner Absonderung von dem Anderen. Die Grenze ist aber als die erste Negation, so sind beide begrenzte, endliche an sich selbst. Jedoch ist jedes auch als sich auf sich affirmativ beziehend die Negation seiner Grenze; so stößt es sie als sein Nichtsein unmittelbar von sich ab, und qualitativ davon getrennt setzt es sie als ein *anderes Sein* außer ihm, das Endliche sein Nichtsein als dies Unendliche, dieses ebenso das Endliche.

is the non-finite—a being in the determinateness of negation. Contrasted with the finite, with the sphere of affirmative determinatenesses, of realities, the infinite is the indeterminate void, the beyond of the finite, whose being-in-itself is not present in its *determinate* reality.

The infinite as thus posited over against the finite, in a relation wherein they are as qualitatively distinct others, is to be called the *spurious infinite,* the infinite of the understanding, for which it has the value of the highest, the absolute Truth.[1] The understanding is satisfied that it has truly reconciled these two, but the truth is that it is entangled in unreconciled, unresolved, absolute contradiction; it can only be brought to a consciousness of this fact by the contradictions into which it falls on every side when it ventures to apply and to explicate these its categories.

This contradiction occurs as a direct result of the circumstance that the finite remains as a determinate being opposed to the infinite, so that there are *two* determinatenesses; *there are* two worlds, one infinite and one finite, and in their relationship the infinite is only the *limit* of the finite and is thus only a determinate infinite, an *infinite which is itself finite.*

This contradiction develops its content into more explicit forms. The finite is real determinate being which persists as such even when transition is made to its non-being, to the infinite; this, as has been shown, has only the first, immediate negation for its determinateness relatively to the finite, just as the finite as opposed to that negation has, as negated, only the significance of an other and is, therefore, still [only] *something.* When, therefore, the understanding, raising itself above this finite world, ascends to its highest, to the infinite, this finite world remains for it on *this* side, so that the infinite is only set *above* or *beyond* the finite, is *separated* from it, with the consequence that the finite is separated from the infinite; each is *assigned a distinct* place—the finite as determinate being here, on *this* side, and the infinite, although the *in-itself* of the finite, nevertheless as a beyond in the dim, inaccessible distance, *outside* of which the finite is and remains.

As thus separated they are just as much essentially *connected* by the very negation which separates them. This negation which connects them—the *somethings* reflected into themselves—is the limit of the one relatively to the other, and that, too, in such a manner that each of them does not have the limit *in it* merely relatively to the other, but the negation is their *being-in-itself*; the limit is thus present in each on its own account, in separation from the other. But the limit is in the form of the first negation and thus both are limited, finite in themselves. However, each as affirmatively self-related is also the negation of its limit; each thus immediately repels the limit, as its non-being, from itself and, as qualitatively separated from it, posits it as *another being* outside it, the finite positing its non-being as this infinite and the infinite, similarly, the finite. It is readily conceded that there is a necessary transition from the finite to the infinite—necessary through the determination of the finite—and that the finite

1. *Das Schlecht-Unendliche* is also known as the Bad Infinite.

Daß von dem Endlichen zum Unendlichen notwendig, d. h. durch die Bestimmung des Endlichen übergegangen und es als zum Ansichsein erhoben werde, wird leicht zugegeben, indem das Endliche zwar als bestehendes Dasein, aber zugleich *auch* als das *an sich* nichtige, also sich nach seiner Bestimmung auflösende bestimmt ist, das Unendliche aber zwar als mit Negation und Grenze behaftet bestimmt ist, aber zugleich auch als das *Ansich*seiende, so daß diese Abstraktion der sich auf sich beziehenden Affirmation seine Bestimmung ausmache, nach dieser hiermit das endliche Dasein nicht in ihr liege. Aber es ist gezeigt worden, daß das Unendliche selbst nur *vermittels* der Negation, als Negation der Negation, zum affirmativen Sein resultiert und daß diese seine Affirmation, als nur einfaches, qualitatives Sein genommen, die in ihm enthaltene Negation zur einfachen unmittelbaren Negation und damit zur Bestimmtheit und Grenze herabsetzt, welches dann ebenso als widersprechend seinem Ansichsein, aus ihm ausgeschlossen, als nicht das Seinige, vielmehr seinem Ansichsein Entgegengesetzte, das Endliche, gesetzt wird. Indem so jedes an ihm selbst und aus seiner Bestimmung das Setzen seines Anderen ist, sind sie *untrennbar*. Aber diese ihre Einheit ist in dem qualitativen Anderssein derselben *verborgen*, sie ist die *innerliche*, die *nur zugrunde* liegt.

Dadurch ist die Weise der Erscheinung dieser Einheit bestimmt; im *Dasein* gesetzt ist sie als ein Umschlagen oder Übergehen des Endlichen zum Unendlichen und umgekehrt; so daß das Unendliche an dem Endlichen und das Endliche an dem Unendlichen, das Andere an dem Anderen, nur *hervortrete*, d. h. jedes ein eigenes *unmittelbares* Entstehen an dem Anderen und ihre Beziehung nur eine äußerliche sei.

Der Prozeß ihres Übergehens hat folgende ausführliche Gestalt. Es wird über das Endliche hinausgegangen in das Unendliche. Dies Hinausgehen erscheint als ein äußerliches Tun. In diesem dem Endlichen jenseitigen Leeren, was entsteht? Was ist das Positive darin? Um der Untrennbarkeit des Unendlichen und Endlichen willen (oder weil dies auf seiner Seite stehende Unendliche selbst beschränkt ist) entsteht die Grenze; das Unendliche ist verschwunden, sein Anderes, das Endliche, ist eingetreten. Aber dies Eintreten des Endlichen erscheint als ein dem Unendlichen äußerliches Geschehen und die neue Grenze als ein solches, das nicht aus dem Unendlichen selbst entstehe, sondern ebenso vorgefunden werde. Es ist damit der Rückfall in die vorherige, vergebens aufgehobene Bestimmung vorhanden. Diese neue Grenze aber ist selbst nur ein solches, das aufzuheben oder über das hinauszugehen ist. Somit ist wieder das Leere, das Nichts entstanden, in welchem ebenso jene Bestimmtheit, eine neue Grenze, angetroffen wird — *und so fort ins Unendliche.*

Es ist die *Wechselbestimmung des Endlichen und Unendlichen* vorhanden; das Endliche ist endlich nur in der Beziehung auf das Sollen oder auf das Unendliche, und das Unendliche ist nur unendlich in Beziehung auf das Endliche. Sie sind untrennbar und zugleich schlechthin Andere gegeneinander; jedes hat das Andere seiner an ihm selbst; so ist jedes die Einheit

is raised to the form of being-in-itself, since the finite, although persisting as a determinate being, is at the same time *also* determined as *in itself* nothing and therefore as destined to bring about its own dissolution; whereas the infinite, although determined as burdened with negation and limit, is at the same time also determined as possessing *being-in-itself,* so that this abstraction of self-related affirmation constitutes its determination, and hence finite determinate being is not present in it. But it has been shown that the infinite itself attains affirmative being only *by means of* negation, as the negation of negation, and that when this its affirmation is taken as merely simple, qualitative being, the negation contained in it is reduced to a simple immediate negation and thus to a determinateness and limit, which then, as in contradiction with the being-in-itself of the infinite is posited as excluded from it, as not belonging to it, as, on the contrary, opposed to its being-in-itself, as the finite. As therefore each is in its own self and through its own determination the positing of its other, they are *inseparable.* But this their unity is *concealed* in their *qualitative* otherness, it is the *inner* unity which only lies at their base.

This determines the manner in which this unity is manifested: posited in *determinate being,* the unity is a changing or transition of the finite into the infinite, and vice versa; so that the infinite only *emerges* in the finite and the finite in the infinite, the other in the other; that is to say, each arises *immediately* and independently in the other, their connection being only an external one.

The process of their transition has the following detailed shape. We pass from the finite to the infinite. This transcending of the finite appears as an external act. In this void beyond the finite, what arises? What is the positive element in it? Owing to the inseparability of the infinite and the finite—or because this infinite remaining aloof on its own side is itself limited—there arises a limit; the infinite has vanished and its other, the finite, has entered. But this entrance of the finite appears as a happening external to the infinite, and the new limit as something that does not arise from the infinite itself but is likewise found as given. And so we are faced with a relapse into the previous determination which has been sublated in vain. But this new limit is itself only something which has to be sublated or transcended. And so again there arises the void, the nothing, in which similarly the said determinateness, a new limit, is encountered—and *so on to infinity.*

We have before us the alternating determination of the *finite* and the *infinite;* the finite is finite only in its relation to the ought or to the infinite, and the latter is only infinite in its relation to the finite. They are inseparable and at the same time mutually related as sheer others; each has in its own self the other of itself. Each is thus the unity of itself and its other and is in its determinateness *not* that which it itself is, and which its other is.

It is this alternating determination negating both its own self and its negation, which appears as the *progress to infinity,* a progress which in so many forms and applications is accepted as something ultimate beyond which thought does not go but, having got as far as this 'and so on to infinity', has usually

seiner und seines Anderen und ist in seiner Bestimmtheit Dasein, das *nicht* zu sein, was es selbst und was sein Anderes ist.

Diese sich selbst und seine Negation negierende Wechselbestimmung ist es, welche als der *Progreß ins Unendliche* auftritt, der in so vielen Gestalten und Anwendungen als ein *Letztes* gilt, über das nicht mehr hinausgegangen wird, sondern angekommen bei jenem "*und so fort* ins Unendliche" pflegt der Gedanke sein Ende erreicht zu haben. — Dieser Progreß tritt allenthalben ein, wo *relative* Bestimmungen bis zu ihrer Entgegensetzung getrieben sind, so daß sie in untrennbarer Einheit sind und doch jeder gegen die andere ein selbständiges Dasein zugeschrieben wird. Dieser Progreß ist daher der *Widerspruch*, der nicht aufgelöst ist, sondern immer nur als *vorhanden* ausgesprochen wird.

Es ist ein abstraktes Hinausgehen vorhanden, das unvollständig bleibt, indem *über dies Hinausgehen* nicht selbst *hinausgegangen* wird. Es ist das Unendliche vorhanden; über dasselbe wird allerdings hinausgegangen, denn es wird eine neue Grenze gesetzt, aber damit eben wird vielmehr nur zum Endlichen zurückgekehrt. Diese schlechte Unendlichkeit ist an sich dasselbe, was das *perennierende Sollen*; sie ist zwar die Negation des Endlichen, aber sie vermag sich nicht in Wahrheit davon zu befreien; dies tritt *an ihr selbst* wieder hervor als ihr Anderes, weil dies Unendliche nur ist als *in Beziehung* auf das ihm andere Endliche. Der Progreß ins Unendliche ist daher nur die sich wiederholende Einerleiheit, eine und dieselbe langweilige *Abwechslung* dieses Endlichen und Unendlichen.

Die Unendlichkeit des unendlichen Progresses bleibt mit dem Endlichen als solchem behaftet, ist dadurch begrenzt und selbst *endlich*. Somit wäre es aber in der Tat als die Einheit des Endlichen und Unendlichen gesetzt. Aber auf diese Einheit wird nicht reflektiert. Sie ist es jedoch nur, welche im Endlichen das Unendliche und im Unendlichen das Endliche hervorruft, sie ist sozusagen die Triebfeder des unendlichen Progresses. Er ist das *Äußere* jener Einheit, bei welchem die Vorstellung stehenbleibt, bei jener perennierenden Wiederholung eines und desselben Abwechselns, der leeren Unruhe des Weitergehens über die Grenze hinaus zur Unendlichkeit, das in diesem Unendlichen eine neue Grenze *findet*, auf derselben aber sich sowenig halten kann als in dem Unendlichen. Dieses Unendliche hat die feste Determination eines *Jenseits*, das nicht erreicht werden kann, darum weil es nicht erreicht werden *soll*, weil von der Bestimmtheit des Jenseits, der *seienden* Negation nicht abgelassen wird. Es hat nach dieser Bestimmung das Endliche als ein *Diesseits* sich gegenüber, das sich ebensowenig ins Unendliche erheben kann, darum weil es diese Determination eines *Anderen*, hiermit [eines] ein Perennierendes, sich in seinem Jenseits wieder, und zwar als davon verschieden, erzeugenden *Daseins* hat.

c. Die affirmative Unendlichkeit

In dem aufgezeigten herüber- und hinübergehenden Wechselbestimmen des Endlichen und Unendlichen ist die Wahrheit derselben an sich schon *vorhanden*, und es bedarf nur des Aufnehmens dessen, was vorhanden ist. Dies Herüber- und Hinübergehen macht die äußere Realisation des Begriffes aus;

reached its goal. This progress makes its appearance wherever *relative* determinations are pressed to the point of opposition, with the result that although they are in an inseparable unity, each is credited with a self-subsistent determinate being over against the other. The progress is, consequently, a *contradiction* which is not resolved but is always only enunciated as *present.*

What we have here is an abstract transcending of a limit, a transcending which remains incomplete because *it is not itself transcended.* Before us is the infinite; it is of course transcended, for a new limit is posited, but the result is rather only a return to the finite. This spurious infinity is in itself the same thing as the perennial ought; it is the negation of the finite it is true, but it cannot in truth free itself therefrom. The finite reappears *in the infinite itself* as its other, because it is only in its *connection* with its other, the finite, that the infinite is. The progress to infinity is, consequently, only the perpetual repetition of one and the same content, one and the same tedious *alternation* of this finite and infinite.

The infinity of the infinite progress remains burdened with the finite as such, is thereby limited and is itself *finite.* But this being so, the infinite progress would in fact be posited as the unity of the finite and the infinite; but this unity is not reflected on. Yet it is this unity alone which evokes the infinite in the finite and the finite in the infinite; it is, so to speak, the mainspring of the infinite progress. This progress is the *external* aspect of this unity at which ordinary thinking halts, at this perpetual repetition of one and the same alternation, of the vain unrest of advancing beyond the limit to infinity, only to *find* in this infinite a new limit in which, however, it is as little able to rest as in the infinite. This infinite has the fixed determination of a *beyond,* which cannot be reached, for the very reason that *it is not meant* to be reached, because the determinateness of the beyond, of the *affirmative* negation, is not let go. In accordance with this determination the infinite has the finite opposed to it as a being *on this side,* which is equally unable to raise itself into the infinite just because it has this determination of an *other,* of a *determinate being* which perpetually generates itself in its beyond, a beyond from which it is again distinct.[2]

(c) Affirmative Infinity

In this alternating determination of the finite and the infinite from one to the other and back again, their truth is already implicitly *present,* and all that is required is to take up what is before us. This transition from one to the other and back again constitutes the external realization of the Notion. In this real-

---

2. The text of the Meiner historical-critical edition of the 1832 version of the Doctrine of Being differs slightly from that of the Suhrkamp edition at this point. It reads: "weil es diese Determination eines *Anderen*, hiermit eines perennirenden, sich in seinem Jenseits wieder und zwar als davon verschieden, erzeugenden *Daseyns* hat." Even though Miller's translation was published several years before the Meiner edition, it captures the sense of the Meiner text well and so has not been revised. A more accurate translation of the Suhrkamp text (which is the one reprinted here) might be: "it has this determination of an *other,* of a *determinate being* which generates itself, as something perpetual, in its beyond, a beyond from which it is again distinct."

es ist in ihr das, aber *äußerlich*, außereinanderfallend *gesetzt*, was der Begriff enthält; es bedarf nur der Vergleichung dieser verschiedenen Momente, in welcher die *Einheit* sich ergibt, die den Begriff selbst gibt; — die *Einheit* des Unendlichen und Endlichen ist, wie schon oft bemerkt, hier aber vornehmlich in Erinnerung zu bringen ist, der schiefe Ausdruck für die Einheit, wie sie selbst wahrhaft ist; aber auch das Entfernen dieser schiefen Bestimmung muß in jener vor uns liegenden Äußerung des Begriffes vorhanden sein.

Nach ihrer nächsten, nur unmittelbaren Bestimmung genommen, so ist das Unendliche nur als das *Hinausgehen* über das *Endliche*; es ist seiner Bestimmung nach die Negation des Endlichen; so ist das Endliche nur als das, worüber hinausgegangen werden muß, die Negation seiner an ihm selbst, welche die Unendlichkeit ist. In *jedem liegt* hiermit die *Bestimmtheit* des *Anderen*, die nach der Meinung des unendlichen Progresses voneinander ausgeschlossen sein sollen und nur abwechselnd aufeinander folgen; es kann keines gesetzt und gefaßt werden ohne das andere, das Unendliche nicht ohne das Endliche, diese nicht ohne das Unendliche. Wenn *gesagt* wird, was das Unendliche ist, nämlich die Negation des *Endlichen*, so wird das Endliche selbst mit *ausgesprochen*; es kann zur Bestimmung des Unendlichen *nicht entbehrt* werden. Man bedarf nur zu *wissen, was man sagt*, um die Bestimmung des Endlichen im Unendlichen zu finden. Vom Endlichen seinerseits wird sogleich zugegeben, daß es das Nichtige ist, aber eben seine Nichtigkeit ist die Unendlichkeit, von der es ebenso untrennbar ist. — In diesem Auffassen können sie nach ihrer *Beziehung* auf ihr *Anderes* genommen zu sein scheinen. Werden sie hiermit *beziehungslos* genommen, so daß sie nur durch das "*Und*" verbunden seien, so stehen sie als selbständig, jedes nur an ihm selbst seiend, einander gegenüber. Es ist zu sehen, wie sie in solcher Weise beschaffen sind. Das Unendliche, so gestellt, ist *eines der beiden*; aber als *nur* eines der beiden ist es selbst endlich, es ist nicht das Ganze, sondern nur die eine Seite; es hat an dem Gegenüberstehenden seine Grenze; es ist so das *endliche Unendliche*. Es sind nur *zwei Endliche* vorhanden. Eben darin, daß es so vom Endlichen *abgesondert*, damit als *Einseitiges* gestellt wird, liegt seine Endlichkeit, also seine Einheit mit dem Endlichen. — Das Endliche seinerseits, als für sich vom Unendlichen entfernt gestellt, ist *diese Beziehung auf sich*, in der seine Relativität, Abhängigkeit, seine Vergänglichkeit entfernt ist; es ist dieselbe Selbständigkeit und Affirmation seiner, welche das Unendliche sein soll.

Beide Betrachtungsweisen, die zunächst eine verschiedene Bestimmtheit zu ihrem Ausgangspunkte zu haben scheinen, insofern die erstere nur als *Beziehung* des Unendlichen und Endlichen aufeinander, eines jeden auf sein Anderes, und die zweite sie in ihrer völligen Absonderung voneinander halten soll, geben ein und dasselbe Resultat; das Unendliche und Endliche nach der *Beziehung* beider aufeinander, die ihnen äußerlich wäre, aber die ihnen wesentlich, ohne die keines ist, was es ist, enthält so sein Anderes in seiner

ization is *posited* the content of the Notion, but it is posited as *external*, as falling *asunder*; all that is required is to compare these different moments which yield the *unity* which gives the Notion itself; the *unity* of the infinite and the finite is—as has often been remarked already but here especially is to be borne in mind—the one-sided expression for the unity as it is in truth; but the elimination, too, of this one-sided determination must lie in the externalisation of the Notion now before us.[3]

Taken according to their first, only immediate determination, the infinite is only the *beyond* of the *finite*; according to its determination it is the negation of the finite; thus the finite is only that which must be transcended, the negation of itself in its own self, which is infinity. In *each,* therefore, there lies the *determinateness of the other,* although according to the standpoint of the infinite progress these two are supposed to be shut out from each other and only to follow each other alternately; neither can be posited and grasped without the other, the infinite not without the finite, nor the latter without the infinite. In *saying* what the infinite is, namely the negation of the *finite,* the latter is itself included in what is *said;* it cannot be dispensed with for the definition or determination of the infinite. One only needs to *be aware of what one is saying* in order to find the determination of the finite in the infinite. As regards the finite, it is readily conceded that it is the null; but its very nullity is the infinity from which it is thus inseparable. In this way of conceiving them, each may seem to be taken in its *connection* with its other. But if they are taken as *devoid of connection* with each other so that they are only joined by 'and', then each confronts the other as self-subsistent, as in its own self only affirmatively present. Let us see how they are constituted when so taken. The infinite, in that case, is *one of the two;* but as *only* one of the two it is itself finite, it is not the whole but only *one* side; it has its limit in what stands over against it; it is thus the *finite infinite.* There are present only *two finites.* It is precisely this holding of the infinite *apart* from the finite, thus giving it a *one-sided* character, that constitutes its finitude and, therefore, its unity with the finite. The finite, on the other hand, characterized as independent of and apart from the infinite, is that *self-relation* in which its relativity, its dependence and transitoriness is removed; it is the same self-subsistence and affirmation which the infinite is supposed to be.

The two modes of consideration at first seem to have a different determinateness for their point of departure, inasmuch as the former is supposed to be only the *connection* of the infinite and the finite, of each with its other, and the latter is supposed to hold them apart in complete separation from each other; but both modes yield one and the same result: the infinite and the finite viewed as *connected* with each other—the connection being only external to them but

---

3. I read the following account of the "unity" of the finite and the infinite as departing from Hegel's otherwise strictly immanent development of the categories by providing an external *comparison* of finitude and infinity; see chapter 22, below, p. 415 and Hegel, *SL* 146/1: 161 (253). On my interpretation, Hegel's immanent analysis of the progress to infinity starts again on p. 253 with the paragraph beginning: "In the first place, the negation of the finite and infinite which is posited in the infinite progress […]."

eigenen Bestimmung, ebensosehr als *jedes für sich* genommen, *an ihm* selbst betrachtet, sein Anderes in ihm als sein eigenes Moment liegen hat.

Dies gibt denn die — verrufene — Einheit des Endlichen und Unendlichen, die Einheit, die selbst das Unendliche ist, welches sich selbst und die Endlichkeit in sich begreift, — also das Unendliche in einem andern Sinne als in dem, wonach das Endliche von ihm abgetrennt und auf die andere Seite gestellt ist. Indem sie nun auch unterschieden werden müssen, ist jedes, wie vorhin gezeigt, selbst an ihm die Einheit beider; so ergeben sich zwei solche Einheiten. Das Gemeinschaftliche, die Einheit beider Bestimmtheiten, setzt als Einheit sie zunächst als negierte, da jedes das sein soll, was es ist in ihrer Unterschiedenheit; in ihrer Einheit verlieren sie also ihre qualitative Natur; — eine wichtige Reflexion gegen die Vorstellung, die sich nicht davon losmachen will, in der Einheit des Unendlichen und Endlichen sie nach der Qualität, welche sie als außereinander genommen haben sollen, festzuhalten, und daher in jener Einheit nichts als den Widerspruch, nicht auch die Auflösung desselben durch die Negation der qualitativen Bestimmtheit beider sieht; so wird die zunächst einfache, allgemeine Einheit des Unendlichen und Endlichen verfälscht.

Ferner aber, indem sie nun auch als unterschieden zu nehmen sind, so ist die Einheit des Unendlichen, die jedes dieser Momente selbst ist, in jedem derselben auf verschiedene Weise bestimmt. Das seiner Bestimmung nach Unendliche hat die von ihm unterschiedene Endlichkeit an ihm, jenes ist das *Ansich* in dieser Einheit, und diese ist nur Bestimmtheit, Grenze an ihm; allein es ist eine Grenze, welche das schlechthin Andere desselben, sein Gegenteil ist; seine Bestimmung, welche das Ansichsein als solches ist, wird durch den Beischlag einer Qualität solcher Art verdorben; es ist so ein *verendlichtes Unendliches.* Auf gleiche Weise, indem das Endliche als solches nur das Nicht-Ansichsein ist, aber nach jener Einheit gleichfalls sein Gegenteil an ihm hat, wird es über seinen Wert, und zwar sozusagen unendlich erhoben; es wird als das *verunendlichte* Endliche gesetzt.

Auf gleiche Weise wie vorhin die einfache, so wird vom Verstande auch die gedoppelte Einheit des Unendlichen und Endlichen verfälscht. Dies geschieht hier ebenso dadurch, daß in der einen der beiden Einheiten das Unendliche als nicht negiertes, vielmehr als das Ansichsein angenommen wird, an welches also nicht die Bestimmtheit und Schranke gesetzt werden soll; es werde dadurch das Ansichsein herabgesetzt und verdorben. Umgekehrt wird das Endliche gleichfalls als das nicht Negierte, obgleich an sich Nichtige, festgehalten, so daß es in seiner Verbindung mit dem Unendlichen zu dem, was es nicht *sei*, erhoben und dadurch gegen seine nicht verschwundene, vielmehr perennierende Bestimmung verunendlicht werde.

Die Verfälschung, die der Verstand mit dem Endlichen und Unendlichen vornimmt, ihre Beziehung aufeinander als qualitative Verschiedenheit festzuhalten, sie in ihrer Bestimmung als getrennt, und zwar absolut getrennt zu behaupten, gründet sich auf das Vergessen dessen, was für ihn selbst der Begriff dieser Momente ist. Nach diesem ist die Einheit des Endlichen und Unendlichen nicht ein äußerliches Zusammenbringen derselben noch eine

also essential to them, without which neither is what it is—each contains its own other in its own determination, just as much as each, taken *on its own account,* considered *in its own self,* has its other present within it as its own moment.

This yields the decried unity of the finite and the infinite—the unity which is itself the infinite which embraces both itself and finitude—and is therefore the infinite in a different sense from that in which the finite is regarded as separated and set apart from the infinite. Since now they must also be distinguished, each is, as has just been shown, in its own self the unity of both; thus we have two such unities. The common element, the unity of the two determinatenesses, as unity, posits them in the first place as negated, since each is supposed to be what it is in its distinction from the other; in their unity, therefore, they lose their qualitative nature—an important reflection for rebutting that idea of the unity which insists on holding fast to the infinite and finite in the quality they are supposed to have when taken in their separation from each other, a view which therefore sees in that unity *only* contradiction, but not also resolution of the contradiction through the negation of the qualitative determinateness of both; thus the unity of the infinite and finite, simple and general in the first instance, is falsified.

But further, since now they are also to be taken as distinct, the *unity* of the infinite which each of these moments is, is differently determined in each of them. The infinite determined as such, has present in it the finitude which is distinct from it; the former is the *in-itself* in this unity, and the latter is only determinateness, limit in it; but it is a limit which is the sheer other of the in-itself, is its opposite; the infinite's determination, which is the in-itself as such, is ruined by the addition of such a quality; it is thus a *finitized infinite.* Similarly, since the finite as such is only the negation of the in-itself, but by reason of this unity also has its opposite present in it, it is exalted and, so to say, infinitely exalted above its worth; the finite is posited as the *infinitized* finite.

Just as before, the simple unity of the infinite and finite was falsified by the understanding, so too is the double unity. Here too this results from taking the infinite in one of the two unities not as negated, but rather as the in-itself, in which, therefore, determinateness and limitation are not to be explicitly present, for these would debase and ruin it. Conversely, the finite is likewise held fast as not negated, although in itself it is null; so that in its union with the infinite it is exalted to what it is not and is thereby infinitized in opposition to its determination as finite, which instead of vanishing is perpetuated.

The falsification of the finite and infinite by the understanding which holds fast to a qualitatively distinct relation between them and asserts that each in its own nature is separate, in fact absolutely separate from the other, comes from forgetting what the Notion of these moments is for the understanding itself. According to this, the unity of the finite and infinite is not an external bringing together of them, nor an incongruous combination alien to their own nature in which there would be joined together determinations inherently separate and opposed, each having a simple affirmative being independent of the other and

ungehörige, ihrer Bestimmung zuwiderlaufende Verbindung, in welcher an sich getrennte und entgegengesetzte, gegeneinander Selbständige, Seiende, somit Unverträgliche verknüpft würden, sondern jedes ist an ihm selbst diese Einheit, und dies nur als *Aufheben* seiner selbst, worin keines vor dem anderen einen Vorzug des Ansichseins und affirmativen Daseins hätte. Wie früher gezeigt, ist die Endlichkeit nur als Hinausgehen über sich; es ist also in ihr die Unendlichkeit, das Andere ihrer selbst, enthalten. Ebenso ist die Unendlichkeit nur als Hinausgehen über das Endliche; sie enthält also wesentlich ihr Anderes und ist somit an ihr das Andere ihrer selbst. Das Endliche wird nicht vom Unendlichen als einer außer ihm vorhandenen Macht aufgehoben, sondern es ist seine Unendlichkeit, sich selbst aufzuheben.

Dies Aufheben ist somit nicht die Veränderung oder das Anderssein überhaupt, nicht das Aufheben von *Etwas*. Das, worin sich das Endliche aufhebt, ist das Unendliche als das Negieren der Endlichkeit; aber diese ist längst selbst nur das Dasein als ein *Nichtsein* bestimmt. Es ist also nur die *Negation*, die sich in der *Negation aufhebt*. So ist ihrerseits die Unendlichkeit als das Negative der Endlichkeit und damit der Bestimmtheit überhaupt, als das leere Jenseits bestimmt; sein Sichaufheben im Endlichen ist ein Zurückkehren aus der leeren Flucht, *Negation* des Jenseits, das ein *Negatives* an ihm selbst ist.

Was also vorhanden ist, ist in beiden dieselbe Negation der Negation. Aber diese ist *an sich* Beziehung auf sich selbst, die Affirmation, aber als Rückkehr zu sich selbst, d. i. durch die *Vermittlung*, welche die Negation der Negation ist. Diese Bestimmungen sind es, die wesentlich ins Auge zu fassen sind; das Zweite aber ist, daß sie im unendlichen Progresse auch *gesetzt* sind und wie sie in ihm gesetzt sind, — nämlich noch nicht in ihrer letzten Wahrheit.

Es werden darin *erstens* beide, sowohl das Unendliche als das Endliche, negiert, — es wird über beide auf gleiche Weise hinausgegangen; *zweitens* werden sie auch als unterschiedene, jedes nach dem anderen, als für sich positive gesetzt. Wir fassen so diese zwei Bestimmungen vergleichend heraus, wie wir in der Vergleichung, einem äußeren Vergleichen, die zwei Betrachtungsweisen — des Endlichen und Unendlichen in ihrer Beziehung und ihrer jedes für sich genommen — getrennt haben. Aber der unendliche Progreß spricht mehr aus, es ist in ihm auch der *Zusammenhang* der auch Unterschiedenen gesetzt, jedoch zunächst nur noch als Übergang und Abwechslung; es ist nur in einer einfachen Reflexion von uns zu sehen, was in der Tat darin vorhanden ist.

Zunächst kann die Negation des Endlichen und Unendlichen, die im unendlichen Progresse gesetzt ist, als einfach, somit als auseinander, nur aufeinander folgend genommen werden. Vom Endlichen angefangen, so wird über die Grenze hinausgegangen, das Endliche negiert. Nun ist also das Jenseits desselben, das Unendliche, vorhanden, aber in diesem *entsteht* wieder die Grenze; so ist das Hinausgehen über das Unendliche vorhanden. Dies zweifache Aufheben ist jedoch teils überhaupt nur als ein äußerliches Geschehen und Abwechseln der Momente, teils noch nicht als *eine Einheit gesetzt*; jedes dieser Hinaus ist ein eigener Ansatz, ein neuer Akt, so daß sie so auseinanderfallen. — Es ist aber auch ferner im unendlichen Progresse deren *Beziehung*

incompatible with it; but each is in its own self this unity, and this only as a *sublating* of its own self in which neither would have the advantage over the other of having an in-itself and an affirmative determinate being. As has already been shown, finitude *is* only as a transcending of itself; it therefore contains infinity, the other of itself. Similarly, infinity *is* only as a transcending of the finite; it therefore essentially contains its other and is, consequently, in its own self the other of itself. The finite is not sublated by the infinite as by a power existing outside it; on the contrary, its infinity consists in sublating its own self.

This sublating is, therefore, not alteration or otherness as such, not the sublating of a *something*. That in which the finite sublates itself is the infinite as the negating of finitude; but finitude itself has long since been determined as only the *non-being* of determinate being. It is therefore only *negation* which *sublates* itself in the *negation*. Thus infinity on *its* side is determined as the negative of finitude, and hence of determinateness in general, as the empty beyond; the sublating of itself in the finite is a return from an empty flight, a *negation* of the beyond which is in its own self a *negative*.

What is therefore present is the same negation of negation in each. But this is *in itself* self-relation, affirmation, but as return to itself, that is, through the *mediation* which the negation of negation is. These are the determinations which it is essential to keep in view; but secondly it is to be noted that they are also *posited* in the infinite progress, and how they are posited in it, namely, as not yet in their ultimate truth.

In the first place, both the infinite and the finite are negated in the infinite progress; both are transcended in the same manner. Secondly, they are posited one after the other as distinct, each as positive on its own account. We thus compare these two determinations in their separation, just as in our comparison—an external comparing—we have separated the two modes of considering the finite and the infinite: on the one hand in their connection, and on the other hand each on its own account. But the infinite progress expresses more than this; in it there is also posited the *connection* of terms which are also distinct from each other, although at first the connection is still only a transition and alternation; only a simple reflection on our part is needed to see what is in fact present.

In the first place, the negation of the finite and infinite which is posited in the infinite progress can be taken as simple, hence as separate and merely successive. Starting from the finite, the limit is transcended, the finite negated. We now have its beyond, the infinite, but in this the limit *arises* again; and so we have the transcending of the infinite. This double sublation, however, is partly only an external affair, an alternation of the moments, and partly it is not yet posited as a *single unity;* the transcending of each moment starts independently, is a fresh act, so that the two processes fall apart. But in addition there is also present in the infinite progress their *connection*. First there is the finite, then this is transcended and this negative or beyond of the finite is the infinite, and then this negation is again transcended, so that there arises a new limit, a *finite*

vorhanden. Es ist *erstlich* das *Endliche*; *dann* wird darüber hinausgegangen, dies Negative oder Jenseits des Endlichen ist das Unendliche; *drittens* wird über diese Negation wieder hinausgegangen, es entsteht eine neue Grenze, wieder ein *Endliches*. — Dies ist die vollständige, sich selbst schließende Bewegung, die bei dem angekommen, das den Anfang machte; es entsteht *dasselbe, von dem ausgegangen worden war*, d. i. das Endliche ist wiederhergestellt; dasselbe ist also *mit sich selbst zusammengegangen*, hat nur *sich in seinem Jenseits wiedergefunden*.

Derselbe Fall ist in Ansehung des Unendlichen vorhanden. Im Unendlichen, dem Jenseits der Grenze, entsteht nur eine neue, welche dasselbe Schicksal hat, als Endliches negiert werden zu müssen. Was so wieder vorhanden ist, ist *dasselbe* Unendliche, das vorhin in der neuen Grenze verschwand; das Unendliche ist daher durch sein Aufheben, durch die neue Grenze hindurch, nicht weiter hinausgeschoben, weder von dem Endlichen entfernt worden — denn dieses ist nur dies, in das Unendliche überzugehen — noch von sich selbst, denn es ist *bei sich angekommen*.

So ist beides, das Endliche und das Unendliche, diese *Bewegung*, zu sich durch seine Negation zurückzukehren; sie sind nur als *Vermittlung* in sich, und das Affirmative beider enthält die Negation beider und ist die Negation der Negation. — Sie sind so *Resultat*, hiermit nicht das, was sie in der Bestimmung ihres *Anfangs* sind; — nicht das Endliche ein *Dasein* seinerseits und das Unendliche ein *Dasein* oder *Ansichsein* jenseits des Daseins, d. i. des als endlich bestimmten. Gegen die Einheit des Endlichen und Unendlichen sträubt sich der Verstand nur darum so sehr, weil er die Schranke und das Endliche wie das Ansichsein als *perennierend* voraussetzt; damit *übersieht* er die Negation beider, die im unendlichen Progresse faktisch vorhanden ist, wie ebenso, daß sie darin nur als Momente eines Ganzen vorkommen und daß sie nur vermittels ihres Gegenteils, aber wesentlich ebenso vermittels des Aufhebens ihres Gegenteils hervortreten.

Wenn zunächst die Rückkehr in sich ebensowohl als Rückkehr des Endlichen zu sich wie als die des Unendlichen zu sich betrachtet wurde, so zeigt sich in diesem Resultate selbst eine Unrichtigkeit, die mit der soeben gerügten Schiefheit zusammenhängt; das Endliche ist das eine Mal, das Unendliche das andere Mal als *Ausgangspunkt* genommen, und nur dadurch entstehen *zwei* Resultate. Es ist aber völlig gleichgültig, welches als Anfang genommen werde; damit fällt der Unterschied für sich hinweg, der die *Zweiheit* der Resultate hervorbrachte. Dies ist in der nach beiden Seiten unbegrenzten Linie des unendlichen Progresses gleichfalls gesetzt, worin jedes der Momente mit gleichem abwechselnden Vorkommen vorhanden und es ganz äußerlich ist, in welche Stelle gegriffen und [welches] als Anfang genommen werde. — Sie sind in demselben unterschieden, aber auf gleiche Weise das eine nur das Moment des anderen. Indem sie beide, das Endliche und das Unendliche, selbst Momente des Progresses sind, sind sie *gemeinschaftlich das Endliche*, und indem sie ebenso gemeinschaftlich in ihm und im Resultate negiert sind, so heißt dieses Resultat als Negation jener Endlichkeit beider mit Wahrheit das Unendliche. Ihr Unterschied ist so der *Doppelsinn*, den beide haben. Das Endliche hat den

again. This is the complete, self-closing movement which has arrived at that which constituted the beginning; what arises is the *same* as that from which the movement *began*, that is, the finite is restored; it has therefore united *with itself,* has in its beyond only found *itself* again.

The same is the case with the infinite. In the infinite, the beyond of the limit, there arises only another limit which has the same fate, namely, that as finite it must be negated. Thus what is present again is the *same* infinite which had previously disappeared in the new limit; the infinite, therefore, through its sublating, through its transcending of the new limit, is not removed any further either from the finite—for the finite is only this, to pass over into the infinite—or from itself, for it has arrived *at its own self.*

Thus, both finite and infinite are this *movement* in which each returns to itself through its negation; they *are* only as *mediation* within themselves, and the affirmative of each contains the negative of each and is the negation of the negation. They are thus a *result,* and consequently not what they are in the determination of their *beginning*; the finite is not a *determinate being* on *its* side, and the infinite a *determinate being* or *being-in-itself,* beyond the determinate being, that is, beyond the being determined as finite. The reason why understanding is so antagonistic to the unity of the finite and infinite is simply that it presupposes the limitation and the finite, as well as the in-itself, as *perpetuated*; in doing so it *overlooks* the negation of both which is actually present in the infinite progress, as also the fact that they occur therein only as moments of a whole and that they come on the scene only by means of their opposite, but essentially also by means of the sublation of their opposite.

If, at first, the return into self was considered to be just as much a return of the finite to itself as return of the infinite to itself, this very result reveals an error which is connected with the one-sidedness just criticised: first the finite and then the infinite is taken as the *starting point* and it is only this that gives rise to two results. It is, however, a matter of complete indifference which is taken as the beginning; and thus the difference which occasioned the *double* result disappears of itself. This is likewise explicit in the line—unending in both directions—of the infinite progress in which each of the moments presents itself in equal alternation, and it is quite immaterial what point is fixed on or which of the two is taken as the beginning. They are distinguished in it but each is equally only the moment of the other. Since both the finite and the infinite itself are moments of the progress they are *jointly or in common the finite,* and since they are equally together negated in it and in the result, this result as negation of the finitude of both is called with truth the infinite.[4] Their difference is thus the *double* meaning which both have. The finite has the double meaning of being first, only the finite *over against* the infinite which stands

4 The Meiner edition has *Momente des Processes* instead of *Momente des Progresses.* The meaning of these lines is not affected by this change.

Doppelsinn, erstens nur das Endliche *gegen* das Unendliche zu sein, das ihm gegenübersteht, und zweitens das Endliche und das ihm gegenüberstehende Unendliche *zugleich* zu sein. Auch das Unendliche hat den Doppelsinn, *eines* jener beiden Momente zu sein — so ist es das Schlecht-Unendliche — und das Unendliche zu sein, in welchem jene beiden, es selbst und sein Anderes, nur Momente sind. Wie also das Unendliche in der Tat vorhanden ist, ist [einerseits,] der Prozeß zu sein, in welchem es sich herabsetzt, nur *eine* seiner Bestimmungen, dem Endlichen gegenüber und damit selbst nur eines der Endlichen zu sein, und [andererseits,] diesen Unterschied seiner von sich selbst zur Affirmation seiner aufzuheben und durch diese Vermittlung als *wahrhaft Unendliches* zu sein.

Diese Bestimmung des wahrhaft Unendlichen kann nicht in die schon gerügte *Formel* einer *Einheit* des Endlichen und Unendlichen gefaßt werden; die *Einheit* ist abstrakte bewegungslose Sichselbstgleichheit, und die Momente sind ebenso als unbewegte Seiende. Das Unendliche aber ist, wie seine beiden Momente, vielmehr wesentlich nur als *Werden*, aber das nun in seinen Momenten *weiter bestimmte* Werden. Dieses hat zunächst das abstrakte Sein und Nichts zu seinen Bestimmungen; als Veränderung Daseiende, Etwas und Anderes; nun als Unendliches, Endliches und Unendliches, selbst als Werdende.

Dieses Unendliche als In-sich-Zurückgekehrtsein, Beziehung seiner auf sich selbst, ist *Sein*, aber nicht bestimmungsloses, abstraktes Sein, denn es ist gesetzt als negierend die Negation; es ist somit auch *Dasein*, denn es enthält die Negation überhaupt, somit die Bestimmtheit. Es *ist* und *ist da*, präsent, gegenwärtig. Nur das Schlecht-Unendliche ist das *Jenseits*, weil es *nur* die Negation des als *real* gesetzten Endlichen ist, — so ist es die abstrakte, erste Negation; *nur* als negativ bestimmt, hat es nicht die Affirmation des *Daseins* in ihm; festgehalten als nur Negatives, *soll* es sogar *nicht da*, soll unerreichbar sein. Diese Unerreichbarkeit ist aber nicht seine Hoheit, sondern sein Mangel, welcher seinen letzten Grund darin hat, daß das Endliche als solches *als seiend* festgehalten wird. Das Unwahre ist das Unerreichbare; und es ist einzusehen, daß solches Unendliche das Unwahre ist. — Das Bild des Progresses ins Unendliche ist die gerade *Linie*, an deren beiden Grenzen nur das Unendliche [ist] und immer nur ist, wo sie — und sie ist Dasein — nicht ist, und die zu diesem ihrem Nichtdasein, d. i. ins Unbestimmte *hinausgeht*; als wahrhafte Unendlichkeit, in sich zurückgebogen, wird deren Bild der *Kreis*, die sich erreicht habende Linie, die geschlossen und ganz gegenwärtig ist, ohne *Anfangspunkt* und *Ende*.

Die wahrhafte Unendlichkeit so überhaupt als *Dasein*, das als *affirmativ* gegen die abstrakte Negation gesetzt ist, ist die *Realität* in höherem Sinn als die früher *einfach* bestimmte; sie hat hier einen konkreten Inhalt erhalten. Das Endliche ist nicht das Reale, sondern das Unendliche. So wird die Realität weiter als das Wesen, der Begriff, die Idee usf. bestimmt. Es ist jedoch überflüssig, solche frühere, abstraktere Kategorie wie die Realität bei dem Konkreteren zu wiederholen und sie für konkretere Bestimmungen, als jene an

opposed to it, and secondly, of being the finite and *at the same time* the infinite opposed to it. The infinite, too, has the double meaning of being one of these two moments—as such it is the spurious infinite—and also the infinite in which both, the infinite and its other, are only moments. The infinite, therefore, as now before us is, in fact, the process in which it is deposed to being only *one* of its determinations, the opposite of the finite, and so to being itself only one of the finites, and then raising this its difference from itself into the affirmation of itself and through this mediation becoming the *true* infinite.

This determination of the true infinite cannot be expressed in the *formula*, already criticised, of a *unity* of the finite and infinite; *unity* is abstract, inert self-sameness, and the moments are similarly only in the form of inert, simply affirmative being. The infinite, however, like its two moments, is essentially only as a *becoming*, but a becoming now *further determined* in its moments. Becoming, in the first instance, has abstract being and nothing for its determinations; as alteration, its moments possess determinate being, something and other; now, as the infinite, they are the finite and the infinite, which are themselves in process of becoming.

This infinite, as the consummated return into self, the relation of itself to itself, is *being*—but not indeterminate, abstract being, for it is posited as negating the negation; it is, therefore, also *determinate* being for it contains negation in general and hence determinateness. It *is* and *is there*, present before us. It is only the spurious infinite which is the *beyond*, because it is *only* the negation of the finite posited as *real*—as such it is the abstract, first negation; determined *only* as negative, the affirmation of *determinate* being is lacking in it; the spurious infinite, held fast as only negative, is even *supposed to be not there*, is supposed to be unattainable. However, to be thus unattainable is not its grandeur but its defect, which is at bottom the result of holding fast to the *finite* as such as a *merely affirmative being*. It is what is untrue that is unattainable, and such an infinite must be seen as a falsity.[5] The image of the progress to infinity is the *straight line*, at the two limits of which alone the infinite is, and always only is where the line—which is determinate being—is not, and which goes *out beyond* to this negation of its determinate being, that is, to the indeterminate; the image of true infinity, bent back into itself, becomes the *circle*, the line which has reached itself, which is closed and wholly present, without *beginning* and *end*.

True infinity taken thus generally as *determinate* being which is posited as *affirmative* in contrast to the abstract negation, is *reality* in a higher sense than the former reality which was *simply* determinate; for here it has acquired a concrete content. It is not the finite which is the real, but the infinite. Thus reality is further determined as essence, Notion, Idea, and so on. It is, however, superfluous to repeat an earlier, more abstract category such as reality, in connection with the more concrete categories and to employ it for determinations

5. This does not mean, however, that the bad infinite and the infinite progress do not exist, but simply that they are not truly infinite. See chapter 21, below, pp. 406–8, 411.

ihnen selbst sind, zu gebrauchen. Solches Wiederholen, wie zu sagen, daß das Wesen oder daß die Idee das Reale sei, hat seine Veranlassung darin, daß dem ungebildeten Denken die abstraktesten Kategorien, wie Sein, Dasein, Realität, Endlichkeit, die geläufigsten sind.

Hier hat die Zurückrufung der Kategorie der Realität ihre bestimmtere Veranlassung, indem die Negation, gegen welche sie das Affirmative ist, hier die Negation der Negation [ist]; damit ist sie selbst jener Realität, die das endliche Dasein ist, gegenübergesetzt. — Die Negation ist so als Idealität bestimmt; das Ideelle ist das Endliche, wie es im wahrhaften Unendlichen ist, — als eine Bestimmung, Inhalt, der unterschieden, aber nicht *selbständig seiend*, sondern als *Moment* ist. Die Idealität hat diese konkretere Bedeutung, welche durch Negation des endlichen Daseins nicht vollständig ausgedrückt ist. — In Beziehung auf Realität und Idealität wird aber der Gegensatz des Endlichen und Unendlichen so gefaßt, daß das Endliche für das Reale gilt, das Unendliche aber für das Ideelle gilt, wie auch weiterhin der Begriff als ein Ideelles, und zwar als ein *nur* Ideelles, das Dasein überhaupt dagegen als das Reale betrachtet wird. Auf solche Weise hilft es freilich nichts, für die angegebene konkrete Bestimmung der Negation den eigenen Ausdruck des Ideellen zu haben; es wird in jenem Gegensatze wieder zu der Einseitigkeit des abstrakten Negativen, die dem Schlecht-Unendlichen zukommt, zurückgegangen und bei dem affirmativen Dasein des Endlichen beharrt.

Der Übergang

Die Idealität kann die *Qualität* der Unendlichkeit genannt werden; aber sie ist wesentlich der Prozeß des *Werdens* und damit ein Übergang, wie des Werdens in Dasein, der nun anzugeben ist. Als Aufheben der Endlichkeit, d. i. der Endlichkeit als solcher und ebensosehr der ihr nur gegenüberstehenden, nur negativen Unendlichkeit ist diese Rückkehr in sich, *Beziehung auf sich selbst, Sein*. Da in diesem Sein Negation ist, ist es *Dasein*, aber da sie ferner wesentlich Negation der Negation, die sich auf sich beziehende Negation ist, ist sie das Dasein, welches *Fürsichsein* genannt wird. [A]

which are more concrete than it is in its own self. Such repetition as to say that essence, or the Idea, is the real, has its origin in the fact that for untrained thinking, the most abstract categories such as being, determinate being, reality, finitude, are the most familiar.

The more precise reason for recalling the category of reality here is that the negation to which it is opposed as the affirmative is here negation of the negation; as such it is itself opposed to that reality which finite determinate being is. The negation is thus determined as ideality; ideal being [*das Ideelle*] is the finite as it is in the true infinite—as a determination, a content, which is distinct but is not an *independent, self-subsistent* being, but only a *moment*. Ideality has this more concrete signification which is not fully expressed by the negation of finite determinate being. With reference to reality and ideality, however, the opposition of finite and infinite is grasped in such a manner that the finite ranks as the real but the infinite as the 'ideal'; in the same way that further on the Notion, too, is regarded as an 'ideal', that is, as a *mere* 'ideal', in contrast to determinate being as such which is regarded as the real. When they are contrasted in this way, it is pointless to reserve the term 'ideal' for the concrete determination of negation in question; in that opposition we return once more to the one-sidedness of the abstract negative which is characteristic of the spurious infinite, and perpetuate the affirmative determinate being of the finite.

Transition

Ideality can be called the *quality* of infinity; but it is essentially the process of *becoming*, and hence a transition—like that of becoming in determinate being—which is now to be indicated. As a sublating of finitude, that is, of finitude as such, and equally of the infinity which is merely its opposite, merely negative, this return into self is *self-relation, being*. As this being contains negation it is *determinate*, but as this negation further is essentially negation of the negation, the self-related negation, it is that determinate being which is called *being-for-self*. [R]

Part Three

Commentary and Discussion

Chapter Fourteen

Being, Nothing, and Becoming

Part 3 of this study provides a commentary on and discussion of the text contained in part 2. The issues addressed by Hegel in the introductory essay presented in chapter 9—"With What Must the Science Begin?"—have already been extensively considered in part 1. The following chapters will thus concentrate on the main text of the *Logic* presented in chapters 10 to 13. My hope is that what I have to say here will help readers to understand both the specific details and the broader philosophical relevance of Hegel's arguments.

From Being to Becoming

One might think that philosophy ought to begin with the concept of "beginning" itself. Yet for Hegel such a concept is, paradoxically, too complex to serve as the real beginning of thought. The concept of "beginning" (*Anfang*) is that of "a nothing from which something is to proceed" (*SL* 73/1: 73 [181]). It thus takes for granted from the start that what is being thought is the beginning *of* something yet to emerge. At the start of philosophy, however, we cannot assume that there will be anything beyond what we start with. We cannot assume, therefore, that what we start with is in fact the *beginning* of anything further. All we may understand there to be is sheer indeterminate being, which may or may not prove later to be, or to have been, the beginning of something more.

Hegel's account of being begins not with a full sentence but with a sentence fragment: "*being, pure being*, without any further determination" (*SL* 82/1: 82 [193]). In this way, Hegel indicates through his language that what we are to focus on is not a determinate subject of discourse or "thing" nor a predicate of some assumed thing (such as the "Absolute") but rather utterly indeterminate being. Such being is to be thought of not as existence or nature but as sheer being as such—what Hegel calls "indeterminate immediacy." As we saw in chapter 4, these words are intended by Hegel to bring to mind not the explicit *negation* of determinacy or mediation but being that is *indeterminately immediate*. Such being is so indeterminate, indeed, that it has no "determination" or "content" of its own that would set it in explicit contrast to anything else. It is not "positivity" in opposition to "negativity" or "actuality" in opposition to "possibility" but pure and simple being.[1]

1. See Hegel, *SL* 93/1: 96.

Such being is abstract, but it is not a mere illusion for Hegel as it is, for example, for Nietzsche. On the contrary, it is sheer *immediacy* itself. It is the least we can understand thought to be and the least we can understand there to be at all. Such being is that with which we are most familiar but which we rarely, if ever, reflect upon: the sheer *isness* of things, here considered by itself in abstraction from all relation to things or anything else as sheer, indeterminate being.

At this point, Hegel confronts us with the first of many surprising paradoxes: for he maintains that by virtue of its utter indeterminacy pure being is actually no different from *nothing* at all: "being, the indeterminate immediate, is in fact *nothing* (*Nichts*), and neither more nor less than *nothing*" (*SL* 82/1: 83 [195]). Of all Hegel's statements in the *Logic*, this is the one that has perhaps invited the most ridicule and elicited the greatest misunderstanding. In Hegel's view, however, it is trivially true: pure being is utterly indeterminate and vacuous and as such is completely indistinguishable from sheer and utter nothingness. This is not to say that we are wrong to talk of pure being in the first place. There is being; it is all around us and is, minimally, pure and simple *being*, whatever else it may prove to be. Insofar as it is *pure* being, however, it is so utterly indeterminate that logically it vanishes into nothing. Presuppositionless philosophy is thus led by being itself to the thought of its very opposite.

This nothing that pure, indeterminate being itself proves to be is not just the nothingness to which we frequently refer in everyday discourse. We often say that there is "nothing" in the bag or "nothing" on television when what we mean is that the specific things we desire are not to be found and what there is is not what we are interested in. Such everyday nothingness is merely the absence of this or that specific thing (say, a ball), that is at the same time the presence of something else (say, the air). By contrast, the nothingness Hegel has in mind in the *Logic* is the absolute "lack" or "absence" of anything at all, or sheer and utter nothing. It is not even the pure void of space or the empty form of time, but is *nothing whatsoever*: "*nothing, pure nothing*. . . . complete emptiness, absence of all determination and content," or what Hegel also refers to as the sheer "not" (*SL* 82–83/1: 83–4 [195]).

Hegel maintains, however, that such absolute, radical nothingness has its own immediacy. After all, it *is* sheer and utter nothingness and as such *is* intelligible to thought. Nothingness is, indeed, nothing but the sheer *immediacy* of nothingness itself; there is nothing else to it. As this immediacy, Hegel contends, it is indistinguishable from pure indeterminate *being*. This is not to say that we are mistaken to think of it as nothing in the first place. Pure nothing is *nothing* whatsoever, but it is so purely and immediately nothing that it vanishes logically *into* empty immediate being. Just as pure being vanishes logically into nothing, therefore, pure nothing equally vanishes logically back into being. This means, of course, that pure being and pure nothing not only vanish but also prove to be ineliminable since each one disappears into, and so immediately revives, the other.

Unpalatable though it may be to some, the unavoidable conclusion to which presuppositionless logic leads us is that "*pure being* and *pure nothing* are . . . the same" because both are equally indeterminate and vacuous (*SL* 82/1: 83 [195]). Yet Hegel also insists that being and nothing are not simply the same but are immediately different from one another: being is *being*, and nothing is *nothing*. As such, Hegel tells us, they are "absolutely distinct" (*absolut unterschieden*) (*SL* 83/1: 83 [195]).[2] They do not just constitute one and the same indeterminacy, therefore, but form *two* radically different indeterminacies whose difference is, however, indeterminable. The fact that being and nothing are indistinguishable in their immediate difference is evident in their immediate *disappearance into* one another. On the other hand, the fact that they are immediately different in their indistinguishability is evident in the immediate disappearance of each into the *other*. In Michael Rosen's words, they are "non-identical indiscernibles."[3]

Being and nothing are utterly different from one another but collapse logically into one another because of the indeterminate immediacy of their difference. Since each one collapses into the *other*, however, each proves, as I noted above, to be ineliminable and irreducible. Yet each one proves to be irreducible precisely *as* vanishing into the other. The recognition of this fact brings about a subtle but important shift in the way being and nothing are to be thought. For we can now no longer say simply that being and nothing vanish into one another, but we have to understand each one to be nothing but its own vanishing or collapse. They do not just *disappear* into the other but *are* such disappearing.

Being and nothing thus both prove to be absolutely necessary and to be endlessly generated by one another. Yet neither has a separate stable identity apart from its vanishing since logically each vanishes straight away into the other. This vanishing that each one is is its own utter *indeterminacy*—indeterminacy now understood not just as sheer *being* or *nothing* but as radical instability and fluidity. The name Hegel gives to this "immediate vanishing of the one in the other" is *becoming* (*Werden*). Pure indeterminate being is not just being or nothing, therefore, but becoming; nothing, in turn, cannot just be sheer and utter nothing but must also be its own vanishing, or becoming.

Presuppositionless philosophy has to begin with sheer being, but it evidently cannot stop there because sheer being immediately proves to be not just being but becoming. This is not to say that it is now wrong to talk of "being." Being *is;* it is—or, rather, proves to be—absolutely irreducible. What Hegel's philosophy shows, however, is that logically, purely by virtue of being "being," being turns out to be "becoming." Becoming is thus what being is *in truth:* immediacy as the restless vanishing and reemergence of itself.

---

2. See Hegel, *EL* 141/188 (§88).

3. Rosen, *Hegel's Dialectic and Its Criticism*, p. 152.

Misunderstandings

The opening of the *Logic* is remarkably simple, but it has met with considerable misunderstanding and so evidently needs further clarification. The first thing to note is that Hegel's account of pure being is both conceptual and ontological. It shows that the bare thought of being mutates into the thought of becoming *and* that being itself turns out to be becoming. The fact that the *Logic* advances an ontological thesis does not mean, however, that it describes a temporal or historical process. As finite beings, we must unfold in time all that being entails and so must think first of being, then of nothing, and then of becoming. In so doing, however, we are not claiming that pure being itself vanishes and develops into becoming *over time*. We are claiming that pure being proves to be *logically* or *structurally* unstable—that it turns out logically to be nothing but vanishing and becoming.[4]

Hegel's *Logic* unfolds what it means and is to be, not just what *we* understand being to be. In the process, it demonstrates that pure being itself entails further, more complex structures or determinations, but it does not show that being leads over time to such determinations. Later in Hegel's system—for example, in the philosophy of history—we will learn that there are in fact developments in time (such as the emergence of consciousness) that are codetermined by the logical character of being. The task of the *Logic*, however, is not to describe such temporal developments but simply to lay out before us all that being logically must be.

In moving from being to nothing and back again in thought, we are certainly thinking in time, but what we are thinking is the *logical* collapse of being and nothing into one another and the corresponding *logical* transformation of each into becoming. In other words, we are setting out the logical "history" of being. Logically, being proves not just to be being after all but to be becoming; becoming, accordingly, is nothing but the structural instability that being immediately proves to be. Later in the *Logic* and in the *Philosophy of Nature*, being gradually shows itself to be much more determinate—to be the realm of finite things in space—and in the process, becoming mutates into the temporal coming-to-be and passing-away of such things. At the moment, however, we do not have temporal change and development in mind. All we have in view is sheer indeterminate becoming as such, or being as utter instability.

In the *Logic*, being and nothing are initially pure and indeterminate, but they soon prove to be much more determinate and complex than mere *being* and *nothing* (or becoming). Being will mutate logically into reality, being-something, actuality, and ultimately, space, whereas nothing, or the simple "not," will mutate into negation, otherness, negativity, and ultimately, time. In each one, however,

---

4. See D. Duquette, "Kant, Hegel, and the Possibility of a Speculative Logic," in *Essays on Hegel's Logic*, p. 8.

being and nothing as such will be preserved. "Nowhere in heaven or on earth," Hegel writes, "is there anything which does not contain within itself both being and nothing" (*SL* 85/1: 86). Indeed, every further determination *of* being and nothing will simply be a more complex and intimate interrelation *between* being and nothing.

The key to understanding Hegel's *Logic* is to distinguish carefully what is true of being *qua* pure *being* from what is true of, for example, being *qua* reality or being-something and to avoid reducing one category or determination of being to another. There will clearly be structural affinities between such determinations since less determinate ones are contained in more determinate ones, but there will also be significant differences that are not to be overlooked.[5]

To be finite, as we will see later, is to cease to be. Finitude thus incorporates into its structure the vanishing of immediate being into nothing. Yet to be finite involves more than simply *being* and its vanishing. Over and above sheer being, finitude entails being "something" in relation to "others" and being subject to "change." Thus, although all finite things are destined to pass away by virtue of the fact that they *are* at all, there is a clear determinable difference between their structure as existing things and their nonexistence. Being a finite thing is definitely not the same as utter nothingness.

Sheer indeterminate being is, however, logically indistinguishable from nothingness. Or, rather, there is an immediate difference between pure being and pure nothing that is indeterminable and so immediately evanesces. We can say of pure being, therefore, that it is identical to nothingness because pure being considered by itself is quite indeterminate. But we cannot say of finite things that they are just nothing or that their existence and nonexistence are indistinguishable because finitude has a determinate logical structure that is clearly different from that of pure nothingness.

In Hegel's view, it is the failure to respect this difference that often prompts people to pour scorn on the beginning of the *Logic*. For readers all too often assume that Hegel is equating the being and nonbeing of concrete, *determinate* things. According to Hegel, such readers draw the following facile conclusion: "being and non-being (*Nichtsein*) are the same, therefore it is the same whether this house is or not, whether these hundred dollars are part of my fortune or not." As Hegel notes, however,

> this inference from, or application of, the proposition [that being and nothing are the same] completely alters its meaning. The proposition contains the pure abstractions of being and nothing; but the application converts them into a determinate being and a determinate nothing. But, as we have said, the question here is not of determinate being. (*SL* 85–6/1: 87)

5. See Hegel, *SL* 840/2: 569.

Hegel's point is that utterly *indeterminate* being is logically indistinguishable from—though also irreducible to—sheer nothingness. He is not claiming that existing things cannot be distinguished from nonexisting things or that it makes no difference to me whether I exist or not. He is highlighting the slippery, evanescent character of indeterminate immediacy as such, not denying the reality of *determinate* objects. As we shall see, all determinate things share in the slipperiness of indeterminate being to some extent since they are modes of being; for this reason, they are subject to negation, destruction, and death. But what they are is not exhausted by such indeterminacy since they are also concrete determinate things with a definite logical and, indeed, empirical character. Those who mock Hegel for denying the clear difference between the existence and nonexistence of determinate things are thus themselves guilty of blurring distinctions because they fail to distinguish between the logical character of pure being as such and that of determinate being. Indeed, Hegel's critics fail to notice—or mischievously choose to ignore—that at the start of the *Logic* Hegel cannot possibly be erasing the distinction between the existence and nonexistence of determinate things because he has not yet demonstrated that pure being actually entails any determinacy at all.[6]

Hegel and Nothing

Another charge that might conceivably be leveled at Hegel—although he does not mention it himself—is that he is a nihilist for whom all there "is" is *nothing*. According to this view, when Hegel asserts that pure being is nothing, he is not telling us anything about being as such but is replacing the *fiction* of "being" with the true idea of sheer and utter nothingness. He is saying that there never is any being to begin with but that ultimately there only ever "is" nothingness. To my mind, this is not, and cannot be, Hegel's position. When he states that being is in fact nothing, he is not denying that there is any being in the first place. On the contrary, he is affirming that there *is* being, but he is pointing out that insofar as it is utterly indeterminate and immediate, being vanishes logically into nothing. Yes, we are brought to consider nothingness—sheer and utter nothingness without any trace of being at all. But we are brought to consider such nothingness by the indeterminacy of pure, immediate *being*. Hegel is thus not a nihilist who rejects the very idea of being but an ontologist—albeit one of a highly original kind. Moreover, Hegel's ontology does not merely run aground on the sandbank of nothingness because sheer and utter nothingness itself proves to be indeterminate being. Being is thus actually irreducible and so does not just vanish into nothing but proves logically to *be* its own vanishing or becoming.

---

6. On this misunderstanding of Hegel, see Harris, *An Interpretation of the Logic of Hegel*, p. 97; Stace, *The Philosophy of Hegel*, pp. 137–8; and J. M. E. McTaggart, *A Commentary on Hegel's Logic* (Cambridge: Cambridge University Press, 1910), pp. 15–16.

Hegel's apparent "nihilism" actually turns out to be a stage in the logical transformation of being into becoming.

This is not to say that Hegel interprets nothingness from the start as a mode of being. The nothing Hegel has in mind is absolute nothingness—no space, no time, no "presence," no determinacy, no "things," no *being* whatsoever but the pure and utter *not*. By virtue of its very purity and *immediacy* as sheer nothingness, however, such nothingness is itself indistinguishable from indeterminate being. It, too, is, logically, the vanishing of itself into its absolute other. So even if Hegel were a total nihilist and completely rejected the very idea of being, he could not remain one, because nothingness would itself slip ineluctably into being and make him an ontologist.

An important consequence of this dialectical slippage of nothing into being, as Cynthia Willett and George Cave have both pointed out, is that speculative philosophy could just as easily have begun with nothing as with being.[7] Hegel begins with being because what is left once all our presuppositions have been suspended is the sheer being of thought itself—thought *as* sheer being. It turns out, however, as Cave notes, that "Being has no ontological priority over Nothing," because "Being and Nothing vanish *immediately* into one another."[8] We could, therefore, have begun with nothing, as Hegel himself states: "that . . the beginning should be made with nothing (as in Chinese philosophy), need not cause us to lift a finger, for before we could do so this nothing would no less have converted itself into being" (*SL* 99–100/1: 105 [197]). I stress that this is *not* because Hegel has loaded the dice in favor of being from the start. The nothingness that Hegel considers in the *Logic* is sheer nothingness without a trace of being whatsoever. By virtue of its utter purity as *nothing*, however, such absolute nothingness proves to have an *immediacy* of its own and so to be indeterminate being. Nihilism thus converts itself into ontology, whether it wishes to or not, through its insistence on its own purity.

An Immediate, Indeterminate, but Ineliminable Difference

As I have noted, Hegel's opening analysis of being and nothing is quite simple: pure being is so indeterminate that it is nothing at all, and nothing is so purely and immediately negative that it is being. The principal difficulty confronting the reader of this simple dialectical account is that being and nothing have no stable, determinate identity but shimmer with irreducible duplicity. We are used to—or at least believe we are used to—a world of stable, identifiable objects. It is thus hard for us to get our minds around the dialectical shimmering and flickering of pure being and nothing. Yet if Hegel is right, being and nothing as such

7. C. Willett, "The Shadow of Hegel's *Science of Logic*," in *Essays on Hegel's Logic*, p. 88, and G. P. Cave, "The Dialectic of Becoming in Hegel's Logic," *The Owl of Minerva* 16, 2 (Spring 1985): 157.

8. Cave, "The Dialectic of Becoming in Hegel's Logic," p. 159.

are nothing but this shimmering. This is not to say that Hegel believes the whole world of nature and history keeps slipping in and out of being as if someone were switching existence on and off like a light. But Hegel does believe that pure being and pure nothing vanish logically into one another, and as we shall see, he believes that such restless vanishing constitutes a moment of, though does not exhaust, the world of finite, determinate things.

In order to comprehend this unstable indeterminacy of being and nothing, one must recognize that they are ineliminably *different* and that each one vanishes into its *other*. As several commentators have pointed out, *being* and *nothing* are not just two words for the same thing or thought but are two *different* determinations.[9] The significant point, however, is that the difference between them is utterly immediate and is not further specifiable or determinable because they are both indeterminate. As Hegel remarks, "if being and nothing had any determinateness by which they were distinguished from each other then . . . they would be determinate being and determinate nothing, not the pure being and pure nothing that here they still are." The difference between being and nothing thus cannot be stated or defined but can only be "meant" (*gemeint*) (*SL* 92/1: 95).[10]

Günther Maluschke concludes from this that there is no intrinsic *logical* difference between being and nothing at all but that their difference is "extralogical," or formed by subjective opinion (*Meinen*) alone.[11] To my mind, however, this is not Hegel's position. It is true that he maintains that the difference between being and nothing "exists (*besteht*) not in themselves but in a third, in subjective *opinion*" (*SL* 92/1: 95). As I understand Hegel, however, what he is claiming is that there is no definite, stable difference between being and nothing in themselves and that only subjective opinion can keep them clearly apart. This is quite compatible with the claim that being and nothing are themselves logically—though unstably and indeterminably—different. Indeed, as we have seen, Hegel insists explicitly that they are "absolutely distinct," and elsewhere he calls them "incompatibles" (*Unverträgliche*) (*SL* 83, 91/1: 83, 94 [195]).

Hegel's position, as I understand it, is that there is an immediate *logical* difference between being and nothing—being is being and nothing is nothing—but that this difference just as immediately vanishes, only to reemerge as it vanishes. This disappearing difference cannot be defined, but it can be *meant* or, one might even say, *intuited*. Hegel thus cannot be accused of utterly eliminating even the difference between pure being and pure nothing, let alone that between concrete existence and nonexistence. What he invites us to think is an irreducible difference that vanishes the moment it is thought—the moment it *is*—

9. See, for example, Johnson, *The Critique of Thought*, p. 19, and Pöggeler, ed. *Hegel*, p. 80.

10. Miller's translation has "fancied or imagined" for *gemeint*.

11. G. Maluschke, *Kritik und absolute Methode in Hegels Dialektik* (*Hegel-Studien* Beiheft 13) (1974) (Bonn: Bouvier Verlag, 1984), p. 163.

because it is simply immediate and indeterminate. The lesson for the rest of the *Logic* will be that any difference that is not just to vanish will have to be more than just immediate.

The Transition from Being to Nothing

In the paragraph on becoming Hegel says of both being and nothing that "each immediately *vanishes in its opposite*" (*SL* 83/1: 83 [195]). Yet at the start of the same paragraph, he writes that "being—does not pass over but has passed over—into nothing, and nothing into being" (*daß das Sein in Nichts und das Nichts in Sein—nicht übergeht, sondern übergegangen ist*). Is there a contradiction between the use of the present and perfect tenses in these two sentences? Is Hegel both affirming and denying that there is an actual transition from being to nothing and back again? I believe not. What the remark at the beginning of the paragraph indicates is that the transition is in each case *immediate*. There is not first being and then later the vanishing of being into nothing, but pure being vanishes immediately—and so *has* vanished—the moment it is thought, indeed the moment it *is*. As Gadamer puts it, "being and nothing exist solely as passing over or as transition itself, as Becoming."[12] If, Hegel writes, there are those "who are reluctant to recognize either one or the other as only a *transition* (*Übergehen*) of the one into the other," then "let them state *what* it is they are speaking of, that is, put forward a *definition* of being and nothing and demonstrate its correctness" (*SL* 92/1: 96). Hegel is confident, however, that this challenge cannot be met.

By virtue of being pure transition into the other, being and nothing are both *becoming*. As Alan White notes, "what is thought in 'Becoming' is precisely the movement from Being to Nothingness and from Nothingness to Being."[13] Yet Michael Theunissen points out that Hegel appears to draw a distinction between the ideas of "transition" and "becoming."[14] Hegel states that "*transition* (*Übergehen*) is the same as becoming (*Werden*) except that in the former the two [being and nothing], from one of which transition is made to the other, are pictured (*vorgestellt*) more as resting outside one another, the transition taking place *between* them" (*SL* 93/1: 97).[15] In these lines, however, Hegel is not denying that the transition of being and nothing into one another constitutes becoming. He is simply warning his readers that, unlike the word "becoming," the word "transition" can seduce us into misconstruing the movement at issue as one between two quite *separate* and enduring categories. For Hegel, there can be no such transition "between" being and nothing precisely because neither is anything apart from the transition into the other. This transition, or movement, that being and nothing

12. Gadamer, *Hegel's Dialectic*, p. 89.
13. White, *Absolute Knowledge*, p. 37.
14. Theunissen, *Sein und Schein*, p. 119.
15. Translation revised.

each is is all that Hegel means by "becoming." Becoming is thus not actually distinct from transition at all but is simply "this movement (*Bewegung*) of the immediate vanishing of the one in the other" (*SL* 83/1: 83 [195]).

I should add that the fact that being and nothing both vanish in this way does not mean that they are in any sense unthinkable. Hegel is not asserting that both vanish *before* they can even be thought. He is claiming that they can and must be thought since they are both ineliminable, but that logically what they are thought to be, and what they *are*, is nothing but their *vanishing*. The fact that they vanish the moment they are thought does not demonstrate that their immediacy somehow eludes our grasp. Rather, it reveals that logically the immediacy of the one *is* its own vanishing into the equally vanishing immediacy of the other. Logically, pure being *is* nothing but its vanishing and so *is* nothing but becoming, and the same is true of sheer and utter nothing.

Why Do Being and Nothing "Move"?

One common misunderstanding of the *Logic* is that it describes not the logical movement of being and nothing—or of the categories of being and nothing—themselves but the *experience* undergone by the philosopher as he or she endeavors to render each one intelligible. On this reading of the *Logic*, being does not itself vanish logically into nothing. What happens is simply that *we* inevitably move from thinking of being to thinking of nothing when we try to bring pure being into focus. The origin of this kind of misreading is to be found in the work of Schelling, Trendelenburg, and Kierkegaard.

Schelling insists that Hegel's attribution of immanent movement to pure being "means no more . . . than that the *thought* which begins with pure being feels it is impossible for it to stop at this most abstract and empty thing of all." For Schelling, as I suggested in chapter 3, "the compulsion to move on" in the *Logic* does not derive from pure being itself; it "has its basis only in the fact that thought is already used to a more concrete being . . . and thus cannot be satisfied with that meagre diet of pure being in which only content in the abstract but no determinate content is thought." He concludes from this that "the concept [of being] for its own part would lie completely immobile if it were not the concept of a thinking subject," that is, if it were not thought by such a subject.[16]

Kierkegaard also takes the view that concepts do not move by themselves and calls Hegel's introduction of movement into logic "a sheer confusion of logical science." With a noticeably raised eyebrow, Kierkegaard remarks that "it is surely strange to make movement fundamental in a sphere where movement is unthinkable; and to make movement explain logic, when as a matter of fact logic cannot explain movement."[17] Kierkegaard's source for this apparent truism is not

16. Schelling, *On the History of Modern Philosophy*, p. 138.

17. Kierkegaard, *Concluding Unscientific Postscript*, pp. 99–100.

Schelling but Trendelenburg. Trendelenburg insists that he takes Hegel very seriously. He maintains, however, that "he who is strict enough to hold the presuppositionless dialectic of pure thought to its word, and really attempts to proceed without any presupposition and purely, soon sees that it remains immovable and that its productions are still-born." Concepts move in the *Logic* only because Hegel smuggles in a principle derived from nature—that of "*local* motion"—and uses it to animate the categories artificially. Without importing this principle, Trendelenburg argues, "thought would not move from its place."[18] Trendelenburg does not share Schelling's specific explanation for the movement of categories in the *Logic*, but he agrees that those categories move, or appear to move, only because of the way they are thought by the philosopher, not because of any logical feature of their own.

In my view, nothing in the text of the *Logic* supports Trendelenburg's claim. Nor is there any evidence to back up Schelling's assertion that the speculative philosopher moves from pure being to other categories because of some nostalgia for the concreteness of life that is missing from the thought of pure being. There appears, however, to be some evidence to support the general view that speculative logic is moved from one category to another by the activity of the philosopher rather than the categories themselves. At one point in the *Logic*, Hegel writes that it is *reflection* (*Reflexion*) that "declares" being to be nothing and so "equates" the two categories (*SL* 99/1: 104 [195]). This seems at least to suggest that we move from the thought of pure being to that of nothing only because reflection *experiences* pure being as vacuous, not because pure being logically converts itself into nothing.

Wolfgang Wieland interprets the "move" from being to nothing along these lines. According to him, the category of pure being turns out to be something other than it purports to be "when one makes use of it or even thematizes it." The opening move of the *Logic* thus presupposes "that one has undertaken the attempt to determine pure being. Only as a result of this attempt does the category of nothing offer itself to the systematic progression."[19] Without this effort on the part of the philosopher to employ or render determinate and intelligible the category of being, it would seem that that category would forever remain that of pure being.

As Henrich has pointed out, however, any reading that understands the move from being to nothing to be prompted by the activity of the philosopher must be mistaken because it turns speculative logic into a *phenomenological* logic—an account of what happens when pure being is thought *by us*, not an account of the logical character of pure being *itself*.[20] Hegel states clearly in the *Encyclopedia Logic* that the categories "investigate themselves" and that dialectic dwells

18. Trendelenburg, *The Logical Question in Hegel's System*, p. 189.
19. Wieland, "Bemerkungen zum Anfang von Hegels Logik," p. 201, my translation.
20. Henrich, "Anfang und Methode der Logik," p. 82.

"within" them (*EL* 82/114 [§41 Add. 1]). If this is the case, they must be understood to develop or "move" because of their own *logical* character, not because of the way we think of them or experience them. As Henrich puts it, "reflection on their being thought (*Gedachtsein*) cannot count as the moving principle of their progress."[21]

This is not to deny that thought or reflection has to render explicit and "experience" for itself the dialectic implicit in each category, but this dialectic must be inherent in the categories *themselves*. Reflection does, indeed, "declare" being to be nothing, but it does so only because pure being *itself* vanishes logically into nothing.[22] Hegel does not claim merely that our thought slips from one category to another as it tries to render them determinate (as Wieland claims); nor does he assert that our thought passes from one category to another as it struggles to get back to the concreteness of life (as Schelling claims); nor does he simply and arbitrarily import the idea of motion into his treatment of the categories (as Trendelenburg claims). On the contrary, he uncovers the dialectic at the logical heart of being itself.

The Dialectic of Being and Nothing Reexamined

We now have to consider in more detail why exactly pure being does immediately slip away into nothing (and so prove to be nothing but its own vanishing, or "becoming"). The simple answer is that being does so because it is utterly indeterminate. Hegel makes this clear in both the *Logic* and the *Encyclopedia Logic*. In the former, he argues that, since being is "pure indeterminateness and emptiness" "there is *nothing* to be intuited in it" (*SL* 82/1: 82 [193]); in the latter, he confirms this conclusion by stating that "only in this indeterminacy, and because of it, is being *nothing*" (*EL* 139/186 [§87]). To my mind, however, the way in which this argument is often understood by commentators is much more problematic than is generally recognized. Consider the following restatements of Hegel's argument.

According to Stace's account:

> Being . . . is the highest possible abstraction. . . . Because being is thus utterly empty, it is therefore equivalent to nothing. The thought of nothing is simply the thought of the absence of all determination. When we think of anything we can only think it by virtue of its having this or that determination, size, shape, colour, weight, etc. What has no determinations of any kind is an absolute emptiness, nothing. And because being is by its very definition the absence of all determination, it is nothing.[23]

---

21. Henrich, "Anfang und Methode der Logik," p. 82.

22. This refines the position set out in Houlgate, "Schelling's Critique of Hegel's *Science of Logic*," p. 123.

23. Stace, *The Philosophy of Hegel*, p. 135.

McTaggart argues as follows:

> Pure Being, says Hegel .. has no determination of any sort. Any determination would give it some particular nature, as against some other particular nature—would make it X rather than not-X. It has therefore no determination whatever. But to be completely free of any determination is just what we mean by Nothing. . . . And thus we pass over to the second category.[24]

Lastly, here is a more recent account of Hegel's argument by Friederike Schick:

> The first determination of being is "indeterminacy and emptiness" . . . It does not have difference within itself or with respect to anything else. For thought, however (which is here not yet distinguished from intuition), it is thus—nothing. If thought otherwise means distinguishing, that is, determining, then nothing is to be thought where nothing is given to be determined and distinguished.[25]

On the surface, these three restatements of Hegel's position seem reasonable and accurate enough: they all say that pure being lacks determination and for that reason is actually nothing at all. Yet, one should note that in each case the argument as it is presented has a very significant condition. For Stace, it is that "when *we* think of anything *we* can only think it by virtue of its having this or that determination." Given this condition, Stace argues, "what has no determinations of any kind is . . . nothing." Schick takes the same condition for granted: "if *thought* otherwise means distinguishing, that is, *determining*, then nothing is to be thought where nothing is given to be determined and distinguished." Accordingly, we are told, being is nothing "for thought" (*für das Denken*). Finally, McTaggart presupposes that "to be completely free of any determination is just what *we* mean by Nothing." On this condition, he contends, "we pass over" from being to nothing. In each case, then, being is nothing only because its utter lack of determination makes it nothing *for us*. It is evident, however, that this way of interpreting Hegel's argument renders the vanishing of being into nothing wholly contingent upon our need for determinacy and our assumption that one can talk of being (rather than nothing) only when such determinacy is encountered. *We* can only think in terms of determinacy, and if we encounter no such determinacy, *we* judge that there is nothing to be thought. For *us*, therefore, pure being cannot but be equivalent to nothing at all.

But this raises the following obvious question: *given this reading*, would be-

---

24. McTaggart, *A Commentary on Hegel's Logic*, p. 15.

25. F. Schick, *Hegels Wissenschaft der Logik—metaphysische Letztbegründung oder Theorie logischer Formen?* (Freiburg/München: Verlag Karl Alber, 1994), p. 118, my translation.

ing still vanish into nothing if it were thought by an intelligence that does *not* constantly seek determinacy and assume that an absence of determinacy is the total absence of being, or nothing at all? Surely the answer must be no. For if we were to give up the idea that there is no being without determinacy (as the modern demand for radical self-criticism requires us to do), then there would no longer be any compelling reason to equate pure, *indeterminate* being with the absence of being altogether, or nothing. Being would certainly lack all determination, but this would provide no ground for thinking of it as nothing because we could no longer take it for granted that the absence of determinacy is the absence of being as such. In other words, nothing of *being* would be lost by pointing out that pure being is nothing *determinate*; one would simply be considering being from a different perspective. Pure being would be indeterminate immediacy, and "nothing" would be one and the same being, only now conceived specifically as the absence of determinacy. There would be no vanishing of the one into the other; *we* would simply turn our attention from one to the other and back again.

The interpretations of the opening of the *Logic* provided by Stace, Schick, and McTaggart may seem at first sight to restate accurately Hegel's argument, but they clearly cannot do so because they make the transition from being to nothing contingent upon *our* habits of thought and so fail to explain why pure being *itself* should vanish logically into nothing. Furthermore, there is a fatal incoherence to the argument as Stace and others present it. For on the one hand, we are required to begin speculative logic with the thought of pure being as such with no further determination. Yet on the other hand, the claim that the absence of determination is nothing whatsoever implies that there is being only where there is determinacy. We are thus able to argue that pure being is nothing only because we simultaneously set aside *and* hold on to the idea that all being entails *determinacy* and so is determinate being.

Note that it is not just a matter here of our operating with the idea of indeterminate being yet remaining familiar with the idea that being entails determinacy. As we saw in chapter 4, there is nothing objectionable about retaining such a double perspective, provided that the two perspectives do not both play a role in moving the logic forward.[26] The problem with the reading of the *Logic* that I am considering here is that the idea that being is indeterminate *and* the idea that being entails determinacy are both operative in the logical account itself: for pure, indeterminate being is said to be the absence of being—that is, nothing—only by virtue of the fact that it is the absence of determinacy.

To my knowledge, Henrich was the first to note that this manner of interpreting Hegel's account of being is unsatisfactory. According to Henrich,

> this transition [from being to nothing] would not be understood in Hegel's sense at all, if one tried to interpret it in the following way: We

---

26. See above, pp. 84–6, 101–2.

> first think of the indeterminate immediacy of being. Then we notice (*bemerken*) that we have thought a completely empty immediacy, and we now characterize (*bezeichnen*) this immediacy in virtue of its emptiness as nothing.[27]

Henrich does not say which commentators he has in mind here, but in my view his point clearly applies to the three I have quoted above.

Now it might be argued that McTaggart, in contrast to Stace and Schick, does not define being *as* the absence of determinacy or *as* empty of content, but just focuses on pure being as such and notes—correctly—that pure being *in fact* lacks determinate content. Little would be gained from pointing this out, however, if the move from being to nothing is still made contingent upon our failure to encounter in pure being the determinate content with which *we* are familiar and which *we* require for there to be more than just nothing. Being and nothing would not disappear of their own accord into one another; rather, our thought would oscillate back and forth between the two as it attends now to the pure immediacy before it and now to that immediacy's emptiness.

Moreover, on this account, being would be excluded by nothingness—and so be understood to vanish—only on the basis of our *assumption* that the absence of determinacy is in fact the absence of being. At the outset of speculative logic, however, this very assumption is meant to be abandoned along with all other assumptions about being and thought. Indeed, only by abandoning it can we think of indeterminate *being* in the first place. As I suggested above, therefore, this problematic reading can explain the dialectical slippage of pure being into nothing only by simultaneously suspending *and* retaining the idea that determinacy is needed for being.

To recapitulate: Hegel's argument at the start of the *Logic* is not, and cannot be, that pure being is nothing because it is defined as lacking—or in fact lacks—the determinacy and concreteness with which *we* are familiar from ordinary experience and which *we* require for there to be an object of thought. Such an argument cannot be Hegel's because it makes the move from being to nothing depend wholly on *our* assumption that the absence of all determinateness or content leaves us with nothing. Hegel, by contrast, argues that pure being vanishes into nothing through its *own* indeterminacy, quite independently of any assumptions we might make. But how exactly are we to understand this vanishing? Why does it occur?

Being vanishes into nothing, according to Hegel, because it is so indeterminate in itself that logically *it is not even the pure being that it is* and so is in fact the absence of being. Pure being vanishes, in other words, not because it fails to meet our standard of intelligibility or because it is experienced by us as nothing but because its own utter indeterminacy prevents it logically from even being

27. Henrich, "Anfang und Methode der Logik," pp. 87–8.

pure and simple being. Hegel makes this particularly clear in these lines from the *Logic*: "because being is devoid of all determination whatsoever (*das Bestimmungslose*), it is not the (affirmative) determinateness which it is; it is not being but nothing" (*SL* 99/1: 104 [195–7]). This, then, is the *logical* reason why pure being vanishes—one that is independent of the way in which we may or may not experience such being. Hegel does not deny that at the beginning of the *Logic we* have to hold fast the thought of pure being in its sheer immediacy; pure being does not just jump up from nowhere and confront us.[28] He insists, however, that logically being dissolves *itself* into nothing through its own purity and indeterminacy and is not merely found by us to be nothing when we try to determine it or render it intelligible.

Note that the transition from being to nothing occurs *immediately*. It is not mediated by any comparison we might make between pure being and "what we mean by nothing"; nor does pure being harbor within itself a distinct, identifiable "ground," "cause," or "condition" of nothingness.[29] Being vanishes immediately into nothing because the very indeterminacy of being *itself* means that logically being is not even the being it is. As Hegel puts it, "because *being* is posited only as immediate, therefore *nothing* emerges (*bricht hervor*) in it only immediately" (*SL* 99/1: 104).[30]

On this reading, it should be noted, nothingness is not merely the absence of being by virtue of being the "absence of all determination"—a position that conflates being and determinacy. Nothingness is, rather, the *immediate* absence of being as such; it is the sheer lack of being into which pure being itself immediately vanishes. It is, as Hegel says, quite simply "not being, but nothing" (*SL* 99/1: 104 [197]).[31] McTaggart takes the alternative view of Hegelian nothingness that I reject. According to him, Hegel "means by Not-Being, as he meant by Nothing, not the mere denial of Being, but the assertion of the absence of all determination."[32] In support of McTaggart's interpretation one could point out that Hegel does say of pure being that it is nothing because "just as little is anything (*etwas*) to be thought in it" as intuited (*SL* 82/1: 83 [193]). The problem, however, is that equating "nothing" with the absence of "anything" or "something" makes it difficult to think of pure being as vanishing purely by itself—without any reference to any other category—into nothingness.

---

28. As we saw in chapter 3, it is the understanding (*Verstand*) that holds fast to the thought of pure being at the start of the *Logic*; see above, p. 65.

29. See Hegel, *SL* 103/1: 109, and Henrich, "Anfang und Methode der Logik," p. 88.

30. See also Burbidge, *On Hegel's Logic*, p. 39.

31. This is made particularly clear in the first edition of the *Science of Logic*. See G. W. F. Hegel, *Wissenschaft der Logik. Erster Band: Die Objektive Logik (1812/1813)*, eds. F. Hogemann and W. Jaeschke, *Gesammelte Werke*, vol. 11 (Hamburg: Felix Meiner Verlag, 1978), p. 53: "das Nichts ist hier die reine Abwesenheit des Seyns [Seins]" ("nothing is here the pure absence of being").

32. McTaggart, *A Commentary on Hegel's Logic*, p. 16.

On the one hand, if nothing is understood primarily as the absence of something and for that reason is taken to be the absence of being, then being is effectively equated with being-*something*. But if this is the case, then there can be no pure *being* that is not something in the first place, and so there can be no vanishing of such being into nothing. Rather, one simply has the absence of something that is nothing from the start. On the other hand, we may accept that the absence of something constitutes pure indeterminate *being* just as much as nothing. After all, being is thought as pure and indeterminate at the start of the *Logic* precisely by not being thought of as a "thing." This means, however, that being does not disappear from view when we point out that it is not "something" or a determinate entity and so call it "nothing." Such nothingness is simply being, or the "absence of something," under a different description.

In neither case, then, is pure being actually thought to *vanish*. In the first case, it cannot be thought at all since being is identified with being-something. In the second case, being remains when nothing is thought since nothing is the very same "absence of something" as being. Yet Hegel states clearly and unequivocally that both being and nothing do vanish into their opposites: "their truth is . . . this movement of the immediate vanishing (*Verschwinden*) of the one in the other" (*SL* 83/1: 83 [195]). We can make sense of Hegel's claim, in my view, only if nothingness is understood not just as the absence of "something" or "determinacy" but as the immediate absence of being as such that is entailed by the sheer indeterminacy of pure being itself. Indeed, on my reading, "nothing" is simply the name we give to the complete and utter *vanishedness* of being. Being is thought, but it is too indeterminate even to be being and so immediately vanishes; what is left is nothing.

This is not to deny that nothingness is indeed the absence of determinacy, or sheer "indeterminacy." But it is to maintain that nothingness is the absence of determinacy (and of finitude, quantity, content, space, and so on) because it is the absence of being as such, *not the other way around*. Accordingly, when Hegel says that pure being is "pure indeterminateness and emptiness" and so is nothing, he means not only that pure being lacks determinacy (which is perfectly true), but also that it is so indeterminate in itself that logically it is not actually *being* at all. For this reason, Hegel concedes, "should it be held more correct to oppose to being, *non-being* (*Nichtsein*) instead of nothing, there would be no objection to this so far as the result is concerned, for in *non-being* the relation to *being* is contained" (*SL* 83/1: 84 [195]). The important point is that nothingness should not just be conceived as "the nothing of a particular something" (*das Nichts von irgend Etwas*) but as the absence of all being whatsoever.

Having said this, Henrich is right to note that at the start of the *Logic* nothingness may not actually be conceived as the *explicit* negation of being—as *Nicht-sein*—because this would turn nothingness into a mediated category constituted by its opposition to another and so would make of it more than *simple*

nothingness.[33] Nothingness *is*, indeed, the absence of being. Yet it may not be defined as such because to do so would be to include being in nothing as excluded by it. Nothingness is the sheer and utter absence of being, so all reference to being must be absent from it. Consequently, it must be understood purely and simply as *nothing*. "We are concerned first of all," Hegel writes, "not with the form of opposition . . . but with the abstract, immediate negation: nothing, purely on its own account (*das Nichts rein für sich*), negation devoid of any relations—what could also be expressed if one so wished merely by 'not' (*Nicht*)" (*SL* 83/1: 84 [195]). It is by virtue of such immediacy, of course, that pure nothing immediately vanishes back into being.

The opening dialectic of being in the *Logic* is straightforward, but it harbors various traps for the unwary. Readers need to distinguish carefully between the way in which being and nothing are defined and what they are: they *are* utterly indeterminate, but they are not defined as—and must not be confused with the category of—"in-determinacy" itself. Readers must also distinguish between the way pure being is experienced by the philosopher and the intrinsic logic of pure being itself. If these distinctions are respected, then Hegel's account of being will be seen to be quite intelligible: pure being immediately vanishes into nothing because it is so pure and indeterminate that logically it is not even the very being it is.

Hegel's Immanent Critique of the Idea of Purity

Robert Pippin suggests that in beginning with pure being Hegel is only pretending to accept and entertain a concept he actually considers to be impossible. The whole point of German Idealism, Pippin contends, is "the denial of the possibility of immediacy, or an intuitive apprehension of pure being," so Hegel obviously cannot begin with the successful thought of immediacy or pure being itself. The dialectical move from being to nothing thus does not show us how *being* is to be understood. On the contrary, "the thought of 'nothing' is . . . just the thought *that* the thought of being designates no possible object of thought."[34]

It should be clear that I do not share this interpretation of the opening of the *Logic*. In my view, Hegel does not implicitly reject the very idea of immediacy or pure being from the start but rather sets out to establish what pure being *is*. The ensuing account demonstrates that logically pure being is not just pure *being* after all but the vanishing of itself into nothing (and back again), or what Hegel calls *becoming*. In the course of this account, however, Hegel reveals what pure being *itself* proves to be and so unfolds its own true nature. In the

33. Henrich, "Anfang und Methode der Logik," p. 88.

34. Pippin, *Hegel's Idealism*, pp. 183–4.

words of the *Encyclopedia Logic*, the progression from being to nothing to becoming and beyond is "the *going-into-itself* (*Insichgehen*) of being, its own deepening into itself" (*EL* 135/181 [§84]).

The *Logic* thus presents being itself in its immanent logical self-determination. Yet by proving that being is not just pure being but becoming, the *Logic* at the same time provides a thorough critique of the reduction of being to *pure being* by thought. Indeed, by unfolding the truth implicit in being and each subsequent category, Hegel shows how all the categories determine their own limits, reveal their own inadequacies, and so subject themselves to an autonomous, immanent critique. In speculative logic, therefore, "the activity of the forms of thinking, and the critique of them, [are] united within the process of cognition" (*EL* 82/114 [§41 Add. 1]).

The idea that Hegel's *Logic* combines the presentation and the critique of the categories has been explored most extensively by Michael Theunissen in his seminal and magisterial work, *Sein und Schein*. Theunissen argues that, for Hegel, pure being and nothing lack truth not because they are still "undeveloped determinations" but because they are "unreal, and thus illusory" (*unwirklich, also Schein*).[35] On my reading, by contrast, Hegel's immanent critique does not show pure being to be a mere illusion but reveals pure being rather to be a radical *underdetermination* of being's true character. Similarly, speculative logic shows that the sheer "not" or nothing is an underdetermination of negation, negativity, and otherness. Hegel's contention, therefore, is that there *is* being and immediacy but that such being is not *merely* being but also becoming, determinacy, finitude, and so on. Equally, there "is" the not or nothingness, but this not is not *merely* nothing but also determinacy, negation, difference, and so on. Moreover, sheer being and nothing both prove themselves to be more than they immediately are, *through* what they immediately are.

Hegel's challenge to Parmenides is thus not that the latter clings to the illusion of pure being (as Nietzsche would argue) but that he actually fails to think pure being itself in its utter purity and indeterminacy. By distinguishing sharply between being and nothing and insisting that being is utterly free of negation, Parmenides neglects to attend closely enough to what *being* itself proves to be; for he fails to recognize that being in fact "is not what it should be, if it is not this pure negation, . . . nothing."[36] Hegel claims with startling boldness that any philosopher who insists absolutely that being is simply being and that nothing is simply nothing remains under the spell of Parmenides and subscribes to what Hegel calls "a system of identity" (*SL* 84/1: 85). As I indicated in chapter 2, the dialectic of pure being thus provides a critique not only of Parmenides but of the

35. Theunissen, *Sein und Schein*, p. 100. All translations of passages from Theunissen's book are my own.

36. Hegel, *VLM* 77, my translation.

whole tradition that he spawned, including most obviously Spinoza. That dialectic also calls into question the familiar conviction that "nothing comes from nothing" and lends support to the Judeo-Christian idea that being is created from nothing. Judaism and Christianity often picture this creation as a specific event in time rather than as an eternal ongoing occurrence. Nevertheless, for Hegel they articulate in an imaginative form the truth that being is always being generated and "created" through negation (*SL* 84/1: 85).

It is important to remember, however, that Hegel is led to his "Judeo-Christian" conception of being and nothing not by any prior assumption that there is a divine creator but by his logical demonstration that pure being and pure nothingness prove to be nothing but their immediate vanishing into one another. Indeed, an important key to Hegel's dialectic as a whole is the insight that all *purity* is essentially the process of its own disappearance and loss. This is not to say that the idea of pure being is utterly illusory after all. Hegel's point is more paradoxical and profound than that. His point is that *ultimately* being is *not* pure being or pure immediacy precisely because *insofar as it is* pure and simple being it undermines itself logically and turns out to be the instability of becoming. In Hegel's view, there *is* immediate being; it is all around us. This being has a character that belongs to it by virtue of the fact that it is purely and simply *being* and nothing else. In being purely what it is, however, being proves paradoxically but logically not *just* to be pure being but to be its own vanishing or becoming. In this respect, Hegel's speculative analysis comes close to deconstruction, for both call into question the idea of unblemished purity. Hegel does not, however, regard purity as rendered impossible by the differential conditions of its possibility but understands it to undermine itself. In Hegel's speculative logic, there is nothing *other* than pure being at work. Yet such being constantly undermines, negates, and—as we shall see—"others" itself and so shows that ultimately it is not utterly *pure* being but the complex realm of finitude and nature. Hegel's critique of unblemished purity is wholly immanent rather than quasi-transcendental and, in my view, is all the more trenchant for that.[37]

The self-dissolution of pure being could be said to constitute the *tragic* nature of being. Being negates itself simply through being what it is just as heroes and heroines, such as Macbeth and Antigone, destroy themselves through their own actions.[38] Ontological tragedy for Hegel is not the brutal incursion of nothingness into being but the conversion or slippage of being and nothing into one another through their own nature and "action." (As we saw in chapter 2, it is above all the recognition of this "tragic," dialectical dimension to being that distinguishes Hegel from Plato.)[39] This slippage, or dialectical conversion, is not

37. See chapter 5, above.

38. See Houlgate, *Hegel, Nietzsche, and the Criticism of Metaphysics*, pp. 198–213, and chapter 20, below, p. 374.

39. See above, pp. 42–3.

driven or determined by any necessity prior to being but is the very *happening* of being itself—the happening that Hegel names "becoming." In the next chapter we will examine Hegel's account of becoming more closely and explain why becoming is necessarily the becoming of determinate being.

Chapter Fifteen

From Becoming to Determinate Being

Becoming

In the previous chapter we examined Hegel's account of indeterminate being—the account with which presuppositionless logic begins—and we saw that because of its utter indeterminacy such being vanishes logically into nothingness. Hegel's claim is not that *we* equate pure being with nothing because it lacks the determinacy and concrete content that *we* expect to find in an object of thought. His claim rather is that pure being vanishes of its own accord into nothing because it is so indeterminate in itself that it is not even unquestionably the pure *being* that it is. Sheer being does indeed lack the multifaceted determinacy and content with which we are familiar from ordinary experience, but it vanishes logically into nothing because, as utterly indeterminate being, it turns out to lack even the minimal "determinacy" or "content" of being itself.

According to Hegel, however, pure nothingness in turn immediately vanishes back into indeterminate being because of its purity and immediacy as sheer nothingness. Being and nothing thus both prove to be ineliminable because each one vanishes into, and so revives, the other. They are ineliminable, however, purely as *vanishing* into one another—a vanishing or transition that Hegel names "becoming." The word "becoming" in speculative logic thus does not merely name the slippage of *our* thought from one concept to another. Becoming is, rather, the *truth* (*Wahrheit*) of being and nothing themselves; it is what each logically proves to be (*SL* 83/1: 83 [195]).[1] *Pace* Pippin, therefore, Hegel *is* affirming a "Heraclitean vision" of being. Indeed, he shows that such a vision is made necessary by Parmenides's conception of pure being, suitably refined and purified, and by the very immediacy of being itself.[2]

The becoming that is now the focus of our attention is not the becoming *of* anything in particular. It is not the process of change undergone by a given object, nor is it a process of development leading to a definite goal. It is simply unspecified, unlocated becoming in general or indeterminate becoming as such. Such becoming cannot be a process undergone by *something* because specula-

---

1. See also Hegel, *EL* 144/192 (§88 Add.): "Becoming is simply the positedness of what being is in its truth."

2. See Pippin, *Hegel's Idealism*, p. 189. See also Hegel, *EL* 144/193 (§88 Add.).

tive logic has not yet shown that being entails being something. All we know is that being is no more nor less than becoming. Nor should being itself be regarded as the subject or substrate of which "becoming" is predicated. Being is not *that which* becomes but is nothing but becoming itself: being as sheer dialectical fluidity and instability. The statement that "being is becoming" is thus a speculative proposition, not an ordinary predicative judgment: it discloses the very nature of being itself.[3]

It is tempting to picture such objectless, agentless becoming as the empty flow of time. This temptation should, however, be avoided. Time for Hegel is the vanishing of spatial existence,[4] but being has not yet shown itself to be spatial, so becoming cannot yet be equated with time. Becoming will, indeed, prove to be temporality (in the *Philosophy of Nature*), but at the beginning of the *Logic* this has not yet been established, so we may not import the idea of time into becoming. Becoming must be conceived simply as the indeterminate vanishing and reemerging that, logically, being proves to be. Hegel does not, therefore, understand becoming from the start within the presupposed horizon of time. He shows, rather, that becoming is itself the logical "ground" of time since it is the pure vanishing that later turns out to be time and consequently explains why there is time at all. As Errol Harris puts it, "time presupposes becoming; becoming does not presuppose time."[5]

It is important to remember when reading the *Logic* that Hegel does not suffer from some extreme form of philosophical myopia. He recognizes that things in the world have many varied characteristics. Take, for example, the tree in my garden. It is a horse chestnut adorned with green leaves and playing host to numerous scampering squirrels. More abstractly, it is located at a specific position in space and is subject to seasonal—and so temporal—change. More abstractly still, it has form, content, and quantity and is a finite thing. Even more abstractly, it is something, it is determinate, it becomes, and it *is*. To say that it is and that it becomes is not, of course, to say very much, but it is nevertheless true. Hegel's principal concern in the *Logic* is to determine precisely what, if anything, follows from the simple *being* of things without regard to their spatio-temporal or empirical qualities. He wants to know specifically what it means—what it *is*—to "be." He addresses this question by deliberately abstracting from all the other features that characterize things in the world—their empirical qualities, their spatio-temporality, even their being-something and being-determinate—and simply considering indeterminate being as such. This being immediately proves to be becoming, and (as we learn later in the *Logic* and in the *Philosophy of Nature*) this becoming in turn proves to be all that we have set to one side: determinacy, finitude, spatio-temporality, and empirical contingency. The phi-

3. See chapter 4, above, pp. 93–5.

4. Hegel, *EPN* 34/48 (§258).

5. Harris, *An Interpretation of the Logic of Hegel*, p. 96.

losopher can only demonstrate that becoming must entail all these other ways or levels of being, however, by focusing on the distinctive logical character of becoming as such and of each subsequent level of being and establishing what it is about each one that requires it to mutate logically into a more complex level. For this reason, Hegel ignores the apparently obvious truth that all becoming is in time and focuses on the minimal logical structure of becoming as such—a structure that leads logically to becoming's temporalization but that is logically "prior" to time itself. Unlike Heidegger, therefore, Hegel does not just take time for granted but *proves* that becoming must be temporal.

Becoming as such entails the vanishing of being into nothing and of nothing into being. Hegel points out that becoming thereby comprises *two* processes, which he calls "ceasing to be" and "coming to be," or *Vergehen* and *Entstehen*. In the latter, "*nothing* is immediate, that is, the determination starts from nothing which relates itself to being," and in the former, "*being* is immediate, that is, the determination starts from being which changes into nothing" (*SL* 105/1: 112 [197–9]). Cynthia Willett suggests that Hegel's word for "becoming"—*Werden* —means "growing, arising, and progressing" and so privileges the positive moment of coming-to-be over that of ceasing-to-be.[6] It is clear, however, that Hegel understands becoming to be in equal measure coming-to-*be* and coming-*not*-to-be. Neither has priority over the other, but both are constitutive of becoming. Becoming is no more (and no less) positive than it is negative. Indeed, the two processes must be absolutely inseparable since each one immediately entails the other.

> The one is *ceasing-to-be* (*Vergehen*): being passes over into nothing, but nothing is equally the opposite of itself, transition into being, coming-to-be (*Entstehen*). This coming-to-be is the other direction: nothing passes over into being, but being equally sublates itself and is rather transition into nothing, is ceasing-to-be. (*SL* 106/1: 112 [199])

As Stace notes, this does not mean that all specific changes in nature are reversible: "that a leaf turns from green to yellow does not necessitate its changing back from yellow to green."[7] Becoming has not yet shown itself to be natural change, so we cannot extrapolate from what Hegel says about becoming to what he might say about nature. Hegel's argument does mean, however, that—in a manner to be further specified—all coming-to-be entails a ceasing-to-be of *some* kind and that all ceasing-to-be entails a coming-to-be. There is no pure genesis that does not involve a process of corruption and no pure destruction that is not a process of generation. Once again, Derridean (or, indeed, Nietzschean) echoes resound from Hegel's speculative logic.

Becoming is the indissoluble unity of its two constituent processes and so is

6. Willett, "The Shadow of Hegel's *Science of Logic*," p. 90.
7. Stace, *The Philosophy of Hegel*, p. 136.

in fact *one* process of coming-to-be and ceasing-to-be. This process is not just taken for granted by Hegel but is what being and nothing both turn out logically to be. As John Burbidge points out, "the category *becoming* [thus] has as components of its connotation the two previous categories of *being* and *nothing*."[8] It should be noted, however, that being and nothing are constitutive of becoming in two subtly different senses at one and the same time. On the one hand, insofar as each is nothing but its own immediate *vanishing*, each is the *process* of becoming: being is ceasing-to-be, and nothing is coming-to-be. On the other hand, insofar as each is its own vanishing into *the other*, each is merely one *moment* of the very process it proves to be. Being and nothing thus not only each constitute respectively one of the two processes in which becoming consists, but they also both occur in the specific process that *each one* is. That is to say, being is one moment of ceasing-to-be along with nothing, and nothing is one moment of coming-to-be along with being. This is because ceasing-to-be is *being*-as-vanishing-into-*nothing*, and coming-to-be is *nothing*-as-vanishing-into-*being*. In becoming, therefore, being and nothing both reduce themselves to moments *of* the processes they each individually constitute (*SL* 105/1: 112 [197]). We will encounter this perplexing logical relation again (or relations that are very similar) later in the *Logic*—in particular when we consider the account of finitude and infinity. Here, however, we meet this relation in its simplest form.

Hegel draws attention to this relation when he says of being and nothing that each proves to be not just itself but the "unity" (*Einheit*) of itself and its other. "Becoming," he writes, "contains being and nothing as *two* such unities, *each* of which is itself a unity of being and nothing" (*SL* 105/1: 112 [197]). There is a danger in putting the point this way, however, for it may seduce us into thinking of being and nothing as somehow coexisting in becoming as its component "parts." Being and nothing clearly do not, and cannot, coexist in becoming because becoming is nothing but the *vanishing* of one into the other. One emerges—or comes to be—only through the disappearance of the other, so there is never an instant when they are both "present." To the extent that the word "unity" causes us to think of being and nothing as belonging *together* in becoming—as standing, as it were, side by side—and obscures the fact that becoming is in fact an "*unrest* of *incompatibles*," it is, as Hegel himself remarks elsewhere, an "unfortunate word" (*SL* 91/1: 94). It is certainly true that being and nothing are both *moments* of the particular mode of becoming they each prove to be, but one must remember that they come to be such moments only insofar as they *vanish* into one another. Indeed, each one comes to be such a moment through *having disappeared*.

Hegel understands becoming as the disappearance, or "vanishing" (*Verschwinden*), of being and nothing because that is the only conception of becoming that arises in presuppositionless philosophy (*SL* 83/1: 83 [195]). No other

---

8. Burbidge, *On Hegel's Logic*, p. 40.

conception of becoming is permitted if we are to remain rigorously self-critical philosophers. Hegel argues, however, that conceiving becoming in this manner requires us to understand becoming itself as collapsing logically into determinate being, or *Dasein*. We shall now consider why this should be.

The Emergence of Determinate Being

The precise reason why pure becoming should lead to determinate being has eluded many commentators. Gadamer, as we saw in chapter 4, can do no more than appeal to the ordinary connotations of the word "becoming" to render the transition intelligible. "It lies in the very meaning of Becoming itself," we are told, "that it reaches determinacy in that which finally has become."[9] This appeal to the ordinary meanings of words does nothing, however, to make it clear why becoming *logically* entails determinate being. Paul Johnson fares no better than Gadamer and simply asserts, with no supporting proof, that "the processes of coming-to-be and ceasing-to-be *presuppose* something which comes-to-be and ceases-to-be, . . . which is determinate being."[10] Note that Johnson not only fails to provide an immanent derivation of determinate being but also assumes without any explanation that being "determinate" entails being "something."

The account provided by Charles Taylor is equally weak. Taylor notes that for Hegel "pure being turns out to be pure emptiness, nothing; and reciprocally, this nothing which is purely indeterminate is equivalent to pure being." He infers from this, however, that "the notion of pure being frustrates its own purpose" because "we cannot characterize reality with it alone," as if it were obvious that the category of pure being is intended to "characterize *reality*" in the first place, as opposed to simply being the thought of pure being. As a result of the evident inadequacy of the category of pure being, Taylor concludes, "we are forced to move to a notion of being as determinate, as having some quality and not another."[11] Taylor thus makes no attempt to show how the concept of pure being *itself* turns into that of determinate being (by first turning into that of becoming) but simply asserts that we are "forced" to think of being as determinate. Moreover, as far as I can tell, he never explains why we are constrained in this way or why we should not be "forced" to adopt some other conception of things. Taylor claims that Hegel's derivation of determinate being is "solid" or, at least, more solid than that of becoming. To my mind, however, Taylor's Hegel does not actually *derive* the idea of determinate being at all but simply takes it for granted that "being can only be thought as determinate."[12]

When we look at Hegel's text itself, we see that he makes no reference to the ordinary meaning of the term "becoming" or to any alleged presuppositions of

9. Gadamer, *Hegel's Dialectic*, p. 87.
10. Johnson, *The Critique of Thought*, p. 21, my emphasis.
11. Taylor, *Hegel*, p. 232.
12. Taylor, *Hegel*, p. 232.

becoming. He argues, rather, that pure becoming collapses immanently through its own logical structure into determinate being. The first thing we need to note, in order to understand why this logical collapse should occur, is that all vanishing of being and nothing into one another entails the pure and absolute *difference* between the two immediacies. As I suggested in chapter 3, the initial disappearance of being into nothing is what first generates an explicit difference between the two. Being and nothing are not given from the start as two distinct categories; all we have initially is pure being alone, without relation to any other category. A difference arises, however, as being vanishes and leaves nothing in its wake.[13] The difference between being and nothing thus emerges in the very movement in which it disappears—that is, in the very movement in which pure being *itself* proves logically to be nothing at all.

This difference is preserved when nothing slides immediately back into being; for in proving to be indistinguishable from being, nothing turns into its absolute opposite. Hegel argues, indeed, that being and nothing vanish and pass over into one another only insofar as they are absolutely different. Without this pure difference, there would be no transition of each into its *other*, no vanishing of either one into its *opposite*, and so no logical transformation of both into becoming. Thus, "becoming as such *is* only through their distinguishedness (*Unterschiedenheit*)" (*SL* 106/1: 113 [199]).[14]

If being and nothing were simply the same indeterminacy under a different name, then neither would become anything different in taking on the name of the other. All we would encounter would be the dreary repetition of the same indeterminacy. Being and nothing are not simply the same, however, but are immediately different. Furthermore, each vanishes *into* its other. In this way each becomes something different and so proves itself to be becoming as such.[15]

Yet it is not enough simply to point out that becoming depends on the absolute difference between being and nothing: for becoming is principally the process whereby being and nothing show themselves to be utterly *indistinguishable*. Yes, they are immediately different; but their vanishing into one another is pre-

13. See J. Biard *et al.*, eds. *Introduction à la lecture de La Science de la Logique de Hegel. I. L'Etre* (Paris: Aubier, 1981), p. 59. See also above, p. 65.

14. See also Hegel, *EL* 144/192 (§88 Add.).

15. Although being and nothing are described here as "other" than one another, they do not exhibit explicitly within themselves the logical structure of "otherness." "Otherness" emerges as an intrinsic feature of what there is only later in the *Logic*. Nevertheless, since being is pure *being* and nothing is pure *nothing*, these two immediacies *are* in fact "other" than one another. Here we see a good example of the way later categories can be used to explain what happens to earlier categories. Note, however, that the subsequent logical development of being and nothing into moments of determinate being depends purely on what is implicit in the logical structure of becoming, that is, of the vanishing that being and nothing each is. That development does not rely in any way on illegitimately anticipating the logical structure of "otherness" itself.

cisely the collapse of the pure *difference* between them. It shows that they are not actually other than one another at all. Indeed, in Hegel's view, their vanishing signals the collapse of the very difference by virtue of which each is understood to vanish into its *other* in the first place. Their vanishing, as the vanishing of the *difference* between them, thus brings all vanishing into *another*—and so becoming itself—to a halt. This is without doubt one of the most difficult dialectical moves in the *Logic*, but its logical necessity is clear to see. Being and nothing can each be said to vanish into its *other* only insofar as it is absolutely different from that other. But in vanishing into its other each proves that it is *not* different from that other after all. The vanishing of one into the other is thus the vanishing of the very difference between them. With the vanishing of that difference, however, all vanishing into what is absolutely "other" necessarily ceases, and with it all becoming.

This is the logical core of Hegel's "deconstructive" analysis of becoming. Being and nothing start out by vanishing, but precisely by virtue of vanishing into one another they show themselves to be indistinguishable and so no longer to be purely *other* than one another at all. This means that there can no longer be any vanishing or transition of *one* into the *other*. That in turn means that there can no longer be any becoming. All there can be is the undifferentiatedness and "sameness" of the two. Logically, therefore, being and nothing do not vanish endlessly into one another but settle into simply being indistinguishable. The vanishing of being and nothing turns out to be not merely the vanishing of each into the other but the vanishing of the very difference between them and so the vanishing of both of them into their mutual indistinguishability.

This is not to say that vanishing and becoming never occurs. It is to say that becoming necessarily entails its own cessation. Logically, becoming must cease because it is the vanishing of being and nothing into one another that leads to their pure and absolute difference *having vanished* and thus to the end of their movement of vanishing. "Heraclitean" becoming, in other words, is the vanishing and ceasing of the very vanishing that it is:

> Being and nothing are in this equilibrium only as vanishing moments; yet becoming as such *is* only through their distinguishedness. Their vanishing, therefore, is the vanishing of becoming or the vanishing of the vanishing itself (*Verschwinden des Verschwindens selbst*). Becoming is an unstable unrest which settles into a stable result. (*SL* 106/1: 113 [199])[16]

The "stable result," to which Hegel refers here is the definitive "vanishedness" (*Verschwundensein*) of the pure difference between being and nothing, or the newly established indistinguishability of the two.

---

16. See also Hegel, *EL* 146/195 (§89 Add.). Miller has "Being and nothing are in this unity."

Yet what has just been said should not be taken to imply that the immediate difference between being and nothing is completely eliminated. What results from the logical collapse of becoming in on itself is the indistinguishability of *being* and *nothing*. These two immediacies are still logically distinct and irreducible. They are, however, no longer *purely* and *absolutely* distinct—in the sense that each one excludes, and disappears in the face of, the other—but are now fused *together* in their immediate difference. Their indistinguishability is thus in fact their absolute *inseparability*; indeed, it can appropriately be called their *unity*. Being and nothing no longer pass over *into* one another and disappear but have proven themselves to *be* both indistinguishable and inextricable. As Richard Winfield puts it, "each immediately cancels itself as a *sequence*"[17]; each comes to be a moment that does not simply disappear as the other one arises but that coexists—indissolubly—with the other. Each thus ceases to be purely itself and also ceases to be the sheer vanishing and reemergence of its purity and comes to the point at which its purity has been definitively *lost* in an intimate unity with the other. Being proves to be both being *and* nothing (or the "not") together as one, and so, too, does nothing.

One should note that the purity of being and nothing disappears—or is lost—much more radically in this settled unity of being and nothing than in the restless to-ing and fro-ing of becoming. Insofar as being and nothing are moments of becoming, each one does indeed lose its purity, sheer immediacy, and apparently inviolable independence and become logically bound up with the other. On the other hand, each reduces itself to such a moment of becoming by vanishing *altogether* and so reinstating the other in its *purity*. The purity of being and nothing is thus actually preserved in its very vanishing. Becoming is the *total* loss of that purity that is *not* actually the loss of such purity at all since each one ceases to be purely itself by immediately vanishing into the purity of the other.

As Hegel points out, however, becoming is precisely the process in which the utter purity of—and pure difference between—being and nothing disappears. It is thus implicitly not only the vanishing of being *into* nothing and of nothing *into* being but "the vanishing of being and nothing generally" (*das Verschwinden von Sein und Nichts überhaupt*) (*SL* 106/1: 113 [199]). Pure being and pure nothing truly vanish, however, only when they do not constantly reappear. This happens when they cease vanishing *into* one another and come to be irrevocably *united* with—or, one could say, "contaminated" by—one another. In proving themselves to be such a unity, being and nothing prove themselves no longer to be *purely* what they are. Their purity does not, however, just disappear temporarily, only to reemerge immediately in its very vanishing. In the settled unity of being and nothing—or what Hegel calls "determinate being" (*Dasein*) —pure being and pure nothing have both disappeared for good.

17. Winfield, *Overcoming Foundations*, p. 68, my emphasis.

Fundamentalist "Heracliteans," who would deny that becoming leads logically to determinate being and who would prefer to cling to pure becoming, thus not only fail to let becoming be what it is—the vanishing of its own vanishing—but also, effectively, refuse to allow the purity of being and nothing genuinely to pass away. This is because the process of becoming can be sustained only through the constant reemergence of purity. Recall that becoming is generated by nothing other than the purity of being and nothing: it is the pure indeterminacy of being and the pure immediacy of nothing that causes each one to vanish into, and thereby *become*, the other. In the absence of such purity, there would be no more becoming, no more vanishing—at least as it has been understood so far. To put it another way, once the purity of being and nothing *has* vanished, it can no longer *continue* to vanish because the purity that first spawned its own vanishing has gone. This is the point that is reached when becoming settles into the unity of being and nothing. In this unity, being and nothing are no longer *purely* themselves because each is inseparable from the other. For this reason, there is no more becoming. Indeterminate becoming can only be preserved, therefore, by refusing to let the purity of being and nothing undermine itself. It would appear that from the Hegelian point of view there is a much deeper complicity between unrelenting "Heracliteans" and "Parmenideans" than either group acknowledges.

Schelling's Interpretation of Hegel

Cynthia Willett has claimed that Hegel "stabilizes" becoming as determinate being, or *Dasein,* only by privileging the positive side of becoming and, like Aristotle, equating becoming with "coming-to-be" or "genesis." Were Hegel to keep similarly in view the negative side of becoming—ceasing-to-be, or what Willett calls the "Heraclitian notion of transitoriness"—he would, we are told, be faced with a notion of becoming that "paralyzes" his system and prevents any further development of the dialectic. If both aspects of becoming were taken fully into account, Willett explains, speculative logic could not move from becoming to determinate being because, "as Aristotle justly claims, an ambiguous starting point renders motion impossible and yields only paralysis."[18]

It should be evident, however, that Willett seriously distorts Hegel's account of becoming. Hegel does not effect the transition from becoming to determinate being by interpreting becoming "positively" as "genesis and development." On the contrary, he understands determinate being to emerge because he interprets both coming-to-be and ceasing-to-be *negatively* as vanishing through their own internal logic into determinate being. Moreover, speculative logic is not "paralyzed" by taking seriously both coming-to-be and ceasing-to-be but is carried forward to determinate being by the immanent collapse of both of them.

18. Willett, "The Shadow of Hegel's *Science of Logic*," pp. 85, 91.

Like Gadamer and Johnson, Willett tries to identify something other than the logical character of becoming itself as the motor that moves us on to a new category. As we have seen, however, the move from becoming to determinate being does not occur because Hegel presupposes that becoming must always result in "something" or because he harbors some quasi-Aristotelian desire to understand the world positively as a fruitful course of development. Becoming leads to determinate being quite simply because logically it is the *vanishing* of the very difference between being and nothing that sustains it and so cannot but issue in the undifferentiatedness, or *unity*, of being and nothing—the unity that constitutes determinate being. The move to determinate being is thus rendered necessary by the wholly immanent and autonomous vanishing and cessation of becoming itself. All we need to do is *let* becoming occur; if we do that, becoming will undermine itself in simply being what it is and will give way through its own logic to determinate being.

Becoming is spawned and sustained by the pure difference between being and nothing: it is the vanishing of each one into the *other*. Yet, precisely because it is the vanishing of each into the other, becoming is the collapsing and vanishing of the pure difference between them. Logically, therefore, becoming leads to its own demise and issues in the inseparability or unity of being and nothing. McTaggart understands this move well:

> Being and Nothing only exist in Becoming as disappearing moments. But Becoming only exists in so far as they are separate, for, if they are not separate, how can they pass into one another? As they vanish, therefore, Becoming ceases to be Becoming, and collapses into a state of rest, which Hegel calls Being Determinate.[19]

One philosopher who appears not to understand how determinate being arises in speculative logic, however, is Schelling.

Even a cursory glance at the contents page of Hegel's *Logic* reveals that the category of pure being leads first to that of becoming and then to that of determinate being. For Schelling, by contrast, Hegel can only move from being to becoming in the first place by thinking of being as already determinate in some way. He thus not only fails to explain why becoming should lead to determinacy

19. McTaggart, *A Commentary on Hegel's Logic*, p. 17. See also Stace, *The Philosophy of Hegel*, p. 139, and Burbidge, *On Hegel's Logic*, p. 41. It should now be clear why Hegel's account of pure becoming deviates from what Michael Forster takes to be Hegel's "official method" (see Forster, "Hegel's Dialectical Method," p. 155). Forster claims that Hegel is committed in advance to uniting every concept with its contrary. This, however, is not the case: Hegel is committed simply to rendering explicit what is implicit in each category. Consequently, in his analysis of becoming he does not show becoming and some contrary category to be united in determinate being (as Forster thinks he should). He demonstrates, rather, that becoming leads immanently—*by itself*—to determinate being. See chapter 2, above, pp. 33–4.

but seriously distorts Hegel's account of the move from being to becoming. Schelling explains the transition from being to becoming in the following way.[20]

First of all, the speculative philosopher anticipates the goal of full being (as "concept," "Idea," and ultimately, nature) and judges that the meager concept of pure being with which the *Logic* begins falls short of that goal. The proposition "Pure being is nothing" is thus reread as saying that "Pure being is *still* (*noch*) nothing" or that "it is *not yet* (*noch nicht*) real being."[21] By being recast as *not yet* real being in this way, pure being is understood not just as nothing but as harboring the possibility of real being which is yet to be fulfilled, that is, as "being *in potentia*." With the interpolation of the word "yet" (*noch*), Schelling maintains, pure being is thus understood as lacking, but also as promising, something which has yet to be. That is to say, pure being is thought as pointing beyond itself and as heralding real being which is *to come*. In this way, Schelling claims, the transition is made by the Hegelian philosopher from the thought of pure being to the thought of coming-to-be, or *becoming*. One moves from pure being to becoming, therefore, not by understanding pure being as pure, indeterminate being but by understanding it as *not yet* real being and so as pointing forward to the future *coming* of that real being itself. In Schelling's view, it is only "with the help of this *yet* [that] Hegel gets to *becoming*."[22] Hegel's dialectic develops, therefore, because pure being is understood already to be the "concept" (*Begriff*) in its abstract form, though not yet the full "concept" to come.

The significant point to note here is that, for Schelling, in being thought as "being *in potentia*," pure being is conceived as "no longer being in general, but rather *determinate* being."[23] We move from being to becoming, therefore, only because being is already regarded as determinate—as *not yet* amounting to, but nevertheless promising, real being. The sequence of categories, on Schelling's reading, is thus "being, determinate being, becoming," not "being, becoming, determinate being." In conceiving of the categories in this way, however, Schelling has no way to explain how becoming itself becomes determinate.

Schelling's interpretation of the *Logic* has been hugely influential even on critics of Hegel who do not explicitly acknowledge their debt to Schelling. The idea that Hegel's dialectic moves forward "thanks to the play of the *already* and the *not-yet*" governs the whole of Derrida's reading of Hegel in *Glas*, for example.[24] It is what enables Derrida to suggest that at every stage in its development Hegelian spirit is always already what it is but also not yet what it is and so is

---

20. For a more extensive study of Schelling's critique of Hegel's account of becoming, see also Houlgate, "Schelling's Critique of Hegel's *Science of Logic*."

21. Schelling, *On the History of Modern Philosophy*, pp. 140–1.

22. Schelling, *On the History of Modern Philosophy*, p. 141.

23. Schelling, *On the History of Modern Philosophy*, p. 141, my emphasis.

24. Derrida, *Glas*, p. 201.

never actually at one with itself but always, as it were, both ahead of and behind itself. It is apparent, however, that Schelling's interpretation is, to say the least, cavalier. No category in the *Logic* mutates into another one because it is "not yet" the concept, Idea, or nature to come. Each one mutates immanently and presuppositionlessly into subsequent categories—without anticipating any goal whatsoever or "already" harboring the promise of such a goal. This is clearly true, as we have just seen, of the transformation of being into becoming and determinate being, and in my view, it remains true throughout the *Logic*.

The only evidence Schelling can adduce that Hegel does conceive of being as "not yet" what is to come is a passage from the *Encyclopedia Logic* in which Hegel writes that "the matter [itself] *is not yet* (*noch nicht*) in its beginning, but the beginning is not merely its *nothing*: on the contrary, its *being* is already there, too" (*EL* 143/190 [§88]). Schelling neglects to note, however, that Hegel is talking here not about the category of pure being but about the concept of "*beginning*" itself. He is showing that the very concept of "beginning" anticipates what is not yet present but is yet to come, namely, that of which the beginning is the beginning; he is not understanding pure *being* itself as "not yet real being." Schelling's reading of Hegel is here, once again, decidedly cavalier.

There is another passage that might appear to lend support to a "Schellingian" way of reading the *Logic* but that Schelling himself does not mention. This is contained in the short section that precedes Hegel's opening analysis of being. Hegel does not use the words "not yet" in this section, but he does appear to suggest that pure being is already determinate because it starts out opposed to determinacy and so is actually *determined* as indeterminacy from the outset (*SL* 81/1: 82 [193]). This appearance is, however, deceptive. Hegel is careful to say that at the start pure being is only *implicitly* (*an sich*), not explicitly, opposed to determinate being; explicitly, it is simply pure being by itself. Furthermore, he states that determinate being *steps*, or *comes* to stand, over against pure being ("*tritt [dem Sein] gegenüber*"), not as Miller's translation suggests, that determinate being actually stands over against pure being from the beginning. Indeterminacy thus only comes *retrospectively* to constitute the distinctive "determinacy" of pure being once being and becoming have mutated logically into determinate being and there is a new notion of being available with which to contrast the initial category of pure being.[25] Pure being is not *determined* from the outset as indeterminate-rather-than-determinate or, indeed, as anything else. This passage does not, therefore, lend any support to a "Schellingian" reading after all.

The idea of determinacy arises in the *Logic* for no other reason than that being in its purity turns out to be a vanishing purity and that very vanishing itself collapses into the unity of being and nothing that constitutes determinate being. Determinacy emerges, in other words, only because pure being is *lost*. This is

25. See chapter 16, below, p. 305.

the point I wish to emphasize above all but that is missed by readers such as Schelling. Speculative logic does not move from being and becoming to determinacy because the philosopher is unable to live with the indeterminacy of being or the restlessness of becoming: there is no nostalgia for the concrete and the living, no desire for permanence, order, and stability, at work in Hegel's *Logic*. Pure being and becoming mutate and develop into determinate being for no other reason than that they undermine themselves logically and in so doing slip into determinacy, as it were, despite themselves.

Pace Klaus Hartmann, therefore, sheer indeterminacy *does* generate determinacy purely by itself; it is not irrevocably at odds with determinacy.[26] This is not because it is already "determined" from the start as indeterminacy but because it *vanishes*—immanently and necessarily—*into* determinacy. It is thus the vanishing of being and becoming as such that explains why there is any determinacy at all.

The transition from becoming to determinate being is, of course, a logical one, not one that occurs over time. Hegel is not describing the gradual emergence of form and order over millions of years out of some primordial chaos but is demonstrating that the structure of pure becoming renders determinate being *logically* necessary. (He is thereby also showing that the *concept* of becoming leads to that of determinacy). It is vital to remember that pure becoming is not the process of coming-to-be and passing away in time. It is nothing but the sheer logical instability that pure being itself proves to be. What Hegel has now shown is that being cannot *just* be sheer instability precisely because logically such instability collapses of its own accord into determinate being.

This is not to say that we are wrong to conceive of being as becoming and instability in the first place. There is being, and being as such is necessarily vanishing and unstable. We have now learned, however, that logically being is not definitively unstable because it is vanishing that itself vanishes. Such radical vanishing does not leave us merely with nothing but, for the reasons we have considered above, issues in determinate being. Determinacy is thus made necessary by the very instability, or "happening," of being itself. This collapse of being and becoming into determinate being is not a one-off event that occurred some time in the past; it is the *universal* logical fate of being and becoming. In the next chapter we will examine the intricate logical structure of determinate being itself more closely.

---

26. See Hartmann, "Hegel: A Non-Metaphysical View," p. 105: "how could the absence of determination lead to richness?"

Chapter Sixteen

Determinate Being

The Simple Oneness of Being and Nothing

The lesson of Hegel's *Logic* so far is that being must be *determinate*. This is because being proves to be becoming, and becoming logically settles into the unity of being and nothing that constitutes determinate being. Being cannot just be *pure* being, therefore, because it renders itself "impure" and determinate through its own immanent logic: it necessarily impurifies and determines itself. The occurrence of determinate being is thus not an accident but the inevitable consequence of the fact that being and nothing (or the "not") prove to be inseparable. Everything Hegel has to say about determinate being follows directly from its being the complete unity, or "simple oneness" (*das einfache Einssein*), of being and nothing (*SL* 109/1: 116 [203]).

At its simplest, then, determinate being, or *Dasein,* is being that is one with nothing, or the not. It is not just being as such but "being-that-is-*not* . . . " Of course, we say of pure being, too, that it "is not" nothing, "is not" becoming, and indeed "is not" determinacy. We do so, however, in order to hold everything but sheer being at bay and to conceive of being in its utter purity. Determinate being, by contrast, is explicitly defined *as* "being-that-is-not . . . " Its logical structure fuses being and the not together into one.

We must remember, however, that being and nothing are immediately different even in being one and the same. Their oneness is the inseparability of *two* immediacies: *being* is indissolubly connected with the *not*. This not with which being is intimately bound up thus has a character of its own. It is, however, itself inseparable from being. Consequently, it is no longer purely negative but is not-being or nonbeing (*Nichtsein*). Determinate being is not just the unity of being and the not, therefore, but the unity of being and nonbeing. As Hegel puts it, "determinate being (*Dasein*) . . . is, in general, being with a non-being such that this non-being is taken up into simple unity with being" (*SL* 110/1: 116 [203]).[1]

The moment of nonbeing that is here united with being is called by Hegel "determinateness" or "determinacy" (*Bestimmtheit*). As we saw earlier, pure nothing is also—albeit implicitly—nonbeing since it is the sheer opposite of be-

1. See Winfield, *Overcoming Foundations*, pp. 70–1.

ing and so lacks any being whatsoever.[2] Pure nothing is not *explicitly* nonbeing, however, but simply lacks all being in fact. Pure nothing is *not* being, but it is not to be confused with *non*-being as such. Determinacy, by contrast, is explicitly nonbeing. For this reason, however, it does not, and cannot, simply lack being. It is, rather, the overt negation of being that is *inseparable* from the being it negates. Indeed, Hegel's claim is that no not can be defined *as* explicitly negating or excluding being without including it as excluded. Determinacy is the first of a whole array of negatives to be encountered in the *Logic* that, in contrast to pure nothing, include the moment of being within themselves.

In Hegel's view, it is solely the presence of this determinacy, or nonbeing, in being that turns the latter into *determinate* being. This is obvious in English but somewhat less so in German. Employing German terms, Hegel's claim is that *Dasein* is distinct from pure *Sein* only because of the presence in it of *Bestimmtheit* and thus is *bestimmtes Sein*. The logical point is the same in either language—that *Dasein* is distinguished from pure being by its inclusion of nonbeing—but German-speaking speculative philosophers come to associate *Dasein* explicitly with "determinacy," or *Bestimmtheit,* slightly later than their English-speaking counterparts (or, at least, later than those who choose to translate *Dasein* as "determinate being").

Having noted a difference between being and nonbeing in determinate being, we must not forget that together they form *one* unity and immediacy. In fact, in determinate being, being is so intimately united with nonbeing that the two are completely coextensive. Determinate being, consequently, is being that, in being, *is* at the same time nonbeing; indeed, only by virtue of being *non*-being as much as being is it determinate being. Hegel himself puts the point like this: "because of the immediacy of the oneness of being and nothing in determinate being, they do not extend beyond each other; so far as determinate being is in the form of being, so far is it non-being, so far is it determinate" (*SL* 111/1: 117 [205]). Hegel goes on to state that "determinateness has not yet severed (*abgelöst*) itself from being." He notes, in fact, that determinacy will never sever itself from being because "the truth which from now on underlies them as ground is the unity of non-being with being; on this as ground all further determinations are developed" (*SL* 111/1: 118 [205]).

The category of determinate being is clearly not an easy one to hold in mind, but the difficulties that it presents are forced on us by the peculiar circumstances of its logical genesis. To understand what Hegel is asking us to think here, we must bear in mind that being and nothing are *two* immediacies that have collapsed into *one*. Insofar as they are two, we must conceive of them as inseparable: being must be conceived as "being-that-is-not . . . ," or "determinate being," and the not that is here combined with being must be conceived in turn as nonbeing, or "determinacy." Insofar as being and the not are one, however, we must

---

2. See Hegel, *SL* 83/1: 84 (195), and chapter 14, above, pp. 279–80.

conceive of determinate being not just as being that is combined with a not but as being that *is* itself nonbeing. That is to say, determinate being must be conceived as being that is completely congruent with and indistinguishable from nonbeing or determinacy. In order to do full justice to determinate being, it should thus be conceived as "being-that-is-not-being" or, more simply, as *being nonbeing*.

There is, of course, a profound ambiguity in such expressions, for they could mean either "being that consists in not being something *else*" or "being that consists in not being *being itself*." As we shall see, Hegel believes that determinate being proves to be equivalent to both of these. It turns out to involve being other than and limited by something else *and* being finite or ceasing to be through simply being what one is. The further logical development of determinate being thus unpacks the ambiguous implications inherent in being determinate. For the moment, however, we must set all such implications to one side because we have not yet demonstrated that determinate being entails anything beyond itself. All we may do is focus our attention on being that consists in being nonbeing. This may not be a very informative concept, but at this stage of the *Logic* it is the only one we are allowed to entertain.

Determinate Being Further Clarified

We might well ask ourselves at this point what on earth Hegel's concept of determinate being has to do with determinacy as we normally understand it. When we think of something as determinate, or as being definitely what it is, we normally associate with that thought a whole range of properties and qualities that lend specificity to the thing concerned. We think of it as having a particular color, texture, and size and interacting in a variety of distinctive ways with other things. This object is determinate because it is green rather than red, made of metal rather than wood, my car rather than yours, and so on. Its determinate character patently does not consist in simply being "nonbeing."

We should remember, however, that Hegel is outlining the minimal logical structure of determinacy. Being, in Hegel's logical story, has only just shown itself to be determinate at all, so we cannot expect to learn from his account any more than what determinate being must be *at first* or *at least*. We should not expect to discover everything that is required for things to be determinate in the concrete, empirical sense with which we are familiar. It may well be that empirical determinacy demands specificity of color, texture, and size. What Hegel's speculative logic shows, however, is that before it can entail any of these things determinate being must consist minimally in being *not-being* or *nonbeing*. We will discover a little later in the *Logic* that this means being *other* than—and so not being—something else (and thus also being something in its own right). For the moment, however, we do not yet know that this is the case; indeed, we do not know precisely what is entailed by "being not-being." All we know is that if we understand being to be anything less than this—if, say, we

understand it to consist in simple *being* without a trace of not-being anywhere—then we deprive being of all determinacy whatsoever and render it utterly indeterminate and vacuous. We thus know that being's determinacy stems minimally from the moment of not-being that it harbors within itself, however that not-being is further to be understood. This may not be to know very much and may still leave us with an abstract, *indeterminate* conception of determinacy; but it is at least to make a start.

To my mind, the fact that, minimally, determinate being does not even entail being *something* disqualifies John Burbidge's expression, "a being," from being an adequate translation of *Dasein*.[3] *Dasein*, for Hegel, is not *a* being; nor is it, as Errol Harris puts it, "a stable entity."[4] It is simply a general way of being: *being* determinate. Strictly speaking, determinate being does not initially consist in being differentiated in any way at all. Being and nonbeing are the two moments of determinate being; but determinate being itself consists in the *unity* or *oneness* of these moments, not in any clear, stable difference between them or in any difference from anything else. So what is it about being nonbeing that constitutes *determinacy* as we normally understand it? Is there any overlap between our ordinary conception of determinacy and Hegel's minimal philosophical conception?

I believe there is. It lies in the fact that before all else determinate being is the *settled* unity of being and nothing. Becoming is the restless vanishing of being and nothing into one another. Determinate being, however, is—to use Lakebrink's apt phrase—the "pacified unity" (*befriedete Einheit*) of being and nothing that immediately results from their transition into one another.[5] In my view, it is this settledness enjoyed by being and the not together that initially and minimally constitutes *determinate* being. The sheer indeterminacy of pure being and nothing showed itself in their restless vanishing—in their never being what they are but always coming to be the other. Determinate being arises when being and the not cease vanishing in this way and settle down into a stable unity in which they constitute—definitely and unequivocally—one and the same thing: namely, being-that-is-not-being.

In spite of the etymology of the German word *Dasein*, determinate being is not being at a certain place, or being *there*, since being has not yet shown itself to be spatial. *Dasein* should thus not be translated as "being-there."[6] Nor, as we

---

3. Burbidge, *On Hegel's Logic*, p. 46. Note that, although Burbidge translates *Dasein* as "a being," he does not conceive of it as related to "something else" but as "immediate and isolated from all relations."

4. Harris, *An Interpretation of the Logic of Hegel*, p. 101.

5. B. Lakebrink, *Kommentar zu Hegels "Logik" in seiner "Enzyklopädie" von 1830.* Band 1: *Sein und Wesen* (Freiburg/München: Verlag Karl Alber, 1979), p. 115, my translation.

6. As it is in the Hackett translation of the *Encyclopedia Logic*. See Hegel, *EL* 145 (§89).

have seen, is determinate being initially equivalent to being something, or even to being differentiated at all (to being A *rather than* B). To begin with, determinate being is simply being that is settled, at rest, and tranquil. It is being that is definitely *being* and that does not vanish the moment it is. The price being has to pay for this definiteness, however, is that it is indistinguishable from the nothing or the not that is also definite. Being is only determinate, in other words, in definitely being *not-being*—the same not-being that the not now definitely is.

Aufhebung

Becoming, for Hegel, is the dialectical process in which pure being and pure nothing are actually engaged in vanishing. Determinate being, by contrast, is what immediately results from this vanishing: the speculative unity in which their purity and pure difference have vanished.[7] Another way of putting this is to say that becoming is the process of "sublating" pure being and nothing—the movement of their *Aufhebung*—whereas determinate being is the resulting state of their being, or having been, sublated—their *Aufgehobensein*.

Before we continue with our examination of *Dasein*, we must consider briefly Hegel's concept of *Aufhebung*, which he declares to be "one of the most important concepts in philosophy." *Aufhebung*, Hegel says, is "a fundamental determination which repeatedly occurs throughout the whole of philosophy." When something is *aufgehoben,* or sublated, it is negated, but it is not annihilated altogether. Rather, it is deprived of its independence and brought into "unity with its opposite" (*SL* 107/1: 113–14 [201]). What is sublated thus continues to be but at the same time loses its immediacy and so no longer remains purely itself. In the first act of *Aufhebung* in the *Logic*, being and nothing cease being purely what they are, vanish into one another, and then settle into their unity with one another—the unity that constitutes determinate being.

In the course of this *Aufhebung*, Hegel argues, being and nothing are transformed—or, rather, transform themselves—into new determinations. They start out as pure being and pure nothing. As immediately vanishing into one another, they then transform themselves into the two opposed forms of becoming: ceasing-to-be and coming-to-be. By settling just as immediately into their indissoluble unity, they transform themselves further into determinate being and the moment of nonbeing contained within it that renders being determinate. *Aufhebung*, for Hegel, is precisely this process whereby being and nothing lose their purity and thereby *change* into more complex determinations.

At the same time, Hegel points out, what results has in each case "*in itself* the *determinateness from which it originates*" (*SL* 107/1: 114 [199]) and so preserves within it both *being* and *nothing*. Becoming thus comprises ceasing-to-be

7. On dialectic and speculative unity, see Hegel, *EL* 128–132/172–7 (§§81–2).

and coming-to-be, each of which is the vanishing of being or nothing into the other. Similarly, determinate being is the oneness of being and nonbeing, the latter itself being the settled unity of being and nothing. It is very important to recognize, as we noted in the last chapter, that being and nothing not only mutate into new configurations of themselves but also remain *moments* of those new configurations—that is, determinations that are no longer purely "for themselves" but related to and connected with one another. Hegelian *Aufhebung* is both the process of mutation *and* the process of becoming a moment undergone by being and nothing. *Aufhebung* thus does not cast anything aside; as the absolute, immanent "method" of speculative philosophy, it carries everything along with it (*SL* 840/2: 569).[8] What gets lost is merely the purity of a category—the idea that a category is purely and simply itself *and nothing more*.

Hegel believes that every subsequent determination will similarly preserve its predecessors as moments of itself. This is why the Idea and then nature will be said to contain all previous categories. Natural objects are not just finite objects. Nevertheless, they are *at least* finite objects, just as they are something, are determinate, become, and *are*. Indeed, natural objects are simply what being, becoming, determinacy, and finitude ultimately prove to *be*. The logic that requires there to be a realm of natural objects does not derive from some transcendent, alien authority, therefore, but stems from finitude, determinacy, and being that turn themselves into moments constitutive of and contained within such objects. Being, remember, is not a mere fiction: there *is* being. The fundamental paradox, however, is that such being, by virtue of simply being *being*, logically turns into—and so turns out to be—the being *of* determinate, finite, natural things. So far we have witnessed the initial stage of that process wherein being proves to be the being of determinacy as such.

The first thing to be said about *Aufhebung*, then, is that it is a process of negation *and* preservation at one and the same time. The second thing to be noted is that it is nothing beyond the process of *self*-impurification that is initiated and undergone by the categories and forms of being concerned. *Aufhebung* is not an "external" act of negating categories or of raising them up into a "higher" unity carried out by thought. Nothing is done by the philosopher to the categories to sublate them, nor is any unity presupposed as that *into which* categories are "taken up." Furthermore, *Aufhebung* is a process without any goal or *telos*. It is not guided by any will to synthesize or to overcome differences or by any desire to make strife and conflict yield to harmony and reconciliation. Nor, *pace* Derrida, is it driven by any "economic" interest in reappropriating and drawing profit from absolute loss.[9] *Aufhebung*, for Hegel, is simply the process whereby purity slips away into, and is lost in, impurity—impurity that consists in not just

8. Although becoming has for the moment disappeared completely, it will reemerge later as a moment of "change" and "finitude."

9. Derrida, *Glas*, p. 133.

being what one is but in being inextricably bound to another. It is the process whereby initially independent, self-sufficient immediacies constitute a unity *that was never there before* by collapsing into inseparability.

Hegel is certainly an advocate of the "unity of opposites." His post-Nietzschean critics are right about that. He advocates unity, however, not because he wants to "overcome" difference in the name of some preferred harmony, but because he believes that *pure* difference—and the purest difference is between being and nothing—is unsustainable and necessarily collapses *through itself* into unity and impurity.

Derrida tries to resist Hegelian *Aufhebung* by suggesting that there is always a risk of a "pure loss" that never leads to new meaning in which old differences are *aufgehoben.*[10] He suspects that Hegel denies this risk because he is incapable of thinking "without *relève*" and so can only think any loss, death, or nothingness *within* a system already skewed in favor of *Aufhebung*. To my mind, however, Derrida misunderstands Hegel's position. Hegel is not advocating a system oriented in advance toward unity, resolution, and *Aufhebung*. He is a philosopher of *Aufhebung* because he believes that purity—whether the purity of being or of nothing—undermines, "deconstructs," or sublates *itself* and thereby renders itself impure. From a Hegelian point of view, Derrida's critique itself rests on clinging—*impossibly*—to a notion of pure loss or the purely negative that is ultimately unsustainable.

Hegelian *Aufhebung* and Derridean deconstruction are by no means the same: Hegel sets out the immanent self-undermining of pure being, whereas Derrida points to, among many other things, the play of unresolvable differences that (he thinks) make possible and render impossible any idea of pure being. The two philosophers do, however, share a common belief that the idea of pure being is problematic. What I wish to stress is that Derrida misunderstands Hegelian *Aufhebung* by failing to see that it represents a much more thorough suspension of purity than deconstruction. This is because for Hegel *Aufhebung,* or self-impurification, is the immanent fate not only of pure being but also of the *pure* "loss," or nothing, to which Derrida himself points in the attempt to disrupt the process of *Aufhebung*. In Hegel's view, both pure being and pure nothing render themselves impure. The initial result of this movement into impurity is the indissoluble unity of being and nothing, or *Dasein*, to the analysis of which we now return.

Quality, Negation, and Reality

We have seen that determinate being consists in being nonbeing. It *is*, but insofar as it is, it is *non*-being. In it, its constituent moments of being and nonbeing are perfectly fused into one. Determinate being is thus not pure being but being

10. Derrida, *Margins of Philosophy*, p. 107.

that is coextensive with determinacy. Yet determinate being is not only *being* that is determinate but also determinacy-that-*is*. This may seem to be a redundant point to make, but if we are to understand everything that is entailed by a concept, we must render all its aspects explicit—however minimal the differences between them may be. This means that we must here pay equal attention to the fact that determinate being is a mode of *being* and to the fact that it is *determinacy* (or nonbeing) in the form of being.

Our explication of the idea of determinate being has followed a certain rhythm. First, we noted that it is *being*-that-is-not. Then we noted that the not with which being is united is itself connected with being and so is nonbeing. This means that determinate being is in fact to be conceived as being-that-is-non-being. To conceive of determinate being in this way, however, is to understand it principally as a new, transformed mode of *being*—as being that has been infused with the negative. Yet the intimate connection of being and nonbeing in *Dasein* means that the latter is not just *being* in a new guise but also the *not* in a new guise. In other words, determinate being is just as much nonbeing or determinacy that enjoys being as it is being that enjoys determinacy. Indeed, only when determinate being has been conceived in both of these ways is it understood to be fully *determinate* being. Determinate being is not just a modified form of being, therefore, but being that is completely congruent with determinacy-that-*is*. Admittedly, this is a somewhat abstract way to understand determinate being, but it is the way we are required to understand it by the development of speculative logic so far.

The name that Hegel gives to determinacy-that-*is*, or *seiende Bestimmtheit*, is "quality" (*SL* 111/1: 118 [205]).[11] Quality, for Hegel, is thus nothing but definiteness and settledness that enjoys being. Several commentators have pointed out that quality as Hegel conceives it is actually identical with determinate being as such. Quality as determinacy-that-is *is* at the same time being-that-is-determinate. Determinate being does not, therefore, underlie or support quality in the manner of Lockean substance, nor can it be said to "have" quality as a thing has properties that may change without affecting the fundamental character of the thing itself.[12] Quality is utterly inseparable from determinate being. One might say that it is *what* determinate being is; indeed, as Harris puts it, it is nothing but the latter's "*what*." If one takes away quality, one takes away determinate being itself.[13]

The hard thing to get one's mind around here is the fact that quality is not

---

11. See also Hegel, *EL* 146/195 (§90).

12. Lakebrink, *Kommentar zu Hegels "Logik,"* p. 118, and G. Rinaldi, *A History and Interpretation of the Logic of Hegel* (Lewiston, N.Y.: The Edwin Mellen Press, 1992), p. 148.

13. Harris, *An Interpretation of the Logic of Hegel*, p. 101. See also Stace, *The Philosophy of Hegel,* p. 141.

yet understood as the quality or property of *something*. We still do not know that being entails being something, so we cannot regard quality as attached to something in the manner of a predicate. Hegel's claim is simply that being as such is qualitative. It is not indeterminate but, rather, *determinate* being—being that is *what* it is, is characterized in a certain way, and thereby is quality. If it should turn out that being does entail being something after all, then any "something" will be, to use Spinoza's language, a particular mode or instance *of* such qualitative being.

Now that the idea of qualitative being has emerged in the *Logic*, indeterminacy itself may be said retrospectively to constitute the "quality" of pure being (see *SL* 81/82 [193]). Pure being is not explicitly qualified being, however, because it is not explicitly *determined* as in-determinate being. This, indeed, is what makes it utterly *indeterminate* in fact. Determinate being, by contrast, is explicitly determinate and qualitative, because it unites being and nonbeing openly within itself.[14]

With the recognition that determinate being is *quality*, being at last comes to be understood as genuinely determinate. Determinate being consists not just in *being* that is determinate, or *Dasein*, but also in affirmative *determinacy*, or quality. The one is inseparable from—indeed, indistinguishable from—the other. There can therefore be no determinate difference *between* determinate being and quality because together they constitute what it is to be determinate. Accordingly, determinate being is undifferentiated being, or pure and simple quality.

McTaggart assumes that where there is quality there is automatically a plurality of qualities.[15] To my mind, however, quality not only is not plural when we first encounter it but is not differentiated in itself at all. Quality is determinate being, and being determinate initially means being settled and definite; it does not mean being differentiated from something else. One might say that it consists in being *this*, but does not yet involve being explicitly this *rather than* that. Quality is not initially distinguished from anything other than itself but simply *is* what it is.

Hegel goes on to show, however, that the intrinsic logic of quality does generate a difference in quality after all (though not an internal "plurality"). There are actually two kinds of quality. Why should this be the case? To understand why, we first need to note that even in being conceived as quality or affirmative *determinacy* the moment of nonbeing is not given equal prominence to that of being. So far we have understood *Dasein* to be *being* that is determinate and determinacy that *is*, but as Hegel points out, this is in each case to conceive it in a "one-sided" way as *being*. *Dasein* is, however, just as much negative as affirmative and so is "equally to be posited in the determination of nothing" (*SL* 111/1: 118 [205]). What does this mean? It means that quality has to be conceived not

14. See chapter 15, above, p. 295.

15. McTaggart, *A Commentary on Hegel's Logic*, pp. 21–2.

only as determinacy that *is*, or determinacy in the form of being, but also as *determinacy* that is. Or to put it another way, quality must be understood not only as nonbeing that is *being* but also as *non-being* that is being. Quality results when being and nothing cease vanishing into one another and settle down into their unity that constitutes definite, determinate being. Quality, however, is not just being that has become determinate but also the *not* that has become determinate. If the not is itself to be determinate, however, it cannot simply be the moment of nonbeing or determinacy that is incorporated into determinate being and thereby renders being determinate. Nor can it just be quality, or determinacy that *is* and enjoys *being*. It must gain a settled character or identity as clearly *negative*, that is, as *nonbeing* or *determinacy* that is. It must be negative, rather than simply affirmative, quality. The name that Hegel gives to quality with the accent on nonbeing rather than on being is *negation* (*Negation*) (*SL* 111/1: 118 [207]).[16]

With the idea of negation, a *difference* opens up in quality itself. Quality as such is simply determinacy that *is*, but quality immediately differentiates itself as negation from the simple, affirmative quality that it is. Simple, affirmative quality thereby changes its logical status, for it is no longer *all* of quality but comes to be one mode of quality alongside negation. In this way, quality takes on two distinct forms.

Quality with the accent on being—in contrast to nonbeing—is named by Hegel *reality* (*Realität*).[17] Quality is thus not simply undifferentiated determinate being after all but is reality *or* negation. Reality, it should be noted, is not just being as such, but neither does it yet entail being something, being finite, or being spatio-temporal. Reality is simply being that is determinate and settled—no more and no less. Similarly, negation is neither pure nothing nor something but falls between the two. Negation is simply nothing, or the not that has come to be stable and determinate—the not that definitely is negative. Indeed, the word "negation" names nothing other than the quality of *being negative*.[18]

Negation, for Hegel, is not principally an act or operation performed by thought on concepts or by things on one another. It is a form of determinate being or, if you like, a way of being: being negative in contrast to being real. *This* is real, we say, but *that* is mere negation. By saying this, we do not mean that

16. Whereas the word "negation" (*Negation*) refers to one type of quality, namely, *non-being*-that-is, the word "negative" (*Verneinung*) refers to the specifically negative moment in such negation; that is, to the "non-" in "non-being-that-is." As Hegel puts it, the "negative" is "the determinate element of a determinateness" (*das Bestimmte einer Bestimmtheit*). Since determinateness (*Bestimmtheit*) was earlier said to be simple nonbeing (*Nichtsein*), the "determinate element" therein—or the "negative"—must be the "non-" or "not-" (*Nicht-*) taken by itself.

17. See also Hegel, *EL* 147/196 (§91).

18. Winfield, by contrast, understands negation not to be the quality of being negative but rather to be "what quality in general is not" or "the nonbeing of quality." See Winfield, *Overcoming Foundations*, pp. 71–2.

there is nothing there; we mean that what there *is* is negative in quality rather than positive. It may not yet be perfectly clear what "being negative" actually involves. Some may even claim that it is an incoherent notion: for how can anything *be* "negative"? Nevertheless, despite such reservations, we know that whatever it may turn out to mean negation must be acknowledged to be a quality of being because determinate being logically has shown itself to entail negation as much as reality. The speculative philosopher cannot reject a category because its implications are not yet clear or because it is suspected of leading to undesirable consequences or because it appears to violate our customary expectations. He or she has to accept what being shows itself to be and wait patiently for the further implications of each category to reveal themselves. It may trouble some to think of negation as a quality or way of being, but the speculative philosopher has no alternative but to acknowledge that that is indeed what negation *is*.

Reality and negation coexist as two kinds of quality or two different qualities of being. There is a sense, however, in which negation comes before reality logically. This is because negation first introduces the difference between itself and reality into quality. Quality as such is undifferentiated determinate being. By virtue of the fact that it is equally negation, however, qualitative *being* is converted into reality in contrast to negation. Reality is thus quality in its original sense but now distinguished from the other quality—negation—*by* negation itself. Negation does perform an operation of its own therefore: it turns quality in general into *real* quality, or quality that is distinct from mere negation. Hegel draws attention to this work of negation, I believe, when he writes that through the emergence of quality as negation "the immediate or *affirmative* [*seiend*] determinateness is posited as a differentiated, reflected determinateness" (*SL* 111/1: 118 [205–7]).[19]

Through this split into reality and negation, determinate being at last comes to consist in being *differentiated*. We now see that being determinate does not mean just being settled or being *this*, but also being this *rather than* that—specifically, being real *rather than* negative or negative *rather than* real. Determinate being still does not consist in being something, nor does it consist in a plurality of qualities, but it has at least shown itself to entail a contrast between being real and being negative.

This is the first point in the *Logic* at which a determinate—as opposed to immediate and vanishing—difference has been thought. Being and nothing vanish into one another because each is an utterly indeterminate immediacy; reality and negation, by contrast, are definitely different because each is determinately what it is. As Hegel puts it, "in quality as determinately present, there *is* distinction—of reality and negation" (*SL* 114/1: 122 [207]). Note that the relation between negation and reality is also significantly different from that between quality as such and determinate being. The latter are identical; there is no determinate

19. Translation revised.

difference between them because neither is fully determinate in itself. It is impossible for either to be fully determinate by itself because determinate being consists both in being that is determinate *and* in determinacy-that-is, or quality. Determinate being is thus *nothing less than* quality itself.

Negation and reality, by contrast, are not simply two moments that go together to constitute determinate being as a whole but rather two forms *of* determinate, qualitative being itself, or two qualities of being. The difference between them is thus between one form of genuinely determinate being and another. Accordingly, each in differing from the other is itself determinate: each is what it is. They must therefore be *determinately* different. Indeed, they are the first determinations that can conceivably be determinately different because they are the first to be forms of *determinate being.* They must therefore be the minimal constituents of determinate difference as such, whatever else such difference may turn out to involve.

Determinate difference always consists at least in the difference between what is real and what is negative. Such difference may well turn out to involve more than this. Nevertheless, before we can distinguish one natural object from another or one color from another, we must understand the basic difference between being real, or definitely *being* what one is, and being *negative.* This is not to say that we have to be able to understand the difference between what actually exists in space and time and what is merely imaginary. It is to say simply that in order to draw any determinate distinction at all (even between two imaginary objects) we must at least be able to understand the qualitative difference between *being this* and *not* being this (or being *not*-this).

We saw earlier that determinate being consists in being *settled*, or in enjoying being that is definite and that does not immediately disappear into nothing. We have now seen that determinate being also involves being *differentiated* as real rather than negative or as negative rather than real. One might well protest at this point, however, that Hegel has gone through an enormous amount of trouble to prove something obvious and trivial. Surely it does not take a long-winded German philosopher to convince us that there is a difference between *being* a chair and *not* being a chair. Anyone can tell that being real and being a mere negation are different. True enough, but ordinary consciousness can do no more than take this obvious insight for granted. What Hegel has done is to explain why reality and negation are different without simply assuming this to be the case. As we are about to see, his convoluted derivation of the difference between reality and negation also demonstrates that that difference, though determinate, is rather more problematic than people ordinarily believe.[20]

20. The previous analysis has, I hope, demonstrated that the distinction between reality and negation is generated immanently by the logical structure of determinate being (*Dasein*) itself. *Pace* Theunissen, that distinction is not merely the product of our "objectifying thinking." See Theunissen, *Sein und Schein*, p. 231.

Real Negation and Negative Reality

Being and nothing immediately vanish into one another because each is *purely* itself. Being is sheer being that is utterly indeterminate and so is in fact nothing at all; nothing is purely and immediately nothing and so is actually indeterminate being. Reality and negation, by contrast, do not vanish into one another but are determinately different because each is itself *determinate.* We learn from this that sustainable difference cannot be pure difference. Reality and negation are, indeed, immediately different as affirmative and negative, but their difference is stabilized by the fact that "both are determinate being" (*SL* 111/1: 118 [207]). Neither is pure being or pure nothing, but each one is the settled unity of being and nonbeing or determinacy. Each one is quality, or determinacy-that-is. The difference between them lies in the fact that each one is quality with a different "accent." In other words, each is determinate *in a different way*.

Reality is simply quality itself—or "original" quality—that has come to be one kind of determinate being rather than all of it: "quality with the accent on *being*." It consists therefore in being settled, in definitely *being* what it is. Negation, by contrast, is *non*-being that is. It consists not just in being what it is but in being explicitly and definitely *negative*. More specifically, it consists in *not* being affirmative quality or reality. Negation's quality thus actually resides in *differing* from reality.

Hegel does not draw attention to the point, but it is clear that in the asymmetrical difference between reality and negation the two basic ways of being determinate so far identified have emerged as two different qualities of being. The determinacy that consists in being settled and definite has crystallized out as reality, and a second kind of determinacy that consists in being differentiated has separated itself from such reality as negation. In contrast to what we initially thought (namely that determinacy is simply settled being), determinacy thus turns out to involve *either* being settled and real *or* being differentiated and negative. In the final paragraph of the section on *Dasein*, however, Hegel points out that this difference between reality and negation is not quite as clear-cut as it appears to be.

The reason for this is not hard to see. On the one hand, reality is determinate not only by virtue of being what it is but also by virtue of differing from—and so *not* being—mere negation. It is therefore intrinsically *negative* in itself. On the other hand, negation is determinate not just because it differs from—and so is not—reality but also because it *is* the quality it is, namely, negation. It is therefore irreducibly *real*. Reality is thus not sheer positivity—even though it appears to be—because "it contains determinateness and therefore also negation." Conversely, negation is not purely negative—not merely the lack of reality—but "is a *determinate* being, a quality, only determined with a non-being," the quality of *really* being negative (*SL* 111/1: 118 [207]). This is not to say that reality and negation vanish into and endlessly supplant one another like being

and nothing. Reality and negation remain different qualities: "the distinction cannot be omitted, for it *is*" (*SL* 115/1: 123 [207]). Each one is what it is and does not simply disappear into its opposite. The important point to note, however, is that, in being and remaining what it is, each at the same time *includes* the other. Each is, indeed, itself and not the other, but neither is *purely* itself because each harbors the other within itself. Reality is reality precisely because it is also negation, and negation is negation precisely because it is also reality. This is not simply how *we* understand them but an irreducible logical feature of each one itself.

What we learn from the *Logic*, therefore, is that in neither of its forms is determinate being purely and simply what it is. There is reality and negation, but each bears within itself more than it is. The principal consequence of this complicity between reality and negation is that we can finally acknowledge Hegelian determinate being to have the structure that is most commonly attributed to it by commentators. Readers will perhaps have noticed that I have so far avoided describing determinate being as "being that *is* what it is in *not* being what it is not." This is the most familiar way to construe determinate being in Hegel's *Logic*. Errol Harris, for example, writes that "only in virtue of distinction from what it is not, is any quality precisely what it is—or, for that matter, anything at all."[21] I have shied away from such statements up to now because nothing about determinate being has so far warranted making them. Determinate being has shown itself to consist first in being settled and then in being differentiated as real *or* negative. Until now, however, it has not determined itself to consist in being real *as* negative. Now, though, we have recognized that determinate being can only take the form of reality at all by virtue of *not* being mere negation and thus by virtue of being negative in itself.

We have also noted that negation can be a quality in its own right only insofar as it is *real*. This means that there is actually no negation by itself, floating free and independent, but that all negation is inseparable from *reality*—just as all reality is inherently negative.[22] Determinate being takes the form of real and negative quality. We have now seen, however, that each quality actually incorporates the other. Determinate being cannot consist in simply being real *or* negative, therefore, but must always involve being real *and* negative together. In other words, it must entail being settled and differentiated at the same time. Genuine determinate being is the fusion of these two different qualities.

Here at last we reach Hegel's "classical" conception of determinate being: it is being that is real only by virtue of being the *negation* of negation that is in turn real being. *Dasein* thereby shows itself to be, in a much fuller sense than was initially the case, being-that-is-*not*-being. Originally, the moment of not-being that constitutes being's determinacy lends stability to *being*; it renders being determinate and allows it to be what it is. Such not-being has no distinctly

21. Harris, *An Interpretation of the Logic of Hegel*, p. 102.

22. See Theunissen, *Sein und Schein*, p. 232.

negative character but is, as it were, absorbed in being. Now, by contrast, the moment of not-being, or determinacy in being, has mutated into *negation,* or determinacy that is explicitly negative. Being turns out to be determinate, therefore, not merely through *being* what it is but also through clearly *not* being what it is not. We may believe that all identification is immediate—that we simply open our eyes and identify what we see as "red" or "chair." If Hegel is right, however, we only understand what red really is by noting what distinguishes it from green, yellow, and so on. We have to draw such distinctions because we can understand there to be anything determinate at all only by differentiating what is before us from what it is not.[23]

Indeed, being can only *be* what it is by not being what it is not. Negation is not just a device that we employ to characterize things contrastively, as Pippin claims.[24] Negation is a quality of being itself; it is what being *is*. Being is real only because it is negative in itself and actually excludes certain qualities. As we shall soon see, this will turn out to mean that all determinate reality must be related to and distinguished from *something* else. That lesson, however, is yet to be learned. All we know at the moment is that there is no reality that is not in some way informed by difference and negation—no purely positive finite thing or divine *ens realissimum*—for without negation reality would not be *determinate* being at all but would evaporate into nothing. As Hegel writes: "reality is quality, determinate being; consequently, it contains the moment of the negative and is through this alone the determinate being that it is" (*SL* 112/1: 119).

Determinacy and negation are essential to being. There is no immediacy, finitude, nature—or post-modern "pure difference"—without it. As we shall see in the next chapter, however, being determinate is by no means all there is to being.

---

23. As I noted in chapter 6 (p. 142, above), this does not mean that we have to establish the way in which a thing differs from *everything* else before we can identify it at all. A thing is thought to be determinate the moment it is distinguished from anything that is not it. Having said this, it is, of course, true that our understanding of the determinacy of something grows the more we recognize how it differs from other things. For Hegel (as becomes clear in the doctrine of essence), things are themselves distinguished from everything else, because they are all unique (see *SL* 418–24/2: 47–55). Consequently, the more we comprehend of these differences, the more we understand of things. This does not mean, however, that we have to know how something differs from everything else before we can understand it to be determinate at all. We begin to recognize something as determinate as soon as we say that it is this, *not* that.

24. Pippin, *Hegel's Idealism*, p. 188.

Chapter Seventeen

Something and Other

From Determinate Being to Something

In his *Logic* Hegel demonstrates that being turns out to be much more than pure being alone. So far we have learned that being proves to be sheer instability or becoming, and that that instability in turn collapses logically into determinate being. Determinate being is simply logical stability, or the settled unity of being and nonbeing. In its more developed form, it proves to be being that is what it is in not being what it is not. Being determinate, according to Hegel, thus involves being real *and* negative at the same time.

Hegel's account of determinate being is immanent and presuppositionless because it draws on no familiar assumptions about determinacy or definiteness but arises through a consideration of sheer indeterminate being. Hegel now proceeds to demonstrate that determinate being itself mutates logically into *something*. The analysis so far has been inevitably—and for some, perhaps, infuriatingly—abstract. Now we will at last have something to think about.

Kant famously maintains that "something" is itself the most abstract concept we can entertain. In the Jäsche *Logik* he states that "the *most abstract* concept is the one that has nothing in common with any distinct from itself," and he argues that "this is the concept of *something* (*Etwas*), for that which is different from it is *nothing*, and it thus has nothing in common with something."[1] For Kant, then, the least we can think of—without thinking of nothing—is neither being nor becoming but something, or as he puts it in the Blomberg *Logik*, "a possible thing."[2] "Nothing" cannot count as a moment of any such something precisely because it is excluded by the very idea of something. Yet neither does "being" belong to the thought of something, in Kant's view, since it is merely the "positing"—or actual setting there before us—of that which has *already* been conceived as something (in general and in particular) (*CPR* 567/572 [B 626]). According to Kant, we think first of something and then determine—by reference to sensuous experience—whether or not it *is*.

In marked contrast to Kant, Hegel will show that the category of some-

1. I. Kant, *Lectures on Logic*, trans. and ed. J. M. Young (Cambridge: Cambridge University Press, 1992), p. 593; *Schriften zur Metaphysik und Logik*, 2: 525–6. See also Winfield, *Overcoming Foundations*, p. 73.

2. Kant, *Lectures on Logic*, p. 207.

thing—far from being the most abstract and basic concept we can entertain—is actually derived from the even more primitive determinations of being, nothing, reality, and negation and incorporates these within itself as its moments.[3] Being, for Hegel, is thus not merely the positing of that which is already a possible something; being gives rise to the very possibility of something in the first place by turning through its immanent logic *into* the realm of somethings. Being, not possible thinghood, comes first logically, in Hegel's view, because the categorial and ontological structure of "something" is made necessary by the logical self-transformation of being itself—a process that religion pictures as the work of God. In this respect, for all his evident indebtedness to Kant, Hegel remains a disciple of Spinoza.

Philosophers such as Leibniz and Schelling have posed the question: why is there something rather than nothing? Hegel's answer is simple: there has to be something because logically nothing slides into being, being transforms itself into determinacy, and being's irreducible determinacy in turn proves to be something. So what is it about determinate being that yields something?

Hegel's explanation of the logical move to something is brief, but I believe that it can be made intelligible. Like the transition from becoming to determinate being, it rests on the self-undermining—and consequent partial *loss*—of a difference that being has shown itself to entail. The difference concerned in this case is not the immediate one between being and nothing but the *determinate* one between reality and negation. (Hegel also mentions in this context the difference between determinate being and its quality or determinacy. Since these categories—which are not determinately different anyway—themselves give rise to the difference between reality and negation, it suffices to examine this latter difference.)

The difference between reality and negation is not a difference between things but between *qualities* of being. Reality is the quality of being what one is, and negation is the quality of being negative. Before he reaches the end of his account of *Dasein*, Hegel claims that being determinate consists minimally in being real *or* negative. He then points out, however, that this difference between qualities undermines itself logically, because reality and negation both contain one another. Reality is itself negative because it is *not* mere negation, and negation is in turn affirmative and real because it *is* the quality it is. The difference between reality and negation is thus not absolute but is a difference between two qualities that inhabit one another and *together* constitute all determinate being. Determinate being consists, therefore, not just in being real *or* negative but in being real *as* negative and being negative *as* real.

This is not to say that there is no difference at all between reality and nega-

---

3. As I noted in chapter 16, becoming is for the moment absent from determinate being, but it reemerges as a moment of something later in the *Logic*, when something turns out to be subject to change. See chapter 16, above, note 8 (p. 302), and chapter 17, p. 327.

tion. As Hegel puts it, "the distinction cannot be omitted, for it *is*" (*SL* 115/1: 123 [207]). We now see, however, that reality and negation are not just two opposed qualities but make up the two different sides of any being that is determinate—that is, of any quality. This means, in other words, that there is after all only *one* way of being determinate and *one* quality of being: one that involves being both real *and* negative at the same time. Reality and negation are in truth merely the constitutive *moments* of such determinate being.

Yet are they just moments that are to be found in all quality? Cannot a distinction still be drawn between the specific quality of being real and that of being negative? Indeed—albeit only up to a point. For in each case we are actually dealing with *one and the same* quality or determinacy, though with a different "accent." As Hegel writes, "reality itself contains negation, is determinate being. . . . Similarly, negation is determinate being" (*SL* 115/1: 122 [207]). Even though they differ, therefore, real quality and negative quality both entail the same fusion of reality and negation that constitutes all determinate being. Each includes both itself and the other as its moments. (The fact that all determinate being consists in the same quality of being real-and-negative reinforces the idea that "quality is completely unseparated from determinate being.")

Whether reality and negation are understood as different qualities or different moments of all quality, the difference between them falls *within* determinate being. It is a difference internal to the only way of being determinate there is. Consequently, it is one in which determinate being differs from, and relates to, nothing but *itself*. Recognizing this marks an important turning point in the unfolding of determinate being: for it now becomes apparent that determinate being is in truth inwardly differentiated, *self-relating* determinacy. This is a new dimension to determinate being that we have not encountered before. We saw earlier that determinate being is quality and that quality differentiates itself logically into reality and negation. What we have now learned is that reality and negation themselves prove to be moments or modes of self-relating quality.

Hegel is not claiming that determinate being simply reverts at this point to its original undifferentiated condition. He is arguing that it acquires a new logical identity that comes from having first been *differentiated* into two distinct qualities. Determinate being is self-relating determinacy only because it contains an internal difference between itself as real and itself as negative, and it contains this internal difference only because there is first—logically, not temporally—a qualitative difference between reality and negation that then undermines, or "sublates," itself and in so doing reconstitutes determinate being as a single, simple quality that is equally real and negative. If determinate being had never split into two different qualities, it would never prove to have any internal difference at all and so would not now relate to itself. The distinctive logical "history" of determinate being is thus as follows: "what is . . . in fact present is determinate being in general, distinction in it, and sublation (*Aufheben*) of this distinction." The fact that determinate being gains a new identity through being differentiated

is further indicated by Hegel when he writes that it is simplicity that is "*again* equal to itself" (*SL* 115/1: 123 [207]).

It should now be clear what Hegel means when he says that sublated difference, or difference-that-has-been-undermined, is "determinate being's *own* determinateness" (*die eigene Bestimmtheit des Daseins*). Hegel's claim is that such sublated difference is what determinate being is *in truth*. Determinacy does not reside merely in logical stability or in qualitative difference but in difference that is not sheer difference after all but self-relation. To be determinate, therefore, is to relate to oneself in being both real and negative.

Yet sublated difference is determinate being's *own* determinateness in another sense, too. It is not only *Dasein*'s true or proper character but also the character or determinacy that *Dasein* has on its *own*, purely because of what it is in itself. Reality and negation are different qualities that owe their determinacy as much to one another as to themselves: each is what it is by virtue of the other's presence within it. Determinate being has now turned out, however, not just to be differentiated quality—not just to be reality *as opposed to* negation—but to be sublated difference, or difference that is at the same time *self-relation*. Determinate being owes *this* character—as self-relating quality—purely to itself, not to anything else. It is determinate being's *own* character or determinacy—the one that belongs to it purely because it is determinate being. Indeed, there is nothing else to which determinate being could be indebted, for there is nothing beyond or outside of determinate being.

As we know, determinate being does not possess the quality of self-relation from the start. Initially, it is nothing but the unity of being and nonbeing. It comes to enjoy its own true character, however, by developing logically through its different moments *into* self-relating determinacy. In retrospect, it thus becomes apparent that determinate being overall is the logical process of *coming into its own* and of displaying its true colors late in the day. It is not initially what it is but develops into its true form. Determinate being is not explicitly defined as development, but it can clearly be described in this way. The development of *Dasein* that we have examined so far is, of course, purely logical not temporal. All we know at the moment is that *logically* determinate being must prove to be more than simple quality if it is to be truly determinate. In the *Philosophy of Nature* and *Philosophy of Spirit*, however, we will see that being must develop temporally and historically, too. The historical development of consciousness from servitude to freedom is thus prefigured by the logical structure of determinate being as such.

To recapitulate: we have seen that determinate being consists logically in sublated difference, or difference-as-self-relation. We may not yet know all that this entails, but we know that we cannot conceive of determinate being as anything less than this. It is crucial to note that determinate being preserves the moment of difference within its self-relation: *Dasein* can relate *to* itself only insofar as it preserves an internal difference *between* itself and itself. The qualita-

tive difference between reality and negation is not illusory but definite and determinate. Where there is determinacy, there must be at least two different qualities, or one quality with two different "accents"; there cannot just be one simple identity. Those two qualities or modes of quality are, however, now understood to fall *within* self-relating determinacy. There is genuine determinacy, therefore, only where there is self-relating determinacy that is both real and negative within itself. Consequently, true determinate being must possess a differentiated logical "interior" and be what Hegel calls *Insichsein,* or "being-within-self" (*SL* 115/1: 123 [207]).

No previous logical determination has enjoyed being-within-self because none has taken the form of self-relating, self-enclosed being within which more abstract moments are preserved. Pure being and nothing are utterly indeterminate and have no moments of their own. Becoming does have moments but only because it is the vanishing *of* being and nothing into one another. Similarly, determinate being initially is merely the unity or inseparability of being and nonbeing. None of these ways of being takes the form of simple *self-relation*, or constitutes a sphere of "ownness," within which moments can be contained, so none exhibits *Insichsein*.

As *Insichsein,* or self-relating determinacy, Hegel maintains, determinate being is not just quality in general but constitutes *something* (*Etwas*). Neither pure being nor becoming nor simple quality constitutes something; only quality that relates to itself and forms a self-enclosed logical "space" of its own is something. In saying this, Hegel is defining anew what it is to be something. He is claiming that, whatever else we may normally understand by the word, from the perspective of presuppositionless philosophy "something" is simply *self-relating* determinacy. There is—for the moment, at least—nothing more to something than that.

The fact that there is something is thus not contingent, in Hegel's view, but logically necessary. There must be something because being must be determinate, and determinacy is necessarily self-relating quality *within* which different moments are contained. There can be no determinacy or quality by itself, therefore, but all quality must form itself into something.

Note that, for Hegel, the word "something" does not name *that which* relates to itself, for that which relates to itself is determinacy or quality. Determinacy constitutes something only insofar as it is *self-relation* as such rather than that which enters into such self-relation. There is thus no something before there is any self-relating; there is only qualitative determinacy. Being-something, or "somethingness," consists in self-relation itself: "something is . . . simple self-relation in the form of being" (*SL* 115/1: 123 [207]).

This is clearly a rather bare and austere conception of "something" that fails to capture the richness of the things we normally regard as something. Hegel is still working at a very abstract and minimal level, however, and is not yet interested in explaining what constitutes the empirical things with which we are familiar. He is concerned to clarify the minimal logical difference between simply

being determinate and being something, and his claim is that the difference lies in the fact that something is self-relating, rather than merely stable and differentiated, determinacy. Self-relation may not be enough to constitute things as we know them, but without it there would be no somethings at all.

The Negation of Negation

In proving to be something, determinate being does not vanish or cease being determinate altogether. It remains determinate being but is no longer *merely* determinate. This is because it has acquired a new dimension that is not characteristic of mere determinacy as such, namely, self-relation. Determinacy as such consists in being stable or real and in being differentiated or negative. It consists in *being* what it is and in *not* being what it is not. Something retains these characteristics but is not reducible to them. It is real being, but real being that is self-relating. It is also negation, but again negation that is self-relating. Self-relating negation, however, is necessarily "self-negating" negation because it is negation that is not *mere* negation after all. Accordingly, Hegel defines something as "the *first negation of negation*" (*SL* 115/1: 123 [207]). This is a concept of some complexity.

Simple negation, for Hegel, is quality that is explicitly negative *rather than* affirmative. It thus forms one moment or "side" of a difference. Indeed, it consists explicitly in "differing from . . . ," since it is negation only as the negation of reality. Something is still negation, insofar as it is determinate at all, but it is not simple negation. This is because something consists specifically in "relating to itself" rather than "differing from . . . ." It is crucial to note that the reason why something is not simple negation is that it is *self-relation*. Self-relation comes first logically, and only by virtue of relating to itself (and not just differing from . . .) is something the *negation* of simple negation—or "negativity"—rather than simple negation itself (*SL* 116/1: 124 [209]). Self-relation is thus what turns something into a different kind of negation from "original" negation.

There is, however, a problem lurking in what I have just said: for something can only be self-relation in the first place by virtue of being self-relating determinacy or negation. Negation can only relate to itself, however, insofar as it is the "negation of negation." We appear, therefore, to be in a vicious circle. Negation must first be the negation of negation in order to be self-relating negation. Yet only when it is self-relating negation can it be the negation of negation, or negation that is *not* mere negation after all. This vicious circle dissolves, however, when we recall that we have actually encountered the "negation of negation" in *two* different forms so far.

Reality is also the negation of negation, since it is real only in *not* being negative. Reality is negative, however, in precisely the same sense as negation itself. Reality is just negation *again*; it is the negation of negation as the repetition of negation. For this reason, the difference between reality and negation is in fact the relation of negation to itself. *That which* relates to itself is simple negation. By virtue of relating to itself, however, negation takes on a new quality

that it does not possess as simple negation. For it now becomes negation as *self-relating* rather than as "differing from . . . ." It is this mutation of negation into a new form that turns it into the negation of negation in the second sense. For negation is now *not* just simple negation—or the mere repetition of simple negation—but self-relating determinacy, or *something*.

When we consider the phrase "negation of negation," we must distinguish carefully between its two meanings. It can refer either to the first, simple negation of negation (found in reality) in which negation is merely duplicated, *or* to the second, more profound negation of negation (found in something) through which negation is deprived of its purely negative character. Readers will note that Hegel himself refers to the latter as the "*first* negation of negation." This is because the negation of negation that is found in reality is not really the *negation* of negation at all but merely its repetition. Only with something do we encounter the genuine negation of negation because only in something does negation actually lose its negative character.[4]

---

4. Theunissen maintains that the "negation of negation" involved in something does not constitute *self-relating* negation, as Hegel claims. It is, he says, "eine Negation der Negation ohne Selbstbezüglichkeit." Theunissen argues that what is negated in the emergence of something is the difference inherent in determinate being but that what negates this difference is an act of *Aufheben* that is *other* than this difference. There is thus no relation of negation or difference to *itself* in this case. He argues further that, although the quality of negation is hereby negated (since it is one side of the negated difference), it is not itself the moment that negates that difference. Once again, therefore, something cannot be thought (with Hegel) as self-relating negation. See Theunissen, *Sein und Schein*, pp. 155, 230–1, 293.

In my view, by contrast, something does indeed involve self-relating negation. The difference inherent in determinate being is one in which the quality of negation differs from and relates to *itself* (because negation differs from reality that is also negative). Furthermore, it is precisely by virtue of relating to itself that negation proves *not* just to be differentiated, determinate being, but something.

There is, however, some truth in Theunissen's position. He is right to suggest that negation does not come to constitute a self-relation *through negating itself*. Indeed, negation does not actually *negate itself* here at all. As I understand it, negation initially relates to itself not because it truly negates itself but rather because it duplicates itself (in relating to reality). Negation is self-relating, therefore, without being genuinely self-negating. Once it has become self-relating negation, however, it is no longer mere negation. Its status as mere negation is thus *negated*. Yet it is negated by virtue of the fact that it is self-relating, not by virtue of being negation *tout court*. Negation is thus not actually negated by *itself* but rather by the self-relation that it has become.

To sum up: negation clearly proves to be the "negation of negation." However, it relates to itself *prior* to being genuinely negated, and insofar as it is then negated, it does not, strictly speaking, relate to or negate *itself*. As Henrich points out, negation will not come to constitute self-relation *through* genuinely negating itself until it turns into otherness and change; see D. Henrich, "Formen der Negation in Hegels Logik," in *Seminar: Dialektik in der Philosophie Hegels*, pp. 219–20, and chapter 17, pp. 329–30.

Winfield's Account of Something

The logical transition from determinate being to something is no more mysterious—some might say, no *less* mysterious—than any other in the *Logic*. It is, however, a transition that eludes the comprehension of many commentators. Johnson makes no attempt to explain it at all but simply writes that "the concepts of something and something else . . . come up for consideration here."[5] Taylor resorts to the idea of "instantiation" to make sense of the transition. According to him, determinate being must entail being something because quality must be instantiated *in* something. But on what basis does he make this claim? Certainly not on the basis of Hegel's actual argument. Taylor gives the game away with this remark: "it might be thought," he concedes, "that the argument is getting a bit loose here, for we seem to be bringing in facts which may be well-attested by common sense, but which are not shown to be necessary features of being." He thus admits that he is not explaining how determinate being *logically* entails being something but is substituting his own "common sense" account; however, such an account not only is illegitimate but also fails to shed any light on the specific logical structure of "something."[6]

By contrast, Burbidge recognizes that the idea of something arises because a difference in determinate being is dissolved. He notes correctly that "something" is the name for "reconstituted identity." Yet, strangely, he then explains the logical structure of something by reference to the English word, "something." "Something," he says, "refers to the determinate quality 'some' and the basic reality 'thing' but integrates them into a unity." In saying this, however, Burbidge not only neglects to point out that the German word "etwas" does not have the same connotation as its English equivalent but also fails to make it clear that what is distinctive about something for Hegel is the fact that it is "simple *self-relation* in the form of being."[7]

Giacomo Rinaldi also overlooks this crucial feature of something by appearing to equate being something with being determinate or "differing from . . . ." For Rinaldi, something "is nothing more than a quality *excluding* from itself 'another' quality."[8] The problem is that this reading defines something from the start as the simple *negation* of that which differs from it and so obscures the fact that something is actually the negation of simple negation by virtue of being *self-relating* determinacy. What is distinctive about something for Hegel is precisely that it is not merely determinate or negative but, as he puts it in the *Encyclopedia Logic*, "reflected *into itself*" (*EL* 146/195 [§90]). Something is thus not defined primarily by its difference from its negation but exhibits a certain *indifference* to what differs from it because it is folded or closed in on itself. To put

5. Johnson, *The Critique of Thought*, p. 23.
6. Taylor, *Hegel*, p. 234.
7. Burbidge, *On Hegel's Logic*, p. 47.
8. Rinaldi, *A History and Interpretation of the Logic of Hegel*, p. 148, my emphasis.

it simply, what is characteristic of something above all is that it is *itself*, not that it is the negation of what it is not.[9]

Something is also reduced to determinacy and negation by Winfield, who otherwise offers one of the more sophisticated accounts of the opening of the *Logic*. The move to something, according to Winfield, goes like this: reality and negation are first distinguished as two moments of determinate being. Reality is "quality insofar as it is," whereas "negation is the nonbeing of quality." Negation is not initially to be understood as the *quality* of being negative—Winfield and I disagree on this point—but is simply the opposite of quality, or "nondeterminate being." As such, negation is quite *other* than quality; indeed, it is sheer otherness itself. Otherness is thus "simply what quality is not." Yet otherness in fact turns out to be a quality of its own after all, since it is what it is and has (real) quality as its own negation. Otherness is thus "a determinate being in its own right." This contrast between quality and otherness, we are told, "provides the conceptual resources for categorizing something." This is because in quality and otherness we encounter "*a* qualitative being distinct from another qualitative being." Each one is thus something over against its other.[10]

There are, in my view, two problems with Winfield's account. The first is that, like Rinaldi, Winfield appears to equate being something with simply being determinate. Something, for him, is "a determinate being that is distinguishable by virtue of its *contrastive* relation to another determinate being."[11] As I have emphasized, however, this way of conceiving something overlooks the fact that something is first and foremost self-relating determinacy and *not* determinate, differentiated being as such. For Hegel, something does not arise because of a contrast.

The second problem is that Winfield is led to the idea of something by the specific contrast between quality and *otherness*, whereas Hegel himself makes no reference to otherness in the account of determinate being we have been analyzing. The text of the doctrine of being included in this study is taken from the second edition of the *Logic* published in 1832. In the first edition of the *Logic*, published 1812–16, however, Hegel does identify determinacy or nonbeing with otherness (*Anderssein*).[12] The transition from determinate being to something in the first edition differs, accordingly, from that in the second edition. Hegel first distinguishes determinate being's relation to otherness—its "being-for-other" (*Sein für Anderes*)—from its "being-in-itself" (*Ansichsein*) and then recognizes that both of these moments form a single self-relating unity, or *something*.

9. Note that something is not to be understood in a *wesenslogisch* sense as reflected into itself out of its other but rather as relating immediately to itself. For Hegel's discussion of *Reflexion* in the doctrine of essence, see *SL* 401/2: 27: "reflection-into-self is essentially the presupposing of that from which it is the return."

10. Winfield, *Overcoming Foundations,* p. 72.

11. Winfield, *Overcoming Foundations,* p. 72, my emphasis.

12. Hegel, *Wissenschaft der Logik. Erster Band: Die Objektive Logik* (1812/1813), pp. 60–1.

Winfield refers explicitly to the first edition when he introduces the idea of otherness, but he otherwise follows the second edition by moving straight from quality to something and only touching on being-for-other and being-in-itself *after* the relation between something and its other has been discussed. Yet even if Winfield had adhered to the first edition throughout—as, for example, do Biard, *et al.*—his claim that something is defined by its contrast with its negation would still not find any textual support: for even in the first edition Hegel understands something to be "simple relation to *itself*."[13] The difference between the two editions is simply that in the first determinate being relates to itself in being differentiated into being-for-other and being-in-itself rather than reality and negation.

In the second edition Hegel drops the idea of otherness from his account of determinate being, presumably because he came to recognize that otherness can only be thought as being-other-than-*something* and so cannot precede the category of "something" itself. In the second edition, therefore, there is no mention of otherness until the idea of something has been introduced. Negation and reality are described as "other" than one another before we come to the thought of something, but neither is *defined* as otherness. There can only be genuine otherness as such once there is something. But why is otherness introduced at all? Why is something necessarily in relation to what is other?

The Derivation of Otherness

It has to be said that Hegel does not provide as clear an answer to this question as he might. His derivation of the category of "other" is contained in the last, rather cryptic paragraph of 2.A.c (*SL* 116/1: 124 [209]). There is not much to go on in this paragraph, but I believe that we can reconstruct what Hegel has in mind. The principal thing to note is that Hegel derives the idea of otherness from the logical structure of something itself. He does not refer back to the analysis of *Dasein* and argue that something stands in relation to what is other simply because it is *determinate* and therefore necessarily differentiated from another. If he were to do so, he would not only risk reducing being-other-than-something to being-the-*negation*-of-something but also would fail to show why something's *somethingness* in particular, rather than its determinacy, requires that it be related to what is other.

Hegel's claim is that something is necessarily related to an other because of what it is to be something as such. Something doubles *itself* into something and its other, just as determinate being differentiates itself into real and negative quality. Hegel is, of course, arguing that the structure of something *logically* entails a relation to other. He is not describing a temporal process of doubling whereby an empirical object actually generates another from within itself as, for example, when a fertilized egg produces multiple versions of itself by cell division.

13. Hegel, *Wissenschaft der Logik. Erster Band: Die Objektive Logik (1812/1813)*, p. 66: "einfache Beziehung auf *sich selbst*," my emphasis.

So why should something logically entail a relation to what is other? The first thing to understand is that being something is a way of *being*. Something certainly includes reality and negation within itself, but they coalesce to constitute self-relating, self-identical determinate *being*. Hegel insists on this point: "something *is*, and *is*, then, also a determinate being (*Daseiendes*)" (*SL* 116/1: 124 [209]). Since it includes negation, something is, of course, also self-relating negation. Such self-relating negation, as we saw above, is negation that is not *mere* negation precisely because it is self-relation. It is negation that is something rather than mere determinacy. In ceasing to be simple negation or determinacy and proving to be self-relating, negation thus loses its explicitly negative character and constitutes a new way of *being*, namely, being something.

Yet if something arises through the coalescence of reality and negation and each of these moments has equal weight, then the result must not only be affirmative but also negative. In other words, it must not only be *self-relating* negation but also self-relating *negation*. But this confronts us with a problem. On the one hand, such self-relating *negation* must be constitutive of something since it is determinacy that relates to itself. On the other hand, something as such, as we have seen, is a way of *being*, whereas self-relating *negation* is a way of being explicitly *negative*. In constituting something, therefore, self-relating negation must at the same time constitute that which is *not* something as the latter has so far been defined. This non-something cannot, however, be the simple, direct *negation* of something because it consists in negation that relates to itself and is reflected or folded in on itself. This something that is *not* something but nevertheless relates to itself is identified by Hegel as the *other* of something: "the second is equally a *determinate* being, but determined as a negative of the something—an *other* (*Anderes*)" (*SL* 116/1: 124 [209]). Earlier categories have been described as "other" than one another, but only now do we encounter otherness itself.

Being other, for Hegel, is being explicitly negative but, in so doing, relating immediately to itself. Otherness does not, therefore, consist simply in differing from what it is not; the other also enjoys an identity of its *own* constituted by its self-relation. Reality and negation are the two inseparable sides of a difference: each is what it is in *not* being the other. Something and other are also distinguished by virtue of being explicitly affirmative or negative, but they differ above all because each relates to itself and, as it were, turns its back on the other, not because they confront one another directly. They differ because, as Hegel puts it, they are "indifferent" (*gleichgültig*) to one another and are folded in on themselves (*SL* 116/1: 125 [211]).[14]

---

14. The fact that otherness is not mere negation might explain why some post-Hegelians are tempted to try to understand otherness without reference to negation at all. In so doing, however, they overlook the fact that negation is an irreducible moment and precondition of otherness. Hegel does not accept the view that "otherness logically precedes the possibility of negation" (see Gasché, *The Tain of the Mirror*, p. 92).

It is important to note that Hegel finds otherness within the logical structure of something itself. Something logically doubles itself and differentiates its other from itself. It does so because its own structure is inherently contradictory. On the one hand, something is self-relating determinate *being* that results from the contraction of reality and negation into one simple determinacy. On the other hand, precisely because it is the unity of reality and negation, something must be just as much negative as positive. Something must thus take the form of self-relating *negation.* Yet such explicitly negative being is constitutive not simply of something but of something that is precisely *not* the something we initially encounter. In other words, it is constitutive of something *other* than that first, affirmative something.

Like reality, therefore, something entails its own negation. Unlike reality, however, something relates primarily to *itself* and entails a negation that relates in turn primarily to *itself.* The negation that logically must always haunt something thus falls *outside* the interior logical "space" of something itself. That, indeed, is what it means to be *other* than something rather than merely *different.* Negation is a constitutive moment that falls within something, but the otherness that something necessarily brings with it must form an interior sphere of its own that stands *apart* from something. The paradox that Hegel uncovers in something is that something's *own* logical structure requires that it must also take the form of, and so be accompanied by, that which is *other* than itself.

For Hegel, then, there is never just something by itself with nothing else besides. There is always something *and* an other. Being cannot take the form of just one thing but must entail at least two spheres of self-relation. Hegel is clearly not a monist in any straightforward sense.[15] Furthermore, as we are about to see, otherness proves not only to lie outside something but also to be a characteristic *of* something itself.

---

15. Strictly speaking, Hegel has not yet proven that there must be more than *two* things. McTaggart is thus wrong to claim that Hegel introduces the idea of "plurality" at this point in the *Logic*; see McTaggart, *A Commentary on Hegel's Logic*, pp. 23–4. At the end of the section on finitude, Hegel will show that the demise of one finite thing gives rise to another and another *ad infinitum*; see *SL* 136/1: 148 (237). But he will not prove that there must be many things *together* until we reach the section on being-for-self; see *SL* 164-84/1: 182–208. (It is also in this section that we encounter the idea that being can take the form of things in a void—an idea that anticipates the claim in the *Philosophy of Nature* that there is empty space between things.) Nevertheless, Hegel will eventually demonstrate that there are many things and not just two, and for that reason I will talk in the following chapters of what characterizes *every* something and *every* finite thing. Note that the logical development of Hegel's argument at this stage does not depend upon the idea of plurality. The argument is carried forward purely by what is inherent in the relation between something and *another.*

Something and Other

Hegel has demonstrated so far that being is not mere logical instability (becoming) or mere logical stability (determinate being) but logical self-relation (something). Being something has not yet shown itself to entail being spatio-temporal and material, but it is the most concrete form of being we have encountered up to this point. Hegel now proceeds to show that being something and being other are in fact interchangeable determinations. Something and its other are both *something* and are both *other* than one another. This adds a layer of complexity to the relation between the affirmative and negative aspects of being that we have not met before.

Pure being and nothing vanish *into* one another: each in being purely itself immediately gives way to the other. Therein lies their utter indeterminacy and instability. Reality and negation, by contrast, have a stable, determinate character; neither vanishes into or simply gives way to the other, but each retains an identity over against the other. Each is definitely what it is and *not* the other. Nevertheless, even though they differ, each incorporates the other within itself. Unlike being and nothing, and like reality and negation, something and other do not vanish into one another either but enjoy a stable identity of their own. Yet, *unlike* reality and negation, something and other also exhibit a degree of *indeterminacy* in their very determinacy. This is because each one, in being what it is, is also immediately its other. Reality certainly includes negation within itself, but something *is* itself other—namely, other than something else. This is what gives something and other a certain indeterminacy and renders them stable and unstable at the same time: something is something and not an other, and yet something is itself the other of its other. This indeterminacy stems, I believe, from the fact that something and other are self-relating: for in relating to itself each one ceases being merely or straightforwardly *determinate*. If this is right, then the reemergence of indeterminacy is the necessary effect of being *something* at all. Indeterminacy is not, however, the only characteristic of pure being that reemerges with something. As we shall see, something will also exhibit a distinctive *becoming* of its own, namely, change.

Hegel starts his analysis of something and other in 2.B.a by pointing out that not only something but also the other is *self-relating* determinacy and thus something. To be other is to be negative—that is, *not* to be something—but to relate to itself in the process, and insofar as that which is other is self-relating, it is necessarily something of its own. Whatever is other than something is thus always *something* else. Consequently, both something and its other are something.

Yet they are also both other since each is not the something that the other one is. As I have suggested, what is other stands apart from something and enjoys an identity of its own. It is quite independent of something. Yet the other also *depends* on something for its identity since it is simply that which is *not* something. Although it is not merely the negation of something—since it is a self-relating logical sphere of its own—the other is at least the negation of

something. Paradoxically, therefore, the other enjoys its own independent identity in relation to, and thanks to, something outside it. It is the "other" because there is something apart from it that it is not. To be other is thus always to be other-*than*-something, for if there were not first something, there would be no other.[16] Such otherness now characterizes both something *and* its other because each has something outside it which it is not. Each is *other* than the other something. Where there are two somethings—and for Hegel there are always at least two—each one must be the other of the other since each differs from, and so is *not*, what the other one is.

It is crucial to recognize that each something is an other by *comparison* with something that is there first. That is to say, each is an other *because of the other.* Were either—*per impossibile*—to stand completely alone, it would simply be something, not an "other." Only the presence of another something turns something into that which is other itself:

> Otherness thus appears as a determination alien to the determinate being thus characterized . . . , partly because a determinate being is determined as other only through being *compared* by a Third, and partly because it is only determined as other on account of the other which is outside it, but is not an other on its own account (*SL* 118/1: 126 [213]).

Such a comparison is not, however, an arbitrary act carried out by "external" reflection. On the contrary, something is intrinsically exposed to being determined as the other of another since it is logically impossible that it should stand alone. As Hegel writes, "there is no determinate being which is determined only as such, which is not outside a determinate being and therefore is not itself an other." Another way of putting the point is to say that every something is *intrinsically* vulnerable to being *externally* compared with another by a third party. Even though Hegel seems to violate the requirement that philosophy be strictly immanent with his talk of comparison by a "Third," his account of something remains rigorously immanent, because the necessary possibility of such comparison is derived from the logical structure of something itself.[17]

To recapitulate: something and its other are both something, and each is an other by virtue of not being what the other is. Consequently, Hegel tells us, something and its other are in fact "the same": "there is so far no distinction between them." The other is a something, and something in turn is an other. Hegel

16. See Doz, *La logique de Hegel et les problèmes traditionnels de l'ontologie*, p. 65.

17. This argument proves that logically something and its other are both "other" in *comparison* with one another whether or not there is actually a third party there to compare them. It does not prove that there must be such a third party and so does not constitute Hegel's proof that there must be more than two things. All we know at this point is that something and its other are intrinsically vulnerable to being compared by a third party *if there should be one*. See chapter 17, note 15 (p. 323).

now reminds us, however, that being other does not just consist in *not* being something else. It also consists in being *self-relating* determinacy. What is other stands apart from something and enjoys its *own* identity. Moreover, it enjoys an identity as an *other*, not just as something. Something and its other are separate spheres of being, each with a character and an integrity of its own.

Something is clearly constituted by its relation to itself, not by its relation to what differs from it. Indeed, it is related to something else only insofar as it is already independently something. The other is more explicitly relational and negative since it consists precisely in not-being-something. Yet it does not consist merely in differing from something but also forms a separate, self-contained sphere of being. This is true, Hegel believes, of anything that is other than another. Every something, as we have seen, is an other by comparison with something else; *as* an other, however, it has an identity of its own that sets it apart from something. This has a rather surprising consequence: for it means that every other must actually be the other it is—or exhibit "otherness" (*Anderssein*)—*in itself*, quite apart from anything else. This does not mean that we are wrong to say that something is other by comparison. Things are, indeed, other by comparison because they require the presence of something in order to be other at all. Yet that which is other cannot be other *merely* by comparison with something else: for *as* an other it necessarily has a character of its *own* that makes it specifically other, rather than something. It must therefore also be other "in its own self." As Hegel puts it: "the other as at first posited, although an other in relation to the something, is nevertheless also an other on its own account, apart from the something (*für sich außerhalb desselben*)" (*SL* 118/1: 126 [213]).

This is a somewhat difficult idea to grasp. Surely, to be other is always to be "other-than . . . ." How can anything be other purely in itself? Hegel has shown, however, that to be other is to be separate and unrelated, to stand apart as other. Consequently, it cannot involve merely being other-*than* . . . , but must also entail simply being *other*—being other in its own right. This separation or "isolation" of otherness from something is not, as Theunissen contends, the result of an act of abstraction by "objectifying thought" but is a logical feature of otherness itself.[18] It is implied by what it is to be *other*, rather than merely different.

This is not to say that there are now two distinct ways of being other. For Hegel, there is one way of being other that entails both being other-than . . . *and* being other in its own right. Something is certainly other than something else by comparison because being other consists in not-being-something. Yet, at the same time, being other entails being *separately* and *independently* not-something. Otherness, in other words, is the negation of something that stands apart from something. As other *than* something, the other's identity is tied to and dependent upon the presence of something, but as *other*, it is quite separate from something. The other is thus dependent and independent at the same time.

18. Theunissen, *Sein und Schein*, p. 263: "das vergegenständlichende Denken."

Whether we like it or not, being other entails being other in and by itself. Something and its other—which are both other than one another—must therefore be other in themselves, too. In being quite simply other, however, they do not cease being other-*than* . . . . They remain—comparatively—other than one another. Yet Hegel believes that the connection between being other and being other-than must also go much deeper than that: for something and its other must also be "other-than . . . " in their separate, quite *unrelated* otherness. They must be "other-than . . . " purely within themselves. Logically, Hegel concludes, this can only mean that each is other than *itself*. This in turn means not only that each is other than the *something* it is but that each is other than the very *other* it is.

For Hegel, to be something is to be an other and to be other within oneself. To be other within oneself is to be other *than* oneself. This in turn means being other than the other that one is. But, of course, it also means being other than *that* other, and being other than *that* other, and so on. To be other is thus constantly to negate or "other" oneself into something different or into another other. As Burbidge puts it, therefore, something "can only *be* other in itself by *becoming* other than itself."[19] This process of becoming other (*Anderes*) or of othering oneself is the process of *change* or *alteration* (*Veränderung*): "the other simply by itself is the other in its own self, hence the other of itself and so the other of the other—it is, therefore, that which is absolutely dissimilar within itself, that which negates itself, *alters* itself (*das sich Verändernde*)" (*SL* 118/1: 127 [213]). According to Hegel, then, something necessarily changes. It does so not because it is in time nor because it is transformed by other things but because logically it is otherness in itself and, *as* other, must be endlessly other than itself.[20]

Change: Hegel contra Kant and Aristotle

With the emergence of the idea of change, being once more proves to be becoming. It is no longer pure becoming, however, but what Hegel calls "concrete" becoming (*SL* 116/1: 124 [209])—the becoming of *something*. Since something is self-relating stable being, the becoming it exhibits is itself stable. It does not merely vanish, therefore, but is irreducible; it is definite, determinate becoming. This is because it is the becoming *of* the determinate being into which pure becoming logically vanishes.

It is important to note that Hegel understands change without reference to time. Change does not depend upon the temporality of things—it cannot do so because being has not yet proven to be temporal—but arises from the intrinsic

---

19. Burbidge, *On Hegel's Logic*, p. 48.

20. The young Kant, by contrast, argues in the *Nova Dilucidatio* that "if . . . a change occurs it must be the case that it arises from an external connection." See I. Kant, *Theoretical Philosophy, 1755–1770*, eds. D. Walford and R. Meerbote (Cambridge: Cambridge University Press, 1992), p. 38.

logical structure of something. Indeed, the fact that logically something must change is itself part of what makes time necessary. Hegel's account of change also differs from more traditional accounts because he does not assume that change requires a permanent substrate. Kant argues that all change or "alteration" (*Veränderung*) involves the exchange (*Wechsel*) of determinations or predicates that inhere in an underlying substance. The substance itself endures, but the determinations replace one another and so come to be and pass away (*CPR* 303/239 [B 230]). In arguing in this way, Kant follows Aristotle, who claims in the *Physics* that in all change or becoming "there must always be an underlying something, namely that which becomes."[21]

Kant and Aristotle conceive of change like this, of course, because they assume from the outset that what there is—or, in Kant's case, what is knowable—are substances in which certain properties inhere. They make this assumption, Hegel would claim, because their thought is governed by the structure of judgment. They take for granted that what there is—or is knowable—are objects of judgment *about* which certain things can be said and *to* which certain predicates may be applied.

As we know, Hegel does not accept that thought is essentially judgment but begins from the simple thought of being. Such being is not substance or the substrate of properties but sheer indeterminate immediacy. Hegel demonstrates in the *Logic* that such indeterminate being entails being something and that something necessarily consists in change. Change, for Hegel, is thus not a property of some presupposed "underlying" thing but what something itself proves to *be*. No dimension of something remains unaffected by change, but something *is* the process of change through and through.

This is not to say that something preserves no identity through change. However, the identity it comes to enjoy—at least as a mere something—consists purely in the continuity established *by* its self-othering. That identity is nothing apart from that process of self-othering but is one that something *acquires* through changing itself. Something *is* only in becoming *other*, but in becoming other it comes to be itself.[22]

Change and Self-Relation

In proving to be change, something shows itself to be the negation of negation in a new way. Reality is the negation of negation insofar as it is real by virtue of *not* being mere negation. As we have seen, however, reality merely duplicates or mirrors simple negation in differing from it. Something is the first genuine negation of negation insofar as it is negation that has deprived itself of its explicitly

21. *The Complete Works of Aristotle*, ed. J. Barnes, 2 vols. (Princeton, N.J.: Princeton University Press, 1984), 1: 324 (190a14).

22. See Rinaldi, *A History and Interpretation of the Logic of Hegel*, pp. 148–9.

negative character by being self-relating. Something is *self-relating* negation and, therefore, no longer overtly negative. That is to say, it is negation that is no longer just the negation that reality incorporates.

In the other, self-relation itself takes on a more overtly negative character: it is self-relation that is *not* something. The other's negative character remains muted, however, since the other does not directly confront and oppose something but forms a self-relating sphere of its own *apart* from something. The other is negation—or not-being-something—that has withdrawn into itself. Note also that the negative moment that principally characterizes the other is directed against *something*, not against simple negation. The other is thus the self-relating "negation of something," not a new "negation of negation."

As change, the other becomes even more explicitly negative. It does so by turning against itself and constantly becoming *another* other. As change, the other thus reveals itself to be a new "negation of negation," after all. For now not only is the other not something, but it is not even the other—or self-relating *negation*—that it is. Accordingly, the changing other, or the other that is the other of the other, is the "self-negating" other or negation (*das sich Negierende*) (*SL* 118/1: 127 [213]).

If something is the first genuine negation of negation, then change is the second. This second negation of negation differs from the first in one very important way. In the first, the two negations involved are not the same. The negation that is negated—negation$_1$—is simple negation, the negation included in reality. Something is the negation of negation$_1$, because it is self-relation rather than this simple negation. As the *negation* of negation, something is thus not just simple negation once again, but something new. Something, we might say, is the negation$_2$ of negation$_1$. The negation that specifically constitutes something does not, therefore, relate to itself through negating negation. On the contrary, it negates negation only because it is *already* self-relating negation, namely, the self-relating negation that simple, or *real*, negation proves to be. The logical sequence goes like this: (a) in differing from reality, simple negation—negation$_1$— relates to itself and so constitutes something; (b) something is thus self-relation, not mere negation; (c) something is thus the negation$_2$ of negation$_1$; (d) yet something is not self-relation *by virtue of* being the negation$_2$ of negation$_1$ because the negation that something *is* and the negation that something is *not*, are not the same.

Change, by contrast, is the genuine negation of negation through which negation does relate to itself. This is, first, because, in change, the other—which is the form that negation now takes—is other than *itself*, and second, because in becoming other than itself, the other merely comes to be *other* again. In change, the other genuinely negates the other that it is: it ceases being that other and becomes another one. In so doing, however, it becomes other once more; indeed, it *remains* other. As Hegel points out, the other "remains identical with itself, for that into which it alters is the other, and this is its sole determination" (*SL* 118/1:

127 [213]).[23] This does *not* mean that change never actually occurs. Something, as it is here conceived, is otherness within itself and does indeed become *other* than itself. The problem is that change can occur—and continue to occur—only insofar as something carries on being other. Change is thus necessarily the eternal recurrence of otherness—the recurrence of the *same* old other. Each new way of being other is other than the one it displaces, but it remains just another way of being *other*. In becoming other than itself, the other thus remains identical to itself. Or, rather, it *comes to be* identical with itself since it proves to be the same other only in negating, othering, or changing itself. The other constitutes itself as self-identical *through* the process of change and self-negation.

Something as such is the genuine negation of negation by virtue of being self-relating. The changing something, by contrast, comes to be self-relating or self-identical in a new way by virtue of being the genuine negation of the negation or, more accurately, the other of the other. To my mind, therefore, Henrich is right to assert that change is the first genuine negation of negation that actually *constitutes* (*herstellt*) self-relation.[24] We have now reached an important point of transition in the *Logic*. For we have learned that something and its other are not only self-relating determinacy but also determinacy that establishes its identity through change. In changing, something constantly settles into a new identity or, as Hegel puts it, "unites with its own self" (*geht . . . mit sich zusammen*) (*SL* 118/1: 127 [213]). The process described by Hegel whereby change leads to self-identity is, of course, a logical one. Spatio-temporal objects may well also gain new identities through changing in time, but we do not yet know this to be the case. For the moment, all Hegel is concerned to show is that by virtue of being change something must *logically* give itself an identity that we have not encountered so far.

The identity we shall now consider arises through the constancy of change rather than the immediate vanishing of pure becoming. Nevertheless, the move from change to this new identity obviously echoes the logical process whereby pure becoming settled into determinate being. Indeed, the transition we are now witnessing is one in which something—which is defined by *not* being merely determinate but rather self-relating—proves to be explicitly *determinate* after all, or at least begins to exhibit determinacy. In the next chapter, we shall examine more closely what it means for something to be incipiently determinate.

---

23. See Burbidge, *On Hegel's Logic*, p. 48.

24. Henrich, "Formen der Negation in Hegels Logik," p. 219. See also Theunissen, *Sein und Schein*, p. 261, and chapter 17, note 4, above. This is not to say—as Theunissen appears to claim—that there cannot be later in the *Logic* a further genuine negation of negation that constitutes a self-relation but does not involve "becoming-other." It simply means that self-othering is the *first* genuine negation of negation we have met so far that actually constitutes or establishes self-relation. See Theunissen, *Sein und Schein*, pp. 292–3.

Chapter Eighteen

Being-in-Itself and Being-for-Other

Why Something Comes to Be Determinate Through Change

In the last chapter we saw that being something, as opposed to merely being determinate (or, indeed, merely *being*), entails being self-relating determinacy. It also entails standing in relation to *another* thing that is in turn self-relating. Something is thus itself *other* than something else. It is necessarily one of two.

Insofar as each one is an other, however, it is not merely related to but also stands apart from its counterpart. As *other* than something else (rather than simply different from it), it constitutes a wholly separate, self-relating sphere of being. As such, Hegel argues, it must have a character of its own that makes it precisely an *other* rather than just something. The other must therefore be "an other on its own account, apart from the something" (*SL* 118/1: 126 [213]).

Yet, even though it is other within itself, the other must still be thought of as other-*than* . . . , since otherness remains a comparative quality. This means that that which is other on its own account must still be other than something else. According to Hegel, it also means that in its utter separateness the other must be other than *itself*—other than the something and the other that *it* is. For Hegel, the other must therefore be "the other of the other." But then, of course, it must also be the other of that other, and the other of that other, and so on. That is to say, the other must constantly *become* other than itself, must "other" itself into another other, and so be subject to *change*. Change is thus an irreducible feature of every something—not because everything is in time but because logically each something, insofar as it is other, is the process of becoming other than itself.

Yet, Hegel points out, in this process of becoming other, the other always remains—or rather comes to be—the *same* other. In negating itself and becoming another other, the other simply returns again and again to being the *other* that it is. Consequently, "what is altered is not determined in any different way but in the same way, namely, to be an other." In its self-negation the other continues being itself, preserves an identity through the process of change, and so constitutes itself as a self-identical *something*.

Recall that Hegel is here analyzing the minimal logical structure of change. He is not considering empirical change but rather the purely formal process of becoming-other-than-one-is that is involved in any empirical change. And he is

pointing out that in this formal process of becoming other the other *remains* the other that it is and so proves to be not just *other* but *something* identifiable. This, Hegel argues, leads to a new conception of something that we have not previously encountered: for something has now to be thought as that which is self-relating only insofar as it is *not* pure and simple *otherness*.

Initially, something was understood to be purely self-relating. Then it was conceived as other than something else. Finally, it was conceived as being other "on its own account" and thereby as "othering" itself or changing. Now we have reached a more complex conception of something. Something is now recognized to be that which preserves—or, indeed, attains and establishes—its identity in the process of being and becoming other. Furthermore, it is that which preserves itself by virtue of *negating* or "sublating" the very otherness and self-othering that it is. Being "something" and being "other" are thus not just two separate, self-enclosed ways of being, after all. Rather, being something itself consists in *not-just-being-other*. Hegel gives precise expression to this new conception of something in these somewhat compressed lines:

> [The other] is thus posited as reflected into itself with sublation of the otherness (*mit Aufheben des Andersseins*), as a self-identical something from which, consequently, the otherness, which is at the same time a moment of it, is distinct and does not appertain to the something itself. (*SL* 119/1: 127 [213])[1]

Plucked at random from Hegel's text, this sentence would be difficult if not well-nigh impossible to comprehend. In the context of the logical development of the concept of something, however, the meaning of the sentence is clear. Something is "reflected into itself"—that is to say, it is self-relating and self-identical; however, it is self-identical only by virtue of *not* being sheer otherness—that is to say, through "the sublation of otherness." There is something, therefore, because in changing the other not only becomes other than itself but "others" or negates itself into something self-identical. In Hegel's view, sheer otherness itself constitutes something. This is not because Hegel fails to take otherness seriously. It is because he understands otherness to be wholly and utterly *other* and so even to be other than the sheer otherness it is.

Note that otherness is now seen to be an irreducible, constitutive moment of something. There is no something without the movement of othering or change, since something preserves and constitutes itself *in* the very process of change. Yet being something is at the same time different from simply being other because something subsists insofar as sheer otherness negates itself. Otherness is thus a moment of something and yet is also logically distinct from it. In other words, otherness, or being-other (*Anderssein*), is that quality in the *negating* of which something consists.

1. Translation revised.

At this point something at last acquires explicit determinacy because it is conceived as the explicit negation of otherness. A determinate something enjoys its positivity or "affirmative being" by virtue of *not* being merely negative or "other." It should be noted, by the way, that something is here conceived as the negation of otherness as such; its positivity consists, therefore, in not being the otherness that it is itself *and* in not being the otherness that lies outside it—that is, in not being another something. Indeed, in what follows, this exclusion of the other something takes center stage. Something certainly gains determinacy by not just being endless change but exhibiting a definite identity through change. Its identity is rendered truly determinate, however, only when it clearly marks itself off from another thing outside it. For that reason, Hegel will now pay particular attention to the fact that something is what it is in not being *something else* even though he is alerted to this aspect of something by the self-negating character of change within the thing.

The new-found determinacy of something, Hegel points out, is double-edged. On the one hand, it distinguishes being something from being other; on the other hand, it also binds something to otherness and that which is other, for something is what it is only through its negative *relation* to what is other. We will now look in more detail at the ambiguous determinacy of something.

The Difference Between Being-in-Itself and Being-for-Other

At the beginning of 2.B.a.2 Hegel writes that "something *preserves* itself in its negative determinate being (*Nichtdasein*)" (*SL* 119/1: 127 [213]).[2] Negative determinate being clearly is determinate being with a negative rather than affirmative character. It is "negation" and, more specifically, the self-relating negation that constitutes "otherness." Hegel's claim, therefore, is that something preserves its own identity "in its otherness"; that is, in being other than itself (and so changing) and in being other than other somethings. At the same time, something preserves its identity only by *distinguishing* itself from otherness. Being something entails *not* being merely changeable and, even more importantly, *not* being something else.[3]

Something at this point in the logical development thus proves to have two defining characteristics. It is something by virtue of being self-relating determinacy (this is the original character of something) and also by virtue of *not simply being other*. As Hegel points out, otherness therefore belongs to the logical structure of something as that from which something differentiates itself: "otherness is at once contained in it and also still *separate* (*getrennt*) from it." This means that something is inextricably bound up with the very otherness from which it differs; indeed, it is tied to otherness *by* the fact that its identity depends on differing from such otherness. Something is thus inseparably *related* to

2. Translation revised.
3. See Burbidge, *On Hegel's Logic*, p. 48.

otherness, specifically to the otherness of the other outside it. In Hegel's words, something is necessarily *being-for-other* (*Sein-für-Anderes*).

The word "for" here does not indicate that something exists for the benefit or enjoyment of another. It indicates simply that something is related to another as such. By characterizing something itself as being-for-other, Hegel is pointing out that such other-relatedness—or, to use Burbidge's term, "other-directedness"—is not merely a contingent feature of things, but their necessary and irreducible quality or structure.[4] Things are not related to others just because those others happen to be there but because everything is itself other-directed. Later in the *Logic* Hegel will spell out all that such other-directedness entails, including the capacity to bring about effects in others and susceptibility to the causal influence of those others in turn. For the moment, however, all he is concerned to note is that other-relatedness is a constitutive feature of each thing itself.

Hegel goes on to remark, however, that something is not only related to its other but is also distinguished from that other. After all, something is something precisely through *not* being what is other. Something is determinate, therefore, insofar as it stands over against other things and constitutes a distinct sphere of *self*-relation and *self*-identity: being something entails being withdrawn into oneself and exhibiting an identity quite separate from that of any other. To the extent that something is determinate and definitely not an other, it must thus enjoy being that is distinctively its own, or what Hegel calls *being-in-itself* (*Ansichsein*) (*SL* 119/1: 128 [215]).

Earlier in his analysis, Hegel introduced the concept of "being-within-self" (*Insichsein*) (*SL* 115/1: 123 [207]). This is the quality exhibited by any something insofar as it relates to itself at all and constitutes a sphere of ownness, or interiority. The quality of being-*in*-itself to which Hegel now draws attention is subtly different from such being-*within*-self. It is not just interiority as such—which is possessed by every something—but the interior dimension of something that definitively differs from that of another thing: the being that is proper to that thing alone. Since something's being-in-itself shuts out all that is other than the thing, it also excludes any *relation* to what is other. It is the simple selfhood of the thing—what the thing is in itself—as opposed to the way the thing relates to other things. Something is what it is in itself, therefore, insofar as it is "self-related in *opposition* to its relation to other" (*SL* 119/1: 128 [215]). That is to say, something's being-in-itself is distinct not only from that of every other thing but also from the thing's own being-for-other.

Note that the two aspects of something with which we are now confronted represent features of something that we have already encountered, only in an intensified form. Something is initially understood to stand in an irreducible relation to something else but in such a way that each is separate from and indifferent to the other. One might say that something and its other are initially related

4. Burbidge, *On Hegel's Logic*, p. 49.

as two *unrelated*, self-enclosed spheres of being that, as it were, merely stand next to one another. Insofar as we regard what we encounter to be "something" and "other," and nothing more than this, we thus focus on their separateness and what Hegel calls the "unrelatedness of their determinateness" (*SL* 119/1: 128 [215]). Such indifference, or lack of relation between something and its other, is not imported into their relation by us but is entailed by their logical structure; that is, by the fact each is primarily *self*-related and something *apart* from its other.

Now, however, something has proven to be not only self-relating and separate but also determinate: it has shown itself to be *this* only insofar as it is clearly *not* that. In the process both the relatedness *and* the unrelatedness of something and other have become more intense. Something is now understood not just to stand indifferently next to an other but to be explicitly other-related because it preserves its identity only by differing in certain specific ways from something else. As a consequence, it is taken out of itself and connected—precisely through such differences—much more explicitly with other things. In Hegel's language, it is understood to be there *for* the other in a variety of (as yet unspecified) ways. At the same time, since something is recognized to have a character of its own that is *not* that of any other, it is also understood to be withdrawn into itself and so removed from all relation to and contact with others. Its separateness and unrelatedness are thereby heightened. By becoming determinate, something gains much greater definition and distinctness, but it does so only by being pulled in two different directions at the same time.

The Relation Between Being-in-Itself and Being-for-Other

For Hegel, things must possess a distinct character of their own (or "being-in-itself") if they are to be determinate. Equally, however, they must also be differentiated from, and so related to or "for," an other thing. These two qualities of being—being-in-itself and being-for-other—are irreducible moments of every something. It should be noted that they are not themselves to be regarded as *something* and *something else*. There is not something we call "being-in-itself" and something else we call "being-for-other." Rather, these two qualities of being are "*moments* of one and the same something" (*SL* 119/1: 128 [215]). They are aspects of something, not two separate somethings themselves. To think of intrinsic being as *something other* than other-relatedness and so to reify the two is, according to Hegelian logic, a category mistake.

This is not to deny that the categories of "something" and "other" are still significant for Hegel. Being still has to be conceived as at least the relation between something and its other in which both are changing yet also self-identical. The focus has now shifted, however, from that "relationless" relation itself to the ambiguity inherent in each something (or, if one prefers, in each *other* insofar as it is also something). In Hegel's view, each something must have its own proper character or being-in-itself. The concept of "being-in-itself" or being *an*

sich is thus not a fiction for Hegel, as it is for Nietzsche. It is an important concept that captures a fundamental aspect of what it is to be something. Equally, however, each something is irreducibly relational. Things do not stand alone in splendid isolation, but each one relates to, and interacts with, others in its own distinctive way.

Since being-in-itself and being-for-other are not themselves something and something else but moments of every something, they are not simply separate from one another. Rather, they are bound together or related through negation. As Hegel writes: "each . . . contains within itself its other moment which is distinguished from it" (*SL* 119/1: 128 [215]). How is this relation between them to be understood?

Being-in-itself is the quality that something enjoys not simply because it is something as such (and so self-related) but also because it is definitively *not* something else. Such being-in-itself, Hegel explains, is "self-relation, equality with itself . . . only as the non-being of otherness (*als Nichtsein des Andersseins*)." As we have already indicated, however, a thing's being-in-itself is not only clearly differentiated from the defining character of other things; it is also explicitly distinguished from the thing's own relation to others. This is because something's being-in-itself is its *ownmost* being—the being it enjoys insofar as it is simply itself and *not* related to anything else. This difference between something's being-in-itself and its other-relatedness is not merely accidental but is actually constitutive of being-in-itself: a thing enjoys its ownmost being in itself only insofar as this is explicitly distinguished from the thing's relation to other things. Without being related to others, something could not possess any distinctive being *in itself* because there would be nothing about a thing against which to mark off its *own proper* being. The thing would simply be something.[5]

The point Hegel is making here is, I believe, an important one. When we talk of what something is *in itself*, we do not just have in mind the thing's overall character, but we introduce a distinction between two different dimensions of the thing. We point to that dimension of the thing that most properly defines and characterizes it, that dimension in which it is simply itself. But such a dimension cannot be identified unless it can be distinguished from another aspect of the thing wherein the thing is not simply itself. The only aspect of something in which it is not purely and simply itself is its relation to other things. Since a thing's being-in-itself has to be distinguished from another aspect of the thing if it is not just to be conflated with the thing's overall character, it can thus only be distinguished from the thing's being-for-other. Indeed, for Hegel, what something is in itself is nothing but the identity it enjoys in *contrast* to its other-relatedness. In Hegel's own words, "in so far as something is *in itself* (*an sich*) it is withdrawn from otherness and being-for-other" (*SL* 120/1: 128 [215]). But, of course, this means that something's being-in-itself is inseparably *related* to and

5. See Findlay, *Hegel: A Re-Examination*, p. 160.

tied to the thing's being-for-other. Without the latter, there could not be the former: for being-in-itself is simply "the *non-being* of being-for-other."

Conversely, something can be related to other things only if it has a character of its own that clearly distinguishes it from those other things to which it relates. Insofar as something is other-related, it is not just what it is in itself; it lacks being that is simply its *own*, because its being consists in relating to something *else*. Yet other-relatedness is inseparable from being-in-itself because it is the other-relatedness *of* something that is otherwise determinate in itself. Being-for-other is thus "negative determinate being which points to being-in-itself as to its own being which is reflected into itself, just as, conversely, being-in-itself points to being-for-other" (*SL* 120/129 [215]). Each of the two aspects of something points to the other, therefore, and together they make up the determinate character of something—the character that something exhibits in its very process of change.

The Identity of Being-in-Itself and Being-for-Other

In 2.B.a.3 Hegel goes on to show that the distinction between what something is in itself and what it is for others is not actually as hard and fast as it appears at first sight. This is because in each case we are dealing with one and the same something. We noted above that there are not two wholly separate spheres of being: being-in-itself and being-for-other. These qualities of being are merely moments or aspects of one self-relating, self-identical something. This means that it is the *same* something that is what it is in itself and that stands in relation to other somethings. This in turn means that something must be what it is in itself *in* its relations to others and must stand in relation to others *as* what it is in itself. To say this is not simply to erase the distinction that has just been made: there is, indeed, a difference between something in itself and its relations to other things. The point to note, however, is that the way something relates to others is not utterly separate from what it is in itself: the thing is not one thing in its external relations and a quite different thing in its ownmost being. The thing is the same thing in both cases. Its being-for-other, in other words, is nothing but the other-relatedness *of* its ownmost being. It is the way its being *in itself* relates to—and so is *for*—others. Hegel puts the point like this:

> that something also has in *it* (*an ihm*) the same character that it is *in itself* (*an sich*), and, conversely, that what it is as being-for-other it also is in itself—this is the identity of being-in-itself and being-for-other, in accordance with the determination that the something itself is one and the same something of both moments, which, therefore, are undividedly present in it. (*SL* 120/1: 129 [217])[6]

Note that in this sentence Hegel introduces a new term, *an ihm*, into his analysis.

6. Translation revised.

This term is distinguished from the closely related *an sich* in the following way. *Sich* is the German third person reflexive pronoun and is the word one uses when talking about the relation something bears to itself. One says of someone brushing his teeth, for example: "Er putzt *sich* die Zähne." This makes it clear that the person is brushing his own teeth (not someone else's). To speak of what something is *an sich* is thus to talk of the thing viewed, as it were, from its own perspective—the thing as it is in itself.

By contrast, the word *ihm* is the normal German third person singular pronoun (in the dative case). If, for example, I want to say of an animal that "I give it water," I say: "Ich gebe *ihm* Wasser." The word *ihm* is used, therefore, when we have in mind the thing viewed, as it were, from the perspective of other things. The difference between *sich* and *ihm* is thus equivalent to that between the English words *itself* and *it*.

The philosophical point Hegel wants to make by means of these words is that whatever qualities something has in *itself*, it necessarily has in *it*; they are located nowhere other than in *this* thing. But if they are indeed in *it*, then they are in the thing not just as it is from its own "private" perspective but also as it is from the "public" perspective of others. That is to say, the qualities something possesses in itself also belong to it just as much for, or in relation to, others.

> Something is *in itself* (*an sich*) in so far as it has returned into itself out of the being-for-other. But something also has *in itself* (*an sich*) (here the accent falls on *in*) or in *it* (*an ihm*), a determination or circumstance in so far as this circumstance is outwardly *in it*, is a being-for-other. (*SL* 120/1: 129 [215–17])[7]

There can therefore be nothing about something that does not enter into relation with an other but remains hidden from view. If something has a quality in itself, then that quality is in *it*—in the one, self-identical thing that it is; however, that means that it must be an evident quality of that thing for others. What something is in itself is necessarily manifest in its relation to others because we are always dealing with the same thing. This is not to deny that there is a difference between the thing *as* it is in itself and *as* it relates to others: that difference has proven to be necessary and cannot now be removed. We can distinguish, for example, between the chemical composition of grass itself and the different effects it has on the stomach of a cow and that of a human being. Hegel's point is simply that we are dealing with *one and the same* thing in each case.

Hegel's Logical Critique of Kant's Concept of the "Thing in Itself"

Hegel's logical analysis of something is obviously anti-Romantic in its implications. For him, there is no precious, secluded "inner" realm within beings that is not available for others to see. In 2.B.a.3, however, Hegel draws on his logical

---

7. Translation revised.

analysis to mount a brief but trenchant critique not of Romanticism but rather of the Kantian notion of the "thing in itself."

In chapter 6, I considered the criticism of Kant's notorious concept presented by Hegel before the science of logic proper gets underway. In the introduction to the *Logic* and in the introductory paragraphs of the *Encyclopedia*, Hegel's stated objection to Kant's concept of the thing in itself is that it is an "abstraction" (*Abstraktum*) (*SL* 62/1: 60). I argued, however, that it is not merely the abstractness of Kant's concept that troubles Hegel. What Hegel criticizes is the fact that Kant's concept of the thing in itself is the concept of an abstract *object*—of "something alien and external to thought." The real problem is that, in abstracting, Kant remains mired in the perspective of consciousness and simply formulates the thought of "the object (*Gegenstand*), inasmuch as *abstraction* is made of all that it is for consciousness, of all determinations of feeling, as well as of all determinate thoughts about it" (*EL* 87/120–1 [§44]). Kant's failure, therefore, is not just that he abstracts but that in so doing he fails to suspend the ordinary assumption that thought relates to objects and so fails to begin from the utterly indeterminate thought of sheer, immediate being. That is to say—though Hegel himself does not put it quite like this—Kant's notion of the thing in itself is in fact not abstract enough.

The criticism of Kant that Hegel now presents from within his science of logic is subtly different from the one just outlined. Although Hegel urges that we must initially give up the idea that thought always relates to objects "over there" and instead simply attend to the thought of immediate being, he has shown in the course of the *Logic* that being itself proves to be a realm of somethings or "objects" (in the broad sense)—objects that later, in the *Philosophy of Nature*, will prove to be spatio-temporal, physical, chemical, or organic objects. In this sense, Hegel's speculative philosophy confirms the ordinary view that we relate to a world of things "over there" (and, indeed, all around us) even though it begins by suspending that view. However, the speculative understanding of things set out in the *Logic* and *Philosophy of Nature* differs from the ordinary view of things in one significant respect. The speculative philosopher does not regard such things as simply confronting us and requiring us, as it were, to cross over to them so that we can discover what they are like. The speculative philosopher understands things to be real, independent objects whose fundamental ontological structure is identical with, and so contained in, the *thought* of "being something," "being finite," and "being spatio-temporal." We do not need to gain "access" to things, therefore, in order to discover their ontological structure, but we can discover that structure by simply rendering explicit what is implicit in the thought of being as such. "Thinghood" is not just something that comes at us from the outside but something we understand a priori to be inherent in the sheer being or "that-ness" of which thought is minimally aware. The point to remember, however, is that thought would never have recognized that it can determine the character of things a priori if it had not first *given up* the assumption that things stand over against

thought—an assumption that embroils thought in all the traditional epistemological problems of "access" that Hegel's onto-logic avoids.

One of the things that speculative onto-logic reveals about things is that they are inseparably related to other things and, indeed, that their ownmost being in themselves enters into such relations. A thing's intrinsic nature does not stand aloof or remain hidden from the outside world but manifests itself fully *in* the thing's interaction with that world. Viewed from the perspective of this speculative conception of something in itself, Hegel argues, Kant's notion of the thing in itself is, indeed, a pure abstraction.

Now, of course, in one sense Kant specifically intends the concept of the thing in itself to be an abstraction, insofar as it is the thought of that which lies beyond ordinary experience. Nevertheless, Kant understands the concept to bring to mind that which, though inaccessible to us, is *logically* possible. Hegel's own, presuppositionless analysis of the structure of "something" shows, however, that Kant's concept of the "thing in itself" is *not* actually the concept of a logically possible something after all.

Kant states in the *Critique of Pure Reason* that "through mere relations no thing in itself (*Sache an sich*) is cognized" because the concept of such a thing is specifically the concept of a thing in abstraction from all relations in which it is known to enter (*CPR* 189/89 [B 67]). Kant thus believes that one can abstract a thing in thought from its spatio-temporal and empirical-causal relations and still conceive of it as a possible *thing* or *object*. One may not conclude that there are actually such things, but the thought of such things is conceivable and sustainable. By contrast, Hegel demonstrates in his presuppositionless *Logic* that what a thing is in itself necessarily stands in relation to other things—whether that thing is merely conceived to be possible or actually exists. In this way, he shows that the thought of a thing in itself, in abstraction from all relations, is *not* actually sustainable after all. From Hegel's point of view, the problem with Kant's concept of the "thing in itself" is thus that it is too abstract to count as the thought of any possible or actual *something*. "Things are called 'in themselves' in so far as abstraction is made from all being-for-other," Hegel writes; but this means that they are thought as "devoid of all determination, as nothings (*Nichtse*)" (*SL* 121/1: 130 [217]).

Hegel's criticism of Kant's concept of the "thing in itself" at this point in the *Logic* is not simply that it is an abstract concept—Kant knows that, and Hegel's own concept of being is abstract, too—but that its degree of abstractness prevents it from counting as a concept of *something*. It is too abstract to establish the real *or* logical possibility of the thing it pretends to conceive. Kant's concept is, indeed, a profoundly deceptive thought, for it purports to open up the possibility of things, or dimensions of things, beyond what we experience but fails to bring to mind anything determinate. (To the extent that it does succeed in bringing anything to mind, all that can be—though Kant fails to recognize this—is simply the sheer being of thought itself.)

If we put this criticism together with the one we discussed in chapter 6, we see that Hegel actually has a two-pronged criticism to make of Kant's concept of the thing in itself. On the one hand, that concept demonstrates that Kant does not abstract enough because it shows that he does not abstract from, or suspend, the idea that thought always relates to objects or from the idea that thought alone can only entertain the logical possibility of objects and never intuit being itself. On the other hand, Kant's concept of the thing in itself is too abstract to count as the thought of a possible thing at all even though it pretends to be such a thought.

In my view, the first of these charges is without doubt justified. It might be argued, however, that Hegel's second charge does not quite hit the mark. Does not Hegel perhaps overestimate the extent to which Kant conceives of things in themselves in abstraction from all relations? Such things are clearly conceived by Kant in abstraction from what he regards as all *known* relations—that is, from all spatio-temporal and empirical-causal relations. Yet a remark Kant makes on B 59 of the *Critique of Pure Reason* suggests that he may not conceive of things in themselves as lacking all relationality whatsoever: referring to the "things we intuit," Kant writes: "nor [are] their relations so constituted in themselves (*an sich selbst*) as they appear to us" (*CPR* 185/83). One could also point out, of course, that Kant conceives of things in themselves as the "intelligible" (i.e., nonempirical and nonverifiable) "cause of appearance" and, in that sense, as related to the knowing mind (*CPR* 381/330 [B 344]). If this represents Kant's considered view, then Hegel's argument that the thing in itself is conceived by Kant as utterly nonrelational and thus too abstractly to count as a thing at all would actually miss its target.

This objection to Hegel's critique of Kant is, however, itself beside the point. For Hegel has proven that things relate to other things precisely *as* they are in themselves. Their ownmost nature manifests itself *in* these relations and does not remain hidden from view. Kant may well acknowledge a degree of relationality in things as they are in themselves, but he also insists that what they are in themselves does *not* manifest itself in their relation to us. Indeed, he is quite unambiguous on this point:

> We have therefore wanted to say that all our intuition is nothing but the representation of appearance; that the things that we intuit are not in themselves what we intuit them to be (*daß die Dinge, die wir anschauen, nicht das an sich selbst sind, wofür wir sie anschauen*). (*CPR* 185/83 [B 59])

It may well be true that Hegel misrepresents the Kantian thing in itself when he claims that it is utterly nonrelational. Yet it is also the case that by asserting that things do not appear as they are in themselves Kant adheres to an abstract concept of the thing in itself that clearly falls short of the true speculative concept of being-in-itself developed by Hegel.

Yet Kantians may still want to argue that Hegel's critique misses the mark: for one might claim that Kant does not start from the concept of the thing in itself but begins, rather, from a certain understanding of sensibility. To focus, as Hegel does, on Kant's concept of the thing in itself without regard to his doctrine of sensibility is thus seriously to distort Kant's position and to indulge in a distinctively Hegelian form of abstraction.

There is without doubt some merit to this Kantian rejoinder. Kant makes it quite clear that the notion of the thing in itself—or the "negative noumenon"—is not an independent concept but merely the correlate of his understanding of sensibility. It is the concept we are required to entertain once we recognize that our sensibility or way of intuiting is not the only possible one and so cannot be assumed to reveal to us the inner nature of things themselves. As Kant puts it,

> The concept of a noumenon, i.e., of a thing that is not to be thought of as an object of the senses but rather as a thing in itself (*Ding an sich*) . . . is not at all contradictory; for one cannot assert of sensibility that it is the only possible kind of intuition. Further, this concept is necessary in order not to extend sensible intuition to things in themselves, and thus to limit the objective validity of sensible cognition. (*CPR* 362/304 [B 310])

In the Transcendental Aesthetic Kant starts from the idea that human sensibility rests on two forms of intuition—space and time—that are universal and necessary for us and so are a priori. Since they are a priori, Kant contends, they must have their source in the constitution of our own mind. Furthermore, since this is the case, they cannot at the same time reveal to us the nature of things as they are in themselves: "for neither absolute nor relative determinations can be intuited prior to the existence of the things to which they pertain, thus be intuited *a priori*" (*CPR* 176/70 [B 42]). In short: the forms of intuition are the forms in which *we* intuit things, and so they cannot let us see what *things* themselves are like.

In drawing this latter conclusion, Kant presupposes that the only conceivable way in which I *could* know what things are like in themselves would be if their properties could somehow "migrate into my faculty of representation."[8] This is in fact impossible since things affect us and so cause sensations to arise in our minds but do not transmit their properties directly into my head. Nevertheless, if such "migration" were possible, we would be able to know things in themselves; indeed, that would be the *only* way in which we could know the intrinsic nature of things. To put Kant's point in its simplest form: we could only know *about* things themselves *from* those things themselves. Whatever has its source in us thus cannot in principle reveal to us the nature of things themselves. The forms of intuition—space and time—are the a priori forms of *our* intuiting;

8. I. Kant, *Prolegomena to Any Future Metaphysics That Will Be Able to Present Itself as a Science*, trans. P. G. Lucas (Manchester: Manchester University Press, 1953), p. 38 (§9).

therefore, they cannot by definition also be forms intrinsic to things themselves but can only be the conditions under which we know things. "We can accordingly speak of space, extended beings, and so on [and time], only from the human standpoint" (*CPR* 159/70 [B 42]).

Now, if we are to make sense of the idea that we intuit things in a way that is specific to us, we must concede that things are—or, at least, must be thought to be—quite different in themselves from the way we perceive them. Hence we must frame the thought of the "thing in itself." The idea that things in themselves do not manifest their ownmost nature in the way they appear to and are known by us is thus an essential correlate of the idea that our sensibility is essentially limited.

> The concept of a noumenon is therefore merely a boundary concept, in order to limit the pretension of sensibility, and therefore only of negative use. But it is nevertheless not invented arbitrarily, but is rather connected with the limitation of sensibility. (*CPR* 362/305 [B 311])

We do not know that there are any things in themselves or noumena, but we must entertain the thought or concept of such things, and we must conceive them to be quite different from the way we perceive them because space and time are merely the limited forms of *our* intuition.

The concept of the thing in itself, or negative noumenon, is thus not a free-standing concept that Kant develops for its own sake. It is a concept that plays a definite epistemic role: namely, to remind us that the conditions under which we intuit things are merely the conditions under which *we* intuit things and may not be regarded as the ontological conditions of things as they truly are. To the extent that Hegel neglects the epistemic context within which Kant posits the idea of the thing in itself and focuses on Kant's concept in the abstract, his critique cannot but fail to miss its mark.

That, at least, is how Kantians might regard Hegel's critique. In my view, however, such Kantians would overlook the profound challenge that Hegel's *logical* account of being-in-itself poses to Kant's whole *epistemic* position. We may well accept Kant's claim that the concept of the thing in itself is the necessary correlate of his doctrine that the a priori forms of intuition are merely the conditions under which we intuit things. Yet we may nevertheless point out that Hegel has shown that the Kantian conception of the thing in itself is itself an unsustainable abstraction. Furthermore, we may go on to note that since that concept is unsustainable the epistemic idea that it accompanies—namely, that our mode of sensibility is necessarily limited to us—must be unsustainable, too. The charge that Hegel misses the point by ignoring the epistemic function to be played by the concept of the "thing in itself" does not let Kant off the hook. On the contrary, it exposes Kant to the countercharge that his own epistemic position is rendered untenable by the logical deficiencies of his concept of the thing in itself.

In Hegel's view, what something is in itself necessarily stands in relation to other things and manifests itself *in* such relations. Indeed, it is logically and ontologically impossible for the ownmost nature of things *not* to manifest itself in the relations into which those things enter: even when something seeks to deceive us, it still reveals itself in so doing. This means, therefore, that the way things appear to us, and are known by us, must disclose their nature in themselves. This means, in turn, that the necessary forms in which we intuit things—space and time—cannot merely be the forms in which *we* intuit things but must also be forms that reveal the nature of things themselves *in some way*. Of course, by itself this does not prove that things in themselves must be *spatio-temporal* in particular. It may well be that viewing the world through rose-colored spectacles necessarily reveals something of the world in itself, but that does not mean that the world is necessarily rose-colored. It does mean, however, that the world should not be thought necessarily *not* to be rose-colored. If something of the world in itself must disclose itself in the a priori forms of our intuiting, it could therefore be the case that the world is in fact spatio-temporal itself. It cannot be the case that just because space and time are the a priori forms of our intuition they necessarily do not belong to the world.

Hegel does not doubt that space and time are the a priori forms of our intuiting. His point against Kant is that that fact does not prevent the true nature of things themselves becoming manifest in those forms. Nor, therefore, does it prevent things being spatio-temporal in themselves.[9] It will, however, have to be proven independently that space and time do in fact belong to objects themselves; indeed, in the *Philosophy of Nature* Hegel does precisely that.

In my view, Hegel's logical critique of Kant's concept of the thing in itself is not invalidated simply because it does not explicitly address that concept's epistemic role in Kant's transcendental philosophy. On the contrary, Hegel's logical critique exposes as untenable both Kant's concept *and* the epistemic doctrine of necessarily "limited human sensibility" that it complements. For Hegel, it cannot be true that the a priori forms of space and time reveal nothing of things in themselves because *logically* things cannot *not* reveal their intrinsic nature in the way they are known. This by itself may not prove that things in themselves are necessarily spatio-temporal, but it does prove that space and time cannot be known definitively to be *merely* the forms in which *we* intuit things and so to have no existence or meaning beyond our experience. That is to say, it proves that human sensibility is not necessarily limited by the fact that it is subject to a priori conditions.

Kant maintains that his concept of the thing in itself is the necessary correlate of his epistemic doctrine that human sensibility is necessarily limited. We have now seen that Hegel's logical critique of Kant's concept of the thing in itself renders that epistemic doctrine untenable. This brief encounter between

9. Hegel, *EPM* 198/253 (§448 Add.).

Kant and Hegel thus shows that the latter's complex analyses in the *Logic* are far from being irrelevant to the concerns of other philosophers. On the contrary, they call into question the abstractly conceived categories that all too often inform their thought.

Hegel and Nietzsche on "Things in Themselves"

One thinker who takes a view of things strikingly similar to Hegel's is Nietzsche. Like Hegel, Nietzsche believes that things are what they are in relation to other things. He dismisses as fiction the idea that there is a dimension to things that is utterly separate from their relation to other things. Nietzsche's position is set out with exemplary concision in this passage from his *Nachlaß*:

> The properties of a thing are effects on other "things": if one removes other "things," then a thing has no properties, i.e., there is no thing without other things, i.e., there is no "thing-in-itself."[10]

Yet closer inspection of this passage reveals a significant difference between Nietzsche and Hegel. Both agree that "there is no thing without other things" and that no thing stands alone purely by itself. Hegel, however, would not endorse Nietzsche's final blanket judgment that "there is no 'thing-in-itself.'" For Hegel, as for Nietzsche, there is indeed no thing in itself if by that one has in mind a thing abstracted from all relations, but in his view that does not mean that there is no thing in itself whatsoever because a thing in itself, properly understood, is not to be equated with a thing abstracted from all relations. On the contrary, things are what they are in themselves *in* their relations to other things. In spite of certain similarities, therefore, Nietzsche and Hegel adopt quite different positions. Nietzsche retains an abstract conception of the thing in itself but asserts that that concept is a mere fiction. Hegel, by contrast, develops an alternative, more complex conception of something in itself, on the basis of which he argues that things *do* enjoy an intrinsic character of their own in their very relations to other things.

Once again, Hegel's logical analyses alert us to the fact that another philosopher is operating with an uncritically assumed abstraction. Indeed, it is evident that Nietzsche's ostensibly radical rejection of the very idea of a "thing in itself" depends entirely on his retention of such an abstraction. From Hegel's point of view, therefore, Nietzsche throws the baby out with the bath water because he cannot see that there is any baby to be saved. All he sees is the murky, bathwatery concept of the thing in itself, abstractly conceived. Hegel's achievement, in my view, is to have shown—*contra* Nietzsche—that relationality is in fact inseparable from being-in-itself and that there is thus no reason to reject as fictional the idea of the thing in itself merely because "there is no thing without other things."

10. Nietzsche, *The Will to Power*, p. 302 (§557).

For Hegel, things do have a specific character in themselves that distinguishes them from other things. This intrinsic character has an integrity of its own and is not merely reducible to the way (or ways) in which the thing relates to others. A flower, for example, cannot merely consist in smelling sweet to my nose and feeling soft to my touch, but must have a form and qualities of its own that make it that which relates to other things in certain ways. *Pace* Nietzsche, a thing cannot consist simply in its "effects" on other things but must have a distinctive character through which it exercises those effects.

The distinction between being-in-itself and being-for-other is thus preserved by Hegel. The unexpected twist in his account, however, is that the thing in itself itself stands in relation to others—that something's own intrinsic being is manifest in its relations. The difference between something's being-in-itself and its other-relatedness is thus not an absolute one: what the thing is in itself, it is for others, and what is for others is the thing as it is in itself. The thing is the *same* thing in either case. It may be that Nietzsche would have further objections to this idea that all things enjoy an "identity" of their own. All that I wish to point out here is that Nietzsche is not entitled to reject the idea of the thing in itself on the grounds that "things" are thoroughly relational. After Hegel, being something in itself and being other-related are no longer to be understood as absolutely mutually exclusive.

The intrinsic nature of a thing, as it reveals itself in and determines the thing's relations to others is what Hegel calls the *determination* (*Bestimmung*) of the thing. Things do not just have an intrinsic character, therefore; they have a specific determination—a specific way of being what they are and, as it were, asserting their own identity *in* their encounters with others (see *SL* 122/1: 131 [219]).

Hegel's Method: A Reminder

Before we turn to consider the determination of things, I want briefly to remind the reader of an important feature of Hegel's method. Hegel is unfolding, or rendering explicit, various ways of being that are immanent in being as such. So far we have learned that being entails becoming, determinacy, being something or other, and being something both in itself and in relation to other things. Each way of being, or category, Hegel maintains, is implied and rendered necessary by the one that precedes it. As we proceed through the logical analysis, we thus learn that what being is first thought to be is actually an underdetermination of being. Being is first thought as pure being, but we soon recognize that it is not *merely* being after all but becoming, determinacy, and being something. Our understanding of the nature and structure of being is thus revised by the very nature of being itself.

It is important to remember, however, that in this process of categorial revision categories as they are first conceived are not simply rejected or set to one side in favor of later ones. Each something remains a way of *being* and remains

determinate; "being" and "determinacy" are irreducible logical components of any something. It is just that being something is shown not to be reducible to being or to being determinate. To put it another way, each category is preserved as *aufgehoben* in the later ones.

One needs to bear this in mind particularly in the current discussion of something: for it is easy to imagine—falsely—that once we have reached the idea that something is essentially other-directed any idea that things are separate from one another simply falls away. We now know that something is not *just* a separate, self-enclosed sphere of being but that it has a distinct character of its own that is in direct and necessary relation to other things. To think of something as merely a separate "something" and to neglect a thing's being-in-itself and being-for-other is thus severely to underdetermine what it is to be something. But it is not *wrong*. No something is merely something, but every something is at least a separate something. It remains true, therefore, that the table on which I write is "something" even though it is also a finite, spatio-temporal object with specific physical and chemical properties. It also remains true that, *insofar as* this table is something, it is quite separate from this computer (which is something else). A detailed account of the table and the computer would examine how each relates to the other, but it should not overlook the fact that each is at one level a separate thing.

The principal aim of Hegel's *Logic* is to derive the various ways, or categories, of being from one another and, ultimately, from the indeterminate concept of being as such. Included in that aim, however, is the intention to alert us to what is involved in each way of being in turn. It is as if Hegel is providing multiple conceptual cross-sections of things and showing what it is for something to exhibit *this* conceptual structure rather than another. Of course, one conceptual structure entails and leads logically to another, and the world in which we live exhibits the whole array of ways of being that are set out in the *Logic* and in the *Philosophies of Nature* and *Spirit*. It is vital, however, to understand what each individual category in turn involves. That way, we learn not only what it is to be a concrete object in the world but also what characterizes a thing *insofar as* it is something, *insofar as* it is finite, *insofar as* it is quantitative, and so on. In other words, we gain an understanding of all the *different* ways of being that make up the things that are.

The whole picture that emerges at the end of the *Logic* and then at the end of the *Philosophies of Nature* and *Spirit* is certainly important. But one comprehends the whole only by appreciating precisely what is involved in each of the different ways of being that constitute that whole. The hallmark of Hegel's philosophy is not only the presentation of a grand synthesizing vision but also the subtle and precise attention to detail.

Chapter Nineteen

Determination, Constitution, and Limit

Determination and Determinacy

It is important to distinguish the category of determinacy, or determinateness (*Bestimmtheit*), from that of determination (*Bestimmung*). Determinateness, as we saw in chapter 16, is simply the moment of "nonbeing" (*Nichtsein*) that renders all being stable and definite. By contrast, determination is considerably more complex. Hegel defines determination in the apparently incomprehensible sentence cited in the introduction to this study:

> Determination is affirmative determinateness as the in-itself with which something in its determinate being remains congruous in face of its entanglement with the other by which it might be determined, maintaining itself in its self-equality, and making its determination hold good in its being-for-other. (*SL* 123/1: 132 [221])

This sentence may appear at first sight to be rather intimidating (indeed, unintelligible), but it is actually quite clear and precise. A determination is the "affirmative determinateness," or quality, of something. It is that aspect of something by virtue of which something is itself and *not* an other. It is something-as-determinate. Now something, as we have seen, is determinate insofar as it enjoys intrinsic being of its own or being-in-itself (*Ansichsein*) and insofar as it relates to others. The determination of something is the fusion of these two ways of being. It is not, therefore, merely a thing's intrinsic being by itself but, rather, the intrinsic being of something preserved "in face of its entanglement with the other." Indeed, it is the specific quality or character that something manifests or asserts in its relation to an other.

As an example (borrowing a phrase from Fichte), Hegel mentions the determination of humanity (*die Bestimmung des Menschen*), which he claims is "thinking reason." That which characterizes humanity's proper nature and distinguishes us from the animals, Hegel maintains, is thought (*Denken*). Thought, however, is not a purely inner quality of which each individual alone is aware. It is a quality that exhibits itself in and suffuses our dealings with others (whether we act in explicit accordance with the dictates of reason or not). Thought is our *determination*, therefore, because it is the defining character of humanity evident in our relations to others.

Determination and Constitution

At the start of 2.B.b.2 Hegel draws attention to an important feature of the categories of quality. In the field of the qualitative, he writes, "differences in their sublated form as moments also retain the form of immediate, qualitative being relatively to one another" (*SL* 123/1: 133 [221]). That is to say, differences are not eliminated just because they are shown not to be absolute. "Being" remains immediately different from "nothing," or the "not," even though the two prove to be inseparable. Similarly, even though being-in-itself proves to be inextricably linked to being-for-other and so transforms itself logically into something's determination, there is still a qualitative difference between the two ways of being since being-in-itself is not simply reducible to other-relatedness.

Something's being-in-itself does not just consist in a collection of ways of relating to *others* but is its specific way of being *itself*. It is the distinctive quality or identity that makes something *this* unique thing rather than another. Being-in-itself, in other words, is that quality by virtue of which each thing is something of its own, *whatever* its relations to others may be. It is crucial to bear in mind this lingering difference between something's intrinsic character and its other-relatedness when considering the category of "determination." For a thing's determination is not coextensive with its other-relatedness but is the being-in-itself, or identity, that a thing asserts *in* its relations to others (***in*** *seinem Sein-für-Anderes*). The word "in" indicates that a thing's determination informs but does not completely overlap with or exhaust its other-relatedness.

The fact that this difference is preserved has a further significant consequence. It means that something's being-for-other cannot be reduced to the other-relatedness *of* the thing's ownmost being. This, in turn, means that there must be another dimension of the thing's being-for-other that remains distinct from its ownmost being. That is to say, there must be an aspect of the way something relates to other things that is informed and determined *not* by what something is in itself but by something *else*. As Hegel puts it, "that which something has *in it* (*an ihm*) . . . divides itself" and includes that which "is also *its* determinate being, but does not belong to the something's in-itself." The other-relatedness of something that is not determined by something's own character is its *constitution* (*Beschaffenheit*). If the constitution of something is not governed by what the thing itself is, it can only be determined by the *other* things to which something relates. Accordingly, Hegel writes, "constituted in this or that way, something is involved in *external* influences and relationships" (*SL* 124/1: 133 [223], my emphasis).

For Hegel, then, something is always related to another something; that relation is partly governed by the character of the thing concerned and partly by the other thing to which it relates. Nothing can avoid asserting its own determination in its relations with others, but equally nothing can avoid being constituted in ways that are beyond its control by other things that surround it. Every something is thus vulnerable by its very nature to being influenced and affected by

other things for the simple reason that it necessarily stands in a relation to another that is not determined purely by what *it* is in itself.

Hegel is sometimes taken to be a philosopher who privileges interiority and inner identity above all else. True, he acknowledges that there is always something other than identity (for example, difference, or nature as the other of thought); however, so the story goes, any such other is invariably subordinated to the interests of identity. Its role, we are told, is to mediate and make possible the identity of things and of thought. It is as if everything in Hegel's universe aspires to emulate the master in the *Phenomenology*, who consumes or utilizes natural objects for his own ends and puts the slave to work in the service of his own self-satisfaction.

This reading of Hegel is very common, especially among commentators inspired by Nietzsche, Heidegger, or Derrida. Christina Howells, for example, maintains that "Hegel is a predatory philosopher," and contends that "a frontal attack on him is bound to fail because of the way the dialectic transforms all opposition into a negative, antithetical moment in an ongoing synthetic process."[1] A much more subtle but nevertheless similar view of things is advanced by David Krell, who asserts that for Hegel "*Er-Innerung* [remembrance] calls to mind not only a particular faculty or power of spirit but the *method*, the fundamental *way*, of all things on, above, and below the Earth—the way of interiorization."[2] Both interpreters paint essentially the same picture: everything in Hegel's world endeavors to absorb what is other *into* its own self-identity.

It is clear from Hegel's remarks on constitution, however, that this popular interpretation of his philosophy is seriously misleading. Hegel certainly does not deny that things enjoy an identity of their own. He insists, however, that things are also vulnerable to being constituted in certain ways by *other* things. Moreover, the influence of other things is not simply put to work by something in the service of its own self-determination. On the contrary, external influences make of a thing precisely something other than what it is determined to be by its ownmost nature. This vulnerability to external influence is not merely a contingent feature of something—a feature that something might or might not exhibit depending on the circumstances. Hegel claims that it is a necessary feature of every something: "it is the quality of something to be open to external influences and to have a *constitution*" (*SL* 124/1: 133 [223]). Indeed, such exposure to the outside is immanent in the very structure of something. In my view, this insight turns the more familiar picture of Hegel on its head. For far from arguing that everything absorbs (or tries to absorb) what is external and other into itself, Hegel maintains that everything within itself is open to the *outside*.

Since external influences make of a thing something other than what it is de-

1. Howells, *Derrida: Deconstruction from Phenomenology to Ethics,* p. 85.

2. D. F. Krell, *Of Memory, Reminiscence, and Writing: On the Verge* (Bloomington: Indiana University Press, 1990), p. 205.

termined to be by its intrinsic nature, such influences introduce "othering," or change (*Veränderung*), into the thing: "in so far as something alters, the alteration falls within its constitution; it is that *in* the something which becomes an other." We saw earlier that something changes by virtue of the fact that it is itself always other than itself. Such change is proper to the thing and, indeed, is the process in the course of which something acquires and exhibits an identity of its own. We have now encountered a new dimension of change within the thing—change brought about by other things. Something thus suffers externally induced, as well as internal, change. Since this new mode of change is determined by *other* things, it affects only the constitution of the thing and leaves the thing's ownmost nature untouched. Something thus continues to manifest its own determination in its relations to others even though it is, in another respect, affected and (re-)constituted by those others.

There are, therefore, still *two* dimensions to every something: what belongs to it in itself and what belongs to it because of its contact with others. Hegel insists that something retains its intrinsic nature *however* it may be constituted by those others: "the something itself preserves itself in the alteration which affects only this unstable surface of its otherness, not its determination" (*SL* 124/1: 133 [223]). The important point, however, is that these two aspects are both evident in the thing's dealings with others. According to Hegel, the internal structure of things and their changing surface characteristics are both equally apparent.

The division in something between its intrinsic nature and its other-relatedness has thus subtly transformed itself into a distinction between two sides of its other-relatedness: its determination and constitution. We recall that what something is for another is what it has outwardly *in it* (*an ihm*), rather than what it is *in itself* (*an sich*) (though what a thing is in itself is evident *in* what it has outwardly in it). The difference we now see between the two ways in which something is for another can thus be conceived as a difference between the two aspects of what is outwardly *in the thing*. Another way of putting this is to say that the being-of-something-that-is-outwardly-evident-in-it-for-others (in other words, its other-relatedness) has differentiated itself into two contrasting forms. This is the point Hegel is trying to make in these—admittedly rather inelegant—lines: "that which something has *in it* (*an ihm*), is the middle term connecting [its determination and constitution] in this syllogism. Or, rather, the *being-in-the-something* (*Am-Etwas-sein*) showed itself as falling apart into these two extremes" (*SL* 124/133 [223]).

The middle term to which Hegel refers here—something's other-relatedness—can also be described as "*determinateness* as such" (*Bestimmtheit als solche*). It is the simple determinacy that makes something this thing, *not* another. Something is determinate in being what it is in itself, but it is also determinate—indeed, is all the more so—in *relating to another* from which it differs. The principal claim that Hegel is making at this point in his analysis is that the determinacy of something with respect to its other has now taken on two forms:

one that is governed by itself and one that is governed by the other things to which it relates. The thing is distinctive and determinate either way, but in the latter case it is constituted as a determinate something *by* what is other than it.

The Identity of Determination and Constitution

Hegel now proceeds to show that this distinction between something's determination and constitution actually undermines, or "deconstructs," itself. It will not disappear altogether, but it turns out not to be quite as clear cut as it initially seems.

Let us first consider the logical mutation of something's determination into that which is constituted. This logical move is made necessary by the very structure of determination itself. The determination of something is its intrinsic nature insofar as it manifests itself in the thing's relations to others. By virtue of this simple fact, however, the determination is itself "open to relationship to other," and this openness to the other undermines the purity of the determination itself. Something's being-for-other is qualitatively different from its being-in-itself: it does not form the inner identity of the thing concerned but connects it inextricably with *another* something. The fact that what something is in itself informs its being-for-other means, therefore, that it is itself placed in direct contact with whatever is other than the thing. As Hegel puts it, the unity of being-in-itself and being-for-other necessarily "brings the otherness into . . . the determination." But, of course, this means that something's being-in-itself (and thereby its determination) is itself vulnerable to being determined or reconstituted by the other to which it relates. To sum up: insofar as the determination of something is its ownmost nature exhibited in its relations to another, it cannot be governed solely by the thing itself after all but must always risk becoming part of the constitution of the thing—a constitution determined by the other to which the thing relates.

The quasi-Derridean insight to which Hegel is led at this point in the text is this: there is no aspect of something's ownmost being that is protected from the influence of another thing and that is consequently invulnerable to being constituted anew by that other, because there is nothing in the thing that does not stand in direct relation to another. External influence does not just transform the surface of things; it goes to the very heart of things and can transform even what things are in their innermost selves. In Hegel's view, therefore, there is and can be no ownmost ownness that is wholly a thing's *own*: for what something is in itself is always open to being reconstituted by another. External influences can permeate things through and through, and there is nothing that can be done to prevent this. (But note that, unlike Derrida, Hegel reaches this conclusion through a wholly *immanent* study of being.)

Does this mean that things turn out to enjoy no identity of their own at all? Has the very idea of being-in-itself now been exposed as an illusion after all? No; there are two reasons why this is not the case. First of all, anything that is

constituted anew by other things must have an identity of its own *on which* those other things can exert their influence. There must be *something* there that is affected by another, and that something must have a defining character of its own. We now know that that character is open to being transformed by other things, but it must be there to start with and set limits to the influence of those other things on it.

Second, and perhaps more importantly, whatever something comes to be through the influence of others itself has a determinacy of its own. Yes, things can be reconstituted at their core by other things, but that process of constitution generates a new something with its own intrinsic character. In Hegel's view, the fact that something is open to external influence—or, indeed, as with a work of art, arises wholly through the activity of another—does not mean that what results lacks any identity. On the contrary, it enjoys an identity of its *own* that has been constituted by *other* things; that identity belongs to it, even if it was not solely responsible for it.

The more precise logical reason why this should be is this: the constitution of something is that dimension of the thing that, through the influence of others, changes and becomes other than what it is. Since it is subject to constant change, it undergoes the same dialectic we encountered in chapter 17 when we considered what it means for something to be utterly other by itself. In becoming other, Hegel pointed out, the other becomes other again and again and so in fact always *remains* the same old other. Logically, therefore, it retains—or acquires—an identity in the very process of becoming other.[3] Hegel claims that the same can be said of the changes that occur in the constitution of something. In being changed, the constitution of the thing always comes to be other than it is and so necessarily exhibits an *identity* in and through such change. This identity is constituted by other things insofar as they transform the character of the thing, but it is no less the thing's own identity for that. The constituted character of something is nothing other than that thing's *own* character—a character that must manifest itself in the thing's relations to others and so form the thing's determination. Hegel's brief account of the logical mutation of something's constitution into its determination goes like this:

> being-for-other isolated as constitution and posited by itself, is in its own self the same as the other as such, the other in its own self, that is, the other of itself; but thus it is *self-related* determinate being, the in-itself (*Ansichsein*) with a determinateness, and therefore a *determination* (*Bestimmung*). (*SL* 124/1: 134 [223])

We now see that the determination and constitution of something are not simply distinct but, rather, two profoundly interrelated aspects of one and the same something. On the one hand, something has a determination of its own that sets

3. See Hegel, *SL* 118–19/1: 127 (213), and chapter 17, above, pp. 328–30.

limits to the ways in which other things can transform it: unlike paper, water cannot be set alight by the application of heat but can only be brought to the boil. The constitution of something thus depends not just on the character of the other things to which the thing relates but also on the thing's own determination which co-determines how it may be affected by others. As Hegel words it, "the determining (*Bestimmen*) from outside is at the same time determined by the something's own, immanent determination (*Bestimmung*)." On the other hand, the determination of something is itself vulnerable to being changed and reconstituted by other things: "the constitution belongs to that which the something is in itself; something alters with its constitution."[4]

Identity and "ownness" are not just fictions, for Hegel, but real. Things do enjoy an intrinsic character or determination of their own that makes them what they are as opposed to something else and that can be distinguished—at least initially—from the qualities they are given by other things. What follows from Hegel's logical analysis of something, however, is that the intrinsic character of something itself undergoes change—change brought about by the thing's internal dynamic *and* by the influence of other things. The identity of something is thus not absolutely immune to reconstitution by other things and so is at most *relatively* stable: now we say that the fence itself is made of wood and the paint has been applied by us, but now we say that the paint forms part of what the fence *itself* has come to be.

Of course, other philosophers apart from Hegel including Spinoza and Kant have argued that things stand in a relation of thoroughgoing reciprocal influence with one another. What distinguishes Hegel's position is the fact that he derives the necessity for such reciprocal influence from the very idea of being something. Something relates to, influences, and is influenced by another thing, not because it is a finite mode of extension causally connected to other such modes, nor because it is spatio-temporal and governed by the category of "reciprocal causality," but quite simply because it is *something* at all. For Hegel, being other-related and open to the influence of others is built logically into the very structure of something as such.

The category of something, it is true, is rather bare and primitive. One is not saying very much when one says that there is "something" over there on the table. Hegel shows, however, that the category of something—and, accordingly, *being* something—entails much more than one might first suppose. Above all, he shows that every something is irreducibly relational—regardless of whether it is a physical, chemical, organic, or conscious entity. This is because things must be determinate, and all determinacy—being this, *not* that—sets the things concerned in relation to others. Every something is "open to relationship to other," therefore, because its own being and identity is logically inseparable from *negation*.

---

4. See Burbidge, *On Hegel's Logic*, p. 50.

Here it is worth noting a fundamental difference between Hegel and Kant. Kant also accepts that things—at least as they are experienced by us—stand in a relation of reciprocal influence. In his view, this is due to the fact that although objects of experience are known a priori to be spatially and temporally related, the relative position of objects in space and time can be established only if they are understood to exercise causal influence on one another (*CPR* 304–19/241–63 [B 232–62]). Kant insists, however, that no thing in itself, in abstraction from the conditions under which it is known, is *intrinsically* related to others purely by virtue of being what it is. This is not to deny that things in themselves might stand in some kind of relation to one another;[5] but it is to maintain—as Kant contended throughout his philosophical career—that any relations there might be between things in themselves or purely intelligible objects are established by God and are not rooted in the very structure of things as such.

In the chapter on the Amphiboly of Concepts of Reflection in the first *Critique*, Kant states unambiguously that

> in an object of the pure understanding only that is internal that has no relation (as far as the existence is concerned) to anything that is different from it. The inner determinations of a *substantia phaenomenon* in space, on the contrary, are nothing but relations, and it is itself entirely a sum total of mere relations. (*CPR* 369/313 [B 321])

Kant held the same conception of things or substances in themselves throughout his career, both before and during his "critical" period. In his *Inaugural Dissertation* (1770), for example, he argued that

> if a plurality of substances is given, the *principle* of a possible *interaction* between them *does not consist in their existence alone*, but something else is required in addition, by means of which their reciprocal relations may be understood. For they do not necessarily relate to anything else simply in virtue of their subsistence, unless, perhaps, they relate to their cause.[6]

And in his *Nova Dilucidatio* (1755) he made essentially the same point:

> finite substances do not, in virtue of their existence alone, stand in a relationship with each other, nor are they linked together by any interaction at all, except in so far as the common principle of their existence, namely the divine understanding, maintains them in a state of harmony in their reciprocal relations.[7]

Kant's "neo-Leibnizian" conception of "objects of the pure understanding" —that is, objects not as we know them but as we must think them to be in them-

5. See chapter 18, above, p. 341.
6. Kant, *Theoretical Philosophy, 1755–1770*, p. 402 (§17).
7. Kant, *Theoretical Philosophy, 1755–1770*, p. 40 (Prop. XIII).

selves—is by no means obviously absurd. Surely, if we consider a thing in abstraction from all spatio-temporal and empirical-causal relations and think of it purely by itself, is it not evident that it will be understood to lack all relationality? How can something taken purely *by itself* be conceived as relating to something *else*?

Hegel's claim, however, is precisely that every something—conceived in abstraction from space, time, and empirical causality—is other-related purely through itself. This is because, in Hegel's view, every something is rendered determinate by *negation*. Something does not just relate to another thing because that other happens to lie next to it in space or because God creates all things in preestablished harmony; something relates to another because *logically* it is determinate, negative, and therefore relational in *itself*. That is to say, "something *through its own nature* (*aus sich selbst*) relates itself to the other" (*SL* 125/1: 135 [225]). Paradoxical though it may seem, Hegel's claim is thus that if there were—*per impossibile*—only one thing in the universe the logical structure of that one thing would by itself require that there be at least two somethings and that each stand in a relation of negation, difference, and (as we see in the account of determination and constitution) reciprocal influence to the other.[8]

Limit

The analysis of something's determination and constitution has revealed that there is nothing in a thing that is not in direct relation to its other. The relation to the other permeates the whole of something. This relation is one in which each something brings about changes in the constitution of the other—that is, one in which each something actively *negates* the other in some way. Yet something negates the other not only by changing it but also by differing from—and so not being—that other. Indeed, something can change—or make something *other* of —the other to which it relates only to the extent that it is itself other than—and so is *not*—the other to which it relates. If it were no different from the other, it could not bring to bear on that other anything that is *other* than that other, and so it could not change, or "other," that other into something new. One thing's ability to negate—that is, alter—the constitution of another depends upon the fact that it negates—that is, differs from—that other.

Consequently, if something is, at the very core of its being, in a direct relation of reciprocal influence with its other, it must also, at the very core of its being, differ from and *negate* that other, too. Something in its ownmost being must relate negatively, in both senses, to its other: it must influence and be influenced by its other *and* at its heart it must *not be* that other. This, I take it, is what Hegel means when he writes that negation is now recognized to be "*immanent* in the somethings" (*SL* 125/1: 134–5 [225]).

---

8. See Hegel, *EL* 148/197 (§92 Add.): "In something we at once hit upon the other, and we know that there is not only something, but also something else."

To say that negation is immanent in every something is to say that something is *through and through* the negation of its other, that there is nothing about something that is not the negation of its other. It is to say that something is something at all only insofar as it is in every respect *not-its-other*: "the negation of its other is . . . the quality of the something, for it is as this sublating of its other that it is something" (*SL* 125/1: 135 [225]). This is not to reduce something to mere negation or determinacy. Something is and remains self-relating negation or the negation of negation. At the same time, however, we now see that in being self-relating or double negation something must also be the *simple* negation of its other.

Hegel notes that this renders something determinate in a way that simply being "something" does not. Insofar as a thing is merely something, it is just like any other something. Each one is something, and of course, each one is other than its other. There is thus an element of structural indeterminacy built into simply being "something." When something is conceived as the thorough *negation* of its other, however, it acquires much greater determinacy: it is clearly *this* something, *not* any other one. Since something is through and through the negation of its other, it excludes the other from itself completely. It is not at all the other to which it relates; this something is, indeed, the point at which any other something ends.

Something conceived in this way is, as Hegel puts it, "*the ceasing of an other in it*" (*das Aufhören eines Anderen an ihm*) (*SL* 126/1: 135 [225]). This is not to say that the two somethings cannot have certain features in common; they may, for example, both be red and be made of wood. The point is that something is determinate only if it is clearly *not* red and wooden in the way that another one is; that is, only if it shuts out from itself whatever the other is. To understand something and its other in this way, Hegel maintains, is to think of each as constituting the *limit* or *boundary* (*Grenze*) of the other. Presuppositionless logic thus leads to the conclusion that something must not only relate to and influence but also limit and be limited by its other.

The logical structure of the limit is complicated, even by Hegel's unusual standards. First of all, the limit is the moment of radical negation in any something that marks it off completely from any other. Such negation is to be regarded as the *limit* because it is the point in this something at which another something stops. It is that aspect of something that makes it this and definitely *not* that. Second, however, the limit binds something to its other because it is the moment of not-being-the-*other* that belongs to something itself. Something is tied to the other, therefore, because it is only in limiting the other that something is what it is. Furthermore, if the limit is the point at which this something begins and that one stops, it is at the same time the point at which that one begins and this one stops. That is to say, it is the point at which each one marks itself off from and so negates its other. The limit thus actually belongs to both something *and* its other simultaneously. It is their common boundary—the moment of not-being-the-other that each one is.

Third, in limiting its other, something is not only the simple negation of that other but also self-relating negation, or something in its *own* right. In Hegel's words, something "is posited as relating itself negatively to the other and in so doing preserving itself" (*SL* 126/1: 135 [225]). Each something, in limiting the other and sharing a boundary with the other, thus remains something *separate* from the other; it remains quite *other* than the other. Indeed, it is as the other of the other that something is what it is *in itself* (*an sich*). This is the point I believe Hegel is making in one of the more enigmatic clauses in his account: "this other, the being-within-self of the something as negation of the negation, is its *in-itself* (*Ansichsein*)."

Fourth, however, something can be distinguished from another only if it is not merely other than its other but also the definitive *negation* or *limit* of the other. Something is what it is in itself, but "at the same time this sublation [of the other] is *present in it* (*an ihm*) as a simple negation, namely, as its negation of the other something external to it." Something is a *determinate* something, therefore, only if limits and negates its other.

If we put all of these points together, we see that something that limits its other is separate from but also connected to that other (precisely by being distinguished from it), and that the limit is for this reason a highly complex logical structure. Hegel summarizes the basic features of the limit in this typically concise sentence:

> There is a *single* determinateness of both [something and its other], which on the one hand is identical with the being-within-self of the somethings as negation of the negation, and on the other hand, since these negations are opposed to one another as other somethings, conjoins and equally disjoins them through their own nature, each negating the other: this determinateness is *limit*. (*SL* 126/1: 135 [225])[9]

In order to understand the structure of the limit properly, it is vital to remember that the limit constitutes the simple *determinacy* of *something*. To appreciate precisely what this involves, however, one must keep in mind that there is a logical distinction between being "determinate" and being "something." Determinacy, we recall, consists in simple negation—what Hegel calls "the *first* negation" (*SL* 116/1: 124 [209]). Something, by contrast, is not mere determinacy, but *self-relating* negation—double negation, or "negativity." As Hegel

9. See Rinaldi, *A History and Interpretation of the Logic of Hegel*, p. 151. In contrast to Paul Guyer, I do not believe that the limit deprives things altogether of their "independence" (*Selbständigkeit*) but rather that things prove to be independent *in* being limited. Something limited, for Hegel, is something of its *own* in *not*-being-another; it is both positive and negative—a meadow as not-wood. This is because the limited thing is both a self-relating something *and* the determinate negation of another at the same time. See P. Guyer, "Hegel, Leibniz und der Widerspruch des Endlichen," in *Seminar: Dialektik in der Philosophie Hegels*, p. 257.

emphasizes in 2.A.c, "*something* is the negation of the negation in the form of *being*" (*SL* 116/1: 124 [209]). In drawing this distinction between simple and double negation, Hegel is not merely playing with words. He is pointing out that something must be determinate—and so entail negation—but cannot just be this, for it is *self-relating* being that is something of its *own*. Something is negation or determinacy that is *not* just negation, after all. This is, admittedly, an unusual way of conceiving of something. In presuppositionless philosophy, however, it is the only way we are permitted to conceive of something.

With the recognition that something is the limit or simple negation of its other, we have now reached the thought that something is not purely and simply something—not just self-relating being—but something *determinate*. As we have seen, the process whereby something proves to be determinate is logically necessary. Yet it leads to a new category—that of limit—that is structurally ambiguous. The limit is problematic precisely because it constitutes the determinacy of that which, by definition, is *not* mere determinacy: namely, *something*. This tension within the very structure of a determinate, limiting, and limited something pulls something in two different directions at once.

On the one hand, the moment of determinacy or negation—the limit—belongs irrevocably to something itself. Something as the negation of negation is at the same time the simple *negation* of its other; this is why Hegel says that "there is a *single* determinateness . . . , which is identical with the being-within-self of the somethings as negation of the negation." On the other hand, as the negation of negation, something is *not* the very negation that it is; it is not just the limit of another but is a self-relating something in its own right. Logically, therefore, something differentiates itself from the limit it necessarily shares with others and places itself "beyond" or "outside" that limit. And yet, it is only in limiting, and being limited by, its other that it is a determinately distinct something at all. A determinate something is thus structurally at odds with the very limit that makes it what it is. Its determinacy and its "somethingness" are inseparable, and yet they work against one another: something is one with its determinacy or limit, and yet at the same time it is *not* one with it. This is not just a problem with our concept of the limit. In Hegel's view, it is an ontological tension or ambiguity within the very nature of a determinate, limiting/limited something. Indeed, as we shall see, it is a tension that will transform something logically into a *finite* thing.

Different Degrees of Determinacy

Before we proceed to examine the limit in more detail, we must consider another problem that readers of this study may have noticed. We have said that something becomes determinate in being limited. Yet did we not also say earlier that something becomes determinate in differentiating itself into being-in-itself and being-for-other? If something is determinate in both cases, what exactly is new about the idea of something as the limit of another?

It has to be said that the differences between these categories, or subcategories, of something are subtle. In fact McTaggart admits that "the subtlety of the distinctions at this point is so great that I must confess to having only a very vague idea of what is meant."[10] In my view, however, if we pay close attention to the way Hegel conceives each category, we can detect significant differences between them.

"Something" and "other," we recall, are defined as self-relating being, determinacy, or negation. Being "other" is more overtly negative than being "something," but both entail self-relation above all. That is why we think of something and its other as quite separate from one another.

Something comes to be thought as *determinate* when it is thought not just as something in general but as something-that-is-*not*-what-is-other. This occurs at the end of the analysis of the "other on its own account" (in the final paragraph of 2.B.a.1). What emerges here is the distinction between something's being-in-itself and its being-for-other. These two aspects of something render something determinate because they explicitly incorporate the *negation* of otherness into something. Something is for another—or in relation to another—to the extent that "it is essentially *one* with it and essentially *not one* with it." Equally, something's being-in-itself is the "*non-being* of being-for-other" (*SL* 119–20/1: 127–8 [215]).[11]

This is where the problem arises: how does this form of something's determinacy differ from that represented by the limit? The answer, I think, lies in the fact that insofar as something is split into being-in-itself and being-for-other, it is incipiently determinate but not fully determinate. Something is, indeed, determinate and negative, but not yet as thoroughly and overtly determinate as it is when it is limited.

The mark of the fact that something's determinacy is only beginning to emerge in being-in-itself and being-for-other is the fact that the moment of negation explicitly present in something is at the same time tempered, indeed partially concealed. Something, understood as it is in itself and for another, is conceived not merely as something in general but as the determinate negation of otherness. Yet that moment of negation in something is present in a curiously muted form: something is distinguished from, and so negates, its other insofar as it *relates* to its other and also *withdraws* from its other into *itself.*

Relating to and withdrawing from an other are both ways of *not*-being-the-

10. McTaggart, *A Commentary on Hegel's Logic*, p. 26.

11. In §92 of the *Encyclopedia Logic* Hegel appears to distinguish being-in-itself from determinacy suggesting that being-in-itself is not actually part of the determinacy of something. In §91, however, he equates being-in-itself with the "*being* of quality as such" and defines quality itself as "*affirmative* (*seiend*) determinacy" (translation revised). It is clear, therefore, that he does regard being-in-itself as part of the determinacy of something, although he also recognizes that it is rendered indeterminate if it is thought in complete abstraction from the thing's being-for-other. See *EL* 147–8/196–7.

other, but they are ways of not being the other that are actually *affirmative* rather than fully negative. As Hegel notes in 2.B.b.3, "being-for-other is the indeterminate, affirmative (*affirmative*) community of something with its other"; it consists, as it were, in reaching out to the other rather than shutting the other out (*SL* 126/1: 135 [225]). Similarly, although something's being-in-itself does shut out all that is other than the thing, it does so simply by withdrawing from the other into the thing's own self-relating being rather than by going out of its way to actively exclude the other. To draw an analogy with human behavior: something in itself turns its back on the other and looks only to itself; it does not seek out the other in order actively to push it away.

In being what it is in itself and for another, something is without doubt determinate and so *not* an other, but it is not the negation of the other in a thoroughly negative way. Its distinctive determinacy consists in positively *being* the something that *it* is rather than another; that is to say, it consists in possessing an intrinsic identity of its own and in relating to others in a distinctive manner. That determinacy does not consist in altogether *negating* the other and *excluding* the other from itself.

The limit, by contrast, makes something positively what it is *and* at the same time turns it into the utter negation of its other. What happens when something reveals itself to be limited is thus that the moment of negation in something's determinacy becomes fully apparent. Something in the limit no longer possesses mere being for another, but "the *non-being*-for-other becomes prominent, the qualitative negation of the other" (*SL* 126/136 [225]). Despite his diffidence about his own interpretive skills, McTaggart understands this point well. He also recognizes that through its limit something gains a "certain stability and exclusiveness."[12]

The logical development of the idea of something is thus the process whereby something proves to be not just positively what it is but positive *and* negative in equal measure. That development passes through the following stages: (1) In something as such, the moment of negation or determinacy is contained but is concealed because something is negation that is *not* just negation but rather *self-relating* negation. At this stage, something is an indeterminate something in general. (2) In something as it is in itself and for an other, the moment of negation or determinacy is made explicit: something is here conceived as being itself in *not* being an other and so is understood to be a determinate something. Yet that moment of negation lacks a thoroughly negative edge because something distinguishes itself from, and thereby "negates," its other by being positively *itself* and communicating in a positive way with its other rather than by excluding that other altogether. (3) In something with a limit, the moment of negation or determinacy becomes explicit as thoroughly *negative*. The limiting and limited something is thus both self-relating negation *and* at the

12. McTaggart, *A Commentary on Hegel's Logic*, p. 27. See also Hegel, *VLM* 88.

same time the simple negation and exclusion of its other. It is something as *fully* determinate.

The transition from stage 2 to stage 3 is made necessary, as we have seen, by the categories of determination and constitution. In its determination, something remains positively itself, though the difference between its being-in-itself and its being-for-other begins to collapse. In its constitution, by contrast, something is subject to change by an other. With this idea that something is changed by another (and changes it in turn), the relation between something and its other is itself transformed from one of predominantly positive communication and openness into one of *active negation*. This is because in bringing about change in an other something makes of that other precisely what it is *not* through itself.

Something conceived merely as relating to another is already the negation of that other in the sense that it differs from that other. Yet that negation, difference, and determinacy takes a peculiarly positive form: something differs from its other by being *open* to—or *for*—that other in a distinctive way. Once something is understood to induce changes in its other, however, that positive relation to the other takes on a much more overtly negative character. Something with a constitution is thus a properly *negative* something.

When the determination and constitution of the thing are shown to collapse into one another, the thing is revealed to be thoroughly negative at its very core since it proves to be subject to change by others in every aspect of its being and to change those others in turn through every aspect of its being. Something is thereby understood to be a positively self-relating something *as* the direct, untempered negation of its other. Now, insofar as something is the thorough negation of its other, it must differ completely from that other. That means that it must exclude the other totally from itself. That, in turn, means that the other must actually *cease* where something itself begins. Something must thus be the *limit* of the other. In this way, the moment of simple negation, latent in the very structure of something as the negation of negation, is finally brought out into the open, and something acquires complete determinacy in utter distinction (though also utter inseparability) from its other. As we are about to see, however, this determinacy is decidedly ambiguous.[13]

The Ambiguous Nature of the Limit

Something is subject to change through the agency of others; what it is in itself is not hermetically sealed off from the outside but is vulnerable to modification by other things. Insofar as something is fully determinate, however, it marks itself off from and thereby *delimits* the other that acts upon it. Hegel begins his

---

13. Taylor is thus right to point out that the difference between the "contrastive" and "interactive" senses of negation is "elided" in the category of limit. In contrast to Taylor, however, I see nothing illegitimate in this elision because Hegel demonstrates that in constitution difference itself becomes *active* negation. See Taylor, *Hegel*, p. 236.

detailed analysis of the logical structure of such limiting in 2.B.b.3.α. The limiting to which he refers here is first and foremost the limiting of the *other* to which every something relates. Every something excludes its other from itself and so is, as it were, where that other stops, where the other no longer is. Something's own being is thus "the *non-being* of the other" and in this sense is the other's limit (*SL* 126/1: 136 [227]).

Note that Hegel is here examining what it means for something to limit its other *qualitatively* rather than merely spatially. Something is its other's qualitative limit when its own defining quality—*what* it is—excludes the defining quality of the other however the two may be spatially related. In the *Encyclopedia Logic*, Hegel gives the following example of what he has in mind: "this piece of land is . . . a meadow and not a wood or a pond, and this is its qualitative limit" (*EL* 148/197 [§92 Add.]); Stace similarly points out that "the boundary lines between species and species are qualitative limits."[14] Of course, contrasting qualities may also be set beside one another in space: this meadow may lie next to that wood.[15] Nevertheless, what Hegel is concerned with at this point is not spatial limitation as such but the way in which something's being a meadow, as Mure phrases it, "stops it from being any other sort of land."[16]

Something, then, is through and through the limit of its other.[17] Yet, of course, the other is also something in turn and as such must limit the first something: if being a meadow stops something being a wood (at least as long as its quality is not changed), then being a wood equally stops something being a meadow. Insofar as something limits another, therefore, it is itself *limited* by that other thing. In other words, the other is where the first something stops, and so the other is the "*non-being of that something*."

Moreover, the first something is limited by its other in precisely the respect in which it limits that other itself. Although we are dealing with two somethings, there is, in Hegel's view, *one* limit that distinguishes and connects them. The limit at which the other stops and gives way to something is thus the very point at which that something itself stops and gives way to the other. It is the point at which *both* stop and so are equally limited. This does not mean that something ceases to limit the other. It means simply that, in limiting the other, something is itself limited and negated: the limit of A is *at one and the same time* the limit of B. Their shared limit is where each one ceases being what it is. As Hegel puts it, the limit is "not only non-being of the other, but non-being equally of the one and of the other something, consequently of the something as such" (*SL* 126/1: 136 [227]).

---

14. Stace, *The Philosophy of Hegel*, p. 143.

15. See Harris, *An Interpretation of the Logic of Hegel*, p. 103.

16. Mure, *A Study of Hegel's Logic*, p. 47. Theunissen, by contrast, believes that Hegel does conceive of the limit in spatial terms; see *Sein und Schein*, p. 269.

17. See Hegel, *EL* 148/197 (§92 Add.): "limit totally permeates everything that is there." See also Taylor, *Hegel*, p. 236, and Lakebrink, *Kommentar zu Hegels Logik*, p. 122.

Hegel immediately reminds us, however, that the limit is not just where something stops. It is also that by virtue of which something *is* what it is and not another thing. "It is true," he concedes, "that something, in limiting the other, is subjected to being limited itself." Nevertheless, he points out, "*through the limit something is what it is, and in the limit it has its quality*."

There is, therefore, an evident tension within the logical structure of something limited: for something *is* what it is only by means of a limit at which it *ceases* to be what it is. In other words, something *is* thanks to its own, as well as to the other's, *nonbeing*. The limit, as Hegel puts it, is thus "the mediation through which something and other each as well *is*, as *is not*." It is the point at which something stops and so is not what it is, *and yet* it is that through which something is what it is. If something were not bounded and so brought to a stop by another, it could never be a determinate something. In the *Encyclopedia Logic*, Hegel reminds us that this is true of human beings as well as natural objects:

> Humans who want to be actual (*wirklich*) must be *there* (*dasein*), and to this end they must limit themselves. Those who are too fastidious toward the finite achieve nothing real at all, but remain in the realm of the abstract and peter out (*EL* 148/197 [§92 Add.]).[18]

The necessity of being limited has been derived immanently from the logical structure of the determinate something. We have now learned, however, that something cannot actually *be* a determinate something at all unless it has a limit. This does not mean that Hegel's previous analysis of something must have tacitly presupposed the idea of limit all along. Hegel argues that the logical structure of something considered without reference to the idea of limit proves *by itself* that something must be limited. He first shows us that something must have being-in-itself, being-for-other, a determination, and a constitution, and he then shows—through a purely immanent analysis of something so understood—that, in truth, something has these features and is what it is only insofar as it is also *limited*. The fact that the limit, or *nonbeing*, of something is essential to its *being* is thus established by the complex determinate being of something itself.

Hegel tells us that the ambiguous relationship—described in 2.B.b.3.α—between something and its limit is the "outward manifestation" of the fact that the two actually have conflicting logical structures. We drew attention to this difference above (see pp. 358–9), but now Hegel himself refers to it explicitly. "The limit," he writes, "is simple negation or the *first* negation, whereas the other is, at the same time, the negation of the negation, the being-within-self of the something" (*SL* 126–7/136 [227]). Something can be determinate only insofar as it is the simple negation of its other. Yet, insofar as it is *something* (or other), it is double negation and so is *not* the simple negation that it is. This means in turn that insofar as it is the simple negation of its other, something stops being the something that it is and thus is limited. There is, therefore, a fundamen-

18. See Hegel, *VLM* 88.

tal *difference* between being "something" and being "determinate" and "limited," even though something proves necessarily to be a limited thing. Something is what it is by means of its limit, and yet at its limit it *ceases* to be what it is.

In 2.B.b.3.β Hegel looks more closely at the tangled relation between something and the limit. If the limit is where something ceases and so *is no longer*, then the *being* of something must actually lie this side of the limit itself. As Hegel words it, "something has its determinate being (*Dasein*) *outside* (or, as it is also put, on the *inside*) of its limit," and "the other, too, because it is a something, is outside it." The being and nonbeing of something thus "fall outside each other." This in turn means that the limit must be the midpoint *between* what each something *is*. "Limit," Hegel says, "is the *middle (Mitte) between* the two of them in which they cease." Indeed, he claims, the limit is other than both something and its other, which, as a result, "have their determinate being *beyond* each other and *beyond* their limit." Something is what it is *by means of* its limit, but *in itself* it lies on this (or that) side of the limit (*SL* 127/1: 137 [227]).

This important conclusion is made necessary by the logical structure of the limit itself: if the limit is the common point at which something and its other both *cease*, it must fall between what each of them *is* and so form a boundary between them. This boundary is qualitative rather than spatial: it is simply the point at which meadow and wood both stop being what they are. Such a boundary can, of course, also take a spatial form—there may actually be a physical border between meadow and wood—but it is the qualitative limit that Hegel has in mind here. The limit thus *detaches* itself logically from whatever something and its other are and shows itself to be other than the two spheres of being between which it falls. It is the qualitative boundary between them constituted by the ceasing or "the nonbeing" of each.

It is very important to recognize, however, that the limit is not a third "thing" in addition to something and its other. There are only two things in the relation we are considering, and the limit is simply the boundary that is common to both of them. As Burbidge notes, it is "the point of *transition* where one becomes the other" or the "mutual point of contact" that conjoins and disjoins them.[19] As such, the limit belongs to both something and its other, just as the line conjoining two squares belongs to both.

Yet, if this is the case, how can a limit or boundary be said to lie "between" two things? Strictly speaking, it cannot lie between two things since it forms an integral part of them, but it can be said to lie between what each of them *is*. In order to understand Hegel's claim at this point in the analysis, we must draw a distinction between, on the one hand, something and other as wholes and, on the other hand, what each of these things *is*, or the simple *Dasein* of each. The limit that separates two things from one another (and thereby connects them) does not fall outside or between those things taken as wholes but belongs inseparably to

19. Burbidge, *On Hegel's Logic*, p. 51, my emphasis.

them. At the same time, however, the limit is the point at which each thing stops being what it is, and as such, it must be distinguished from what each one *is* in itself. Consequently, the limit may be said to lie between the positive *being* (*Dasein*) or quality of one thing and the equivalent *being* of another, and the positive being of each thing may be said to lie on either side of that limit.

The limit is definitely not a third thing falling between something and its other but is simply the point of transition from one to the other—the point of logical (though not necessarily spatial) contact between them. Nevertheless, the limit is the point at which each thing stops—the *nonbeing* of each thing—that lies between what each one *is*. The two things *are* what they are, therefore, within—or on the other side of—their common boundary. Representational thinking, or *Vorstellung*, latches on to the idea that the limit falls between what each thing is but holds it to be altogether separate from those things themselves. Consequently, it turns the point of transition between them into an actual *thing*: it imagines that between two things there is always a line, a fence, or a hedge—an image that, of course, just raises the further problem of how to conceive of the limit between any two of these three things.[20] The limit cannot be such a third thing, however, because it is not *other* than something and its other *in the full sense* but is simply their common *negation,* or *Nichtsein*. The limit cannot, therefore, "other" itself into being something. It is merely the joint coming-to-a-stop or ceasing-to-be that lies between what each thing *is* but that equally forms an essential ingredient of each thing as a whole. It is the mutual boundary *through which* each one is what it is. Picture thinking ignores this fact by turning the limit into a third thing and so fails to see that logically the limit is a deeply contradictory structure.[21]

The contradiction at the heart of the limited thing is this: something is what it is within or this side of its limit, but without the limit something cannot *be* a distinct, determinate thing. Neither thing is what it is purely through its own being, therefore, but each needs to be limited and so to come to a stop in order to be a determinate thing at all. As Hegel puts it in his 1808 *Philosophical Encyclopedia*, something and its other

> are (1) distinct from the Limit or from their difference which is their middle (*Mitte*), outside of which they are something. But (2) the Limit belongs to them because it *is their limit*.[22]

---

20. See Rinaldi, *A History and Interpretation of the Logic of Hegel*, p. 151.

21. The only sense in which the limit of something might be said to be genuinely other than that something is insofar as it belongs to the *other* something by which the first something is limited—though in truth the limit belongs to both somethings equally.

22. G. W. F. Hegel, *The Philosophical Propaedeutic*, trans. A. V. Miller, eds. M. George and A. Vincent (Oxford: Blackwell, 1986), p. 128 (§20); G. W. F. Hegel, *Nürnberger und Heidelberger Schriften (1808–1817)*, ed. E. Moldenhauer and K. M. Michel, *Werke in zwanzig Bänden*, vol. 4 (Frankfurt am Main: Suhrkamp Verlag, 1970), p. 14.

Hegel alerts us to the intrinsic ambiguity of the limit right at the start of his account: the limit, he says, "manifests itself . . . as an entanglement and a contradiction (*Verwicklung und Widerspruch*)" (*SL* 126/1: 136 [225]). This contradiction is not just in our concept of the limit but in the very structure of *being* limited. On the one hand, the limit is the point between the being or *Dasein* of something and its other at which both cease. Insofar as the limit is the *nonbeing* of each, it does not belong to their being as such but falls between what each one is. What each is thus lies within, or on the other side of, their common boundary. On the other hand, the limit is nothing apart from the two things it conjoins and disjoins but belongs irreducibly to both of them. It is the common boundary at which each thing stops and through which each gains a definite identity.

Consequently—to put the point in its simplest form—the limit, which does *not* belong to the simple being of something, *does* belong to the thing's overall identity because it is the *nonbeing* of the thing through which alone the thing is what it is. A thing finds its identity and being, therefore, not just in being what it is but also in having a limit at which it stops being what it is—a limit at which its own being is brought to a halt and negated by that of another.

From Being Limited to Being Finite

The limit has proven to be a necessary moment of both something and its other and yet to be different from, and so not to belong to, their being as such. In the closing paragraphs on the limit (at 2.B.b.3.γ), Hegel examines the two characteristics of the limited something that necessarily follow from the analysis he has just carried out: the fact that something is what it is beyond or within its limit, and the fact that it has no determinate being without its limit.

What something is in itself lies within its boundary. Hegel points out, however, that something as it is within or beyond—and so *apart* from—its boundary is actually an "unlimited" something, or mere determinate being (*Dasein*) as such. It is not nothing, but it lacks the genuine determinacy that comes from being *limited* by another. Accordingly, it has no proper specificity and is not clearly distinguished from anything else. It is simply something or other as such, *just like any other thing*. The very respect in which something is purely what it is thus fails to confer on it an identity that is distinct from that of anything else. That is to say, the determinate being that something enjoys within its boundary fails by itself to make it properly *determinate*.[23]

But, of course, we have seen that something does not just lie within or beyond its boundary but is what it is *by virtue of* that boundary. Something is not just an indefinite, unlimited something, therefore, but is something *with* a definite limit. It is, as Hegel inelegantly puts it, "immediate determinate being . . . now posited with the determinateness as limit" (*SL* 127/1: 137 [227]). It is through this limit that something gains its specificity and is this rather than that.

23. See Burbidge, *On Hegel's Logic*, p. 51.

Hegel points out, however, that the limit does not actually distinguish and specify a thing as much as it first appears, either, because the limit is the *common* boundary between two things. It thus gives each thing the same logical form: that of being a *limited* something. Since the limit is equally the limit of the one and of the other, it turns each into the mirror image of the other and so effectively deprives each of its specificity.

If we revert to the idea that what each thing is actually lies *within* its boundary, we are immediately confronted once again by the fact that such inner being beyond the limit no more differentiates one thing from another than does its being limited. It appears, therefore, that we have reached an impasse. Only as limited is something determinate and definitely distinguished from another thing; as limited, it is what it is *within* its limit but also *through* its limit; either way, however, it proves to be the same as its other and so not to be a determinate, specific thing after all. The logical structure of being limited is thus contradictory for two reasons. On the one hand, something with a limit is what it is both within (or beyond) and through its limit. On the other hand, as we now recognize, being limited deprives something of the very determinacy it confers upon the thing. Something and its other prove to be no more clearly differentiated as limited than they are as mere "something" and "other."

Indeed, something and its other prove to be *identical*: within their limit they are both determinate being as such (or simply something), and through their limit they are both limited. Yet being determinate as such and being limited constitute two *different* ways in which something and its other are the same. Accordingly, Hegel refers to determinate being and the limit as the "double identity" of the two things involved. His point is not, as Miller's mistranslation suggests, that being determinate as such and being limited are themselves identical with one another but that each constitutes a different way in which something and its other are identical.[24] Indeed, it is vital to note that determinate being as such—the being that something and its other enjoy within their limit—and being limited are *not* identical themselves, but are "the negative (*das Negative*) of each other." The limit, after all, is the *negation* or *nonbeing* of both something and its other; it is the point at which their being ceases and so neither is what it is.

Since something and its other have now shown themselves to be identical, what commands our attention is no longer the relation between the two. The focus of attention switches rather to the relation that is equally constitutive of both of them: namely, that between their determinate being and their nonbeing or limit. This is not to say that something and its other now disappear from view.

24. Hegel writes: "diese doppelte Identität beider, das Dasein und die Grenze," not "diese doppelte Identität beider, des Daseins und der Grenze." This makes it clear that determinate being (*Dasein*) and the limit (*Grenze*) are each the identity of something and other, not that Hegel has in mind the identity *of* determinate being and the limit themselves. See Hegel, *SL* 127/1: 137 (226–7).

We are, however, led by the logical structure of their relation to one another—a relation in which each limits the other—to consider the relation between being and nonbeing that is the same in both of them. That is to say, our attention is now directed toward the contradictory logical structure that characterizes *every* limited thing.

As we recall, the principal contradiction at the heart of being limited is this: something's being lies within or beyond that limit, and yet something is what it is only *through* that limit. Hegel notes that this means that every limited thing actually "points beyond itself" in being what it is: for insofar as something is what it is only through its limit, what it is *apart* from that limit must point *beyond* itself to that very limit as the real core of the thing's being. This means, in turn, that the being that something enjoys this side of its limit logically entails its own *nonbeing* or *coming-to-an-end* and so necessarily negates itself. Self-transcendence and self-negation are therefore intrinsic features of any limited thing:

> something has its determinate being only in the limit, and . . . since the limit and the determinate being are each at the same time the negative of each other, the something, which *is* only in its limit, just as much separates itself from itself and points beyond itself to its non-being (*über sich hinaus auf sein Nichtsein weist*), declaring this is to be its being and thus passing over into it. (*SL* 127/1: 137 [229])

This quality of being what one is only in pointing and leading beyond one's being to one's own nonbeing is the quality of *finitude*. Finitude, for Hegel, is thus built into the very fabric of being. This is because being necessarily entails being something limited, and

> something, with its immanent limit, posited as the contradiction of itself, through which it is directed and forced out of and beyond itself, is the *finite* (*das Endliche*). (*SL* 129/1: 139 [229])

In the next chapter, we will examine more closely what finitude involves.

Chapter Twenty

Finitude: Limitation and the Ought

Being Limited and Being Finite

Hegel is certainly not the first philosopher to maintain that the world is made up of finite things. Yet he may well be one of the first to demonstrate *why* there is finitude without resorting explicitly to the theological notion of "creation." Like Spinoza, Hegel starts from what he deems to be most universal and then goes on to claim that this universal does not just subsist by itself but is immanent in particular, finite things. Hegel differs from Spinoza (at least initially, in the doctrine of being) by understanding things to be self-relating *being* rather than "modes" of self-grounding "substance." The more important difference between the two philosophers, however, is that Hegel actually *derives* the idea of finitude logically from what he takes to be most universal, whereas Spinoza does not.

Spinoza asserts in his *Ethics* that "from the necessity of the divine nature there must follow infinitely many things in infinitely many modes," but he never tells us why this should be.[1] Indeed, he does not explain why substance should have any attributes or modes at all; he simply assumes that it does (inheriting the idea from predecessors, such as Descartes) and asserts that finite modes must be caused by the nature of substance as well as by one another.

Hegel, on the other hand, explains why there should be finite things by showing in precise detail how pure being *determines itself* to be finitude. Finitude for Hegel is not just a given feature of things that we must take for granted; it is a quality of things that can be proven to be inherent in—and so derivable from—being as such (through the very same logical development that proves the category of finitude to be inherent in the nature of thought). Hegel thus demonstrates a priori what Spinoza simply presumes: namely, that being is not merely undifferentiated Parmenidean unity but a realm of particular, finite things.

In Hegel's view, things must be finite because they are determinate and, as such, bear within themselves the ineliminable moment of *negation*. Finitude, indeed, is simply "the development of this negation" or "qualitative negation pushed to its extreme" (*SL* 129/1: 139–40 [231]). Taylor is thus quite correct when he writes that for Hegel "the very determination which reality must have

1. *A Spinoza Reader,* p. 97 (Ethics I P16).

in order to be tends to annul it."[2] Hegel's argument, we recall, is this: something is determinate, not only by virtue of being what it is in itself and therein relating to another but also through definitively excluding and setting a limit to any other. In limiting its other, however, something is itself limited by that other; it is brought to a halt and negated by the very thing it excludes from itself. Something is determinate, therefore, only insofar as it *ceases* being what it is at some point, namely, wherever it differs qualitatively from (or is bounded spatially by) another. Being determinate certainly entails *being* a self-relating thing and so is not a purely negative quality. Hegel insists, however, that determinacy is at least partly negative because it entails *stopping* where another begins. Determinate being is being that comes to an end at some point and there meets its limit, and that limit in turn is simply the nonbeing of something that enables it definitely to be the thing it is.

For Hegel, then, "something only is what it is *in* its limit and *through* its limit" (*EL* 148/197 [§92 Add.]).[3] Since the limit is where something ends and is no longer, however, what that thing *is* must actually lie to this side of the limit itself. Something must have a being of its own *within* the boundary it shares with another thing. And yet, as we know, without that limit—*apart* from that limit—the thing is not a clearly defined determinate thing but simply determinate being, or something, as such: something is properly determinate only through its limit. The conclusion we must draw, therefore, is this: even though something does have a being of its own within its boundary, that being does not exhaust the thing's identity; a thing is not just what it is apart from whatever limits it, but it is determinate only as *limited*. What something is within its limit thus necessarily points beyond itself to that very limit as that which truly lets the thing *be* what it is. In other words, the core of a limited thing's being is not simply its being as such but passes over logically into its *nonbeing*. Logically, something is what it is, only insofar as it *stops* being what it is.

This is not just a judgment that we make about something. Hegel is not claiming merely that we first identify something with what it is within its limit and then correct that assessment as we become aware of the role played in constituting the thing by its limit. Hegel's claim is that what something is on this side of the limit *itself* points to the limit—to the thing's nonbeing—as the real core of its being. That is to say: logically, a thing's being negates itself. For Hegel, therefore, even though something is limited by another, its being actually passes over *of its own accord* into its nonbeing. Something meets its limit and its end *through itself*, and its own being thereby comes to be one with its ceasing-to-be and ending. It is this logical characteristic of the determinate, limited something that renders it *finite* because the finite is nothing but that which comes to an end simply through being what it is: *das Endliche*. We can now see

2. Taylor, *Hegel*, p. 238.

3. Translation revised.

why Hegel calls finitude "qualitative negation pushed to its extreme": finitude is simply the quality of ending that is implicit in the fact that something is rendered determinate by its *negation* (in all of its senses).

It is important to note that finitude is not just another name for being limited. Finitude is a quality inherent in being limited but logically distinct from it: it is not the quality of being negated by another but rather of passing over into nonbeing through simply being what one is, or of ceasing to be through one's own nature. Many commentators, however, overlook this difference and equate being finite with being limited. Stace, for example, maintains that "to be finite means to be limited *by something else*," and McTaggart writes that "the idea of a Limit is . . . the idea of Finitude, since they both mean that the limited thing has a nature of its own, and that its nature is in subjection to an Other."[4] This position is also held by Spinoza, who states in the *Ethics* that "that thing is said to be finite in its own kind that can be limited by another of the same nature."[5] Hegel, by contrast, makes it eminently clear that "finite things are not merely limited" (*SL* 129/1: 139 [231]). This is well recognized by Johnson, who writes that "finitude, for Hegel . . . means not only that a thing is limited, but that its being is just as much non-being[;] that is, it is, but equally, it is destined to pass out of existence."[6]

As I indicated above, the principal difference between being limited and being finite is that the former entails being brought to a halt or negated by something else, whereas the latter involves coming to an end through one's own being. Finite things can thus be said to *negate themselves*. As Hegel puts it, "finite things *are*, but their relation to themselves is that they are *negatively* self-related and in this very self-relation send themselves away beyond themselves, beyond their being" (*SL* 129/1: 139 [231]). Finitude for Hegel is not a relation between one thing and another; it is a relation between the being and the nonbeing of one and the same thing. Finitude—to appropriate Heidegger's term—is every thing's *own* being-towards-death.

Even though finitude is not reducible to being limited, Hegel believes it is implicit in the very nature of being limited. Every limited thing is finite, therefore, and every finite thing is limited. Indeed, the connection between being limited and being finite is intimate. As we saw in the last chapter, this is because the being that something limited enjoys this side of its limit *itself* passes over into that limit and so into its own nonbeing. There is also another way, however, to explain the connection between being limited and being finite. That is by reflecting on the logical process that gave rise to the necessity of the limit in the first place.

---

4. Stace, *The Philosophy of Hegel*, p. 143, and McTaggart, *A Commentary on Hegel's Logic*, p. 28. See also Mure, *A Study of Hegel's Logic*, p. 48.

5. *A Spinoza Reader*, p. 85 (*Ethics* I D2).

6. Johnson, *The Critique of Thought*, p. 25.

As we know, a thing is limited by *another* thing. It is limited by another, however, by virtue of what it is *in itself*. Remember that a thing is in contact with other things not simply because there are other things out there but because a thing's intrinsic being is itself other-related. Something is thus constituted or determined by another thing because its *own* nature renders it vulnerable to such constitution: "the determining from outside is at the same time determined by the something's own, immanent determination" (*SL* 125/1: 134 [223]). This means that something is limited by others because its very nature as a determinate thing is to be so limited; limits are not only imposed on something from the outside but are actually the thing's *own* limits. As Burbidge notes, "the *limit* is inherent in *a being*."[7]

The idea that something has its own limits is, however, ambiguous. On the one hand, it means that it lies in the thing's own nature to be brought to a stop by *another*; on the other hand, it means quite simply that it lies in a thing's *own* nature to come to an end. This latter quality of coming to an end by oneself through simply being what one is is the quality of being finite. Finitude is implicit in being limited, therefore, because being limited, and so coming to a stop, is itself part of a thing's ownmost being.

To repeat: things are intrinsically and necessarily limited by other things, but at the same time they bring themselves to a limit or end that is their very *own*—an end that has its source in their own being, regardless of the way they may be affected by other things. This is the ineliminable finitude of things.

Now, to say that a finite thing ceases to be through its own being is not to deny that finite things do stand in relation to other things and that they can be changed in their innermost being by the others to which they relate. Nor is it to deny that such externally induced change can go so far as to destroy the thing altogether. Hegel's point, however, is that a thing is vulnerable to such external change and destruction by virtue of having a *constitution* rather than by virtue of being *finite*. The fact that a something is other-related is what exposes it to dangers from the outside; by contrast, the fact that the thing is finite exposes it to internal decay and consigns it to a death that is properly its own. The finitude and other-relatedness of something can, of course, work together to destroy the thing: a thing's internal structure and organization can breakdown autonomously, and at the same time, it can be crushed by something outside it (think, for example, of the Roman Empire). Indeed, a thing's *own* finitude can itself include increased vulnerability to *external* destructive forces. It is important to recognize, however, that for Hegel finitude is the being-toward-death that a thing bears within itself and that a finite thing will come to an end even if externally-induced changes are not great enough by themselves to destroy it.

By the way, the difference between being limited and being finite is not, as

7. Burbidge, *On Hegel's Logic*, p. 52.

Theunissen contends, that limits are spatial whereas finitude is temporal.[8] As we have seen, the limit that Hegel has been discussing so far is qualitative, rather than spatial: it is the boundary between this quality in one thing and that quality in another, whatever may be their spatial relation to one another (though, to be sure, such a limit can be a spatial one, too). It is also evident that finitude, as Hegel conceives it, is not grounded specifically in the temporality of things. Being has not yet proven itself to involve time and will not do so until we reach the philosophy of nature. Finitude is made necessary, therefore, not by temporality but by the *logical* structure of something—the fact that a determinate thing's being necessarily passes over into its nonbeing. As Taylor rightly points out, Hegel "wants to show from *conceptual necessity* what we know from experience . . . , viz., that all things not only can in principle but do effectively pass away."[9]

There is no doubt that being limited and being finite provide the logical foundation for—and in that sense prefigure—being spatial and temporal. At this point, however, they are not conceived in explicitly spatio-temporal terms. The difference between being limited and being finite is a purely logical one: being limited entails being negated by another, whereas being finite entails negating oneself or coming to an end on one's own. It is far from clear at this point in Hegel's philosophy why being limited spatially would mean that something only exists for a limited period of time (though Hegel does explain this connection in the *Philosophy of Nature*). It is eminently clear, however, why being limited by another logically entails bringing oneself to an end: anything that is limited by another necessarily has a limit of its *own*.

Finitude, or bringing oneself to an end, is the *tragic* quality at the heart of all being. "In tragedy," Hegel argues in the *Aesthetics*, "the individuals destroy themselves through the one-sidedness of their otherwise solid will and character" and so suffer "self-prepared destruction" (*ein selbstbereitetes Verderben*).[10] A tragic fate is one that we bring about through our own action, not one that is simply inflicted on us by others. It is true that Hegel believes we may be able to avoid the specific fate of Antigone or Macbeth by taking a broader view of our position in life and so overcoming our "one-sidedness." It is also clear, however, that for Hegel tragedy is unavoidable at a deeper level: for however broad-minded or virtuous one may be, every finite thing ultimately consigns *itself* to death or destruction simply by being what it is. In *Waiting for Godot*, Beckett has Pozzo exclaim with acerbity to Vladimir: "one day we were born, one day we'll die, the same day, the same second. . . . They give birth astride of a grave, the light gleams an instant, then it's night once more."[11] Hegel's view of the in-

8. Theunissen, *Sein und Schein*, p. 269.

9. Taylor, *Hegel*, p. 237, my emphasis.

10. Hegel, *A* 2: 1199, 1: 579/3: 527, 2: 202. See also Houlgate, *Hegel, Nietzsche, and the Criticism of Metaphysics*, p. 209.

11. S. Beckett, *En attendant Godot* (Paris: Les Éditions de Minuit, 1952), p.126. Translation taken from A. Alvarez, *Beckett* (London: Fontana/Collins, 1973), p. 87.

nate mortality of things—though reached through purely rational speculation—is no less sobering:

> the being as such of finite things is to have the germ of decease as their being-within-self: the hour of their birth is the hour of their death. (*SL* 129/1: 140 [231])[12]

The idea that everything is born to die—and to die, as it were, by its own hand—is one that clearly separates Hegel from Spinoza, whom he otherwise resembles so closely. Spinoza does not deny that finite modes are vulnerable to destruction. He argues, however, that all such destruction is wrought upon things by *other*, more powerful things. There is nothing intrinsic in things themselves that would destroy them: things are not consigned to nonbeing by their very own being. External interference is the sole source of death:

> For the definition of any thing affirms, and does not deny, the thing's essence, *or* it posits the thing's essence, and does not take it away. So while we attend only to the thing itself, and not to external causes, we shall not be able to find anything in it which can destroy it.[13]

In this respect, as I noted in chapter 2, Spinoza remains a pupil of Parmenides, for whom being is sheer *being* without any immanent principle of self-negation (see *SL* 83–4/1: 84–5). Spinoza may well accept that determinate being—including being limited and being finite—entails negation or, as Hegel famously insists, that "*omnis determinatio est negatio*" (*SL* 113/1: 121). He believes, however, that all such negation has its source in the presence and action (i.e., the greater power) of other things, never in the things themselves.[14] In Hegel's view, by contrast, negation—and finitude—is woven into the very fabric of a thing's being.

Finitude and Self-Negation

Negation, in Hegel's view, is present in something right from the start. It is, however, concealed in the logical structure of something as such and only becomes apparent when something proves to be explicitly determinate. Something as such, we recall, is defined by Hegel as *self-relating* being or negation; it is determinate being or negation that is *not* just that because it relates positively to itself and so constitutes a realm of being of its own. Insofar as something is not mere negation, its negative character is immersed in and covered over by its quality of relating-to-itself.

As we have seen, however, something proves not just to be self-relating being but also to be an explicitly *determinate* something. This determinacy con-

---

12. See also Hegel, *EL* 149/198 (§92 Add.): "The living die, and they do so simply because, insofar as they live, they bear the germ of death within themselves."

13. *A Spinoza Reader*, p. 159 (*Ethics* III P4).

14. See *A Spinoza Reader*, pp. 88, 214 (*Ethics* I P8 Schol. 1, IV P32 Dem., Schol.), and Harris, *An Interpretation of the Logic of Hegel*, pp. 105, 122 (note 21).

sists in not being—and so limiting—another, but also in being limited in turn by that other. The determinacy of something thus requires that something have a clear limit at which it *stops* being what it is. This means that a determinate something is one that is overtly *negative*, as well as positively self-relating. Specifically, it is negative with respect to an *other*, which it negates and by which it is itself negated. In the limited thing, therefore, the moment of negation, which is immersed in the structure of something, comes out into the open. The self-relating—and thus double—negation that every something is proves to be at the same time the simple negation of, and being-negated-by, an other thing.

We have seen, however, that implicit in the very quality of being limited by another is the quality of coming to an end by oneself. That is to say, implicit in the structure of being negated by another is the quality of *negating oneself* and thereby being finite. In the finite thing, therefore, being determinate entails not only relating to other things in various ways but also being limited in one's own right by one's own being; it means being destined to end purely by being the *something* that one is. In proving itself to be finite, something in its very self-relation proves itself to be *self-negating* being.

Such self-negation may be said to be implicit in something from the outset since something as such is the negation of negation, or negation that is *not* just negation after all. Yet, initially, as we know, something does not actually and explicitly negate *itself.* On the contrary, it is the negation$_2$ of negation$_1$, and it is this only because it is positively self-relating being.[15] At the start, then, the moment of self-negation is merely *implicit* in something and is hidden by the positive self-relation of the thing. The finite thing, by contrast, is explicitly self-negating. In proving itself to be finite, therefore, something is showing itself to be explicitly what it is implicitly. It is taking on a new character, but it is also revealing more fully its inherent nature. As Theunissen puts it, "the concept of finitude expresses the *truth* about determinate being," namely, that it is intrinsically self-negating.[16]

It is true that something also proved to be overtly self-negating when it showed itself to be the process of change. Indeed, Hegel refers to the changing thing explicitly as *das sich Negierende* (*SL* 118/1: 127 [212]).[17] In changing, however, something merely negates or "others" itself into another form of itself and so continues in being. It does not negate its being as such and pass over into definitive nonbeing. In that sense, its activity of self-negation is tempered: in retrospect, it does not *thoroughly* negate what it is. The finite thing, by contrast, is thoroughly self-negating, for it destroys its own being completely. Only as finite, therefore, does something fully reveal its negative character.

Note that, in revealing itself to be finite and self-undermining, something

15. See chapter 17, above, p. 329.

16. Theunissen, *Sein und Schein*, p. 267, my emphasis.

17. See chapter 17, above, p. 329.

does not lose its original character. It remains something positive; indeed, it cannot come to an end—and so be finite—unless it *is* something to begin with. Furthermore, a finite something continues to be irreducible to simple determinacy and simple negation. As *something*, it is not just determinate and negative but is *self-relating* being, and as *finite*, it is not just a determinate, negative something either but is a *self-negating* thing. Finitude, after all, is different from, and irreducible to, being limited by and being determinate with respect to another. The finite something thus remains a self-relating thing; now, however, its relation to itself is both positive *and* negative at once: "finite things *are*, but their relation to themselves is that they are *negatively* self-related" (*SL* 129/1: 139 [231]).

At this point we must make sure that we do not get ahead of ourselves. Note that the finite thing is something that explicitly negates its own *being*: in being what it is, the finite thing comes to an end. It is clear, however, that finitude does not render explicit all that is implicit in something. In particular, it does not entail the idea that something is the explicit *negation* of the very *negation* it is. This will come to the fore later in the *Logic*. In the doctrine of essence, for example, being shows itself, in Hegel's words, to be "negation with the negation" or "the movement of nothing to nothing" or what he calls *Reflexion* (*SL* 399–400/2: 24). By that point in the analysis, being will be understood to be sheer and utter negativity and to consist simply in *not-being-negative*.

The idea of change did not take us quite that far. The changing thing is, indeed, the negation of the very negation it is but only insofar as it is the *other* of the *other* that it is. It turns out to consist, therefore, in being-other-than-purely-other rather than just *not*-being-merely-*negative*. Nor does the finitude of something take us as far as utter negativity—or, at least, it has not yet done so.[18] What has so far become apparent in the finite thing is not that something is the fully explicit negation of *negation* but simply that it is thorough *self*-negation as such. In negating itself, as we have seen, the finite thing negates its own *being* as a thing; indeed, its being negates itself and passes away. Such finitude is not, however, all that is implicit in something. There is more to be revealed including the sheer negativity or reflexivity inherent in things (and the identity or rationality [*Begriff*] that is constituted by such negativity). This will emerge, however, only when we work through what is entailed by simply negating oneself as such—that is, by negating one's own being.

The Contradictory Character of Finitude

To repeat: the finite thing is something, or the negation of negation, not as the explicit negation of *negation* but as the explicit negation of its own *being*. Here lies the basic contradiction at the core of all finitude—the real contradiction that every finite thing itself *is*. Paul Guyer maintains that the contradiction within fi-

---

18. For an account of the way in which finitude begins later to exhibit sheer negativity, see chapter 20, pp. 389–90 (including note 33), and chapter 21, below, pp. 394–5.

nite things is between their purported independence as discrete things and their actual, intrinsic interrelatedness.[19] To conceive of the contradictoriness of the finite in this way, however, is to ignore the fact that finitude is a relation to oneself rather than to other things. Hegel writes that the finite something is "the contradiction of itself, through which it is directed and forced out of and beyond itself" (*SL* 129/1: 139 [229]). By this he does not mean that it is cast out of its self-enclosed independence into relation with others—that has already taken place in the analysis of being-for-other, constitution, and limit—but that a thing's *own* being points beyond itself to, and passes over into, its *own* nonbeing.

In the second of the opening paragraphs of 2.B.c, in the course of contrasting being limited with being finite, Hegel presents this contradiction in a particularly sharp form. Insofar as things are limited, he writes, "they still have determinate being outside their limit" (albeit one that does not exhaust what they are). Insofar as things are finite, however, they have no such being apart from their limit or nonbeing but "non-being constitutes their nature and being" (*SL* 129/1: 139 [231]). The very core of their being is *nonbeing*. Yet this sharply contradictory way of defining finitude actually risks misleading readers of the *Logic*. After all, finitude is not sheer and utter nonbeing but a way of *being* that leads to its own nonbeing. A finite thing's being is not simply reducible to nonbeing but remains different from it. This is why Hegel says that finitude "has gone back to the abstract *opposition* of nothing and ceasing-to-be as opposed to being" (*SL* 129/1: 140 [231], my emphasis). Yet Hegel also claims that the being of the finite thing is absolutely *inseparable* from nonbeing.

This difference between, and inseparability of, being and nonbeing in the finite something is captured in the idea that finite things in their being necessarily *pass over into* nonbeing. This is the real contradiction in finite things: "they *are*, but the truth of this being is their *end*." As we have seen, such finitude is immanent in being limited: for the very being that lies *within* the limit points *beyond* itself to its nonbeing and so brings itself to its limit and its end. Finitude as a logical structure is not the same as being limited, but the finite thing is simply the limited thing viewed from a subtly different point of view.

Hegel insists that the process of coming to an end is not a contingent feature of a finite thing that it may or may not exhibit depending on the circumstances: "its ceasing to be is not merely a possibility, so that it could be without ceasing to be." On the contrary, finite things necessarily come to an end because of what they are. Indeed, the being of finite things is nothing but this ceasing to be and passing over into nonbeing: what they are *is* the process of ending. This is because finite being is intrinsically self-negating being: it negates itself simply through being what it is. It is thus being that *consists* in bringing itself to its own limit and end. Overall, of course, there is more to things than just this ceasing-to-be; things have an intrinsic character, relate to others in various ways, and as

19. Guyer, "Hegel, Leibniz und der Widerspruch des Endlichen," p. 258.

we learn later in the *Logic* and in the *Philosophy of Nature*, have a specific physical, chemical, or organic makeup. Insofar as they are *finite*, however, they are nothing other than their own ceasing to be.

In finitude, we thus encounter once again the logical character of *becoming* (*Werden*)—only with this twofold difference. In pure becoming, there is not yet *something* that becomes, and the process of becoming is two-way: from being to nothing and back again. Being finite, by contrast, is a quality of, or process exhibited by, something, and it is a resolutely one-way process: namely, the passing of something's being into nonbeing, or something's coming to an *end*. As Hegel puts it, "the finite . . . is itself this, to be determined or destined to its end, but *only* to its end" (*SL* 130/1: 140 [231]). Being finite is hereby also explicitly differentiated from merely being subject to change. Hegel reminds us that change (or "othering") and other forms of negation, such as being related to, constituted by, and limited by other things, are compatible with the continuing being of something: "negation in general, constitution and limit, reconcile themselves with their other, with determinate being (*Dasein*)." Something can thus change within itself or be reconstituted by another thing and remain in being. Being finite, on the other hand, is ultimately incompatible with remaining in being because it leads to the definitive *end* of the thing concerned. The finite thing, as Hegel puts it, "is posited as inseparable from its nothing, and is thereby cut off from all reconciliation with its other, the affirmative." For this reason, Hegel writes that "negation [is] *fixed in itself*, and it therefore stands in abrupt contrast to its affirmative." This does not mean that finitude is a quality that somehow lies outside the thing it affects. It means that the finitude inherent in things is *opposed* to their being insofar as it puts an end to that being.

Finitude, then, is absolutely at odds with a thing's being. It is important to remember, however, that it is also one with that very being itself: insofar as something is finite, its being consists in nothing but passing away and ending. As Theunissen points out, therefore, finite things do not just end up coming to an end but begin to end "from the very start."[20] Johnson also puts the point well: "finite things *are*, only in so far as they will one day cease to be, and they begin to pass away at the same time as they come into being."[21] Finite things, for Hegel, as for Beckett's Pozzo, are born "astride of a grave." They are inherently contradictory, because their innermost being and determination is actually *not* to be: "the determination or destiny (*Bestimmung*) of finite things takes them no further than their *end*" (*SL* 130/1: 140 [231]).

Finitude and the Understanding

Hegel clearly takes finitude very seriously. He does not regard it as a figment of our imagination, nor does he hold that it is immediately "absorbed" wherever it

20. Theunissen, *Sein und Schein*, p. 269.
21. Johnson, *The Critique of Thought*, p. 25.

is found into some all-embracing and all-consuming absolute. According to Hegel, being proves to be a realm of irreducibly finite things, and he makes no attempt to conceal the "sadness" (*Trauer*) that this thought is bound to elicit in us. Having said this, Hegel does not regard being as constituting a world of *pure* finitude. As we shall see in the next chapter, he believes that finite things constitute an *infinite* process of being. Such infinity is nothing apart from finitude, however, and is generated by the irreducible finitude and passing away of things itself. Hegel proves to be a philosopher of the infinite *because* he is a philosopher of the finite, not in spite of that fact. To take finitude seriously, therefore, is not to cling on to it in its purity but to let it show itself to be more than it is. From Hegel's perspective, those who insist that finitude is a realm of transitoriness and perishing *and no more than this* do not actually take finitude seriously enough, for they do not render explicit all that finitude itself entails. Such people are firmly wedded to the "understanding" (*Verstand*) rather than being followers of presuppositionless thought or reason.

Understanding, we recall, holds that each category and way of being is purely what it is and should not be confused with its opposite (see *EL* 125/169 [§80]). It insists that finitude is finitude, not infinity, and that reality is reality, not negation. As we saw in chapter 3, such understanding actually plays an important role in presuppositionless philosophy itself by bringing to mind what is specific to each new category. Indeed, presuppositionless thought begins with an act of abstraction by the understanding wherein it suspends its assumptions about concepts and the world and focuses on the category of pure being. Such understanding, however, is no more than a *moment* within radically self-critical thought that proves to be not just understanding but also dialectical and speculative reason. What Hegel considers at this point in his discussion of finitude is understanding that stands apart *by itself*—understanding that sets itself up as the highest instance of thought.

Hegel writes that the category of "finitude" is "the most stubborn category of the understanding." This is not merely because the understanding clings to it most resolutely but because more than any other category we have encountered so far it actually *invites* the understanding to cling to it in its purity. The logical structure of being finite will itself eventually mutate into that of infinity; first and foremost, however, the finite invites thought to resist any such move and to conceive of the finite as purely finite. Why should it do this? Because the finite does no more than come to an end. It is not reborn after its demise but is lost forever once it has ceased to be; it is, and then it is no more. Built into the finite is thus what Hegel calls "the refusal (*Verweigern*) to let itself be brought affirmatively to its affirmative, to the infinite, and to let itself be united with it" (*SL* 130/1: 140 [231]). This is not to say that finite things have any choice in the matter but that their very being *insists*—like some inverted Spinozan *conatus*—on coming to an irreversible close. Finite things do not let themselves be renewed or revived once they have passed away.

This conception of finitude is, by the way, quite compatible with Hegel's Christian faith. For Hegel—as for the theologian, Eberhard Jüngel—the heart of Christianity is the belief that we can be "reborn" in this life through a loving acceptance of our frailty and mortality; it is not the hope that conscious life as we know it will continue after we have died.[22]

For Hegel, then, the understanding is right to conceive of the finite as the process of simply *ending* since the finite encourages the understanding to conceive of it in this way. What the understanding by itself fails to comprehend, however, is this: just because finite things are irreducibly finite and do nothing but come to an end, this does not mean that they do not participate in any way in infinity. That which is purely finite and nothing more is not for that reason opposed to the infinite. On the contrary, as we will see, being *purely* finite is precisely what makes the finite give rise to, or pass over into, infinity. This dialectic is lost on the understanding. For the understanding, if X is purely and simply X and nothing more, then that is all that X is. It is utterly absurd to claim as Hegel does that, because X is purely and simply X, it is also non-X or Y. Yet we have seen throughout the *Logic* so far that such a dialectic lies at the heart of being: being is nothing precisely because it is pure being, and something is other than itself because it is something. The same will turn out to be true of the finite: the finite will lead to and participate in the infinite precisely because it is purely finite and *nothing more*.

For Hegel, therefore, the understanding goes wrong not in insisting that the finite is purely finite but in holding on to this thought to the exclusion of its opposite. Yet let us not be too hasty. At this stage in the *Logic*, are we actually justified in criticizing the understanding for clinging to the thought of pure finitude? After all, we have not actually demonstrated that pure finitude does lead to the infinite, and there is as yet no compelling reason to believe that it will. Later, we may well be justified in criticizing the understanding for failing to appreciate how finitude gives way to infinity, but strictly speaking, we should not raise that criticism at this point since we cannot fault the understanding for neglecting to anticipate a logical move that remains to be demonstrated. So do we have any grounds *now* for faulting the understanding? Hegel believes that we do.

The understanding can be criticized even at this point, in Hegel's view, because it actually *fails* to think what it claims to think, namely, the process of sheer passing away. It fails in this regard because, precisely by clinging on to pure and simple passing away, it turns it into something *enduring* and *eternal*—that is, into that which is not just pure passing away after all. The understanding, as I have noted, is not wrong to formulate the thought of pure finitude in the first place; it goes wrong, however, because it "persists (*verharrt*) in this sadness of finitude by making non-being the determination of things and at the same time making it

22. See Houlgate, *An Introduction to Hegel,* pp. 265–6, and E. Jüngel, *Tod* (Gütersloh: Gütersloher Verlagshaus Mohn, 1979), pp. 150–2, 160.

imperishable and *absolute*" (*SL* 130/1: 140 [231]). The understanding is open to criticism, therefore, because it violates its own conception of finitude, regardless of the way Hegel may conceive of it now or later. This is not, of course, to maintain that the understanding ends up regarding individual finite things as eternal. It is, however, to assert that the understanding fails to think of finitude as such as involving nothing except ceasing to be and passing away, as soon as it insists that finitude *remains* nothing but such ceasing to be.

Another way of putting the point is to say that the understanding renders pure finitude absolutely limitless, or *infinite*. Presuppositionless philosophy introduces the thought of finitude without any prior reference to infinity; something proves to be finite not because it falls short of the infinite (which has not yet been derived) but simply because it has its own intrinsic limit. By contrast, the understanding that sets itself up as the highest authority opposes finitude to infinity from the outset: the finite is that which is *not* absolute and unending. As soon as it is set in absolute opposition to the infinite, however, the finite in Hegel's view is made to share in the very infinity or "absoluteness" that it is meant to exclude and so is no longer utterly opposed to the infinite after all.

> Being, absolute being, is ascribed to the infinite; confronting it, the finite thus remains held fast as its negative; incapable of union with the infinite, it remains *absolute* on its own side. (*SL* 130/1: 141 [233], my emphasis)

As Theunissen puts it, the understanding "absolutizes" (*verabsolutiert*) the finite in the very act of trying to preserve its sheer and utter finitude.[23]

The reason why Hegel criticizes the understanding at this point in the text is thus not because it thinks of the finite as purely finite rather than as passing over into the infinite. Hegel criticizes the understanding here because it actually fails to think of the finite as truly *finite* at all: from the start, it insists that the finite is *always* the process of ceasing to be and so turns it into that which is not purely finite after all but also infinite and unending.[24] Hegel's own strategy, by contrast, is to avoid assuming *either* that the finite persists as finite unendingly *or* that the finite leads logically to the infinite and simply to think finitude as such, letting it unfold its own logical implications, whatever they may be. As we shall see later, finitude does mutate logically into infinity. It does not do so, however, because the infinite is presupposed as the horizon in relation to which finitude must be thought or because the understanding artificially "infinitizes" the finite. Finitude turns into infinity, in Hegel's view, of its own accord: because it is *sheer* ceasing to be and as such must even *cease* being the very ceasing-to-be that it is and so prove to be unending, infinite being (*das Unendliche*).

Both the understanding and presuppositionless thought, or reason, conceive

---

23. Theunissen, *Sein und Schein*, p. 270.

24. See Theunissen, *Sein und Schein*, p. 274.

of finitude as constitutive of infinity. Understanding does so, however, because it clings—willfully—to finitude as that which persists absolutely. Presuppositionless thought, on the other hand, is more open-minded: it simply attends closely to the logical structure of finitude and *lets* it be the sheer ceasing that it is. Accordingly, such thought even lets finitude *cease* being sheer ceasing-to-be and thereby become infinite being. The difference between an abstract conception of the finite (favored by the understanding) and a presuppositionless, rational conception thus depends on "whether in thinking of the finite one holds fast to the *being* of finitude and the *transitoriness* continues to be, or whether the *transitoriness* and the *ceasing-to-be cease to be*" (*SL* 130/1: 141 [233]).[25] Hegel's wording here inevitably reminds us of his analysis of pure becoming: just as becoming can be pure becoming only by coming to be determinate being, so finitude can be pure and simple finitude, or ceasing-to-be, only by turning logically into infinity. In the next chapter we will consider precisely how and why this logical transition takes place. Before that, however, we must look more closely at the internal logical structure of finitude itself.

Limitation and the Ought

In 2.B.c.β Hegel reminds us that a finite thing is not just something that passes away but something that also has a determination, constitution, and limit. McTaggart asserts that it is actually quite "useless" to draw such fine distinctions between the various aspects of something because nothing new is learned thereby: the idea of "constitution" for him is no different from that of "something and other," and "Limit is identical with finitude."[26] In Hegel's view, however, it is essential to draw such distinctions if we are to tease out all the intricate implications of being "something." Furthermore, only if we pay careful attention to the subtle ways in which the relation between a thing's intrinsic nature (or *Ansichsein*) and its other-relatedness (or *Sein-für-Anderes*) changes as we turn from its determination and constitution to its limit can we understand the complex internal structure of a finite thing. This becomes apparent in the dense opening lines of the second paragraph of 2.B.c.β.

The first thing to remember as we read this paragraph is that the determination (*Bestimmung*) of something is the thing's intrinsic nature in relation to *other* things. The fact that something has a determination thus brings other-relatedness into the thing's ownmost being. As Hegel himself puts it, the determination of something "already contained otherness as belonging to the something's *in-itself*" (*SL* 131/1: 142 [233]). We must also remember, however, that, in addition to its determination, something has a constitution that is not under its control but is vulnerable to alteration by the other things to which it relates.

25. Translation revised.

26. McTaggart, *A Commentary on Hegel's Logic*, p. 28. McTaggart himself translates *Beschaffenheit* as "modification," rather than "constitution."

There is a difference, therefore, between the other-relatedness of a thing that is rooted in and determined by the thing's ownmost being and that which is at the mercy of those things that surround it. This difference is what Hegel alludes to—somewhat obliquely, it has to be said—in the following sentence: "the externality of the otherness is on the one hand in the something's own inwardness, on the other hand it remains, as externality, distinguished from it, it is still externality as such, but present *in* the something (*an dem Etwas*)."

Yet Hegel goes on to show that there is no *absolute* distinction between a thing's determination and its constitution. This is because, on the one hand, that determination can itself be transformed through the agency of other things, and on the other hand, the thing acquires a new intrinsic identity and determination precisely by being reconstituted in this way. The logical consequence of this "collapse" of determination and constitution into one another is that each thing proves to be open to being reconstituted and negated by *others* in its *ownmost* being. As we have seen, this in turn leads immediately to the thought that each thing in every aspect of its being is *limited* by another in some way.

It is important to recognize that something must be limited by another because its determination and constitution are inextricably fused together and in this way the quality of being negated by—and of negating—another is brought into the very heart of the thing. This, I take it, is what Hegel means when he writes that, "since the otherness is determined as *limit*, . . . the otherness immanent in the something is posited as the connection of the two sides." The "two sides" that are connected in the limited thing are not only its determination and constitution but also its determination and its *limit* itself. The limit, after all, is not merely a contingent feature of something, or an optional extra without which it could perfectly well be what it is. The limit belongs to the thing *itself*, indeed, to what the thing is *in itself*: something is intrinsically and necessarily limited by another. Furthermore, when the limited thing is recognized to be finite, it is understood not only to be limited by something else but also to have a limit that is wholly its *own* (see p. 373, above). The limit is thus wholly immanent in the finite thing; it belongs completely to the thing's own *determination*. That is to say, the finite thing is limited both *in* itself and *by* itself and is destined to reveal that intrinsic limit in its relations with others.

Yet, we must not forget that the intrinsic limit of something is a limit *on* the thing's ownmost being; as we saw in the last chapter, the limit is the point at which something ceases being what it is in itself. The limit that is immanent in the finite thing is, therefore, profoundly contradictory. It is the moment of nonbeing that forms an integral part of a thing's ownmost being; yet at the same time, it is directly at odds with, and negates, the thing's being and determination.

Now, insofar as the limit is at odds with a thing's intrinsic being, that being is in turn at odds with, and negates, its own limit. After all, something has an intrinsic being of its own that does *not* consist in mere nonbeing or in merely being limited. The finite something with an immanent limit is thus one in which its

being and *nonbeing* are in unavoidable tension with one another. Even though it is intrinsically consigned to nonbeing, its determination and ownmost nature consist not just in nonbeing but precisely in *being what it is*; the finite thing is meant both not to be *and* to be, and it is pulled in these two conflicting directions by the one and the same inner nature. Hegel presents the tension at the heart of the finite thing as follows:

> the unity with itself of the something . . . is its relation turned towards its own self, the relation of its *intrinsic* (*an sich seiend*) determination to the limit immanent in the something, a relation in which this immanent limit is negated (*SL* 131/1: 142 [235]).[27]

Hegel notes that the finite thing hereby reveals itself to be self-negating in a new sense: for not only does it negate its own being and cease to be, but its intrinsic being or determination also works against, and so negates, its own limit and ceasing-to-be:

> the self-identical being-within-self thus relates itself to itself as [to] its own non-being, but as negation of the negation, as negating the non-being which at the same time retains in it determinate being.

When a limit is understood to be intrinsic to something, and to be a limit *on* the thing's very being, and to be resisted by the thing itself, it is understood to be that thing's *limitation* (*Schranke*). The finite thing's limitation is not the limit imposed on it by something else but that aspect of the thing's *own* character that actually prevents it from being what it intrinsically is and, ultimately, stops it being what it is at all.

Every finite thing, in Hegel's view, bears its limitation within itself. It is important to note, however, that limitations are not simply *found* in things, like other qualities; rather, a thing's own determination sets up, or "posits," its inherent limit *as* its limitation. The reason why this should be is obvious: it is only because a thing's determination entails *being* what it is that any limit or nonbeing is turned into that which *restricts* it and *prevents* it from fulfilling its determination. By itself the thing's own limit simply marks the point at which it ends. That end point is, however, transmuted into a hindrance—or, indeed, a threat—to the thing by the thing's intrinsic insistence on being what it is. In other words, the thing itself posits its inherent limit as the negation of its own determination, and so as a *limitation* on it. In so doing, we should note, the thing's own determination distinguishes itself from that limitation and so negates it in turn.

Hegel now points out that this act of negation on the part of the thing is actually "two-edged" (*zweischneidig*): for it not only turns the limit into a negative but also turns the determination itself into a negative, namely into the *negation of the limit*. In distancing itself from its limitation, therefore, the thing's deter-

27. Translation revised.

mination, or being-in-itself, comes to be defined—and so bounded—by that very limitation itself. This brings about a significant change in the determination of the thing.

As such, the determination of something is what the thing is in itself as it manifests itself in its relations to others; it is the positive quality of the thing or what the thing itself *is*. Insofar as the thing is finite, as we have seen, this determination turns out to have its own limit; the determination remains something positive, but its own ceasing to be is now built into it. What we have now discovered, however, is that the determination of something does not just harbor its own limit within itself and does not just suffer being brought to an end by that limit but asserts itself *against* that limit. It is this assertion of itself that logically turns the limit into that which restricts and inhibits it, that is, into its *limitation*. This self-assertion by the thing has, however, a strange dialectical consequence, for it actually *deprives* its determination of the very being it seeks to defend. This is because it transforms the determination, which is the intrinsic *being* of the thing, into the mere *negation of its limit or nonbeing*. Insofar as it distinguishes itself from and affirms itself against its limitation, therefore, the determination of the thing alters its logical status. Logically, it mutates into intrinsic being that is no longer intrinsic *being* as such but rather the thing's intrinsic *not-just-being-limited*. That which something "is" intrinsically but which it cannot actually *be* in any straightforward sense is, Hegel tells us, what something *should* be or *ought* to be. "This *in-itself*, therefore, as the negative relation to its limit (which is also distinguished from it), to itself as limitation, is the *ought* (*Sollen*)" (*SL* 132/1: 143 [235]).

In Hegel's view, that aspect of something that distinguishes itself from the limitation inherent in the thing is no longer its ownmost being or determination in the full sense but what the thing should be. Yet why is the determination of something logically forced out of being into merely "oughting to be" as soon as it differentiates itself from the thing's limitation? Why is it not just rendered *determinate* in contrast to its limitation? The answer lies in the fact that the limitation is intrinsic to the thing's *being*; it belongs inseparably to what something *is* in itself. Since every aspect of the thing's being is touched by an irreducible, immanent limitation, the dimension of the thing that differentiates itself from its limitation necessarily marks itself off from all that the thing actually *is*. Consequently, it cannot share in the thing's being as such. It must, therefore, be reduced to a mere "ought-to-be"; that is, to intrinsic "being" that does not actually consist in being at all but rather in mere not-being-limited. Logically, the determination of the thing, or what it intrinsically is, deprives itself of being because it sets itself against the limit that is inherent in everything the thing *is*.

For Hegel, then, beyond a thing's intrinsic limitation, there is also what the thing should be. Something has a limitation not just because its *being* is destined to end but because in itself it is not what it *should be*. In falling short in this way, however, every finite thing also points beyond its limitation *to* what it

should be as the standard it fails to meet. In this sense, Hegel argues, every finite limited thing transcends its own limitation to some degree. This, he claims, is a necessary condition of having a limitation at all:

> In order that the limit which is in something as such should be a limitation, something must at the same time in its own self transcend the limit, it must in its own self *be related to the limit as to that which is not* (*als auf ein Nichtseiendes*). (*SL* 132/1: 143 [235])[28]

Insofar as a thing is merely limited by another thing, Hegel reminds us, "the determinate being of something lies inertly indifferent, as it were, *alongside* its limit" (even though the thing only is what it is through the limit). Insofar as it is a finite thing in general, its being points beyond itself to its limit or nonbeing, and so brings itself to an end. Insofar as it is a finite thing with a limitation, however, its being points beyond even the limit or limitation that is immanent in it and so transcends itself completely. Yet this does not mean that the finite thing *is* actually anything beyond the finite thing that it is. It transcends its own limited being only in the sense that it *should* be more than mere "ceasing to be" or "failing to be." This "should" remains, however, unfulfilled precisely because the finite thing is irrevocably limited and so marked by and consigned to *nonbeing*. As Burbidge puts it, "the *ought* struggles against its *limitation*; [but] the limitation *resists* any such pressure."[29]

The Limitation of the Ought Itself

Taylor contends that Hegel introduces the ideas of limitation and the ought "to allow a reference to the errors of Kant and Fichte, whose ethics and metaphysics is bound up with the notion of a goal which we are bound to seek but can never realize."[30] Findlay, on the other hand, argues that this part of Hegel's logical analysis simply shows "how much Hegel conceived of the world on anthropomorphic and personal lines: the most insignificant patch of colour is for him an analogue of self-conscious Spirit."[31] Findlay's suspicion is that, because human beings are conscious that they should be different from the way they are (for example, through their sense of moral obligation), Hegel attributes a similar "ought-to-be" to all finite things. In my view, however, Hegel is not guided in this part of the *Logic* by the intention to criticize other philosophers, nor is he merely projecting human characteristics on to things; he is simply drawing out the logical and ontological implications of being *finite*.

To be finite, for Hegel, is to be infected with nonbeing at one's very core. It entails being intrinsically limited in one's being and therein suffering a funda-

---

28. Translation revised.
29. Burbidge, *On Hegel's Logic*, p. 53.
30. Taylor, *Hegel*, p. 239. See also McTaggart, *A Commentary on Hegel's Logic*, p. 29.
31. Findlay, *Hegel: A Re-Examination*, p. 162.

mental limitation. That limitation cannot, however, exhaust the thing's identity; it must be a limitation on, and so be distinct from, a thing's intrinsic determination. The finite thing, after all, is what it *is*, not just ceasing and failing to be. Yet insofar as the thing's determination distinguishes itself from the thing's intrinsic limitation, it actually uncouples itself from the intrinsic *being* of which that limitation is an essential part. It thus transforms itself logically into a "not-being-limited" that has no share in the thing's actual being but constitutes, rather, what the thing *should* be. Finite things must, therefore, harbor within themselves the moment of "oughting to be," because their intrinsic being (*Ansichsein*) or determination (*Bestimmung*) is necessarily divided against itself. Things are intrinsically limited and so shot through with nonbeing, and yet they are intrinsically *not* just limited. Since what they actually *are* is inseparable from limitation, however, their intrinsic not-being-limited cannot itself form part of what they are. It must, therefore, constitute what they *should* be.

Now finite objects "should" be all manner of things. This pen, for example, should write well (given its make), but in certain ways it does not do so, and without doubt it will end up not doing so; similarly, this apple should taste sweet (given its variety), but it will also end up not doing so. The general "should" in all things, however, is simply that they should *be* what they are. As finite, they are consigned to nonbeing and so will ultimately come to an end; this is a limitation on them, however, because as things they should simply *be* the things they are. The fundamental paradox, for Hegel, is thus that what finite things actually *are* entails *failing* to be what they are in various ways and *ceasing* to be and so is shot through with *nonbeing*; whereas their intrinsic nature and determination—namely, *simply being what they are*—is what *should* characterize them but (because of their limitation) does *not* characterize them in fact. In other words, the core of a finite thing's being is *nonbeing*; and what it should be but is not is unambiguous *being*. No wonder Hegel thinks that finite things are inherently self-contradictory.

The logical structure of the "should" in finite things is especially complicated. This is because the "should" both differs and is inseparable from a thing's limitation: something can *ought-to-be* only in contrast and in relation to its limitation. This is what Hegel has in mind when he writes that the "should" "contains the determination in double form." On the one hand, the "should" contains the thing's "*intrinsic* (*an sich seiend*) determination counter to the negation," that is, in contrast to its limitation. On the other hand, the "should" also contains the thing's "non-being which, as a limitation, is distinguished from the determination, but is at the same time itself an intrinsic determination" (*SL* 132/1: 143 [235]).[32] That is to say, the "should" itself contains—in the sense of being inherently related to—the thing's intrinsic limitation. Consequently, just as a thing has a limitation by virtue of falling short of what it should be, so it bears within

32. Translation revised.

itself an "ought-to-be" only because intrinsically it has, but is also more than, its limitation. The two aspects of the finite thing depend upon one another. Indeed, each is the explicit negation of the other. As burdened with a limitation, the thing is *not* as it should be; conversely, what it should be is *not* to be burdened with a limitation.

Now, as we recall, what something is intrinsically first reduces itself to what something merely should be because logically it detaches itself from the thing's actual limited being. In the process, the thing's limitation proves to be the negation of whatever that thing should be. What something should be turns out, therefore, to be the negation of that which is itself the negation of it. I noted earlier that the finite, limited thing turns out to be self-negating in a much more developed sense than is the case in the simple process of change (see pp. 376–7). This has now become even more apparent: the finite thing proves to be not only the negation of its own *being* but also the negation of the *negation* that it is, or what Hegel later calls the "negative of the negative" (*SL* 136/1: 148 [237]). This is because the finite thing not only ceases to *be* but in ceasing to be also fails to be what it *ought* to be.[33]

Yet does not this conception of finitude risk depriving the finite thing of any being whatsoever? If the finite thing turns out to consist above all in "not-being-negative," to what extent can we continue to say that there *is* a finite thing at all? Hegel does not address this question directly, but it is clear what the answer must be. We must remember that the finite thing is still *something*: it has quality, an intrinsic character or determination, and a constitution. In this sense, it is rich in being. What Hegel considers at this point in his analysis, however, is what happens to this being insofar as the thing is specifically *finite* (rather than determinate, an other, open to being constituted anew, and so on). We have seen that two things happen: first, the being of the thing turns out to entail its own ceasing to be, and second, the being of the thing turns out to have a limitation built into it *and* at the same time (but in another respect) to transform itself logically into a mere ought-to-be. The point to remember here is that, in exhibiting this structure, the finite thing does not evaporate altogether into mere limitation and "oughting to be" and so does not become a purely *virtual* thing. It remains determinate and real. What occurs is simply that the real, determinate, intrinsic being of the thing *adds to itself* the element of "oughting to be," as soon as it distinguishes itself—as it must—from its intrinsic limitation. The logical structure

---

33. In this sense, the finite thing clearly begins to exhibit the sheer negativity that will turn out to characterize things in the doctrine of essence (see p. 377, above). It is true that at this point there remains a difference between the two negations concerned (one is the ought and the other is the limitation). However, once the ought has itself proven to be a limitation on the thing (see p. 393), the finite thing will be unequivocally the negation of the very negation it is, or the negation that negates *itself*. Note that the finite thing still remains the negation of its being since it is the negation of the specific negation that its own intrinsic *being* proves to be.

of finitude does not replace that of being something but supplements it. *Insofar as* the thing is finite, it proves to be the somewhat shadowy relation between its limitation and its "ought." Yet the finite thing is not purely and simply *finite*: over and above its ceasing to be, being burdened by limitation and "oughting to be," it retains all the qualities it has as *something*. The finite thing still has positive qualities of its own, which it asserts in its relations to other things and which are subject to change by those things in turn. As specifically finite, however, it also passes away into nonbeing and falls short of what it should be.

The *finite* thing is still the finite *something* (with all that that entails). Consequently, the limit that besets the thing is first of all a limit on the thing's real *being*, not merely a limitation with respect to what the thing should be. It is the actual being of the thing that is limited by another thing and of its own accord ceases to be what it is. That limit mutates into a limitation, however, because the thing's own being sets itself against its inherent limit and in so doing transforms itself logically into being that *should not* just be subject to negation but *should be* what it is. It is vital to note that only through this subtle change in the thing's intrinsic being does the limit come to inhibit the thing from being what it should be rather than just stop it being what it *is*. The first logical move is made by the thing's intrinsic being in relation to its limit.

The fact that this move is made indicates that the "should" is not something alien to the thing but is simply the thing's *own being* insofar as it sets itself against, and points beyond, the very limit that makes it what it is. In passing from the consideration of what it *is* to be something to the consideration of what something *should* be, Hegel is not leaving ontology behind and entering the realm of ethics. He is simply disclosing the strange, unreal form that logically the being of finite things itself takes on. For Hegel, "oughting to be" is part of what every finite thing is; it is simply that thing's very own being or quality extending "virtually" beyond its limited actuality.

Hegel is quite clear that what the thing should be is not some ideal standard brought to bear on the thing from the outside but is inherent in the thing itself. It is the thing's own character that has turned itself into a mere "should be" by distinguishing itself from the thing's actual limitation and so depriving itself of the only real being that it can have. As Hegel writes, "the being-in-itself of the something in its determination *reduces itself* (*setzt sich . . . herab*) therefore to an *ought-to-be* through the fact that the same thing which constitutes its in-itself is in one and the same respect a *non-being*" (*SL* 133/1: 144 [237]).[34] It is for this reason, by the way, that "what ought to be *is*, and at the same time *is not*." The "should" encompasses what the thing is but *not* what it actually is.

For Hegel, then, the "ought" can and must be derived from the "is" since one and the same quality or set of qualities constitutes both what something is *and* what it ought to be. The difference is that a thing's quality constitutes what the

34. My emphasis on "reduces itself."

thing ought to be, insofar as it negates and disavows, rather than suffers, its essential limitation.

To repeat: Hegel is not claiming that all finite things must be judged to be deficient when measured against an external standard. Their fault is not that they fail to live up to an ideal set for them by others but rather that they fail to live up to what they themselves intrinsically are and ought to be because they are what they are only *imperfectly*. The criterion that they ought to, but do not, meet is immanent within them. It is their own "essence," "form," or as Hegel often calls it, "concept" (*Begriff*) (see *EL* 99/136 [§51]). This even applies to human beings who fall short of—or who believe they fall short of—certain moral standards. Those standards may, of course, be wholly artificial, but insofar as they require us to act freely out of a sense of duty and respect for our fellow human beings (as Kant argues), "it is in the true sense my *own* objectivity that I bring to fulfilment in doing so."[35] Inanimate things are, of course, unaware that they are restricted in any way or that they should be anything other than they are. Human beings, by contrast, are often acutely conscious that they have an obligation to improve themselves—for example, that they should be fully and explicitly free—and can feel pain in the knowledge that they fall short of what they should be (*EL* 105/144 [§60]).

Hegel is sometimes regarded as a philosopher who dismisses the very idea that we should acknowledge obligations or feel that we should do or be anything at all. His sole interest, it is said, is in determining what *is*, not what ought to be. In support of this interpretation, one could cite the following passage from the *Encyclopedia Logic:*

> Who is not smart enough to be able to see around him quite a lot that is not, in fact, how it ought to be? But this smartness (*Klugheit*) is wrong when it has the illusion that, in its dealings with objects of this kind and with their "ought" (*Sollen*), it is operating within the [true] concerns of philosophical science. This science deals only with the Idea—which is not so impotent that it merely ought to be, and is not actual—and further with an actuality of which those objects, institutions, and situations are only the superficial outer rind. (*EL* 30/49 [§6])

It is evident from this passage that philosophy for Hegel attends to and discloses what being *is*, not what moralists and social critics think it ought to be. The problem for those who read passages such as this in isolation, however, is that the analysis carried out in the *Logic* proves that the ought is itself a necessary structural feature of what there actually *is*. The "ought," for Hegel, is an ontological category. The fact that a thing should be anything at all beyond what it actually is is due not merely to human interpretation but to the very nature of finitude: every finite thing harbors within *itself* its own "should" or *Sollen*. What

35. Hegel, *PR* 161/251 (§133 Add.), my emphasis.

something should be is simply what it is intrinsically but what it constantly fails—and eventually ceases—to be in fact. This even applies to the most primitive forms of being, such as stones:

> Because the stone does not think, does not even feel, its limitedness is not a limitation *for it*, that is, is not a negation in it for sensation, imagination, thought, etc., which it does not possess. But even the stone, as a something, contains the distinction of its determination or in-itself and its determinate being, and to that extent it, too, transcends its limitation; the concept (*Begriff*) which is implicit in it contains the identity of the stone with its other. (*SL* 134/1: 145–6)

Chemicals also exhibit a certain limitation and ought-to-be. In their case, the limitation is not simply that each one is imperfectly what it is but that, as acids and bases, they stand isolated from one another when they should be united. Their readiness to combine with one another is thus interpreted by Hegel as their internal drive to overcome their limitation:

> This ought (*Sollen*), this obligation to transcend limitations, is present in both acid and caustic base in such a degree that it is only by force that they can be kept fixed as (waterless, that is, purely non-neutral) acid and caustic base.

Nor does Hegel deny that human beings are correct in feeling an obligation to be free, rational, and responsible beings:

> Duty is an ought directed against the particular will, against self-seeking desire and capricious interest and it is held up as an ought to the will in so far as this has the capacity to isolate itself from the true. Those who attach such importance to the ought of morality and fancy that morality is destroyed if the ought is not recognised as ultimate truth . . . do not see that as regards the finitude of their sphere the ought receives full recognition (*daß für die Endlichkeit ihrer Kreise das Sollen vollkommen anerkannt wird*). (*SL* 136/1: 147–8)

Hegel's complaint against Kant and Fichte—who both accord a central place in their philosophies to the ideas of limitation and of obligation—is not that they value the sense of "ought" at all but that they do not allow us to progress any further than that sense of "ought." In Hegel's view, neither Kant nor Fichte acknowledges sufficiently the extent to which human beings can fulfil their determination to be free, rational, and ethical beings and thereby actually *be* what they ought to be (see *EL* 150/200 [§94 Add.]).

Yet, why should finite beings, such as ourselves, seek to be anything more than beings who *should*, but never actually do, transcend their moral, epistemological, and ontological limitations? Why not just be content with remaining beings who are finite and flawed but who feel a strong obligation to better themselves? The reason, in Hegel's view, is that being confined to what we *should*

be is itself a fundamental *limitation*, and by the logic of all limitation, it should itself be transcended. Finite things not only bear within them what they should be, as well as their intrinsic limitation; they also carry the obligation and drive to become more than merely finite beings forever spanned between their limitations and their "ought."

The "ought," or "should," in things constitutes a limitation in its own right in two senses. First, the specific character that something should have limits the thing because it prevents it from being anything else and so restricts its possibilities. (This only counts as a genuine limitation of a thing, however, if one accepts that everything is born not just to change but to become a wholly different thing—a point that as yet has not been established.)[36] Second, what something should be is limited precisely to the extent that it lacks real being. The thing has certain limitations insofar as it fails to live up to what it should be. At the same time, the very fact that what the thing should be can only ever be what it *should* be is itself a fundamental limitation because it prevents the thing from ever *being* what it should. If human beings, for example, are confined to being obligated to be free and rational but can never fulfil that obligation, that restricts them just as much as their actual unfreedom and irrationality do. So even though something points beyond its limitation by virtue of the fact that it should be this or that, the fact that it only *should* be this or that limits it anew. "As the *ought*, something is *raised above its limitation*," Hegel writes, "but conversely, it is only as the *ought* that it has its limitation."

The finite thing thus suffers a limitation in both aspects of its being: in being the limited thing it actually is *and* insofar as it should—but only *should*—be more than a merely limited thing. "The limitation of the finite is not something external to it," Hegel comments; "on the contrary, its own determination is also its limitation; and this latter is both itself and also the ought-to-be" (*SL* 133/1: 144 [237]).

Yet every finite thing points beyond its limitation insofar as it should not just fail to be what it intrinsically is. This means, however, that every finite thing should not be restricted to merely "oughting to be" what it is intrinsically. Every finite thing—by virtue of its own logical structure—should be more than just a limited thing that *should* be unambiguously what it is but never is. In other words, finite things should be more than just *finite*. That does not imply that they should leave their finitude behind altogether. As we have seen, to be is to be irreducibly and irreversibly finite; finitude is no illusion for Hegel but hard, inescapable reality. At the same time, however, in being irreducibly finite, things should not be *merely* finite. They should participate in, and be moments of, nonfinite or *infinite* being. In 2.B.c.γ, indeed, Hegel argues that finite things not only should share in infinite being, but do actually constitute infinity in their very finitude.

36. But see chapter 21, below, p. 397.

Chapter Twenty-one

Through Finitude to Infinity

Finitude ad Infinitum

Every finite thing has its intrinsic character: it is this pen or this book, and so on. Yet it is in the contradictory position of failing in many ways to be what it is intrinsically because of its various limitations and imperfections. These imperfections, however, constitute what the thing actually *is*. What something is *intrinsically*, therefore, can only be what it *should* be. Indeed, what something should be is simply what it is intrinsically aside from the various limitations that mar it. Most things do not confront any conscious obligation to become anything other than they actually are. Yet a certain "should-be" is immanent in all things as the internal standard that they set for themselves and that they cannot but fail to live up to.

For Hegel, then, both the ought and its corresponding limitation belong to the thing: "their relation to each other is the finite itself which contains them both in its being-within-self (*Insichsein*)" (*SL* 136/1: 148 [237]). Yet Hegel reminds us that these two moments are also "qualitatively opposed." As limited, something is *not* as it should be, and what it should be is *not* subject to limitation. Accordingly, "limitation is determined as the negative of the ought and the ought likewise as the negative of the limitation." Insofar as it is finite, therefore, the thing is "the negative of the negative"; its being consists in *not* just being its own *non-being* or failure to be what it should be.

This is not to deny that each side of the finite thing is more than merely negative. The thing's limitation is part of what the thing actually is; similarly, what the thing should be is what it is intrinsically, insofar as this has detached itself logically from the thing's actual being. Both the ought and the limitation are thus bound up in some way with the thing's *being*. Nevertheless, in itself each one is the negative of the other. So what the finite thing *is* is inseparable from the fact that it is also the "negative of the negative" (*das Negative des Negativen*).[1]

It is important to keep in mind the finite thing's internal "negativity," as we

1. Hegel makes no distinction here between "negative" and "negation." Indeed, earlier he describes the finite thing as the "negation of the negation," too (*SL* 132/1: 142 [235]). For a definition of the "negative" in the sense of *Verneinung* rather than *das Negative*, see *SL* 111/1: 118 (207) and chapter 16, above, note 16 (p. 306).

turn to consider what happens when the thing ceases to be. Hegel writes that the demise of a finite thing results in the "negative as such" (*das Negative überhaupt*). When a finite thing ceases to be, it does not simply undergo minor changes but is destroyed altogether. It passes from being into sheer and utter *nonbeing*. Nonbeing, we recall, initially constitutes the determinacy of something; here, however, it signals a thing's total dissolution. The "negative" to which Hegel refers here is thus the lack of being that is left when a finite thing meets its end.

Earlier in the text, however, Hegel indicates that the demise of a finite thing cannot simply leave *nothing* whatsoever in its wake. "If," he writes, "the finite is not to pass away in the affirmative, but its end is to be grasped as the *nothing* (*Nichts*), then we should be back again at that first, abstract nothing which itself has long since passed away" (*SL* 131/1: 141 [233]). The finite thing cannot disappear into nothing according to this passage because logically there cannot be any pure nothingness. As we saw at the start of the *Logic*, sheer nothing, or the "not," immediately vanishes into being and so becomes a moment of determinate being and something. The disappearance of a finite thing must, therefore, leave a "negative," or lack of being, that is not simply nothing—or purely *negative*—but, rather, *something*. It has been proven, however, that every something is necessarily finite and consigned to nonbeing. The disappearance of one finite thing must, therefore, result in the presence of another *finite* thing.

There is also another reason why this should be the case. The resultant something is characterized above all by the fact that it is *not* just *nonbeing*. That is to say, it consists in being the "negative of the negative." But, of course, that is precisely the mark or intrinsic "determination" of a *finite* thing: for such a thing ought to be what it is but, due to its limitation, sadly is not; yet it is *not* mere limitation or *negation* precisely because it has an intrinsic character that it should manifest. Once again, therefore, we see that what results from the passing away of the finite thing is nothing but another finite thing:

> The finite is . . . inwardly self-contradictory; it sublates itself, ceases to be. But this its result, the negative as such, is (a) its very *determination* (*Bestimmung*); for it is the negative of the negative. (*SL* 136/1: 148 [237])

The demise of something finite certainly results in the "negative as such," or the absence of the being that was there. Yet it does not lead to nothing, or the sheer absence of any being whatsoever. It leads, rather, to a negative—the nonbeing of the finite something—that is not just negative but something in its own right. This something that arises when another one ceases to be and that is itself constituted by not-just-being-negative is a *new* finite thing. So, with the ending of one finite thing, finitude as such does not come to an end. The finite has rather "become in the first instance only *another* finite which, however, is equally a ceasing-to-be as transition into another finite, and so on to *infinity* (*ins Unendliche*)."

There are two things to be noted about this necessary sequence of finite things. The first is that it marks the point in Hegel's analysis at which finitude or ceasing-to-be proves to be identical with the process of change. Things do, indeed, come to a definitive end, but their end is always their transformation into something else. This is brought out particularly clearly in the *Encyclopedia Logic*, where Hegel explicitly connects the two ideas: "in virtue of its quality, *something* is first *finite* and secondly *alterable* (*veränderlich*), so that the finitude and alterability belong to its being" (*EL* 148/197 [§92]). A lucid summary of Hegel's reason for identifying finitude and change at this point is given by Taylor:

> A finite thing goes under of necessity. But in going under it does not simply disappear. The negation from which it suffers is itself a determinate one, and hence in breaking up it is replaced by another determinate thing—e.g., wood which is burnt becomes smoke and ash. In any case, we cannot think of determinate things as just disappearing, because being as we saw must be determinate, and since Being is an indispensable concept, so is *Dasein*.[2]

The second point is that this process of ceasing-to-be and changing into another finite thing is endless and so *infinite*. The process of simple change as such, analyzed in chapter 17, may be described as "endless" insofar as it entails something constantly becoming other than itself. Strictly speaking, however, change alone cannot constitute an *infinite* process because it does not involve a chain of finite things that, in contrast to the individual things themselves, *does not end*. Now, however, change can be thought as infinite and unending. This is because the things concerned do not merely change but cease to be and in *ending* give way to—by changing into—other things *without end*. There can, therefore, be no infinity without *finite* things—no going on forever without definitive, irreversible ceasing-to-be.

The idea of infinity is not introduced arbitrarily at this point by thought but is generated by finitude itself. The finite turns out to be infinite not because the unbridled understanding holds on to it and renders its ceasing-to-be artificially absolute and "imperishable," but because finite being itself, in its very ceasing to be, ceases to be *mere* ceasing to be and proves to be the *unending* process of giving rise to new finite things. Of course, the philosopher has a role to play in the emergence of the idea of infinity. His role, however, is simply to *let* the infinity inherent in finitude itself come explicitly to the fore.

As we shall see later, Hegel does not regard this unending generation of finitude as true infinity. Thought is not in error, however, when it claims that finite things give rise to one another *ad infinitum*. Such endlessness is a real characteristic of finite being. Indeed, it constitutes the very process of the world.

---

2. Taylor, *Hegel*, p. 242.

Through Finitude to Infinite, Self-Relating Being

Hegel's first infinity consists in nothing but endless finitude. There is infinity because one finite thing leads to another finite thing and another and another endlessly. Hegel now points out, however, that contained in this infinite sequence of finite things is a second infinity that is qualitatively different from finite being.

We do not need to look beyond finitude itself for this new infinity. We simply need to look more closely at what occurs when one finite thing gives way to another. In Hegel's view, "closer consideration of this result shows that the finite in its ceasing-to-be, in this negation of itself[,] has attained its being-in-itself (*Ansichsein*), is *united with itself* (*mit sich selbst zusammengegangen*)" (*SL* 136/1: 148 [237]). But how exactly does this yield a new sense of infinity? To answer this question, we need to look specifically at what Hegel means when he says that "the finite . . . has attained its being-in-itself." The implication behind this remark is that, in ceasing to be, something does not just violate but also *fulfills* its determination. Its determination, we recall, is both to be what it is and *not* to be what it is. In ending, therefore, a thing not only fails to be what it should be but, in another sense, comes to be precisely what it should be, namely, nonbeing. As we have seen, however, when a finite thing meets its demise, it actually becomes another thing: wood, for example, becomes smoke and ash when burnt. If it is the determination of a thing to pass away, then it must also be the determination of something to become something else. This is not to say that wood is born to become ash in particular, but it is to say that wood is born eventually to become something other than wood. In ceasing to be, therefore, a finite thing is not simply *ceasing* to be what it is but is in fact fulfilling its own determination. It is realizing a tendency inherent in what it *is*, namely, that of becoming something *other* than it is. This means, however, that, in ceasing to be, a finite thing is actually revealing a previously hidden dimension of its own being and so is in fact coming to be *itself* in another guise. Its being continues beyond its demise—albeit in a radically transformed mode.[3]

This, I take it, is what Hegel means when he says that in ceasing to be the finite is actually "united with itself": the finite in ceasing to be not only gives way to *another* thing but at the same time gives way to a continuation of its *own* being. In passing away, therefore, finite things themselves form a process of continuous, unending being. Such being is *infinite* because it always *is* and never ceases to be even though individual, finite things must pass away.

Note that this second infinity does not consist—like the first—in endlessly becoming something *else* but rather in being that is never anything but *itself*. Such infinity is being that is and remains itself beyond itself—that is, beyond any finite instance of itself. It is, as Hegel puts it, being that always "unites with

3. See Maluschke, *Kritik und absolute Methode in Hegels Dialektik*, p. 172; Stace, *The Philosophy of Hegel*, p. 147; Theunissen, *Sein und Schein*, p. 277.

itself" or that is "indeterminate self-relation" (*SL* 137/1: 148–9 [237–9]). This infinite being is not to be found by going on for ever and ever, whether in space or time or in counting. It is encountered wherever one finite thing gives way to another: for it is simply the being that *in* the demise of any finite thing turns out not to come to an end after all. Infinity in Hegel's second sense should thus not be confused with the infinite series or totality of finite things but should rather be understood as an altogether different *kind* of being from finite being—albeit one that is found within the realm of finitude itself. It is being that, in contrast to finite being, does *not* end but always *is*. Or to be more precise, it is being that constantly constitutes itself as unending in and through the demise of finite things. This last point is particularly important: for it reminds us that, although Hegel's second infinite is qualitatively different from endless finitude, it is found within and at every stage of such endlessness.

Theunissen points out that there is a significant shift in Hegel's text concerning the subject of "uniting with oneself" or "relating to oneself." First we are told that it is the finite that unites with itself, but then Hegel states that the infinite itself is "*being* which has restored itself out of limitedness" (*SL* 137/1: 150 [239]). According to Theunissen, only the first statement is warranted by Hegel's account; by contrast, Hegel does not properly justify the claim that infinite being itself relates to itself or unites with itself in any way.[4] In my view, however, Theunissen overlooks the fact that for Hegel both processes are one and the same. The finite, in ceasing to be and becoming another, comes to be itself in another guise, but it constitutes thereby a quite different kind of being from mere finitude, namely, infinite being, or being that does not end. The reason why Hegel shifts from one way of speaking to another is thus that he is following the logical shift in the very structure of finitude itself. None of this implies that finite things continue forever as the specific things that they are. Rather, the process whereby finite things cease to be is itself the process whereby being proves to be infinite, and every finite thing contributes through its own demise to the continuous constitution of that infinite, never-ending being.

However we look at a finite thing, Hegel believes, we are unable to dissociate from it infinite being or the quality of uniting-with-itself. If we consider its internal structure, for example, we note that the ought points beyond its limitation but constitutes therein a limitation of its own. Accordingly, Hegel writes, "it is the same thing; in going beyond itself, . . . it equally only unites with itself." Similarly, if we consider the fact that one finite ends and becomes another finite and another and so on, we note that it always comes to be another *finite* and so establishes a continuous, *unending identity* throughout the process of change. Although this identity is borne by a chain of finite things, it nevertheless constitutes infinite being in the second Hegelian sense. Hegel makes this point especially clear in the *Encyclopedia Logic:*

4. Theunissen, *Sein und Schein*, pp. 280, 293.

> In its relationship to an other, something is already an other itself vis-à-vis the latter; and therefore, since what it passes into is entirely the same as what passes into it—neither having any further determination than this identical one of being an *other*—in its passing into another, something only comes together *with itself*; and this relation to itself in the passing and in the other is *genuine Infinity*. (*EL* 150–1/200–1 [§95])

As I have noted, the infinite to which Hegel draws attention at this point does not consist in the endless generation of new finite things but is rather the self-same being that continues and relates only to itself *in* all such othering. Hegel is adamant that there is no such infinite being apart from, before, or outside the process of change and death undergone by finite things. The infinite does not precede or underlie the finite, nor does it manipulate things from on high. It is simply the unending being that is formed *by* the passing into one another of finite things. Since infinite being is inseparable from the *process* of the world, such being cannot simply *be* infinite. It must constantly prove to be infinite and unending in the process whereby finite things themselves end. Indeed, it must constantly *constitute* itself as infinite. Infinite being always *is* what it is and never ends, but this is only because it always *proves itself* to be infinite and never ending. Hegel's infinite is, consequently, dynamic rather than static. As Hegel puts it, it must be "posited as *being* and *becoming*" (*SL* 137/1: 149 [239]).

Burbidge identifies infinity—at least, initially—solely with the "intellectual activity" involved in moving from the thought of limitation to that of the ought.[5] It is evident, however, that Hegel understands infinity to be what finite being *itself* turns out to be. Yet in the second sense we have encountered, it is a different kind of being from finite being since it is not mere negation or ceasing-to-be but unambiguously *affirmative* being—being that *is*, and never is not.

Hegel and Descartes

Infinity, by definition, is being that does not come to an end. In Hegel's second sense, however, infinite being does not not end because there will always be another finite thing but rather because it *is* and is absolutely. Nothing detracts from its being at any point or stops it being what it is. It is being without limitation. Yet infinite being is not just pure, immediate being. Hegel writes that "the infinite *is*, and more intensely so than the first immediate being," because it is what being turns out to be in truth (*SL* 137/1: 150 [239]). Being can turn out to be infinite, however, only insofar as it remains as finite things cease to be. In other words, being proves to be infinite only by grace of the finite. Indeed, as we have seen, it is the unending being that finitude *itself* comes to constitute as it ceases to be mere ceasing-to-be.[6]

---

5. Burbidge, *On Hegel's Logic*, p. 53.
6. See Doz, *La logique de Hegel et les problèmes traditionnels de l'ontologie*, p. 67.

Hegel insists, *contra* Kant, that it is not our faculty of reason that gives rise to the idea of the infinite or unconditioned but finite being itself: "it is the very nature of the finite to transcend itself, to negate its negation and to become infinite" (*SL* 138/1: 150 [239]). It is also clear that Hegel derives the idea of infinity from that of finitude, rather than the other way around. In this respect, he differs strikingly from Descartes.

In the third Meditation Descartes argues that God must exist because God is the only possible source of the idea that I, as a finite intellect, entertain of him. Descartes assumes that "there must be at least as much reality in the efficient and total cause as in the effect of that cause." The idea in my mind of an infinite being must, therefore, have as its cause a real being that is itself infinite rather than one that is merely finite. Consequently, an infinite being—which for Descartes can only be God—must exist.[7]

In the course of presenting this argument, however, Descartes considers a possible objection to it. Could it be that I do not have a true idea of the infinite at all but arrive at "my perception of the infinite . . . merely by negating the finite"?[8] Descartes immediately counters this objection by asserting that the idea of the finite itself presupposes that of infinity. I could not produce an idea of infinity simply by negating the finite because I could not form the idea of the finite in the first place unless I could understand what it means to fall short of the infinite. My idea of the infinite must come first—implicitly, if not explicitly—and so must be a "true" idea whose cause must be a really existing God.

For Descartes, it is clear that "my perception of the infinite, that is God, is in some way prior to my perception of the finite, that is, myself." Indeed, it is actually the implicit precondition of the doubts that Descartes expresses in the first Meditation. Descartes can doubt the existence of God—and so require that God's existence be proven—only because he assumes from the start that the I is finite and liable to error, *in contrast to God*. "For how could I understand that I doubted or desired—that is, lacked something—and that I was not wholly perfect, unless there were in me some idea of a more perfect being which enabled me to recognize my own defects by comparison."[9]

Hegel's conception of the relation between the finite and the infinite is the exact opposite of Descartes's. In Hegel's view, we are first led by the very nature of being to the idea that being is finite, and this occurs without any contrast being drawn between finite and infinite being. Being is finite according to Hegel not because it lacks the characteristics of some presupposed infinite being but simply because it brings *itself* to an end. Finite being is determinate, limited being that is what it is and, in being, finishes. Its limitation, or "imperfection," is that it fails to be unambiguously what *it* is intrinsically as this particular thing,

7. *The Philosophical Writings of Descartes*, 2: 28, 32; 1: 202.

8. *The Philosophical Writings of Descartes*, 2: 31.

9. *The Philosophical Writings of Descartes*, 2: 31; 3: 338.

not that it falls short of infinite perfection. Indeed, the idea of the infinite itself arises only because finite things turn out to constitute unending being in their very process of decay and death.

Hegel thus takes seriously the idea that infinite being is in-finite, or *non*-finite, being that can be understood only *after* we have understood what it is to be finite. Descartes, by contrast, assumes that infinite being is purely positive being that must be comprehended before any knowledge of the finite can be obtained. Note that the dispute between Hegel and Descartes does not just concern which idea we must entertain first. It also concerns how the finite and the infinite themselves are to be understood. For Hegel, the fact that being first proves to be finite and only after this reveals itself to be infinite means that infinite being must be understood as constituted by the disappearing of finite things themselves. It is simply the being that continues *in* the transformation of one finite thing into another. For Descartes, on the other hand, not only does the idea of the infinite precede the idea of the finite in our minds, but infinite being itself precedes and transcends finite being in reality. According to Descartes, although infinite being—God—creates and sustains all finite things in being, it nevertheless has, or at least had, an existence *apart* from finite things.

As I argued earlier in this study, Hegel is profoundly influenced by the Cartesian conviction that all assumed certainties must be suspended before we may begin philosophy. It has now become apparent, however, that concerning the particular relation between the finite and the infinite, Hegel is a follower of Spinoza rather than Descartes, for he believes that there can be no true infinity outside, beyond, or apart from finitude. By contrast, many post-Hegelians, including most notably Levinas, prefer to follow Descartes and to regard infinity as transcending, rather than as immanent in, finite being.

A Contradiction in the Infinite

For Hegel, the finite is not rendered infinite by an "alien force" (*fremde Gewalt*) such as human understanding but turns out to constitute infinite being through its own internal logic (*SL* 138/1: 150 [241]). Infinite being is being that is not finite; it arises, however, as Rinaldi remarks, because logically the finite *negates itself* into affirmative, unending being.[10] There is infinite being, therefore, because finite being is itself *not* merely *negative* being and so is the "negation of negation."

As we know, something (*Etwas*) is the "negation of negation" right from the start: it is negation that relates to itself and so is not mere negation after all. To begin with, however, something is double negation as affirmative, self-relating being. Yet the moment of *negation* embedded in something becomes more and more explicit as Hegel's logical analysis of something develops. First of all, something shows itself simply to be distinguished from, but also related to, something else. Then it proves to be the overt negation of that other as its *limit*. Then

10. Rinaldi, *A History and Interpretation of the Logic of Hegel*, p. 152.

something reveals itself to be the negation of its own being, or to be a *finite* thing. Lastly, it turns out to be the negation of the negative that it itself is, by transcending its own limitation through its own ought-to-be. Now we see that this very self-negation at the heart of all finitude—which renders every finite thing structurally contradictory—turns finite being into that which is *not* merely finite after all, namely, infinite, unending being.

The category of the infinite bears some similarity to that of something, since in each case we encounter the "negation of negation" that is at the same time affirmative, *self-relating* being.[11] There is, however, an important difference between the two categories. Something is the first, most primitive form of self-relating negation; it is simple determinacy, or negation, that forms a sphere of its own over against another such self-relating sphere of being, or something else. Infinite being is also "self-relation" (*Beziehung-auf-sich*) (*SL* 137/1: 149 [239]), but it does not constitute *something* in relation to something *else*. It is, rather, the being that is, and relates to itself, in every something and through the fact that every something comes to an end. This significant difference explains why Hegel states right at the start of his account of the infinite that "the forms of *determinate being* (*Dasein*) find no place in the series of those determinations which can be regarded as definitions of the absolute." This is not to deny that the categories of determinate being—something, other, being-in-itself, being-for-other, determination, constitution, and limit—capture real features of what there is, but it is to emphasize that they only represent ways of being *finite* and do not characterize infinite, absolute being as such. As Hegel puts it, "the infinite . . . is held to be absolute without qualification."

One of the central lessons of Hegel's *Logic* is thus that the infinite must not be understood as *something*, or as a sphere of its own, over against and limited by something *else*. Infinite being is not something other than, or apart from, finite being but is one with it. It is simply the affirmative, unending being that finite things together constitute, or what finitude proves to be in truth: "the finite is only this, through its own nature to become itself the infinite. The infinite is its *affirmative determination* (*Bestimmung*), that which it truly is in itself" (*SL* 138/1: 150 [241]).

With this insight, however, our understanding of the world undergoes a dramatic shift. For in proving to be infinite, unending being, finite being turns out in truth *not* to be *finite* being after all. That is to say, finitude ceases to be fini-

11. The logical move from finitude to infinity (as self-relating being) does not, however, follow the pattern of the move from *Dasein* to something but resembles rather the move whereby the pure other others itself into self-relating being; see Hegel, *SL* 118–19/1: 127 (213) and *EL* 151/201 (§95). Indeed, this move from the finite to the infinite is the second point in the *Logic* at which the genuine negation of negation *constitutes* (rather than presupposes) affirmative self-relation; see chapter 17, above, p. 330. The differences between the two moves are, of course, due to the fact that we are dealing with the pure other in one case and the finite in the other case.

tude as such as soon as it reveals itself to constitute infinite being. Hence Hegel ends 2.C.a with the following bold statement: "the finite has vanished in the infinite, and what *is*, is only the *infinite*."

Theunissen objects that by understanding infinite being to supplant finitude altogether Hegel contradicts his stated belief that infinite being is nothing apart from finite being itself. If infinite being arises only because *finite* being continues in some way beyond its own demise, then surely finite being itself must remain if there is to be continuing infinite being. "For in order to be able to transcend itself, the finite would have to remain preserved as the subject."[12]

Theunissen, however, overlooks the fact that it is the very identity of finite and infinite being that causes the former—at least initially—to disappear. Were infinite being something other than finite being, then the two could coexist side by side; however, infinite being is not anything other than finite being but is simply what finite being *itself* proves to be. Insofar as finite being constitutes infinite being, it takes on a wholly *different* quality; it reveals itself *not* to be finite being after all but to be infinite being. Since, however, there is no realm of the finite *beyond* this newly revealed infinity, such infinite being must be *all* that there actually is. Being, or the realm of changing, finite things, must thus prove to be purely *infinite* being and nothing else.

Yet, in 2.C.b, Hegel points out that this cannot be the whole story: for, logically, infinity is not only what finitude proves to be but also the immediate *negation* of the finite. Infinite being has a character and quality of its own that is *not* that of finite being. Insofar as it is identical with the process of finitude, however, infinity does not differ *explicitly* from finitude. This means that it is not in-finite in the full sense. How, then, can infinite being come to be explicitly what it is implicitly? In Hegel's view, it can do so only by clearly differentiating itself from the finite in which it is immanent. Infinite being can do this, however, only by setting finite being definitively *outside* itself as that which is quite distinct from it. If infinity is to be properly infinite, therefore, it may not simply supplant the finite but must actually *preserve* the finite over against itself, as that by contrast with which it acquires an identity of its own. A moment ago, we learned that all there is is infinite being. We have now learned that there must also be finite being apart from such infinite being since infinite being can be explicitly in-finite only through marking itself off *from the finite that is there.*

This insight brings about a further dramatic shift in our understanding of infinity. For it means that, logically, infinite being must transform itself into precisely what it is not supposed to be, namely, something *other* than finite, determinate being:

> As thus in the form of simple being and at the same time as the *non-being* of an *other*, it [the infinite] has fallen back into the category of

12. Theunissen, *Sein und Schein*, pp. 281–2. See also McTaggart, *A Commentary on Hegel's Logic*, p. 30.

> *something* (*Etwas*) as a determinate being in general—more precisely, into the category of something with a limit, because the infinite is determinate being reflected into itself, resulting from the sublating of determinateness in general, and hence is determinate being *posited* as distinguished from its determinateness. (*SL* 138/1: 151 [241])

Infinite being thus turns out to be just as contradictory as finite being. On the one hand, infinite being is simply what finite being is in truth, and so is all that there truly is. On the other hand, infinite being itself requires that there also be finite being from which it can clearly and explicitly differentiate itself: "the *immediate being* of the infinite resuscitates (*erweckt . . . wieder*) the *being* of its negation, of the finite again which at first seemed to have vanished in the infinite." The finite thus cannot simply disappear into infinite being, as we first thought, but must remain as that which is other than the infinite. In the light of this latter idea, it appears that Descartes and his epigones may not have been quite as mistaken as we initially thought.

The Bad Infinite

Remember that Hegel is not describing a temporal process of development here. He is unpacking what is *logically* implicit in the nature of infinite being. This is (a) that infinite being is simply that which finitude proves in truth to be, and (b) that in order to be explicitly in-finite, infinity must set itself apart from finite being as something other than the latter. As we are now about to see, however, in distinguishing itself from the finite in this way, infinite being logically deprives itself of the very quality that makes it infinite in the first place and turns itself into determinate, *finite* infinity.

In the second paragraph of 2.C.b, Hegel points out that though they are necessarily other than one another finitude and infinity are not *purely* other than or indifferent to one another. On the contrary, they are intimately related to one another. After all, it is still true that every finite thing is intrinsically destined to transform itself, and to be transformed, into something different and so to generate unending, infinite being. Infinite being is thus what all finite being itself intrinsically is and should come to be explicitly:

> determinate [finite] being is posited with the *determination* to pass over into its *in itself*, to *become* infinite. Infinity is the nothing of the finite, it is what the latter is *in itself*, what it *ought to be* (*dessen Ansichsein und Sollen*), but this ought-to-be is at the same time reflected into itself, is *realized*. (*SL* 139/1: 151 [241])

Infinite being is not only that which differentiates itself from finite being and gives itself a character and being of its own; it is at the same time the "other" to which all finite being points from within *itself*.

Yet as we have just seen, infinite being is also the immediate "*negation* . . . of

the finite." Infinity is that form of being to which finitude points but that consists specifically in *not* being finite. This is not to deny that infinity is affirmative, self-relating being in its own right. It is to note, however, that infinite being is explicitly in-finite only insofar as it is related negatively *to the finite*. Indeed, its own affirmative character must itself consist in not-being-the-finite-in-any-way or in transcending-the-finite. Understood like this, Hegel says, infinite being proves to be simply the "beyond of the finite" or the "non-finite" (*das Nicht-Endliche*) (*SL* 139/1: 152 [243]). Logically, therefore, infinity cannot just be the continuous being that finite things themselves generate; it must also come to be something that lies beyond finite things and to which their own being constantly refers.

Hegel famously names this transcendent infinite the "bad," or "spurious," infinite (*das Schlecht-Unendliche*). The word "bad" is not to be understood in a moral sense. Hegel is not arguing—at this point, at least—that the idea of a transcendent infinite leads to atheism or corrupts public morals. He deems the transcendent infinite to be "bad" simply because it is not actually *infinite* at all. To say this is not (yet) to claim that the bad infinite falls short of the conception of true infinity that will be reached later in the *Logic*. That conception has yet to be developed and so cannot be employed at this point as a standard of criticism. The bad infinite is bad, in Hegel's view, because it falls short of what infinity has already proven to be.

Infinite being, in the second sense we encountered, is being that is not finite and does not end. It is being that does not take the form of something in relation to something else but that is immanent in and continues through all finite things. Infinite being thus has no limit or boundary with respect to anything else: it is unbounded being. We have now discovered, however, that insofar as it explicitly differentiates itself from finitude and so comes to be genuinely *in-finite*, infinity proves to be precisely what initially it is not supposed to be, namely, *something other* than finite being. As such, it necessarily sets a limit to finite being: it is the form of being in which there is no longer any finitude. But, of course, this means that it must be bounded by such finite being in turn: finite being must be where infinity stops. By differentiating itself from finite being and so becoming properly in-finite, infinity actually turns itself into that which is *not* infinite after all, but limited. In so doing it establishes two distinct qualities or "realms" of being.

Infinity is not limited just by finitude, however, but also gives *itself* a boundary at which it comes to an end by setting itself in relation to that which is not infinite. After all, the reason why there is finitude outside the infinite is that infinite being by its very nature is the negation of finitude and must come to be explicitly what it is implicitly. Infinity thus imposes a limit on itself, thereby giving itself an endpoint, and so is not merely limited but *finite*. To be finite, we recall, is not necessarily to bring oneself to an end over time but is just to come to a stop through what one is oneself. Bad infinity stops itself being simply infinite and unending by running up against finite being; in this sense, bad infinity

logically is finite infinity. Accordingly, as Hegel puts it, "*there are* two worlds, one infinite and one finite, and in their relationship the infinite is only the *limit* (*Grenze*) of the finite and is thus only a determinate infinite, an *infinite which is itself finite*" (*SL* 139–40/1: 152 [243]).[13] The bad infinite is bad, therefore, not for moral reasons but quite simply because it is a limited, *finite* infinite.

Note that the idea of bad infinity is not artificially engendered, as Theunissen claims, by "representation" or *Vorstellung*—or, indeed, by the understanding—but is inherent in the very nature of infinity as such.[14] Infinity itself must prove to be bad, or finite, infinity because it must *distinguish* itself explicitly from the finitude that constitutes it and so turn itself into the determinate negation of, or something other than, finitude itself. On my reading then, Hegel does not dismiss the idea of the bad infinite out of hand as a fiction or an error of thought. On the contrary, he demonstrates that, logically, infinite being must take the form of that which transcends the finite. As we shall see, being "badly," or abstractly, infinite is by no means the only way to be infinite. Nevertheless, it is one important and necessary way of being infinite. Accordingly, though we may not start out from Descartes's idea of the infinite, we must recognize that there is some truth in his idea because there must be "bad" infinite being that transcends finitude.

An example of actual bad infinity may be found in light (at least, as Hegel conceives it). Light, for Hegel, is not a particular thing but is that "immaterial matter" that makes particular things manifest and brings them into "universal interrelation"; it is what he calls "pure making manifest" or "the universal making-visible (*Sichtbarmachen*) of objects as such."[15] Hegel describes light in terms that are otherwise used to characterize infinite being, clearly suggesting that he regards it as infinite in some sense. He calls it "*pure identity*-with-self" or material "ideality."[16] Indeed, he refers to light explicitly as "infinite self-externality," "infinite expansion," and "infinite spatial dispersion."[17] (This is because it immediately spreads out to fill the whole of space with "absolute velocity"—which, by the way, is not to deny that the propagation of light takes time.)[18]

Yet light is also distinct from the objects it illuminates:

> light, as the universal physical identity, enters into relation with matter qualified by the other moments of the concept (*Begriff*), in the first place, as *different* from it and therefore as something else, external to it; such matter, being thus the negative of light, is specified as *dark*.[19]

---

13. See also Rinaldi, *A History and Interpretation of the Logic of Hegel*, p.153.

14. See Theunissen, *Sein und Schein*, p. 280.

15. Hegel, *EPN* 93, 88, 91/119, 112, 116 (§§276 and Add., 275 Add.), and *A* 2: 808/3: 31, translation revised.

16. Hegel, *EPN* 87, 91/111, 116 (§§275–6).

17. Hegel, *EPN* 91–2, 88/116–17, 113 (§§276, 275 Add.).

18. Hegel, *EPN* 87, 94/112, 120 (§§275 Add., 276 Add.).

19. Hegel, *EPN* 94–5/121 (§277).

Indeed, Hegel notes that light not only differs from dark matter, but "exists independently in an individualized form," namely, as stars.[20] In both these senses, light is thus a limited, finite reality, even though it is also "infinite expansion." As such, light clearly exhibits the structure of "bad" infinity.

Furthermore, not only is light distinct from matter, but it is at the same time matter *itself* that has distinguished itself from the finite, "dark" bodies in which it inheres. This is not to say that the matter running through, and continuing in, every finite body itself takes the explicit form of light. The matter in bodies, for Hegel, is being that fills space in time. It repels other such matter and is subject to gravity; it is heavy and definitely not "light" in either sense of the word. Nevertheless, in Hegel's view, light is what arises insofar as matter, or the filling of space in time, *distinguishes itself* from heavy bodies and acquires an identity of its own. Light is thus nothing but matter that has separated itself off from things as the "pure *existent* force of space-filling" or "pure materiality which is everywhere present." It is, Hegel writes, "the abstract self (*Selbst*) of matter" that is "*absolutely weightless*."[21] In this sense, as well, light shows itself to be "bad infinity" because it is simply what is generated when infinite spatio-temporal, material being sets *itself* over against the finite things in which it otherwise inheres.

It is true that Hegel does not cite light in the *Logic* as an explicit example of bad infinity. In the *Philosophy of Nature*, however, he comes very close to doing so when he refers to light as "the *abstractly infinite* (*abstrakt-unendlich*) reflection-into-self."[22]

Another example of actually existing bad infinity is human consciousness or thought itself, insofar as it understands objects to be fundamentally distinct from itself. Consciousness, or the "I," Hegel writes, is the "infinite self-relation of mind (*Geist*)." It is infinite because it is not bounded by the things to which it relates but can discern within them its own concepts and laws. Like light, with which Hegel explicitly compares it, consciousness thus reveals and manifests whatever it encounters; indeed, it reveals not just their surface but also their inner nature and structure. Yet also like light, consciousness is clearly distinguished from the things to which it relates: "the pure abstract freedom of mind lets go from it its specific qualities . . . to an equal freedom as an independent *object*."[23] Consciousness may well be infinite, therefore, but it is at best abstractly or "badly" infinite. By contrast, presuppositionless thought, for which being is not just "over there" but that which is disclosed *within* thought itself, may be said to be truly infinite and unbounded.

Hegel acknowledges, then, that there is bad infinity in the world. As we shall see later, however, he does not believe that all infinity is irreducibly bad or fi-

---

20. Hegel, *EPN* 89/114 (§275 Add.).
21. Hegel, *EPN* 87, 91/112, 116 (§§275 Add., 276).
22. Hegel, *EPN* 95/121 (§277), my emphasis.
23. Hegel, *EPM* 153/199 (§413).

nite. The unself-critical understanding (*Verstand*), by contrast, regards bad infinity as "the highest, the absolute Truth" (*SL* 139/1: 152 [243])—and for this reason, of course, does not consider it to be altogether *bad*. For the understanding, therefore, all infinity by its very nature transcends the realm of the finite, and is none the worse for so doing. There is no other infinite but one that lies beyond, and so is radically other than, the finite:

> When . . . the understanding, raising itself above this finite world, ascends to its highest, to the infinite, this finite world remains for it on *this* side, so that the infinite is only set *above* or *beyond* the finite, is *separated* from it, with the consequence that the finite is separated from the infinite. (*SL* 140/1: 153 [243])

In Hegel's view, the understanding cannot see past this opposition between the finite and the infinite. For it, finite being is irredeemably finite and nothing more, whereas the infinite is simply that which is distinct from the finite. The problem with this view of things, however, is that it reduces all infinity to something *finite* and so never thinks *beyond* finitude after all (and in this sense actually renders finitude all-encompassing and "infinite").

It is crucial to note that Hegel does not reject the idea of the bad infinite out of hand. Philosophers of the understanding are in his view not completely wrong. Hegel accepts that "there is Understanding in nature, i.e. the forms of the Understanding exist in it," and, as I have suggested, this includes the form of bad infinity.[24] This is not to say that absolute reason, or "God," may be understood as something other than finite being, as Descartes believes, but it is to accept that light and human consciousness, for example, may be understood as "finite infinities." The error of the understanding, according to Hegel, thus does not lie in thinking that there is infinity beyond finite things. It lies in never suspecting that infinity could be anything *other* than that which lies beyond and is bounded by the finite.

Yet, at this stage of the *Logic*, why should anyone argue that infinity is anything more than bad infinity? Has not Hegel demonstrated precisely that infinite being must give itself the form of finite infinity? And has he not thereby confirmed the standpoint of the understanding? What reason can he adduce at this point in order to call the understanding's conception of the infinite into question? There are two reasons. First of all, the qualitative infinity that is constituted by the transformation of one thing into another has not simply disappeared from the scene: matter, for example, does not stop taking the form of weighty, dark matter just because it takes on the separate form of light. The understanding can be criticized, therefore, for overlooking what qualitative infinity is initially. Secondly, the very idea of the bad infinity itself leads logically to further, more complex forms of infinity. We must move beyond the infinite of the un-

---

24. Hegel, *EPN* 93/119 (§276 Add.).

derstanding, therefore, because other kinds of infinity are implicit in, and made necessary by, that finite infinity itself.

The Progress to Infinity

In his derivation of the next form of infinity, Hegel first reminds us that the finite and the (finite) infinite are not just separate from one another but are bound together by their common boundary. Each one is the qualitative limit of the other: where one begins, the other stops. Yet each one not only limits—and is limited by—the *other* but also limits *itself* by setting itself in relation to its other. This, indeed, is what makes each one finite rather than merely limited: for the finite is being that has its limit and endpoint in itself. Hegel sums up these points in the following lines:

> this negation which connects them . . . is the limit of the one relatively to the other, and that, too, in such a manner that each of them does not have the limit *in it* (*an ihm*) merely relatively to the other, but the negation is their *being-in-itself* (*Ansichsein*); the limit is thus present in each on its own account, in separation from the other . . . thus both are limited, finite in themselves (*an sich selbst*). (*SL* 140/1: 153 [243])

Finite being, therefore, is, in itself and quite apart from infinite being, finite-not-infinite; conversely, spuriously infinite being, in itself and quite apart from finite being, is infinite-not-finite. Limiting and being limited by the other form part of the separate, intrinsic identity of each.

At the same time, of course, each one is qualitatively distinct from the *other*: finite being is not infinite being and vice versa. Each of the two types of being thus pushes the other outside itself, or in Hegel's words, "each . . . immediately repels the limit, as its non-being, from itself and . . . posits it as *another being* outside it, the finite positing its non-being as this infinite and the infinite, similarly, the finite." Consequently, the finite is *in itself* the negation of an other that lies wholly *outside* it, and the same is true of the bad infinite. To put it another way, each one from within itself *excludes* the other.

Yet the relation between these two ways of being is even more complicated than I have suggested because logically each one *turns into* the other from which it is then immediately excluded. Consider the finite first. The finite becomes infinite being because it "bring[s] about its own dissolution" and therein, as we have seen, constitutes continuous, unending being. Such infinite being is thus what finite being is intrinsically, what finite being by its very nature is meant to become. Yet as we know, infinite being immediately differentiates itself from and *excludes* finite being from itself. Finite being thus turns into infinite being from which it is immediately shut out.

Now consider the infinite. Insofar as it differentiates itself from the finite as its "immediate negation," infinity reduces itself to limited, finite infinity. In placing itself beyond finitude, the infinite thus turns into the opposite form of being from which infinity itself is excluded.

Hegel concludes from this analysis that the finite and the infinite are "inseparable" (*untrennbar*) since each turns of its *own* accord into the *other*, or as Hegel himself puts it, "each is in its own self and through its own determination the positing of its other." He also notes, however, that their inseparability, or "unity," is concealed (*verborgen*) by the fact that each is radically different from the other and so excluded by the other into which it mutates. This means that although the finite and the infinite are intimately connected they do not occupy the same logical space: the presence of the one rules out that of the other. Accordingly, their inseparability takes the form of the immediate "transition" or "flipping over" (*Umschlagen*) of one into the other that displaces it. Like pure being and nothing, "each arises *immediately* and independently in the other, their connection being only an external one": finite being proves to be infinite being, but infinite being in turn then proves to be finite.

The process of transition to which Hegel draws attention here is inherent in the structure of the bad infinite and leaves the bad infinite intact. All Hegel has done is point out that finite being in passing away flips over logically into infinite being which then immediately turns itself back into something finite. This brings out the dynamic character of the bad infinite more clearly than occurred earlier, but it does not take us beyond the bad infinite itself to a new conception of infinity. A new conception of infinity does arise, however, when we note that the finite being to which the *infinite* reduces itself must be subject to the same negation as the finite that first turns into infinite being. There are two reasons why infinity's own finitude should be negated and transcended.

First, as finite and limited, it must point beyond itself to further infinite being. Second, the logical structure of infinity itself demands that it not just lie beyond the finite to which it is *initially* opposed. If infinity is the utter negation of the finite, then it must lie beyond *all* finitude including the finite to which it reduces *itself*.

This logical requirement that the finite infinite must point to infinity beyond itself brings about a significant change in the infinite: for the bad infinite ceases to enjoy a settled identity and initiates a process of continual self-transcendence and self-negation. Hegel describes this process as follows: The finite points beyond itself and passes over into infinite being, but the infinite into which it passes sets itself apart from that finite, thereby limiting it and being limited by it and so proving to be a new *finite* in its own right. As a result, Hegel writes, "the infinite has vanished and its other, the finite, has entered" (*SL* 141/1: 154 [245]). This new finite then demands to be transcended in turn and points beyond itself to a new infinite. This new infinite once more reduces itself to something finite by virtue of the simple fact that it transcends the finite that gave rise to it. Once again, however, this new finite points beyond itself to the infinite and so on *ad infinitum*.

Hegel names this process of endlessly transcending the finite the "progress to infinity" (*Progreß ins Unendliche*) (*SL* 142/1: 155 [245]). It can be represented as follows:

Finite → Infinite (Finite) → Infinite (Finite) → Infinite (Finite) → . . .

This process does not arise merely because the finite and the infinite flip over into one another. It arises more specifically because infinity may not be confined to a spurious, finite condition but logically must exceed even its *own* finitude.

This infinite progress clearly mirrors the first infinity we encountered. That initial infinity, we recall, did not consist in being that is qualitatively different from finite being but lay rather in the endless series of *finite* things—that is, in one finite thing giving way to another and another and so on. That endless series can be represented as follows:

Finite → Finite → Finite → Finite → Finite → . . .

The difference between the two infinite series is this: in the first case, the finite points beyond itself to nothing but more finitude, whereas in the second case, the finite points beyond itself to an *infinite* that lies beyond all finitude including the finite that it thereby constitutes. Apart from this, there is no difference between the two series, both of which may therefore be regarded as forming the same "progress to infinity" understood in a subtly different way.

It appears, then, that the various senses of infinity identified by Hegel are all intimately connected with one another. The first infinite series of finite things harbors within itself qualitatively infinite being because finite things in ceasing to be do not just lead to ever more finite things but also constitute continuous, unending being. Such qualitatively infinite being must, however, differentiate itself explicitly from finitude and so turn itself into the bad infinite. This bad infinite must then point beyond itself to further infinity that proves in turn to be finite and so to point beyond itself *ad infinitum*. We have, it seems, come full circle or, rather, spiraled around to a new conception of infinity that renders explicit an aspect of the first infinity that was not initially apparent.

This new progress to infinity not only leads from one bad infinity to another but constitutes thereby what one might call a *tedious infinity*. This is precisely because it leads beyond the finite to the same finite infinity again and again and again. As Hegel puts it, "the progress to infinity is . . . only the perpetual repetition of . . . one and the same tedious (*langweilig*) *alternation* of this finite and infinite" (*SL* 142/1: 155 [247]).[25] Like the first bad infinite, this infinite progress is a real feature of being, not just an illusion generated by abstract thought. Matter, for example, is infinitely divisible to the point of tedium.[26] Hegel has no objection, therefore, to understanding certain aspects of the world as progressing to infinity. He takes issue, however, with those—such as Fichte—who regard the tedious infinite as "something ultimate beyond which thought does not go"

---

25. See also Hegel, *EL* 150/199 (§94 Add.).

26. Hegel, *SL* 198/1: 227. Similarly, the progression of musical notes (*Töne*) can be considered infinite in this sense, in Hegel's view; see *EL* 172/228 (§109 Add.).

(*SL* 142/155 [245]). Their error, in Hegel's view, is that they can see no further than endlessness and so reduce all infinity to the tedious (or the bad) infinite.

Infinity takes the form of the tedious infinite, according to Hegel, insofar as it is both irreducibly *related* to and completely *other* than finitude. Infinity must explicitly differentiate itself from the finite since it is implicitly the *negation* of the finite. This means that it must both preserve its relation to the finite and set itself quite apart from the finite. Logically, therefore, infinity must take the form of that-which-lies-*beyond*-the-finite. In so doing, however, the infinite reduces itself to a finite, limited infinite. Yet since its infinity consists precisely in lying beyond the finite, it must transcend even its own finitude. But, of course, this again just renders it finite once more, and so on to infinity. This is what Hegel has in mind, I believe, when he states that "the progress makes its appearance wherever *relative* determinations are pressed to the point of opposition, with the result that although they are in an inseparable unity, each is credited with a self-subsistent determinate being over against the other."

Whether one has in mind infinitely divisible matter or the infinite freedom and perfection after which moralists strive, the infinite that lies beyond all finitude—including its *own* finite manifestation—is, in Hegel's view, structurally ambiguous. It is infinite insofar as it is radically different from the limited, finite being that it exceeds; yet it is not infinite precisely because it is bounded and limited by that which it exceeds. Such an infinite is not, therefore, unequivocally infinite at all. It *should* be infinite but constantly fails to live up to its promise. This is true of the infinite that begins beyond this point or beyond that point or beyond that point: it can never be the unalloyed infinite that, due to its transcendence of the finite, it ought to be, but it always consists in more and more finitude. As Hegel puts it, "this spurious infinity is in itself the same thing as the perennial ought (*Sollen*); it is the negation of the finite it is true, but it cannot in truth free itself therefrom" (*SL* 142/1: 155 [247]). We saw in the last chapter that finite things ought to be what they are intrinsically but, due to their limitations, fall short of the standard they set for themselves. We have now seen that there is also a certain kind of infinity that ought to be, but fails to be, infinite: namely, the systematically transcendent, or excessive, infinite.

In retrospect, of course, one can say of the first bad infinite—found, for example, in light—that it, too, only *ought* to be infinite but is in fact finite. After all, that first bad infinite is not merely *limited* by the finite but is itself something *finite* and is thus beset with an intrinsic limitation—namely, the limitation of failing to be the infinite it should be. To begin with, however, the fact that it only ought to be infinite is merely *implicit* in the bad infinite; its principal explicit characteristic is that it *limits*, and is limited by, the finite. Only when the bad infinite points openly beyond its own limited, finite infinity does it explicitly reveal that it ought to be infinite rather than finite. The moment that the bad infinite manifests its inherent ought-to-be-infinite is thus the moment at which it

inaugurates the progress to infinity.[27] Indeed, that infinite progress is simply the expression of the fact that the finite infinite always "strives"—unsuccessfully—to be properly infinite.

Not only does the infinite that lies beyond all finitude reduce itself to a mere ought-to-be, but the whole tedious *progress* to infinity itself can be said to be that which only *ought* to be infinite. Such an infinite progression is not a mere illusion but is found in many aspects of nature and human consciousness. Nevertheless, the infinity that it exhibits is ultimately no different from the first infinity we encountered, namely, that which consists in endless *finitude*. As a form of infinity, the infinite progress should constitute being that is qualitatively different from finitude, but it never succeeds in doing so and remains, in Burbidge's words, "qualitatively the same as the *finite*."[28] As Harris recognizes, it is the process in which "the finite *ought to be* transcended, but never is."[29]

To repeat: qualitative infinity ought to be found beyond the finite, but it never is because what lies beyond the finite can only be more finitude. Yet, in another sense, one could say that in fact the radically transcendent infinite ought *not* to be found beyond the finite at all, precisely because it is defined as lying *beyond* wherever we are, and beyond that point, and beyond that point, and so on. From this point of view, the progress to infinity is the endless reaching out to an "infinite" that is necessarily endlessly deferred. "This infinite," Hegel writes, "has the fixed determination of a *beyond*, which cannot be reached, for the very reason that *it is not meant* to be reached (*weil es nicht erreicht werden soll*)" (*SL* 142/1: 156 [247]).

In Hegel's view, we are restricted to this systematically elusive infinite—one that repeatedly proves to be finite and constantly relocates itself beyond its own finite incarnation—as long as we refuse to *let go of* (*ablassen von*) the idea that the infinite is the simple *negation* of the finite. For it is the idea that the infinite is quite simply *not* the finite that places the infinite out of reach beyond the realm of the finite in which we live and so prevents infinity from ever *being* the infinite it promises to be. True, the infinite itself demands to be understood as the negation of finitude. If we adhere fixedly to that conception of the infinite, however, we will never understand infinity to be anything other than finite infinity or infinity that endlessly—and fruitlessly—seeks to evade its own finitude. But why should we want to entertain any other conception of the infinite? Because closer attention reveals a different kind of infinity to be immanent in the infinite progress itself. In the next chapter, we will consider the nature of this new form of infinity.

27. See Burbidge, *On Hegel's Logic*, p. 53.

28. Burbidge, *On Hegel' s Logic*, p. 55.

29. Harris, *An Interpretation of the Logic of Hegel*, p. 109.

Chapter Twenty-two

True Infinity

Opening Remarks

Infinity is the new quality of being that finitude, through its demise, comes to constitute. Yet infinite being is also the *negation* of finitude. It shows itself explicitly to be this negation by distinguishing itself from the finite. In so doing, however, as we have seen, infinity succeeds only in reducing itself to something finite. Nevertheless, as the negation of the finite, infinity must logically lie beyond all finitude, including even its own. This logical necessity fails, however, to secure a distinct identity for infinite being, for it simply engenders an endless progress to infinity wherein all finitude points beyond itself to being that *should* be infinite but that always turns out to be more finitude that points beyond itself, and so on. Insofar as infinity distinguishes itself sharply from and places itself beyond the finite, it thus proves to be little different from the first infinity we encountered: namely, one that is not qualitatively distinct from finitude at all but that consists in finitude that goes on forever.

Remember that what Hegel is describing is not a historical process whereby infinite being changes over time from endlessness into immanent infinity and then into bad infinity and finally into the progress to infinity. He is not arguing that at the dawn of time infinite being was nothing more than the endless sequence of finite things and that later it transformed itself into the other forms of infinity. He is unpacking the *logical* implications inherent in the very nature of infinity and thereby disclosing the various forms that infinite being logically must take. In other words, he is showing us what infinite being necessarily proves to be. Hegel ends his discussion of infinity by arguing that the last form we have encountered—the endless progress to infinity—turns out to contain within itself *true* infinity after all: "in this alternating determination of the finite and the infinite from one to the other and back again, their truth is already implicitly *present*, and all that is required is to take up what is before us" (*SL* 143/1: 156 [247]).

Hegel does not, however, proceed immediately to explain how and why true infinity is inherent in the progress to infinity. He first returns to the earlier idea of the bad infinite in order to show that an important aspect of the true infinite can already be glimpsed within it. What Hegel has in mind, specifically, is the *unity* of the infinite and the finite. As we shall see later, the true infinite is by no means

reducible to this unity. Accordingly, Hegel states that "the *unity* of the infinite and the finite is . . . the *one-sided* expression for the unity as it is in truth."[1] Nevertheless, the true infinite does entail such unity (properly understood), and Hegel now points out that this unity is in fact already latent in the bad infinite.

Hegel also makes it clear, however, that the bad infinite does not lead by itself directly to the idea of the unity of the infinite and the finite. By itself, as we have seen, it leads to the idea of the infinite progress. The unity of the infinite and the finite becomes apparent, we are told, only if the philosopher undertakes an "external" comparison of the bad infinite and the finite and draws conclusions of his own on the basis of what he sees (*SL* 146/1: 161 [253]). In the first few pages of 2.C.c, therefore, Hegel departs from his method of letting one category mutate logically into another and instead offers his own reflections on the nature of the infinite. In this way, he anticipates part of what will later be disclosed when he continues his immanent analysis of the progress to infinity. Since that later analysis has to be wholly immanent, however, he will have to set aside what he learns from his "external" consideration of the bad infinite before he turns to the infinite progress itself. Much of what Hegel has to say about the unity of the infinite and the finite is interesting and important; but it may not be used to carry forward the presuppositionless account of infinity. Indeed, it can be skipped without detriment to the coherence and continuity of Hegel's overall argument. The reason Hegel discusses the idea of the "unity" of the finite and the infinite at this point is not to move his logical analysis forward but to show that the idea does not deserve to be utterly dismissed and to criticize the understanding for distorting it.[2]

The "Unity" of the Finite and the Infinite

In comparing the finite and the (bad) infinite, Hegel first notes that they have something very important in common: each actually includes the other within itself. The infinite is nothing but the transcending, or negation, of the *finite*, and the finite is nothing but the pointing to, or negating itself into, the *infinite*. Consequently, "neither can be posited or grasped without the other, the infinite not without the finite, nor the latter without the infinite" (*SL* 143/1: 157 [249]). From the standpoint of the infinite progress (at least, as it has been understood so far), the finite and the infinite are meant to exclude one another and "to follow each other alternately." External comparison of the two reveals, however, that "in *each* . . . there lies the *determinateness of the other*."

---

1. My emphasis. See also Hegel, *EL* 152/202 (§95).

2. The comparison undertaken here between the finite and the infinite is not one that is required by the immanent development of being itself but one that is initiated by Hegel. By contrast, it is *immanent* in the very idea of something and its other that each is *comparatively* other than the other; see chapter 17, above, p. 325, and Hegel, *SL* 118/1: 126 (213).

This is particularly obvious, Hegel claims, in the way in which we speak of the infinite: for "in *saying* what the infinite is, namely the negation of the *finite*, the latter is itself included in what is *said*." To recognize that the infinite and the finite are inseparable, therefore, "one only needs to *be aware of what one is saying*." Hegel's external comparison of the categories of the finite and the infinite thus goes hand in hand with close attention to the *language* in which we formulate the definition of those categories.

The infinite and the finite are each included in the other because each one is in necessary relation (*Beziehung*) to its other. What happens, however, if we consider each one as quite distinct and separate from its opposite? Do we—paradoxically—discover a similar intimate connection between the two? Hegel believes that we do.

Even if we take the infinite by itself as one of the two categories, we necessarily discern its opposite—the finite—within it. This is because "it is not the whole but only *one* side," and so "it has its limit in what stands over against it" and "is thus the *finite infinite*" (*SL* 144/1: 157–8 [249]). Separating the infinite off from the finite does not actually preserve the infinite in its purity. On the contrary, "it is precisely this holding of the infinite *apart* from the finite, thus giving it a *one-sided* character, that constitutes its finitude and, therefore, its unity with the finite."

On the other hand, if we consider the finite purely by itself, quite apart from the infinite, we necessarily take away from it the very quality that renders it finite. This is because the only way we can abstract from the fact that the finite constitutes *infinite* being is by abstracting from the fact that it comes to a definite end and so passes into further *finite* being without end. If we detach finite being from infinity altogether, therefore, what we are left with is simply self-relating being that is no longer explicitly finite. But this means that we find in the finite "the same self-subsistence and affirmation which the infinite is supposed to be." Just like the infinite, the finite by itself thus turns out to be inseparable from its opposite.

Whether the finite and the infinite are taken by themselves or in their relation to one another, they cannot but be understood as including one another within themselves. Hegel states, therefore, that his external comparison of the two categories yields "the decried unity (*Einheit*) of the finite and the infinite"—a unity that constitutes a new form of infinite or unbounded being "which embraces both itself and finitude." (As will become apparent later, this new infinite is the true infinite, albeit abstractly conceived.) This unity is not a third category over and above the finite and the infinite themselves. It is simply the unity with its other that each one is *within itself*. Accordingly, Hegel says, "we have two such unities," each of which is the same new infinity.

Hegel notes that, insofar as each category is this unity with its opposite, it necessarily ceases being quite distinct from, or other than, its opposite. It loses its separate character and is thus "negated" (*negiert*) (*SL* 144/1: 158 [251]). Ex-

actly what this means is by no means completely clear and will not become clear until we move to the further immanent analysis of the infinite progress. What is clear, however, is that for Hegel the finite and the infinite cannot possess the same quality or character insofar as they are included in the other that they possess insofar as they are distinct from or other than one another. In other words, to the extent that each forms an intrinsic part of and so is united with its other, it can no longer be conceived as *other* than its other at all.

Hegel believes that this insight—incomplete though it is—suffices to allow us to formulate a criticism of "representational thinking" (*Vorstellung*), or the unbridled understanding (*Verstand*). Such thinking, according to Hegel, holds the finite and infinite apart as separate spheres, or kinds of being. Furthermore, to the extent that it acknowledges that the finite and the infinite do in fact belong together, it connects them as two *separate* categories, or ways of being. The understanding treats the finite and the infinite rather like two bricks that can be cemented together but that nonetheless remain separate; it does not recognize that the character of each one is *negated* and changed to the extent that it is united with its other. For the understanding, therefore, there is only one relation between finitude and infinity, namely, that of being *other* than one another; this relation governs them whether they are taken separately or together. For Hegel, by contrast—based on the comparison he undertakes here, if not yet on the immanent analysis of the infinite progress—there are *two* relations between the finite and the infinite: one that makes them distinct spheres of being, namely, that of being other than one another, and a second that characterizes their unity, or "being-included-in-one-another." We do not yet know all that this second relation entails, but we do know that it is *not* the relation of one *something* to *another*. Insofar as the understanding conceives of the unity of the finite and the infinite as the unity of two separate kinds of being, it thus distorts, or "falsifies" (*verfälscht*), the true idea of their unity (*SL* 145/1: 159 [251]). Hegel believes that his own comparison of the finite and the infinite demonstrates this even before it is confirmed by the purely immanent analysis of the progress to infinity.

Hegel goes on to explain that although the infinite and the finite both include their opposites within themselves they are nevertheless united with one another in two *different* ways. The infinite is affirmative, intrinsic being (*Ansichsein*) but is rendered finite—and thereby "united" with finitude—by the fact that it has its own limit vis-à-vis the finite. The finite, on the other hand, is being that is consigned to nonbeing, but it is rendered infinite by virtue of being contrasted with the infinite—as the "negation of the in-itself" or *Nicht-Ansichsein*—and so being invested with an unchanging and unending identity of its own.

Once again, Hegel argues, the understanding distorts and misrepresents each form of unity. To the extent that the understanding accepts that the infinite beyond the finite is indeed limited by and inseparable from the finite, it assumes that this limit does not in any way compromise or negate the infinite's *infinity* as such. The infinite remains infinite beyond the limit that it *also* has with respect

to the finite. In Hegel's own words, the understanding takes the infinite "not as negated, but rather as the in-itself, in which, therefore, determinateness and limitation are not to be explicitly present" (*SL* 145/1: 159 [251]).

Similarly, the understanding assumes that the *finitude* of the finite is not compromised by the fact that the finite is conceived as purely, unalterably, and so infinitely finite. In its unity with the infinite, "the finite is . . . held fast as not negated"; it remains finite *in spite of* being invested with a certain infinity. This, I believe, is the sense behind one of Hegel's most complex sentences: insofar as the finite is united with infinity by the understanding, Hegel writes, it is "infinitized in opposition to (*gegen*) its determination as finite, which instead of vanishing, is perpetuated."

Hegel again contends that the understanding distorts the unity of the finite and the infinite because it insists that, even insofar as they are united with one another, "each in its own nature is separate, in fact absolutely separate from the other." It will not let go of the idea that the infinite and the finite are "qualitatively distinct," and in this respect it does not really accept that the two kinds of being form a *unity* at all. As a result, the understanding overlooks what Hegel regards as a crucial fact: namely, that each category turns out to include its other within itself because each one, of its own accord, *negates* and undermines its own separate identity:

> each is in its own self this unity, and this only as a *sublating* (*Aufheben*) of its own self. . . . As has already been shown, finitude *is* only as a transcending of itself; it therefore contains infinity, the other of itself. Similarly, infinity *is* only as a transcending of the finite; it therefore essentially contains its other and is, consequently, in its own self the other of itself. (*SL* 145-6/1: 160 [253])

The fault of the understanding is thus not only that it reduces infinity to bad (or tedious) infinity but also that it does not fully comprehend the unity of the finite and the infinite inherent in bad infinity. That is to say, the understanding does not properly understand what is implicit in the "infinite of the understanding." Or as Hegel puts it, the understanding "forget[s] what the concept (*Begriff*) of these moments is for the understanding itself" (*SL* 145/1: 160 [251]).

As I have already remarked, Hegel does not spell out at this stage all that the negation of the finite and the infinite involves. It is clear, however, that the finite and the infinite should no longer be conceived just as *other* than one another but must be conceived as *negating themselves into* one another. This dialectical moment at the heart of both finitude and infinity is what the understanding fails to comprehend or, at least, to take seriously.

For Hegel, dialectical self-negation is common to both the finite and the infinite. Furthermore, insofar as the finite and the infinite do differ from one another—and Hegel insists that there is always a difference, if not always a relation of otherness, between them—each is simply the *negation* of the essentially

negative character of the other. The finite is negative because it brings itself to an end, and the infinite is negative because it is *not* the finite but—at least, at this stage—an empty "beyond." In differing from the other, therefore, each one negates the negation that the other is. Consequently, the finite and the infinite are *both* self-negating *and* the negation of another negation. "What is therefore present," Hegel writes, "is the same negation of negation in each" (*SL* 146/1: 160 [253]).

At the same time, however, through negating themselves and one another, the finite and the infinite come together to constitute *one* sphere of being that relates affirmatively to *itself*. What is actually present, therefore, is "*in itself* self-relation, affirmation, but as return to itself, that is through the *mediation* which the negation of negation is."

This conclusion is by no means arbitrary and subjective but is based on a study of the logical structure of finitude and infinity itself. Nevertheless, it is reached by undertaking an external *comparison* of the two categories, not by simply following where the structure of the bad infinite itself leads us (which, as we know, is to the idea of the infinite progress). Hegel compares the finite and the infinite and detects (a) that they are each *negated* (in some as yet unspecified way) through being united with the other and (b) that, insofar as they are self-negating and the negation of one another, they constitute together one realm of affirmative, self-relating being (whose nature is as yet also unspecified). Hegel now points out that these two ideas are in fact explicitly contained in, or "posited" (*gesetzt*) by, the infinite progress itself. If we examine the progress to infinity, we will thus learn in more detail what it means for the finite and the infinite to be *negated* in such a way that together they constitute *self-relating* being.

Yet we can, of course, continue to *compare* the way in which the finite and the infinite appear in the infinite progress. What we discern by so doing, Hegel claims, is that both the finite and the infinite are transcended and negated but that both also follow one another as positively distinct categories. Hegel immediately points out, however, that this is by no means all that is *logically* contained in the infinite progress itself: for "in it there is also posited the *connection* (*Zusammenhang*) of terms which are also distinct from each other." The finite and the infinite are connected in the infinite progress by virtue of the fact that they pass over *into* one another. It is because each is this transition (*Übergang*) into the other that each is negated but also generated anew in the progress to infinity.[3] Hegel now turns to consider the immanent logical structure of the progress to infinity in order to discover precisely what such transition entails.

To ensure that the analysis is indeed rigorously immanent, however, we must begin from the infinite progress as it emerged at the end of the last chapter. This means that we must set to one side what we have just learned through comparing the finite and the bad infinite. Above all, we must leave behind the

---

3. See Maluschke, *Kritik und absolute Methode in Hegels Dialektik*, p. 181.

specific idea that the finite and the infinite form a *unity* together. When *we* compare the two categories, *we* can see that one is included in, and so united with, the other. As we saw in the last chapter, however, this unity is "concealed" (*verborgen*) in the infinite progress itself (and in the bad infinite).[4] The finite and the infinite do not occupy the same logical space in the infinite progress but pass over into and supplant one another; in that sense, they fail to exhibit any explicit "unity" or togetherness. Indeed, the progress is generated precisely by the endless transition of the one into the *other*. A rigorously immanent study of the infinite progress may thus not start by invoking the "unity" of the finite and the infinite but must focus purely on their transition into one another. The idea of the unity of the two categories may be considered only if it is made necessary by the infinite progress itself. From now on, then, the work of external comparison ceases, and immanent logical analysis recommences. The "simple reflection" that Hegel says is needed in order to "see what is in fact present" in the infinite progress is not itself a further act of comparison but simply the activity—demanded of us throughout the *Logic*—of rendering explicit what is implicit in the category at hand (*SL* 146/1: 161 [253]).

The Progress to Infinity Further Considered

Hegel now examines the progress to infinity more closely. This progress starts from the finite (since being proves to be finite before it proves to be infinite) and, as we have seen, this finite immediately points beyond itself to, and passes over into, the infinite. This infinite, however, is bounded by the finite that it transcends, and so itself immediately turns into something finite. As such, it points beyond itself to the infinite, which once more proves to be bounded and finite. This process whereby the finite points beyond itself to yet another finite goes on endlessly.

In the course of this process, however, finitude is not just endlessly repeated. It also proves to be other than, or more than, mere *finitude* as such. This is because in pointing and passing *beyond* itself it simply joins, or "unites," with *itself* once again and so turns out to be unending being: "what arises is the *same* as that from which the movement *began*, that is, the finite is restored; it has therefore united *with itself*, has in its beyond only found *itself* again" (*SL* 147/1: 161–2 [255]). The same is true of the infinite that lies beyond the finite. This infinite proves to be limited and finite itself and so in turn points beyond itself to the infinite once more. "Spuriously" infinite being thus points beyond itself to, and passes over into, *itself*. Like the finite, therefore, such infinite being proves to be genuinely unending being, or being that beyond itself "has arrived *at its own self*."

Yet have we not encountered this logical move before? Did not the finite

4. See chapter 21, above, p. 410, and Hegel, *SL* 141/1: 154 (245).

prove to be qualitatively infinite in the first place by fulfilling its own determination and so "uniting with itself," as it changed into something else? And did not this infinite being then distinguish itself from the finite and so take the form of the bad infinite? If we have now returned to a similar conception of infinity, is there not a danger that we will be led once more to the bad infinite and, indeed, that we will be cast over and over again into the progress to infinity? Not necessarily, for there is a subtle difference between the move that we have just made and the one made at the start of the account of the qualitative infinite.

Finitude initially gives rise to qualitatively infinite being because it comes to be itself in a new guise when it passes away and turns into something else. The finite thing does, indeed, meet its demise and so issue in *another* thing, but in the process its *own* being continues in a new form. The finite thus unites immediately with itself when it mutates into a wholly other thing. The infinite being that emerges in this process is in turn nothing but the immediately self-relating being that is constituted through the demise of the finite. This infinite being is itself immediately different from finitude as such because the finite as *finite* consists specifically in self-negation and the constant passage into something *else*. In passing away but continuing to be itself in a new guise, the finite thus establishes an utterly different kind of being: one that does *not* change or come to an end. Since it is the immediate negation of finitude, infinite being explicitly differentiates itself from finite being and takes the form of bad infinity. We are led to the bad infinite and then to the infinite progress, therefore, because infinite being is initially immediately self-relating being that is immediately distinct from finitude as such.

In the infinite progress, however, the finite and the infinite do not constitute infinite being by simply continuing in another form and so uniting *immediately* with themselves. Each one unites with itself *by means of* its utter negation. Finite being does not just unite with itself in further finitude but joins together with itself in the *infinite* being by which it is transcended. Similarly, infinite being unites with itself by virtue of being *finite* and so pointing beyond itself to further infinite being. Finite and spuriously infinite being thus unite with themselves in and through the other, or negation, that excludes them. In the infinite progress, therefore, finite and infinite being do not constitute immediately continuous, self-relating being but prove to be the "*movement* in which each returns to itself *through its negation*." Consequently, "they *are* only as the *mediation* within themselves, and the affirmative of each contains the negative of each and is the negation of the negation."

Insofar as each is this movement of uniting with itself, each constitutes unending, *infinite* being. Such infinite being is not, however, immediately self-relating being; it is thus not immediately *distinct* from finite being that constantly negates itself into something else. On the contrary, the infinite being we now encounter is explicitly *mediated* being: it is the movement of uniting-with-self that the finite and the (bad) infinite each proves to be *by virtue of* the fact

that each is equally its negation. Since it is explicitly mediated by the self-negation of the finite and the bad infinite, this new infinite, self-relating being cannot set itself apart from the finite and the bad infinite as immediately different from them but must incorporate them explicitly within its own logical structure. This new infinity is thus not just the bad infinite once again but promises to be truly infinite.

Note that this new infinity emerges because the finite and the bad infinite are *negated* in three related ways. First of all, as we have just mentioned, the finite and the infinite negate themselves into their opposites and so allow one another to unite with themselves and thereby to constitute infinite being. Secondly, although they start out as distinct categories or kinds of being, the finite and the infinite prove, in the course of the infinite progress, *not* just to be distinct kinds of being after all and so lose their initial character. This is because they end up constituting the same process of uniting-with-self-in-the-other—and thus the same infinite, self-relating being—as one another. This, I believe, is what Hegel means when he says that the finite and the infinite are now understood to be "a *result*, and consequently not what they are in the determination of their *beginning*" (*SL* 147/1: 162 [255]).

Thirdly, the finite and the infinite cease being merely distinct from one another not only because they turn out to be the same process of uniting-with-self as one another but also because each one proves to be an integral *moment* of the process that the other one is. Each must be a moment of the other's process or movement because each unites with itself *only through the other*. If each is in fact an irreducible moment of the other, however, they cannot simply be distinct from or other than one another.

In the progress to infinity, finite and infinite being are both transformed or negated in these three ways and so necessarily exhibit a new logical character. They reveal themselves not just to be *something* in relation to something *else* but rather to be different *moments* of the *process* that each one also is. According to Hegel, the fact that each is negated in this way is what is overlooked by the understanding. As we saw above (see pp. 416–17), Hegel came to a similar conclusion earlier on the basis of his external comparison of the finite and the infinite—though it remained unclear just what it meant for each to be "negated." His criticism of the understanding has now been reinforced and clarified by his immanent analysis of the infinite progress, for we now know that the finite and the infinite are negated in that progress by being turned into *moments*:

> The reason why understanding is so antagonistic to the unity of the finite and the infinite is simply that it presupposes the limitation and the finite, as well as the in-itself, as *perpetuated*; in doing so it *overlooks* the negation of both which is actually present in the infinite progress, as also the fact that they occur therein only as moments of a whole (*Momente eines Ganzen*).

True Infinity

So far the finite and the (bad) infinite have *each* been understood to unite with and "return into" themselves through their negation. From this perspective, therefore, there are two processes of uniting-with-self in the progress to infinity: one initiated by the finite and the other by the infinite. Hegel notes, however, that these two processes are not actually distinct from one another. After all, the process whereby the infinite unites with itself is *itself* the process whereby the finite unites with itself since each is at the same time its opposite. The finite and the infinite thus in fact constitute *one and the same* process of uniting-with-self-in-the-other. Yet this is not the only respect in which the two are identical. Each one constitutes self-relating being by negating and pointing beyond itself and by uniting with itself in that beyond. Insofar as each one is specifically *that which* negates itself and points beyond itself in this process of uniting with self, each is a *moment* of the process rather than the whole process itself. Moreover, they are moments in exactly the same way.

This does not mean that we now have to reject completely the idea that the finite and the bad infinite are other than one another. We now see, however, that that idea only captures part of the truth, for the finite and the bad infinite turn out to form one and the same process of uniting-with-self and to be in equal measure a moment of this process. Hegel argues that this insight now opens up a new way of differentiating finite from infinite being. There is, he notes, a logical difference between the self-negating *moments* of the process we are considering and the *process* itself. Since they are self-negating, these moments are both finite; by contrast, the process of uniting-with-self is constitutive of infinite, unending being. This difference between a "moment" and the "process" to which it belongs does not characterize the relation between the finite and the *bad* infinite. It does, however, characterize the relation between, on the one hand, the finite and the bad infinite taken together and, on the other hand, the new infinite that we have seen emerge in this chapter. Up to this point, we have seen that the infinite is rendered finite by virtue of being *other* than the finite. What we now learn is that both the finite and the bad infinite are finite by virtue of being *moments* of the process of uniting-with-self that alone is *true* infinity:

> Since both the finite and the infinite itself are moments of the process they are *jointly or in common the finite*, and since they are equally together negated in it and in the result, this result as negation of the finitude of both is called with truth the infinite. (*SL* 148/1: 163 [255])[5]

It is apparent that we now have two senses of "finitude": to be finite is to be something in relation to something else but also to be a moment of a proc-

5. Translation revised.

ess.[6] Similarly, infinity takes the form both of the bad infinite and of the truly infinite process generated by the bad infinite and the finite. This process constitutes truly infinite being because it is the movement in which being always unites with itself and because it is not *bounded* in any way by the finite or the finite infinite but includes them as its own moments. The true infinite is simply the process of always-relating-to-self to which finitude itself gives rise.[7]

The development of the idea of the infinite has actually taken us through *five* conceptions of the infinite: from endlessness to immediate, qualitative infinity to bad infinity to the progress to infinity to true infinity. Each form of infinity is a necessary stage in the logical process whereby infinite being develops into true infinity. Hegel summarizes this logical process as follows:

> The infinite . . . is, in fact, the process in which it is deposed to being only *one* of its determinations, the opposite of the finite, and so to being itself only one of the finites, and then raising this its difference from itself into the affirmation of itself and through this mediation becoming the *true* infinite. (*SL* 148/1: 163 [257])

It is important to recognize that the true infinite is *different* from the finite. Hegel's point, however, is that the true infinite cannot be something *other* than the finite because it is the process generated by the finite in which the finite is a constitutive moment. In Hegel's view, therefore, we can understand the nature of true infinity only when we give up the idea that "differing from" always amounts to "being other than." Finite things are certainly other than one another. There is also a form of infinite being that is other than the finite, namely, bad infinity. True infinity cannot be *other* than the finite, however, because it is by definition *not* a finite something. In order to comprehend true infinity, we thus need to develop an idea of difference that is different from "being other than." Precisely such an idea of difference is to be found in the relation between a process and its moments. A moment of a process is not the whole process itself and so can be distinguished from it. Such a moment is not *other* than the process, however, nor is the process other than it, since that moment is a moment *of* the process itself. In this sense, as Lakebrink puts it, otherness "disappears" (*verschwindet*) in the true infinite.[8] This does *not* mean, as many of Hegel's subsequent critics have charged, that the other is "absorbed" into or "digested" by some preexisting Absolute. It means simply that the finite—which is always something or other—

---

6. Maluschke notes that Hegel thus distinguishes between an "untrue" and a "true" finitude, as well as between an "untrue" and "true" infinity. See *Kritik und absolute Methode in Hegels Dialektik*, p. 169.

7. On the idea of the true infinite as process, see Lakebrink, *Kommentar zu Hegels "Logik,"* p. 130; Rinaldi, *A History and Interpretation of the Logic of Hegel*, p. 155; Theunissen, *Sein und Schein*, p. 294.

8. Lakebrink, *Kommentar zu Hegels "Logik,"* p. 124.

turns itself into a *moment* of an infinite process to which finite being itself gives rise.

Note that the relation between a process and its moments yields not only a new form of difference but also a new form of unity. It is tempting to conceive of unity as the unity between one thing and another; this is a temptation to which, as we know, the understanding succumbs. The unity of the finite and the true infinite cannot be conceived in this way, however, because they are not two separate realms of being. Nevertheless, they do form a unity insofar as a process is inseparable from its moments. In retrospect, therefore, Hegel was quite justified in discussing the "unity" of the finite and the infinite at the start of 2.C.c. What was missing from that discussion, however, was a clear sense of the form that such a unity must take. Hegel's immanent analysis of the infinite progress has now made good that deficit.

We have, of course, encountered the idea of a "moment" before. Being and nothing, for example, proved to be moments of pure becoming. Hegel's claim now is that concrete finite things must also be conceived as moments of truly infinite being. True infinity is not, however, merely the endless succession of changing, finite things or the progress to infinity. True infinity is the process in which being comes to *unite with itself*—and only with itself—in and through the self-negating of finite things. This process occurs within the process of endless change, but is by no means reducible to it.

As Doz points out, however, this concept of truly infinite being is still quite abstract.[9] True infinity is the least we can now understand being to be; but the idea that being is *infinity* does not take us all that far. We can shed more light on Hegel's understanding of being's infinity, however, by looking ahead to what truly infinite being will later turn out to entail. Later in Hegel's system, we learn that being is truly infinite insofar as it unites with itself and relates to itself by becoming *conscious* of itself. True infinity thus proves to be not just the endless series of occurrences in space and time but the process whereby being brings itself to self-consciousness (and so to life) and so becomes *spirit*.

Hegel argues throughout his philosophy that this process is a rational one but that it is not under the sway of any divine or rational necessity beyond nature and humanity. It is the process whereby being—that is, natural and human being—determines itself through its own inherent logic to become self-conscious. Stace is thus right to claim that "genuine infinity means self-determination."[10] The *logos* or "Idea" at work in this process cannot be controlled or manipulated by human beings but "bloweth where it listeth" (John 3:8). Human beings can, however, come to understand that logic, and bring their hearts, minds, and bod-

9. Doz, *La logique de Hegel et les problèmes traditionnels de l'ontologie*, p. 69.

10. Stace, *The Philosophy of Hegel*, p. 146. See also Mure, *A Study of Hegel's Logic*, pp. 49–50, and McTaggart, *A Commentary on Hegel's Logic*, pp. 34–5.

ies into accord with its dictates. In this way, we become willing agents of infinite, self-determining reason.[11]

This infinite reason within nature and human history working toward self-consciousness (and, ultimately, freedom) is what religion pictures as "God." For Hegel, then, God does not transcend the finite world, as Descartes would have us believe, but lives and moves *within* the finite world. "God" is simply the infinite rational process whereby being achieves "unity with itself" in self-consciousness and self-knowledge. One should remember, however, that this conception of true infinity goes further than we are entitled to go on the basis of what we have learned so far in the *Logic*. I mention it here merely to indicate what comes later in Hegel's system. Insofar as true infinity is nothing more than simple *infinity*, it does not entail any explicit progress toward self-consciousness or freedom; it is simply being that, in the demise of finite things, comes to unite with itself. It is important to note, however, that the very fact that being does prove to be truly infinite and self-relating means that there is a nisus toward self-consciousness within the logical structure of being itself. The fact that self-consciousness emerges in the world thus cannot be purely accidental because it is made necessary by being's inherent *infinity*.

Taylor maintains that true infinity is the "whole system of finite things and their relations."[12] This definition is helpful because it reminds us that true infinity is nothing beyond the finite things that actually exist. True infinity is the process that is actually occurring here and now. It does not transcend the world or systematically exceed our comprehension but "*is* and *is there*, present before us" (*SL* 149/1: 164 [257]). Yet Taylor's description also misses an important aspect of true infinity that manifests itself explicitly in the later idea that infinity is the process leading to self-consciousness and freedom. True infinity is not only an "ordered whole" (to use another of Taylor's descriptions)[13] but also implicitly a process of *development*. That is to say, it is not just being that continues and remains in the demise of finite things but being that *comes to* unite with itself through the self-negation of the finite. It is being that *emerges* as unified—indeed, that emerges as the very process of uniting with itself. To be sure, conceiving of being as infinity falls a long way short of conceiving it as structured, rational development, or "concept" (*Begriff*). We will not reach that conception of being until the last part of the *Logic*. Nevertheless, insofar as we understand being to be truly infinite, we conceive of it not merely as stasis but as a primitive, abstract form of development constituted by the demise of finite things. This is because, to employ the language of the *Phenomenology*, truly infinite be-

11. On the relation between reason and contingency in Hegel's philosophy, see Houlgate, "Necessity and Contingency in Hegel's *Science of Logic*," pp. 47–9. See also chapter 6, above, p. 118.

12. Taylor, *Hegel*, p. 241.

13. Taylor, *Hegel*, p. 240.

ing is not just substance, but substance that is always becoming *subject* (see *PhS* 14/28).

This is one of the things that distinguishes true infinity from the immediate qualitative infinity that we encountered earlier. Whereas immediate infinity comes to *continue* as finite things pass away, truly infinite being continuously *comes to* unite with, and relate to, itself. Truly infinite being, in other words, is more overtly progressive and developmental than immediate infinity. As we have seen, the other difference between these two forms of infinity is that true infinity explicitly preserves the finite within it as its constitutive moment, whereas immediately infinite being—though immanent in the finite—is immediately *different* from finitude itself and so logically must detach itself from finitude. There is, of course, an intimate connection between the two ways in which these two forms of infinity differ. Truly infinite being is necessarily developmental because it always has to emerge from the finite that it retains as an irreducible moment of itself. By contrast, immediate infinity is simply continuous, self-relating being, because it owes its genesis to the fact that the finite *ceases* being merely finite and does not just come to an end after all.

Hartnack is thus wrong to claim of the true infinite that "the finite is absorbed into the infinite and therefore ceases to exist as a finite element." The finite disappears—albeit temporarily—in *immediately* infinite being but not in *truly* infinite being.[14] In my view, Rinaldi gets it right when he says that the true infinite "does not exclude the finite from its self-identity, but posits it as an essential 'moment' of its own."[15]

Having distinguished between immediately and truly infinite being, we must avoid the temptation to treat them as wholly separate from one another. They are, rather, two kinds of infinity manifested by one and the same realm of being. Being can be understood as infinite because it *remains* when finite things pass away and so is not finite itself. (This is the infinity that Spinoza discerns.) Or being can be understood to be infinite because it *comes to* unite with itself—and eventually comes to consciousness of itself—through the self-negation of finite things. We are dealing with the same being in each case, understood in a subtly different way. In nature, as we learn in the *Philosophy of Nature*, being is immediately infinite as matter, spuriously infinite as matter that distinguishes itself from gravity and heaviness to become light, and truly infinite as matter that turns into organic (and then conscious) life.

---

14. See J. Hartnack, *An Introduction to Hegel's Logic*, trans. L. Aagaard-Mogensen, ed. K. Westphal (Indianapolis: Hackett Publishing, 1998), p. 24. The line that Hartnack quotes in support of his claim—"the finite has vanished in the infinite and what *is*, is only the *infinite*"—is actually taken from the section on the immediate infinite; see Hegel, *SL* 138/1: 150 (241).

15. Rinaldi, *A History and Interpretation of the Logic of Hegel*, p. 154.

Infinity and Ideality

To recapitulate: truly infinite being is nothing apart from finitude but is simply the process whereby *finite* things constitute being that unites with itself. For Hegel, there is only *one* process going on—the process of true infinity, or "substance becoming subject"—and finite things including human beings are the sole agents that carry that process forward. Expressed in religious language, God's work in the world is carried out by human beings who negate, or "die to," themselves and so bring themselves into loving unity with one another. This is not to say that we create and control that "divine" process but rather that our activity *is* that "divine" process.

In the more technical vocabulary of Hegelian logic, true infinity is *self-relating* being that is one with finite, *self-negating* being. As we know, something (*etwas*) is self-relating being; a finite something is self-negating being; and immediately infinite being is the immediately self-relating being that finite, self-negating being constitutes but that is immediately *different* from such self-negation. In true infinity, self-relating being becomes explicitly *identical* with self-negating, finite being. In true infinity, therefore, the positivity and negativity at the heart of being are perfectly fused. Furthermore, the logical implications of being a *finite something* are rendered fully explicit. True infinity is not itself "something" in relation to something else, yet it is the process that must occur if there is something at all. It is what is made necessary by the very nature of *things*.

In constituting true infinity—or the process whereby being unites itself with itself—finite things, according to Hegel, take on a new quality: that of being *ideal* (*ideell*). This is not to say that finite things manifest exquisite beauty in this process or that they turn out to be ultimately unreal. Hegel means simply that such things are transformed from being fundamentally separate objects to being *moments* of a process: "ideal being is the finite as it is in the true infinite—as a determination, a content, which is distinct but is not an *independent, self-subsistent* being, but only a *moment*" (*SL* 149–50/1: 165 [259]). The defining characteristic of a "moment" in Hegel's view is that it does not have a separate identity of its own but gains its character from the role it plays within the whole that it helps to constitute. Hegel argues that all finite things, as well as being separate from one another, turn out to be moments in this sense. In other words, all finite things turn out to be *ideal*. Presuppositionless philosophy thus proves to be unabashed idealism:

> The proposition that the finite is ideal (*ideell*) constitutes idealism. The idealism of philosophy consists in nothing else than the fact that the finite is not to be recognized as something true (*ein wahrhaft Seiendes*). Every philosophy is essentially an idealism or at least has idealism for

> its principle, and the question then is only how far this principle is actually carried out. (*SL* 154–5/1: 172)[16]

When reading these lines, it is important to recognize that Hegel is not now denying that finite things exist; he is not depriving them of "true" being in that sense. The whole argument of the *Logic* so far has demonstrated that being must take the form of finitude and that such finitude is absolutely irreducible. Indeed, finite things are essential to infinite being: without the one, one could not have the other. Yet precisely because finite things do constitute infinite being, finitude as such cannot exhaust what there is. What being is *in truth*, therefore, is not mere finitude but infinite being that includes finite being as its indispensable moment. Hegel declares finite things to be ideal not because he regards such things as mere figments of our imagination but because he denies that finitude *alone* makes up what there truly is.

Finite things are undeniably real, but they are also ideal insofar as they constitute mere "moments" of truly infinite, self-relating being. Ideality, for Hegel, is thus a quality exhibited by actual finite things themselves; it is an aspect of their ontological structure: their being moments-of-a-process. In other words, Hegel's idealism is just as much a full-blooded realism (in the ordinary sense of the word). Indeed, Hegel states explicitly that "the opposition of idealistic and realistic philosophy has no significance" (*SL* 155/1: 172).

Hegelian idealism should not, therefore, be confused with either Berkeley's or Kant's "subjective" idealism according to which empirical objects as we experience them exist merely *for the knowing mind*. Both Berkeley and Kant insist that the material objects we see are "empirically real": that is to say, they occupy definite positions in space and time, obey definite laws of nature, and behave in ways that can be predicted by any intelligent observer. Nevertheless, Berkeley and Kant also insist that empirical objects as we know them do not exist outside of human experience. The known empirical world is simply the world *of* our shared experience and is thus mind-dependent or, in Hegel's terms, "subjectively" ideal.[17]

By contrast, Hegel rejects the idea that things are in any sense mind-dependent. In the *Logic* he argues that finite things in general are made necessary by the very nature of *being* itself, not by the structure of the human mind. It is also clear from the *Philosophy of Nature* and the *Philosophy of Spirit* that empirical objects exist independently of the mind and that the human mind itself is born into a world that is already populated by concrete finite things. Such things are nevertheless "ideal" for Hegel precisely because they constitute moments of the *real process* that leads to the emergence of human consciousness.

---

16. Translation revised.

17. Kant differs from Berkeley, of course, by pointing to what he takes to be the a priori conditions of experience and by arguing that we must think of ourselves as affected by objects in themselves.

Hegel thus believes in the ontological or structural "ideality" of things, but he is clearly not a subjective idealist.[18] Indeed, he claims that subjective idealists often overlook the genuine ideality of things to which he wishes to draw attention. This is because they frequently treat things simply as law-governed *finite* objects of experience and fail to detect within the world they encounter any genuinely *infinite* movement toward self-consciousness. In Hegel's own words,

> subjective idealism . . . concerns only the *form* of conception according to which a content is mine. . . . Such idealism is [merely] formal because it disregards the *content* of imagination or thought, which content in being imagined or thought can remain wholly in its finitude. (*SL* 155-6/1: 173)[19]

The account of Hegel's idealism presented here differs significantly from that offered by Pippin. For Pippin, Hegel's idealism is the doctrine that "there is and must be a kind of spontaneous, positing reflection necessary for the determinacy of any determinate being to be accounted for."[20] Hegelian idealism, on this reading, is thus not a theory about what there *is* but rather a theory about the conceptual conditions of human judgment itself and of possible objects of judgment.[21] This is not to say that Pippin's Hegel believes that objects in themselves are mind-dependent; for Pippin, Hegel is committed to the idea that there are independently existing objects. Hegel is an idealist, however, because he holds that a network of spontaneously generated, nonempirical concepts provides the conditions under which alone we can *judge* something to be a determinate object of a certain kind.

Now I agree with Pippin that Hegel does, indeed, argue that certain a priori categories structure our thought and experience. For reasons that I have outlined earlier in this study, however, I believe that Hegel also retains what Pippin calls the "precritical" notion that a category is a "purely rational determination of the real."[22] Hegel is an idealist, in my view, because he regards *ideality* as just such a determination of the real. That is to say, he is an idealist not merely because he understands our judgments about things to have pure conceptual conditions but because he understands ideality, or "being-a-moment-of-a-process," to be an *on-*

---

18. See L. Heyde, *The Weight of Finitude: On the Philosophical Question of God*, trans. A. Harmsen and W. Desmond (Albany: SUNY Press, 1999), p. 138: "That the finite is, in fact, ideal, does not mean that it is not real or only a sort of representation."

19. Hegel also recognizes, of course, that the idea of "divine" purpose in nature and history plays an important role in Kant's philosophy. The fact that Kant regards purpose as merely a regulative idea of human reason rather than a constitutive feature of being itself means, however, that from Hegel's point of view Kant remains mired in finitude. See Hegel, *EL* 103–4/141–2 (§§57–8).

20. Pippin, *Hegel's Idealism*, p. 216.

21. Pippin, *Hegel's Idealism*, pp. 243, 246, 248.

22. Pippin, *Hegel's Idealism*, p. 180.

tological structure, or a quality that is exhibited by things themselves independently of our thought or judgments about them. On my reading, Hegel claims that thought can determine from within itself both how being must be understood *and* what being is in itself. He proves to be an idealist because he demonstrates that being must take the form of irreducibly *real* finite things that turn themselves into *ideal* moments of the process of true infinity.

For Hegel, all finite things are moments of the process of uniting-with-itself that being proves to be. Later in his philosophy, however, he shows that some finite things are more explicitly ideal, or "momentary," than others. Human beings, for example, form deeply intimate bonds with one another in which they cease being merely separate entities and acquire a new, shared identity. In such bonds of unity—in marriage or the state—human beings become moments of the whole that they together constitute. They do not actually have to die to join together in this way, but they do have to give up, or "negate," the autonomy and independence on which they otherwise insist. The whole that is thereby constituted is nothing beyond the finite individuals that make it up, even though it has a structure and integrity (and sometimes laws) of its own that those individuals must understand, recognize, and promote if it is to flourish. Such a whole can thus be considered to be instance of true *infinity*. This is not to deny that marriages and states break up or go into decline and in this sense are finite. They exhibit the quality of infinity, however, insofar as they are unified, self-relating wholes—and, indeed, processes—that are nothing beyond their constitutive moments. If the state or the family sets itself against its members, of course—as it often can—it becomes a *bad* infinity.

The individuals who join together to form families and states may themselves be said to enjoy or embody true infinity insofar as they find their own identities recognized, affirmed, and expanded by the other people to whom they relate. Infinite being is being that is not limited or brought to a halt by another but that always relates to itself. Since individuals in families and states find their identity, and so unite with and relate to themselves, in and through other people, they are in fact concrete instances or embodiments of truly infinite being. When I am in love, Hegel says, "I do not wish to be an independent person in my own right and . . . if I were, I would feel deficient and incomplete." I thus give up the idea that I am a wholly separate person and look to gain a new identity in communion with the other whom I love. Indeed, in genuine love "I find myself in another person, . . . I gain recognition in this person, who in turn gains recognition in me."[23] Love is the incarnation of true infinity, therefore, because it is a relation to another person in which one's identity is not simply limited by that other but in which one finds or "unites with" oneself in the other. As persons and as bodies occupying different regions of space, people remain separate from one another; as lovers, however, they not only become ideal moments of the

23. Hegel, *PR* 199/308 (§158 Add.).

bond of love that they form but also gain a sense of being unbounded and "infinite" in their togetherness. In the *Encyclopedia Logic*, Hegel writes that "this relation to itself . . . in the other is *genuine infinity*" (*EL* 151/201 [§95]). Hegel's philosophy reveals that examples of such infinity are to be found throughout human society and history.

Finite things are moments of the infinite process that being as a whole proves to be: the process of coming to unite with itself that ultimately issues in life and human consciousness. Finite human beings are also moments of various social and historical structures, such as marriage and the state, that embody the logical structure of infinity. Furthermore, individual human beings can also exhibit the quality of infinity themselves insofar as they "find themselves"—and so unite with themselves—in various ways in and with other people. For Hegel, therefore, finite human beings can and do enjoy infinite, or "eternal," life. Such infinity does not, however, consist in the endless continuation of existence beyond death. It consists in what Hegel memorably calls "*pure* self-recognition in absolute otherness" (*PhS* 14/29)—a self-recognition that one finds in love, in communal life, and also in knowledge of the world around one but that one enjoys only as long as one is alive. Such self-recognition in the other is thus a quality of *infinite* life that every human being can enjoy for a limited, *finite* amount of time. For Hegel, this qualitatively infinite but quantitatively finite life is the true goal of all human endeavor; indeed, it is the inherent aim of all being.[24]

Hegel and Levinas

Hegel's account of true infinity does not bring his philosophy as a whole to an end. There are another seven hundred pages in the *Logic* alone, and then we face the *Philosophy of Nature* and the *Philosophy of Spirit*. Nevertheless, the account of infinity is the place at which I have chosen to conclude my commentary on the *Logic* because it marks a significant turning point in the logical development of the idea of being. Indeed, in the *Encyclopedia Logic*, Hegel claims that the true infinite is the "basic concept of philosophy"—the concept that will be developed further throughout, and that will inform, the rest of Hegel's philosophical system (*EL* 152/203 [§95]). To the frustration of some readers, perhaps, I shall thus conclude my study of Hegel's *Logic* at the very point at which Hegel's account of the true character of being is really just beginning.

As I have already noted, there is something rather abstract about Hegel's notion of true infinity. The idea that being "unites with itself" in the passing away of finite things does not seem to have taken us a whole lot further than the idea that being is pure and simple being. We are still a long way from the more concrete ideas of being as reason, nature, or history. Yet, we have come further than

24. On Hegel's understanding of "eternal life," see Houlgate, *An Introduction to Hegel*, pp. 265–6.

we might think, for Hegel's account of true infinity has taught us something very important that will stay with us for the rest of our philosophizing.

Hegel's account of true infinity teaches us that, if we are to come to a proper understanding of the truth, we must learn to think of being as a process of development. We must also be prepared to let go of the idea that everything is to be conceived as *something* in relation to something *else*. In Hegel's world, there are certainly *things* that interact with other things. In his view, however, it is not sufficient to conceive of such things merely as "things" or as "other" than one another. One must also recognize that they constitute ideal *moments* of the process of being and, indeed, moments of organized unities, such as states. Put positively, therefore, the decisive insight we gain from Hegel's account of true infinity is that we must understand the world primarily in terms of processes and their moments, because much of what surrounds us will be distorted if we think of it solely as something in relation to its other. This applies in particular to the structure of living organisms and to various forms of human community.

The point is not to abandon altogether the idea that we are separate, finite things, but to recognize that the infinite process of being cannot be something *other* than its constitutive moments (and that the same is true of "infinite" structures, such as the state). Whether we think of it as the process of being as a whole or as a quality exemplified by individual things, true infinity does not lie beyond or over against finite things, nor does it consist in endless finitude. It consists in the process—constituted *by* finite things—whereby being unites with and relates to itself. There have been philosophers before Hegel—most notably, Spinoza—who have entertained a similar conception of immanent infinity.[25] Many more, however, have failed to appreciate the nature of the true infinite. As a result, they run the risk of misrepresenting the character of many of the most important features of our world.

Descartes, for example, understands the only truly infinite being he acknowledges—namely, God—to exceed and transcend the realm of the finite, and several post-Hegelian philosophers including Levinas have endorsed this Cartesian view of infinity. With direct reference to Descartes, Levinas insists that "infinity is characteristic of a transcendent being as transcendent; the infinite is the absolutely other."[26] In this sense, he reduces infinity to what Hegel considers to be the bad infinite. True, Levinas insists that precisely because in-

25. In contrast to Nietzsche, Hegel also understands Plato's "forms" to be immanent in things rather than located in another world. See *SL* 50/1: 44 and *EPN* 9/19 (§246 Add.). From a Hegelian point of view, therefore, Plato's allegory of the cave in the *Republic* distorts the relation between forms and things insofar as it suggests that forms lie "outside" the realm of finite things.

26. E. Levinas, *Totality and Infinity: An Essay on Exteriority*, trans. A. Lingis (Pittsburgh: Duquesne University Press, 1969), p. 49. Similarly, Derrida understands the idea of God to be the idea of the "*wholly other*"; see J. Derrida, *The Gift of Death*, trans. D. Wills (Chicago: University of Chicago Press, 1995), p. 57.

finity does transcend the finite it cannot itself be a finite object of any kind: "to think the infinite, the transcendent, the Stranger, is . . . not to think an object."[27] The infinite is sheer exteriority and otherness and for that very reason is not a thing that we are able to survey, understand, or control. The fact that Levinas's infinite is not *something* does not, however, prevent it from falling short of true infinity. Indeed, Levinas's conception of the infinite comes remarkably close to that attributed by Hegel to the unfettered understanding (*Verstand*). Levinas argues that finite human beings stand in relation to the transcendent infinite—both to the infinite that is God and the infinite that is the "face" of the other human being. Just like the understanding, however, he believes that the relation to the finite does not detract in any way from the sheer, unadulterated *infinity* of the infinite. For the understanding, Hegel claims, the infinite beyond the finite is not "negated" but is rather "the in-itself, in which, therefore, determinateness and limitation are not to be explicitly present, for these would debase and ruin it" (*SL* 145/1: 159 [251]). Similarly, for Levinas, "the Cartesian notion of the idea of the Infinite designates a relation with a being that maintains its total exteriority with respect to him who thinks it. It designates the contact with the intangible, a contact that *does not compromise the integrity of what is touched*."[28] Levinas protests against the reduction of the "infinite" face of the other to that which is conceivable, knowable, and familiar. From Hegel's point of view, however, Levinas's conception of the infinite is itself a product of a reductive understanding that sees nothing in the infinite but that which utterly *transcends* the finite.

As we know, Hegel does not altogether dismiss the idea that there is transcendent, or "bad," infinity. In contrast to Levinas (and the understanding), however, he argues that the point of contact between the finite and the bad infinite necessarily limits the infinite and so cannot but compromise and negate its simple infinity. Levinas's infinite may well not be an object or a thing, but the fact that it is conceived to be radically *other* than the finite means that it is necessarily limited by that finite and so is not truly *infinite* at all. The Hegelian objection to Levinas is thus not that there is no transcendent infinity whatsoever but rather that Levinas's transcendent infinity cannot be truly infinite. Indeed, the very fact that it is utterly exterior to the finite is what prevents it from being truly infinite.

The true infinite, for Hegel, is simply the process that is generated by finite things themselves; it is nothing *beyond* them, nor is it an ever-receding goal that things strive to attain. It is the *one* realm of being that there is—this world of finite things and bad infinities—insofar as it constitutes the process of *uniting with itself*. When this process is understood more fully later in Hegel's philosophy, it proves to be one in which being—in and through human being—comes to be *conscious* of itself and of its unity. In contrast to Levinas, therefore, Hegel

27. Levinas, *Totality and Infinity*, p. 49.

28. Levinas, *Totality and Infinity*, p. 50, my emphasis.

is ultimately a philosopher of radical immanence rather than transcendence. As far as the infinite is concerned, he is a follower of Spinoza rather than Descartes. He differs from Spinoza simply because he believes that being is not just eternal substance but *develops* immanently of its own accord into self-conscious being.

Clearly a proper discussion of the differences between Hegel and Levinas would require much subtler attention to the details of Levinas's position and to his distinctively ethical perspective. Nevertheless, one thing does become apparent even from the cursory comparison between the two thinkers undertaken here: however Levinas conceives in detail of infinity, he necessarily fails to bring to mind *true* infinity to the extent that, like the unhappy consciousness, he equates infinity with transcendence. This is because true infinity *logically* cannot be *other* than or lie beyond the finite without being reduced to finitude itself. Hegel and Levinas agree that the infinite differs from the finite. For Hegel, however, any infinite that transcends the finite and so is intrinsically bounded and limited by the finite is necessarily finite itself. Consequently, Levinas's infinite cannot be true infinity.

Levinas is right that "to think the infinite" is "not to think an object."[29] Hegel demonstrates that it is not to think sheer transcendence or otherness either. In his view, the only way to think true infinity is to understand it as the self-relating being that finitude itself in its self-negation and demise comes to constitute. Infinity understood in this way is truly infinite because it is not bounded by finitude but rather lives *in* and *through* finitude itself.

None of this is to assert that Hegel is beyond all criticism from a Levinasian point of view. It is to insist, however, that a Levinasian challenge to Hegel cannot be mounted in the name of infinity because logically no transcendent infinite can be truly infinite. According to Hegel, the nature of true infinity can be uncovered only through detailed, unprejudiced attention to the logical character of being itself.[30] In particular, one begins to comprehend true infinity when one has thought through the implications of being finite and when one is prepared to *let go* of the idea that infinite being is simply the negation of, or other than, finite being. The central lesson of Hegel's *Logic*, in other words, is that one begins to think the true infinite and hence the true nature of being (including human being) when one lets go of the idea of transcendence. This is a logical lesson that, in my view, many post-Hegelians have still to learn.[31]

---

29. Levinas, *Totality and Infinity*, p. 49.

30. In contrast to Maluschke, I do not believe that Hegel is led to the idea of the true infinite by the *image* of the circle. He is led to that idea by the logic inherent in being. See Maluschke, *Kritik und absolute Methode in Hegels Dialektik*, p. 181.

31. On the parallels between Hegel and Nietzsche as critics of transcendence, see Houlgate, *Hegel, Nietzsche, and the Criticism of Metaphysics*, *passim*. See also Theunissen, *Sein und Schein*, p. 284.

Conclusion

Hegel's Logic *as Ontology*

Robert Pippin understands Hegel's project in the *Logic* to be that of determining "the conditions under which any subject must think in order to think objectively at all."[1] For Pippin, the categories set out in the *Logic*, which constitute these conditions, are not determinations of being as such but concepts of self-conscious thought. Pippin's Hegel, accordingly, is not a straightforwardly ontological thinker but a transcendental philosopher who uncovers the "conceptual scheme" that is needed if *we* are to judge anything to be a determinate object.[2]

Hegel's method is also transcendental for Pippin insofar as it starts with the bare thought of being and then *regresses* to ever more fundamental conditions of the successful thought of determinate being. Later categories are thus shown to be the presuppositions of those that precede them in Hegel's system. Pippin's Hegel, it seems, proceeds in a manner similar to Fichte, who "begin[s] with the immediate object of consciousness, . . . and then go[es] on to display the conditions of the same."[3]

In this study I have sought to defend a different conception of Hegel's *Logic*. The categories analyzed by Hegel are, in my view, both forms of thought *and* structures of being as such. Hegel is thus doing straightforward ontology as much as conceptual analysis or transcendental philosophy. Every category in the *Logic*—including that of the bad infinite—is an ontological structure, or an aspect of what there is, as well as a concept that we employ to understand the world. None, therefore, can be dismissed as an utter misconception or error.

I have also tried to show that Hegel's method is immanent and developmental rather than transcendental and regressive. Hegel argues not that later categories constitute the *conditions* of earlier ones, but that they render explicit what is implicit in those earlier categories themselves. His task as a philosopher is thus simply to let each category unfold its own implications and thereby mutate of its own accord into further categories. Finitude is not the precondition of there being something, nor is infinity the precondition of finitude; rather, finite is what every something itself proves to be, and infinity is what finite being itself turns out to constitute.

This process of immanent logical development is presuppositionless, be-

1. Pippin, *Hegel's Idealism*, p. 246.

2. Pippin, *Hegel's Idealism*, pp. 219, 233.

3. J. G. Fichte, *Foundations of Transcendental Philosophy (Wissenschaftslehre) Nova Methodo (1796/99)*, trans. and ed. D. Breazeale (Ithaca: Cornell University Press, 1992), p. 182.

cause it begins from the utterly indeterminate category of pure being and discloses all that is implicit in it. Every category is thus simply a further determination of what it is and means to be. It may seem incredible to some that an utterly indeterminate category should harbor so many other categories within itself, but Hegel labors painstakingly to demonstrate that this is indeed the case. Pure being, he claims, entails becoming, determinacy, being something, being finite, and being infinite. As we have seen, the reason why these more complex structures are implicit in being is that being proves to be not just sheer being after all but the unity of being and the *not:* all subsequent categories are generated by the various ways in which being and the not combine with one another. Being transforms itself logically into a multiplicity of ways of being, therefore, because of the moment of *negation* that it necessarily bears within itself.

Hegel's conception of the categories in some ways overlaps with, but in other ways departs from, our ordinary conception of things. It is important to remember, however, that Hegel understands each category as he does, not because he is seeking deliberately to flout the law of noncontradiction or to throw more conventionally minded readers into confusion but because he believes he is led to that understanding by the very nature of being and thought itself. Hegel argues that something is intrinsically related to other things and that infinity is immanent in finitude quite simply because he believes he is required to do so by the category of pure being from which, in his view, a thoroughly self-critical philosophy must start.

The reader of Hegel's *Logic* who wants to determine the merits of Hegel's enterprise thus has to ask himself or herself three simple questions: (1) Should philosophy try to be radically self-critical and take nothing for granted? (2) If so, should it begin from the thought of pure indeterminate being? (3) If so, does the category of pure being actually give rise to the further categories that Hegel sets out? I am not suggesting that every reader will find it easy to answer these questions; but I believe that these are the questions that must be asked and addressed if one is to come to a considered judgment on the value of Hegel's *Logic*. Hegel's *Logic* is difficult—at times ferociously so—but it is not an essentially mysterious or elusive work. What Hegel is trying to do is quite clear: derive the basic categories of thought and forms of being logically and immanently from a starting point that takes as little as possible for granted. With patience and close attention to Hegel's text, it is also possible to establish how he understands each category that emerges. The reader of Hegel's *Logic* does not face the problem that readers of, for example, Nietzsche encounter: is he being ironic? does he really believe what he says? what is he trying to do to me by saying this or that? The task confronting Hegel's readers is much more straightforward: it is to consider whether it is right to try to determine what is implicit in pure being and, if so, whether Hegel succeeds in each specific case in deriving a category properly. If the answer in each case is "yes," then it seems to me one has no choice but to be persuaded by Hegel's argument.

Schopenhauer accuses Hegel of deliberately befuddling young minds with his dialectical trickery. In my view, by contrast, Hegel—like Aristotle, Leibniz, or Kant—offers us a set of clear and intelligible theses that it is up to us to evaluate: being is not pure *being*, but becoming and determinate being; determinate being does not stand alone as sheer determinacy, but takes the form of something that is separate from but also related to something else; something is by its very nature subject to change and is also open to being reconstituted at its core by other things; things necessarily limit one another and also prove to be finite; finite being in turn gives rise to various forms of infinity; truly infinite being is not something of its own beyond the finite but is simply the process whereby being unites with itself through the demise of finite things—a process, we learn later, that issues in being's coming to consciousness of itself. Not everyone will agree with these theses, but they are surely quite intelligible and capable of being assessed publicly and rationally, just like the claims of most other philosophers. Hegel's *Logic* is not by any means as impenetrable or absurd a text as some would have us believe.

Later in the *Logic* Hegel shows that being takes the form not just of quality but also of quantity, specificity, reflexivity (or mediation), explicit rational development (or *Begriff*), and ultimately nature (or the realm of things in space and time). His conclusion at the end of the *Logic* is that being is in fact never anything less than nature. For Hegel, being does not progress *in time* from indeterminacy through infinity to nature but is always spatio-temporal, natural being. What the *Logic* describes is thus not some imagined temporal or historical process whereby nature emerges but rather the actual *logical* necessity, or rationality, by virtue of which being proves to be nothing less than nature. This rationality, or "logos," within being is always at work requiring that there be something, finitude, infinity, and nature. It is the logos that religion identifies as "God."

This logos also requires that organic life, self-consciousness, and history emerge within nature. It cannot lead immediately to life and self-consciousness, however, because it requires that they emerge only where the appropriate natural conditions prevail. *Logically*, there must be self-consciousness, because this is demanded by the very nature of being—that is, by being's true infinity. Self-consciousness can arise, however, only where natural processes allow this to occur. If one is going to understand Hegel's account of the work of reason or "God" properly, one should thus not stop with his *Logic* but move on to his *Philosophy of Nature*.

Hegel's Logic *as Critical Philosophy*

Hegel's *Logic* not only provides a subtle exposition of what it means to be; it is also a work of philosophical critique. The targets of Hegel's criticism are certain fundamental errors and misconceptions about being and the reduction of one

category to another or to a mere moment of itself. The *Logic* clearly demonstrates that it is an error to believe that there is no such thing as infinity or to deny the reality of change. It also shows that being something should not be reduced to being determinate and that being finite should not be reduced to being limited by something else. These reductions are not simple errors, since they do capture something of the truth: finitude, for example, does indeed involve being limited. They are to be criticized, however, because they overlook what specifically distinguishes a category from the one to which it is reduced: what makes something *finite* rather than merely *limited*.

The *Logic* also shows that categories should not be reduced to mere moments of themselves. Something is self-relating determinacy; but that is not all it is, because it is also related to other things. If we reduce something to that which is simply separate from everything else, then we miss out on an essential aspect of its logical structure. Similarly, true infinity is being that is not finite, but that is not all it is, because it is at the same time the process constituted *by* finite things themselves. If we reduce true infinity to that which is simply *not finite*, then we end up conflating it with bad or finite infinity and so miss out on what makes it truly infinite. In these cases, the problem is that one aspect of a category is taken to be all there is to the category, and so the category as a whole is distorted.

Hegel's criticisms are not advanced in isolation from his speculative exposition of the true character of the categories. That exposition is itself the critique of the reduction of one category to another or to a mere moment of itself. This fusion of exposition and critique is a direct consequence of Hegel's immanent method. How so? That method, we recall, involves showing how one concept is actually implicit in another. When the later concept emerges explicitly—when, for example, "something" proves to be "limited" and "finite"—the earlier concept (in this case, "something") is not replaced or shown to be an error but is revealed to be an *underdetermination* of what is at hand. It is shown to constitute a mere moment of the more complex category or form of being. So a finite thing is still something, but it is not merely something, precisely because it is something finite. Similarly, true infinity is inseparable from finitude. It is not reducible to finitude, however, because it is the process of uniting-with-self (and, ultimately, coming to consciousness of self) that occurs *in* the endlessly changing realm of the finite. In these ways, the very process whereby the true nature of "something" or of "infinity" becomes apparent itself constitutes the critique of attempts—by the understanding or ordinary consciousness—to reduce such categories to anything less than they really are.

Since that process proves categories to be necessary, it also represents a fundamental critique of any attempt to deny altogether that those categories capture what there actually is. Parmenides may deny the reality of change, but Hegel's logical derivation of the categories implicit in being itself shows him to be

wrong. Once again, therefore, speculative analysis and criticism form one and the same process.[4]

In my view, one of the great merits of Hegel's *Logic* is the way in which it exposes the extent to which other philosophies rest on misconceptions or, more frequently, reduced conceptions of certain categories. In the preceding commentary, I have tried to indicate how, in the light of Hegel's analyses, Kant and Nietzsche may be said to operate with a reduced conception of the "thing in itself," how Spinoza may be said to assume a reduced conception of finitude, and how Levinas may be said to presuppose a reduced conception of infinity. Of course, one might wish to argue in response that criticisms of Kant or Levinas based on Hegel's *Logic* are misplaced because they fail to engage directly with the epistemic claims made by Kant or the ethical claims made by Levinas. From the Hegelian point of view, however, the *Logic* is perfectly suited to provide a critique of epistemic or ethical positions, because it exposes the impoverished *categories* that underlie or inform those positions. The rudimentary critique of Levinas sketched in the last chapter is certainly indirect insofar as it ignores all that Levinas has to say about ethical relations. Nevertheless, it is a powerful critique, in my view, because it reveals that Levinas's ethical position is built on a conception of infinity that falls short logically of the concept of true infinity.

What makes Hegel's explicit or implied criticisms of conceptual reduction so trenchant is the fact that they are based on an analysis of categories that is radically self-critical and presuppositionless. Hegel's *Logic* is not founded on any prior commitment to the "Absolute" or to being's "return to itself." It is founded simply on the concern to take nothing for granted and to be wholly open to what thought and being show themselves to be. It is true that being turns out to unite with or relate to itself in the demise of finite things and thus to be truly infinite; it is further true that this might seem to lend credence to the Derridean charge that Hegel's philosophy is oriented from the start toward being's return-to-self and against openness to the other. Yet, *pace* Derrida, the *Logic* is not oriented *in advance* toward being's return-to-self. Being is understood by Hegel to be self-relating, infinite being because that is what pure being—about which no other assumptions are made—*turns out* in truth to be. If one wants to deny that being is ultimately self-relating in this way, then one must either show where Hegel's logical analyses go awry or assume from the start that being is consigned to endless finitude and repetition or conditioned by irreducible differences that render its union with itself impossible. The second option, from my point of view, is a nonstarter, because it is less self-critical and takes more for

4 For an alternative account of the way in which exposition and critique are blended into one in Hegel's *Logic*, see Theunissen, *Sein und Schein, passim*. Theunissen argues in the main that Hegel's speculative exposition shows various categories to be illusions (*Schein*) generated by thought rather than underdeterminations of the truth; see, for example, *Sein und Schein*, p. 100.

granted than Hegel's own procedure. The first option is, however, always a possibility. But it requires the reader to engage closely with Hegel's own arguments. My aim in this study is to help readers of the *Logic* understand those arguments so that they may come to their own assessment of their value.

It would be disingenuous of me to deny that I am persuaded by Hegel's arguments—at least in the early part of the *Logic*. My principal concern, however, is not to cajole people into feeling similarly persuaded. It is to encourage readers to approach the *Logic* with an open mind and to examine the details of Hegel's analyses without having already decided that they are contradictory (and therefore wrong) or governed by some predetermined dialectical method (and so not really presuppositionless at all). The point I am urging is not that one should read Hegel assuming all along that he is right. It is, rather, that one should avoid assuming from the start that he is obviously wrong or that he simply prejudges the issues at hand by adhering to some tacit or explicit "logocentrism."

This study is thus devoted to the *opening* of Hegel's *Science of Logic* in several senses. It discusses the opening chapters of the *Logic* itself. It tries to show that pure being is not conceived by Hegel within the closed framework of a predetermined dialectical method but of its own accord opens out into further categories and ways of being. It also aims to open up Hegel's logic to readers by rendering the project intelligible and the details accessible. In this way, my study will, I hope, open the possibility both of a broader understanding of Hegel's most difficult text and of intelligent, informed criticism.

Charles Taylor says of one of Hegel's arguments (namely, that finitude and self-negation are built into the very structure of determinacy) that "it would be of immense consequence if valid."[5] Taylor himself patently does not think that Hegel's argument is valid. For reasons set out in the preceding commentary, I beg to differ. I believe, however, that Taylor's sentence can be read as a fitting comment on the whole opening section of the *Logic*. All of Hegel's arguments—from his account of pure being to his account of true infinity—would be of immense importance if valid. My hope is that this study will encourage more readers to consider seriously just how valid and important Hegel's arguments actually are.

---

5 Taylor, *Hegel,* p. 238.

Bibliography

Works by Hegel

Hegel's Phenomenology of Spirit, trans. A.V. Miller (Oxford: Oxford University Press, 1977).

G.W.F. Hegel, *Phänomenologie des Geistes*, ed. E. Moldenhauer and K.M. Michel, *Werke in zwanzig Bänden*, vol. 3 (Frankfurt am Main: Suhrkamp Verlag, 1969).

Hegel's Science of Logic, trans. A.V. Miller (Amherst, NY: Humanity Books, 1999).

Hegel's Science of Logic, trans. W.H. Johnston and L.G. Struthers, 2 vols. (London: George Allen and Unwin, 1929).

G.W.F. Hegel, *Wissenschaft der Logik*, ed. E. Moldenhauer and K.M. Michel, 2 vols, *Werke in zwanzig Bänden*, vols. 5, 6 (Frankfurt am Main: Suhrkamp Verlag, 1969).

G.W.F. Hegel, *Wissenschaft der Logik. Erster Teil: Die Objektive Logik. Erster Band: Die Lehre vom Sein (1832)*, ed. F. Hogemann and W. Jaeschke, *Gesammelte Werke*, vol. 21 (Hamburg: Felix Meiner Verlag, 1985).

G.W.F. Hegel, *Wissenschaft der Logik. Erster Band: Die Objektive Logik (1812/1813)*, ed. F. Hogemann and W. Jaeschke, *Gesammelte Werke*, vol. 11 (Hamburg: Felix Meiner Verlag, 1978).

G.W.F. Hegel, *Vorlesungen über Logik und Metaphysik. Heidelberg 1817*, ed. K. Gloy, *Ausgewählte Nachschriften und Manuskripte*, vol. 11 (Hamburg: Felix Meiner, 1992).

G.W.F. Hegel, *Vorlesungen über die Logik. Berlin 1831*, ed. U. Rameil in cooperation with H.-C. Lucas, *Ausgewählte Nachschriften und Manuskripte*, vol. 10 (Hamburg: Felix Meiner, 2001).

G.W.F. Hegel, *The Philosophical Propaedeutic*, trans. A.V. Miller, ed. M. George and A. Vincent (Oxford: Blackwell, 1986).

G.W.F. Hegel, *Nürnberger und Heidelberger Schriften (1808–1817)*, ed. E. Moldenhauer and K.M. Michel, *Werke in zwanzig Bänden*, vol. 4 (Frankfurt am Main: Suhrkamp Verlag, 1970).

G.W.F. Hegel, *The Encyclopaedia Logic*, trans. T.F. Geraets, W.A. Suchting, and H.S. Harris (Indianapolis: Hackett, 1991).

G.W.F. Hegel, *Enzyklopädie der philosophischen Wissenschaften im Grundrisse (1830). Erster Teil: Die Wissenschaft der Logik*, ed. E. Moldenhauer and K.M. Michel, *Werke in zwanzig Bänden*, vol. 8 (Frankfurt am Main: Suhrkamp Verlag, 1970).

Hegel's Philosophy of Nature. Being Part Two of the Encyclopaedia of the Philosophical Sciences (1830), trans. A.V. Miller (Oxford: Clarendon Press, 1970).

G.W.F. Hegel, *Enzyklopädie der philosophischen Wissenschaften im Grundrisse (1830). Zweiter Teil: Die Naturphilosophie*, ed. E. Moldenhauer and K.M. Michel, *Werke in zwanzig Bänden*, vol. 9 (Frankfurt am Main: Suhrkamp Verlag, 1970).

Hegel's Philosophy of Mind. Being Part Three of the Encyclopaedia of the Philosophical Sciences (1830), trans. W. Wallace, together with the *Zusätze* in Boumann's text (1845), trans. A.V. Miller (Oxford: Clarendon Press, 1971).

G.W.F. Hegel, *Enzyklopädie der philosophischen Wissenschaften im Grundrisse (1830). Dritter Teil: Die Philosophie des Geistes*, ed. E. Moldenhauer and K.M. Michel, *Werke in zwanzig Bänden*, vol. 10 (Frankfurt am Main: Suhrkamp Verlag, 1970).

G.W.F. Hegel, *Elements of the Philosophy of Right*, ed. A.W. Wood, trans. H.B. Nisbet (Cambridge: Cambridge University Press, 1991).

G.W.F. Hegel, *Grundlinien der Philosophie des Rechts*, ed. E. Moldenhauer and K.M. Michel, *Werke in zwanzig Bänden*, vol. 7 (Frankfurt am Main: Suhrkamp Verlag, 1970).

G.W.F. Hegel, *Vorlesungen über die Philosophie der Weltgeschichte, Zweite Hälfte*, ed. G. Lasson (1919) (Hamburg: Felix Meiner, 1923).

G.W.F. Hegel, *Aesthetics. Lectures on Fine Art*, trans. T.M. Knox, 2 vols. (Oxford: Clarendon Press, 1975).

G.W.F. Hegel, *Vorlesungen über die Ästhetik*, ed. E. Moldenhauer and K.M. Michel, 3 vols, *Werke in zwanzig Bänden*, vols. 13, 14, 15 (Frankfurt am Main: Suhrkamp Verlag, 1969).

G.W.F. Hegel, *Lectures on the History of Philosophy. The Lectures of 1825–1826*, ed. R.F. Brown, trans. R.F. Brown and J.M. Stewart with the assistance of H.S. Harris, vol. 3: *Medieval and Modern Philosophy* (Berkeley: University of California Press, 1990).

G.W.F. Hegel, *Vorlesungen über die Geschichte der Philosophie. Teil 4: Philosophie des Mittelalters und der neueren Zeit*, ed. P. Garniron and W. Jaeschke, *Ausgewählte Nachschriften und Manuskripte*, vol. 9 (Hamburg: Felix Meiner, 1986).

G.W.F. Hegel, *Vorlesungen über die Geschichte der Philosophie*, ed. E. Moldenhauer and K.M. Michel, 3 vols, *Werke in zwanzig Bänden*, vols. 18, 19, 20 (Frankfurt am Main: Suhrkamp Verlag, 1971).

Hegel: The Letters, trans. C. Butler and C. Seiler (Bloomington: Indiana University Press, 1984).

Other Works

Henry Allison, *Kant's Transcendental Idealism: An Interpretation and Defense* (New Haven: Yale University Press, 1983).

A. Alvarez, *Beckett* (London: Fontana/Collins, 1973).

The Complete Works of Aristotle, ed. J. Barnes, 2 vols. (Princeton: Princeton University Press, 1984).

Samuel Beckett, *En attendant Godot* (Paris: Les Éditions de Minuit, 1952).

Frederick C. Beiser, ed. *The Cambridge Companion to Hegel* (Cambridge: Cambridge University Press, 1993).

Frederick C. Beiser, "Hegel, A Non-Metaphysician? A Polemic Review of H.T. Engelhardt and Terry Pinkard, eds. *Hegel Reconsidered*," *Bulletin of the Hegel Society of Great Britain* 32 (Autumn/Winter 1995): 1–13.

J. Biard et al., eds. *Introduction à la lecture de La Science de la Logique de Hegel. I. L'Etre* (Paris: Aubier, 1981).

Reinhard Brandt, *The Table of Judgments: Critique of Pure Reason A 67–76; B 92–101*, trans. E. Watkins (Atascadero, CA: Ridgeview Publishing, 1995).

Rüdiger Bubner, "Die 'Sache selbst' in Hegels System," in *Seminar: Dialektik in der Philosophie Hegels*, ed. R.-P. Horstmann (Frankfurt am Main: Suhrkamp Verlag, 1978), pp. 101–23.

John Burbidge, *On Hegel's Logic: Fragments of a Commentary* (Atlantic Highlands, NJ: Humanities Press, 1981).

John Burbidge, "Where Is the Place of Understanding?" in *Essays on Hegel's Logic*, ed. G. di Giovanni (Albany: SUNY Press, 1990), pp. 171–82.

Bernd Burkhardt, *Hegels "Wissenschaft der Logik" im Spannungsfeld der Kritik* (Hildesheim: Georg Olms Verlag, 1993).

George P. Cave, "The Dialectic of Becoming in Hegel's Logic," *The Owl of Minerva* 16, 2 (Spring 1985): 147–60.

Ardis Collins, ed. *Hegel on the Modern World* (Albany: SUNY Press, 1995).

Rod Coltman, *The Language of Hermeneutics: Gadamer and Heidegger in Dialogue* (Albany: SUNY Press, 1998).

Jacques Derrida, *Writing and Difference*, trans. A. Bass (London: Routledge and Kegan Paul, 1978).

Jacques Derrida, *Margins of Philosophy*, trans. A. Bass (Brighton: Harvester Press, 1982).

Jacques Derrida, *Glas*, trans. J.P. Leavey and R. Rand (Lincoln: University of Nebraska Press, 1986).

Jacques Derrida, *The Gift of Death*, trans. D. Wills (Chicago: University of Chicago Press, 1995).

The Philosophical Writings of Descartes, trans. J. Cottingham, R. Stoothoff, D. Murdoch, 3 vols. (Cambridge: Cambridge University Press, 1984–91).

George di Giovanni, ed. *Essays on Hegel's Logic* (Albany: SUNY Press, 1990).

André Doz, *La logique de Hegel et les problèmes traditionnels de l'ontologie* (Paris: J. Vrin, 1987).

David Duquette, "Kant, Hegel and the Possibility of a Speculative Logic," in *Essays on Hegel's Logic*, ed. G. di Giovanni (Albany: SUNY Press, 1990), pp. 1–16.

S.M. Emmanuel, ed. *The Blackwell Guide to the Modern Philosophers: From Descartes to Nietzsche* (Oxford: Blackwell, 2001).

Hans-Peter Falk, *Das Wissen in Hegels "Wissenschaft der Logik"* (Freiburg/München: Verlag Karl Alber, 1983).

Ludwig Feuerbach, *Towards a Critique of Hegel's Philosophy*, in *The Young Hegelians: An Anthology*, ed. L. Stepelevich (Cambridge: Cambridge University Press, 1983), pp. 95–128.

Ludwig Feuerbach, "Zur Kritik der Hegelschen Philosophie" (1839), in *Philosophische Kritiken und Grundsätze*, ed. W. Bolin and F. Jodl, *Sämtliche Werke*, vol. 2 (Stuttgart-Bad Cannstatt: Frommann-Holzboog, 1959), pp. 158–204.

J.G. Fichte, *Foundations of Transcendental Philosophy (Wissenschaftslehre) Nova Methodo (1796/99)*, trans. and ed. D. Breazeale (Ithaca: Cornell University Press, 1992).

J.G. Fichte, *Introductions to the Wissenschaftslehre and Other Writings*, trans. D. Breazeale (Indianapolis: Hackett, 1994).

J.N. Findlay, *Hegel: A Re-examination* (1958) (New York: Oxford University Press, 1976).

Michael Forster, "Hegel's Dialectical Method," in *The Cambridge Companion to Hegel*, ed. F.C. Beiser (Cambridge: Cambridge University Press, 1993), pp. 130–70.

Hans-Georg Gadamer, *Hegel's Dialectic: Five Hermeneutical Studies*, trans. P.C. Smith (New Haven: Yale University Press, 1976).

Rodolphe Gasché, *The Tain of the Mirror: Derrida and the Philosophy of Reflection* (Cambridge, MA: Harvard University Press, 1986).

Paul Guyer, "Hegel, Leibniz und der Widerspruch des Endlichen," in *Seminar: Dialektik in der Philosophie Hegels*, ed. R.-P. Horstmann (Frankfurt am Main: Suhrkamp Verlag, 1978), pp. 230–60.

U. Guzzoni, *Werden zu sich. Eine Untersuchung zu Hegels "Wissenschaft der Logik"* (Freiburg/München: Verlag Karl Alber, 1963).

Jürgen Habermas, *Erkenntnis und Interesse* (Frankfurt am Main: Suhrkamp Verlag, 1968).

E.E. Harris, *An Interpretation of the Logic of Hegel* (Lanham, MD: University Press of America, 1983).

Klaus Hartmann, "Hegel: A Non-Metaphysical View," in *Hegel: A Collection of Critical Essays*, ed. A. MacIntyre (1972) (Notre Dame: University of Notre Dame Press, 1976), pp. 101–24.

Justus Hartnack, *An Introduction to Hegel's Logic*, trans. L. Aagaard-Mogensen, ed. K. Westphal (Indianapolis: Hackett, 1998).

Martin Heidegger, *Being and Time*, trans. J. Macquarrie and E. Robinson (Oxford: Blackwell, 1962).

Martin Heidegger, *Hegel's Phenomenology of Spirit*, trans. P. Emad and K. Maly (Bloomington: Indiana University Press, 1988).

Martin Heidegger, *Gelassenheit* (Pfullingen: Verlag Günther Neske, 1959).

Martin Heidegger, *Hegel*, ed. I. Schübler, *Gesamtausgabe*, vol. 68 (Vittorio Klostermann: Frankfurt am Main, 1993).

Dieter Henrich, "Anfang und Methode der Logik," in D. Henrich, *Hegel im Kontext* (Frankfurt am Main: Suhrkamp Verlag, 1971), pp. 73–94.

Dieter Henrich, *Hegel im Kontext* (Frankfurt am Main: Suhrkamp Verlag, 1971).

Dieter Henrich, "Hegels Logik der Reflexion. Neue Fassung," in *Die Wissenschaft der Logik und die Logik der Reflexion*, ed. D. Henrich, *Hegel-Studien* Beiheft 18 (Bonn: Bouvier Verlag, 1978), pp. 203–324.

Dieter Henrich, ed. *Die Wissenschaft der Logik und die Logik der Reflexion*, *Hegel-Studien* Beiheft 18 (Bonn: Bouvier Verlag, 1978).

Dieter Henrich, "Formen der Negation in Hegels Logik," in *Seminar: Dialektik in der Philosophie Hegels*, ed. R.-P. Horstmann (Frankfurt am Main: Suhrkamp Verlag, 1978), pp. 213–29.

Ludwig Heyde, *The Weight of Finitude: On the Philosophical Question of God*, trans. A. Harmsen and W. Desmond (Albany: SUNY Press, 1999).

Rolf-Peter Horstmann, ed. *Seminar: Dialektik in der Philosophie Hegels* (Frankfurt am Main: Suhrkamp Verlag, 1978).

Rolf-Peter Horstmann, "What's Wrong with Kant's Categories, Professor Hegel?" in *Proceedings of the Eighth International Kant Congress*, ed. H. Robinson, 2 vols. (Milwaukee: Marquette University Press, 1995), 1.3: 1005–15.

Stephen Houlgate, "Some Notes on Michael Rosen's *Hegel's Dialectic and Its Criticism*," *Hegel-Studien* 20 (1985): 213–19.

Stephen Houlgate, *Hegel, Nietzsche and the Criticism of Metaphysics* (Cambridge: Cambridge University Press, 1986).

Stephen Houlgate, "A Reply to John Burbidge," in *Essays on Hegel's Logic*, ed. G. di Giovanni (Albany: SUNY Press, 1990), pp. 183–9.

Stephen Houlgate, "Hegel and Fichte: Recognition, Otherness, and Absolute Knowing," *The Owl of Minerva* 26, 1 (Fall 1994): 3–19.

Stephen Houlgate, "Response to Professor Horstmann," in *Proceedings of the Eighth International Kant Congress*, ed. H. Robinson, 2 vols. (Milwaukee: Marquette University Press, 1995), 1.3: 1017–23.

Stephen Houlgate, "Hegel, Kant and the Formal Distinctions of Reflective Understanding," in *Hegel on the Modern World*, ed. A. Collins (Albany: SUNY Press, 1995), pp. 125–41.

Stephen Houlgate, "Necessity and Contingency in Hegel's *Science of Logic*," *The Owl of Minerva* 27, 1 (Fall 1995): 37–49.

Stephen Houlgate, Review of *Die Wesenslogik in Hegels "Wissenschaft der Logik"* by Gerhard Martin Wölfle, *Bulletin of the Hegel Society of Great Britain* 32 (Autumn/Winter 1995): 40–7.

Stephen Houlgate, "Hegel, Derrida and Restricted Economy: The Case of Mechanical Memory," *Journal of the History of Philosophy* 34, 1 (January 1996): 79–93.

Stephen Houlgate, "Absolute Knowing Revisited," *The Owl of Minerva* 30, 1 (Fall 1998): 51–67.

Stephen Houlgate, "Schelling's Critique of Hegel's *Science of Logic*," *The Review of Metaphysics* 53.1 (September, 1999): 99–128.

Stephen Houlgate, "Substance, Causality, and the Question of Method in Hegel's *Science of Logic*," in *The Reception of Kant's Critical Philosophy: Fichte, Schelling and Hegel*, ed. S. Sedgwick (Cambridge: Cambridge University Press, 2000), pp. 232–52.

Stephen Houlgate, "G.W.F. Hegel," in *The Blackwell Guide to the Modern Philosophers: From Descartes to Nietzsche*, ed. S.M. Emmanuel (Oxford: Blackwell, 2001), pp. 278–305.

Stephen Houlgate, *An Introdution to Hegel: Freedom, Truth and History* (1991) (Oxford: Blackwell, 2005).

Christina Howells, *Derrida: Deconstruction from Phenomenology to Ethics* (Cambridge: Polity Press, 1999).

Jean Hyppolite, *Genesis and Structure of Hegel's Phenomenology of Spirit*, trans. S. Cherniak and J. Heckman (Evanston, IL: Northwestern University Press, 1974).

Paul Owen Johnson, *The Critique of Thought: A Re-examination of Hegel's Science of Logic* (Aldershot: Avebury, 1988).

Eberhard Jüngel, *Tod* (Gütersloh: Gütersloher Verlagshaus Mohn, 1979).

Immanuel Kant, *Theoretical Philosophy, 1755–1770*, ed. D. Walford and R. Meerbote (Cambridge: Cambridge University Press, 1992).

Immanuel Kant, *Critique of Pure Reason*, trans. P. Guyer and A. Wood (Cambridge: Cambridge University Press, 1997).

Immanuel Kant, *Kritik der reinen Vernunft*, ed. R. Schmidt (Hamburg: Felix Meiner Verlag, 1990).

Immanuel Kant, *Prolegomena to any Future Metaphysics That Will Be Able to Present Itself as a Science*, trans. P.G. Lucas (Manchester: Manchester University Press, 1953).

Immanuel Kant, *Lectures on Logic*, trans. and ed. J.M. Young (Cambridge: Cambridge University Press, 1992).

Immanuel Kant, *Schriften zur Metaphysik und Logik*, ed. W. Weischedel, 2 vols. (Frankfurt am Main: Suhrkamp Verlag, 1968).

Immanuel Kant, *Critique of Judgment*, trans. W.S. Pluhar (Indianapolis: Hackett, 1987).

Søren Kierkegaard, *Concluding Unscientific Postscript*, trans. D.F. Swenson and W. Lowrie (Princeton: Princeton University Press, 1968).

Wendell Kisner, "*Erinnerung*, *Retrait*, Absolute Reflection: Hegel and Derrida," *The Owl of Minerva* 26, 2 (Spring 1995): 171–86.

David Kolb, *The Critique of Pure Modernity: Hegel, Heidegger, and After* (Chicago: University of Chicago Press, 1986).

David Farrell Krell, *Of Memory, Reminiscence and Writing: On the Verge* (Bloomington: Indiana University Press, 1990).

Bernhard Lakebrink, *Kommentar zu Hegels "Logik" in seiner "Enzyklopädie" von 1830*. Vol. 1: *Sein und Wesen* (Freiburg/München: Verlag Karl Alber, 1979).

Quentin Lauer, *A Reading of Hegel's Phenomenology of Spirit* (New York: Fordham University Press, 1976).

Emmanuel Levinas, *Totality and Infinity: An Essay on Exteriority*, trans. A. Lingis (Pittsburgh: Duquesne University Press, 1969).

Emmanuel Levinas, *Basic Philosophical Writings*, ed. A.T. Peperzak, S. Critchley and R. Bernasconi (Bloomington: Indiana University Press, 1996).

A. MacIntyre, ed. *Hegel: A Collection of Critical Essays* (1972) (Notre Dame: University of Notre Dame Press, 1976).

William Maker, *Philosophy Without Foundations: Rethinking Hegel* (Albany: SUNY Press, 1994).

Günther Maluschke, *Kritik und absolute Methode in Hegels Dialektik* (*Hegel-Studien* Beiheft 13) (1974) (Bonn: Bouvier Verlag, 1984).

J.M.E. McTaggart, *A Commentary on Hegel's Logic* (Cambridge: Cambridge University Press, 1910).

J.M.E. McTaggart, "The Changes of Method in Hegel's Dialectic," in *G.W.F. Hegel: Critical Assessments*, ed. R. Stern, 4 vols. (London: Routledge, 1993), 2: 60–88.

G.R.G. Mure, *A Study of Hegel's Logic* (1950) (Westport, CT: Greenwood Press, 1984).

Friedrich Nietzsche, *Twilight of the Idols/The Antichrist*, trans. R.J. Hollingdale (Harmondsworth: Penguin Books, 1968).

Friedrich Nietzsche, *On the Genealogy of Morals*, trans. W. Kaufmann and R.J. Hollingdale, and *Ecce Homo*, trans. W. Kaufmann (New York: Vintage Books, 1969).

Friedrich Nietzsche, *The Will to Power*, trans. W. Kaufmann and R.J. Hollingdale (New York: Vintage Books, 1968).

Robert Pippin, *Hegel's Idealism: The Satisfactions of Self-Consciousness* (Cambridge: Cambridge University Press, 1989).

Robert Pippin, "Hegel's Idealism: Prospects," *Bulletin of the Hegel Society of Great Britain* 19 (Spring/Summer 1989): 28–41.

Plato, *Phaedo*, trans. D. Gallop (Oxford: Oxford University Press, 1993).

Otto Pöggeler, ed. *Hegel* (Freiburg/München: Verlag Karl Alber, 1977).

The Presocratic Philosophers, ed. G.S. Kirk, J.E. Raven and M. Schofield (1957) (Cambridge: Cambridge University Press, 1983).

Giacomo Rinaldi, *A History and Interpretation of the Logic of Hegel* (Lewiston NY: The Edwin Mellen Press, 1992).

Hoke Robinson, ed. *Proceedings of the Eighth International Kant Congress*, 2 vols. (Milwaukee: Marquette University Press, 1995).

Michael Rosen, *Hegel's Dialectic and Its Criticism* (Cambridge: Cambridge University Press, 1982).

F.W.J. von Schelling, *On the History of Modern Philosophy*, trans. A. Bowie (Cambridge: Cambridge University Press, 1994).

Friederike Schick, *Hegels Wissenschaft der Logik—metaphysische Letztbegründung oder Theorie logischer Formen?* (Freiburg/München: Verlag Karl Alber, 1994).

Arthur Schopenhauer, *The World as Will and Representation*, trans. E.F.J. Payne, 2 vols. (New York: Dover Publications, 1969).

Sally Sedgwick, ed. *The Reception of Kant's Critical Philosophy: Fichte, Schelling and Hegel* (Cambridge: Cambridge University Press, 2000).

A Spinoza Reader: The Ethics and Other Works, ed. E. Curley (Princeton: Princeton University Press, 1994).

W.T. Stace, *The Philosophy of Hegel* (1924) (New York: Dover Publications, 1955).

Lawrence Stepelevich, ed. *The Young Hegelians: An Anthology* (Cambridge: Cambridge University Press, 1983).

David S. Stern, "The Immanence of Thought: Hegel's Critique of Foundationalism," *The Owl of Minerva* 22, 1 (Fall 1990): 19–33.

Robert Stern, ed. *G.W.F. Hegel: Critical Assessments*, 4 vols. (London: Routledge, 1993).

Charles Taylor, *Hegel* (Cambridge: Cambridge University Press, 1975).

Michael Theunissen, *Sein und Schein. Die kritische Funktion der Hegelschen Logik* (Frankfurt am Main: Suhrkamp Verlag, 1980).

F.A. Trendelenburg, *The Logical Question in Hegel's System*, in *G.W.F. Hegel: Critical Assessments*, ed. R. Stern, 4 vols. (London: Routledge, 1993), 1: 182–216.

Alan White, *Absolute Knowledge: Hegel and the Problem of Metaphysics* (Athens, OH: Ohio University Press, 1983).

Wolfgang Wieland, "Bemerkungen zum Anfang von Hegels Logik," in *Seminar: Dialektik in der Philosophie Hegels*, ed. R.-P. Horstmann (Frankfurt am Main: Suhrkamp Verlag, 1978), pp. 194–212.

Cynthia Willett, "The Shadow of Hegel's *Science of Logic*," in *Essays on Hegel's Logic*, ed. G. di Giovanni (Albany: SUNY Press, 1990), pp. 85–92.

Richard Winfield, *Reason and Justice* (Albany: SUNY Press, 1988).

Richard Winfield, *Overcoming Foundations: Studies in Systematic Philosophy* (New York: Columbia University Press, 1989).

Gerhard Martin Wölfle, *Die Wesenslogik in Hegels "Wissenschaft der Logik"* (Stuttgart-Bad Cannstatt: Frommann-Holzboog, 1994).

Allen W. Wood, *Hegel's Ethical Thought* (Cambridge: Cambridge University Press, 1990).

Allen W. Wood, "Reply," *Bulletin of the Hegel Society of Great Britain* 25 (Spring/Summer 1992): 34–50.

Index